# Other A to Z Guides from The Scarecrow Press, Inc.

# The A to Z
# of the Vietnam War

Edwin E. Moïse

*The A to Z Guides, No. 9*

The Scarecrow Press, Inc.
Lanham, Maryland • Toronto • Oxford
2005

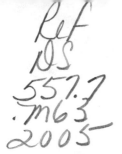

# SCARECROW PRESS, INC.

Published in the United States of America
by Scarecrow Press, Inc.
A wholly owned subsidary of
The Rowman & Littlefield Publishing Group, Inc.
4501 Forbes Boulevard, Suite 200, Lanham, Maryland 20706
www.scarecrowpress.com

PO Box 317
Oxford
OX2 9RU, UK

*The A to Z of the Vietnam War* is a revised paperback edition of the *Historical Dictionary of the Vietnam War*, by Edwin E. Moïse, published by Scarecrow Press in 2001.

British Library Cataloguing in Publication Information Available

The hardback version of this book was previously cataloged by the Library of Congress as follows:

Moise, Edwin E., 1946–
    Historical dictionary of the Vietnam War / Edwin E. Moise.
        p. cm. — (Historical dictionaries of war, revolution, and civil unrest ; no. 17)
    Includes bibliographical references and index.
    1. Vietnamese Conflict, 1961–1975—Dictionaries. I. Title. II. Series.
DS557.7 .M63 2001
959.704'3'03—dc21                                    2001042943

ISBN 0-8108-5333-7 (pbk. : alk. paper)

# Contents

# Editor's Foreword

All wars are complex, but few are so complex as the Vietnam War. It was fought, in the narrowest sense, as a war between two sides in South Vietnam, one obviously backed by North Vietnam and more distantly China and the Soviet Union, and the other by the United States and a loose coalition of allies. It spilled over from South Vietnam to North Vietnam, Laos, and Cambodia, with ramifications further afield. The goals of the two Vietnamese sides were straightforward: one struggled to throw off foreign encroachment and unify Vietnam under Communist rule, the other to preserve a non-Communist South Vietnam. It was the interaction of the Vietnamese with other groups both in the region and worldwide, and the methods used in the struggle, that made the war so complex. There were few pitched battles; most of the fighting took place in distant villages or in the jungle, more rarely in the cities; it took place in dozens of places at once. One side engaged mainly in guerrilla warfare, while the other, also out in the field, basically counted on advanced weaponry. Even the point of who won, let alone why, is unclear. It is true that the North defeated the South and its allies, but soon broke with its own supporters and eventually turned to capitalism and its former enemies to develop the country's economy. Despite the incredible complexity, much of the literature (let alone the films) simplified ruthlessly, and still does so now.

This *Historical Dictionary of the Vietnam War* attempts to sort things out, to make them more clear, but without oversimplifying what is inherently complex. Rather, and this is an advantage of the format, it focuses on the essential elements, presenting significant persons (military and political), armed units, battles and confrontations, weapons, places, and events. They are described succinctly in the dictionary. The long course of the war—as well as the events that foreshadowed it and its aftermath from 1975 to the present—is traced in the chronology. The introduction, while providing an overall view, endeavors to avoid rather than foster simplistic conclusions. Following the dictionary is a bibliography, which includes works on the war as a whole and aspects thereof. Some of these works are excellent, others less so, but all constitute a serious effort at understanding the Vietnam War.  While reading more about the subject, it would be wise to keep this historical dictionary at hand, to look up some of the details while trying to form one's own understanding.

It is obviously harder to write about a hotly debated and deeply controversial subject like the Vietnam War than most of the wars further back in history or some more recent ones, which actually were simpler and more straightforward.  The endeavor must be approached carefully and objectively, without falling into the opposite extreme of blurring events and claiming there were no rights and wrongs.  This has been done uncommonly well by Edwin E. Moïse, a professor of history at Clemson University, where he gives courses on Vietnam and the history of warfare, among other subjects.  In addition to this, he has written extensively on the region.  His first books were *Land Reform in China and North Vietnam* and *Modern China: A History*.  More recently, Dr. Moïse turned his attention to the Vietnam War, first with a number of articles and then a major book: *Tonkin Gulf and the Escalation of the Vietnam War*.  His knowledge of the region's social, political, and military history are indispensable in this series on warfare.

Jon Woronoff
Series Editor

# Notes for the Reader

In each entry in this dictionary, words in **bold** type indicate the titles of other entries. When several consecutive words are in bold type, bear in mind the possibility that this indicates the titles of several entries. Thus when the entry on Binh Dinh province states that "the U.S. 1st **Cavalry Division (Airmobile)** established its base at An Khe" in the province in 1965, this directs the reader's attention to three entries: "Airmobile," "Cavalry," and "Division."

The code names of military operations and projects are given in italics; thus Operation *Linebacker*, Operation *Lam Son 719*.

Most Vietnamese names are in three parts; some are in two. The family name comes first. Thus President Ngo Dinh Diem of the Republic of Vietnam was the son of Ngo Dinh Kha. When a name is not given in full, it is the personal name (the last of the three parts) that is used, even for formal purposes. Thus we refer to Diem or President Diem, not to Ngo or President Ngo. The only exception in general usage is Ho Chi Minh, who is referred to as Ho, not as Minh.

Best usage, followed in this dictionary, calls for Vietnamese names to be alphabetized under the family name. This can cause difficulty, however, for readers who have seen a reference to "President Diem" and want to look him up, but have no way to tell they they should be searching for him under the name Ngo. Some English-language books deal with this by alphabetizing under the personal name. This volume instead has an index that lists Vietnamese names both ways; thus "Ngo Dinh Diem" will be found under the letter N, and "Diem, Ngo Dinh" under the letter D in the name index.

Cambodian and Laotian names also are alphabetized under their first component. When Cambodian names are abbreviated, the last component is used (or occasionally the last two; Sisowath Sirik Matak can properly be called Sirik Matak, but not just Matak). When Laotian names are abbreviated, however, the first component is used. Laotian Prime Minister Souvanna Phouma can be called Souvanna, but not Phouma.

The standard organizational structure of U.S. Army forces in Vietnam was for a division to be made up of three brigades. Usually these were the 1st, 2d, and 3d, but the 23d Infantry Division was made up of the 11th, 196th, and 198th Infantry Brigades. Brigades were made up of battalions, battalions of companies, and companies of platoons. A company was designated by a letter. A division, brigade, or platoon was designated by a number. The designation of a battalion was more complex; it would be a numbered component of a regiment, but the regiment was not an actual unit; its only existence was in the nominal affiliation of battalions to it. In written documents, the number of the battalion would be separated from the number of the (purely theoretical) regiment by a slash. Thus the 1st Battalion of the 12th Infantry Regiment would be the 1/12 Battalion. Looking at the overall structure, we might identify a soldier as belonging to the 2d Platoon, Company C, 1/12 Battalion, 2d Brigade, 4th Infantry Division.

In some U.S. Army units formally designated "cavalry" (though they did not ride horses), the term "squadron" was used instead of "battalion," and "troop" instead of "company."

In the United States Marine Corps and in Vietnamese forces on both sides in the war, the regiment was an actual functioning unit, playing the role of the brigade in the U.S. Army structure. The structure was division-regiment-battalion-company-platoon.

In this work, Vietnamese born north of the 17th parallel, the line that separated North from South Vietnam from 1954 to 1975, will be called "North Vietnamese" or "northerners." Those born south of the 17th parallel will be called "South Vietnamese" or "southerners." The reader is warned that some works, especially those written by Vietnamese, use the terms "North Vietnamese" and "South Vietnamese" to refer to people born in the northernmost (Bac Bo, Bac Ky, Tonkin) and southernmost (Nam Bo, Nam Ky, Cochinchina) of the three sections into which Vietnam had been divided before 1954. They refer to those born in the large area in between (Trung Bo, Trung Ky, Annam) as "Central Vietnamese."

In an ultimate sense the Communist forces in South Vietnam were a single structure under a single high command, but it is useful to distinguish within this structure between units of the People's Army of Vietnam (PAVN, which Americans often called the North Vietnamese Army or NVA) that had been sent into South Vietnam from the North, and Viet Cong units, created within South Vietnam primarily through recruitment within South Vietnam. Too much should not be made of the distinction. Many South Vietnamese served in PAVN units, and many North Vietnamese, especially in the later portions of the war, served in Viet Cong units. This dictionary will use the phrase "Communist forces" to designate units the identity of which is unclear, and mixed groups of PAVN and non-PAVN Communist units.

Metric units of measurement and distance have been used where possible in this dictionary, but where the sources use the English units, and conversion into metric units would have created a danger of either inaccuracy or a spurious and misleading precision, it has seemed best to use the English units. When figures are given in tons, these are short tons, equal to 2,000 pounds or 907.2 kilograms. Miles are statute miles equal to 5,280 feet or 1.609 kilometers, unless nautical miles (1.852 kilometers) are specified.

# Acronyms and Abbreviations

| | |
|---|---|
| a.k.a. | also known as |
| AAA | Anti-Aircraft Artillery |
| ABC | American Broadcasting Company |
| ABCCC | Airborne Battlefield Command and Control Center |
| ACAV | Armored Cavalry Assault Vehicle (APC) |
| ADVON | Advanced Echelon |
| AFV | American Friends of Vietnam |
| AGM | Air-to-Ground Missile |
| AID | Agency for International Development |
| AIM | Air Intercept Missile |
| AP | Associated Press |
| APC | Armored Personnel Carrier |
| ARM | Anti-Radiation Missile *or* Anti-Radar Missile |
| ARVN | Army of the Republic of Vietnam |
| ASA | Army Security Agency |
| ASPB | Assault Support Patrol Boat |
| BLT | Battalion Landing Team |
| BNR | Body Not Recovered |
| CAP | Combined Action Platoon |
| CAP | Combat Air Patrol |
| CAS | Euphemism ("Controlled American Source" or "Combined Area Studies") for Central Intelligence Agency |
| CBS | Columbia Broadcasting System |
| CBU | Cluster Bomb Unit |
| CCC | Command and Control, Central (SOG) |
| CCN | Command and Control, North (SOG) |
| CCS | Command and Control, South (SOG) |
| CDNI | Committee for the Defense of National Interests |
| CIA | Central Intelligence Agency |
| CICV | Combined Intelligence Center, Vietnam |

| | |
|---|---|
| CIDG | Civilian Irregular Defense Groups |
| CINCPAC | Commander in Chief, Pacific |
| CJCS | Chairman, Joint Chiefs of Staff |
| CNO | Chief of Naval Operations |
| COMINT | Communications Intelligence |
| CORDS | Civil Operations and Revolutionary Development Support |
| COSVN | Central Office for South Vietnam |
| CTZ | Corps Tactical Zone |
| CV | Aircraft Carrier (U.S. Navy) |
| DAO | Defense Attaché Office |
| DCI | Director of Central Intelligence |
| DD | Destroyer |
| DEROS | Date Eligible for Return from Overseas *or* Date of Expected Return from Overseas |
| DIA | Defense Intelligence Agency |
| DMZ | Demilitarized Zone |
| DOD | Department of Defense |
| DOS | Department of State |
| DRV | Democratic Republic of Vietnam |
| ECM | Electronic Countermeasures |
| ELINT | Electronic Intelligence |
| FAC | Forward Air Controller |
| FANK | Forces Armées Nationales Khmères, the Cambodian Army from 1970 to 1975 |
| FAR | Forces Armées Royales, the Laotian Army |
| FARK | Forces Armées Royales Khmères, the Cambodian Army up to 1970 |
| FLIR | Forward Looking Infrared Radar |
| FSB | Fire Support Base |
| FULRO | Front Unifié de la Lutte des Races Opprimées |
| FUNK | Front Uni National de Kampuchea (National United Front of Kampuchea), the coalition between the Khmer Rouge and Prince Sihanouk, established in 1970 to fight the government of Lon Nol. |
| GP | General Purpose |
| GRUNK | Gouvernement Royal d'Union Nationale de Kampuchea, the coalition led nominally by Prince Sihanouk, and actually by the Khmer Rouge, that fought Lon Nol from 1970 to 1975. |

| | |
|---|---|
| GVN | Government of Vietnam (State of Vietnam, Republic of Vietnam) |
| H&I | Harassment and Interdiction |
| HES | Hamlet Evaluation System |
| HMAS | Her Majesty's Australian Ship |
| HUMINT | Human Intelligence |
| ICC | International Control Commission |
| ICCS | International Commission for Control and Supervision |
| ICEX | Infrastructure Intelligence Coordination and Exploitation (often written Intelligence Coordination and Exploitation *or* Infrastructure Coordination and Exploitation) |
| ICP | Indochinese Communist Party |
| INR | Bureau of Intelligence and Research (State Department) |
| IVS | International Voluntary Services |
| JCS | Joint Chiefs of Staff |
| JUSPAO | Joint U.S. Public Affairs Office |
| KIA | Killed in Action |
| KIA/BNR | Killed in Action/Body Not Recovered |
| KPRP | Khmer People's Revolutionary Party |
| LAW | Light Antitank Weapon |
| LBJ | Lyndon Baines Johnson |
| LBJ | Long Binh Jail |
| LDNN | Lien Doi Nguoi Nhai (Frogman Unit) |
| LLDB | Luc Luong Dac Biet (RVN Special Forces) |
| LOH | Light Observation Helicopter (pronounced "Loach") |
| LRP | Long-Range Patrol (pronounced "Lurp") |
| LRRP | Long-Range Reconnaissance Patrol (pronounced "Lurp") |
| LS | Lima Site |
| LST | Landing Ship, Tank |
| LVTP | Landing Vehicle Tracked, Personnel |
| LZ | Landing Zone |
| MAAG | Military Assistance Advisory Group |
| MACSOG | Initially Military Assistance Command, Special Operations Group; *later* Military Assistance Command, Studies and Observations Group (SOG) |
| MACV | Military Assistance Command, Vietnam |
| MAF | Marine Amphibious Force |
| MAP | Military Assistance Program |

| MEDCAP | Medical Civic Action Program |
| MEDEVAC | Medical Evacuation |
| MIA | Missing in Action |
| MIKE | Mobile Strike |
| MOS | Military Occupational Specialty |
| MP | Military Police |
| MPC | Military Payment Certificate |
| MR | Military Region |
| MSUG | Michigan State University Group |
| NCO | Non-commissioned Officer |
| NFLSV | National Front for the Liberation of South Vietnam (NLF) |
| NKP | Nakhon Phanom |
| NLF | National Liberation Front |
| NSA | National Security Agency |
| NSC | National Security Council |
| NVA | North Vietnamese Army (PAVN) |
| NVN | North Vietnam |
| OB | Order of Battle |
| OCO | Office of Civil Operations |
| OPLAN | Operations Plan |
| PA&E | Pacific Architects and Engineers |
| PAT | People's Action Team |
| PAVN | People's Army of Vietnam (DRV) |
| PBR | Patrol Boat, River |
| PCF | Patrol Craft, Fast (Swift Boat) |
| PEO | Programs Evaluation Office |
| PF | Popular Forces |
| PFIAB | President's Foreign Intelligence Advisory Board |
| PGM | Motor Gunboat |
| PHILCAG | Philippines Civic Action Group |
| PIOCC | Province Intelligence and Operations Coordinating Center |
| PL | Progressive Labor Party |
| PLAF | People's Liberation Armed Forces |
| POL | Petrol, Oil, and Lubricants |
| POW | Prisoner of War |
| PRC | People's Republic of China |
| PRG | Provisional Revolutionary Government of the Republic of South Vietnam |

| | |
|---|---|
| PRP | People's Revolutionary Party |
| PRU | Provincial Reconnaissance Units |
| PSDF | People's Self-Defense Force |
| PSYOPS | Psychological Operations |
| PT | Motor Torpedo Boat (Patrol Torpedo) |
| PTSD | Post-Traumatic Stress Disorder |
| PX | Post Exchange |
| RAAF | Royal Australian Air Force |
| RD | Revolutionary Development, *later* Rural Development |
| RF/PF | Regional Forces/Popular Forces |
| RLAF | Royal Lao Air Force |
| RLG | Royal Lao Government |
| RMK-BRJ | Raymond Morrison-Knudsen - Brown & Root, Jones |
| ROC | Republic of China |
| ROE | Rules of Engagement |
| ROK | Republic of Korea |
| ROTC | Reserve Officer Training Corps |
| RPG | *Ruchnoy Protivotankovy Granatomet* (light anti-tank grenade launcher) |
| R&R | Rest and Recuperation *or* Rest and Recreation |
| RVN | Republic of Vietnam |
| RVNAF | Republic of Vietnam Armed Forces |
| SAM | Surface-to-Air Missile |
| SAR | Search and Rescue |
| SAVA | Special Assistant for Vietnamese Affairs (CIA) |
| SDS | Students for a Democratic Society |
| SEAL | Sea, Air, Land (U.S. Navy special units) |
| SEATO | Southeast Asia Treaty Organization |
| SECDEF | Secretary of Defense |
| SF | Special Forces |
| SIGINT | Signals Intelligence |
| SITREP | Situation Report |
| SLAR | Side-Looking Airborne Radar |
| SMM | Saigon Military Mission |
| SOG | Special Operations Group, *later* Studies and Observations Group |
| SOP | Standard Operating Procedures |
| STD | Strategic Technical Directorate (RVN) |

| STRATA | Short-Term Roadwatch and Target Acquisition |
| SVN | South Vietnam |
| TACAN | Tactical Air Navigation |
| TAOR | Tactical Area of Operational Responsibility |
| TDY | Temporary Duty |
| TERM | Temporary Equipment Recovery Mission |
| UDT | Underwater Demolition Team |
| UN | United Nations |
| UPI | United Press International |
| U.S. | United States |
| USA | United States Army |
| USAF | United States Air Force |
| USARV | United States Army, Vietnam |
| USIA | United States Information Agency |
| USMC | United States Marine Corps |
| USN | United States Navy |
| USO | United Services Organization |
| USOM | United States Operations Mission |
| USSAG | United States Support Activity Group |
| USSR | Union of Soviet Socialist Republics |
| VC | Viet Cong |
| VCI | Viet Cong Infrastructure |
| VMC | Vietnam Moratorium Committee |
| VNA | Vietnamese National Army |
| VNAF | Vietnamese Air Force (RVN) |
| VNMC | Vietnamese Marine Corps (RVN) |
| VNN | Vietnamese Navy (RVN) |
| VVAW | Vietnam Veterans Against the War |
| WIA | Wounded in Action |
| WP | White Phosphorus |

Vietnam, Laos, and Cambodia

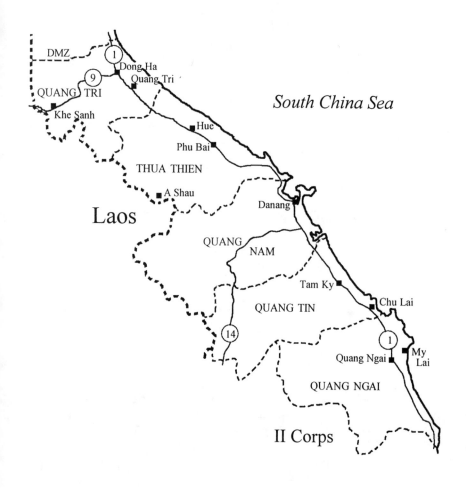

**I Corps**, as it existed from late 1964 onward. Quang Ngai province had been part of II Corps from 1962 to 1964.

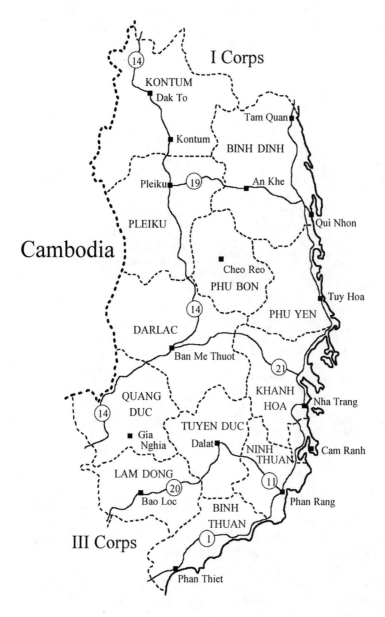

I Corps

14
KONTUM
Dak To

Tam Quan

Kontum

BINH DINH

Pleiku  19  An Khe

PLEIKU

Cambodia

Qui Nhon

Cheo Reo
PHU BON

14

Tuy Hoa

PHU YEN

DARLAC

Ban Me Thuot

21

QUANG
DUC

KHANH
HOA

Nha Trang

14

TUYEN DUC

Gia
Nghia  Dalat

NINH
THUAN

Cam Ranh

LAM DONG

20
Bao Loc

11

BINH
THUAN

Phan Rang

1

III Corps

Phan Thiet

**II Corps**, 1967 onward. Cam Ranh, before becoming a separate unit, had been part of Khanh Hoa province. The provinces from Darlac and Khanh Hoa southward had been part of III Corps from 1962 to 1964.

Cambodia

■ Bu Dop

Loc
Ninh■

Phuoc Binh/
■ Song Be (14)

■ An
Loc

PHUOC / LONG

II Corps

*War Zone*
*C*

BINH
LONG

TAY NINH

BINH [DUONG]

■ Tay
Ninh

Lai Khe■

*War Zone*
*D*

LONG
KHANH

(13)

(1)

Cu Chi ■

HAU NGHIA

Bien Hoa

BINH TUY

■ Xuan Loc

(1)

GIA
DINH

■Saigon

BIEN
HOA

LONG
AN (4)

*Rung*
*Sat*

PHUOC TUY

■ Ham Tan

IV Corps

■ Tan An

● Phuoc Le

Vung Tau

**III Corps**, from 1964 onward. Up to 1962, III Corps had extended much farther to the southwest than the borders shown, taking in the whole of the Mekong Delta. From late 1962 to late 1964, III Corps had extended much farther to the northeast than the borders shown.

Hau Nghia province had been created in 1963, from portions of Long An, Tay Ninh, and Binh Duong provinces. Long An, in turn, had been created in 1957, by the amalgamation of Tan An province with part of Cholon province.

**IV Corps**, mid-1960s onward. Bac Lieu had formerly been part of Ba Xuyen. Most of Chau Doc had formerly been part of An Giang; the western part of Chau Doc had been part of Kien Giang. Chuong Thien had been part of Phong Dinh. Sa Dec had been part of Vinh Long. Go Cong had been part of Dinh Tuong.

1 U.S. Marines walking along a dike between flooded rice fields.

2 Two soldiers of the 1st Cavalry Division (Airmobile) advance through elephant grass, Landing Zone X-Ray, Ia Drang Valley, November 1965.

**3** A marine firing a 7.62-mm M60 machine gun, Hue, 1968.

**4** A quad 50 (four .50-caliber machine guns) mounted on a truck.

5 A 155-mm towed howitzer.

6 This 175-mm self-propelled gun, with its longer barrel, had a greater range.

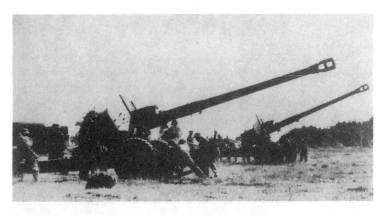

**7** A long-range PAVN weapon, the 122-mm field gun.

**8** An ARVN unit in Cambodia, 1970. *Right:* standard M-113 Armored Personnel Carrier. *Left foreground:* a variant, the M-557, used as a command vehicle.

**9** Marines running to board a UH-34 helicopter in 1965.

**10** A CH-47 Chinook hovers after delivering ammunition to Fire Support Base razor, Quang Tri province. 105-mm howitzers at bottom left.

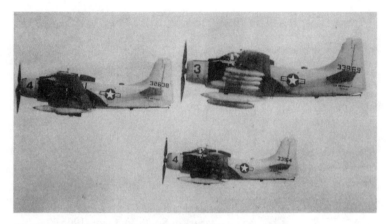

**11** Three A-1E Skyraiders over South Vietnam, 1965.

**12** The OV-10 Bronco, used by forward air controllers.

**13** A B-52 releases bombs on a target in South Vietnam, 1965.

**14** An F-4B Phantom II. The Phantom was the main Navy fighter in the war; it also flew bombing missions.

**15** A 500-pound bomb, dropped by an A-6 Intruder, hits a bridge in North Vietnam in April 1968. Note the craters near the road from previous air strikes.

**16** The Communists moved considerable loads by bicycle, on the Ho Chi Minh Trail and elsewhere.

**17** Soviet-made 122-mm rockets could be fired from simple, crude launchers.

## Photo Credits

1, 9: Jack Shulimson and Charles M. Johnson, *The Landing and the Buildup, 1965* (Washington, D.C.: History and Museums Division, Headquarters, U.S. Marine Corps, 1978), pp. 109, 26.

2: John M. Carland, *Combat Operations: Stemming the Tide, May 1965 to October 1966* (Washington, D.C.: Center of Military History, 2000), p. 121.

3: Jack Shulimson, *The Defining Year, 1968* (Washington, D.C.: History and Museums Division, Headquarters, U.S. Marine Corps, 1997), p. 203.

4, 6: Gary L. Telfer, Lane Rogers, and V. Keith Fleming, Jr., *Fighting the North Vietnamese, 1967* (Washington, D.C.: History and Museums Division, Headquarters, U.S. Marine Corps, 1984), pp. 222, 220.

5: Jack Shulimson, *An Expanding War, 1966* (Washington, D.C.: History and Museums Division, Headquarters, U.S. Marine Corps, 1982), p. 281.

7, 8: Joel D. Meyerson, *Images of a Lengthy War* (Washington, D.C.: Center of Military History, 1986), pp. 154, 200.

10: Charles R. Smith, *High Mobility and Stand-Down, 1969* (Washington, D.C.: History and Museums Division, Headquarters, U.S. Marine Corps, 1988), p. 69.

11, 12, 13: John Schlight, *The War in South Vietnam: The Years of the Offensive, 1965–1968* (Washington, D.C.: Office of Air Force History, 1988), pp. 47, 294, 83.

14, 17: Edward J. Marolda, *By Sea, Air, and Land: An Illustrated History of the U.S. Navy and the War in Southeast Asia* (Washington, D.C.: Naval Historical Center, 1994), pp. 117, 256.

15: Naval Historical Center, photograph NAH-002819.

16: John D. Bergen, *Military Communications: A Test for Technology* (Washington, D.C.: Center of Military History, 1986), p. 382.

# Chronology

## 1954

July 20–21     The Geneva Conference produced the Geneva Accords, ending the First Indochina War.

September 8     The Southeast Asia Treaty Organization (SEATO) was established.

September 10     Premier Ngo Dinh Diem attempted, unsuccessfully, to dismiss General Nguyen Van Hinh, chief of staff of the Vietnamese National Army.

October 9–10     The French handed over Hanoi to the People's Army of Vietnam (PAVN).

November 19     The withdrawal of PAVN troops from Laos was completed.

      General Nguyen Van Hinh left Vietnam; Ngo Dinh Diem acquired effective control of the Vietnamese National Army.

## 1955

March 29     Brief outbreak of shooting in Saigon between Diem's forces and those of the Binh Xuyen.

April 28–May 2     Diem fought and decisively defeated the Binh Xuyen forces in the Saigon area.

May 13     French forces withdrew from the city and port of Haiphong.

May 16     The last French forces withdrew from North Vietnam.

May 18     Deadline, under the Geneva Accords, for movements of military personnel and civilians between North and South Vietnam.

June 5     The Vietnamese National Army began a major offensive against the Hoa Hao in the Mekong Delta, which achieved quick success.

July 16     Ngo Dinh Diem declared his refusal to discuss preparations for the 1956 elections called for by the Geneva

## 1955 (cont.)

|  | Accords. |
|---|---|
| October 23 | Ngo Dinh Diem held a referendum, in which Bao Dai was deposed as chief of state. |
| October 26 | The State of Vietnam became the Republic of Vietnam. |

Mid-1955 to mid-1956: A radical land reform campaign (begun on a small scale late in 1953) spread to most of North Vietnam.

## 1956

| April 13 | Hoa Hao General Ba Cut was captured by government forces; he was executed in July. |
|---|---|
| July 20 | The date on which the Geneva Accords had called for national elections to be held in Vietnam. |
| August | Le Duan wrote "The Revolutionary Line in the South," arguing that Diem would have to be overthrown by revolution. |
| October 30–31 | Lao Dong Party leaders publicly repudiated the errors of land reform in North Vietnam. |
| November 2–14 | Catholics rioted in Quynh Luu district of Nghe An province, in North Vietnam. |

## 1957

| August 10 | Raid by Viet Cong forces on Minh Thanh, in Thu Dau Mot province. |
|---|---|
| September 18 | Raid by Viet Cong forces on the Trai Be lumbering camp, Bien Hoa province. |
| October | The Viet Cong established armed propaganda units in eastern and western Nam Bo, and in the Central Highlands. |
|  | Unit 250, a battalion-sized Viet Cong force, was established in War Zone D. |
| December 15 | Two Pathet Lao battalions went to the Plain of Jars to be integrated into the Royal Laotian Army. |

## 1958

| May 1 | The Bajaraka Movement was founded among the Montagnards. |
|---|---|
| August 10 | A Viet Cong enlarged company, C.1000, raided Dau Tieng, about 70 kilometers northwest of Saigon. |

# 1959

| | |
|---|---|
| January | The Cor tribe rebelled in Quang Ngai province. |
| January 12–21 | The 15th Plenum of the Lao Dong Party Central Committee decided to initiate a guerrilla war in South Vietnam. But dissemination and implementation of the decision did not occur until May. |
| May 6 | The Republic of Vietnam issued Law 10/59, creating special military tribunals which could issue death sentences. |
| May 18 | The 2d Pathet Lao Battalion retreated eastward from the Plain of Jars, evading absorption into the Royal Lao Army. |
| May 19 | Group 559 was established to reopen the Ho Chi Minh Trail. |
| July 8 | Two U.S. advisers were killed by a Viet Cong attack on their quarters at Bien Hoa. |
| July 23 | Premier Phoui Sananikone ordered the arrest of Pathet Lao leaders in Vientiane. |
| August 28 | Montagnards in Tra Bong district, in the western part of Quang Ngai province, rebelled under Communist leadership. |
| September 12 | The Democratic Republic of Vietnam (DRV) established Group 959, to provide military aid to the Pathet Lao forces in Laos. |
| December 31 | A right-wing group led by Phoumi Nosavan seized power in Laos. |

# 1960

| | |
|---|---|
| January | Guerrilla warfare erupted on a broad scale in South Vietnam. |
| January 17 | The Ben Tre uprising. |
| Night of January | 26: Three Viet Cong infantry companies and a sapper company overran the base of the 7th Regiment of the Army of the Republic of Vietnam (ARVN) 5th Division at Trang Sup, seven kilometers from Tay Ninh City. |
| March | The "Declaration of Former Resistance Fighters" called for the overthrow of Ngo Dinh Diem and his family. |
| April 30 | The "Caravelle Group" released a call, dated April 26, for reform in South Vietnam. |

## 1960 (cont.)

| | |
|---|---|
| May 24 | The Pathet Lao leaders imprisoned in Vientiane escaped. |
| August 9 | A coup led by Kong Le placed a neutralist government in power in Laos. |
| September 5–10 | The Lao Dong Party's Third Congress publicly endorsed the idea of an armed revolution against Ngo Dinh Diem in South Vietnam. |
| September 26 | The Pathet Lao seized power in Sam Neua, in northeast Laos. |
| October 20 | Attacks on government outposts along Route 14 north of Kontum began a major Viet Cong offensive in the Central Highlands. |
| November 11 | A coup led by Nguyen Chanh Thi almost succeeded in overthrowing Ngo Dinh Diem. |
| December 9–16 | Phoumi Nosavan's forces overthrew the neutralist government in Laos. |
| December 15 | A Soviet airlift of supplies and weapons for Pathet Lao and neutralist forces in Laos began. |
| December 20 | The National Liberation Front (NLF) was founded. |
| December 31 | There were approximately 900 U.S. military personnel in South Vietnam. |

## 1961

| | |
|---|---|
| January | An offensive by Pathet Lao and PAVN troops in Laos achieved substantial gains in the Plain of Jars and Xieng Khoang province. |
| January 20 | John F. Kennedy was inaugurated president of the United States. |

Late April or early May: PAVN forces took Tchepone, in southern Laos.

| | |
|---|---|
| May 3 | A cease-fire was signed in Laos, but combat did not cease. |
| May 11 | National Security Action Memorandum (NSAM) 52: President Kennedy declared it was U.S. policy to prevent the Communist domination of South Vietnam, and sent additional U.S. advisers. |
| May 16 | First session of the Geneva Conference on Laos. |

June 16–July 17: The Staley Mission to Vietnam. Dr. Eugene Staley recommended a substantial expansion of the ARVN.

| | |
|---|---|
| October 11 | Ngo Dinh Diem requested that the U.S. send combat |

# 1961 (cont.)

troops to South Vietnam.

President Kennedy ordered an air commando squadron to Vietnam for Project *Farm Gate*; it arrived in November.

October 18–November 2: The Taylor-Rostow Mission to Vietnam.

October
: The Central Intelligence Agency (CIA) approached Montagnard leaders to begin what became the Civilian Irregular Defense Groups (CIDG) program.

November 22
: President Kennedy approved NSAM 111, rejecting the Taylor-Rostow recommendation of U.S. ground combat troops, but sending additional advisers, helicopter units, etc.

December 11
: Two companies of U.S. Army H-21 helicopters arrived in Vietnam.

December 23
: The U.S. helicopters for the first time carried ARVN troops on a combat operation.

December 31
: There were approximately 3,200 U.S. military personnel in South Vietnam.

# 1962

February 8
: Military Assistance Command, Vietnam (MACV), was established.

February 27
: Two Vietnamese Air Force pilots bombed the Presidential Palace in Saigon.

March 22
: Operation *Sunrise*, establishing strategic hamlets in Binh Duong province, began.

April 15
: A U.S. Marine helicopter squadron arrived in Vietnam.

May 6
: Communist forces took Nam Tha, in northwest Laos.

May–October
: ARVN forces with M-113 armored personnel carriers, supported by U.S. helicopters and aircraft, inflicted serious casualties on Viet Cong forces in the northern Mekong Delta.

June 11
: Representatives of the Left, Right, and neutralists in Laos agreed to form the Second Coalition Government, headed by the neutralist Prince Souvanna Phouma.

July 23
: The Geneva Accords of 1962 declared Laos a neutral country, and called for the withdrawal of all outside military forces.

## 1962 (cont.)

September 14    The ship *Phuong Dong 1*, of Group 759, brought the first major shipment of munitions to reach South Vietnam from North Vietnam by sea.

On or about October 10: Ngo Dinh Diem gave Colonel Huynh Van Cao, commander of the ARVN 7th Infantry Division, a reprimand for being overly aggressive in combat.

December 31    There were approximately 11,300 U.S. military personnel in South Vietnam.

## 1963

January 2    The Battle of Ap Bac.

January 3    Viet Cong forces overran the Plei Mrong CIDG camp.

March 30    Combat broke out between neutralist and Pathet Lao forces in Laos.

April 19    The Pathet Lao took the airfield on the Plain of Jars from the neutralists.

May 8    Government troops fired on a crowd of Buddhist protesters in Hue.

June 11    Buddhist monk Thich Quang Duc committed public suicide in Saigon.

July 1    Operation *Switchback*, transferring the CIDG from CIA to military control, was completed.

August 21    Ngo Dinh Nhu's Special Forces raided Buddhist pagodas, arresting and beating many monks.

August 24    A State Department message instructed Ambassador Henry Cabot Lodge, in Saigon, to demand that President Diem dismiss his brother Nhu, and suggested that if Diem refused, the United States might have to turn against Diem.

September 1    Thich Tri Quang and two other radical Buddhist monks took refuge in the U.S. Embassy in Saigon.

October 5    Another monk committed suicide in Saigon; three newsmen photographing the event were beaten by police.

November 1    A military coup overthrew Ngo Dinh Diem. Diem and his brother Nhu escaped from the Presidential Palace and went into hiding.

November 2    Diem and Nhu surrendered to the forces that had carried out the coup, and were promptly killed.

# 1963 (cont.)

| | |
|---|---|
| November 22 | John F. Kennedy was assassinated; Lyndon B. Johnson became president of the United States. |
| December 15 | MACV and CIA together produced *OPLAN 34A*. |
| December | The Ninth Plenum of the Lao Dong Party Central Committee decided on a major intensification of the war in South Vietnam. It is not clear whether the Ninth Plenum decided to send PAVN units made up of North Vietnamese to South Vietnam. If this decision was made, it was not implemented quickly. |
| | Forces of Phoumi Nosavan and Vang Pao, working together, occupied the southern part of the Plain of Jars. They then attacked the northern part. |
| December 31 | There were approximately 16,300 U.S. military personnel in South Vietnam. |

# 1964

| | |
|---|---|
| January 16 | President Johnson approved a modified version of *OPLAN 34A*, less ambitious than the original. |
| January 24 | The Special Operations Group (SOG) was established. |
| January 30 | General Nguyen Khanh seized power in a bloodless coup in Saigon. |
| April 18 | A rightist coup overthrew Souvanna Phouma in Laos, but U.S. pressure put Souvanna back in office on April 23. |
| May 2 | The small U.S. aircraft carrier *Card* was sunk by sappers in Saigon. |
| Mid-May | A major Communist offensive in the Plain of Jars and nearby areas devastated Kong Le's neutralist forces. |
| Night of July 30–31: | An *OPLAN 34A* raid shelled the islands of Hon Me and Hon Ngu off the coast of North Vietnam. |
| July 31 | The U.S. destroyer *Maddox* began a *Desoto* Patrol along the coast of North Vietnam. |
| August 2 | Three DRV torpedo boats attacked the *Maddox* northeast of Hon Me (first Tonkin Gulf incident). |
| August 4 | The U.S. destroyers *Maddox* and *Turner Joy* mistakenly reported that they were under attack by DRV torpedo boats (second Tonkin Gulf incident). |
| August 5 | Operation *Pierce Arrow*: air strikes against targets along |

## 1964 (cont.)

|  | the coast of North Vietnam. |
|---|---|
| August 7 | The U.S. Congress passed the Tonkin Gulf Resolution. |

September 20–28: FULRO organized a rebellion by Montagnard troops in several CIDG units near Ban Me Thuot.

| November 1 | Viet Cong forces mortared Bien Hoa Air Base. |
|---|---|
| November 4 | Tran Van Huong took office as premier of the Republic of Vietnam. |
| November 22 | Police broke up a demonstration against Tran Van Huong in Saigon. Other demonstrations followed. Martial law was declared on November 26. |
| December 6 | A major Viet Cong offensive began in the An Lao Valley, Binh Dinh province. |
| December 14 | Operation *Barrel Roll*, U.S. bombing of Communist transportation lines in eastern Laos, began. |
| December 24 | The Viet Cong planted a bomb at the Brink Hotel (U.S. officers' quarters), in Saigon. |

December 28, 1964 to January 3, 1965: The 4th Vietnamese Marine Battalion and the 35th ARVN Ranger Battalion suffered devastating casualties in the Battle of Binh Gia.

| December 31 | There were about 23,300 U.S. military personnel in South Vietnam. |
|---|---|

## 1965

| January 27 | The Armed Forces Council deposed Prime Minister Tran Van Huong. |
|---|---|
| February 7 | Viet Cong attack on Pleiku. |
| February 7–8 | Operation *Flaming Dart*: air strikes against targets in the southern part of North Vietnam. |
| February 10 | A bomb planted at a U.S. billet at Qui Nhon killed 23 American and seven Vietnamese personnel. |
| February 11 | Operation *Flaming Dart II*. |
| February 13 | President Johnson approved Operation *Rolling Thunder*. But there were delays, and the first *Rolling Thunder* air strike was not flown until March 2. |
| February 16 | Phan Huy Quat was appointed Republic of Vietnam (RVN) premier, but General Nguyen Khanh as head of the Armed Forces Council held more real power. |
|  | A North Vietnamese trawler, delivering weapons and |

# 1965 (cont.)

|  |  |
|---|---|
|  | ammunition to Viet Cong forces, was sunk at Vung Ro. |
| February 19 | Four B-57 Canberra bombers conducted the first overt U.S. bombing mission in South Vietnam. |
| February 19 | General Lam Van Phat, encouraged by Colonel Pham Ngoc Thao, attempted a coup in Saigon. |
| February 20 | General Nguyen Khanh and the "Young Turks" defeated the attempted coup. |
| February 21 | The "Young Turks" deposed General Khanh as head of the Armed Forces Council. |
| March 8 | Two U.S. Marine Battalions landed at Danang, assigned to guard the Danang air base. |
| March 24 | The first anti-war "teach-in" occurred at the University of Michigan. |
| March 25–27 | The Lao Dong Party's 11th Plenum decided to try for a quick victory in the South, while preparing for the possibility of a major expansion of U.S. forces in South Vietnam. |
| April 2 | The first bombing of Ham Rong Bridge. |
| April 3–4 | The first direct combat between U.S. and DRV aircraft; MiGs shot down two U.S. F-105s on April 4 near the Ham Rong Bridge. |
| April 17 | The first really large demonstration against the war in Washington, D.C. |
| May 3–12 | The 173d Airborne Brigade arrived in Vietnam, initially assigned primarily to guard Vung Tau on the coast, and the Bien Hoa Air Base. This was the first major U.S. Army ground combat unit in Vietnam. |
| May 10–11 | Song Be, capital of Phuoc Long province, was overrun by Viet Cong forces. |
| May 13 | U.S. bombing of North Vietnam was halted, without public announcement. |
| May 18 | U.S. bombing of North Vietnam resumed. |
| June 8 | The United States announced that General William Westmoreland had been authorized to commit U.S. troops to combat under certain circumstances. |
| June 12 | Phan Huy Quat resigned as RVN premier. |
| June 17 | The first two MiGs were shot down by U.S. aircraft |

# 1965 (cont.)

|  |  |
|---|---|
| | over North Vietnam. |
| June 18 | The first B-52 strike in Vietnam was flown, hitting targets in War Zone D northeast of Saigon. |
| June 19 | Nguyen Cao Ky became RVN premier, and Nguyen Van Thieu became chief of state. |
| June 26–30 | The 173d Airborne Brigade, an Australian battalion, and RVN forces conducted a joint operation northwest of Saigon, going into War Zone D. |
| July 24 | First U.S. jet shot down by a surface-to-air missile in North Vietnam. |
| July 26 | President Lyndon Johnson decided not to mobilize the reserves, or declare a national emergency, to provide manpower for the growing U.S. combat role in Vietnam. |
| July 28 | President Johnson announced that the number of American military personnel in South Vietnam would be increased from 75,000 to 125,000. |
| August 18–24 | U.S. Marine forces attacked a Viet Cong force along the coast of Quang Ngai province in Operation *Starlite*. |
| August 27 | The first 1,000 men of the 1st Cavalry Division (Airmobile) arrived at An Khe. The remainder of the division arrived in September. |
| September 2 | The Viet Cong 9th Division was formed in Nam Bo, and the 3d Division in Military Region 5. |
| October 19 | PAVN forces began an unsuccessful attack on Plei Me, southwest of Pleiku in the Central Highlands. |
| October 23 | The 1st Cavalry Division began Operation *Silver Bayonet* in Pleiku province. |
| November 14–18: | *Silver Bayonet* led to major battles in the Ia Drang Valley, at Landing Zones X-Ray and Albany. |
| December 8 | The A Luoi and Ta Bat Special Forces camps, in the A Shau Valley, were abandoned. |
| December 24 | U.S. bombing of North Vietnam was halted; the halt lasted 37 days. |
| December 31 | There were about 184,300 U.S. military personnel in South Vietnam. |

# 1966

January 7–14   Operation *Crimp*, an attack on Communist forces in the Cu Chi area, particularly the Ho Bo Woods.

January 24 to March 6: Operation *Masher* (name later changed to *White Wing*) in Binh Dinh province.

January 28 to February 9: Operation *Double Eagle* near the coast in the southern part of Quang Ngai province.

January 31   U.S. bombing of North Vietnam resumed.

February 19 to March 1: Operation *Double Eagle II* about 55 kilometers southeast of Danang, near Tam Ky in Quang Tin province.

March 4–7   Operation *Utah* south of Chu Lai.

March 10   The A Shau Special Forces camp, the last U.S. position in the A Shau Valley, was overrun by PAVN forces in a bloody battle.

General Nguyen Chanh Thi was dismissed as ARVN commander of I Corps. This triggered a major uprising by Buddhists, centered in Danang and Hue, lasting until June.

March 20–25   Operation *Texas* south of Chu Lai.

March 26 to April 6: Operation *Jackstay* in the Rung Sat.

April 24 to May 17: The U.S. 1st Infantry Division went into War Zone C, in Tay Ninh province, in Operation *Birmingham*.

April 12   The first B-52 raid on North Vietnam hit the Mu Gia Pass.

June 2 to July 13: The U.S. 1st Infantry Division and the ARVN 5th Division conducted Operation *El Paso II* on the eastern edge of War Zone C.

June 3–13   There was heavy fighting between the 1st Brigade of the 101st Airborne Division and the PAVN 24th Regiment in Kontum province, in Operation *Hawthorne*.

June 7–30   Operation *Liberty*, a pacification sweep and clear by the 3d Marine Division, in the Danang area.

June 18–27   U.S. Marines landed on the coast of Phu Yen province, II Corps, in Operation *Deckhouse I*. This was coordinated with Operation *Nathan Hale*, involving troops of the U.S. 101st Airborne Division and 1st Cavalry Division, which began in the same area on June 20.

# 1966 (cont.)

June 29        The United States bombed fuel storage facilities in the Hanoi and Haiphong areas.  This was the first time targets within five nautical miles of the center of Hanoi had been bombed.

June           The PAVN established the Route 9–Northern Quang Tri Front and brought in main-force units from North Vietnam, to pull the Americans out into the jungle and reduce the U.S. threat in the Tri-Thien lowlands and in Military Region 5.

July 7 to August 2: Operation *Hastings* near the Demilitarized Zone, in Quang Tri province.

August 3, 1966 to January 31, 1967: Operation *Prairie*, just south of the Demilitarized Zone in Quang Tri province.

September 14   Operation *Attleboro* began, initially on a small scale, in Tay Ninh province.  It expanded dramatically before ending on November 24.

September      Elements of the 1st Cavalry Division began Operation *Thayer* in Binh Dinh province.

October 2–24   The 1st Cavalry Division interrupted *Thayer* to conduct an impromptu operation, *Irving*, in Binh Dinh.

October 25     The 1st Cavalry Division began Operation *Thayer II* in Binh Dinh; it lasted until February 12, 1967.

December 31    There were about 385,300 U.S. military personnel in South Vietnam.

# 1967

January 2      The United States set a trap for North Vietnamese fighter aircraft, Operation *Bolo*.

January 8–26   Operation *Cedar Falls* in the Iron Triangle north of Saigon.

February 11    The 1st Cavalry Division began Operation *Pershing* in Binh Dinh province; it lasted to January 19, 1968.

February 22 to May 14: Operation *Junction City*, in War Zone C, northern Tay Ninh province.  This was the largest operation of the war so far, involving 22 U.S. and four ARVN battalions.

February 24 or 25: U.S. artillery in South Vietnam for the first time shelled North Vietnam.

# 1967 (cont.)

February 27   U.S. aircraft dropped mines into some rivers and minor harbors in North Vietnam.

March 20   For the first time, PAVN heavy artillery in Vinh Linh shelled U.S. positions south of the Demilitarized Zone.

April 24 to May 5: The "Hill Fights" around Khe Sanh.

April 24   First U.S. air strikes against airfields used by MiGs in northern North Vietnam.

May 4   Lang Vei CIDG camp was heavily damaged by a PAVN attack.

June 2   A Soviet freighter, the *Turkestan*, was hit during an air strike on the minor North Vietnamese port of Cam Pha.

August 9–29   Hearings before the Preparedness Investigating Subcommittee of the Senate Armed Services Committee gave a forum for senior military leaders to protest restrictions on the bombing of North Vietnam.

August 11   U.S. aircraft bombed the Doumer Bridge in Hanoi.

September 3   Nguyen Van Thieu was elected president of the Republic of Vietnam.

October 21   A peaceful anti-war rally of about 50,000 people in Washington, D.C., was followed by a march on the Pentagon that led to considerable violence.

November 3–22   Heavy fighting between U.S. and PAVN troops around Dak To, in northwestern II Corps.

December   The U.S. 25th Infantry Division began Operation *Yellowstone* in War Zone C.

December 31   There were about 485,600 U.S. military personnel in South Vietnam.

# 1968

Night of January 20 to morning of January 21: attacks began on Khe Sanh and on U.S. positions along Route 9.

January 22   Operation *Niagara*, massive U.S. bombing of PAVN forces around Khe Sanh, began.

January 24   PT-76 light tanks attacked Royal Lao Army troops on Route 9 in Laos west of Lang Vei, in the first known combat action by PAVN armored vehicles.

January 30   The first wave (premature attacks) of the Tet Offensive began shortly after midnight.

# 1968 (cont.)

| | |
|---|---|
| January 31 | The main wave of the Tet Offensive began shortly after midnight. |
| February 7 | PAVN forces with PT-76 light tanks overran Lang Vei. |
| February 25–26 | The last Communist troops were cleared from Hue. |
| February 28 | General Earle Wheeler reported to President Johnson that an additional 206,000 troops were needed for Vietnam. |
| March 16 | The My Lai Massacre. |
| March 31 | President Johnson announced that he would not run for re-election, and that the United States would stop bombing the northern part of North Vietnam in an effort to get peace talks started. |
| April 1–15 | Operation *Pegasus* reopened Route 9 to Khe Sanh. |
| April 3 | The DRV announced its willingness to negotiate. Martin Luther King Jr. was assassinated. |
| April 19 to May 17: | Operation *Delaware*, a U.S. and ARVN raid into the A Shau Valley. The ARVN component was called *Lam Son 216*. |
| April 24 | The Lao Dong Party Politburo met to assess the results of Tet, and decided to continue pushing the offensive. |
| May 4 | The second phase of the 1968 General Offensive began; again there were heavy attacks against Saigon. |
| May 13 | Preliminary peace talks began in Paris. |
| May 19 | Viet Cong rockets struck Saigon. |
| May | 2,169 U.S. military personnel were killed by enemy action, the highest for any single month of the war. |
| August | The Politburo met and decided to carry out a third phase of the General Offensive; this lasted from August 17 to September 30. |
| August 4–19 | Operation *Somerset Plain*, a U.S. and ARVN raid into the A Shau Valley. |
| August 26–29 | The Democratic Party's national convention in Chicago was marred by conflicts over the war, both in the streets and in the convention hall. |
| October 31 | The United States announced a total halt to the bombing and shelling of North Vietnam. |
| November 2 | Operation *Search Turn* began in Kien Giang province; |

## 1968 (cont.)

|  |  |
|---|---|
|  | this was the first of the *SEALORDS* barrier campaigns. |
| December 1 | The U.S. 9th Infantry Division began Operation *Speedy Express* in the Mekong Delta. |
| December 31 | There were about 536,100 U.S. military personnel in South Vietnam. |

## 1969

| January 20 | Richard Nixon was inaugurated president of the United States. |
|---|---|
| January 25 | First plenary session of the Paris peace talks. |
| March 1 | Operation *Massachusetts Striker*, aimed at the southern and central parts of the A Shau Valley, began. |
| March 17 | The U.S. 11th Armored Cavalry began Operation *Atlas Wedge* against troops of the PAVN 7th Division in the Michelin Rubber Plantation, north of Saigon. |
| April | The number of U.S. military personnel in South Vietnam peaked at about 543,000. |
| May 8 | At the Paris peace talks, the National Liberation Front (NLF) presented a 10-point program for resolving the war. |
| May 9 | The RVN announced it was willing to discuss at least three of the NLF's 10 points. |
| May 10 | U.S. and ARVN troops inserted into the northern A Shau Valley in Operation *Apache Snow*. They began attacking "Hamburger Hill" (Dong Ap Bia) on May 11, and finally took it on May 20. |
| May 14 | President Nixon proposed simultaneous phased withdrawal from South Vietnam of U.S. and PAVN troops. |
| June 8 | Nixon met with Thieu on Midway Island, then announced 25,000 U.S. troops would be withdrawn from Vietnam by August 31. |
| June 10 | The formation of the Provisional Revolutionary Government of the Republic of South Vietnam (PRG) was announced. |
| June 18–21 | Students for a Democratic Society, which had been the leading student anti-war organization, was destroyed by factional infighting at its last national convention. |
| June 28 | Communist forces won full control of the Plain of Jars. |

# 1969 (cont.)

| August | Hmong, Thai, and Royal Laotian Army forces regained the Plain of Jars. |
| September 2 | Ho Chi Minh died. |
| October 15 | Vietnam Moratorium Day: anti-war demonstrations occurred in many towns. |
| November 13 | The story of the My Lai Massacre (March 16, 1968) appeared in major American newspapers. |
| November 15 | A huge anti-war demonstration in Washington, D.C., and a large one in San Francisco. |
| December 31 | About 475,200 U.S. military personnel remained in South Vietnam. |

# 1970

| February 10–27 | PAVN and Pathet Lao forces launched a major offensive, and took the Plain of Jars. |
| March 18 | Prince Norodom Sihanouk of Cambodia was overthrown in a coup led by General Lon Nol. |
| March 20 | ARVN ground forces began small incursions into Cambodia. |
| April | Fire Support Base Ripcord was established in Thua Thien province, in the expectation that it would be used as a base for operations into the Da Krong and A Shau Valleys. |
| April 23 | The Republic of Vietnam, with the approval of the United States, sent three planeloads of weapons to Cambodia for Lon Nol's forces. |

April 28 to May 1: Communist forces took the town of Attopeu and the surrounding area, in southern Laos.

| April 30 | ARVN ground forces began a much larger incursion into the "Parrot's Beak" area of Cambodia. |
| May 1 | U.S. ground forces began a major incursion into the "Fishhook" area of Cambodia. There were quick demonstrations of protest in the United States. |
| May 4 | National Guardsmen killed four students during anti-war protests at Kent State University, in Kent, Ohio. |
| May 9 | Large anti-war demonstration in Washington, D.C. |
| May 24 | Operation *Freedom Deal*, a campaign of bombing directed against targets in eastern Cambodia, began. |

# 1970 (cont.)

June 24  The Senate voted to repeal the Tonkin Gulf Resolution.

July 22–23  Fire Support Base Ripcord in western Thua Thien province, threatened by strong PAVN forces, was abandoned.

November 21  An unsuccessful effort to rescue U.S. prisoners of war from Son Tay, in North Vietnam.

December 22  Both houses of Congress passed a foreign aid bill containing a Cooper-Church amendment forbidding U.S. ground troops or military advisers in Cambodia.

December 29  Both houses of Congress passed a defense appropriations bill that included a Cooper-Church amendment forbidding commitment of U.S. ground troops in Laos or Thailand.

December 31  About 334,600 U.S. military personnel remained in South Vietnam.

# 1971

January 30  Operation *Dewey Canyon II*, the U.S. preliminary to *Lam Son 719* (the ARVN drive into Laos), began.

February 8  ARVN troops crossed the border into Laos, on the ground and by helicopter, in Operation *Lam Son 719*.

February 13  Communist forces attacked Long Cheng, Vang Pao's base in Laos.

March 31  Lieutenant William Calley was sentenced to life imprisonment for the My Lai Massacre.

May 2–5  Anti-war demonstrations in Washington, D.C., led to more than 12,000 arrests.

May 15 to June 11: Communist forces established control of the Bolovens Plateau in southern Laos.

June 13  *The New York Times* began publication of the Pentagon Papers.

July 1  The NLF presented, in Paris, a seven-point peace proposal.

July  An offensive by Vang Pao's forces, with substantial Thai support, took much of the Plain of Jars.

August 17  The Cambodian Army began Operation *Chenla 2*, going north from Phnom Penh to reopen Route 6 to Kompong Thom. By December the operation was failing disastrously.

# 1971 (cont.)

| | |
|---|---|
| August 20 | Charging fraud, Duong Van Minh withdrew from the RVN presidential race, leaving Nguyen Van Thieu un-opposed. |
| October 3 | Nguyen Van Thieu won re-election as president of the Republic of Vietnam. |
| October 8 | The U.S. 101st Airborne Division ended Operation *Jefferson Glenn* in Thua Thien province, the last major offensive operation involving U.S. ground troops. |
| October 26 | Anti-war demonstrations by the "Mayday Tribe" in Washington, D.C.; over 300 were arrested. |
| December 8 | The last Australian combat troops withdrew from Viet-nam. |
| December 18–20 | A major Communist offensive in the Plain of Jars area. |
| December 26–30 | Operation *Proud Deep Alpha*: more than 1,000 sorties against North Vietnam. |
| December 31 | About 158,120 U.S. military personnel remained in South Vietnam. |

# 1972

| | |
|---|---|
| January 13 | President Nixon announced that the number of U.S. military personnel in Vietnam would be cut to 69,000 by May 1. |
| February 21 | President Nixon began his visit to the People's Repub-lic of China. |
| March 30 | PAVN forces began the Easter Offensive with attacks from the Demilitarized Zone (DMZ) into northern Quang Tri province. |
| April 2 | RVN forces abandoned the northern part of Quang Tri. |
| April 4 | The United States sent more B-52s to Southeast Asia. |
| April 6 | The United States initiated Operation *Freedom Train*, a systematic bombing campaign against North Vietnam. |
| April 8 | Communist forces besieged An Loc, in northern III Corps. |
| April 16 | The United States bombed the Hanoi-Haiphong area. |
| April 22 | Peace Action Day: substantial anti-war demonstrations in New York, San Francisco, Los Angeles, and other locations. |
| April 23 | PAVN forces used Sagger wire-guided anti-tank mis- |

**1972 (cont.)**

|            | siles for the first time in South Vietnam. |
|------------|--------------------------------------------|

April 24 PAVN forces took Dak To and nearby Tan Canh.

April 28 PAVN forces took Dong Ha, in Quang Tri province.

May 1 RVN troops abandoned Quang Tri City.

May 2 For the first time, a helicopter was shot down in South Vietnam by a Strela shoulder-launched missile.

May 8 President Nixon announced that the United States was mining North Vietnam's harbors. The actual mining began at the moment Nixon spoke, but due to the time zone difference between Vietnam and the United States, the date the mining began was May 9.

May 14 PAVN troops began an attack on Kontum, which very nearly succeeded on May 25–27.

June 28 The RVN launched a counterattack into Quang Tri province.

July 24 United Nations Secretary General Kurt Waldheim appealed to the United States to stop bombing dikes in North Vietnam. The United States denied bombing dikes.

August 12 The 3/21 Infantry, the last U.S. ground combat battalion in Vietnam, was deactivated.

September 15 RVN troops completed the recapture of Quang Tri City.

September 30 The last U.S. Air Force fighter-bomber squadron based in Vietnam withdrew. (Squadrons based in Thailand continued to bomb targets in Vietnam.)

October 11 Henry Kissinger and Le Duc Tho agreed on the outline of a peace agreement, and agreed on October 30 as the date for the formal signing of the agreement.

October 13 Ben Het fell to PAVN forces.

October 18–23 In discussions with Kissinger, President Thieu rejected the draft peace agreement.

October 20 The DRV accepted the American position on those portions of the draft peace agreement which had still been in dispute between the DRV and the United States

October 22 President Nixon ordered a halt to bombing and shelling north of the 20th parallel.

October 26 Kissinger publicly announced "Peace is at hand."

## 1972 (cont.)

| | |
|---|---|
| November 7 | Nixon was re-elected president. |
| November 20 | Kissinger asked Le Duc Tho for massive changes in the October draft peace agreement. |
| November 22 | For the first time, a B-52 was downed by a surface-to-air missile. |
| December 18–29 | Operation *Linebacker II*, heavy bombing of the northern part of North Vietnam. |
| December 21 | The DRV and PRG delegations walked out of the Paris peace talks in protest against *Linebacker II*. |
| December 28 | Nguyen Van Thieu issued a decree abolishing most political parties in South Vietnam. |
| December 31 | About 24,000 U.S. military personnel remained in South Vietnam. |

## 1973

| | |
|---|---|
| January 4 | Peace talks resumed in Paris. |
| January 8 | Talks between Le Duc Tho and Kissinger resumed in Paris. |
| January 12–13 | Kissinger and Tho reached essential agreement in Paris. |
| January 15 | The United States announced a halt to all bombing and shelling of North Vietnam. |
| January 27 | U.S., DRV, RVN, and PRG representatives signed the Paris Peace Agreement. |
| January 28 | The cease-fire was supposed to take effect at 8:00 a.m. Saigon time. U.S. participation in combat ended on schedule; combat among the Vietnamese continued. |
| February 21 | An "Agreement to Restore Peace and Achieve National Conciliation in Laos" was signed in Vientiane. |
| February 22 | Systematic U.S. bombing of Laos ended. |
| March 29 | The withdrawal of U.S. military forces from South Vietnam was officially completed, and MACV was replaced by the Defense Attaché Office (DAO). The DAO had 50 U.S. military personnel; about 150 U.S. Marines also remained in South Vietnam as security guards for the U.S. Embassy and consulates in Bien Hoa, Nha Trang, and Danang. |
| April 16 | The last U.S. bombing mission in Laos. |

## 1973 (cont.)

June 13        U.S., DRV, RVN, and PRG representatives signed an agreement on implementing the Paris agreement.

August 15      U.S. bombing of Cambodia was halted.

October 16     The Nobel Committee announced that it had awarded the Nobel Prize for Peace jointly to Henry Kissinger and Le Duc Tho.

## 1974

August 6       The U.S. House of Representatives voted to set the level of U.S. military aid for South Vietnam for fiscal year 1975 (which had begun July 1) at $700 million, instead of the $1 billion requested by President Nixon.

August 9       Richard Nixon resigned, and Gerald Ford became president of the United States.

September 8    The People's Anti-Corruption Movement, founded in August by right-wing Catholic priest Tran Huu Thanh, issued its first major public statement, denouncing the government as massively corrupt, and making specific accusations of corruption against several members of President Thieu's family.

September 30 to October 8: The Lao Dong Party Politburo met and decided that the Communist conquest of South Vietnam could be completed during 1976. The main focus of offensive actions during 1975 was to be the Central Highlands.

October        There were demonstrations against government corruption in Saigon.

October 30     President Thieu, in an effort to conciliate the anti-corruption movement, dismissed three of his four corps commanders.

December 13    Major Communist attacks on government positions began in Phuoc Long province, northern III Corps.

December 18, 1974 to January 8, 1975: The Lao Dong Party Politburo, meeting with other leaders, reaffirmed the previous plan to finish the war in 1976, but decided also to draw up plans for the possibility that the ARVN might weaken sufficiently to allow completion of the war during 1975.

# 1975

| | |
|---|---|
| January 6 | Communist forces won full control of Phuoc Long province. This was the first time the ARVN had permanently lost a province in South Vietnam. |
| | Communist forces took the peak of Nui Ba Den, in Tay Ninh province. |
| January 27 | The last convoy of cargo boats successfully to reach Phnom Penh from Vietnam. |
| January 28 | President Ford asked the Congress to increase the level of U.S. military aid for South Vietnam, during the current fiscal year, from $700 million to $1 billion. |
| March 10 | The PAVN began a major attack against Ban Me Thuot, in the Central Highlands. |
| March 12 | PAVN forces took Ban Me Thuot. |
| March 14 | President Thieu ordered that ARVN forces in Pleiku and Kontum provinces retreat to the seacoast. |
| March 17–19 | The ARVN Airborne Division was moved from I Corps south to the Saigon area, and RVN Marines were pulled out of Quang Tri province. |
| March 18 | The Lao Dong Party Politburo decided to complete the conquest of South Vietnam during 1975. |

Night of March 19–20: PAVN forces took Quang Tri City.

| | |
|---|---|
| March 22 | Gia Nghia, capital of Quang Duc province in southwestern II Corps, fell to Communist forces. |
| March 24 | The province capitals of Quang Ngai and Quang Tin, the two southernmost provinces of I Corps, fell to Communist forces. |
| March 26 | Communist forces occupied Hue and Chu Lai. |
| March 30 | Communist forces occupied Danang. |
| March 31 | The Lao Dong Party Politburo decided to attempt to take Saigon by the end of April. |
| April 1 | Communist forces occupied Qui Nhon, capital of Binh Dinh. ARVN forces abandoned Nha Trang. |
| | Lon Nol left Cambodia. |
| April 2 | Communist forces occupied Nha Trang. |
| April 3 | Communist forces occupied Cam Ranh. |
| April 4 | Operation *Eagle Pull* began, evacuating Americans and some people of other nationalities from Phnom Penh. |

# 1975 (cont.)

| | |
|---|---|
| April 9–20 | Battle of Xuan Loc. |
| April 10 | President Ford asked Congress for $722 million additional aid for Saigon. |
| April 12 | The last stage of Operation *Eagle Pull*: helicopters evacuated the remaining Americans, and some people of other nationalities, from Phnom Penh. |
| April 17 | Khmer Rouge forces occupied Phnom Penh in the morning. In the afternoon, they began to expel from the city its entire population; the city was emptied within a few days. |
| April 21 | President Nguyen Van Thieu resigned; Vice President Tran Van Huong succeeded him. |
| April 27 | The RVN National Assembly voted to make General Duong Van Minh president; Minh took office April 28. |
| April 28 | The Communists bombed Tan Son Nhut airport, using captured American-made A-37 light attack aircraft. |
| Night of April 28–29: | PAVN bombardment of Tan Son Nhut airport ended landings by fixed-wing aircraft. |
| April 29–30 | Operation *Frequent Wind*: helicopter evacuation of Americans, and a large number of Vietnamese, from Saigon. |
| April 29 | The last U.S. military deaths in the Vietnam War: two Marines were killed in the PAVN bombardment of Tan Son Nhut Air Base, and two officers were killed when their helicopter, participating in the evacuation, crashed into the sea near an aircraft carrier off the coast. |
| April 30 | Communist forces entered Saigon, and Duong Van Minh's government surrendered. |
| May 12 | An American container ship, SS *Mayaguez*, was seized by a Khmer Rouge gunboat. |
| May 15 | The crew of the *Mayaguez* were released from Kompong Som. Eighteen U.S. Air Force and Marine personnel died in a rescue effort at Koh Tang Island, where the United States had mistakenly believed the crew was being held. |
| May 16 | The U.S. government extended to South Vietnam the embargo on U.S. trade that had long been in effect for North Vietnam. |

## 1975 (cont.)

December 3        The Pathet Lao formally proclaimed the People's Democratic Republic of Laos.

## 1976

April 28          The U.S. Congress passed a bill that would temporarily have lifted the embargo on U.S. trade with Vietnam, but President Ford vetoed this bill on May 7.

July 2            North and South Vietnam were formally joined to become the Socialist Republic of Vietnam.

November 15       The United Nations Security Council voted 14-1 to admit Vietnam to the United Nations, but the one vote against was a United States veto that blocked the measure.

## 1977

September 20      Vietnam was admitted to the United Nations.

## 1978

December 25       Vietnam invaded Cambodia.

## 1979

January 7         Vietnamese forces took Phnom Penh. They installed in power a government headed by Heng Samrin.

February 17       China invaded Vietnam; Chinese forces withdrew in March.

## 1982

June 22           Cambodian leaders in exile agreed to form the Coalition Government of Democratic Kampuchea. Norodom Sihanouk became president. Khieu Samphan of the Khmer Rouge (the strongest guerrilla resistance against the Vietnamese-backed government) became vice president. Son Sann, head of a weaker non-Communist guerrilla force, became prime minister.

## 1985

January 14        Hun Sen became prime minister of the Vietnamese-backed government in Cambodia.

August 22         Vietnam announced that all Vietnamese troops would

## 1985 (cont.)

be withdrawn from Cambodia by the end of 1990.

November 19–December 4: Personnel of the United States and the Socialist Republic of Vietnam for the first time conducted a joint excavation of the site where a U.S. plane had crashed during the war, looking for remains.

## 1986

December 15–18 The Sixth Congress of the Communist Party of Vietnam made Nguyen Van Linh general secretary of the party, and began the policy of *Doi moi* (Renovation), allowing more private enterprise.

## 1989

September 26 Vietnamese troops withdrew from Cambodia.

## 1991

October 23 The contending Cambodian factions, and 18 foreign governments, signed in Paris an agreement to make peace in Cambodia. A United Nations peacekeeping force was to supervise Cambodia until free elections were held in 1993.

November 14 Norodom Sihanouk returned to Cambodia; he became president of Cambodia on November 20.

## 1993

May 28 Voting ended in Cambodian national elections. Prince Norodom Ranariddh's United National Front for an Independent, Neutral, Peaceful Cambodia (Funcinpec) got 45.5 percent of the vote. Hun Sen's Cambodian People's Party got 38.2 percent.

June 18 Ranariddh and Hun Sen agreed to share power equally in the Cambodian government.

October 5 Vietnam became eligible for World Bank and Asian Development Bank loans.

## 1994

February 3 The U.S. economic embargo against Vietnam, already somewhat looser than it had been in the 1980s, was ended.

## 1995

| | |
|---|---|
| January 28 | The United States and Vietnam established low-level diplomatic relations, with "liaison offices" in one another's capitals. |
| July 11 | Full diplomatic relations were established between the United States and Vietnam. |
| July 28 | Vietnam joined the Association of Southeast Asian Nations (ASEAN). |

## 1997

| | |
|---|---|
| July 6 | Hun Sen ousted his co-premier, Prince Norodom Ranariddh, from the Cambodian government. |
| August 15 | The Cambodian government reached an agreement with Khmer Rouge leader Ieng Sary. |
| September 15 | Norodom Sihanouk announced an amnesty for Ieng Sary and his followers. By early November, large numbers of Khmer Rouge troops were coming over to the government side. |

## 2000

| | |
|---|---|
| March 13–15 | William Cohen became the first U.S. secretary of defense to visit Vietnam since the end of the Vietnam War. |
| July 13 | The United States and Vietnam signed a bilateral trade agreement, intended to expand trade and investment. The agreement had come close to signature in 1999, but had been blocked by Vietnamese officials who felt that opening the Vietnamese economy to foreign penetration would threaten state-owned enterprises. |
| November 16–19: | William Clinton became the first U.S. president to visit Vietnam since the end of the Vietnam War. |

## 2001

| | |
|---|---|
| February 2 | Montagnards in Pleiku protested Vietnamese encroachment on Montagnard lands, especially for the creation of coffee plantations. |
| February 6 | Larger Montagnard protests in Buon Ma Thuot (Ban Me Thuot). |
| December 10 | The trade agreement between Vietnam and the United States, which had been ratified by the United States on October 16 and by Vietnam on November 28, went into effect. |

## 2001 (cont.)

December 31    Vietnam's exports to the United States for 2001 were U.S. $1,053 million. Vietnam's imports from the United States were $460 million.

## 2002

February 8    The United Nations broke off negotiations with the government of Cambodia over the establishment of an international tribunal to try former leaders of the Khmer Rouge for genocide. A UN spokesman said that the UN had failed to obtain adequate guarantees of the independence, impartiality, and objectivity of the tribunal.

December 31    Vietnam's exports to the United States for 2002 were $2,395 million. Vietnam's imports from the United States were $580 million.

## 2003

January 6    The United Nations and the government of Cambodia resumed negotiations over establishment of an international tribunal.

November 9    General Pham Van Tra began the first official visit to the United States by a minister of defense of the Socialist Republic of Vietnam.

November 19:    The guided missile frigate USS *Vandegrift* arrived in Ho Chi Minh City, for the first visit to Vietnam by a U.S. warship since the end of the Vietnam War.

## 2004

October 4    The Cambodian parliament ratified an agreement with the United Nations for the establishment of an international tribunal to try former leaders of the Khmer Rouge.

October 7    Norodom Sihanouk announced his abdication as king of Cambodia.

# Introduction

Many wars are confusing while they are going on, but few remain so puzzling, even when one has the advantages of hindsight, as Vietnam. When United States Marine battalions landed at Danang in 1965, they represented the richest, strongest, and most technologically sophisticated power in the world. Most Americans expected a comparatively quick victory over poorly equipped guerrillas. What followed was a bloody international conflict that devastated Vietnam and neighboring Cambodia and Laos, making these small, poor countries centers of world attention. It seriously affected American culture and the image of the United States both among its own people and abroad. It ended finally, in 1975, with Communist victory. There is little agreement today even about what happened, much less why it happened.

## Overview of the War

The Vietnam War or Second Indochina War, which began in 1959 and 1960 with small guerrilla struggles in South Vietnam and Laos, was in many ways an outgrowth of the First Indochina War, which had ended in 1954.

Vietnam stretches a thousand miles southward from the Chinese border along the east coast of the Southeast Asian peninsula, but it is narrow from east to west; overall the country is about the size of Norway. Vietnam and its smaller neighbors to the west, Laos and Cambodia, were conquered by France in the late 19th century, and combined to form French Indochina. Following World War II, a struggle broke out pitting the French against the Viet Minh, a Vietnamese nationalist movement under Communist leadership. The fighting spread to some extent into Laos and Cambodia. In the later stages of this war, from 1950 to 1954, the Viet Minh got aid from the People's Republic of China (PRC) and the Soviet Union, while the French got aid from the United States. The French maintained a substantial superiority in firepower throughout the war, but the Viet Minh had more popular support, which was crucial in guerrilla

1

fighting. The State of Vietnam, a nominally independent Vietnamese government aligned with the French, was so clearly a French puppet that it could not win nearly the degree of popular support that the Viet Minh enjoyed.

In 1954, the French realized they were losing the war and negotiated the Geneva Accords. These accords left Prince Norodom Sihanouk firmly in power in Cambodia, but they failed to resolve the struggles between Communist and anti-Communist forces in Vietnam and Laos. The accords said Vietnam was to be temporarily split at the 17th parallel; Viet Minh armed forces were to go to the North and the forces of the French and the State of Vietnam were to go to the South. The division was supposed to be temporary; North and South were to be re-united in 1956 following internationally supervised elections.

The State of Vietnam, with its capital in Saigon, renamed itself the Republic of Vietnam (RVN) in 1955, consolidated its control in South Vietnam, refused to hold the 1956 elections, and set vigorously to work hunting down the Communists in the South. The United States hoped that Vietnam could be kept indefinitely split, with the RVN under President Ngo Dinh Diem in the South and the Democratic Republic of Vietnam (DRV), controlled by the Lao Dong (Workers') Party—the Communist party of Vietnam—in the North with its capital at Hanoi. But the Lao Dong Party still had many followers in the South. In 1954, the Communists had controlled far more of the South than the State of Vietnam did; they had pulled most of their armed forces out on the promise that they would have the opportunity to win power there through elections. It should have been no surprise when the Lao Dong Party decided in 1959 to return to a policy of armed struggle in the South, authorizing the remaining Communists in South Vietnam to launch a guerrilla war against the government.

Some of the South Vietnamese who had been in the Viet Minh in 1954, who had gone north after the signing of the Geneva Accords, were sent back to South Vietnam beginning in 1959, along what was called the Ho Chi Minh Trail. They joined with Communist elements who had remained in the South after 1954, and others who hated Ngo Dinh Diem, to form the guerrilla movement that Americans called the Viet Cong. Despite being greatly outgunned—the United States provided far more weaponry to the Army of the Republic of Vietnam (ARVN) than the DRV could give the Viet Cong—the guerrillas grew steadily in strength. Ngo Dinh Diem was almost as inept militarily as he was politically, and in 1963, the United States encouraged ARVN officers to overthrow Diem.

The original struggle between the Viet Cong and the ARVN was altered by large-scale outside intervention on both sides: American troops (plus some furnished by South Korea, Australia, Thailand, New Zealand, and the Philippines) supporting the ARVN, and soldiers of the People's Army of Vietnam (PAVN, which Americans often called the North Vietnamese Army or NVA) supporting the Viet Cong. In 1966 the PAVN began deliberately staging relatively conventional battles against American forces; PAVN troops would fortify hills near the Demilitarized Zone (DMZ) separating North from South Vietnam, or near the Laotian border, and in effect invite the Americans to attack. When the pressure became too great, the PAVN forces could retreat across the border out of South Vietnam. The United States was willing to fight such battles both because the great superiority of American firepower ensured the PAVN would lose far more men than the United States did, and because most American generals were eager to fight as close to a conventional war in Vietnam as they could manage. The PAVN was willing because the advantage of defending fortified positions allowed them to inflict substantial casualties on the Americans, and because these battles drew American attention and resources out to the hills along the border, away from the densely populated areas near the coast.

The intensity of combat reached a peak in the first half of 1968, during and after the "Tet Offensive" launched by Communist forces at the end of January. Casualties for the Communist forces, especially the South Vietnamese personnel of the Viet Cong, were very heavy during 1968. The overall strength of the Communist forces, and the proportion of southerners within those forces, declined dramatically. By this time, however, American public support for the war was also fading. Instead of making a massive effort to finish off the weakened enemy, the United States began to withdraw troops from Vietnam in 1969. American participation in ground combat was small by 1971 and ended during 1972, though the United States continued to provide air support for the ARVN. The balance of power, which had swung against the Communist forces in 1968, was beginning to swing back by the time they launched the Easter Offensive in 1972.

In January 1973, a peace agreement was signed in Paris, which was supposed to end the war. It did end American participation in combat, but the struggle among the Vietnamese went on. With no more Americans in combat, American interest in the war, and American willingness to finance the ARVN, faded. A massive Communist offensive in 1975, carried out mainly by PAVN rather than Viet Cong troops, brought final

Communist victory.

The extension of the war into Laos right from its beginning, and into Cambodia somewhat later, had a dual character. Vietnamese Communist forces used bases and supply lines in Laos and Cambodia to support their war in South Vietnam, but they also provided aid and training to local revolutionary movements, the Pathet Lao in Laos and the Khmer Rouge in Cambodia. The Khmer Rouge established Communist rule in Cambodia a few weeks before the final Communist victory in South Vietnam; PAVN and Pathet Lao forces did so in Laos a few months later.

The war was a subject of intense controversy while it was going on. Some of the controversies have been resolved, but many issues, even the most fundamental, are still hotly contested. What follows is only a brief summary of some of the areas of dispute.

## Debates over the Origin of the War

In the late 1950s, the level of anti-government violence in South Vietnam was relatively low. It increased in some areas in 1959; it increased very dramatically, in a great many areas, in 1960. In December 1960, the National Front for the Liberation of South Vietnam, commonly called the National Liberation Front (NLF), was formally established.

For the next 10 years, the public debate about what had happened centered around two major theories. Supporters of the U.S. government argued that the Communist leadership in North Vietnam had been trying to get guerrilla warfare started in the South at least since 1957. Left-wing critics of the war argued that the fighting had been started by people in South Vietnam, reacting against the oppression of Ngo Dinh Diem's government (which fell most heavily on Communists, but was also directed against many other groups). These critics argued that the uprising had begun without the approval and indeed against the wishes of the Communist leaders in Hanoi, who had urged the southerners to limit themselves to peaceful political struggle, and had not endorsed the guerrilla war until September 1960, when it was already vigorously in progress.

In the 1970s it was realized as a result of research by Jeffrey Race[1] that both of these theories had been mistaken. The leaders in Hanoi had forbidden guerrilla warfare in 1957 and 1958, but they changed their policy at the Fifteenth Plenum of the Lao Dong Party Central Committee, in the first half of 1959. There remains confusion as to whether this occurred in January or May of 1959, and more needs to be learned about the limited amount of violence, short of guerrilla warfare, that had been permitted by party policy even before the Fifteenth Plenum. It is also unclear why U.S. government officials, many of whom had been aware of the 1959 turning point long before Race's work was published, had not put this knowledge into the public debate.

## The Nature of the War: Political

Debate over the fundamental nature of the war—the identity of the participants—began in the 1960s and shows no sign of abating. Some argue that the United States intervened in Vietnam to defend South Vietnam from North Vietnamese conquest; others argue that the United States was trying to suppress a revolutionary movement within South Vietnam.

Right from the beginning of the war, the Communist and anti-Communist sides in the war had each attempted to portray itself as a force defending the self-determination of the South Vietnamese people against the outside interference of the other side.

The Communist leadership in Hanoi made elaborate efforts to pretend that it was not controlling the guerrilla war in the South. The National Liberation Front was presented as a coalition of elements in South Vietnam, Communist and non-Communist, working together as equals against their common enemy, Ngo Dinh Diem's dictatorship in Saigon. Even the Communist elements in it went through the motions of severing their ties to Hanoi, establishing a separate Communist party for the South, the People's Revolutionary Party, in 1962. Many members of the American anti-war movement, including some scholars, were fooled to a greater or lesser extent into believing that the NLF guerrillas were less controlled by Communists, and the southern Communists less controlled by Hanoi, than was actually the case.

It is now generally understood that the autonomy of the NLF and of the People's Revolutionary Party were facades. There was only one Communist leadership in Vietnam, that of the Lao Dong Party, and it controlled the guerrilla movement in the South almost as firmly as it did the government in the North. Acceptance of these facts, however, has not caused all those who believed that there was a genuine revolutionary movement in South Vietnam to abandon that belief. Some have instead shifted that belief to a different and much firmer foundation.

The argument today centers on the question of whether North and South Vietnam were one country or two. Those who see two countries see the Communist Party as essentially North Vietnamese, see its activities in South Vietnam as outside interference in that country, and see the South

Vietnamese in it as subordinates or servants of an outside power, North Vietnam. Those who see Vietnam as one country see the South Vietnamese Communists as very important participants in a Vietnamese (not a specifically North Vietnamese) revolutionary movement struggling for control of Vietnam.

The two sides tend to look at different periods of the war for support for their views. In the early years, the guerrillas fighting for the NLF, called the People's Liberation Armed Forces (PLAF) by their supporters and the Viet Cong (VC) by their opponents, were virtually all native-born South Vietnamese. Most had never been outside of South Vietnam; a minority had spent a few years in North Vietnam, and then returned to South Vietnam down the Ho Chi Minh Trail. The officers leading them likewise were virtually all South Vietnamese. The supreme command under which they operated was the Lao Dong Party Politburo in Hanoi, a mixed group of North and South Vietnamese. Le Duan, first secretary of the Lao Dong Party throughout the war, had been born in South Vietnam; so had Premier Pham Van Dong. On the other side, the soldiers of the Army of the Republic of Vietnam (ARVN) were mixed North and South Vietnamese. The officers leading them were mixed North and South Vietnamese. The leaders of the government in Saigon commanding them were mixed North and South Vietnamese. Looking at the whole structures from bottom to top, it is plain that while neither the guerrillas nor those supporting the government were purely South Vietnamese, the guerrillas were much closer to being purely South Vietnamese.

The United States began to put significant numbers of Americans into combat in South Vietnam in 1962; the Communists began to put significant numbers of North Vietnamese into combat in 1964. For the next several years the flow of Americans into South Vietnam was much larger than the flow of North Vietnamese soldiers of the People's Army of Vietnam (PAVN); the proportion of native-born South Vietnamese remained significantly higher among the forces on the Communist side in South Vietnam than among the forces on the anti-Communist side, at least through the middle of 1967 and perhaps significantly beyond that point. Those arguing that there was an indigenous revolutionary movement within South Vietnam can therefore find considerable support for their position in the facts of the period from 1959 to 1967.

A substantial increase in the commitment of PAVN troops to South Vietnam beginning in late 1967, and massive casualties to the South Vietnamese guerrillas, especially in the prolonged period of heavy fighting that began with the Tet Offensive of 1968, reduced the proportion of native-born South Vietnamese among the Communist forces. Then, in 1969, the U.S. forces began to withdraw, leaving South Vietnamese a steadily increasing proportion of the forces fighting on the anti-Communist side. In the last years of the war, the forces fighting for Saigon were overwhelmingly South Vietnamese, while the Communist forces in South Vietnam were predominantly North Vietnamese. Those who argue that the war was an effort by North Vietnam to conquer South Vietnam find their best evidence in this period, though they often exaggerate, claiming that the South Vietnamese component of the Communist force had been effectively destroyed in the Tet Offensive of 1968, and that the Communist forces were essentially all North Vietnamese from that point on.

One of the advantages of those who argue that Vietnam was basically one country was that this was the official position of the Republic of Vietnam, the government the United States was supporting in Saigon, which from the beginning of the war to its end said that North and South should never have been separated (it blamed the Communists for causing this division), and that the two halves of Vietnam should some day be reunited.

## The Nature of the War: Military

Some within the United States government felt that the main Communist threat in Vietnam came from organized military units, and that this threat should be met by fairly conventional military tactics. Others focused on Communist guerrillas, and stressed the need for unconventional methods of "counterinsurgency." The first group believed in applying the massive weight of American firepower, including air power; some spokesmen for the latter group said (perhaps exaggerating a bit for rhetorical effect) that the best weapon to use when fighting guerrillas is a knife.

The advocates of conventional tactics had the upper hand from the beginning, since the U.S. military was dominated by officers trained for conventional warfare. The U.S. Military Assistance Advisory Group under General Samuel Williams had been training the ARVN as a rather conventional military force, and had not shown much interest in the special characteristics of guerrilla warfare, in the late 1950s.

The early 1960s were the high point of counterinsurgency doctrines. President John F. Kennedy supported the advocates of counterinsurgency in the U.S. Army Special Forces, giving them more resources and more autonomy than the Army's top leadership would otherwise have been likely to allow them, and the Central Intelligence Agency (CIA) then brought substantial numbers of Special Forces troops to South Vietnam to recruit, train, and lead thousands of local personnel in the Civilian Irregular Defense Groups (CIDG) and some other smaller organizations. The Strategic Hamlets, copied from a program that had helped the British suppress Communist guerrillas in Malaya in the 1950s, were introduced on a broad scale in 1962 and 1963.

In 1963, however, control of the CIDG was transferred from the CIA to the military, which soon made them much more like regular military forces than they had formerly been. The Strategic Hamlet program had by 1964 become a disastrous failure. Then, in 1965, the United States began flooding Vietnam with conventionally trained military personnel, and while counterinsurgency did not disappear, it could not compete; it became a minor adjunct to the regular military effort. The dominant elements in the U.S. military regarded Viet Cong guerrillas as a minor adjunct to the more conventional Communist forces, and in 1967 they even made a formal decision that U.S. military intelligence should not try to estimate how many people were in the Viet Cong village militia.

Counterinsurgency revived in importance after 1968, with Operation *Phoenix* attacking the Communists' administrative structure and an effective land reform campaign bidding for peasant loyalty. But counterinsurgency still did not become as important, relative to conventional military effort, as it had been in the early 1960s.

Disputes between advocates of the two approaches continued after the war, and were intermingled with disputes over the nature of the Communist forces. Authors like Major Andrew Krepinevich and former CIA Director William Colby, regarding the Vietnam War as a guerrilla war, have argued that the United States made a mistake overemphasizing conventional military tactics.[2] Authors like Colonel Harry Summers and General Phillip Davidson have argued, on the other hand, that the Communist forces that mattered were the conventional units of the PAVN, and that the United States made a mistake overemphasizing operations against guerrillas.[3]

## The Air War

The conflicting views of the nature of the war discussed above have contributed to disagreements about the way the United States used air power. But a much older argument has also played a role: that between the advocates of strategic and tactical bombing. Tactical bombing is directed against the enemy armed forces on the battlefield, or against forces and facilities close enough to the battlefield to provide direct and immediate support for the enemy forces on the battlefield. Strategic bombing attacks targets relevant to the overall power of the enemy nation, such as oil refineries, weapons factories, or the homes of the workers who make the weapons, rather than attacking individual military units or the facilities that support individual units. The U.S. Air Force was dominated by men who believed that strategic bombing was the best use of air power.

Those who believed in strategic bombing, and those who believed that the real enemy the United States was fighting in Vietnam was the government of North Vietnam, tended to believe that the most significant use of U.S. air power would be attacks on the heart of North Vietnam. They were sorely disappointed. President Lyndon Johnson (1963–1969) was concerned that bombing in the northern half of North Vietnam, especially in the areas of Hanoi and Haiphong, and in the immediate vicinity of the Chinese border, could trigger direct intervention in Vietnam by the Soviet Union or the PRC. He was very reluctant to approve any bombing in these areas, and to the extent he approved it, he kept the tightest personal control of it. His often-quoted statement "They can't bomb an outhouse without my permission" describes his attitude toward the use of air power in the northern half of North Vietnam. In April 1968, Johnson halted all bombing of the northern part of North Vietnam. It did not resume on any significant scale until 1972, and even if one includes the bombing of 1972, Hanoi was never subjected to anything like the pounding that had been applied to every North Korean city during the Korean War, and to almost every German and Japanese city during World War II. Looking at the northern part of North Vietnam, one sees a restricted use of air power.

Those who believed in tactical bombing, and those who thought that the war was essentially a struggle against the guerrillas in South Vietnam, looked at areas closer to the battlefields in the South, and saw a very different picture. An enormous weight of U.S. bombing was applied in South Vietnam, and in the areas of Laos through which the Ho Chi Minh Trail carried supplies and reinforcements from North Vietnam to Communist forces in the South. South Vietnam became by a wide margin the most heavily bombed country in the history of the world, and Laos became the second most heavily bombed. The White House, furthermore, left the details—the choices of which targets were to be hit in South Vietnam and along the Ho Chi Minh Trail, and when—pretty much to the military.

The southern part of North Vietnam, especially the area within about 200 kilometers of the DMZ, was intermediate in terms of U.S. policy. Lyndon Johnson approved missions in this area much more readily than he did in the areas further north, and he did not control the missions in such detail. He often approved missions of "armed reconnaissance" in which pilots were authorized to search an area, often quite a large area, and bomb whatever targets of opportunity they found there. The towns of this area were devastated in a fashion that never happened to Hanoi. Bombing was not halted there until October 1968, and the halt was not as absolute as in the area farther north; a significant number of strikes were flown between 1969 and 1971.

## War between Unequal Powers

It is difficult to lay out the strengths of the two sides, both because it is difficult to decide how to define the categories, and because on many issues reliable data are not available.

The population of South Vietnam was estimated at 17 million in 1966. Estimates of the population of North Vietnam varied, but it seems likely that the lower ones, around 18.25 million, were more accurate. To treat these figures as the population bases of the anti-Communist and Communist armies, respectively, would be a mistake; the Communist forces were recruiting vigorously in South Vietnam, and the anti-Communist forces, which had been able to recruit in North Vietnam up to 1954, still contained large numbers of North Vietnamese. The population of the United States was 197 million.

The Democratic Republic of Vietnam was believed in mid-1966 to have regular armed forces of about 250,000 men, almost all Army (the Navy and Air Force were tiny). There were also about 25,000 men in armed public security forces, and about 200,000 in militia and self-defense forces. The North's forces expanded as the war went on.

The Republic of Vietnam was believed early in 1966 to have regular armed forces of 300,000, made up of 264,000 in the Army, 25,000 in the Navy (including Marines), and 11,000 in the Air Force. These were supplemented by almost 25,000 combat troops in the Civilian Irregular Defense Groups, about 260,000 in the Regional Force and Popular Force, and the Police Field Force. RVN forces expanded dramatically as the war went on; by mid-1972 official strengths reached 456,000 for the Army, 42,000 for the Navy, 50,000 for the Air Force, and 17,000 for the Marine Corps. The official strengths of the Regional and Popular Forces had reached 529,000, and they had been joined by another important paramilitary force, the Revolutionary Development Cadres, with over 21,000 men, but the CIDG no longer existed as a separate force.

No good statistics are available for even the organized military units of the Viet Cong, much less their support troops, militias, and paramilitary forces. Official U.S. figures in mid-1964 (just before the first PAVN units made up of North Vietnamese began to arrive in the South) indicated that the Viet Cong had 28,000 to 34,000 men in main-force and local-force units, and about 80,000 guerrillas. The true levels were probably considerably higher than the U.S. estimates at this time, and Viet Cong forces expanded rapidly during the following years.

In mid-1965, the United States armed forces had a strength of 2,653,142. By mid-1968, the demands of the war had increased this to 3,547,429. The number of U.S. military personnel actually in Vietnam peaked at 543,000 in April 1969. But if one adds to these the U.S. personnel of the air bases in Thailand, Okinawa, and Guam from which the United States did much of its bombing of Vietnam, and those of the aircraft carriers off the Vietnamese coast, and so forth, the total for U.S. military personnel in Asia participating in or supporting the war effort was well over 600,000 at the peak.

Aside from the Vietnamese forces on both sides, and the Americans, outside military forces must also be considered. Several nations sent troops to South Vietnam to assist the United States and the ARVN; peak recorded levels for these forces were 50,003 for South Korea; 11,586 for Thailand; 7,672 for Australia; 2,061 for the Philippines; and 552 for New Zealand. The Republic of China sent personnel covertly to South Vietnam; no reliable figures are available. The PRC sent substantial forces—a figure of 170,000 is now widely accepted for the peak strength—to North Vietnam, where they assisted in defense against American air attack. PRC units did not, however, join the ground combat in the South.

The economies of North and South Vietnam were predominantly agricultural, and the official exchange rates of their currencies were artificial. Taking economic figures from the North in *dong* and from the South in *piastres*, and multiplying by the theoretical value of the *dong* and *piastre*, one can compute that in U.S. dollars the gross domestic product of the North was about $1.5 billion in 1965, and that of the South about $1.92 billion. But these figures should be taken only as very rough indicators of the scale of the two economies. Military expenditures on both sides were heavily dependent on foreign aid; the United States was far more generous with aid to Saigon than the Soviet Union and China were in aid to Hanoi. The gross domestic product of the United States in 1965 was $684.9 billion.

Much that seems strange about the Vietnam War arose from the fact

that it was, among other things, a war of attrition between very unbal-
anced opponents. The Communist leaders knew that they could win the
war if all they had to face was the forces of the Republic of Vietnam; the
Communists' problem was to persuade the United States to withdraw from
the struggle. The United States was, however, a very large country, with
more than five times the population of Vietnam as a whole, and more than
nine times the population of North Vietnam. In economic and technologi-
cal terms the imbalance was far greater. According to U.S. government
estimates, the gross domestic product of the United States in 1965 was
more than 400 times that of North Vietnam. Just the amount the United
States spent on the military each year was more than 30 times the entire
gross domestic product of North Vietnam. Without aid from China and
the Soviet Union, the Communist forces in Vietnam would not have had a
chance against the Americans. Even with such aid, they were very severely outgunned; the Chinese and Soviets did not come remotely close to
matching the weapons and supplies the United States poured into Vietnam. The result was what might have been expected: the number of Communist personnel killed by the huge impact of American weaponry was
not just greater but enormously greater than the number of Americans the
Communist forces managed to kill.

This fact has sometimes been obscured by doubts about the honesty of
American "body counts." General Norman Schwarzkopf later commented
that he and the other officers who had served in Vietnam "all know that we
had lied about body count."[4] Captured Communist documents, however,
did not show losses significantly below the level the U.S. forces were
claiming to have inflicted. Many members of the Communist forces were
dying without being counted by the Americans, killed by air strikes, or by
wounds and disease (the Communist forces did not have medical care
nearly as good as that of the Americans; the death rates from serious
wounds, and from disease, were far higher). It seems likely that the number of Communist soldiers who died without ever being counted in American figures at least came close to balancing the number who were falsely
counted, in inflated "body counts."

Approximately 58,000 U.S. military personnel died in the Vietnam War
(including deaths in the war zone by accident and disease, not just deaths
from enemy action). The number of Vietnamese Communist personnel
who died is not known exactly; the problem of figuring out how many
were killed by forces allied with the United States, not just the ARVN but
also the South Koreans and others, makes this especially difficult. But
total deaths among the Vietnamese Communist forces were almost cer-

tainly well over 600,000, in other words more than 10 times the number of American deaths.

Under normal circumstances, the side that loses more men is the loser in a war of attrition, especially if the side that loses more men has the smaller population base. But in Vietnam it was the United States, which suffered much smaller losses out of a much larger population base, that decided the struggle was not worth the cost and pulled out its forces, allowing the Communists to win the war. This paradox has caused much confusion.

Many American officers and officials, during the war, believed that the great discrepancy in casualty levels meant that they were winning the war. Some authors after the war, observing the fact that the Communists won it, have been led to the mistaken conclusion that the Communists must not really have been suffering such heavy casualties. These authors take genuine and important facts about the war—that the sophisticated weaponry of the United States often proved inappropriate to the situation in Vietnam, and that Communist forces were often able to evade combat with the more heavily armed Americans—and greatly exaggerate them, suggesting that high-tech weaponry proved so ineffectual, and that the Communists evaded combat so much of the time, that the Communists overall did not suffer huge losses.

The crucial factor was that the Vietnamese Communist leaders cared far more about South Vietnam than American leaders did. The level of losses that the American forces suffered was enough to make the United States decide the cost was getting too great, and pull out its forces. The Communist leaders, caring much more about what was at stake, were willing to endure much greater losses in order to win. The Communist forces sometimes evaded combat, but often they chose not to do so, pushing their attacks even at very heavy cost in order to inflict the casualties on the Americans that would persuade the Americans to withdraw.

## The Poor and the Uneducated?

A substantial proportion of the troops with which the United States fought the Vietnam War were conscripts, and the conscripts tended to come from the poorer and less educated portions of American society. The Selective Service System had been designed to allow many ways for a young man to avoid conscription. College and university students, and those working in jobs considered to be in the national interest, could postpone or avoid military service. The children of upper- and middle-class families were more able to take advantage of these opportunities than the children of the lower-middle class and the poor. Officially, the justification for this was "manpower channeling": the government was encouraging young men to live their lives in ways the government approved, and rewarded them for doing so by not drafting them. Unofficially, it was suspected that the government was conciliating the more influential elements in society by making it easy for their children to avoid military service.

By the late 1960s, there actually were "draft counselors," people who made a specialty of helping young men find ways to avoid conscription. It was said that a good draft counselor could find a legal way out of the draft for about nine-tenths of his clients, and this was in fact probably true. Men from more prosperous and educated backgrounds could more easily obtain the services of a draft counselor, and perhaps more important, were far more likely to consider the possibility of trying to obtain such services.

The combined result of such factors was that men from prosperous and educated backgrounds were far less likely to be drafted. Both during the war and since its end, many people have said it was grossly unjust that the privileged sectors of society, the ones that had the most influence on government policy and therefore can be presumed to have shaped the decision to fight the war, had left the poorer elements to do the dying.

Recently, however, a number of authors have suggested that the question of who got drafted should not be confused with the question of who fought and died. Many of the most dangerous jobs in the military were performed not by draftees in the enlisted ranks, but by officers who were for the most part volunteers from educated backgrounds. The officers who commanded infantry platoons, and who flew fighter planes over North Vietnam, for example, suffered heavy casualties. Of all the Americans killed in combat in Vietnam, only about 34 percent were draftees.

Some statistical studies have suggested that the average socio-economic level of the Americans who died in Vietnam was not significantly below the average for American society as a whole. The validity of the methods used in these studies has sometimes been disputed, but it is at least unmistakable that the average socio-economic level of those who died in Vietnam was not nearly as low as the average socio-economic level of those who were drafted.

The issue of race was related to that of socio-economic status. There were charges during the war that the Americans dying in Vietnam were disproportionately members of racial minority groups, mainly blacks. These charges were based primarily on figures for U.S. Army casualties in 1965 and 1966, when 20.8 percent of the Army personnel killed by hostile action were black. The percentages were much lower from 1967 onward, and had been much lower for the other services even in 1965 and 1966. Figures covering all the services and the whole length of the war indicate that 12.3 percent of the Americans killed by hostile action were black. Of all the American dead (hostile action and other causes combined), 12.5 percent were black. These figures were only moderately higher than the percentage of blacks among the U.S. male population of military age (about 11 percent). Some authors have treated the high figures for Army casualties in 1965 and 1966 as if they represented all the services and/or the whole length of the war. Some on the other side have tried to make the figures for the proportion of blacks among the dead appear small, by suggesting that the percentage of blacks in the U.S. male population of military age had been higher than 12.5 percent. This suggestion is not supported by U.S. census data.

The time when the proportion of blacks among the casualties was highest, 1965 and 1966, was a time when the U.S. ground combat forces were made up mostly of volunteers. In 1969 and 1970, when the proportion of draftees was much higher, the proportion of blacks among the dead was lower. This suggests that discrimination in the draft was probably not a major factor elevating the proportion of blacks among those who died in Vietnam.

## The Role of the Media

There is a widespread belief that the news media played a crucial role in undermining popular support in the United States for the war. Certainly the media were not as supportive of the war effort as they had been during World War II, and certainly public support for the war would have been greater if the media had been more supportive, but once one gets beyond these obvious truths, one is in a realm of much dispute and numerous myths. Those who felt that the media should have been as supportive as they had been in World War II, and were shocked by what they saw in the media coverage of Vietnam, often in their shock greatly exaggerated the extent to which the media had become critical of the war.

The American media first began to pay significant attention to Vietnam in about 1962. A deep division soon arose. The government of Ngo Dinh Diem had very serious political weaknesses, and was handling the war very ineptly. Reporters who visited strategic hamlets and saw how badly they were being built, and who talked with U.S. military advisers in the field and learned how strong the Viet Cong were becoming, began to file very alarming stories. These reporters were for the most part "hawks." They believed it was right for the U.S. military to be in Vietnam, and that the struggle against the Viet Cong could and should be won. When they pointed out mistakes that were being made, they were hoping those mistakes would be corrected and the Viet Cong defeated. Ambassador Frederick Nolting, however, and General Paul Harkins (commander of Military Assistance Command, Vietnam), believed that the press should be applauding rather than criticizing. They said, and tried to get the press to say, that Ngo Dinh Diem was doing splendidly and was defeating the Viet Cong.

This was not a struggle of the press as a whole against the U.S. government as a whole. Many in the government were on the side of the critical reporters; indeed much of what these reporters wrote, they had been told by U.S. Army officers. And much of the press sided with Nolting and Harkins against the critical reporters; the impulse to accept whatever was said by senior U.S. officals, on subjects like Vietnam, was very strong in the U.S. media during this period.

During 1963, most of the U.S. government became far more realistic in its evaluation of Vietnam. Optimism about Ngo Dinh Diem's political skills was fading by mid-year; optimism about the war in the countryside was fading by the end of the year. There was much less conflict between officials and reporters in 1964. In 1965, with large numbers of American troops directly in combat, the natural tendency of the media to "support our boys" improved government-media relations still further. The common notion that the media sickened the American people by putting scenes of blood and gore into living rooms every evening on the television news is simply false. On most evenings, the news carried no blood and gore from Vietnam.

As the war ground on, however, with casualty levels rising from year to year with no end in sight, the desire of the government to accentuate the positive, to maintain optimism the war was being won, led to increasing conflict with significant elements of the press. The difference between the Johnson administration's statements about the war and what seemed actually to be happening was described as the "credibility gap." When a vigorous effort in the fall of 1967 to persuade the press and the public that the Communist forces were weakening was followed by the Tet Offensive in January 1968, the problem became really serious. The media did not, as has often been said, generally portray the Tet Offensive as having been a Communist military victory. But they did not present it as an American triumph either. The famous documentary by Walter Cronkite,[5] anchor of the CBS evening news and the most influential journalist of the day, is probably typical. Cronkite's overall evaluation of the Tet Offensive was that it had been a stalemate; neither side had won or lost it. This was a political disaster for the Johnson administration; the administration needed for Cronkite to say there had been a decisive American victory. But many authors trying to describe this disaster have suggested, falsely, that Cronkite had described the offensive as a Communist military victory.

Relations between the government and the press worsened during the administration of Richard Nixon. Nixon had disliked the media even before he became president; his inclination was to attack the media in situations in which Kennedy or Johnson would have tried to cajole and manipulate them. There was more negative news about the war to report, as morale and discipline had declined among the American forces in Vietnam, and with the spread of anti-war sentiment in the public, the Congress, and the media, there was more inclination to report it. Probably the greatest extreme of anti-war sentiment in the media was during Operation *Linebacker II*, the "Christmas Bombing," in December 1972.

During the last years of the war, from 1973 to 1975, the American media paid much less attention to the war, but that attention was often negative in tone. The statements of government spokesmen that the ARVN was still strong and still had the ability to win the struggle were so unrealistic as to inspire open expressions of doubt in the media.

Overall, the media appear to have mirrored elite opinion more than they contradicted it. The impression of a sharp difference of opinion has resulted partly from the fact that the public statements of government officials often showed considerably more enthusiasm for the way the war was going than the average official actually felt, and partly from the fact that negative views expressed in the media drew more attention, and were given greater weight in people's later impressions of the media's attitudes, than positive views did.

## Aftermath

The victory of Communism in Indochina in 1975 was not followed by the fall of the rest of Southeast Asia, as some had once predicted. Nor did Vietnam come to be entirely dominated by North Vietnamese. The Socialist Republic of Vietnam, formally proclaimed in 1976, counted a number of southerners, including some who had been leaders of the NLF during the war, among its top leaders. But there were few other bright spots.

It was not surprising that Vietnam after Communist victory was governed as a dictatorship, but few had expected this dictatorship to be so corrupt, and so inept in its management of the economy. Hundreds of thousands of "boat people" fled the country to escape political persecution, ethnic discrimination (especially against the Chinese minority), and simple poverty. Only in the late 1980s did economic reforms allowing more private enterprise begin to lead to rapid economic growth.

The fate of Cambodia was far worse. The Khmer Rouge, who won control of the whole country in 1975, created a nightmare driven by ideological fanaticism. In less than four years, well over one-tenth of the nation's population were executed or died of starvation. A Vietnamese invasion drove the Khmer Rouge from power at the beginning of 1979 and ended the worst horrors, but was unable to establish peace, nor a competent and effective government. The Khmer Rouge remained active as guerrillas in the jungle, hoping to win back their position, until the late 1990s. And even when active guerrilla warfare faded, violence on a smaller scale continued, along with corruption and general misrule.

## Notes

1. Jeffrey Race, *War Comes to Long An* (Berkeley: University of California Press, 1972).

2. Andrew F. Krepinevich, Jr., *The Army and Vietnam* (Baltimore: Johns Hopkins University Press, 1986). William Colby, *Lost Victory: A Firsthand Account of America's Sixteen-Year Involvement in Vietnam* (Chicago: Contemporary Books, 1989).

3. Harry G. Summers, Jr., *On Strategy: A Critical Analysis of the Vietnam War* (Novato, Calif.: Presidio, 1982). Phillip B. Davidson, *Vietnam at War: The History: 1946-1975* (Novato, Calif.: Presidio, 1988).

4. Gen. H. Norman Schwarzkopf, on the ABC television network show *20-20*, March 15, 1991.

5. "Who, What, When, Where, Why: Report from Vietnam by Walter Cronkite," CBS Television Network, February 27, 1968; transcript in Peter Braestrup, *Big Story* (Boulder, Colo.: Westview Press, 1977), vol. 2, pp. 180–89.

# THE DICTIONARY

## - A -

**A-6.** The Grumman A-6 Intruder was a subsonic jet with terrain-following radar that enabled it to bomb with reasonable accuracy even at night or in bad weather. It was flown by **Navy** and **Marine** pilots. The U.S. **Air Force** did not have a plane in Southeast Asia that could match the A-6's night capabilities until a few **F-111s** arrived in 1968.

**A-7.** The Ling-Temco-Vought A-7 Corsair, a single-seat subsonic jet designed to carry relatively heavy bomb loads without costing too much money, entered combat as a U.S. **Navy** aircraft at the end of 1967. It proved highly successful, and was quickly adopted by the **Air Force** also, with some innovations including Heads-Up Display, a system in which instrument data were projected on a screen directly in the pilot's line of sight.

**A SHAU.** In **Thua Thien** province, west of **Hue** near the Laotian border, the A Shau Valley became an important Communist base area after the A Shau **Special Forces** camp was overrun by People's Army of Vietnam (**PAVN**) units on March 10, 1966. In July and August 1967, the A Shau was used as a test area for Operation *Commando Lava*, in which chemicals intended to break up the structure of the soil were dropped from **C-130** aircraft, in the hope that unusually large and impassible mudholes would form on roads in the rainy season. The experiment was not successful. The U.S. 1st **Cavalry Division** made a major raid into the A Shau, Operation *Delaware*, from April 19 to May 17, 1968, to disrupt the base area. The operation was hampered by substantial PAVN fire against the **helicopters** (37-mm anti-aircraft guns and heavy machine guns destroyed 10 helicopters and damaged many others during the initial assault on April 19) and very bad weather, which delayed the landing of additional forces for several days and impeded resupply of the forces on the ground. The operation was quite successful; it captured or destroyed substantial quantities of supplies and equipment including 76 vehicles, and did not suffer massive casualties because most of the PAVN forces in the valley were supply and engineer rather than combat units. A similar raid by two battalions of the 101st Airborne Division and two battalions of the Army of the Republic of Vietnam (**ARVN**), Operation *Somerset Plains*, August 4–19, 1968, was less successful. The United States decided that it would be necessary to establish a permanent presence in the valley, supported by a road from Hue.

Elements of the 101st Airborne began Operation *Massachusetts Striker* on March 1, 1969, aimed at the southern and central portions of the A Shau Valley, and these remained there when U.S. and ARVN troops were inserted into the northern part of the valley on May 10 in Operation *Apache Snow*. Both operations led to heavy fighting, though only the battle for Dong Ap Bia (Hill 937, "**Hamburger Hill**"), May 11–20, has become famous.

Most U.S. and allied forces were pulled out of the A Shau in September 1969, and all were out by October 9. The road leading to the A Shau was abandoned. In December, the road was reopened partway to the A Shau, allowing the U.S. to re-open firebases close enough to the valley to fire into it with long-range **artillery**.

**ABRAMS, CREIGHTON WILLIAMS** (1914–1974). U.S. **Army** general. Born in Springfield, Massachusetts, Abrams graduated from West Point in 1936. He served in World War II in the 4th Armored Division; his tank battalion was the first U.S. unit to break through the German forces encircling Bastogne in December 1944. He commanded the 3d Armored Division 1960–1962.

Abrams was the U.S. Army's vice chief of staff from August 1964 to April 1967. When he was sent to Saigon as deputy commander of **Military Assistance Command, Vietnam** (MACV), in May 1967, it was apparently with the intent that he should spend only a few months as deputy before replacing General **William Westmoreland** as commander of MACV. Something caused a delay, and he served as deputy commander for more than a year before stepping up to commander, though he seems to have been exercising some of the powers of commander starting in April 1968, when the fact that he was going to replace Westmoreland was announced. Abrams was uncomfortable as deputy to Westmoreland, with whom he did not have a good working relationship. This was partly due to policy disagreements. Abrams thought Westmoreland's massive use of American firepower was causing too many civilian casualties, and he thought Westmoreland's stress on big-unit operations going after People's Army of Vietnam (**PAVN**) units in the hills and jungles was not a very effective way to win the war; he felt more emphasis should be placed on strengthening the Army of the Republic of Vietnam (**ARVN**) and on **pacification** of the villages. These differences should not be exaggerated, however; there was far from a total change in policies when Abrams took command in 1968.

In February 1968, Abrams was sent north to command MACV Forward, a headquarters established at **Phu Bai** to control the war in the two northernmost provinces of South Vietnam, **Quang Tri** and **Thua Thien**, where the **Tet Offensive** and the battle of **Khe Sanh** had led to very intense fighting. MACV Forward was formally terminated on March 10, after **Hue** had been retaken and the situation around Khe Sanh had eased, and Abrams returned to Saigon.

After Abrams formally became commander of MACV in June 1968, he promptly ordered U.S. forces withdrawn from Khe Sanh. This was part of a general shift in emphasis away from large-unit operations in the hills and jungles, toward small-unit operations in the more populated areas near the coast. This shift at Abrams's initiative in 1968 only went partway, however; President **Richard Nixon** pushed him considerably farther in June 1969, with a directive to hold down casualties, following public controversy over the Battle of "**Hamburger Hill**" the previous month, during a big-unit operation Abrams had sent into the **A Shau** Valley.

Abrams was sometimes disturbed by the pace of U.S. withdrawals from Vietnam, especially in early 1970, but he did not resist the withdrawals actively, and as they went on, he was generally upbeat about the progress of the ARVN toward becoming able to stand on its own. He urged the extension of U.S. bombing into **Cambodia** in 1969, and during *Lam Son 719*, the 1971 ARVN incursion into **Laos**, he urged the ARVN to advance more rapidly and more deeply into Laos. He was promoted to become chief of staff of the U.S. Army on October 12, 1972, and held that position until his death on September 4, 1974.

**ACHESON, DEAN GOODERHAM** (1893–1971). Secretary of state. Born in Middletown, Connecticut, he graduated from Harvard Law School in 1918, served as private secretary to Supreme Court Justice Louis Brandeis, then went into private practice of the law.

In 1940, Acheson helped draft the constitutional justification for

President Franklin D. Roosevelt's "destroyers-for-bases" deal; the attention this won him led to his appointment as assistant secretary of state for economic affairs from 1941 to 1944, in which capacity he helped to supervise lend-lease. As undersecretary of state from 1945 to 1947, he helped formulate the Truman Doctrine and the Marshall Plan. He then retired briefly from government, but returned to become secretary of state from 1949 to 1953. He opposed massive increases in U.S. aid for Chiang Kai-shek in the last stages of the Chinese Civil War, feeling that no feasible amount of U.S. aid would change the outcome, but he favored U.S. aid to the French in the First Indochina War.

By the time of the Vietnam War, Acheson was a highly respected elder statesman. His relationship with **George Ball**, during the Vietnam War, was an oddity. Acheson was basically a hawk until 1968, but he was willing to work with Ball writing memoranda opposing escalation of the war in 1965. When Acheson finally turned against the war, at the 1968 meeting of the **Wise Men**, this seriously shook President **Lyndon Johnson**.

**ADAMS, SAMUEL A.** (1933–1988). **Central Intelligence Agency** (CIA) officer. Born near Bridgeport, Connecticut, Samuel Adams was descended from the Adams family that had provided two early presidents of the United States. He graduated from Harvard in 1955, served two years in the Navy, and eventually, in 1963, joined the CIA and became an intelligence analyst. At first he worked on Africa, primarily the Congo, but in 1965 he transferred to the Southeast Asia Branch to work on Vietnam.

The crucial moment in Adams' career came early in 1966. He was in Vietnam, doing research on **Viet Cong** morale, and looking in particular at the numbers of deserters and defectors from the Viet Cong as an indication of morale. The number of defectors seemed so large, relative to the U.S. **intelligence** estimates of the total size of the organizations from which these defectors came, as to indicate the Viet Cong were falling apart. But the reality of the battefield indicated clearly that they were not falling apart. Adams checked, and found that the organizations in question had far more people than U.S. intelligence estimates showed. Adams then began to investigate the true size of these organizations.

The Order of Battle reports compiled by military intelligence officers in Saigon reported the strength of Communist main-force combat units in South Vietnam; local-force units; village guerrillas and militia forces; support troops (communications, medical, transport, and other personnel constituting the "logistical tail" of the Communist forces); and the "**infrastructure**," the government personnel who actually administered the substantial portions of South Vietnam that were more or less under Communist control. The Order of Battle reports showed a combined total, for all categories, of slightly less than 300,000; Adams decided the true figure was over 500,000.

There were several inter-agency conferences during 1967, at which military intelligence officers argued for low estimates and CIA officers, including Adams, for higher ones. The military won the dispute; it was decided that the Viet Cong militia would no longer be counted, and the total number of Communist personnel listed in the Order of Battle reports actually dropped instead of being increased.

Adams felt that the intelligence estimates that emerged from these conferences had been grossly dishonest, and that this was an important part of the reason the United States was not better prepared for the **Tet Offensive** a few months later. After leaving the Agency, he published a brief account of the events in *Harper's* in May 1975. His story formed the basis of a major CBS television documentary in 1982, which triggered a lawsuit by General **William Westmoreland**. Adams died in 1988; his book *War of Numbers* was published posthumously in 1994. *See also* ORDER OF BATTLE DISPUTE.

**ADVISERS.** The **Military Assistance Advisory Group** (MAAG) for Indochina was established in 1950, but the United States did not become seriously involved in advising and training the Army of the Republic of Vietnam (**ARVN**) until 1955. Through the late 1950s the United States was hampered by the **Geneva Accords of 1954**, which as originally interpreted limited the number of U.S. military advisers in Vietnam to 342. The United States evaded this limitation to some extent by sending the **Temporary Equipment Recovery Mission** (TERM) to Vietnam; the United States pretended that TERM personnel were not involved in training the ARVN and therefore should not be counted against the 342 limit. In 1960 the accords were re-interpreted to lift the limit to 685. There may have been some evasion of this new limit as well; some sources indicate the United States may have had about 900 military personnel in Vietnam by the beginning of 1961.

Late in 1961, President **John Kennedy** decided to send a much larger number of advisers to Vietnam, enough so that the pretense of compliance with the 685 limit had to be abandoned. Also at this time U.S. military personnel began to be assigned direct combat missions in Vietnam, but a pretense that they were there only as advisers was maintained for several more years. The U.S. **Army Special Forces** A-teams that commanded and led **Civilian Irregular Defense Group** units pretended to be only advisers, and the U.S. **Air Force** pilots who flew bombing missions as part of Project *Farm Gate* had **Vietnamese Air Force** (VNAF) markings on their planes, and had to have a Vietnamese aboard every plane on every mission, so a pretense could be maintained that these were VNAF missions and that the Americans were only aboard for training purposes.

As the war escalated the number of advisers increased only moderately, and they were increasingly overshadowed by the regular U.S. combat units. As the U.S. military began withdrawing from Vietnam in 1969, and the ARVN was expanded to replace U.S. units under **Vietnamization**, the number of advisers was at first increased dramatically to assist the expansion; the strength of the field advisory teams went from about 7,000 at the beginning of 1969 to almost 12,000 by the end of the year, and exceeded 14,000 during 1970. A rapid withdrawal of U.S. Army advisers began in 1971; the **Navy**, Air Force, and **Marines** did not pull advisers out as fast as the Army did.

The effectiveness of advisers varied widely. Few of them spoke Vietnamese, which made it difficult for them to acquire a deep understanding of the Vietnamese organizations they were advising during what was typically a one-year **tour**.

When U.S. military advisers arrived in **Laos** under Project *Hotfoot* in 1959, they were disguised as civilians. Not until 1961, under Project *White Star*, did the United States acknowledge openly that it had military advisers in Laos. They were pulled out in 1962 following the **Geneva Accords of 1962**. In later years, military advice was provided covertly, on a limited scale, through the **Central Intelligence Agency**. Personnel from Laos were also sometimes brought to **Thailand** for training, to get around the prohibition on having U.S. military personnel in Laos to do the training.

There was a U.S. Military Assistance Advisory Group in **Cambodia** from 1955 to 1963, but it was never much involved in advice or training; its role was to supervise delivery of the small quantity of military aid the United States was providing.

The United States sent a few military advisers to Cambodia, very quietly, in May 1970. For the most part, however, U.S. training of

Cambodian military personnel took place in South Vietnam or Thailand, rather than in Cambodia. The Cooper-Church Amendment (*see* **Congress**), which became law in January 1971, forbade the presence of U.S. military advisers in Cambodia.

**AERIAL REFUELING.** KC-135 tanker aircraft, derived from the Boeing 717 (the four-engine 717 of the 1950s, not the two-engine plane designated 717 in the 1990s), provided aerial refueling for U.S. military aircraft.

**AGENT ORANGE.** *See* HERBICIDES.

**AGNEW, SPIRO THEODORE** (1918–1996). U.S. vice president. Born in Baltimore, Agnew attended Johns Hopkins University and then began studying at the University of Baltimore Law School before joining the **Army**, in which he served from 1942 to 1945; he commanded a company in the 10th Armored Division. He completed his law degree in 1947. He entered Republican Party politics, eventually winning election as Baltimore County executive in 1962 and then governor of Maryland in 1966. He was still comparatively unknown in national politics when **Richard Nixon** picked him as his vice-presidential candidate in the 1968 **election**.

Agnew was far more conspicuous than most vice presidents, launching savage attacks on the Democratic Party, the **anti-war movement**, and the media. Alliterative phrases were his trademark; he described his targets as "nattering nabobs of negativism," "vicars of vacillation," and in an extreme case "hopeless, hysterical hypochondriacs of history." He claimed to speak for a "silent majority" of decent, conservative Americans against the radicalism that had emerged from the turmoil of the 1960s, and in fact attained a great deal of popularity.

In 1973, however, a grand jury in Baltimore found proof that Agnew had collected numerous and large bribes as Baltimore County executive and governor of Maryland. Agnew reached an agreement with the prosecutors in October 1973. He pleaded *nolo contendere* and accepted conviction on a charge of failure to pay taxes on his illicit income, but not directly on the charge of bribery; he paid a $10,000 fine; and he resigned the vice presidency. (This bargain did not hold up. In 1981, as a result of a suit filed in civil court on behalf of Maryland taxpayers, he was ordered to pay the State of Maryland the full amount he was found to have collected in bribes—$147,500—plus interest.)

Agnew for years had been a source of strength to the Nixon White House, helping to inspire suspicions of the "liberal media" that have endured to this day. The circumstances of his departure, however, were among the factors weakening the White House, leaving Nixon and then Nixon's successor as president, **Gerald Ford**, unable to obtain the cooperation of **Congress** for their Vietnam policies.

Agnew's memoir *Go Quietly . . . or Else* (1980) claims that he had been innocent of the charges against him, and that he had been forced from office by scheming members of the White House staff.

**AIR AMERICA.** One of the larger "proprietary" airlines, nominally a private corporation, actually controlled by the **Central Intelligence Agency**, Air America was officially created in 1959 (derived from Civil Air Transport) and disbanded in 1976. It played a huge role in the war in **Laos**; its aircraft were the primary means of supply for military units in much of the country. In South Vietnam its operations were significant, but secondary to the operations of **Air Force** and **Army** aircraft. *See also MILL POND.*

**AIR COMMANDOS.** In April 1961, as **counterinsurgency** was becoming at least marginally fashionable within the U.S. Armed Forces, the **Air Force** established a unit that was to specialize in such matters, the 4400th Combat Crew Training Squadron, based at Eglin Air Force Base in Florida, often referred to as *Jungle Jim* or as Air Commandos. In October 1961, a detachment of the Air Commandos was ordered to South Vietnam in Project *Farm Gate*; it began to arrive in Vietnam in November. On July 8, 1963, the *Farm Gate* force, based at **Bien Hoa**, was formally designated the 1st Air Commando Squadron (Composite).

Later in the war, other Air Commando units flew missions in South Vietnam and far more in **Laos**. A small Air Commando team codenamed *Waterpump* was sent to **Thailand** in March 1964 to train pilots of the Royal Lao Air Force. The 56th Special Operations Wing was activated on April 8, 1967, and soon renamed the 56th Air Commando Wing; it was based at Nakhon Phanom in **Thailand** and flew old propeller-driven aircraft on missions over Laos. **C-130** transport planes of the 315th Air Commando Wing were assigned in 1967 to drop chemicals that would break up the structure of the soil and thus create unusually deep and impassible mudholes on dirt roads in the rainy season (*see* Operation *COMMANDO LAVA*).

**AIR CUSHION VEHICLE.** The SRN-5 Patrol Air Cushion Vehicle (PACV), a military version of what in civilian use is usually called a hovercraft, was 39 feet long and 24 feet wide. It could move over land or water, at speeds up to 70 knots. It rode on a cushion of air, held in by rubber skirts on all sides. The first U.S. **Navy** PACVs arrived in Vietnam in 1966. They were tried in Operations *Market Time* and *Game Warden*, but were not effective enough to justify their considerable cost. Their greatest successes were in Operation *Monster*, aimed at **Viet Cong** forces in the **Plain of Reeds** in November 1966, and in the coastal areas of **I Corps** from June 1968 onward. The U.S. **Army** also used air cushion vehicles in Vietnam in the late stages of the war.

**AIR FORCE,** U.S. (USAF). The United States Air Force was dominated by the advocates of strategic bombing, who believed the main role of air power should be to attack the sources of enemy power in the enemy's heartland. It chafed under the restrictions of a war in which it was required to devote more of its efforts to tactical bombing (attacks on enemy military forces on and near the battlefield), but performed its tactical bombing missions, for the most part, with skill. For Air Force actions in the war, *see* **air war**.

General **Curtis E. LeMay,** USAF chief of staff beginning June 1961, strongly advocated escalation of the Vietnam War. By the time General John P. McConnell became chief of staff in February 1965, the escalation was ready to begin, but there were questions as to how it should be done. McConnell urged massive bombing, especially of the northern part of **North Vietnam.** He said this would make a commitment of large ground forces in South Vietnam unnecessary. General John D. Ryan, who became chief of staff in August 1969, and General George S. Brown, who took office in September 1973, did not so conspicuously try to shape policy.

**AIR WAR.** Air power was used in the Second Indochina War on a far larger scale than in any other war in history, and it shaped the conduct of ground operations to a far greater extent than in any previous war. By 1968, the three busiest airports in the world were all in Vietnam: **Bien Hoa, Danang,** and **Tan Son Nhut** in that order.

United States bombers and fighter-bombers expended more than 6,715,500 tons of air munitions in Indochina during this war. More than 3,203,000 tons of this were expended in **South Vietnam** from 1962 to 1973, and 2,093,300 tons in **Laos** from 1964 to 1973, making these the two most heavily bombed countries in the history of the world. Some 880,108 tons were expended in **North Vietnam** from 1964 to 1973, and 539,129 tons in **Cambodia** from 1969 to 1973. A majority of the munitions tonnage fell on South Vietnam in each year from 1962 to 1969, and in 1972; on Laos in 1970 and 1971; and on Cambodia in

1973. There was no year when a majority fell on North Vietnam. Aside from bombers and fighter-bombers, there were also **helicopters**, fixed-wing **gunships**, the **C-130** transport planes that dropped more than 3,700 tons of the huge M-121 and BLU-82 **bombs**, and other aircraft. U.S. and allied aircraft of all types expended a total of about 8,000,000 tons of air munitions of all types, with about half falling on South Vietnam.

This enormous application of aerial firepower not only inflicted heavy casualties on Communist forces, but allowed relatively small U.S. and allied ground units to operate in areas where they could not otherwise have been sent. If they were attacked by forces far too strong for their own weapons to have given them any chance of survival, they could often (not always, but often) be saved by air support.

The United States modified the physical environment of the war by spraying **herbicides** from aircraft to kill trees and brush. Efforts to modify the weather (*see* **weather warfare**) and the structure of the soil (*see* Operation *Commando Lava*) were less successful.

U.S. **Air Force** (USAF) fixed-wing transport planes were carrying 2,732 tons of cargo per day in Vietnam during the peak year, 1968. The peak year for cargo transport by helicopters, which could reach smaller units in the field, was 1969, with an average of 3,533 tons per day. Many positions in isolated locations could not have survived without air supply.

Airmobility—helicopter transport of troops—radically altered the nature of warfare. An **airmobile** unit could be landed in the middle of enemy territory in an organized fashion, not scattered by having the men come down individually by parachute. When men were wounded, **medical evacuation** helicopters carried them to hospitals. Thousands of men suffered wounds that in any previous war would have been fatal, but survived because of the speed with which helicopters brought them to hospitals. Medical evacuation by helicopter also allowed units that had suffered casualties to retain their mobility; they did not need to carry their wounded because the wounded had been sent off into the sky. If enemy forces in an area were too strong, a whole unit could sometimes be picked up and carried to safety.

The American air war in South Vietnam began late in 1961 when USAF pilots were sent to Vietnam under Project *Farm Gate*. **Army** helicopter pilots joined them at the end of the year, and a **Marine Corps** helicopter unit early in 1962 (*see* Project *Shufly*). Their operations were at first kept quiet; the United States maintained a pretense that

U.S. military personnel were in Vietnam only as **advisers**, not to conduct combat operations themselves. The first overt USAF combat missions in South Vietnam were flown on February 19, 1965, by B-57 **Canberra** bombers based at Bien Hoa.

The U.S. bombing campaign against North Vietnam started with sporadic air strikes—the U.S. retaliation for the **Tonkin Gulf incidents** in August 1964, and Operation *Flaming Dart* in February 1965. These were followed by a systematic bombing campaign, *Rolling Thunder*, from March 1965 to October 1968. There were only occasional strikes (*see* **protective reaction**, *Proud Deep Alpha*, **John D. Lavelle**) from then until 1972. Systematic bombing resumed in Operations *Freedom Train* in April 1972, and *Linebacker* beginning in May. *Linebacker II*, the famous "Christmas Bombing," came in the second half of December. All U.S. bombing of North Vietnam was halted in January 1973.

Characterizations of the U.S. air war as limited, and complaints about presidential interference in the choice of targets, refer primarily to North Vietnam, especially the northern half of North Vietnam. **Lyndon Johnson** was very worried about possible reactions by **China** or the **Soviet Union** to U.S. bombing of the northern half of North Vietnam, and he exercised tight personal control over bombing missions there. He allowed the military considerably more freedom in the bombing of the southern **panhandle** of North Vietnam, where all the major towns suffered devastation of a sort never inflicted on **Hanoi**. He allowed great freedom in the bombing of South Vietnam and Laos.

Air-to-air combat occurred mainly over North Vietnam, though there were a few incidents over Laos. The American planes tended to be larger and heavier, with more sophisticated equipment, but with a relatively low ratio of wing area to weight, which limited their maneuverability. The North Vietnamese **MiGs** were smaller, lighter, and more maneuverable. The Americans enjoyed a favorable kill ratio. The airfields from which the MiGs flew were off limits to U.S. bombing until April 1967. Two airfields were bombed on April 24, 1967; raids were authorized against the others gradually over the coming months, and the last, Phuc Yen, was finally bombed on October 25. By late fall of 1967, most of the MiGs had shifted to bases in China.

U.S. aircraft also faced strong ground-based air defenses in North Vietnam (*see* **anti-aircraft artillery**, *Iron Hand*, **Surface-to-Air Missiles**, and *Wild Weasel*).

There were a few U.S. air strikes on Laos in 1964; bombing became systematic and massive in 1965, and remained so until February 22, 1973. The last isolated air strikes were in April 1973. Bombing in Laos fell mainly on the **Ho Chi Minh Trail** in the South, but there was also bombing in northern Laos, supporting the Royal Laotian Army and the **Central Intelligence Agency**'s "Secret Army" of **Hmong** tribesmen in their war against **PAVN** and **Pathet Lao** forces. The CIA's proprietary airline **Air America** provided vital support for the Secret Army. Respecting the fiction of Laotian neutrality, the United States for years avoided openly acknowledging its air war in Laos, but the bombing was not in any genuine sense secret.

When significant U.S. bombing of Cambodia began in March 1969 under Operation *Menu*, it was truly secret. The administration of **Richard Nixon** was determined to prevent the press, the **Congress**, or even most U.S. military officers from learning that it was occurring. Overt bombing of Cambodia did not begin until April 1970 (*see* Operations *Patio, Freedom Deal*). It remained on a limited scale until U.S. bombing of South Vietnam and North Vietnam was halted completely, and bombing of Laos halted almost completely, in January and February 1973. With only Cambodia left to bomb, the United States intensified the bombing there to far higher levels than had ever been attained before. The U.S. **Congress** finally forced a halt to the bombing on August 15, 1973.

**AIRBORNE.** Term used by the U.S. **Army** for troops that could be delivered to the battlefield by parachute or glider. They were considered elite units. In Vietnam, the units officially designated as airborne never used gliders, and hardly ever parachutes; they functioned in practice as regular infantry or as **airmobile (helicopter-**transported) troops. The 173d Airborne Brigade was the first substantial U.S. Army unit sent to Vietnam. It arrived in May 1965, and was initially assigned to the defense of **Bien Hoa**, but by late June was beginning offensive probes into **War Zone D**. It became a sort of "fire brigade," moved around Vietnam to crisis spots. One of its battalions, the 2/503 Infantry, actually parachuted into **War Zone C** on February 22, 1967, during Operation *Junction City*. The 1st Brigade of the 101st Airborne **Division** arrived in July 1965, and the remainder of the division late in 1967. The 3d Brigade of the 82d Airborne Division arrived in February 1968, served initially in the area of **Hue** and later the area of **Saigon**, and departed in December 1969. *See also* AIRBORNE BRIGADE, AIRBORNE DIVISION.

**AIRBORNE BATTLEFIELD COMMAND AND CONTROL CEN-TERS** (ABCCC). Aircraft orbiting usually over **Laos**, coordinating air (and sometimes ground) operations in sections of Laos and **North Vietnam**. RC-47s began doing this work under the code name *Dogpatch* in 1966 and *Alleycat* in 1967. **C-130**s replaced the RC-47s in 1968.

**AIRBORNE BRIGADE, AIRBORNE DIVISION.** When the **Vietnamese National Army** became the Army of the Republic of Vietnam (**ARVN**) in 1955, one of its most important elite units was the Airborne Group, of regimental strength, commanded by **Do Cao Tri**. Tri was replaced by **Nguyen Chanh Thi** in September 1956. In December 1959, the group was expanded to a brigade. In November 1960, Colonel Thi used the brigade in an attempted coup, which almost succeeded in overthrowing President **Ngo Dinh Diem**. **Cao Van Vien** commanded the brigade from this point until December 1964, when he was replaced by **Du Quoc Dong**, a **Nung** from **North Vietnam**.

During 1965, as the brigade's troops were rushed to one crisis point after another, they suffered heavy casualties, and adequate replacements, especially for leadership personnel, were not available. The quality of most battalions in the brigade declined seriously, and after an entire battalion was lost at midyear, General Dong became, for a while, reluctant to risk further casualties. The brigade was expanded to a division in December 1965. General Dong was replaced as division commander by Le Quang Luong in November 1972.

The Airborne Division was part of the general reserve, an elite force available for emergencies or especially important operations, such as the **Cambodian Incursion** and *Lam Son 719*, but there was sometimes a sense that it was too valuable to be risked. President **Nguyen Van Thieu**'s early abandonment of *Lam Son 719* in 1971 may have been inspired partly by fear of unacceptable losses to the Airborne Division, and his decision in March 1975 to move most of the division from **I Corps** (which was seriously endangered) to the **Saigon** area (which was not) helped to trigger the collapse of I Corps and the fall of South Vietnam (*see* **final collapse**).

**AIRMOBILE.** Term used in the U.S. **Army** for troop units that were moved to and on the battlefield by **helicopter**. Some units were specifically designated "airmobile," but airmobility proved so valuable in Vietnam that it came to be used by many units not so designated.

General Hamilton H. Howze was the Army's principal advocate of airmobility from the mid-1950s onward. Howze made only moderate progress until he obtained the support of General **Maxwell Taylor** in 1962. Taylor decided in February 1963 to establish the 11th Air Assault **Division**, under General Harry Kinnard (previously commander of the 101st Airborne Division) to test the new tactics. This unit was a large part of the basis for the 1st **Cavalry** Division (Airmobile), which was sent to Vietnam in August and September 1965, and gave airmobile tactics their first major combat test in the Battle of the **Ia Drang Valley** in November.

**AMERICAN FRIENDS OF VIETNAM** (AFV). An organization dedicated to encouraging and strengthening the American commitment to the **Republic of Vietnam**, established at the end of 1955. The AFV did not aspire to a mass membership. It recruited people of influence, and liked to get people with strong government connections when it could. Members of both houses of **Congress**, and one Supreme Court justice, joined in the 1950s. General **John W. O'Daniel** was chairman of the AFV until 1963. In about 1966, **Henry Cabot Lodge** (U.S. ambassador to Saigon and a power in the Republican Party—he had been **Richard Nixon**'s running mate in the 1960 presidential election) and General **Maxwell Taylor** (former U.S. ambassador to Saigon and former chairman of the **Joint Chiefs of Staff**) jointly became honorary chairmen; they served well into the 1970s.

The AFV initially included anti-Communists from across the American political spectrum, not just conservatives but liberals like Senators **John F. Kennedy** and **Mike Mansfield**, and even Norman Thomas, head of the American Socialist Party. Joseph Buttinger, an Austrian immigrant who still held some of the socialist views of his youth, and who had been sent to **South Vietnam** in 1954 by the International Rescue Committee (a private organization that helped refugees from Communist countries) to aid refugees from **North Vietnam**, was the principal founder of the American Friends of Vietnam. During the 1960s most of the socialists and liberals dropped out, and the AFV shifted to the right.

The American Friends of Vietnam did not have the impact on U.S. policy that some authors have ascribed to it. Its founders wanted to ensure that Dwight Eisenhower's administration made a firm commitment to **Ngo Dinh Diem**, but by the time the AFV actually got organized, the commitment had already been made.

After a long period of quiescence, the AFV revived in late 1964 and early 1965, first urging escalation of American military efforts and then, after President **Lyndon Johnson** had indeed escalated, publicly endorsing what the president had done. The AFV's calls for the United States to bomb North Vietnam apparently had no impact on the president's decision to do so, but its support after the fact did have some effect, increasing public support for the U.S. military effort. For the next few years the AFV released statements, provided speakers to take the pro-war position in debates on the war, and so forth. But by 1967, the White House, disappointed with the impact of the AFV on the public debate, had decided to encourage the establishment of a new group, the Citizens Committee for Peace and Freedom in Vietnam. The AFV hung on to the end of the war, remaining a voice in the arguments over the war, but not a loud one.

**AMTRAC.** The LVTP-5A1 (Landing Vehicle Tracked, Personnel, or Amphibious Tractor) was a U.S. **Marine** vehicle intended for use in amphibious assaults. It could carry as many as 34 troops with crowding; a load of 25 was preferred. The Marines used it in Vietnam for transporting troops and supplies both on land and by water, and for patrolling waterways. Its worst drawback was that its gasoline tanks were in its floor, so land **mines** could easily initiate a lethal fire. Marines often preferred to ride on top of the vehicle and risk enemy rifle fire, rather than ride inside and risk incineration.

**ANTI-AIRCRAFT ARTILLERY** (AAA). By the middle and late stages of the Vietnam War, **North Vietnam** had what is often described as the strongest air defense system in history, though it is important to remember that this is true only in an absolute and not in a relative sense. North Vietnam's air defenses were stronger in 1967 than Germany's had been in 1943, but the attacking aircraft had improved during the intervening years by an even greater margin; North Vietnamese defenses posed less danger to the jet aircraft that were attacking North Vietnam in 1967 than Germany's had to the much slower aircraft attacking Germany in 1943.

The most important component of the North Vietnamese air defenses was anti-aircraft artillery. The 100-mm **radar**-aimed guns, from the **Soviet Union**, could reach altitudes of 30,000 feet and could pose serious dangers to aircraft at altitudes as high as 20,000 or 25,000 feet. The 57-mm guns might be either radar-guided or visually aimed. Smaller visually aimed cannon, 23-mm and 37-mm, could be very dangerous to planes at lower altitudes. The 12.7-mm and 14.5-mm **ma-**

**chine guns** and the rifles of peasant militiamen knocked down few U.S. planes, but were nonetheless significant in deterring U.S. planes from using very low altitudes to dodge the fire of the larger guns.

**ANTI-WAR MOVEMENT.** A few Americans began protesting against the war in Vietnam in 1963; the protest movement attained significant size in 1965. It was made up of a wide variety of people, with widely differing beliefs, including:

1. People who were actually enthusiastic about Communism.

2. People who did not like Communism but opposed the U.S. war effort because they thought a Communist **South Vietnam** was preferable to continued U.S. support for the military dictatorship in Saigon.

3. People who did not like Communism but opposed the U.S. war effort because they did not believe U.S. government charges that the **National Liberation Front** (NLF) was dominated by Communists, and therefore did not think that the U.S. war effort was necessary in order to keep Vietnam from becoming a Communist country. This misunderstanding extended very high in the movement. After the Reverend **Martin Luther King Jr.** was killed, his widow found in his pocket a list of ten commandments in regard to the Vietnam War, which she believed he might have been planning to use in a major anti-war speech. Along with items like not trusting the U.S. government's statistics was "Thou shalt not believe that the enemy's victory means communism."

4. People who had no clear idea of what they wanted to happen in Vietnam, but who were convinced that what the United States was actually doing was wrong.

5. People whose main interest was not in the rights and wrongs of the war, but in its monetary cost, and in their fear that they, or their friends and relatives, might be drafted and sent to fight in Vietnam.

Categories (1) and (2) were very small, though they provided much of the leadership for the anti-war movement. The only forms of anti-war sentiment that became widespread among the American population were those of categories (3), (4), and (5)—sentiments not based on a clear evaluation of the consequences for Vietnam of an American withdrawal.

The first "teach-in" was held at the University of Michigan on March 24, 1965. There had been suggestions that classes be cancelled for a day, but what finally happened was that anti-war professors invited students to come to a series of lectures and talks scheduled not to conflict with regular classes, beginning in the evening and lasting through the night. The organizers were startled when about 3,000 students came. "Teach-ins" were then organized at many other universities.

The first really large protest demonstration against the war was held in Washington, D.C., on April 17, 1965. The main organizing group was **Students for a Democratic Society** (SDS), but many other groups participated. There was much dispute over the SDS policy of "non-exclusion" under which all groups wishing to participate were allowed to do so, even the Communist Party. Many pacifist and moderate left-ist groups had for years refused to participate in any demonstration or political activity that included the Communist Party, or certain Com-munist-leaning or extreme leftist groups, and it was only with diffi-culty that SDS leaders won a grudging acceptance of their non-exclu-sionary policy. The size of the march was disputed, but the number of participants was certainly more than 20,000. Many students rode char-tered buses from distant cities. They marched in an orderly fashion near the White House in the morning, then listened to speeches, and to singers Joan Baez and Judy Collins, in the afternoon.

A peaceful rally of about 50,000 people in Washington on October 21, 1967, was followed by a march on the Pentagon that led to consi-derable violence, with protesters throwing eggs and bottles, and guards clubbing protesters.

The movement never had a tight, unified leadership. In its early years, people of widely differing views were often able to work to-gether in loosely structured organizations, concentrating on their com-mon opposition to the war and not paying much attention to the differ-ences among their opinions. Later, very radical opponents of the war, who were usually critical of the whole capitalist system and not just opponents of the war, became frustrated and unwilling to operate within the framework of large organizations containing many moderates. Some groups of these radicals eventually turned to violence. The assassina-tions in 1968 of **Robert Kennedy** and Martin Luther King Jr., two of the most important anti-war political leaders in the United States, proba-bly encouraged the turn to radicalism and violence by reducing the protestors' faith that they could attain their goals by normal political processes.

The process of radicalization was particularly conspicuous in SDS, by far the most important anti-war organization on college and univer-sity campuses in the early years of the movement. The national organi-zation of SDS was destroyed in June 1969, when its last national convention witnessed a power struggle between the Progressive Labor Party (PL, a Maoist organization), and the group that came to be known as the Weathermen. Local SDS chapters on some college campuses continued to function for a few more months.

Shortly after the breakup of SDS, the Weathermen embarked on a wave of bombings. They were a very small group (probably between 100 and 300 members during the period of the bombings), and very secretive, operating in small cells; this makes it difficult to determine which bombings were really theirs and which were carried out by other groups or individuals inspired by their example. The most famous incident in which they were definitely involved was an accidental detonation in which three of their members were killed while trying to manufacture a bomb in New York City on March 6, 1970. The most famous bombing carried out deliberately against the intended target, the attack on the U.S. **Army**'s mathematical research center on the campus of the University of Wisconsin, in Madison, Wisconsin, on August 24, 1970, in which a graduate student was killed, was carried out not by the Weathermen but by a local group indigenous to the Madison area. Such local groups and the nationally organized Weathermen, between them, did enough bombing to bring considerable discredit on the anti-war movement in general.

Even in the later stages of the war the largest anti-war protests, organized by major anti-war organizations, were usually peaceful and orderly. The ones that turned to violence, with mobs smashing windows and throwing rocks at the police, were usually small local protests, without the guidance of the major leaders of the movement.

After the dissolution of SDS, anti-war organizations were often more ephemeral. The Vietnam Moratorium Committee (VMC), for example, a comparatively moderate organization founded in June 1969, organized the very successful Vietnam Moratorium on October 15 of that year. More people demonstrated against the war that day than had ever done so before, though exact figures are impossible because instead of gathering large numbers in a few places like New York and Washington, the VMC organized hundreds of protests in towns all across the country, many of which had never seen an anti-war demonstration before. It then cooperated with the somewhat more radical New Mobilization Committee to End the War in Vietnam (the "New Mobe," founded in July 1969) to hold a huge demonstration—probably 500,000 people or more—in Washington on November 15. But the Vietnam Moratorium Committee disbanded in April 1970.

On November 15, 1969, besides cooperating with the VMC in Washington, the New Mobe also organized a demonstration of at least 100,000 people in San Francisco, the largest that had yet been held in California. On May 9, 1970, during the huge outburst of anti-war protest on college campuses brought on by the **Cambodian Incursion** and the deaths at **Kent State** University, the New Mobe brought something on the order of 130,000 demonstrators to Washington. They teetered on the edge of major civil disobedience, an effort to block important streets by a massive sit-down, but never quite attempted this. The New Mobe then faded away.

By 1971, demonstrations in Washington were occurring at frequent intervals. From April 19 to 23, **Vietnam Veterans Against the War** (VVAW) organized what it called "Operation Dewey Canyon III, a limited incursion into the country of Congress" (Operations *Dewey Canyon* and *Dewey Canyon II* had been actual military operations in Vietnam that included or assisted "limited incursions" into **Laos**). Crippled veterans, and a few mothers of men who had died in Vietnam, had conspicuous roles. On April 23, the last day of Dewey Canyon III, almost a thousand Vietnam veterans went to the Capitol, intending to return their medals to the government. They found that a fence had been built blocking them from the Capitol steps, so they threw their medals over the fence.

The next day, anti-war organizers brought a huge crowd, about half a million people, to Washington for a peaceful and orderly demonstration against the war. But after that it was the turn of the "May Day Tribe" and associated groups, which brought smaller but still substantial crowds to Washington in early May with the announced intention of blocking the streets and shutting down the city. The government met them with police, National Guardsmen, and Army troops. More than 12,000 people were arrested between May 2 and 5, including most of the leaders of the demonstrations. The largest number, about 7,000, were arrested on May 3, the day the protesters tried to block streets and major bridges. More than a thousand were arrested on May 5 on the steps of the Capitol, where they had gathered to hear speeches by four anti-war members of the House of Representatives. Most of the charges were later dismissed without trial; in many cases the arresting officers had not kept any record specifying the nature of the offense or the location where it was supposed to have taken place.

There were no more huge demonstrations after the spring of 1971, though there were some of very substantial size. On "Peace Action

Day," April 22, 1972, the National Peace Action Coalition and other groups organized demonstrations estimated at 35,000 in New York, 30,000 in San Francisco, 12,000 in Los Angeles, and varying numbers in other cities not only in the United States but also in other countries.

**AP BAC,** Battle of, January 2, 1963. An American aircraft using radio direction-finding gear had located a **Viet Cong** unit in the hamlets of Tan Thoi and Bac, about 20 kilometers northwest of the town of My Tho in the province that the **Republic of Vietnam** called Dinh Tuong and the Viet Cong called by its older name of My Tho, in the **Mekong Delta**. U.S. and **ARVN** officers planned an operation to trap and destroy the Viet Cong force. That force, led by Hai Hoang (born Nguyen Van Dieu), commander of the 261st Battalion (the best Viet Cong unit of **Military Region** 2—Central **Nam Bo**) was far stronger than U.S. and ARVN officers had expected: one company of the 261st Battalion plus one company of the 514th Battalion (the provincial battalion of My Tho), adding up to about 320 men, plus two platoons of local guerrillas. They had a few (probably three) .30-caliber **machine guns**, and a 60-mm **mortar**.

The ARVN force attacking them had greatly superior numbers and weapons. Initially, a battalion of the ARVN 7th Infantry Division landed by **helicopter** to the north of the guerrilla force, while two battalions of **Civil Guards**, and a company of M-113 **armored personnel carriers** carrying a company of ARVN infantry, approached from the south. Later in the day, an additional infantry company was brought in by helicopter, and a battalion of the elite **Airborne Brigade** was dropped by parachute. These troops had the support of helicopter **gunships**, of bombing and strafing by AD-6 **Skyraider**, B-**26**, and **T-28** aircraft, and of 105-mm and 155-mm **artillery**.

The Viet Cong were dug into well-concealed positions in tree lines near the hamlets, facing out across open rice fields. The Americans landed helicopters in one of these fields directly in front of a heavily held tree line; most of the American casualties of the battle (three killed, eight wounded) were crewmen on these helicopters. Part of the airborne battalion that parachuted into the battle late in the afternoon landed in a similar killing zone.

The helicopter gunships fired **rockets** and machine guns into the Viet Cong positions, but otherwise the greatly superior firepower of the ARVN and the Americans was for the most part wasted. The artillery and the fixed-wing aircraft either did not get or did not use information from people on the scene, who knew the location of the enemy, so the artillery shells fell almost at random, while **bombs** and **napalm** were for the most part dropped not on the tree lines in which the Viet Cong were concealed, but on targets more conspicuous to the pilots: the houses of the peasants in the hamlets. The M-113 armored personnel carriers had .50-caliber machine guns, far more powerful than any weapon the guerrillas had, but the gunners had to stand with their upper bodies sticking up out of the vehicles, exposed to enemy fire. The commander of the M-113s hesitated to bring them into the battle at all, and when they finally did attack one of the tree lines, it was in a very uncoordinated fashion, allowing the Viet Cong to concentrate their fire on the machine gunners of one or two vehicles at a time.

General **Huynh Van Cao**, commander of **IV Corps**, was horrified by the ARVN casualties. It seems he decided by late afternoon that the best way to avoid further losses was to allow the Viet Cong to leave the area safely during the night, which they did, having lost 18 men killed and 39 wounded. The ARVN admitted to having lost 63 men killed, and the true figure was closer to 80. The battle quickly became a point of dispute between the American military command and the press. General **Paul Harkins**, commander of **Military Assistance Command, Vietnam** (MACV), said that Ap Bac had been a victory for the ARVN. Several U.S. **advisers**, especially Lieutenant Colonel **John Paul Vann**, senior adviser to the 7th Division, told reporters it had been a disastrous failure. News reports reflecting the opinions of these advisers intensified the hostility that already existed between General Harkins and the reporters.

It is unlikely that Ap Bac caused much change in Viet Cong policy—a decision to form larger and more heavily armed units, capable of fighting this sort of battle, seems already to have been made—but Ap Bac gave the Viet Cong confidence that the new policy was going to work.

*ARC LIGHT.* Code name for air strikes flown by **B-52** bombers.

**ARIZONA TERRITORY.** American nickname for a valley area about 30 kilometers southwest of **Danang** in **Quang Nam** province, notorious for the frequency with which U.S. patrols there were ambushed.

**ARMORED PERSONNEL CARRIERS** (APCs). The M-113 armored personnel carrier (see photograph 8), widely used by both **ARVN** and U.S. forces in Vietnam, was originally intended to transport troops; it was assumed the troops would normally dismount when they reached

the scene of combat. In Vietnam it functioned more as a combat vehicle. This shift in missions called for increased armament. Originally, the standard M-113 had had only a .50-caliber **machine gun**
mounted on it, and the gunner's upper body was exposed to enemy
fire. From 1966 onward, the most common configuration had a .50-
caliber machine gun with a shield to protect the gunner, and also two
7.62-mm machine guns. If all three machine guns were shielded, it
was called an Armored Cavalry Assault Vehicle (ACAV).

Right from the beginning, some M-113s had nonstandard armament. The .50-caliber machine gun might be replaced by a flame
thrower, a 7.62-mm **minigun**, an automatic 40-mm **grenade launcher**,
or a 75-mm, 90-mm, or 106-mm **recoilless rifle**.

The United States began to send M-113 armored personnel carriers
to Vietnam in March 1962, and the ARVN began to use them in combat in the **Mekong Delta** in June. During the next few months, they
showed themselves highly effective as fighting vehicles; their alumi-
num armor was adequate against the light weapons that the guerrillas
were then using, and their .50-caliber machine guns were more powerful than any currently used guerrilla weapon. The **Viet Cong** did
not at first take advantage of the vulnerability of the machine gunners.

At the Battle of **Ap Bac**, on January 2, 1963, the exposed machine
gunners suffered heavy casualties from Viet Cong fire. Soon, shields
were being added to give at least partial protection to the machine
gunners. Soon afterward, however, the Viet Cong began to use weapons capable of piercing the sides of the M-113: heavy machine guns
(.50-caliber and 12.7-mm), 57-mm recoilless rifles, and a shoulder-
launched anti-tank weapon, the **RPG**-2. Penetration of the armored
personnel carrier by any of these weapons threatened not only direct
injury to the crew, but also the possibility of a lethal fire if the gasoline
tank were hit. The transition from the original gasoline-powered M-
113 to the diesel-powered M-113A1, much less vulnerable to fire, occurred mostly during 1967 and 1968.

The worst threat to the M-113 came from large land **mines**. Crews
often placed sandbags on the floors of their vehicles for added protection, sometimes so many that the weight caused significant problems.
Titanium "belly armor" for the bottoms of the vehicles, much lighter
than sandbags and highly effective, became available around 1969.

**ARMY,** U.S. The Army had the largest role in the Vietnam War of any of
the services. When the war was at its peak, about two-thirds of the

U.S. military personnel in Vietnam belonged to the Army. The Army lost 30,900 men killed by hostile action in the war; this was 65 percent of the total for all the services. The headquarters controlling U.S. personnel of all the services in Vietnam—the **Military Assistance Advisory Group** (MAAG) up to 1962, and **Military Assistance Command, Vietnam** (MACV), thereafter—was always headed by an Army general. U.S. Army, Republic of Vietnam (USARV), had its headquarters northeast of Saigon at **Long Binh**, by far the largest Army base in Vietnam.

The U.S. Army had been designed for conventional warfare, and most of its generals were inclined to fight as conventional a war as possible in Vietnam. They had to adapt to some extent to the special demands of guerrilla warfare, but they focused their attention as much as they could on the People's Army of Vietnam (**PAVN**), which was a more conventional force than the **Viet Cong** and could be fought by more conventional means. Even when fighting the Viet Cong, the Army tended to use the tactics and weapons of conventional warfare to the extent it could. General **Samuel Williams** and General **William Westmoreland** were probably the most important exemplars of this conventional mindset. The **Special Forces** were the stronghold of the minority in the Army that was enthusiastic for unconventional tactics.

The total personnel strength of the U.S. Army in mid-1965 was 968,313. The demands of the Vietnam War had increased this to 1,570,186 by mid-1968. President **Lyndon Johnson** decided in July 1965 to accomplish this expansion without a declaration of national emergency, under which the **Reserves** would have been mobilized, and trained soldiers could have been retained in the Army beyond their normal terms of enlistment. Instead President Johnson used the **Selective Service System** to draft huge numbers of young men. Up to this point the Army had been predominantly a volunteer force. In 1965, only 28 percent of the U.S. Army enlisted personnel killed by hostile action in Vietnam were draftees. By 1969 a substantial majority, 62 percent, would be draftees.

General **Harold K. Johnson**, chief of staff of the Army, was horrified when he learned that instead of calling up trained reservists (who would have included trained sergeants and junior officers to provide small-unit leadership), the Army would have to absorb, and try to train in a brief time, huge numbers of civilians. The serious decline of morale and discipline in the Army in the late 1960s has been traced in part to this decision.

Up to early 1965, the Army personnel in Vietnam were predominantly **advisers**, though from 1962 onward there were some belonging to the Special Forces, or to **helicopter** units, who participated directly in combat. The first regular U.S. Army ground combat unit sent to Vietnam, the 173d **Airborne** Brigade, arrived in May 1965. The last Army ground combat unit in Vietnam, the 3/21 Infantry Battalion, was deactivated August 12, 1972.

**ARTILLERY.** The United States used artillery on a massive scale in Vietnam, and assisted the Army of the Republic of Vietnam (**ARVN**) to do likewise. It is believed that over seven million tons of artillery shells were used, though precise figures are not available. It should be borne in mind that most of this weight was the steel of the shell casings, which had to be thick in order to be strong enough to resist the stresses of firing. The standard 105-mm high-explosive shell, for example, used in larger numbers than any other during the war, weighed 33 pounds, but the actual explosive charge inside it was only 4.8 pounds of trinitrotoluene (TNT).

*Howitzers* were designed for economical delivery of shells to moderate ranges; *guns* had longer ranges.

A U.S. **Army** artillery battalion typically had 18 howitzers and/or guns. In July 1969, with U.S. forces in Vietnam near peak strength, most U.S. Army artillery in Vietnam was in 61 battalions:

—105-mm towed howitzers: 31 battalions. When the war began the United States was using the M101A1, which weighed 2,220 kilograms (about 2.45 tons), and could fire four 33-pound shells per minute to a range of 11,000 meters. In 1966, the newer M102 began to arrive. It was much more easily transported, weighing just over 1.5 tons.

—105-mm M108 self-propelled howitzers: two battalions. These had the considerable handicap that they were too heavy to be carried by the Chinook **helicopters** that were used to transport the 105-mm towed howitzers.

—155-mm: seven battalions of towed M114A1 howitzers (see photograph 5), and four battalions of M109 self-propelled howitzers, plus three squadron batteries in the 11th Armored **Cavalry**. These fired a 95-pound shell, at a rate of three rounds per minute, to a range of 14,600 meters (some sources give a longer range for this weapon).

—175-mm guns and 8-inch howitzers, self-propelled, usually found together in the same battalion, and indeed convertible, one to the other, simply by changing barrels on the same chassis: 11 battalions. The rate of fire was slow, one round every two minutes. The M107 175-mm gun (see photograph 6) fired a 147-pound projectile 32,700 meters. The M110 8-inch howitzer fired a 200-pound projectile about 16,900 meters. These were very heavy weapons, weighing 28,165 kilograms and 26,308 kilograms respectively.

—One mixed battalion, 105-mm and 155-mm howitzers.

—Five mixed battalions, 155-mm and 8-inch howitzers.

The U.S. **Marines** used most of the same types of artillery, the 105-mm howitzer, the 155-mm howitzer, the 8-inch howitzer, and in the later stages of the war, the 175-mm gun. In the earlier stages the Marines used one weapon the Army did not, the M53 155-mm self-propelled gun, with a range of 23,500 meters. Do not confuse the 155-mm gun with the much shorter-ranged 155-mm howitzer.

American artillery was overwhelmingly howitzers of moderate range; distant targets could be attacked by aircraft. The **PAVN** preferred longer range guns, in the areas where it could use artillery (these did not include much of **South Vietnam** until 1972). The Soviet-built M46 130-mm field gun fired a 33.4-kilogram shell to a range of 31,000 meters. The PAVN used several Soviet and Chinese 122-mm weapons, with ranges varying from 11,800 to 21,900 meters (see photograph 7). The M37 152-mm howitzer fired a 43.5-kilogram shell to a range that has been variously estimated at 15,800 or 17,260 meters. The PAVN also used captured American-made artillery.

As American troops withdrew from South Vietnam, they handed over a considerable part of their artillery to the ARVN. The ARVN at the end of 1970 had had 1,116 artillery pieces (40 battalions of 105-mm and 15 battalions of 155-mm). By the end of 1971, the ARVN had 1,202 artillery pieces, including 12 175-mm guns. During the first 10 days of the **Easter Offensive** of 1972, however, the ARVN lost 117 artillery pieces, including four 175-mm guns. Many of the lost guns had been captured intact by the PAVN. American officers reported in 1972 that although ARVN artillery units had been trained in the techniques the Americans used, most of them did not bother to use those techniques in practice. They did not conduct registration fire, and the 1st ARVN Division was the only division whose artillerymen bothered to take into account the way atmospheric conditions affected the flight paths of their shells. ARVN artillery fire, while large in volume, tended to be inaccurate.

**ARVN** (Army of the Republic of Vietnam). Formerly the **Vietnamese**

**National Army**, renamed when the State of Vietnam became the **Republic of Vietnam** (RVN) in 1955. It is often called the South Vietnamese Army, though many of its officers and men were actually North Vietnamese. It was heavily influenced by the U.S. **Army**, which provided most of its weapons, trained many of its officers, and placed **advisers** in its units. The United States shaped it as a conventional military force, a less heavily armed version of the U.S. Army. (In the early 1970s, especially the second half of 1972, the United States provided more heavy weaponry; *see* Operation *Enhance*.)

The typical senior officer of the ARVN in the 1960s had become an officer in the French Union Forces in the late 1940s, after training in Vietnam, sometimes supplemented by military schooling in **France**; had transferred to the Vietnamese National Army in the 1950s; and had been sent to the United States for further schooling in the late 1950s, often at the Command and General Staff College, Fort Leavenworth, Kansas.

The ARVN was always heavily influenced by political considerations. **Ngo Dinh Diem**, RVN president from 1955 to 1963, was acutely aware of the danger of a military **coup**, and his choices of officers for key commands were often based more on loyalty than on military competence. His concern increased after Colonel **Nguyen Chanh Thi** almost overthrew him in an attempted coup in November 1960. During the next few years, Diem seems to have decided that heavy combat casualties would make the ARVN unhappy and thus increase the likelihood of a coup. He became determined to hold down casualties, even if this crippled military operations against the **Viet Cong**.

A group of ARVN generals led by **Duong Van Minh** nevertheless overthrew Diem, and killed him on November 2, 1963. ARVN officers dominated the RVN from then until 1975, though civilian prime ministers held nominal power for portions of 1964 and 1965. The ARVN was not a unified force; it was deeply factionalized. The group centering on Duong Van Minh was overthrown by another centering on **Nguyen Khanh** in January 1964, and in the months that followed, various factions plotted to overthrow one another in further coups. A group called the "**Young Turks**" began to emerge in September 1964, and was clearly dominant by February 1965, when it forced Khanh into exile. This group then divided, with **Nguyen Van Thieu** and **Vietnamese Air Force** commander **Nguyen Cao Ky** leading rival factions. Thieu was beginning to get the upper hand by 1967, the year he became president and Ky became vice president, but it was really only in

1968 that Thieu became overwhelmingly stronger than Ky. The structure of power remained comparatively stable from then until the collapse of the RVN in 1975. But effort was required to keep it stable; Thieu had to maintain loyalty by tolerating a great deal of corruption, and by making some personnel decisions on the basis of factional loyalty rather than military competence.

The ARVN was to some extent shoved aside when the United States began pouring combat troops into Vietnam in 1965, but not to as large an extent as Americans sometimes believed. For one thing, American attention tended to focus on the areas where the number of American troops was largest, and not on areas such as **IV Corps** where the ARVN continued to do most of the fighting. For another, there were considerable periods when U.S. official figures seriously understated the level of ARVN casualties, giving a misleading impression that the ARVN was not engaged in heavy combat. This was not a matter of deliberate deception; it was simply that U.S. officers, not familiar with ARVN bureaucratic routines, did not understand where in the ARVN system one needed to go in order to get reasonably complete casualty figures.

Figures for the strength of the ARVN sometimes refer only to the regular ARVN units, and sometimes include the irregular forces associated with it. At the beginning of 1961 there were about 150,000 men in the regular ARVN, and about 60,000 in the **Civil Guard**. By mid-1968 there were 359,959 in the regular ARVN, 197,917 in the **Regional Forces**, and 164,284 in the **Popular Forces**. By mid-1972 there were 456,620 in the regular ARVN, 294,571 in the Regional Forces, and 234,681 in the Popular Forces.

*ATTLEBORO,* Operation. It began on September 14, 1966, as a search-and-destroy operation by elements of the U.S. 196th Light Infantry Brigade in the eastern part of **War Zone C**, in **Tay Ninh** province. It remained relatively small until late October and early November, when elements of the **Viet Cong** 9th Division were discovered to be moving southward from their bases near the Cambodian border, passing both east and west of the *Attleboro* operating area. The operation was then dramatically expanded; portions of the U.S. 1st, 4th, and 25th Infantry **Divisions**, the 173d Airborne Brigade, and some **ARVN** units were committed to it. It ended on November 24, having inflicted heavy casualties on the Viet Cong.

**AUSTRALIA.** In the early to mid-1960s, Australia was more enthusiastic about supporting the U.S. struggle in Vietnam than any of the European allies of the United States. A team of 30 Australian military **advisers** arrived in **South Vietnam** on August 3, 1962. The 1st Battalion, Royal Australian Regiment (1RAR), arrived in June 1965. It was initially assigned to the defense of **Bien Hoa**, but soon was attached to the U.S. 173d **Airborne** Brigade.

From 1966 onward, Australian activities were concentrated mainly in Phuoc Tuy province, on the coast east of **Saigon**. The number of Australian military personnel in Vietnam peaked, at slightly more than 7,600, in 1968 and 1969. **Canberra** bombers of the Royal Australian Air Force expended 26,393 tons of **bombs** in South Vietnam from 1967 to 1971. The Royal Australian Navy also provided **naval gunfire support** along the coast from 1967 to 1971. The guided missile destroyer HMAS *Hobart* was accidentally attacked by a U.S. aircraft near the **Demilitarized Zone** on June 16, 1968; two sailors were killed.

Australia paid the financial costs of its forces in Vietnam, rather than taking U.S. aid for the purpose as some other countries did when providing forces. In the late stages of the war, as the level of Australian political support for the war declined, Australian military forces were pulled out. The last infantry battalion left in March 1972, and most support forces were also out by this time, but there were detachments of engineers, signal corps personnel, and advisers that remained until December 1972.

Australia established diplomatic relations with Hanoi in July 1973, while continuing diplomatic relations with Saigon.

## -B-

**B-26.** The plane that operated in the Vietnam War as the B-26 was a World War II–era plane, but it was not the one that flew in that war as the B-26. During World War II, there were two twin-engined aircraft of approximately the same size: the Martin B-26 Marauder, and the Douglas A-26 Invader. The Martin B-26 was retired from service in the late 1940s, but the Douglas A-26, faster and not requiring such a large aircrew, was kept on and renamed the Douglas B-26. This was the plane that was sent to Southeast Asia in the early 1960s.

Four B-26s belonging to the **Central Intelligence Agency** were sent to Takhli, in **Thailand**, at the end of 1960. Other B-26s supplied by the **Air Force** arrived early in 1961. Plans for these planes to be used in air strikes against Communist forces in Laos, in April 1961 under Project *Mill Pond*, were cancelled at the last minute.

B-26s served in **South Vietnam** for several years with the *Farm Gate* force, but the old planes were hard to maintain, and had structural problems; they were pulled out in 1964. Some B-26s that had been substantially rebuilt became available, under the designation A-26 Counter Invader, in 1966. The A-26 could carry up to five tons of various sorts of ordnance, both under the wings and in the bomb bay, but it also had eight .50-caliber **machine guns** in the nose. A-26s of the 603d **Air Commando** Squadron, based at Nakhon Phanom in **Thailand**, began to be used in 1966 for night attacks on trucks along the **Ho Chi Minh Trail** in **Laos**, in Operation *Big Eagle*.

**B-52 STRATOFORTRESS** (see photograph 13). A large, long-range jet bomber originally designed for delivering nuclear weapons against targets in the Soviet Union, but used very extensively in Indochina. B-52s dropped heavy bomb loads (the average increased from 20.5 tons in 1965 to 25.9 tons in 1971) from very high altitudes. None were ever based within Indochina; they flew at first from Andersen Air Force Base on **Guam**, later also from Kadena Air Base on **Okinawa** and from U-Tapao Air Base in **Thailand**. Their strikes were code-named *Arc Light*.

B-52s were first sent to Guam for possible use in Vietnam on February 11, 1965; their first combat mission, against targets in Binh Duong province of **South Vietnam**, was on June 18, 1965. B-52s began bombing **Laos** in December 1965, **North Vietnam** in April 1966, and **Cambodia** in March 1969, but most B-52 bombing was directed against targets in South Vietnam. By the time bombing ended on August 15, 1973, B-52s had dropped 3,053,914 tons of **bombs** on Indochina, almost as much as all other aircraft combined. *Skyspot*, a system by which **radar** on the ground guided bombing missions, relieving the pilots of the need to identify targets, began to be used to control B-52 missions on July 6, 1966, and was controlling most missions by the end of 1966.

The first time a B-52 was shot down was on November 22, 1972. Fragments from a **surface-to-air missile** detonating close to the aircraft over North Vietnam set it on fire and inflicted other damage, but the crew managed to reach the Thai border before bailing out. The following month, in Operation *Linebacker II*, B-52s were for the first time sent into the most heavily defended areas of North Vietnam, and 15 of them were shot down.

**BAC BO** (Bac Ky, Bac Phan, Tonkin). The northernmost of the three main administrative divisions of Vietnam from the early 19th century up to 1954. The great majority of the population lived in the **Red River Delta**. *Note:* in this dictionary the term **North Vietnam** will be reserved for the northern of the two halves into which Vietnam was divided from 1954 to 1975, an area much larger than Bac Bo, but some authors, especially Vietnamese, call Bac Bo "North Vietnam."

Bac Bo was bombed to some extent from 1965 to 1968 under Operation *Rolling Thunder*, but President **Lyndon Johnson** was very cautious about provoking a reaction from the **Soviet Union** or **China**, and he kept much tighter control over U.S. bombing of Bac Bo than he did over bombing of the southern **panhandle** of North Vietnam. **Richard Nixon** bombed Bac Bo somewhat more heavily in 1972 (*see Linebacker, Linebacker II*).

**BAHNAR.** A **Montagnard** group, speaking a Mon-Khmer language, living in an area extending from **Kontum** to An Khe.

**BAJARAKA** or **BAJARAKO MOVEMENT**. A movement to demand higher status and better treatment for the **Montagnards** of **South Vietnam**, established at a meeting in **Pleiku** on May 1, 1958. The name is derived from the first syllables of the names of the **Bahnar**, **Jarai**, **Rhadé**, and **Koho** tribes. The **Republic of Vietnam** initially tried to suppress the movement, arresting many of its leaders in September 1959, but at times tried to negotiate cooperation.

Members of the Bajaraka Movement were among the primary founders of **FULRO** in 1964.

**BALL, GEORGE WILDMAN** (1909–1994). Government official. Born in Des Moines, Iowa, he graduated from Northwestern University Law School 1933, and practiced law 1935–1942, 1946–1961, 1966–1968, and 1969–1982. He was director of the U.S. Strategic Bombing Survey in London, 1944–1945, and under secretary of state, 1961–1966.

Ball played a crucial role in promoting U.S. support for the **coup** that overthrew **Ngo Dinh Diem** in 1963. In particular, on August 24, 1963, on a weekend when all the top national-security officials were away from Washington and Ball was acting secretary of state, he sent a cable written primarily by **Roger Hilsman** and **W. Averell Harriman**, authorizing U.S. Ambassador **Henry Cabot Lodge**, in **Saigon**, to signal to officers of the Army of the Republic of Vietnam (**ARVN**) that the United States would not object to a coup. Ball was not doing this behind his superiors' backs—he had obtained permission by phone from President **John Kennedy** and Secretary of State **Dean Rusk**—but he was taking advantage of a situation in which he could ask Kennedy and Rusk separately for a decision that probably would not have been forthcoming if all the top officials had met together in Washington in more normal fashion.

From September 1964 through 1965, Ball wrote a series of memoranda expressing doubts that he had had for some time about the very foundation of the U.S. policy in Vietnam. He argued that the war was not being won, that the various sorts of escalation being proposed would not reverse the defeat, and that rather than escalate and lose a big war, the United States should seek a negotiated settlement. Ball showed the first of these memoranda to Rusk, **Robert McNamara**, and **McGeorge Bundy** in the autumn of 1964; he did not begin showing them to President **Lyndon Johnson** until early 1965. He became the "house dove" of the administration, the only strong voice against escalation among the officials Johnson regularly consulted on Vietnam policy. He became increasingly desperate in his fear of further escalation; in a memorandum of January 25, 1966, he told President Johnson he was convinced "that sustained bombing of **North Vietnam** will more than likely lead us into war with Red **China**—probably in six to nine months. And it may well involve at least a limited war with the **Soviet Union**." Later that year, he left the State Department.

Ball served as U.S. ambassador to the **United Nations** for a few months in 1968, but resigned to work for **Hubert Humphrey**'s presidential campaign. He pushed Humphrey to distance himself from President Johnson's Vietnam policy. He was chairman of the Asia Society from 1974 to 1982, during which time he wrote his memoirs, *The Past Has Another Pattern* (1982).

**BAN ME THUOT.** The capital of Darlac province, in the **Central Highlands**, part of **II Corps**. Ban Me Thuot is a major center for the **Rhadé**, a **Montagnard** group. **Route 14** runs southwest from Ban Me Thuot toward **Saigon**, north to **Pleiku** and **Kontum**. The Studies and Observations Group (**SOG**) established Command and Control, South (CCS), which sent covert teams into **Cambodia**, at Ban Me Thuot in 1968.

**FULRO** inspired a mutiny by the **Civilian Irregular Defense Groups** (CIDG) at CIDG camps in the Ban Me Thuot area in September 1964. The mutineers tried to seize the town, but failed.

Ban Me Thuot was one of the places attacked before dawn on January 30, 1968, 24 hours ahead of schedule, in the **Tet Offensive**.

The 320th **PAVN** Division launched a heavy attack on Ban Me Thuot, including **tanks**, in the early morning hours of March 10, 1975. By nightfall the attackers had taken part of the town; by March 12 they had it all. The **ARVN** initially decided to pull troops south from **Pleiku** and **Kontum** to retake Ban Me Thuot, but within days the ARVN was simply abandoning the Central Highlands (*see* **final collapse**). Today the town is called Buon Ma Thuot and is the capital of Dac Lac province, somewhat larger than the wartime Darlac.

**BARREL ROLL**, Operation. Program of U.S. air strikes against Communist transportation lines in eastern **Laos**, both along the **Ho Chi Minh Trail** and farther north, begun on December 14, 1964. At first few missions were actually flown. There was supposed to be no publicity about *Barrel Roll*, but public attention was drawn when two planes were shot down on January 13, 1965.

In April 1965, *Barrel Roll* was restricted to northeastern Laos only; the bombing along the Ho Chi Minh Trail became *Steel Tiger*.

**BEN HET.** Late in 1967, Fire Support Base (FSB) 12 was established at Ben Het, west of **Dak To**, in **Kontum** province, **II Corps**. In May 1968, Ben Het became **Special Forces** camp A-244. Located between Dak To and the point where **Laos**, **Cambodia**, and **South Vietnam** come together, Ben Het was less than 13 kilometers (within long **artillery** range) from the border. It lay across one of the routes by which men and supplies entered South Vietnam from the **Ho Chi Minh Trail**, and **SOG** soon began using it as a launching site for **reconnaissance** teams. It had an airstrip, but during periods of heavy attack fixed-wing aircraft could not land, and Ben Het had to be resupplied by airdrop.

More important than the average A-team camp, it was subject to unusually strong attacks, and sometimes had unusually strong defensive forces assigned to it. Ben Het became the scene of the only direct clash between U.S. and **PAVN** armored vehicles, on the night of March 3–4, 1969, when American M-48 **tanks** defeated an attack on the camp by PAVN PT-76 light amphibious tanks. The best known of the times when Ben Het was besieged, under heavy PAVN attack, was from May 5 to June 29, 1969. The United States had decided earlier that year to allow the **ARVN** to handle the ground combat in that area (with U.S. air and artillery support); ARVN forces had great difficulty and suffered considerable losses working to reopen Road 512 from Dak To to Ben Het, and break the siege.

Ben Het was converted to an ARVN **Ranger** camp on December 31, 1971; it fell to the PAVN on October 13, 1972.

**BEN TRE.** A town in the eastern part of the **Mekong Delta**, southwest of Saigon. It was the capital of the province that the **Republic of Vietnam** called Kien Hoa, but that the **Viet Cong** called by its former name of Ben Tre. The Ben Tre Uprising led by **Nguyen Thi Dinh**, which began on January 17, 1960 in that province, has been treated in Communist histories as a major milestone in the development of the guerrilla movement.

The town of Ben Tre became famous when Associated Press reporter Peter Arnett published the statement made to him by an unnamed U.S. **adviser** that during the **Tet Offensive**, "It became necessary to destroy the town to save it."

**BERRIGAN, DANIEL J.** (1921– ). **Catholic** priest (of the Jesuit order) and anti-war activist. Born in Virginia, Minnesota, Berrigan applied for admission to the Society of Jesus in 1939; he was ordained a priest in 1952. He began agitating against the Vietnam War in 1964. He was an extremely prolific writer, and became one of the most conspicuous public spokesmen for the **anti-war movement**, though his younger brother **Philip Berrigan** was more effective as an organizer of demonstrations.

Early in 1968, the **Democratic Republic of Vietnam** (DRV) decided to release three American **prisoners of war** (POWs) to representatives of the American peace movement. Berrigan was one of the two representatives who went to **Hanoi**, and accompanied the released POWs out of the country. At this time, it was formally illegal for American citizens to travel to Hanoi. The State Department offered to grant Berrigan and the others legal permission to make the trip, but they refused, preferring to go without permission.

Daniel Berrigan served a prison term for participating in the "Catonsville Nine," a group organized by his brother Philip, that destroyed draft board files in May 1968 (*see* **Philip Berrigan**). The Berrigan brothers had made no effort to avoid arrest—indeed they had blatantly courted it, so as to be able to use their trial as a public forum—but when ordered actually to report for imprisonment in April 1970, they refused and became fugitives. Philip was caught quickly, but Daniel remained at large for about four months, vigorously hunted by the Federal Bureau of Investigation (which he taunted by making occasional public appearances) before being caught and imprisoned.

He wrote an autobiography entitled *To Dwell in Peace* (1987), and was also the author of *Night Flight to Hanoi* (1968), *The Trial of the Catonsville Nine* (1970), and other books.

**BERRIGAN, PHILIP FRANCIS** (1923–2002). **Catholic** priest (of the Josephite order) and anti-war activist. Born in Two Harbors, Minnesota, he served in the U.S. **Army** (infantry) in the European Theater during World War II, and was ordained a priest in 1950. He received an A.B. from Holy Cross College in 1950, and an M.A. from Xavier University, New Orleans, in 1961. Philip Berrigan was active in the civil rights movement before he became famous as an opponent of the Vietnam War. His particular target was draft boards. On October 27, 1967, he and three others (the "Baltimore Four") entered a draft board in Baltimore and poured blood over a considerable number of files. While he was awaiting trial for this incident, he, his elder brother **Daniel Berrigan**, and seven others (the "Catonsville Nine") entered a draft board in Catonsville, Ohio, on May 17, 1968, removed a large number of files, and burned them outside where the fire would not imperil the building. They had chosen Catonsville because the draft board there was located in the hall of the Knights of Columbus, and they took this as a symbol of Catholic Church complicity with U.S. government policy.

The Catonsville Nine used their trial as a very effective forum for anti-war propaganda; the judge was more willing than most judges in that era to allow the defendants to make long speeches about their beliefs. All of the Catonsville Nine were convicted, and given sentences ranging from three years (for Philip Berrigan and one other leader in the group) down to two years.

While Philip was in prison, he and six others, the "Harrisburg Seven," were charged with conspiring to kidnap **Henry Kissinger** and plant explosive devices, intended to disrupt the electrical power system, in the steam tunnels under Washington, D.C. In April 1972, Philip Berrigan and Sister Elizabeth McAlister (a nun whom Philip later married) were convicted of smuggling letters in and out of the prison where Philip was being held; the jury was unable to reach a verdict on the other charges against the Harrisburg Seven.

Philip Berrigan was the author of *A Punishment for Peace* (1969) and *Prison Journals of a Priest Revolutionary* (1970).

**BIEN HOA.** Bien Hoa province lay immediately east of **Saigon**. At the beginning of the war it stretched southward to the sea, but by the late 1960s what had been its southern portion had been transferred to **Gia Dinh**. Its capital, also called Bien Hoa, was northeast of Saigon on **Route 1**.

Two U.S. **Army advisers** to the **ARVN** 7th Division were killed in a guerrilla attack on their quarters at Bien Hoa on July 8, 1959; these were the first U.S. advisers killed by hostile action in Vietnam. Bien Hoa Air Base was the first base for **U.S. Air Force** (USAF) combat units in Vietnam; the *Farm Gate* force arrived there late in 1961, and B-57 **Canberra** bombers were sent there in August 1964. A **Viet Cong mortar** attack on November 1, 1964, killed four Americans, destroyed five B-57 bombers, and damaged 15.

As the war expanded, Bien Hoa Air Base did likewise, remaining the largest military air base in Vietnam and becoming the busiest airfield in the world. By the beginning of 1969 the USAF had 220 aircraft assigned there, the U.S. Army had 220, and the **Vietnamese Air Force** (VNAF) had 75.

The headquarters of **II Field Force**, Vietnam (the U.S. Army Command for **III Corps**), and the huge U.S. Army base of **Long Binh**, were in Bien Hoa province a few kilometers east and southeast, respectively, of the town and air base of Bien Hoa. The U.S. 1st Infantry **Division** was briefly based at Bien Hoa after its arrival in Vietnam in late 1965.

**BINH DINH.** A province on the coast of central Vietnam, the northernmost coastal province of **II Corps**. The densely populated rice-growing areas are mostly near the coast, but some of them, such as the An Lao Valley in the northern part of the province, extend into the interior, surrounded by jungle. The intermingling of rice lands with jungle areas helped the Communists create strong bases in Binh Dinh.

The province capital was **Qui Nhon**, on the coast in the southern part of the province. The most important roads were **Route 1**, which ran north to south close to the coast, and **Route 19**, which ran from Qui Nhon west through An Khe and then into **Pleiku** province.

In the autumn of 1965, the U.S. 1st **Cavalry Division (Airmobile)** established its base at An Khe, and the South **Korean** (ROK) Capital Division established its base at Qui Nhon. In January 1966, these units, plus **ARVN** forces, began Operation *Masher* (later renamed *White Wing*), a major effort to destroy Communist forces in the eastern half of Binh Dinh. In September 1966, elements of the 1st Cavalry began Operation *Thayer* in Binh Dinh; when Communist forces were detected in the Hoa Hoi area near the coast, the 1st Cavalry took advantage of the flexibility that airmobility allowed them, scrapped the original plan, and conducted Operation *Irving* from October 2 to 24. Operation *Thayer II* followed, lasting from October 25, 1966, into February 1967. The 1966 operations in Binh Dinh had forced many peasants from their villages;

there were 129,000 people in refugee camps in the province at the end of the year.

The populated areas of Binh Dinh were for the most part considered to have been pacified by 1969, but the situation was becoming shaky again by 1971. In April 1972, three districts were overrun by Communist forces as part of the **Easter Offensive**.

**BINH GIA**, Battle of, December 27, 1964, to January 3, 1965. On December 27, 1964, two **Viet Cong** companies overran Binh Gia, a **Catholic** community in Phuoc Tuy province, about 60 kilometers east of **Saigon**. The 1st and 2d Regiments of the 9th Viet Cong Division were waiting to pounce on whatever forces Saigon sent to the rescue. Saigon sent elite units, **Rangers** and troops of the Vietnamese **Marine Corps** (VNMC); they reoccupied Binh Gia on December 30. On December 31, the 1st Viet Cong Regiment caught the 4th VNMC Battalion in an ambush near Binh Gia; the Marines lost 196 men killed, wounded, or missing, and the battalion was out of combat for three months. On January 3, 1965, the 2d Viet Cong Regiment caught the **ARVN** 35th Ranger Battalion, accompanied by **armored personnel carriers**, in an ambush just as devastating.

**BINH XUYEN.** The organized criminal underground of the **Saigon** area, led by Bay Vien (real name Le Van Vien), the Binh Xuyen allied with the French during the First Indochina War and by 1954 had achieved great wealth and power. The Binh Xuyen had their own military forces, and also controlled the Saigon police force. The Binh Xuyen, the **Hoa Hao**, and the **Cao Dai** (the three are commonly referred to as the "**Sects**," though only the Hoa Hao and Cao Dai were actually religious sects) were strong enough so that when Prime Minister **Ngo Dinh Diem** set out to smash their power early in 1955, it was not obvious whether Diem or the sects would win. Diem won decisively. Most of the Binh Xuyen military units were destroyed; the remnants were driven into remote areas, where within a few years certainly most of them, and probably all of them, came under Communist control.

**BOI LOI WOODS.** A forested area, notorious as a Communist stronghold, west of the **Iron Triangle** and southeast of **Tay Ninh** City in **III Corps**.

*BOLO*, Operation, January 2, 1967. The United States set a trap for North Vietnamese **MiG** fighter aircraft by sending a mission over **North Vietnam** made up of **F-4 Phantom** fighters, armed for air-to-air combat, but using a flight profile, and radio communications, designed to give the impression that they were something more vulnerable to attack by MiGs: a group of **F-105 Thunderchiefs** on a bombing mission. The United States claimed seven MIGs shot down, with no loss of U.S. aircraft.

**BOMBING HALTS.** After the United States began systematic bombing of **North Vietnam**, leaders in **Hanoi** announced that there could be no peace talks as long as the bombing was going on. Not only anti-war agitators but also some U.S. allies and U.S. government officials soon began suggesting that the U.S. halt the bombing, at least temporarily, in an effort to get **negotiations** started. President **Lyndon Johnson** was faced with conflicting advice, some officials urging a bombing halt while others stressed the need for uninterrupted, and indeed substantially expanded, bombing. The United States formed the habit of halting bombing for holidays such as Christmas and **Tet** (the Vietnamese New Year); it was often suggested that one of these holiday truces be lengthened to provide a possible opening toward peace talks.

The first bombing pause began on May 13, 1965. It lasted only five days, and Hanoi was given little or no advance notice that the bombing was going to be halted and that the United States would be awaiting a response—a reduction in combat activity by the **Viet Cong** in the South, or an offer of negotiations. President Johnson does not seem to have had much real hope that Hanoi could make a major change in policy on such short notice.

In November 1965, Secretary of Defense **Robert McNamara** began urging another bombing pause; he was able to persuade Secretary of State **Dean Rusk** and President Johnson, and it began on December 24. Despite pleas from General **William Westmoreland** and Admiral **Ulysses S. G. Sharp** that it be only a Christmas pause, lasting a few days, President Johnson prolonged it to 37 days. Combat activity by Communist forces in **South Vietnam** declined, but there was no real progress toward negotiations, and bombing of the North resumed on January 31, 1966.

On March 31, 1968, President Johnson announced that in an effort to promote negotiations he was halting the bombing of all of North Vietnam "except in the area north of the **Demilitarized Zone** [DMZ] where the continuing enemy buildup directly threatens allied forward positions and where the movements of their troops and supplies are clearly related to that threat." Initially the limit on bombing was set at the 20th parallel, about 350 kilometers from the DMZ, but almost immediately it was moved south to the 19th parallel. The quantity of **bombs** falling on North Vietnam did not decline when the area was restricted; on the contrary the monthly bomb tonnages dropped on this limited area, during this "partial bombing halt," were larger that what the United States had previously been dropping on the whole of North Vietnam.

The preliminaries to the **Paris negotiations** began almost immediately, but produced no quick result. President Johnson halted bombing of all of North Vietnam on November 1, 1968, and **Richard Nixon** continued the bombing halt after he became president in 1969. Until late 1971, Nixon limited U.S. aircraft to **reconnaissance** missions over North Vietnam, and occasional **protective reaction** strikes retaliating for attacks on the reconnaissance missions. In late 1971, the frequency of air strikes increased, due partly to false reports of attacks on reconnaissance aircraft (*see* **John D. Lavelle**, Operation *Proud Deep Alpha*). Systematic U.S. bombing of the North resumed on April 6, 1972, in response to the **Easter Offensive**.

Bombing north of the 20th parallel in North Vietnam was halted again from October 22 to December 17, and from December 30 onward. Bombing of all of North Vietnam ended on January 15, 1973. The **Paris Peace Agreement** ended U.S. bombing of South Vietnam on January 28, 1973. Systematic bombing of **Laos** was halted on February 22, 1973, following conclusion of a peace agreement in that country; the last U.S. air strike in Laos was on April 16. U.S. bombing of **Cambodia** was halted by the U.S. **Congress**, over President Nixon's objections, on August 15, 1973.

**BOMBS.** The most common type of bomb used in Vietnam was the general purpose (GP) high-explosive bomb. About half the weight of such a bomb was actual explosive, and half the weight was the steel case. The 500-pound MK-82 bomb (see photograph 15), for example, contained 192 pounds of explosive; the 750-pound M-117 contained 386 pounds of explosive; the 2,000-pound MK-84 contained 946 pounds of explosive. The most common bomb size in the Vietnam War was 750 pounds, and the 500-pound bomb was the second most common, but 125-pound, 250-pound, 1,000-pound, 2,000-pound, and 3000-pound bombs were also used in significant numbers.

"Snake-eye" bombs had large tail flaps that unfolded after the aircraft released them, to slow their fall. These could be dropped from low altitude; slowing the fall of the bomb gave the plane that dropped it time to get far enough away not to be damaged by the explosion.

"Daisy cutter" bombs used a fuze extender, a long rod attached to the nose of a bomb. When the tip of the fuze extender struck the ground, the bomb would detonate. Detonation while the body of the bomb was still above ground level produced less of a crater, but made the bomb very effective for knocking down trees. Small "daisy cutter" bombs, 500 pounds, were sometimes dropped near roads that the Communist forces were using, to cause trees to fall across the roads and block them. Very large ones, dropped under the code name *Commando Vault* from **C-130** transport aircraft, were used either for the destruction of military targets or for the creation of instant **helicopter** landing zones in the jungle. The first test drops, using five-ton M-121 bombs, were performed in **South Vietnam** in October 1968. Each M-121 cleared an area about 200 feet in diameter. More than 200 were eventually dropped. *Commando Vault* began using an even larger bomb, the 15,000-pound BLU-82, which could create a clearing about 260 feet in diameter, in March 1970. More than 360 BLU-82 bombs had been dropped, in South Vietnam, **Laos**, and **Cambodia**, by the time U.S. bombing was ended in 1973. The **Vietnamese Air Force** (VNAF) dropped an additional 15 of them during the last weeks of the war, in April 1975.

Fuel-air explosive bombs were also used occasionally in Vietnam. These were designed to release a cloud of flammable gas, which was detonated only after it had had time to mix with the air.

A smart bomb is one that is actively guided to its target after leaving the aircraft, rather than simply falling under the influence of gravity. The concept had been tested occasionally in combat beginning late in World War II, but the technology matured to the point of making this a truly effective weapon during the Vietnam War. The AGM-62 Walleye had a television camera in its nose; once it had locked onto the target, it steered itself. It was a glide bomb with a slant range of up to 40,000 feet. Its main disadvantage was that its camera needed daylight, good visibility, and a high-contrast target. Its shaped-charge warhead was effective against pinpoint targets, but was not very large; American pilots were frustrated when direct hits by Walleyes failed to knock down the very strongly built **Ham Rong** Bridge, in Thanh Hoa province. It began combat tests in March 1967, and came into full operational use early in 1968.

Laser guidance proved a more versatile means of steering smart bombs to their targets. Usually, one aircraft would shine a laser on the target, while another dropped the bomb, usually an MK-84 2,000-

pound bomb with a seeker head and steering fins added to allow it to guide itself to the bright spot. The bomb had far more explosive power than the Walleye, and could be used at night and against targets that were not visually conspicuous enough for the television camera in the Walleye to lock onto them. Combat tests began in 1968, but little is known about the early tests and they may not have been very successful. The first combat test of a very successful design was on February 3, 1971, when an **F-4 Phantom** destroyed a 37-mm anti-aircraft gun in Laos, using a bomb equipped with a *Pave Sword* laser-seeker pod. A laser target designator aboard an AC-130 **gunship** provided the bright spot on the target. Smaller **OV-10** aircraft were soon also being equipped with laser target designators. The bomb proved itself during the following months in Laos; in 1972 it was used with spectacular success against considerably more important targets in **North Vietnam**, during Operation *Linebacker*. *See also* **cluster bomb unit**. For the tonnages of bombs dropped on the individual countries of Indochina during the war, *see* **air war**.

**BONG SON PLAIN.** A densely populated area on the coast north of **Qui Nhon** in **Binh Dinh** province of **II Corps**, a Viet Minh stronghold during the First Indochina War, and a **Viet Cong** stronghold again by 1965. Troops of the 1st **Cavalry Division** went into the Bong Son in Operation *Masher* (later renamed *White Wing*) beginning in late January 1966. In an early example of a policy that was later to inspire criticism, the U.S. troops treated the area simply as a battlefield, a place to fight Communist troops (local Viet Cong plus a regiment of the **PAVN** 3d Division), without much effort to win control of the population. When the battle was over, many villages having been destroyed by bombing and **artillery** in the process, the Americans pulled out, allowing the Communists to resume control of the area.

**BOOBY TRAPS.** The Communist forces in Vietnam used booby traps very extensively, the U.S. and **ARVN** forces on a smaller scale. The most common types either used a string or wire a few inches off the ground, which if struck by a man's ankle would cause a grenade or other explosive device to detonate, or else used a camouflaged pit with punji stakes (sharpened bamboo spikes) at the bottom of it, which would impale the foot of anyone who stepped in the pit. *See also* MINES.

**BOUN OUM NA CHAMPASSAK** (1911–1980). A prince of the royal family of Champassak, in southern **Laos**, Boun Oum was educated at the

Lycée Chasseloup-Laubat, in **Saigon**, and became an administrator in Laos. He joined the resistance against the Japanese in 1945. In 1946, he aligned himself with the French, who were then returning to Laos. He was president of the National Assembly, which negotiated national independence in 1949, and prime minister from March 1949 to February 1950.

Prince Boun Oum had a great deal of power in southern Laos. When the neutralists took power in the **coup** of August 1960, Boun Oum became president of the Revolutionary Committee under the banner of which the rightists rallied in southern Laos. After the rightist forces took Vientiane at the end of the year, Boun Oum became prime minister, though **Phoumi Nosavan**, minister of defense, had more real power. Boun Oum was prime minister from December 1960 to June 1962. He represented the rightists in the negotiations that put **Souvanna Phouma** in office as prime minister in the Second Coalition Government in June 1962. He was minister of religion from 1966 to 1972.

**BROWNE, MALCOLM WILDE** (1931– ). Journalist. Born in New York City, he served in the U.S. **Army** from 1956 to 1958, and became a reporter for Associated Press (AP) in 1960. As chief AP correspondent in Vietnam from 1961 to 1965, he was among the journalists who reported serious problems with the government of **Ngo Dinh Diem** and with the conduct of the war, contradicting the optimism of Ambassador **William Nolting** and General **Paul Harkins**. When **Buddhist** dissidents suggested to several reporters that they cover a protest against Diem's government on June 11, 1963, Browne was the only one who bothered to come; his photographs of Buddhist monk **Thich** Quang Duc burning himself alive attracted attention worldwide. He and **David Halberstam** of *The New York Times* shared the Pulitzer Prize in 1964 for their 1963 reporting on Vietnam. From 1965 to 1966, Browne covered Vietnam for the American Broadcasting Company (ABC). He was the author of *The New Face of War* (1965) and *Muddy Boots and Red Socks* (1993).

**BRU.** A **Montagnard** group, speaking a Mon-Khmer language, living in **Quang Tri** province, including the area of **Khe Sanh**.

**BUDDHIST RELIGION.** Buddhism originated in northern India around the sixth century BC. It had arrived in Vietnam by the second century AD. Vietnamese Buddhism is predominantly Mahayana (the school dominant in **China**), but Theravada Buddhism (the school dominant in **Cambodia, Laos, Thailand**, and Burma) also has some influence, especially in the South. In the modern era most Vietnamese have been in some sense Buddhists, though most have not involved themselves in religious affairs on a regular basis.

The **Hoa Hao** Buddhist sect, in the **Mekong Delta**, became politicized and militarized in the 1940s. Mainstream Buddhism, however, remained largely non-political until 1963. On May 7, 1963, when Buddhists in **Hue** were displaying numerous Buddhist flags in celebrations of the birthday of the Buddha, **Catholic** Archbishop **Ngo Dinh Thuc** (brother of President **Ngo Dinh Diem**) persuaded local officials to enforce ordinances of 1957, 1958, and 1962 forbidding the public display of any flag other than that of the **Republic of Vietnam**. The Buddhists, recalling recent and conspicuous displays of Catholic flags, demonstrated in protest. On May 8, in a confrontation in Hue between government troops and a crowd of the Buddhist demonstrators, eight or nine members of the crowd were killed. Government claims that the dead had been killed not by the troops but by **Viet Cong** terrorists were derided. The protests, and government efforts to suppress them, soon spread to **Saigon**.

The protest movement was led mainly by relatively young bonzes (monks), of whom **Thich** (a title for a bonze) **Tri Quang**, Thich Thien Minh, and Thich **Tam Chau** were among the most conspicuous. Some of the older and more conservative bonzes who would in more normal times have been the leaders of Vietnamese Buddhism were uncomfortable, but outrage over government repression made them reluctant to criticize the younger activists. The protest movement attracted even more attention when Thich Quang Duc burned himself alive on June 11 in protest against government actions; photos of Quang Duc, seated with legs crossed, wrapped in flames, were distributed worldwide. Four other bonzes and one Buddhist nun committed suicide during the following months.

Raids on major pagodas on August 21 by troops (generally believed to have been **Ngo Dinh Nhu**'s **Special Forces**, though some claim they were regular **ARVN** troops), who not only arrested hundreds of bonzes but also inflicted savage beatings, further exacerbated the situation. The Buddhist crisis was a major factor in turning large elements both of the ARVN officer corps and of the U.S. government against Ngo Dinh Diem and his brothers, the result being the **coup** of November 1963.

Buddhist activists remained a political force for several more years, coming repeatedly into conflict with the government. Buddhist crowds rioted against **Nguyen Khanh** in late August 1964, and against **Tran**

**Van Huong** beginning in late November. An even larger confrontation began in March 1966, after Premier **Nguyen Cao Ky** removed Buddhist general **Nguyen Chanh Thi** from his position as commander of **I Corps**. Thich Tri Quang led militant Buddhist demonstrations in support of General Thi, and Thi's troops seized **Danang** and Hue, triggering a small civil war. Colonel **Nguyen Ngoc Loan,** head of the National **Police**, coordinated the suppression of the Buddhists, finally completed in June. Conflict between radical bonzes led by Tri Quang and Thien Minh, and more moderate ones led by Tam Chau, began to weaken Buddhist influence around this time.

The radical Buddhists attempted to run candidates for the Senate in the **elections** of September 1967, but were not permitted to do so. They did run candidates in the elections to the House of Representatives the following month, and took 12 seats.

**BUFFALO HUNTER.** Code name for unmanned jet **reconnaissance** drones, 29 feet long, used for aerial photography. Operating at altitudes of 500 to 1,500 feet, they were able to take very clear detailed pictures in areas where North Vietnamese **anti-aircraft** fire would have posed unacceptable risks for piloted aircraft. The 4080th Strategic Reconnaissance Wing began using such drones in Asia in August 1964; it is unclear whether they began to be used specifically over **North Vietnam** at that time, or not until 1965. They were air-launched from modified **C-130** transport aircraft: at first GC-130s, later DC-130s.

They took on a sudden importance in **South Vietnam** after the **Paris Peace Agreement** of January 1973. Aerial photography flights by piloted American aircraft over South Vietnam did not end after the agreement, but they were severely restricted because they were in violation of the clauses of the agreement limiting U.S. military personnel in Vietnam. Photography by *Buffalo Hunter* drones was not a violation of the accords.

**BUNDY, MCGEORGE** "Mac" (1919–1996). Government official, younger brother of **William Bundy**. Born in Boston, to a prominent family (his grandfather was at that time president of Harvard University), McGeorge Bundy attended Groton, then majored in mathematics at Yale and graduated first in his class in 1940. Soon afterward, his interest shifted to international relations. During World War II he joined the **Army**, rising to the rank of captain as a staff officer in the European Theater. In 1953, Harvard appointed him dean of the Faculty of Arts and Sciences.

In 1961, President **John Kennedy** chose Bundy as his special assistant for national security affairs; he served Kennedy and **Lyndon Johnson** in that office until the beginning of 1966. He was at the center of Vietnam policy making under Kennedy, and perhaps even more so during the first years of the Johnson administration, but he only intermittently tried to steer policy; much of the time he simply transmitted to the president the views of other senior officials. Bundy did join **Robert McNamara** in recommending in January 1965 that the United States begin bombing **North Vietnam**. He was in Vietnam on February 7 when the **Viet Cong** attacked **Pleiku**; he urged reprisal air strikes, and he continued to advocate escalation during the next few months, though by the middle of the year he was becoming more restrained.

Bundy left government in 1966; he served as president of the Ford Foundation from 1966 to 1979, where he placed a special emphasis on improving the education of blacks. He began to suggest restraint of U.S. military action in Vietnam privately to President Johnson in early 1967, and he publicly urged de-escalation of the war in October 1968. He did not, however, say that the United States had made a mistake going into Vietnam; he said that while victory in the war was out of reach, preventing a Communist victory remained an attainable and worthwhile goal, which the United States should continue to pursue at reduced force levels. Bundy became a professor of history at New York University in 1979. He worked for the Carnegie Corporation from 1990 to 1996.

**BUNDY, WILLIAM P.** (1917–2000). Government official, elder brother of **McGeorge Bundy**, son-in-law of **Dean Acheson**. Born in Washington, D.C., Bundy earned an A.B. at Yale in 1939 and an M.A. at Harvard in 1940. In the U.S. **Army** from 1941 to 1946, he rose from private to major, working in communications intelligence at Bletchley Park in England. After completing Harvard Law School in 1947, he practiced law in Washington, D.C., from 1947 to 1951. Bundy joined the **Central Intelligence Agency** (CIA) in 1951, serving for a while as staff director at the Office of National Estimates. Nominally he was at the CIA until 1961, but for most of 1960 he was on leave of absence, serving as staff director for President Dwight Eisenhower's Commission on National Goals. He was deputy assistant secretary of defense for international security affairs from January 1961 to November 1963, assistant secretary of defense for international security affairs from November 1963 to March 1964, and assistant secretary of state for Far Eastern affairs from March 1964 to 1969 (the title was changed to East Asian and Pacific affairs in November 1966). In 1964, Bundy was a strong supporter of the use of

U.S. military power in Vietnam; he advocated bombing the North, and wrote preliminary drafts of what eventually became the **Tonkin Gulf Resolution**. He was not a conspicuous participant in the decisions over escalation of the war from February 1965 onward. By mid-1965, he was suggesting moderation of the pace of escalation.

After leaving the government in 1969, Bundy served as editor of *Foreign Affairs* from 1972 to 1984. He was the author of *A Tangled Web: The Making of Foreign Policy in the Nixon Presidency* (1998).

**BUNKER, ELLSWORTH** (1894–1984). Diplomat. Born in Yonkers, New York, he graduated from Yale in 1916. He started work in his father's sugar company as a manual laborer, then moved up to management, and finally was spectacularly successful in running and expanding the company. In 1951, Bunker became U.S. ambassador to Argentina. Later he became U.S. ambassador to Italy and India, and in 1964, U.S. representative to the Organization of American States.

Bunker arrived in **Saigon** as U.S. ambassador to the **Republic of Vietnam** in April 1967. He became a strong advocate of the American war effort in Vietnam, and of General **William Westmoreland**'s methods of fighting it, at a time when many other officials of **Lyndon Johnson**'s administration were beginning to have doubts. He also advocated extending military operations into **Laos** and **Cambodia**. Bunker remained U.S. ambassador in Saigon until March 1973, when he was replaced by **Graham Martin**. He later took on other diplomatic assignments, ending with the negotiation of the Panama Canal Treaty. He retired from government service in 1978 after the signing of that treaty.

**- C -**

**C-4.** Plastic explosive widely used by U.S. troops in Vietnam. It could also be burned instead of detonated, creating a small hot fire for purposes such as heating coffee.

**C-130 HERCULES.** The largest U.S. cargo aircraft frequently used within Vietnam (larger ones flew to Vietnam, seldom within Vietnam), it had four turboprop engines. It had a ramp that lowered in the rear, which could be used to drive vehicles into it, or to dump out large cargoes in flight. The payload for even the first and weakest version, the C-130A, was 33,810 pounds, more than three times that of the C-123K Provider

(10,948 pounds). Later models of the C-130 were even more power-ful. The C-123, however, could use shorter airfields.

The C-130 was the mainstay of cargo transport in Indochina, but it was also adapted to a variety of other uses. It was used as a bomber, dropping huge weapons like the M-121 and BLU-82 out its cargo hatch (*see* **bombs**). It was modified into a **gunship**. It was used to drop various chemicals (*see* **chemical warfare, weather warfare**). In June 1968, C-130 aircraft began functioning as **Airborne Battlefield Command and Control Centers** (ABCCC), coordinating air (and some-times ground) operations in sections of **Laos** and **North Vietnam**. They replaced the RC-47 aircraft that had previously performed this role.

**CA MAU.** The Ca Mau Peninsula formed the southernmost tip of **South Vietnam**. The town of Ca Mau was the capital of the province cover-ing the peninsula. The province had formerly been called Bac Lieu; the **Republic of Vietnam** renamed it An Xuyen, but the Communists sometimes called it Ca Mau. The **U Minh Forest**, straddling the bor-der between An Xuyen and Kien Giang to the north, was a major **Viet Cong** base area.

**CALLEY, WILLIAM LAWS, JR.** (1943– ). Born in Miami, Florida, he attended West Palm Beach Junior College for one year, 1962–1963, with poor grades. He enlisted in the U.S. **Army**, knowing he was about to be drafted, in July 1966; he attended officer candidate school at Fort Benning from March to September 1967, and arrived in Vietnam on December 1, 1967. On March 16, 1968, the company to which he belonged went into the village generally known as My Lai, expecting to find a **Viet Cong** unit there. No Viet Cong were present, but the troops killed a large number of unarmed peasants. Lieutenant Calley had specifically ordered men of his platoon to kill many of these peas-ants (*see* **My Lai massacre**).

The incident was at first successfully covered up, with false reports that the expected Viet Cong unit had indeed been in the village and that a battle against armed Viet Cong soldiers had occurred. Not until April 1969 did a serious investigation begin. Lieutenant Calley was arrested on multiple counts of murder in November 1969. He was convicted on March 29, 1971, on 22 counts of murder, and sentenced on March 31 to life at hard labor, but there was a great deal of public sympathy for him. Many of his sympathizers felt that Calley had been made a scape-goat while higher-ranking officers escaped punishment. Many others misunderstood the nature of the incident, believing that Calley had been punished for the deaths of civilians killed in the crossfire in a battle between U.S. and Communist troops. His sentence was repeatedly reduced. What he actually served was slightly less than three years (April 1971 to February 1974) under house arrest in his apartment at Fort Benning, plus about 11 days in the stockade at Fort Benning, and slightly less than five months (June to November 1974) at Fort Leavenworth, where he did prison labor as a clerk-typist in place of his initial sentence of "hard labor."

**CAM RANH BAY.** A splendid natural harbor on the coast south of **Nha Trang** in southern **II Corps**, Cam Ranh Bay had never been of much importance, because it was in an area having little population and natural resources, until the United States decided to make it one of the four major logistic centers for U.S. forces in Vietnam. Construction on a massive scale began in 1965. A major air base was built on the peninsula between the bay and the South China Sea. This location made it the most defensible major base in **South Vietnam**. It was hardly attacked at all through 1968, but attacks by **rockets** or **mortars** became a serious problem in 1969, and attacks by **sappers** in 1970. Sappers blew up at least 1,500,000 gallons of aviation fuel on May 23, 1971, and 6,000 tons of munitions on August 25, 1971.

Cam Ranh fell to Communist forces on April 3, 1975, during the **final collapse** of the **Republic of Vietnam**.

**CAMBODIA** (Kampuchea). Located between **South Vietnam** and **Thailand**, Cambodia is much less densely populated than Vietnam, with a land area of 181,040 square kilometers (69,900 square miles) and a population estimated at 6,557,000 in 1968. The capital, **Phnom Penh**, is in south-central Cambodia on the **Mekong River**. The only deep-sea port is Kompong Som (sometimes called **Sihanoukville**) on the southwest coast, but Phnom Penh is a port for cargo vessels small enough to come up the Mekong from or through South Vietnam.

The **Khmers** are the dominant people. The most important minorities in modern times have been the Chinese and Vietnamese, but there are also **Chams** in Cambodia, and in the northeast, **Montagnards** closely related to those of the **Central Highlands** of South Vietnam.

The Khmers once ruled a large empire including what is today southern Vietnam. By the 15th century they were weakening militarily, and the Vietnamese pushed down the coast, reaching its southern tip, the **Ca Mau** Peninsula, in the 18th century. The French incorporated Vietnam and Cambodia into French Indochina in the 19th century, and froze the border between them along a line that corresponded approximately but not exactly to the ethnic boundary on the ground; there were areas of predominantly Khmer population on the Vietnamese side of the border, and areas of Vietnamese population on the Cambodian side.

Late in 1949, the French granted token independence to Cambodia, as an "associated state" within the French Union under King **Norodom Sihanouk**. In 1953, Sihanouk was able to pressure the French into handing over a great deal of actual power. French military forces remained in Cambodia, fighting the Viet Minh.

The **Geneva Accords of 1954** gave King Sihanouk (after his 1955 abdication, Prince Sihanouk) essentially uncontested control of Cambodia. The Vietnamese Communists agreed to pull their forces out of Cambodia without obtaining in return any power-sharing role, or real protection from government repression, for their Cambodian comrades.

In April 1955, Sihanouk announced the foundation of a new organization, the Sangkum Reastr Niyum (People's Socialist Community). He intended to use the Sangkum to replace all existing political parties. Some dissolved themselves in favor of the Sangkum. The Democrats and the Pracheachon (political expression of the Communist movement) attempted to contest the national elections of September 1955, but heavy-handed repression (closure of independent newspapers, and beating, arrest, or killing of many anti-Sangkum campaigners), combined with flagrant falsification of the vote count, enabled the Sangkum to take every seat.

This left a lingering hostility between Sihanouk and much of Cambodia's elite, but he was genuinely popular with the mass population at least until 1963. Sihanouk's government was a paternalistic and very personal affair. It was run by his cronies, and he tolerated corruption and incompetence among them, but the peasants at first enjoyed a reasonable degree of economic security, combined with better educational opportunities and medical care than they had ever known, and various other forms of public works. During the 1960s, the mismanaged economy did not grow enough to continue providing security for the growing population.

In 1955, Sihanouk signed an agreement with the United States for the provision of military aid, but almost immediately decided not to accept the U.S. training mission that would normally have accompanied this; instead he chose to have his army trained by the French, and he was not friendly to the United States. The U.S. aid nonetheless continued until 1963.

In the late 1950s, Sihanouk became increasingly friendly to foreign Communist states, granting diplomatic recognition to the People's Republic of **China**. The involvement of the **Republic of Vietnam** (RVN), and of **Ngo Dinh Nhu** in particular, in two plots against Sihanouk in 1959, pushed him farther in this direction. At the same time, however, Sihanouk was becoming firmer in his suppression of Communists within Cambodia.

In 1963, Sihanouk brought more of the economy under government management, renounced U.S. economic and military aid, and further angered the United States by expressing public pleasure at the death of President **John Kennedy**. In 1965, he broke off diplomatic relations with the United States.

In the 1960s, Cambodia came to play several important roles in the Vietnam War. There were areas in Cambodia where **Viet Cong** and **PAVN** forces established bases, comparatively safe from attack by U.S. and **ARVN** forces. Detailed information about the development of these **sanctuaries**—how large they became by particular dates, and how much use was made of them—is scarce. The ones that eventually became most famous as a result of the U.S. and ARVN attacks on them in 1969 and 1970, in the sections of Cambodia opposite **III Corps** and northern **IV Corps** of South Vietnam, seem to have remained limited to small areas immediately adjoining the Vietnamese border up to 1969. In areas farther north, PAVN forces seem to have spread widely in Cambodia at an earlier date.

By 1966, the Viet Cong and PAVN were purchasing massive quantities of rice from Cambodia to feed their forces in South Vietnam. Ammunition, weapons, and supplies also arrived at the port of Sihanoukville, and were trucked along the "**Sihanouk Trail**" to the base areas along the South Vietnamese border, beginning probably in 1964.

In January 1968, the Cambodian Communists usually referred to as the **Khmer Rouge**, led by Saloth Sar (**Pol Pot**), launched a small guerrilla war against the government. The government responded with a general increase in political repression. The Vietnamese Communists, not wishing to disrupt their relations with Sihanouk, did not provide substantial aid to the Khmer Rouge forces.

On March 18, 1969, the United States began Operation *Menu*, the secret bombing of small Vietnamese Communist base areas in eastern Cambodia. Claims that Sihanouk had signalled the Americans ahead of time that he would not object have been questioned, but certainly he did not object seriously; he restored diplomatic relations with the United States in June.

Sihanouk's control of Cambodia had begun to loosen in 1966, and it weakened very seriously in 1969. General **Lon Nol**, who had long controlled the Army and also had a major role in the security police, became prime minister. Prince Sisowath Sirik Matak, who had long opposed Sihanouk's economic policies, became deputy prime minister, with more power that the title suggests. In January 1970, Sihanouk went to France, nominally for medical treatment.

Early in 1970, Cambodian government troops began shelling Vietnamese Communist base areas in Cambodia. On March 11, a government-inspired crowd rioted against the Vietnamese Communist representatives in Phnom Penh. On March 12, Lon Nol demanded that all PAVN and Viet Cong troops leave Cambodia within three days. On March 18, Lon Nol and Sirik Matak carried out a bloodless coup, deposing the absent Sihanouk as chief of state.

Sihanouk responded by allying himself with the Khmer Rouge (previously his deadly enemies) and the Vietnamese Communists against Lon Nol's government. The result was a sudden explosion of warfare in Cambodia. PAVN forces, which had previously kept a low profile to avoid disrupting their arrangements with the Cambodian government and Army, began attacking government forces vigorously, and for the first time provided large-scale aid to the Khmer Rouge. The Khmer Rouge, with this improved access to weapons and with the enormous prestige of Prince Sihanouk aiding their recruiting efforts, grew rapidly. Lon Nol's army also drew many new recruits eager to drive the Vietnamese out of Cambodia—the Cambodian Army expanded within months from about 35,000 to 100,000 men—but they fared poorly against veteran PAVN troops.

U.S. President **Richard Nixon** and RVN President **Nguyen Van Thieu** launched the **Cambodian Incursion** at the end of April. This was partly an effort to save Cambodia from a Communist takeover, but primarily a seizure of the opportunity offered by the crisis, to attack the sanctuaries that had been supporting the Communist war effort in South Vietnam. U.S. troops withdrew from Cambodia at the end of June; ARVN troops remained much longer, and the United States continued to bomb Communist forces in Cambodia. The United States at first provided only small amounts of weapons and ammunition for Lon Nol's forces; an agreement for much higher levels of U.S. aid was signed in August 1970, and actual deliveries were increasing dramatically by

January 1971.

The government was extraordinarily corrupt. Many officers inflated unit rolls with the names of nonexistent troops, and pocketed for themselves the salaries of the "phantom soldiers." Some, including very high officials, sold military supplies to the Communists.

The main Communist forces in Cambodia were four PAVN divisions. Three of these withdrew to Vietnam late in 1972, probably in anticipation of the signing of the **Paris Peace Agreement**. During 1973, relations between the Khmer Rouge and the remaining PAVN troops in Cambodia deteriorated to the point of outright hostility, with some shooting incidents. ARVN operations in Cambodia also diminished after 1971, though they continued on a limited scale until 1974. The reduction in Vietnamese involvement on both sides left the two Cambodian sides—the Khmer Rouge and the government army—to fight one another. They did so with considerable determination, launching attacks and counterattacks rather than letting the war lapse into quiescence as was occurring in **Laos**. This determination, combined with rather inept leadership on both sides, made for a high level of casualties.

After the Paris Peace Agreement terminated U.S. bombing of Vietnam in January 1973, U.S. bombing of Cambodia became far more intense than it had ever been before. The U.S. **Congress** finally halted it on August 15. The Khmer Rouge launched a major effort to take Phnom Penh without waiting for the U.S. bombing to end. American aircraft helped stop this drive, inflicting heavy casualties on the Khmer Rouge forces, but in the process devastated what had been densely populated agricultural areas near Phnom Penh.

Although the Khmer Rouge had not taken the capital, they had taken areas very close to it. They bombarded the city intermittently with **rockets** beginning in December 1973, and with 105-mm **artillery** fire beginning in early 1974.

The greatest threat to Phnom Penh was not this bombardment but the food problem. More than 2,000,000 refugees had flooded into the city, fleeing the devastation of their homes by combat or, increasingly, the brutality of the Khmer Rouge. The food shortage had been serious even when boats were able to bring rice shipments up the Mekong River from South Vietnam. Early in 1975, the Khmer Rouge were able to halt the river traffic, using **mines** made in China. The U.S. delivered what food it could by aircraft landing at Pochentong Airport, but thousands starved.

U.S. Ambassador John G. Dean urged Lon Nol to leave Cambodia, and on April 1 he did so. Dean closed the embassy and left himself on April 12. The Americans departing in Operation *Eagle Pull* took with them some Cambodians who wanted to leave, but there were not in Phnom Penh the large numbers of people desperate to escape that there would be in **Saigon** at the end of that month. The city surrendered on April 17.

The Khmer Rouge under Pol Pot immediately ordered the entire population of Phnom Penh out to the countryside. This provided an early indication of the zealotry with which they would rule Cambodia during the following years. Probably at least a million people had died—executed or simply starved—by the time the Vietnamese intervened, installing at the beginning of 1979 a government that, while not very good by most standards, was at least much better than Pol Pot's had been.

**CAMBODIAN INCURSION,** 1970. The understanding by which Prince **Norodom Sihanouk** of **Cambodia** had allowed Vietnamese Communist forces to use small base areas in eastern Cambodia, along the Vietnamese border, was growing very strained by the beginning of 1970. The bases were growing rapidly, as military reverses in **South Vietnam** forced the **Viet Cong** and **PAVN** to rely less on bases within South Vietnam, and as the bombing of Operation *Menu* forced them to disperse facilities in Cambodia. The understanding broke down completely after the coup of March 18, 1970, which brought General **Lon Nol** to power in Cambodia. The PAVN began providing substantial support for the **Khmer Rouge**—the Cambodian Communist movement—and attacking Cambodian Army positions. U.S. President **Richard Nixon** and **Republic of Vietnam** (RVN) President **Nguyen Van Thieu** decided it was necessary to assist Lon Nol against the Communist threat in Cambodia, and also that the crisis provided an opportunity to launch larger attacks than ever before against the Vietnamese Communist base areas in Cambodia.

The United States and the Army of the Republic of Vietnam (**ARVN**) began providing occasional air and **artillery** support for Cambodian Army units under Communist attack as early as March 20, and ARVN units began limited ground incursions into Cambodia on March 27. But ARVN forces began a much more massive incursion into the **"Parrot's Beak"** area on April 30 (see photograph 8), and U.S. forces into the **"Fishhook"** on May 1. U.S. and ARVN forces crossed at other points along the border over the next few days.

U.S. forces were withdrawn from Cambodia by June 29, 1970. Preliminary figures showing the United States had lost 338 men killed and 1,529 wounded were soon revised upward to show 354 killed and 1,689 wounded. There were also 13 Americans missing. Preliminary figures showing ARVN casualties up to the time of the American withdrawal as 638 killed, 3,009 wounded, and 35 missing may also have been in need of some upward revision. The death in a helicopter crash of **Nguyen Viet Thanh**, commander of **IV Corps** and one of the ARVN's best generals, was also a serious loss.

The United States claimed that 11,369 enemy personnel had been killed and 2,328 captured. Huge quantities of enemy munitions and supplies had been captured or destroyed. Communist logistic systems were seriously disrupted, reducing Viet Cong and PAVN combat capabilities over a substantial area of South Vietnam for an extended period. Public appreciation of the success of the incursion was reduced by President Nixon's mistake of having announced that a major goal of the operation was the destruction of the Communist headquarters for the southern half of South Vietnam, the **Trung uong cuc mien Nam** (COSVN). The Communists had moved this headquarters out of the area targeted by the incursion several weeks before.

The Cambodian Incursion triggered massive protests by the **antiwar movement**. When four students were killed by Ohio National Guardsmen during protests at **Kent State** University, this triggered even larger protests.

ARVN forces remained in Cambodia when the Americans withdrew. After the death on February 23, 1971, of **Do Cao Tri**, the **III Corps** commander who had vigorously pushed combat action in Cambodia, and a serious defeat of an ARVN task force near Snoul in late May, ARVN operations became less aggressive, and stayed closer to the Vietnamese border.

**CAN LAO PARTY.** The Can Lao Nhan Vi Cach Mang Dang (Personalist Labor Revolutionary Party), founded in 1956, was intended to play a role in the **Republic of Vietnam**, under **Ngo Dinh Diem**, somewhat similar to that of the Communist Party in the governments of Communist countries. Diem's brother **Ngo Dinh Nhu** ran it. It had members all through the administration and armed forces, enforcing President Diem's authority and looking for signs of disloyalty. Its membership was secret.

**CAN THO.** The most important town in the **Mekong Delta**, about 140 kilometers southwest of **Saigon**, located where **Route 4** crossed the Hau Giang River (one of the branches of the **Mekong River**). It was the capital of Phong Dinh province (formerly, with slightly different borders, called Can Tho province). The **ARVN** headquarters for **IV Corps** was at Can Tho.

**CANADA.** The **Geneva Accords of 1954** established an **International Control Commission** (ICC) to supervise the accords (officially three commissions, one each for Vietnam, **Laos**, and **Cambodia**), made up of equal numbers of members from neutral **India**, anti-Communist Canada, and Communist Poland, with India furnishing the chairman. The Canadians pushed for the ICC to investigate and denounce Communist violations of the accords, but they claim that they were not so partisan as the Poles, and did not try to block investigation of anti-Communist violations to the extent that the Poles blocked investigation of Communist violations. By the 1960s, the accords had collapsed to such a point that the ICC's only important role was as a facilitator of communication. J. Blair Seaborn, who became the chief Canadian representative on the ICC in mid-1964, carried American messages to Hanoi, threatening that **North Vietnam** would suffer dire punishment if the **Viet Cong** struggle in **South Vietnam** were not restrained.

During the early portions of **Lyndon Johnson**'s escalation of the Vietnam War, the Canadian government agreed with the United States that the problem in Vietnam was caused by Communist aggression and that this must be stopped, but felt the United States was too inclined to choose massive military force as the method of stopping it. Canadian policy was to support American goals in public while urging restraint as to means. Usually the efforts to encourage restraint were kept private, but occasionally they were public, as when Canadian Prime Minister Lester Pearson gave a speech in Philadelphia on April 2, 1965, suggesting a pause in the U.S. bombing of North Vietnam.

By 1972, Canada had become more critical of U.S. policy; the Canadian House of Commons reacted to increased U.S. bombing of North Vietnam in December 1972, Operation *Linebacker II*, by passing unanimously a resolution deploring the bombing. This appears to have been the result of a political bargain; sympathizers of the United States agreed not vote against the resolution, and the sponsors of the resolution agreed to settle for "deplores" when they could have gotten a majority vote for much stronger language.

When the **Paris Peace Agreement** of January 1973 was negotiated, Canada agreed, reluctantly, to be part of the body established to supervise its implementation, the **International Commission for Control and Supervision** (ICCS). This body proved even more helpless than the ICC had been, and Canada was publicly threatening to withdraw as early as March 1973; External Affairs Minister Mitchell Sharp said "Canadians should not take part in a charade." Canada did formally withdraw as of July 31, and was eventually replaced by Iran.

Canada was by far the most common place of refuge for Americans who fled the United States to evade military service. No firm figures exist, but there may have been something on the order of 30,000 draft resisters and deserters in Canada. Much less publicized was the fact that a substantial number of Canadian men, sometimes estimated at 30,000 to 40,000, voluntarily joined the United States armed forces to serve in the Vietnam War.

**CANBERRA.** A twin-engine jet bomber. The American version, the B-57, could carry 7,500 pounds of **bombs**. The British version, the B-20, could carry 6,000 pounds The U.S. **Air Force** (USAF) began to consider sending B-57s to **South Vietnam** early in 1964, and did so in August. They were stationed at **Bien Hoa**. Five of them were destroyed in a Viet Cong **mortar** attack on Bien Hoa on November 1, 1964. They flew the first overt USAF air strikes in South Vietnam on February 19, 1965. **Australia** sent B-20s to Vietnam in 1967. The American B-57s had electronic equipment enabling them to detect the guidance radars of **surface-to-air missiles** (SAMs) and were used for bombing not only in South Vietnam but also along the **Ho Chi Minh Trail**, where SAMs were a threat to aircraft. The Australian B-20s, lacking such equipment, were restricted to South Vietnam.

A variant, the RB-57, was an important **reconnaissance** aircraft, carrying varying combinations of cameras and infrared **sensors**.

**CAO DAI.** The Cao Dai religious sect emerged in 1919 from a spiritualist group in **Nam Bo**, and was always strongest there, though it spread to some extent to other parts of Vietnam and to **Cambodia**. It combined elements from a variety of traditions, venerating not only Buddha and Confucius but also Jesus, Joan of Arc, and others. In the 1940s, it acquired considerable political and military power. By the early 1950s, most Cao Dai leaders were allied with the French. The sect's headquarters was at **Tay Ninh** City north of Saigon, but the Cao Dai "Pope" Pham Cong Tac there did not fully control the various Cao Dai generals.

Early in 1955, what were called the "**Sects**," the Cao Dai and **Hoa Hao** religious sects and the **Binh Xuyen** gangster organization, challenged **Ngo Dinh Diem**'s control of **South Vietnam**. The Cao Dai were not so firm in their opposition to Diem as the Hoa Hao and Binh Xuyen were; Cao Dai General Trinh Minh The was the first major sect leader to rally to Diem. Following Diem's victory (*see* **Sects**), Pham Cong Tac went into exile in Cambodia, where he died in 1961. Most Cao Dai forces rallied to Diem, or disbanded or were destroyed. Considerable numbers of Cao Dai later joined the **Viet Cong**.

After the overthrow of Ngo Dinh Diem in 1963, relations between the Cao Dai and the **Republic of Vietnam** (RVN) improved. In 1975, however, as it became apparent the Communist forces might soon take Tay Ninh, Cao Dai leaders there, who had been firmly allied with the RVN, declared neutrality in an apparent hope later to reach some accommodation with the Communists.

**CAO VAN VIEN** (1921– ). **ARVN** general. Born in Vientiane, **Laos**, a Buddhist, he graduated from the University of Saigon. Vien became an officer under the French in 1949, and in 1953 he was given command of a battalion of the **Vietnamese National Army** in Hung Yen province of the **Red River Delta**. As a lieutenant colonel he became chief of staff to President **Ngo Dinh Diem**'s Special Military Staff in 1956. He was appointed to command the **Airborne Brigade** in November 1960 after the previous commander had attempted a military **coup** against Diem. Vien remained loyal to Diem, and did not participate in the coup that overthrew Diem in 1963, but he nonetheless became chief of staff to the Joint General Staff in 1964. As commander of **III Corps** from October 1964 to September 1965, he was one of the "**Young Turks**." He was chief of the Joint General Staff from September 1965 to 1975. Vien sometimes took on concurrent duties, as commander of the **Vietnamese Navy** (VNN) in September and October 1966, and as minister of defense from January to November 1967. It is suspected that he lasted so long because he was not the sort of general who might exploit his position as chief of the Joint General Staff to carry out a coup. He was long an advocate of a major ground incursion into Laos to cut the **Ho Chi Minh Trail**, a plan eventually implemented in 1971 as Operation *Lam Son 719*. He settled in the United States after the war.

**CARAVELLE GROUP.** Eighteen Vietnamese politicians and officials, who habitually met at the Caravelle Hotel in **Saigon**, signed on April 26, 1960, a manifesto criticizing **Ngo Dinh Diem**'s administration and calling for drastic reforms. **Phan Khac Suu** was their most important leader. Most of them were arrested after the attempted **coup** of November 1960, though Suu seems to have been the only member of the group who had had any involvement in this coup.

**CARVER, GEORGE** (1930–1994). **Central Intelligence Agency** (CIA) officer. Born in Louisville, Kentucky, he grew up in China, where his parents were missionaries. He received a B.A. from Yale in 1950, and a Ph.D. from Oxford University in 1953. He joined the CIA in 1953, and served on Taiwan and then in **South Vietnam**. Carver had to leave Vietnam after the government discovered he had been the CIA liaison with Dr. Phan Quang Dan, a politician who had supported the attempted military **coup** of November 1960. He went to work for the Office of National Estimates. He was very hostile to **Ngo Dinh Diem** in 1963. He joined the special staff for Vietnamese affairs in 1965, and was special assistant for Vietnam affairs (SAVA) to the director of central intelligence from 1966 to 1973.

President **Lyndon Johnson** liked and trusted Carver more than he did most of the people working on Vietnam at the CIA, partly because Carver's views on the war were considerably more optimistic than those of most CIA analysts. When Carver lost his optimism in early 1968 following the **Tet Offensive**, this had a considerable impact on Johnson and some other influential people. But Carver's optimism had bounced back by August 1968.

Carver retired from the CIA in 1979, but in late 1980 was appointed to the "transition team" handling the transition, at the CIA, to the administration of Ronald Reagan.

**CASUALTIES.** There are minor variations in the figures given by various sources for the number of U.S. military personnel who died in the Vietnam War, depending on how many are included of the individuals who were not on the initial lists of the dead compiled shortly after the war, but who were retroactively added to the lists. By 1985, the official figure for the dead was 58,022. Of these, 47,322 were "deaths by hostile action," sometimes called "battle deaths" or "combat deaths." (The figure for combat deaths includes the men **missing in action**, who are believed to be dead, and also the men who died in the **Mayaguez** incident on May 15, 1975, a few days after the war had ended.) The remaining 10,700 were deaths from a variety of causes, including aircraft crashes not caused by the enemy (3,247), vehicular crashes (1,104), drowning (1,020), heart attack and stroke (312), malaria (117), other diseases (506), and suicide (382). When dealing with casualty figures from the war, it is important to distinguish figures for combat deaths from those for total deaths. Approximately 153,000 men were wounded seriously enough to require hospitalization, and an additional 150,000 suffered wounds not requiring hospitalization.

These figures show ratios of combat deaths to deaths from disease, and of wounded men to combat deaths, much higher than in previous wars. In both regards, the reason for the difference was that the medical care available to U.S. personnel in Vietnam was far better than in any previous war.

The number of names on the Vietnam Veterans Memorial, in Washington, D.C., had increased to 58,226 by May of 2001.

Only 30.5 percent of the total U.S. dead were draftees; about 34 percent of the U.S. combat deaths were draftees. The draftees were concentrated overwhelmingly in the **Army**; 50.6 percent of the Army enlisted men who died in Vietnam were draftees. The proportion of draftees among the dead was highest in 1969 and 1970. In 1969, draftees made up 40 percent of all U.S. military personnel killed by hostile action, 62 percent of the Army enlisted men killed by hostile action, and 69 percent of the Army enlisted infantrymen killed by hostile action. The proportion of blacks among the dead was highest in the early years, when the ground combat units were made up mostly of volunteers. The proportion of blacks among the dead declined as the proportion of draftees increased. Overall, blacks accounted for 12.3 percent of the U.S. combat deaths, and 12.5 percent of the total deaths. This was slightly higher than the proportion of blacks among the U.S. male population of military age (*see* **racial tension**).

The common stereotype according to which the United States fought the war primarily with 19-year-olds is not accurate. Of all the U.S. personnel who died in Vietnam, only 20 percent were 19 years old or less. The most common single age at death (24 percent) was 20. Those 21 to 25 years old were 39 percent, and those 26 years old and above were 17 percent of the dead.

The available figures for combat deaths in Vietnam among the forces of the Republic of **Korea** (4,407), **Australia** and **New Zealand** (475), **Thailand** (350), and the **Philippines** (7) are probably accurate.

Reliable figures are not available for casualties among most of the other forces participating in the war, or for civilian casualties. Casualties among the Communist forces were huge. The United States claimed that combat action by U.S. and allied forces killed about 683,000 enemy personnel just between 1965 and 1971. It is plain that some of the "body counts" that went into this total were inflated, but it also is plain that many Communist troops died without ever being counted in American figures. It seems likely that the total number of Communist personnel who died of all causes was at least as high as the number the United States claimed had been killed by combat action. Figures published in Hanoi in 1995 indicate 1,100,000 dead and 300,000 missing among Vietnamese Communist forces from 1954 to 1975; there is no way to tell how many of these would have been northerners and how many southerners. The number of personnel of the **Republic of Vietnam** who died was surely well over 200,000. The number of civilians who died in **North Vietnam** is said to have been about 65,000; the 1995 Hanoi figures place the combined total for North and **South Vietnam** at almost 2,000,000.

**CATHOLIC CHURCH,** in the United States. In the early years of the American involvement in Vietnam, the Catholic Church generally supported U.S. policy. Francis Cardinal Spellman (Archbishop of New York, 1939–1967) was among the most influential backers of **Ngo Dinh Diem**. In the late 1960s, however, a number of Catholic priests became conspicuous spokesmen for the **anti-war movement**. **Philip Berrigan** and his brother **Daniel Berrigan** were the most famous of these, but there was also Father **Robert Drinan**, who won election to the U.S. House of Representatives as an anti-war candidate in 1970. The lay Catholic magazine *Commonweal* also became an important anti-war publication.

**CATHOLIC CHURCH,** in Vietnam. Relations between Catholic and non-Catholic Vietnamese have been uneasy for centuries; one of the reasons the French moved into Vietnam in the 19th century was to protect Catholic missionaries, and Vietnamese Catholics, from persecution by the imperial government. Under colonial rule, the Catholics often lived in separate villages, and the priests had an authority reaching well beyond purely religious matters. During the early 1950s, Catholic communities provided some of the most important Vietnamese allies of the French against the **Democratic Republic of Vietnam** (DRV), the Communist-led government that was fighting against the French.

At the time the **Geneva Accords** separated **North Vietnam** from **South Vietnam**, the premier of the State of Vietnam was **Ngo Dinh**

**Diem**, a very religious Catholic. He was in a weak position; he had few loyal supporters in South Vietnam. Diem, the Catholic hierarchy, and the United States worked together to persuade large numbers of North Vietnamese Catholics to come south in late 1954 and early 1955, when migration was permitted under the Geneva Accords. The atheist doctrines and hostility to Catholicism of the DRV authorities in the North made the persuasion easier. But DRV authorities in some areas, especially Nghe An and Thanh Hoa provinces, blocked the escape of many Catholics. Some of those in Nghe An who had failed to escape rioted or rebelled—the scale of the incident is disputed—in **Quynh Luu** district in November 1956.

The North Vietnamese Catholics who did come south probably numbered more than half a million. Some were settled in strategic areas; some served as government officials or military officers. They became a vital bulwark for Ngo Dinh Diem, who became president of the **Republic of Vietnam** (RVN) in 1955. The RVN was not a Catholic government, but the three most powerful men in it (President Diem and his brothers **Ngo Dinh Nhu** and **Ngo Dinh Can**) were Catholic, as were many other officials, some of whom had converted from Buddhism in what may have been an effort to curry Diem's favor.

In the early 1960s, local militias in some Catholic villages, led by the village priests, were given U.S. assistance under the "Fighting Fathers" program (*see also* **Sea Swallows**).

Diem and his administration managed to get along reasonably well with the Buddhists, the largest religion in South Vietnam, for years. But in 1963 Diem's elder brother **Ngo Dinh Thuc**, Archbishop of **Hue** and notably lacking in tact, persuaded local officials in Hue to forbid Buddhists from displaying Buddhist flags while celebrating Buddha's birthday. Buddhist protests were bloodily suppressed, which triggered larger protests in a cycle that led within six months to the overthrow and death of President Diem (*see* **Buddhist religion**).

The Catholics remained powerful in the government. The conspiracy that overthrew Diem had included not only Buddhists but also Catholics such as Colonel **Nguyen Van Thieu**, who soon became a general, and finally in 1967 president of the Republic of Vietnam. Thieu was a much more pragmatic Catholic than Diem had been; his religious beliefs never caused a crisis. Catholics were especially conspicuous in the Senate elected in 1967.

The Catholic Church was so strongly identified with the anti-Communist cause in Vietnam that Catholicism made an excellent cover for

Communist spies wishing to infiltrate the government, notably **Nguyen Huu Hanh, Pham Ngoc Thao**, and Vu Ngoc Nha (*see* **intelligence**).

The Church for the most part remained a bulwark of Thieu's government until its fall in 1975, but there were Catholic dissidents, notably Father Tran Huu Thanh, whose public campaign to denounce governmental corruption, with particular reference to President Thieu's own family, proved a considerable embarrassment to Thieu in 1974. *See also* CHUNG TAN CANG, HUYNH VAN CAO.

**CAVALRY.** The United States did not use horse-mounted units in Vietnam, but a variety of ground and air units were formally designated "cavalry." Some of these, which were **airmobile** infantry, used the standard U.S. **Army** unit nomenclature of battalion and company. Others, equipped with **helicopters, tanks, armored personnel carriers**, or **air cushion vehicles**, used the unit nomenclature of the old horse cavalry: "squadron" instead of battalion, and "troop" instead of company.

The largest U.S. units designated cavalry were the 1st Cavalry **Division** (Airmobile), which served in many areas of Vietnam from 1965 to 1971, and the 11th Armored Cavalry (often called the "Blackhorse Regiment," though the word "Regiment" was not in its formal title), which served in **III Corps** from 1966 to 1971.

**CENTRAL HIGHLANDS.** Traditionally, almost all the ethnic Vietnamese in central Vietnam (**Trung Bo**) have lived in limited areas near the coast, where the land was flat enough to permit irrigated rice agriculture. Inland from these areas were the Central Highlands, where the thinly scattered population was made up mostly of **Montagnards**. The most important towns in the Central Highlands were (in order from north to south) **Kontum, Pleiku, Ban Me Thuot**, and **Dalat**. Despite the sparsity of the population, the highlands were strategically vital. The Communist capture of Ban Me Thuot on March 12, 1975, and the **ARVN** abandonment of the rest of the Central Highlands a few days later, marked the beginning of the **final collapse** of the **Republic of Vietnam**. *See also* BEN HET, DAK TO, IA DRANG, ROUTE 14, ROUTE 19.

**CENTRAL INTELLIGENCE AGENCY** (CIA). The CIA had two major functions in the Second Indochina War: **intelligence** and covert operations.

On intelligence matters, the CIA had an uneasy relationship with other intelligence agencies, especially those of the military. The head of the CIA was in theory head of the entire U.S. intelligence community, not just one agency, which is why his title was director of central intelligence (DCI), not director of the Central Intelligence Agency. When representatives of the various civilian and military intelligence organizations met to achieve a consensus on some major issue, to be issued as a Special National Intelligence Estimate, the CIA's Board of National Estimates would host the meeting and release the final report. But during the years of heavy combat the military had far more intelligence officers working on Vietnam than the CIA did, and the military often resented CIA intelligence estimates that were more pessimistic than those of the military. Negative CIA evaluations of Operation *Rolling Thunder*, the U.S. bombing of North Vietnam from 1965 to 1968, were particularly resented.

The 1967 **Order of Battle Dispute** attracted much less attention at the time. Military intelligence estimates of Communist personnel in **South Vietnam** were unrealistically low; the CIA argued for several months that these estimates should be increased, before giving in and accepting the military's figures in September 1967 (*see* **Samuel Adams**).

The CIA's charter restricted its intelligence gathering to foreign targets; it was supposed to leave investigation of groups within the United States to the Federal Bureau of Investigation (FBI) and other domestic agencies. Compliance with this restriction may never have been perfect, but violations of it began to expand dramatically in about 1966, when the White House asked the CIA to help the FBI gather information about radical protest groups, especially the **anti-war movement**, within the United States. Evidence of foreign influence and foreign support was particulary desired. DCI **Richard Helms** reported to President **Lyndon Johnson** and other top officials in November 1967 that what was happening was simply an American protest movement, without significant foreign involvement. President Johnson and some of his top advisers, notably **Dean Rusk** and **Walt Rostow**, refused to accept this, as did **Richard Nixon** after he became president in 1969. They had grown up in an era when there really had been significant Soviet influence in and subsidy for left-wing radicalism in the United States; they could not believe that this had ceased to be the case, at a time when left-wing radicals were protesting the American war effort against a Soviet-supported government in North Vietnam. They said the CIA must have missed some crucial evidence, and should keep searching.

In Indochina the CIA often devoted more resources to operations than to the gathering and analysis of information. Some of these were directly American operations, some were under American control but used Asian personnel, and some were controlled by the local governments, mainly the **Republic of Vietnam** (RVN), with the CIA just providing money, weapons, and advice. The CIA tended to see the war in political terms (establishing control of the population, and if possible winning its allegiance) where the U.S. military thought in terms of fighting battles.

**Edward Lansdale**, head of the Saigon Military Mission (actually a CIA operation), conducted sabotage and psychological warfare in North Vietnam in late 1954 and early 1955, and helped **Ngo Dinh Diem** establish and consolidate his authority in South Vietnam.

The CIA had a close relationship with **Ngo Dinh Nhu**, Diem's brother, and during the 1950s helped Nhu build up his **police** forces— the Special Branch operating mainly in the cities and the National Police Field Force mainly in the countryside—and the **First Observation Group**, which during the 1960s would be expanded and renamed the Vietnamese **Special Forces**.

In the early 1960s, the CIA established several programs that were much more under American control; Ngo Dinh Nhu was involved, but he did not control them. They used Asian personnel, trained often by troops of the U.S. **Army Special Forces** or Navy **SEAL**s that the CIA had borrowed. Several of these programs were in the thinly populated jungles and mountains: the large and very important **Civilian Irregular Defense Groups** (CIDG), and the smaller **Trailwatchers** and **Mountain Scouts**. There was also a program of covert paramilitary operations against North Vietnam; some personnel were dropped into North Vietnam by air, while others raided the coast in small boats.

President **John Kennedy** had become less trustful of the CIA's ability to run paramilitary programs after the failed invasion of Cuba at the Bay of Pigs in 1961, however. On June 28, 1961, he had issued a directive, **National Security Action Memorandum 57** (NSAM 57), that if such programs grew to a large size they should be handed over to the U.S. military. This directive was applied to the CIDG, the Trailwatchers, and the Mountain Scouts in 1963, and to the covert raids against North Vietnam at the beginning of 1964 (*see* **SOG**).

In 1963, when the some U.S. officials were supporting Ngo Dinh Diem while others were encouraging the **coup** that overthrew Diem in November 1963, the CIA was for the most part on Diem's side, but

CIA officer Lucien Conein played a crucial role as liaison between the **ARVN** officers plotting the coup and the U.S. ambassador who was encouraging the coup, **Henry Cabot Lodge**.

During 1964, the CIA came up with two new paramilitary programs, the **People's Action Teams** (PATs) to pacify the villages, and the smaller **Counter-Terror Teams** (soon renamed **Provincial Reconnaissance Units** or PRUs) to conduct raids into Communist territory in South Vietnam. The PATs were transferred to military control in 1966; the PRUs remained under CIA supervision into the 1970s.

NSAM 57 was never applied to **Laos**. Under the **Geneva Accord of 1962**, Laos was supposed to be a neutral country, free of foreign intervention. This was massively violated by the People's Army of Vietnam (**PAVN**). The United States waged a large-scale war against the PAVN in Laos, but preferred to conceal this, pretending that it was obeying the Geneva Accord even if the PAVN was not. The CIA was therefore allowed to run as much of the war in Laos as it could handle. The U.S. **Air Force** did almost all the bombing in Laos, but the CIA, mostly working through its proprietary **Air America**, operated many transport planes and **helicopters**. The CIA built up the "Secret Army" of **Hmong** (Meo) tribesmen to a strength of at least 30,000 men; it was the most effective ground force fighting the Communists in Laos. The "Secret Army" even had a few fixed-wing strike aircraft, flown by Hmong pilots. The main base from which the CIA conducted its war effort in Laos was at Udorn, in **Thailand**.

**CHAMS.** The Chams once ruled a substantial kingdom, Champa, along the coast of what is today south-central Vietnam. Champa was conquered by the Vietnamese in the 15th century, and in modern times the Chams have been a relatively small minority group. Their language is of the Malayo-Polynesian family; some are Muslim, while others practice a polytheism containing substantial Hindu elements. The largest concentration of Chams in modern Vietnam was still along the coast, notably in the areas of Phan Rang and Phan Ri, but there were also some whose ancestors had fled inland during or after the Vietnamese conquest of Champa, who were living along the Vietnamese-Cambodian border, and in the interior of **Cambodia** around the Tonle Sap. Some Chams joined **FULRO** in the 1960s.

**CHEMICAL WARFARE.** The most important application of chemicals by the United States was the use of **herbicides**, primarily to kill trees and brush, secondarily to kill crops in enemy-controlled areas.

The United States also made massive use of **CS**, sometimes called "super tear gas," and somewhat more limited use of another **incapacitating agent**, Adamsite (DM), 10-chloro-5,10-dihydrophenarsazine.

The dropping of chemicals from the air to modify the weather (*see* **weather warfare**) and to alter the structure of the soil (*see* Operation *Commando Lava*) were less successful.

The United States denies having used any lethal chemical agents. Allegations made in 1998 that the United States had made occasional use of the nerve gas Sarin (GB), dropped by aircraft in CBU-15 **cluster bomb units**, have not been proven and are generally believed to have been false.

**CHIEU HOI.** The *Chieu Hoi* or "Open Arms" program, initiated in 1963, was intended to encourage Communist personnel in **South Vietnam** to defect to the **Republic of Vietnam**, and to deal with those who did defect, in some cases providing vocational training and assistance in getting jobs. It operated on slender resources until 1965, when the United States began providing more **advisers**, and funding, for the program. Those who defected from the Communist forces under this program were called *hoi chanh*. In 1969, the peak year, there were reported to have been 47,023 *hoi chanh*.

**CHINA.** The Vietnamese have had a very ambivalent relationship with China for most of their history. China conquered the Vietnamese in 111 BC and ruled them for more than a thousand years, until 939 AD; invaded them again in 1406 and remained for a generation; and invaded them briefly in 1788. Many traditional Vietnamese heroes and heroines are remembered for having fought the Chinese, beginning with the Trung sisters, who led a rebellion against China in 39 AD.

The Chinese Communist Party won control of China, and proclaimed the People's Republic of China (PRC), in 1949. From then until the early 1970s, China was cut off from normal contact with much of the world, partly by choice of the Communist government under Mao Zedong (Mao Tse-tung), and partly by a systematic American effort to isolate China from the world. The lack of contact between China and the United States greatly complicated the efforts of the two governments to understand and predict one another's policies toward Vietnam. The widespread American belief that China was planning to conquer all of Southeast Asia, and that the Vietnam War was part of this plan, was an important part of the American motivation for fighting in Vietnam.

China joined the **Soviet Union** in pressing the **Democratic Republic of Vietnam** (DRV) to sign the **Geneva Accords of 1954**, which left the DRV controlling only **North Vietnam**; it had controlled much more of Vietnam. Chinese advisers played an important role in pushing the DRV into disastrous excesses in the **land reform** campaign that began on an experimental scale at the end of 1953, and reached a climax in the first half of 1956.

In the late 1950s and the early 1960s, the alliance between China and the Soviet Union began to collapse in what is known as the Sino-Soviet split. One of the crucial issues was "peaceful coexistence." The Soviets argued that the capitalist and Communist systems could coexist without warfare, and that Communist parties could win power by peaceful, parliamentary means. The Chinese denounced the Soviet leaders as **Revisionists**; they said that war was inevitable as long as capitalism persisted, and that armed revolution remained the primary means by which Communist parties could expect to win power. The DRV leaders in **Hanoi**, who from late 1954 to the beginning of 1959 had required the Communists in **South Vietnam** to rely primarily on peaceful political struggle, had seen how this policy had allowed **Ngo Dinh Diem**'s army and police to devastate the Communist movement in the South. They had concluded by 1959 that only armed revolutionary struggle could save the southern Communists from complete destruction; this naturally inclined them to the Chinese side in the debate over peaceful coexistence. The DRV, however, preferred to remain friendly with, and continue getting aid from, both China and the Soviet Union. It therefore tried to avoid taking sides in the Sino-Soviet dispute. Only briefly, in 1963 and 1964, was the DRV strongly and clearly committed on the Chinese side in the dispute, to such an extent that Vietnamese leaders were openly insulting toward the Soviets and got no significant aid from them. Late in 1964, the DRV's relations with the Soviet Union began to improve again, and during the massive escalation of the war from 1965 onward, the DRV was once again balancing between Beijing and Moscow, obtaining aid from both sides.

The Chinese took the **Tonkin Gulf incidents** of August 1964 as a sign that the war in Vietnam was about to escalate massively, perhaps enough to repeat the pattern of the Korean War, in which U.S. troops had invaded North Korea in retaliation for the North Korean invasion of South Korea, China had intervened to save North Korea from conquest, and the result had been years of bloody fighting between U.S. and Chinese troops in Korea. The Chinese publicly warned that they would defend North Vietnam against American attack. They also sent more troops into the areas of China near the Vietnamese border, strengthened the railroad network there, and built new military airfields, in locations suitable for supporting air combat not only over southern China but also over Vietnam.

The Chinese were aware that there were influential Americans who felt that the United States had made a mistake by not expanding the area of combat in the Korean War into China, and who were suggesting that in the event of a major escalation of the Vietnam War, the United States should spread that war into China. The Chinese took such threats seriously enough to launch, late in 1964, a hugely expensive program to shift industry away from coastal areas into the interior of China, to make it less vulnerable to U.S. bombing. **Lyndon Johnson**, however, remembered clearly what had happened in Korea, and he tried to avoid anything that seemed likely to lead to a Chinese-American war. During Operation *Rolling Thunder* (1965–1968), American aircraft occasionally strayed across the border into China, or encountered Chinese aircraft off the Chinese coast over the Gulf of Tonkin. Twelve American pilots were lost in such incidents; two of these, who had been captured after being shot down, were released by the Chinese in 1973.

China participated in the 1961–62 Geneva Conference on **Laos**, but opposed the **1962 Geneva Accords**, and for the next few years the Chinese advised the Vietnamese Communists to avoid negotiations with the United States, and simply to fight the revolution in South Vietnam through to victory. The Chinese were offended when the DRV announced it was accepting Lyndon Johnson's proposal of peace talks in 1968. Only in the early 1970s did China decide that negotiations between Hanoi and Washington might produce useful results.

Although the Chinese had encouraged the initiation of the war in South Vietnam and urged that it be fought through to victory, they believed it should be as much as possible a local war based on local resources. When the question arose in 1964 of supplementing village guerrillas with more conventional military units, some of which would be North Vietnamese, the Chinese counseled restraint.

The Chinese were unable during the 1960s to furnish the DRV with some of the high-technology weapons that it needed against the Americans, notably **radar**-guided **surface-to-air missiles**, but they were able to furnish many less sophisticated weapons, such as infantry rifles and **anti-aircraft artillery**, and also ammunition, uniforms, and so forth.

The Chinese also placed substantial military forces in North Vietnam, mostly in the area north of Hanoi, beginning in June 1965. There were 130,000 Chinese personnel in North Vietnam by April 1966, and 170,000 during the peak year, 1967. The withdrawal of the Chinese forces occurred mostly during 1969. While in North Vietnam, Chinese personnel had performed three very important functions:

First, military engineer units worked on roads and railroads, especially repairing bomb damage.

Second, anti-aircraft units—many of these arrived in Vietnam in 1967—defended directly against U.S. air attack. Most of these units were kept in the area north of Hanoi, where they saw little actual combat because the United States flew few air strikes there. But the United States almost certainly *would* have flown far more air strikes there if not for the presence of the Chinese. The limited number of anti-aircraft gunners stationed farther south in North Vietnam saw far more combat.

Third, the Chinese troops served as a tripwire, a concrete warning to the United States that an American invasion of North Vietnam could lead to war with China.

The Chinese placed a smaller but still significant military force in the northernmost section of Laos, its maximum size probably between 14,000 and 20,000, nominally a road-building crew. These troops did not intervene in the fighting in Laos. There was occasional mild publicity in the West about the danger that completion of the roads would represent for **Thailand**, but the Chinese were in no hurry to complete them. The purpose of the road project was to provide an excuse for the troops to be in the area, to deter the warring armies in Laos from spreading their war too close to the Chinese border. Completion of the roads would have deprived the troops of the excuse for their presence. The road from Na Sang to Boun Hai was declared complete early in 1978, and most of the troops returned to China at that time. The Laotian government asked early in 1979 that the 1,000 to 2,000 remaining Chinese troops also leave.

In August 1966, Chinese Premier Zhou Enlai proposed to **Pham Van Dong** that China send about 100 advisers to the Communist forces in South Vietnam, but there is no record this proposal was accepted.

When the Soviets resumed shipping significant military aid to the DRV in 1965, China refused to grant them an air corridor across China to do the job with transport planes. The level of hostility in the Sino-Soviet dispute had grown too great for that. But China did allow shipments by rail, and this was the main route by which Soviet weapons reached North Vietnam for the next several years. By early 1967, the quota for shipments of Soviet aid across China was 10,000 tons per month. It is unclear whether shipments of Soviet weaponry across China by rail continued up to, or even beyond, the point when Sino-Soviet hostility led to actual shooting between the two countries on their border (there was a brief flare-up of combat between Chinese and Soviet troops on an island in the Ussuri River, which forms part of the border between the two countries, in March 1969).

Another factor complicating the situation was the Great Proletarian Cultural Revolution, which unleashed incredible chaos in China in the late 1960s. Factional fighting escalated to include the use of automatic weapons in many cities, tanks and artillery in some cities. The Cultural Revolution's disruption of the Chinese rail system impeded the shipment of both Chinese and Soviet weapons to North Vietnam, and trainloads of weapons destined for Vietnam were sometimes plundered by Red Guard factions wanting to use them against one another. But work on matters considered vital for national security was able to continue. In 1967, when much of their country seemed to be sliding into anarchy, the Chinese still managed to transport substantial shipments of both Chinese and Soviet weaponry to the Vietnamese border, to expand very substantially their direct participation in North Vietnam's anti-aircraft defenses, and to build and detonate their first hydrogen bomb.

**Richard Nixon**, although he had been bitterly hostile to the Communist government of China for much of his career, chose as president to open up friendly relations. His national security adviser, **Henry Kissinger**, made a secret visit to Beijing in July 1971, and Nixon himself went there, with massive publicity, in February 1972. One of Nixon's motives was a hope of improving the American position in Vietnam. China firmly refused to bring pressure on Hanoi to be conciliatory in negotiations with Washington, but the opening to China reduced Nixon's worries about Chinese retaliation for Operations *Linebacker* and *Linebacker II* in 1972.

Traditional Vietnamese distrust of the Chinese had kept the relationship between Hanoi and Beijing tense even when Hanoi needed Chinese support the most, between 1965 and 1968. Once the war was over, the alliance collapsed completely; Vietnam became firmly committed to the Soviet side in the Sino-Soviet dispute. China responded to Vietnam's invasion of **Cambodia**, launched in the last days of 1978 to overthrow the **Khmer Rouge**, by launching a substantial Chinese invasion of northern Vietnam in 1979, hoping to draw Vietnamese troops off from Cambodia. *See also* REPUBLIC OF CHINA.

**CHINESE,** ethnic minority in Vietnam. Chinese have been settling in Vietnam sporadically for more than 2,000 years; there was a big wave of settlers (the *Minh huong*) who arrived in the 17th century, and another in the late 19th and early 20th. Some assimilated into Vietnamese society, but many did not. They lived mostly in the towns, with the biggest concentration in **Cholon**, the Chinese section of **Saigon** (officially a separate city adjoining Saigon).

Many Vietnamese resented the Chinese for their dominant role in commerce. When the war opened up new opportunities for huge profits in black-market activities and the narcotics trade, and many of the people who seized these opportunities were Chinese, this resentment may have increased.

The Chinese community as a whole avoided conspicuously committing itself to either side in the struggle for Vietnam, presumably aware of the dangers that such a commitment would pose for a disliked minority group.

After the end of the war, the Communist government of Vietnam decided it would be better off without the ethnic Chinese, and pushed them to leave the country. Many of the "boat people" fleeing by sea were ethnic Chinese who had been urged by the government to leave.

**CHOLON.** The ethnically **Chinese** section of metropolitan **Saigon**, on the southwest side of the city. Officially it was a separate city. Until 1957, Cholon had also been the name of a province immediately west of Saigon.

**CHOMSKY, NOAM AVRAM** (1928– ). Professor of linguistics and anti-war agitator. Born in Philadelphia, he studied at the University of Pennsylvania, where he got his Ph.D. in 1955. He was promptly hired by the Department of Linguistics of the Massachusetts Institute of Technology. He soon became one of the leading theoreticians in the field of linguistics, though not all his colleagues accepted his theories.

During the mid-1960s, he became one of the leading academic spokesmen for the **anti-war movement**. His extreme left-wing political stance—he was bitterly critical not only of the Vietnam War, but of the overall role of the United States in the world during the preceding decades—he backed up with a far more detailed knowledge of the history of the war than was usual among anti-war spokesmen.

**CHU HUY MAN** (1913– ). **PAVN** general. Born in Nghe An province, northern **Trung Bo**, he joined the Communist Party in 1930. He was repeatedly imprisoned by the French. In 1945, Man helped lead the Viet Minh seizure of power in **Quang Nam** province, and afterward he played various roles in central Vietnam, becoming a regiment commander not later than 1951. He was the political officer of the 316th Division during the Battle of Dien Bien Phu in 1954; later that year he was sent to **Laos** to command the PAVN advisers to the **Pathet Lao**. He held several positions in **North Vietnam**, then in January 1961 returned to Laos as head of a PAVN liaison mission to the neutralist forces. In 1964, he was sent to **Military Region** 5 in **South Vietnam**. From 1965 to 1967, Man commanded the **Central Highlands** (B3) **Front**, commanding the PAVN forces in the Battle of the **Ia Drang Valley** in November 1965. From the end of 1967 until 1975 he commanded Military Region 5.

**CHU LAI.** The United States **Marines** began building an air base at Chu Lai, near the coast in southern Quang Tin province, about 85 kilometers south of **Danang**, in 1965. The 1st Marine **Division** was based at Chu Lai from February to November 1966, and the 23d Infantry Division (American) from 1967 to 1971.

**CHUNG TAN CANG** (1926– ). **Vietnamese Navy** (VNN) admiral. Born in **Gia Dinh**, a **Catholic**, Cang became a merchant marine officer in 1948, then went to the VNN Officer School, from which he graduated in 1952. He was briefly operations officer at Navy Headquarters in 1955, then commandant of the Navy Training Center from 1955 to 1957. Cang attended the Amphibious Operations School in Coronado, California, from 1957 to 1958, then served as commanding officer of the minesweeper *Ham Tu* (HQ114) from 1958 to 1959. He took the Command Course at the U.S. Naval War College (1960–1961) between two stints as commander of the River Force (1959–1960 and 1961–1963). As Vietnamese Navy commander from the end of 1963 until April 1965, Cang became one of the "**Young Turks**." He then served as commandant of the Command and General Staff College from 1966 to 1969. He later became **Saigon**-Gia Dinh military governor and concurrently commander of the Capital Military District. At the very end of the war in 1975 he once again became VNN chief of naval operations.

**CHURCH, FRANK FORRESTER** (1924–1984). United States senator. Born in Boise, Idaho, he earned a law degree at Stanford University in 1950. In 1956, he was elected to the U.S. Senate as a Democrat from Idaho; this was his first important public office. His record in the Senate was very liberal. Senator Church, a member of the Foreign Relations Committee, began to dissent from **Lyndon Johnson**'s policies on Vietnam in 1965. He called for disengagement from the war and negotiations with the Communists.

Early in 1970, Church and Senator **John Sherman Cooper** (Republican of Kentucky) jointly sponsored an amendment to a foreign military sales bill, forbidding the use of U.S. government funds for U.S. military operations in **Cambodia**. This passed the Senate in late June by a substantial margin (58–37), but was rejected by the House of Representatives. But two other Cooper-Church amendments, which passed both houses of Congress at the end of 1970 and became law in 1971, forbade the use of U.S. ground troops in **Laos**, Cambodia, and **Thailand**, and forbade even military **advisers** in Cambodia.

In January 1975, the Senate created the Select Committee on Intelligence, with Church as its chairman, to investigate a variety of abuses alleged to have been committed by **intelligence** agencies. Thanks in part to the attitude of Director of Central Intelligence **William Colby**, who startled many of his subordinates at the **Central Intelligence Agency** (CIA) by answering the committee's questions instead of stonewalling, the committee compiled considerable information about such matters as CIA involvement in efforts to assassinate foreign heads of state, distortion of intelligence estimates in Vietnam, and surveillance of political dissidents inside the United States. Senator Church rejected a request from President **Gerald Ford** that the committee's findings not be published.

**CITIZENS COMMITTEE FOR PEACE WITH FREEDOM IN VIETNAM.** An organization founded in 1967 to support U.S. policy in Vietnam. The organizing chairman was Senator Paul Douglas (Democrat of Illinois); the more conspicuous members included former presidents Harry Truman and Dwight Eisenhower, former secretary of state **Dean Acheson**, former chairman of the **Joint Chiefs of Staff** Omar Bradley, former president of Harvard University James B. Conant, and many academics.

The impetus for establishment of the Citizens Committee came from President **Lyndon Johnson**, but the involvement of the White House was kept as quiet as possible.

**CIVIL GUARD** (Bao An). A paramilitary organization in **South Viet-**

**nam**, established in 1955, based on organizations that had existed under the French, with one unit in every district. The units were commanded by officers of the Army of the Republic of Vietnam (**ARVN**). The Civil Guard had about 50,000 men in the late 1950s, but the levels of training and equipment were poor. Part of the problem was a dispute over its proper nature. Until 1960, it was under the Ministry of the Interior, not the Ministry of National Defense. The United States Operations Mission in Vietnam had signed a contract in 1955 to have the Civil Guard trained by police specialists provided by Michigan State University, and U.S. money and equipment for the Civil Guard were funneled through the **Michigan State University Group** (MSUG) until 1959. The MSUG, and Ambassador Elbridge Durbrow, believed that the Civil Guard was properly a police organization, and should be equipped with no more than the light weapons suitable for small-scale anti-guerrilla operations. **Ngo Dinh Diem** and General **Samuel Williams** (commmander of the U.S. **Military Assistance Advisory Group**) thought the Civil Guard should be an essentially military organization, with heavy weapons. Both Diem and Williams seem to have wanted to use militarization of the Civil Guard as a way of getting around the decision of the U.S. government that the ARVN, Diem's regular army, should not be allowed to grow beyond 150,000 men. Diem also wanted to be able to use the Civil Guard as a political counterweight to the ARVN. The dispute kept much weaponry of any sort from reaching the Civil Guard for several years.

U.S. aid revived slightly in the second half of 1959, and the transfer of the Civil Guard to the Ministry of National Defense in 1960 resolved some of the disputes over its nature, though it still was not placed under the Joint General Staff of the Republic of Vietnam Armed Forces. In late 1961 and 1962, the U.S. military finally began handing out large quantities of reasonably modern rifles, automatic weapons, and **mortars** to the Civil Guard. This proved a mixed blessing; the **Viet Cong** were able to capture many of these weapons, and this contributed to a significant expansion of Viet Cong military power beginning in late 1962.

In September 1962, the Civil Guard had a strength of 72,000. It was renamed the **Regional Forces** in 1964.

**CIVIL OPERATIONS AND REVOLUTIONARY DEVELOPMENT SUPPORT** (CORDS), later renamed Civil Operations and Rural Development Support. An organization established in May 1967 to exercise unified control over American **pacification** efforts, military and civilian, in **South Vietnam**. Its head was a deputy to the commander of the **Military Assistance Command, Vietnam** (MACV), and the creation of CORDS meant that pacification had been placed under the control of MACV. The advisory teams responsible for pacification at the province and district levels were composed primarily of military officers; in June 1971 there were 4,924 military **advisers** in CORDS and only 744 civilian advisers. But the role of civilians—usually employees of the State Department—remained significant even at the level of the district and province teams, and civilians became more numerous as one went up the chain of command. Civilians headed CORDS: **Robert Komer** from May 1967 to November 1968, **William Colby** from November 1968 to June 1971, and George Jacobson, a retired **Army** colonel, from then until CORDS was disbanded in 1973. Pacification activities in each province were controlled by the province senior adviser; about half the province senior advisers were military officers, and half civilians. *See also* **Revolutionary Development**.

**CIVILIAN IRREGULAR DEFENSE GROUPS** (CIDG). Military and paramilitary units, at first made up of **Montagnards**. They were organized and led usually by U.S. **Special Forces** soldiers, although detachments of Vietnamese **Special Forces** were often attached to them, and it was policy to try to give the Vietnamese Special Forces control of them.

The program was initiated by the **Central Intelligence Agency** (CIA) in 1961, with permission from the **Republic of Vietnam** (RVN), **Ngo Dinh Nhu** in particular. In October 1961, the village elders of Buon Enao, a **Rhadé** village near **Ban Me Thuot**, in Darlac province, were approached and asked to approve what was initially called the Village Self-Defense Program. The experiment quickly spread to 40 neighboring villages. U.S. Special Forces troops arrived in December, to begin training both "village defenders," later called "hamlet militia," who as the name implies usually remained in their villages to defend them against possible attack, and "strike forces" capable of more mobile operations. The CIA controlled and financed the experiment. By October 1962, 200 villages were involved, and there were 1,500 "strikers" in the strike forces.

In 1962, the United States decided to transfer a variety of programs in Vietnam from CIA to military control. The transfer of the CIDG, called Operation *Switchback*, began in September 1962 and was completed on July 1, 1963. Under CIA control, the CIDG had been primarily a means of establishing control of the areas where the Montagnards lived; the CIDG camps had been based on existing villages, and the strike forces had been small. Under military control, the CIDG was used more like a conventional military force; the strike forces were expanded to about 18,000 men by December 1963, and they began to be used for more offensive operations. CIDG camps began to be established far from the home areas of the recruits, in locations regarded as strategically crucial, especially along the borders of Vietnam. The effort to use the CIDG to support conventional military operations often proved very successful; the CIDG was especially valuable for providing **intelligence**, which could then be used to guide the operations of conventional units. But CIDG units were often misused, put into battles for which their weapons and training were inadequate, and moved around for the convenience of military commanders in ways that undermined their unit cohesion and morale.

There were slightly more than 30,000 men in the strike forces by the end of 1965, and by mid-1967 there were 34,350 in the regular strike forces and 5,700 in mobile strike forces (*see* **Special Forces**). The expansion of the CIDG had involved the recruitment of large numbers of men who were not Montagnards, including **Khmer Krom, Hoa Hao, Chams**, and ordinary Vietnamese.

Communist infiltration of CIDG units could pose serious dangers. The **Viet Cong** force that overran the CIDG camp at Plei Mrong, in **Pleiku** province, on January 3, 1963, apparently had the assistance of 33 members of the camp's strike force. Around 1964, some camps, mainly in **I Corps** and **II Corps**, began to have small special security forces of **Nung**, considered more reliable than the Montagnards who made up the bulk of the personnel.

Efforts to transfer CIDG camps to RVN control began as early as 1962. They were hampered by mutual suspicions between the Montagnards and the Vietnamese. RVN authorities believed, correctly, that some of the Montagnards who had joined the CIDG were supporters of the **Bajaraka Movement**, which was trying to win autonomy for the Montagnards. They felt the U.S. Special Forces had distributed an excessive number of weapons to unreliable tribesmen; the RVN was confiscating weapons from CIDG camps by December 1962. Vietnamese Special Forces (LLDB) officers and men were assigned to lead CIDG units who were, as a U.S. Army history later put it, "not interested in, or even remotely enthusiastic about, the CIDG program."

Rhadé troops in five CIDG camps near Ban Me Thuot rebelled on September 19, 1964, killing 36 LLDB officers and men.

There was a substantial improvement in the quality of the LLDB in 1966 and 1967. This made it possible for the first time during 1967 to give LLDB personnel actual (as distinguished from nominal) command of CIDG camps with some degree of success; up to then camps with Vietnamese commanders had usually been under the de facto command of the U.S. Special Forces "**advisers**" to the camp commanders.

Early in 1970, it was decided that the CIDG units were to be converted to **ARVN Ranger** units, and by the end of 1970 the CIDG program as such had essentially ceased to exist. Some 14,534 CIDG troops had become ARVN Rangers.

**CLAYMORE MINE.** An American anti-personnel weapon, the claymore mine contained a slab of **C-4** plastic explosive, with hundreds of steel pellets on one side of it. When the explosive was detonated, the pellets would be sprayed like the blast of a giant shotgun. They were very effective against personnel caught in the open. Claymore mines were often placed on the perimeters of American bases, facing outward; troops in the bunkers on the perimeter could detonate them when under attack, or simply if they suspected some enemy were sneaking up on them at night.

**CLIFFORD, CLARK MCADAMS** (1906–1998). Secretary of defense. Born in Fort Scott, Kansas, he earned a law degree at Washington University, in St. Louis, in 1928. He practiced as an attorney from 1928 to 1943, then was commissioned a Naval Reserve officer in 1944. Clifford went to the White House in 1945, initially as an assistant to President Harry Truman's naval aide. He quickly became a close friend of President Truman, and an influential adviser on both foreign and domestic policy. As early as 1946 he was a cold warrior, urging a vigorous effort to contain Soviet expansion. Clifford was special counsel to the president from 1946 to 1950. He returned to the private practice of law from 1950 to 1968, but maintained his connections with the government; he served as a member (1961–1963) and then chairman (1963–1968) of the **President's Foreign Intelligence Advisory Board**. He was secretary of defense from February 28, 1968, to January 1969.

Clifford privately and quietly advised President **Lyndon Johnson** against a major commitment of combat forces to Vietnam in early and mid-1965, but once that decision had been made, Clifford became a hawk. He remained one until the beginning of 1968—that was a major reason President Johnson chose him for secretary of defense—but he turned against the war almost immediately after taking that office.

By the summer and fall of 1968, Clifford was urging President Johnson to halt all bombing of **North Vietnam** without waiting for any clear commitment to a quid pro quo from **Hanoi**, simply relying on the threat that the bombing could be resumed if Hanoi took advantage of the halt by increasing support for the combat in the South.

After leaving office, Clifford returned to the practice of law and wrote a memoir, *Counsel to the President* (1991). He also accepted a lucrative position with the Bank of Credit and Commerce International, and was severely embarrassed, though not prosecuted, when illegal activities of the firm came to light.

**CLUSTER BOMB UNIT** (CBU). A bomb that contained a large number of smaller bomblets; it was designed to distribute these bomblets over a wide area. They were used mainly against personnel, rather than objects or structures. The individual bomblet typically was somewhat like a grenade, scattering steel shards or pellets when it detonated. Smaller CBUs contained hundreds of bomblets; larger ones contained over a thousand. The United States used CBUs especially against **anti-aircraft** gunners; the broad spread of the bomblets from a CBU eliminated the need for pinpoint accuracy in the drop, and thus made it unnecessary for the plane to come down dangerously low over the anti-aircraft installation when making the drop.

**COAST GUARD,** U.S. In April 1965, the United States decided to send seventeen 82-foot Coast Guard cutters to Vietnam, to participate in Operation *Market Time*, inspecting vessels off the coast of **South Vietnam** looking for Communist personnel and weapons shipments; the first of them reached Vietnam in July. Their number increased to 26 the following year, and at least four larger (255-foot and 311-foot) cutters were also eventually sent. The Coast Guard vessels were involved in the sinking of six steel-hulled infiltration vessels of substantial size, and the sinking or capture of numerous smaller wooden junks. When the United States pulled out of Vietnam, the Coast Guard cutters were handed over to the **Vietnamese Navy** (VNN) rather than being brought back to the United States.

**COLBY, WILLIAM EGAN** (1920–1996). Director of central intelligence. Born in St. Paul, Minnesota, he graduated from Princeton in 1940, and entered the **Army** as a 2d lieutenant in 1941. He joined the Office of Strategic Services in 1943, and was parachuted into France, behind German lines, in August 1944. He got a law degree from Columbia University in 1947, but then joined the **Central Intelligence Agency** (CIA) in 1950. Colby served in Sweden and Italy before becoming CIA deputy chief of station, **Saigon**, in February 1959; he was promoted to chief of station in June 1960, and remained until 1962.

The most important accomplishment of the CIA in Vietnam during the period Colby was running it was the creation of the **Civilian Irregular Defense Groups** in the **Central Highlands**. He also expanded what had previously been a very small program of covert operations against **North Vietnam**. During the late 1950s, the **Republic of Vietnam** (RVN) had been sending occasional agents north, but they were unobtrusive, and their main purpose was espionage. Colby sent teams trained and armed for sabotage and low-level guerrilla warfare. But by 1962 and 1963, he was becoming disenchanted; too many of the Vietnamese sent north were being lost, for too little result. In 1963, when Colby was thinking of cutting back on raids into the North, the U.S. military decided instead to take control of the program from the CIA and expand it still further (*see OPLAN 34A*). Colby advised against this but his advice was rejected. By this time, he was back in Washington, D.C.; in 1962 he had become deputy chief and then chief of the Far East Division of the Directorate of Plans (which controlled covert operations) at the CIA. He remained chief of the Far East Division through 1967.

Colby returned to South Vietnam in 1968, first as deputy head and then as head of **Civil Operations and Revolutionary Development Support** (CORDS), the agency that had been created in 1967 to exercise unified command over the various elements of the **pacification** program in South Vietnam. As head of CORDS, Colby had the rank of ambassador, and was officially a deputy to the commander of the **Military Assistance Command, Vietnam** (MACV). He returned to Washington in June 1971, became executive director-comptroller of the CIA in 1972, became the CIA's deputy director for plans (he promptly had the title changed to deputy director for operations) early in 1973, and became director of central intelligence in September 1973, at a time when congressional committees were beginning to investigate a variety of scandals in connection with the CIA. His retirement in January 1976 may have been partly a result of President **Gerald Ford**'s displeasure at the extent to which Colby had cooperated with congressional investigators, instead of stonewalling.

In his books *Honorable Men: My Life in the CIA* (1978) and *Lost*

*Victory* (1989), Colby argued that the United States relied too much on the use of conventional armed force in Vietnam, and should have paid more attention to pacification and the political struggle in South Vietnam.

**COLLINS, J[OSEPH] LAWTON** "Lightning Joe" (1896–1987). U.S. **Army** general. Born in New Orleans, Louisiana, he graduated from West Point in 1917, but did not get to Europe until after World War I was over. During World War II he commanded the 25th Infantry **Division** on Guadalcanal, then VII Corps in the Normandy invasion. He was chief of staff of the U.S. Army 1949–1953. He was sent to Vietnam in November 1954, as a special representative with the rank of ambassador. Collins was unable to establish a working relationship with Premier **Ngo Dinh Diem**, and by December 1954 he was seriously considering the possibility the United States should try to have Diem removed from office. During the **Sect** crisis of April 1955, he concluded that Ngo Dinh Diem was hopeless, and he openly recommended that the United States try to persuade Diem to resign. It seemed for a while that the U.S. government might indeed abandon Diem on Collins's recommendation, but between April 28 and May 2, Diem decisively defeated the **Binh Xuyen** in the **Saigon** area, renewing American faith in him. Collins left Vietnam on May 14, 1955. He retired from the Army in 1956.

**COMBAT AIR PATROL** (CAP). Fighter planes assigned to deal with enemy fighters, rather than to attack ground targets. Sometimes called MIGCAP because the threat was **MiG** fighters. U.S. **F-4 Phantoms** were often assigned as CAP, when **F-105 Thunderchiefs** were attacking ground targets in **North Vietnam**.

**COMBAT REFUSAL.** In the later stages of the war, as the average level of morale in U.S. units declined, there were occasional incidents in which U.S. units refused to go on combat missions. The most famous such incident was in August 1969, when some soldiers of the 196th Brigade, 23d Infantry **Division**, briefly refused to continue efforts to fight their way to a crashed U.S. helicopter in the area of the **Que Son Valley**. What may have been the last such incident occurred on April 12, 1972, when Companies A and C of the 2/1 Infantry Battalion, 196th Brigade, were ordered on a patrol west of **Phu Bai**. Company A grumbled but went; about 50 men of Company C refused for an hour and a half to go, but then went. A number of reporters were present, and the battalion commander charged that they had incited the troops in their refusal.

**COMBINED ACTION PLATOON** (CAP). A squad of U.S. **Marines**, a U.S. **Navy** medic, and a platoon of Vietnamese **Popular Forces** (PF) together constituted a CAP. The Marines had better weapons and combat skills, and the ability to call in air and **artillery** support, and **medical evacuation**, on short notice. The PF troops knew the language and the area. This method of **pacification** was both far more effective in excluding Communist forces from the villages than sporadic sweeps by large units would have been, and far less likely to cause civilian casualties. In theory there were supposed to be 15 Americans in a CAP; in practice there were often 10 or fewer.

The program began in August 1965 in villages near **Phu Bai** that until then had been under **Viet Cong** control. By the end of 1966 there were 57 CAPs in three provinces. At the peak of the program in January 1970, there were 114 CAPs spread through the ethnically Vietnamese areas of all five provinces of **I Corps**.

Marine generals like **Lewis Walt** and **Victor Krulak** supported the program strongly, as did **ARVN** General **Ngo Quang Truong**, commander of the ARVN 1st Infantry Division. The U.S. **Army** generals who dominated **Military Assistance Command, Vietnam**, were in many cases less enthusiastic; they felt the Marines would be better employed in large-unit operations than in village defense.

Late in 1970, **Regional Forces** (RF) were increasingly assigned to CAPs in place of PF. The RF were better armed than the PF, but they were less willing to accept Marine direction. Disputes over policies and tactics, between Marine and RF officers, became a significant problem.

The CAP program shrank rapidly during 1970 as part of the overall withdrawal of U.S. Marines from Vietnam. By September, there were CAPs only in **Quang Nam** province. CAPs continued to operate in Quang Nam until mid-1971.

**COMMANDO HUNT,** Operation. A campaign of U.S. air attack against the **Ho Chi Minh Trail** in southern **Laos**, begun on November 1, 1968. Most of the actions carried out under that name had already been occurring under other names before that date.

**COMMANDO LAVA,** Operation. This project used **C-130** aircraft to drop chelating chemicals (a mixture of trisodium nitrilotriacetic acid and sodium tripolyphosphate) to break up the structure of the soil, causing more landslides and deeper and more impassable mudholes on dirt roads in wet weather. The first experimental drops in **Laos** on May 17, 1967, produced mudslides across two Communist roads, and U.S. Ambassador **William Sullivan** was encouraged enough to coin the slogan "make mud, not war," but drops in the **A Shau** Valley in **South Vietnam** beginning on July 20 had less result. Overall, the experiments were not considered successful enough to justify expansion of the program to a large scale.

**COMMITTEE FOR THE DEFENSE OF NATIONAL INTERESTS** (CDNI). An organization of right-wing military officers and officials in **Laos**, mostly quite young, formed in June 1958, partly as a reaction to the very strong showing of left-wing candidates in the May 1958 national **elections**. General **Phoumi Nosavan** led the CDNI's seizure of power in a bloodless **coup** in late December 1959.

**CONGRESS,** U.S. During the Cold War, a consensus had emerged in the American political mainstream, and in the Congress, about the need to take a firm stand against world Communism. This had not, however, implied a consensus about foreign policy; there had never been a time when there were not serious disagreements about particular policies toward particular countries. During the Vietnam War, even the consensus about the need to stand firmly against any expansion of Communism broke down.

As early as the administration of **John Kennedy**, some in Congress were worried that the United States was getting too heavily committed in Vietnam. Senator **Mike Mansfield** in particular repeatedly urged President Kennedy to pull back. Such sentiments, however, were for the most part kept private, not publicized.

During 1964, as **Lyndon Johnson**'s administration came more and more to believe that only an open commitment of U.S. forces to combat could prevent a Communist victory in **South Vietnam**, President Johnson wanted to get some declaration of congressional support for the U.S. commitment in Vietnam. The problem was that a number of senators and representatives opposed the idea of committing U.S. combat forces in Vietnam. In August, President Johnson succumbed to the temptation to use the **Tonkin Gulf incidents**, in which it had been reported that North Vietnamese torpedo boats had twice attacked U.S. naval vessels, to get the Congress to pass the declaration he had been wanting. The **Tonkin Gulf Resolution**, which authorized the president to take any action that was necessary to deal with aggression in Vietnam, passed the House of Representatives unanimously, and the

Senate 98-2, because the Congress was persuaded that President Johnson had no intention of cashing this blank check, and that the practical meaning of the resolution was simply that the Congress stood behind the president in resisting attacks against U.S. ships on the high seas. Some who had voted for the resolution felt betrayed when President Johnson later used it as authorization for massive escalation of the war, and they did not feel committed to support his actions.

The policies for Vietnam advocated by members of Congress ranged from dramatic expansion of the war to immediate withdrawal. The prevalence of anti-war sentiment was somewhat greater among Democrats than among Republicans, and somewhat greater in the Senate than in the House of Representatives.

Probably the most important intervention in the policy process by congressional supporters of the war came in August 1967, when Senator **John Stennis**'s Preparedness Investigating Subcommittee of the Senate Armed Services Committee held hearings that gave top military leaders the opportunity to denounce the restrictions that President Johnson and Secretary of Defense **Robert McNamara** had imposed on the bombing of **North Vietnam**. At the end of the hearings, the committee wrote a report supporting the generals and admirals, which was almost immediately leaked to the press, and the political pressure this generated contributed to a significant loosening of the restrictions.

Members of Congress who complained that they had been tricked into voting for the Tonkin Gulf Resolution were sometimes told that if they did not approve of the war, they had the option of refusing to appropriate the funds for it. Some of them eventually responded by trying to cut off funding, not usually for the war as a whole, but for certain portions of it. They attached amendments to appropriations bills, forbidding the expenditure of U.S. government funds for certain military activities in Indochina. These amendments forbade the use of *any* U.S. government funds for such activities, not just the use of the particular funds being appropriated in the bills to which they were attached. Such efforts were initiated almost always by senators, notably Democrats **Frank Church** of Idaho, Thomas Eagleton of Missouri, Mike Gravel of Alaska, **George McGovern** of South Dakota, and Mike Mansfield of Montana, and Republicans Edward Brooke of Massachusetts, Clifford Case of New Jersey, **John Sherman Cooper** of Kentucky, and **Mark Hatfield** of Oregon.

Many such amendments were proposed; a significant number passed the Senate; few managed also to pass the House of Representatives and become law. The first two full successes were the Cooper-Church Amendments (amendments sponsored by Senators Cooper and Church), both passed by the Congress in December 1970, and signed into law by President **Richard Nixon** in January 1971. One of these, attached to a defense appropriations bill, forbade the use of U.S. ground combat troops in **Laos** and **Thailand**. The other, attached to a foreign aid bill, forbade the use of either U.S. ground combat troops or U.S. military **advisers** in **Cambodia**.

Early in 1973, U.S. bombing of North and South Vietnam and Laos ceased, but the Nixon administration expanded U.S. bombing of Cambodia to record levels. Both houses of Congress attached an amendment to an appropriations bill forbidding all combat activities by U.S. forces "in or over . . . or off the shores of Cambodia, Laos, North Vietnam and South Vietnam" after August 15, 1973. President Nixon signed this into law on July 1, and halted the bombing of Cambodia on schedule on August 15.

There is a widespread belief that the Congress cut off U.S. military aid to South Vietnam during the last stage of the war. This is not correct, although the Congress did reduce the amount of aid. President Nixon had asked the Congress to appropriate $1.45 billion in military aid to South Vietnam for fiscal year 1975 (July 1974 to June 1975); Congress had appropriated $700 million, of which $268 million was for ammunition. President **Gerald Ford** asked on January 28, 1975, for a supplemental appropriation of $300 million; on April 10 he asked for a supplemental appropriation of $722 million. The Congress rejected these requests, but aid based on the appropriation of $700 million continued to flow as long as there was a South Vietnamese government to receive it. (The Department of Defense provided some supplementary aid during this fiscal year beyond that authorized by Congress, shipping for example more than 25,000 tons of ammunition to South Vietnam from surplus stocks elsewhere, the value of which was not counted against the $700 million because it was officially considered to have been surplus.)

**COOPER, JOHN SHERMAN** (1901–1991). United States senator, Republican of Kentucky. Born in Somerset, Kentucky, he graduated from Yale in 1923, attended Harvard Law School from 1923 to 1925, and became a judge in 1928. He enlisted in the U.S. **Army** in 1942, served in the European Theater, and was discharged as a captain in 1946. He had two brief stints in the United States Senate, being elected to serve the two remaining years of an unexpired term in 1946, but losing when he ran for a full six-year term in 1948, and elected to serve the two remaining years of another unexpired term in 1952, but defeated when he ran for a full term in 1954. He served as U.S. ambassador to India and Nepal from 1955 to 1956, then ran once again for the Senate, and this time managed to stay in for 16 years, from 1957 to 1972.

Cooper had become a critic of the Vietnam War by early 1966. In 1970, he and Senator **Frank Church** (Democrat of Idaho) became the most conspicuous and successful figures in efforts to limit the war in Indochina by attaching amendments to appropriations bills, making it illegal to use U.S. government funds to pay for certain types of military operations in certain areas (*see* **Congress**). The Cooper-Church amendments, which passed both houses of Congress at the end of 1970 and became law in 1971, forbade the use of U.S. ground troops in **Laos**, **Cambodia**, and **Thailand**, and forbade even military **advisers** in Cambodia. But Senator Cooper abstained rather than voting for an amendment that Church was sponsoring in 1972, which would have cut off funds for all U.S. combat activities throughout Indochina provided U.S. **prisoners of war** were released. Cooper said this would have left President **Richard Nixon** with too little leverage in peace negotiations.

**COR** (Kor, Core). A **Montagnard** group, very small, sometimes said to be a subgroup of the **Sedang**, living in Quang Ngai province of southern **I Corps**. A Cor attack on government forces in January 1959 has been treated, in some Communist histories, as a crucial step in the beginning of the Vietnam War.

**CORPS TACTICAL ZONES** (CTZ). **South Vietnam** was divided for military command purposes into corps tactical zones, numbered from north to south. Up to 1962 there were three. Late in 1962, IV CTZ or **IV Corps** was created, covering the **Mekong Delta**, the southwest half of what had formerly been **III Corps**. III Corps absorbed the southern third of what had been **II Corps**, which in turn took one province, Quang Ngai, from **I Corps**. The Capital Military District, centered on **Saigon**, was created at this time. Late in 1964, I Corps and II Corps were restored to the boundaries they had had before the change of late 1962; this meant that Quang Ngai was transferred back to I Corps, and that eight provinces were transferred from III Corps back to II Corps.

**I CORPS** (pronounced "eye corps"). *See* map, p. xx. The northernmost of the **corps tactical zones** into which **South Vietnam** was divided. This was the narrowest section of South Vietnam; the distance from the Laotian border to the sea ranged from about 55 to 100 kilometers. For most of the war I Corps included five provinces; from north to south they were **Quang Tri, Thua Thien, Quang Nam**, Quang Tin, and Quang Ngai. (From late 1962 to late 1964, Quang Ngai was part of **II Corps**.) Each of these provinces had a limited area of flat land near the coast with a dense Vietnamese population, and a much larger area of jungle and mountain, thinly inhabited by various **Montagnard** tribes, to the west. Many of the Vietnamese villages along the coast were Communist strongholds dating back to the First Indochina War. The main logistical center for American forces in I Corps, and the biggest air base, were at **Danang** in Quang Nam province.

The U.S. **Marines** who were landed in March 1965 to defend Danang Air Base were the first American ground combat troops sent overtly to Vietnam, and for more than a year the U.S. command left I Corps essentially to the Marines of the 3d Marine Amphibious Force. They emphasized **pacification** of the villages, despite suggestions from **Military Assistance Command, Vietnam** (MACV), that they should be devoting more of their resources to search-and-destroy operations in the jungle.

In 1966, the People's Army of Vietnam (**PAVN**) decided that it needed to initiate more direct combat with American forces in the jungles of South Vietnam, both to impose casualties that would weaken American political will, and to draw U.S. troops away from the densely populated areas along the coast. The northern section of I Corps, along the **Demilitarized Zone** (DMZ) separating Quang Tri from **North Vietnam**, seemed the ideal area. Communist forces there enjoyed short supply lines, and the proximity of North Vietnam and **Laos** allowed them to retreat between battles to partial **sanctuary**—comparatively safe from ground pursuit, though not from air strikes and in some places not from shelling—more easily than Communist forces in most areas of South Vietnam. This area also had more rainfall than most of South Vietnam; this interfered with American use of air power. Dense jungle and hilly terrain provided cover for Communist forces.

PAVN forces began coming across the DMZ to challenge the Marines in northern Quang Tri province in mid-1966. The Marines shifted troops north and west from the coastal lowlands to meet the challenge, and **Army** troops were sent into I Corps both to assist the Marines in fighting the PAVN forces in the hills, and to replace them in lowland areas from which they had withdrawn. I Corps, especially the three northernmost provinces—Quang Tri, Thua Thien, and Quang Nam—soon had more American infantry than any other area of South Vietnam. From 1967 onward, 40 percent of the Americans killed in combat in South Vietnam died just in those three provinces; 53 percent died in I Corps as a whole. There was **guerrilla warfare** in those provinces, but it was supplemented more than in other areas by conventional combat; the Marines repeatedly found themselves assaulting strongly fortified PAVN positions. After May 1967, the line of Marine positions just south of the DMZ also began to be hit by substantial quantities of **artillery** fire from the North. The Americans hit back with artillery, naval gunfire, and air strikes, but without permission to send troops into North Vietnam on the ground, U.S. forces could not impose enough casualties on the PAVN gunners, firing from well camouflaged and fortified positions, to stop the artillery fire.

In February 1968, a headquarters at **Phu Bai** called MACV Forward, headed by General **Creighton Abrams** of the U.S. Army, was created to control the U.S. forces in Quang Tri and Thua Thien. This headquarters was renamed Provisional Corps, Vietnam, in March, and placed under the Marine general who commanded the 3d Marine Amphibious Force (III MAF) and had overall responsibility for U.S. forces in I Corps. Provisional Corps was renamed XXIV Corps in August 1968. In 1970, the relationship was reversed. XXIV Corps, which had controlled only two provinces and had been subordinate to III MAF, was placed over III MAF, given control of all U.S. forces in I Corps, and shifted from Phu Bai to Danang.

**II CORPS.** *See* map, p. xxi. From late 1964 onward, II Corps was by far the largest geographically of the four tactical zones into which **South Vietnam** was divided. It included the coastal provinces (in order from north to south) of **Binh Dinh**, Phu Yen, Khanh Hoa, Ninh Thuan, and Binh Thuan; the provinces bordering **Laos** and **Cambodia** of **Kontum**, **Pleiku**, Darlac, and Quang Duc; and in between these, the provinces of Phu Bon, Tuyen Duc, and Lam Dong. (For fluctuations in boundary up to 1964, *see* **corps tactical zones**.) II Corps was made up mostly of jungles and mountains—the **Central Highlands**—occupied by a thin scattering of **Montagnards**. The ethnically Vietnamese areas, containing most of the population, were restricted mostly to a narrow strip along the coast. The main U.S. logistical centers in II Corps were **Qui Nhon** and **Cam Ranh**, on the coast, but the U.S. did base substantial military forces at locations well inland, especially Pleiku, **Dak To**, and An Khe, in a way it did not do in **I Corps**.

The dispatch of the U.S. 1st **Cavalry Division** to the Central Highlands in 1965 led to the Battle of the **Ia Drang Valley** in Pleiku province, the first direct combat between **PAVN** and U.S. ground troops, in November of that year. In later years the heaviest combat in the Highlands shifted north to Kontum province. The intense battles of November 1967 between PAVN and U.S. troops around Dak To, in Kontum province near the Cambodian border, were a deliberate effort by the PAVN to draw U.S. forces out to the west, away from major centers. U.S. combat actions in the coastal areas of II Corps were mostly in Binh Dinh, where the United States began trying to eradicate the Communists in Operation *Masher* in January 1966, and was still trying to do it in Operation *Washington Green* (1969–1970). More than a third of all U.S. combat deaths in II Corps between 1967 and 1972 occurred in Binh Dinh. In the other coastal provinces, much of the fighting was handled by troops from **Korea**.

From March 1966 to April 1971 the U.S. military command for II Corps was **I Field Force, Vietnam**, with headquarters at **Nha Trang**.

**III CORPS.** *See* map, p. xxii. Initially by far the most important of the tactical zones into which **South Vietnam** was divided, III Corps went through drastic fluctuations in boundary (*see* **corps tactical zones**) before it stabilized at a much-reduced size in late 1964. In this final form it included the Cambodian border provinces (in order from northeast to southwest) of Phuoc Long, Binh Long, **Tay Ninh**, and **Hau Nghia**; the coastal provinces of Binh Tuy, Phuoc Tuy, and **Gia Dinh**; and touching neither the sea nor **Cambodia**, the provinces of Long Khanh, **Bien Hoa**, Binh Duong, and **Long An**. III Corps had substantial ethnically Vietnamese populations spread far into the interior, not just near the coast as in **I Corps** and **II Corps** to its north. The major U.S. bases were mostly well in from the coast (*see* **Bien Hoa, Long Binh, Cu Chi**).

There were numerous **Viet Cong** base areas in III Corps. Some like the **Iron Triangle** not far north of **Saigon** were small enough so the United States could seriously try to destroy them in operations like *Cedar Falls* (January 1967); **War Zone D** was so large that the United States could only try to weaken it with raids like Operation *Uniontown* (early 1968). Communist forces in III Corps were also supported by bases in Cambodia. There was far more ground combat action by U.S.

forces in III Corps than in II Corps, but not as much as in I Corps. The provinces where U.S. forces suffered the heaviest casualties were **Tay Ninh** (containing **War Zone C**) and Binh Duong (containing the Iron Triangle and part of War Zone D).

**IV Corps.** *See* map, p. xxiii. Created in 1962 from what had been the southern half of **III Corps**, IV Corps covered the **Mekong Delta**, the rice bowl of **South Vietnam**. It had more people, and more agricultural land both in absolute quantity and per capita, than any of the other **corps tactical zones**. It was crisscrossed by waterways, including numerous canals as well as the multiple branches by which the **Mekong River** flowed to the sea. Water transport was important both for the civilian inhabitants and for military forces. The U.S. **Mobile Riverine Force**, established in 1967, operated widely in IV Corps (*see also Market Time, SEALORDS,* **River Patrol Force**).

The war was left more to the South Vietnamese, on both sides, in IV Corps than in other areas. Only one U.S. **division**, the 9th, operated there to any large extent, and that for a limited period, 1967 to 1969. There were hardly any **PAVN** troops there until 1968; the United States did not identify any PAVN regiment in IV Corps until the second half of 1969. There was also somewhat less bombing there than in other areas. The heaviest combat for **ARVN** forces, from 1967 onward, was in Kien Hoa and Dinh Tuong provinces, in the eastern part of the delta.

**CORRUPTION.** Corruption in the **Republic of Vietnam** (RVN) had by the mid-1960s reached a level that was very high by Southeast Asian standards, high enough to have a crippling effect. Many officials found that some corruption was unavoidable; their nominal salaries were so low that it would have been impossible to function without supplementing them at least to a small extent, and the payments demanded by their superiors, which had to be made if these officals were to remain in office, required far larger sums. Many province and district chiefs had purchased their positions in the first place. Some officials collected, through bribery and embezzlement, only what was necessary in order to meet expenses; others seized the opportunity to enrich themselves. In the most extreme cases, officials not only embezzled government funds and extorted payments from citizens, but were willing to perform services for the **Viet Cong** in return for bribes, and refused to provide **artillery** support for military units under Communist attack if the units in question were not willing to bribe them for the support.

The collection of taxes of course offered opportunities, but these were eventually surpassed by the administration of American-financed programs for economic development, refugee relief, and military operations.  Many military units had far more men listed on the rosters than were actually serving; the commanding officers pocketed the salaries of the "ghost soldiers," with whom the officers had no contact (they were often dead), and the "potted tree" or "flower" soldiers, with whom the officers had a mutually beneficial relationship: the officers pocketed the men's salaries, and in return protected them from being required actually to serve in the military.

The black market, especially in currency, provided enormous opportunities.  The official exchange rates set a high value on the Vietnamese piastre, and on the semi-money called Military Payment Certificates (MPCs), issued by the American command for the use of American soldiers and not supposed to be in the possession of the Vietnamese.  People who could exchange dollars for piastres or MPCs at the black-market rate, and then exchange them back for dollars at the official rate, could achieve huge profits.

The Communists took advantage of the corruptibility of many government personnel, bribing them to ignore certain Communist activities, and sometimes to release important Communists who had been arrested.

The United States was reluctant to pressure the RVN too hard on the issue of corruption, for fear public discussion of the problem would undermine support for the RVN among the American public.  **Robert Komer** began. and **William Colby** of the **Central Intelligence Agency** continued, a secret program under which they collected files on unusually corrupt officials; they and Ambassador **Ellsworth Bunker** pressed the RVN to dismiss the officials in question.  The results were minimal.

During the war, there was corruption in **North Vietnam**, on a scale far smaller than that in **South Vietnam** but still sufficient to cause resentment and cynicism among those aware of it.  Corruption was almost totally absent in the Communist organizations in the South.  After 1975, as Communist officials (especially in what had been South Vietnam) encountered more lucrative opportunities for corruption than they had ever faced before, the level of corruption increased dramatically.

Corruption among American personnel in Vietnam during the war mainly centered on the black market.  Many Americans profited on a small scale, and some on a large scale, from the black market in MPCs, and from the diversion of goods from the U.S. military's Post Exchange (PX) system, which sold consumer goods to American personnel at very low prices. Some Americans resold these goods on the private market in Vietnam at much higher prices.

**COUNTER-TERROR TEAMS.** Units at the provincial level, sponsored by the **Central Intelligence Agency** (CIA) but under the command of province chiefs, intended to attack the Communist **infrastructure** in South Vietnam. The teams were created by the CIA in 1964, building on previous programs. The Counter-Terror Teams were renamed **Provincial Reconnaissance Units**, in an effort to shake their reputation as assassination squads, in 1966.

**COUNTERINSURGENCY.** The mainstream of U.S. **Army** doctrine in the mid-1950s stressed a very conventional style of warfare, conducted by large units with much use of heavy weapons and air support. In the early 1960s, President **John Kennedy** encouraged a strengthening of unconventional forces suitable for guerrilla or counterguerrilla warfare. Counterinsurgency doctrines stressed "winning hearts and minds" through the provision of services to the peasants, and through propaganda and psychological warfare, as an alternative or supplement to military force. When the advocates of counterinsurgency did use military force they preferred that it be small in scale; men with rifles could apply force with more precision and discrimination than air strikes or **artillery**.

The **Central Intelligence Agency** was much more favorable to counterinsurgency than the U.S. military; within the military, the Army **Special Forces** and the **Marines** tended to favor counterinsurgency more than the main body of the Army, or the **Navy** and **Air Force**, did.

**COUP, in Cambodia.** The degree of U.S. involvement in the coup of March 18, 1970, in which General **Lon Nol** and Prince Sisowath Sirik Matak overthrew Prince **Norodom Sihanouk**, has been disputed. Rumors that the United States had actually provided weapons for the coup appear clearly unfounded. Reports that the **Central Intelligence Agency** had encouraged the coup have more credibility. It seems at least that there had been contact between the coup plotters and some low-level U.S. officers. But it is not clear that higher levels in the U.S. government had known about, or encouraged, the plot.

**COUPS, in Laos.** The rightist government of Phoui Sananikone was replaced by a group of mostly younger rightists associated with the **Committee for the Defense of National Interests** in a bloodless coup on December 25, 1959. Colonel **Phoumi Nosavan**, the main leader of the coup, became minister of defense.

On August 9, 1960, Captain **Kong Le** overthrew the government in which Prince Somsanith was prime minister and General Phoumi Nosavan, minister of defense, the strongest figure. Kong Le's coup placed the neutralist Prince **Souvanna Phouma** in office as prime minister.

In December 1960, troops under the rightist General Phoumi Nosavan, pushing up from southern Laos, drove Souvanna Phouma from Vientiane, and placed Prince **Boun Oum** in office as prime minister.

On April 19, 1964, rightist generals Kouprasith Abhay (Kupasit Aphai) and Siho Lamphouthacoul (Lamphoutacoul, Lanphutthakun) carried out what at first seemed a sucessful coup, arresting Prime Minister Souvanna Phouma (who had returned to office in 1962). American pressure, however, forced them to allow Souvanna to return to power a few days later.

On August 4, 1964, Phoumi Nosavan attempted a coup, but it was quickly smashed by forces of Kouprasith Abhay.

In late January 1965, there were separate coups attempted simultaneously by Phoumi Nosavan and Colonel Bounleut Saycocie. Kouprasith Abhay defeated them both, then used the crisis as an excuse to attack the forces of Siho Lamphouthacoul. Phoumi and Siho had to flee to **Thailand**.

The rightist chief of the Royal Lao Air Force, General Thao Ma, attempted a coup on October 21, 1966, killing 23 people by bombing in the Vientiane area.

General Thao Ma attempted another coup on August 20, 1973, intending to make Boun Oum prime minister once again. But Thao was captured and executed within hours after the attempt began.

**COUPS, in South Vietnam**. Colonel **Nguyen Chanh Thi**, commander of the **Airborne Brigade**, attempted a coup in **Saigon** on November 11, 1960. He very nearly succeeded in overthrowing President **Ngo Dinh Diem**, but Diem was able to keep negotiations going until loyal troops under General **Tran Thien Khiem** could reach Saigon, and the coup collapsed on November 12. The United States remained neutral, rather than opposing the coup.

On February 27, 1962, two **Vietnamese Air Force** (VNAF) pilots attempted to kill Ngo Dinh Diem and his brother **Ngo Dinh Nhu** by bombing the Presidential Palace in Saigon. They failed, although Nhu's wife was injured. One pilot was shot down; the other succeeded in flying to **Cambodia**.

As early as 1961, the United States was so dissatisfied with Diem's leadership that the report of the **Taylor-Rostow Mission** explicitly considered the possibility of encouraging a coup to overthrow Diem, though it recommended against this option. It was not until the **Buddhist** crisis of 1963 that top U.S. officials began to see Diem as such a liability that they were willing seriously to consider overthrowing him.

A coup on November 1, 1963, overthrew Diem. It involved far more people than most coups. The U.S. government knew about, and encouraged, the plot; the U.S. officials most responsible for support of the coup were **W. Averell Harriman** and Ambassador **Henry Cabot Lodge**. Generals **Tran Van Don** (who handled the plotters' liaison with the Americans) and **Duong Van Minh** were its most conspicuous leaders. General **Ton That Dinh** (**III Corps** commander) and Colonel **Nguyen Van Thieu** (5th Division commander) provided most of the actual troops, and Colonel **Nguyen Cao Ky** provided air support. General **Nguyen Khanh** and many others also supported it. Generals Duong Van Minh, Le Van Kim, and Tran Van Don became the new leaders of the government, but they lasted only three months before being overthrown in turn on January 30, 1964, in a coup led by Nguyen Khanh, for which Khanh had obtained advance permission from U.S. General **Paul Harkins**.

Generals Duong Van Duc and Lam Van Phat seized most of Saigon on September 13, 1964, but counter-action by Nguyen Cao Ky, by this time commander of the VNAF, caused their coup to fail. The military handed nominal power to **Tran Van Huong** as premier soon after, but then Nguyen Khanh and a group of younger officers (including Nguyen Cao Ky), called the "**Young Turks**," staged a bloodless coup on December 19. They allowed Huong to resume power on January 9, 1965, then forced him out in another bloodless coup on January 27, replacing him with another civilian, **Phan Huy Quat**, while clearly holding real power themselves.

Military officers, predominantly **Catholic**, attempted a coup, directed more against Khanh and the Young Turks (the holders of real power) than against Premier Quat, on February 19, 1965. The leaders were Colonel **Pham Ngoc Thao**, Brigadier General Lam Van Phat, and Colonel Huynh Van Ton. They were able to seize the radio station, Joint General Staff Headquarters, and **Tan Son Nhut** Airport, but their forces were too weak to offer serious resistance when those of Khanh and the Young Turks moved to retake Saigon. The Young Turks squeezed Khanh out a few days later and forced him into exile. They left Quat in office as premier until June.

**"CREDIBILITY GAP."** A phrase referring to doubts about the reliability of U.S. officials' statements about Vietnam. Some journalists began to use the phrase—at first in private conversation, later in their reporting—during 1965.

**CRONKITE, WALTER LELAND, JR.** (1916– ). Journalist. Born in St. Joseph, Missouri, Cronkite attended the University of Texas in Austin, Texas, in 1935 and 1936, and began working as a reporter for the Scripps-Howard newspapers while a student there. He covered World War II in the European Theater for United Press International. He began working for the Columbia Broadcasting System (CBS) in 1950, and was anchorman of the CBS *Evening News* from 1954 to 1981; this program became more influential when it expanded from 15 to 30 minutes in 1963. In the 1960s, he was sometimes called "the most trusted man in America."

In the early years of the Vietnam War, Cronkite, like most broadcast journalists at the time, generally supported the American war effort. During the **Tet Offensive** of 1968, however, shocked by the discrepancy between what was happening in **South Vietnam** and the U.S. military's claims during the preceding months that the Communist forces were weakening, Cronkite went to Vietnam. CBS broadcast Cronkite's report of what he had found as a half-hour prime-time documentary on February 27. Some today argue that Cronkite's report was fairly moderate. He had not relinquished his belief in the goals of the war; he ended his broadcast by saying that in Vietnam Americans had acted as "an honorable people who lived up to their pledge to defend democracy, and did the best they could." And he did not (as has sometimes been claimed) describe the Tet Offensive as a Communist military victory. What he said was that there had been no clear winner or loser in the Tet Offensive—the Communist forces had suffered a military defeat, but had done great damage, especially to the **pacification** program—and that it seemed unlikely that there would be a clear winner or loser in the war. He predicted a stalemate, leading to a negotiated compromise settlement. Most observers, however, both at the time and today, stressed that for Cronkite, the most influential journalist in the United States, to say publicly that he did not believe the United States could win the war constituted a stunning blow to U.S. policy.

**Lyndon Johnson** is quoted as having said, "If I've lost Cronkite, I've lost middle America."

**CS.** An **incapacitating agent**, ortho-chlorobenzalmalonitrile or ortho-chlorobenzylidenemalonitrile, sometimes called "super tear gas" although it is actually a solid, usually dispensed as a fine powder with a peppery smell. CS was a very powerful irritant, attacking the eyes and respiratory tracts of those exposed, and causing coughing, chest pain, and sometimes nausea. The effects appeared instantly on exposure, and were severe enough to be incapacitating, but the symptoms usually faded after the victim had been in clear air for five or 10 minutes, leaving no permanent ill effects. In the warm, moist conditions often found in the tropics, continuous exposure for an hour or more to a heavy dose of CS could leave second-degree burns on skin. The effects of prolonged exposure on the lungs, and the effects of CS on the lungs of persons having pre-existing lung diseases, were inadequately documented.

The United States began to use CS in military operations in Vietnam in 1963 or 1964, and was using it on a substantial scale by 1966. It could be fired by **grenade launcher** or in **artillery** shells, pumped into underground **tunnels** by an air blower, or dropped from aircraft. U.S. troop units that discovered enemy food stockpiles sometimes mixed CS powder with the rice to make it inedible.

In January 1967, as part of Operation *Cedar Falls*, U.S. forces tried large-scale airdrops of CS in 55-gallon steel drums. The drums were set to explode at treetop height, scattering the CS widely. Thirty such drums, dropped in a line at intervals of about 50 yards, could create a formidable barrier to movement of **Viet Cong** forces on the ground. U.S. sources indicate that by late 1968 and early 1969, the United States was shipping CS to Indochina at an average rate of about 16,000 pounds per day, and presumably expending it at a similar rate. These figures seem consistent with Communist claims that the United States used a total of more than 9,000 tons of CS during the war.

**CU CHI.** Cu Chi District of **Hau Nghia** province, northeast of **Saigon**, was a **Viet Cong** stronghold, and the northern half of the district, which included the **Ho Bo Woods** and the Filhol **Rubber Plantation**, was the site of what was probably the most extensive network of underground **tunnels** in **South Vietnam**. This tunnel complex was the base from which many Communist operations in the Saigon area were supported. The Saigon River was the northeast border of the district; another Communist base, the **Iron Triangle**, was on the far side of the river.

The first major U.S. attack on the Cu Chi base area was Operation *Crimp* (later renamed *Buckskin*), which involved troops of the 1st Infantry **Division**, the 173d **Airborne** Brigade, and the Royal **Australian** Regiment, and began on January 7, 1966. The Americans had not been expecting the tunnels, and at first did not understand how Viet Cong snipers were able to inflict casualties and then disappear to evade retaliation. They eventually found and destroyed some of the tunnels and captured a considerable quantity of documents (one of which, a history of the beginning of the war, became a crucial source for historians of the conflict and was called the "CRIMP Document"), but they failed to eliminate the base area. Indeed, really devastating attacks on the Viet Cong's Cu Chi base did not begin until after the **Tet Offensive** of 1968.

The U.S. military base of Cu Chi, on **Route 1** close to the capital (Cu Chi) of Cu Chi District, was the headquarters of the U.S. 25th Infantry Division. The site was chosen at the end of 1965, and the base established and rapidly expanded to a huge size in 1966. During the early months, there were frequent problems with guerrillas and snipers inside the American perimeter, since the base was being built on top of pre-existing enemy tunnels.

# - D -

*DAGGER THRUST.* Code name for U.S. attacks on **Viet Cong** supply areas and troop concentrations along the coast of **South Vietnam**. The first operation began on September 28, 1965, involving a Battalion Landing Team of the Fleet **Marine** Force, supported by carrier aircraft, and **naval gunfire support** from destroyers. Some of the Marines in *Dagger Thrust* operations came ashore in landing craft, others were carried ashore by **helicopter**.

**DAK TO.** A **Civilian Irregular Defense Group** (CIDG) unit led by a U.S. **Army Special Forces** A-team was placed at Dak To, in **Kontum** province about 25 kilometers east of the **tri-border** where **South Vietnam**, **Laos**, and **Cambodia** come together, early in the CIDG program, probably in 1963. Dak To drew little attention until 1967, when the **PAVN** decided to challenge U.S. forces to large-scale combat in remote jungle areas, to draw American attention and resources away from the coastal lowlands and thus improve the chances of success of the 1968 **Tet Offensive**. Dak To was one of the remote areas chosen; heavy fighting between PAVN units and troops of the U.S. 173d **Airborne** Brigade and 4th Infantry **Division** began there on November 4.

Substantial U.S. forces remained at Dak To into 1969, and after they withdrew it remained an **ARVN** base. It fell to PAVN forces in April 1972, during the **Easter Offensive**, but was retaken in October.

**DALAT.** The southernmost important town in the **Central Highlands**, capital of Tuyen Duc province, Dalat was at a high enough altitude— close to 1,500 meters—to be considerably cooler than most of Vietnam. It had long been a pleasant place where wealthy people had vacation homes. During the war, important conferences were sometimes held there. The French had established a military academy there, which eventually became the **ARVN**'s National Military Academy. The Political Warfare College was also there. Dalat had a university and a nuclear physics research institute. There has been occasional criticism of the American failure to remove the institute's small stock of plutonium before Dalat fell to the **PAVN** in 1975.

**DANANG.** Major city, called Tourane during the colonial period, in **Quang Nam** province on the west bank of the Danang River (Song Hao, Tourane River), where the river flows northward into Danang Bay and the South China Sea. The **Tien Sha** Peninsula, on the east bank of the river, was not formally in the city, but U.S. facilities there are often described as "at Danang."

In the early 1960s, Danang became a center for paramilitary activities. At the **Central Intelligence Agency**'s Hoa Cam training center three kilometers southwest of the city, U.S. **Special Forces** troops trained the **Mountain Scouts** and **Trailwatchers**. **SOG** used facilities in the Danang area from 1964 onward to support covert operations aimed at **North Vietnam** (*see OPLAN 34A*) and **Laos**. SOG established a regional headquarters there, Command and Control, North (CCN), in 1968.

The first regular U.S. ground troop units sent to **South Vietnam** were U.S. **Marines** guarding the facilities of the Marine **helicopter** unit (*see Shufly*) based at Danang. From April 1963 onward, there was a platoon. By late 1964, there was a reinforced company with at least 255 men. On March 8, 1965, two battalions were sent, the first U.S. ground troop units whose arrival in Vietnam had been publicly announced. During the escalation that followed, Danang Air Base expanded to a huge size, and Danang became the main logistics center for the U.S.

forces in **I Corps**. The 3d Marine **Division** was based there from May 1965 to October 1966, and the 1st Marine Division from November 1966 to April 1971.

Danang was one of the centers of an uprising by radical **Buddhists** that began in March 1966. It was one of the points attacked prematurely, in the early morning of January 30, 1968, in the **Tet Offensive**. During the **final collapse** of the **Republic of Vietnam**, the forces defending Danang disintegrated in panic, and Communist forces occupied the city without serious resistance on March 30, 1975.

*DANIEL BOONE,* Operation. Ground raids into **Cambodia** by small **reconnaissance** teams, no more than 12 men, controlled by **SOG**. *Daniel Boone* officially began in June 1967. It was so secret that the teams could not call for air support when in trouble in Cambodia, the way similar teams sent into **Laos** under Operation *Shining Brass* could. Up until late 1968, no more than three members of a team could be American; the rest were Asian.

*Daniel Boone* was renamed *Salem House* in 1969. Americans were not included in the teams sent into Cambodia after June 30, 1970. The shift of the program to Vietnamese control led to its being renamed *Thot Not* in April 1971. From 1970 onward, *Salem House* and *Thot Not* occasionally sent platoon-sized or even multi-platoon units into Cambodia, though small reconnaissance teams, like those which had been sent under *Daniel Boone*, remained the norm.

*DECKHOUSE,* Operation. A series of amphibious landings by the U.S. **Marines'** Special Landing Force, attacking **Viet Cong** base areas in coastal areas. The first four were in 1966. *Deckhouse I*, June 18–27, was in Phu Yen province of **II Corps**. *Deckhouse II* and *IV* were in northern **Quang Tri**, near the **Demilitarized Zone**. *Deckhouse III* was near **Vung Tau** in **III Corps**.

*Deckhouse V* in Kien Hoa province, January 6–15, 1967, was the first major operation by U.S. ground troops in the **Mekong Delta**. *Deckhouse VI*, from February 16 to March 3, 1967, was intended to establish control of the Sa Huynh area in southern Quang Ngai province, a landing point for boats bringing weapons and ammunition to Communist forces.

**DEFENSE ATTACHÉ OFFICE** (DAO). The principal U.S. military headquarters remaining in **Saigon** after **Military Assistance Command, Vietnam**, was disbanded in April 1973. It was commanded by Major General John E. Murray from 1973 to 1974, and by Major General Homer

Smith from 1974 to 1975. It was limited to 50 U.S. military personnel (not counting the substantial force of **Marines** guarding the U.S. Embassy). Almost all of these were logistics officers, who supervised the delivery of U.S. military aid. It also had an **intelligence** role, trying to keep track of the military situation, but as a result of the limitations on U.S. military personnel in Vietnam under the **Paris Peace Agreement** of 1973, DAO intelligence was staffed mostly by civilians. DAO evaluations of the military situation tended to be less optimistic than those of U.S. Ambassador **Graham Martin**.

**DEMILITARIZED ZONE** (DMZ). The **Geneva Accords of 1954** established a demarcation line separating **North** from **South Vietnam**. Its eastern end was the mouth of the Ben Hai (Ben Hat, Cua Tung) River, at the 17th parallel. It followed the winding course of the river generally southwestward to Bo Ho Su, about 60 kilometers from the river mouth and 12 kilometers south of the 17th parallel. From there it ran due east to **Laos**. The accords established a Demilitarized Zone, from which all armed forces were supposed to be excluded, on both sides of the demarcation line. The width of the DMZ varied, in some places about 10 kilometers (five kilometers on either side of the demarcation line), in others significantly less.

When the **Ho Chi Minh Trail** was first established in 1959, it cut across the DMZ. In 1961 it was re-routed to detour around the western end of the DMZ, through Laos. In June 1966, **PAVN** forces of considerable size began crossing the DMZ to challenge the U.S. **Marines** to comparatively conventional battles in the hills of northern **Quang Tri** province, immediately south of the DMZ.

U.S. forces began shelling targets in and north of the DMZ, the bases from which the PAVN supported its forces in the battles just south of the DMZ, in late February 1967. The PAVN responded by using **artillery** in and north of the DMZ for large-scale shelling of U.S. positions south of it. The artillery fire bases the U.S. established just south of the DMZ dueled with PAVN artillery to the north for more than a year. When U.S. bombing of North Vietnam was halted at the end of 1968, this led to a lull in artillery fire across the DMZ, lasting until 1971. The United States handed over the fire bases south of the DMZ to **ARVN** and Vietnamese **Marine Corps** troops under **Vietnamization**; these bases were overrun by a PAVN attack out of the DMZ in the **Easter Offensive** of 1972.

Significant attacks into the DMZ by U.S. and ARVN ground troops were forbidden until May 18, 1967, when an attack going as far as the Ben Hai River began under multiple operational names: Operations *Beau Charger* and *Hickory* for the U.S. Marines involved, and Operation *Lam Son* 54 for the ARVN 1st Division troops. Other such incursions occurred sporadically thereafter.

**DEMOCRATIC REPUBLIC OF VIETNAM** (DRV). The Communist government that ruled **North Vietnam** during the war and had its capital in **Hanoi**. It had been founded in 1945 as a government for all of Vietnam, and its leaders during the war were a mixture of North and South Vietnamese. The cabinet headed by Premier **Pham Van Dong** was less powerful than the Politburo of the **Lao Dong Party**. **Ho Chi Minh**, the founding father of Vietnamese Communism, was the top leader until his death in 1969. **Le Duan**, first secretary of the Lao Dong Party, was the top leader from then through the end of the war, when the DRV became the Socialist Republic of Vietnam, and the Lao Dong Party became the Communist Party of Vietnam.

*DESOTO* **PATROLS**. **Intelligence** gathering missions conducted by U.S. Navy destroyers along the coasts of the **Soviet Union**, **China**, North Korea, **North Vietnam**, and Indonesia, beginning in 1962. The destroyers carried some extra electronic gear, but not nearly as much as would have been aboard a fully equipped electronic intelligence vessel. The first three *Desoto* Patrols in the Gulf of Tonkin, off North Vietnam, were in December 1962, April 1963, and February to March 1964, and were uneventful. The fourth, begun by the *Maddox* on July 31, 1964, led to the very ambiguous **Tonkin Gulf incidents**, which in turn led to the first U.S. air strikes against North Vietnam. The fifth, in September 1964, led to another ambiguous incident (in which it was unclear whether the two destroyers involved had been attacked by North Vietnamese torpedo boats or not). The **Joint Chiefs of Staff** recommended retaliatory air strikes against North Vietnam, but these did not occur.

Another *Desoto* Patrol in the Gulf of Tonkin was planned to begin on February 7, 1965. U.S. officials hoped that this would lead to another incident, which would justify retaliatory air strikes code named *Flaming Dart*. The patrol was cancelled just before it would have begun. *Flaming Dart* was flown on February 7 and 8 in retaliation for a **Viet Cong** attack on **Pleiku**.

*DEWEY CANYON*, Operation. An attack by elements of the 9th **Marines** on a **PAVN** base area in the Da Krong Valley of **Quang Tri** province, beginning on January 22, 1969. As part of this operation, there was a small incursion into **Laos** on the night of February 21–22, and a larger one, lasting several days, soon afterward. When the press learned that the border had been crossed, U.S. spokesmen refused to confirm or deny this explicitly, while implicitly acknowledging that it had occurred.

*Dewey Canyon* inflicted serious losses on the enemy: U.S. figures show 1,617 enemy soldiers killed, five captured, and many weapons, including at least a dozen long-range 122-mm **artillery** pieces, destroyed or captured. But enemy forces were by no means eliminated from the area; when the operation ended on March 18, the last U.S. forces lifted out of the area were under enemy fire as they departed. U.S. losses were reported as 130 killed and 920 wounded.

**DEWEY CANYON II,** Operation. Operation carried out by U.S. forces to support *Lam Son 719*, the **ARVN** effort to cut the **Ho Chi Minh Trail** in southern **Laos**, early in 1971. Its main goals were: to open **Route 9** (the east-west road across **Quang Tri** province) through **Khe Sanh** and up to the Laotian border; to reopen Khe Sanh airstrip for use by **C-130** cargo planes; and to establish U.S. firebases that could provide **artillery** fire support for ARVN troops across the border in Laos. The 1st Brigade of the 5th Infantry **Division** (Mechanized) started west along Route 9 on January 30, 1971, and took Khe Sanh by air assault on January 31, but the airstrip did not become operational until February 12.

**DIKES.** Rice, the main Vietnamese food crop, is grown in shallow water. Land on which rice is grown is usually divided into rectangular fields of modest size, separated by small dikes—low earth walls—to hold the water in (see photograph 1).

In some areas, especially the **Red River Delta** of **North Vietnam**, much larger dikes are required to control rivers and prevent massive flooding. There were some proposals during the war that the United States disrupt the economy of North Vietnam by bombing dams and dikes, but few if any such targets were deliberately attacked.

There were accusations, especially during 1972, by the **Democratic Republic of Vietnam** and by American and European critics of the U.S. war effort (including **United Nations** Secretary General Kurt Waldheim), that the United States had been bombing the dikes of North Vietnam. But the amount of damage was never great enough to render plausible the accusations of a deliberate effort to destroy the dikes. Suggestions by Americans that the North Vietnamese made a deliberate policy of putting **anti-aircraft artillery** on dikes, knowing that the Americans would not bomb them there, also seem unlikely. The favored munition for air strikes against anti-aircraft guns was the **cluster bomb unit**, which would have been completely harmless to a dike.

**DIVISION,** U.S. unit. United States doctrine called for relatively large divisions, larger than those in the armies of most other nations, although the actual number of men in a U.S. division in Vietnam was often considerably below the authorized (theoretical) level. A division typically was made up of three brigades, each having three battalions of infantry, but the division was a combined-arms force. Aside from the nine infantry battalions, the typical U.S. **Army** division in Vietnam had four to six **artillery** battalions, at least a battalion of **helicopters**, about a battalion of armor or armored **cavalry**, assorted **reconnaissance** units adding up to at least a battalion, a medical battalion, a signal battalion, a supply and transport battalion, an engineer battalion, a maintenance battalion, a military **police** company, a military **intelligence** company, an Army Security Agency company to listen in on enemy radio communications, etc. This standard pattern was not an absolute rule; a division could have as many as 11 battalions of infantry, for example.

*The 1st Infantry Division* ("The Big Red One") arrived in Vietnam in October 1965 and remained until April 1970, serving in **III Corps**. Its major operations included efforts to root out Communist forces from **War Zone C** (northern **Tay Ninh** province) in Operations *Attleboro* (September–November 1966) and *Junction City* (February–May 1967). The division headquarters was briefly at **Bien Hoa** when the division first arrived in Vietnam; thereafter it was at Di An and Lai Khe.

*The 1st **Cavalry** Division (**Airmobile**),* commonly called the 1st Air Cavalry or "the Cav," was formally established on July 1, 1965, derived in large part from the 11th Air Assault Division, an experimental unit that had been trying out the concept of airmobility (massive reliance on helicopters for movement of troops). The division was already scheduled for rapid deployment to Vietnam at the time it was created. An advance party arrived by air in late August, and established the division's new headquarters at An Khe, in the highlands of **Binh Dinh** province. The bulk of the division arrived by sea in September.

In late October 1965, elements of the division were sent to the relief of the **Special Forces** camp at Plei Me, in the **Central Highlands** south of **Pleiku**, which was under attack by **PAVN** forces. This was the first significant combat between U.S. and PAVN troops in **South Vietnam**.

Pursuit of PAVN forces westward from Plei Me led to the Battle of the **Ia Drang Valley** in November. The next major campaign was the operation that began as *Masher* and ended as *White Wing*, in Binh Dinh province, from January 24 to March 6, 1966. In January 1968, most of the division was moved north to **I Corps**, where it participated in the battle for **Hue** during the **Tet Offensive**, and in the re-opening of the road to **Khe Sanh** in April 1968. In May and June 1970, the 1st Cavalry Division participated in the **Cambodian Incursion**.

The main part of the division had been withdrawn from Vietnam by the end of April 1971. The division's 3d Brigade remained until June 1972. One battalion of the 3d Brigade, the 1/7 Cavalry, remained until August 1972, forming the core of Task Force *Garry Owen*.

*The 4th Infantry Division* ("Ivy Division") arrived in Vietnam in September 1966, and remained until December 1970. Division headquarters was always in the Central Highlands in **II Corps** (at Pleiku, **Dak To**, or An Khe), and most of the division's operations were in this area, but the division's 3d Brigade and its armored battalion were sent to **III Corps** when the division arrived in Vietnam; they participated in Operations *Attleboro* (September–November 1966) and *Junction City* (February–May 1967) directed against War Zone C in northern Tay Ninh province. The Army finally decided that if they were to be operating in III Corps it would make more sense to have them affiliated with a III Corps division; in August 1967, they were transferred to the 25th Infantry Division, which gave its own 3d Brigade and armored battalion, which had been operating in II Corps, to the 4th Infantry Division in exchange.

*The 5th Infantry Division (Mechanized)* sent only its 1st Brigade to Vietnam, in July 1968. The brigade served in **Quang Tri** province. It played a leading role in Operation *Dewey Canyon II* early in 1971, then returned to the United States in August.

*The 9th Infantry Division* ("Old Reliables") arrived in Vietnam in December 1966 and remained until August 1969, operating in III and **IV Corps**, with headquarters at Bear Cat (southeast of **Saigon**) up to July 1968, and at Dong Tam (near My Tho in the **Mekong Delta**) thereafter. This was the only major U.S. infantry unit to operate in the Mekong Delta. The division's 2d Brigade was the Army component of the **Mobile Riverine Force**, an Army-Navy combined force that operated widely in the Mekong Delta. When the division as a whole left Vietnam in August 1969, its 3d Brigade remained, based in **Long An** province in the northwest part of the Mekong Delta and attached to the 25th Infantry Division. This brigade was pulled out of Vietnam in October 1970.

*The 23d Infantry Division* (Americal) had 11 infantry battalions, instead of the usual nine. It was based at **Chu Lai**, in the southern part of I Corps. It had been created in Vietnam in September 1967, derived from Task Force *Oregon*. There was then some reshuffling of brigades; by early 1968, the Americal contained only one infantry brigade, the 196th, that had been part of *Oregon*. The others had gone to other divisions, and been replaced by two brigades just arriving in Vietnam, the 11th Infantry Brigade and the 198th Infantry Brigade. The 11th Brigade had been sent to Vietnam in December 1967 on a rush basis, without completing the training that would normally have been required before the unit was deployed, and there was further turmoil caused by transfers of personnel, and units, within the brigade early in 1968. One company of this brigade carried out the **My Lai Massacre** on March 16, 1968. In the later stages of the Vietnam War, when there was an overall decline in the morale and the competence of U.S. infantry units in Vietnam, the decline seems to have been more severe in the Americal Division. The division had more than its share of cases in which men refused to engage in combat (*see* **combat refusal**). In December 1969, the recently appointed commander of the 198th Brigade told one of his battalion commanders he believed the 198th was the worst brigade in the whole U.S. Army.

The bulk of the Americal Division had left Vietnam by November 1971; the 196th Infantry Brigade remained as an independent brigade.

*The 25th Infantry Division* ("Tropic Lightning") had long been based in Hawaii, and was specifically trained for tropic warfare; it was a natural candidate for Vietnam. Its 3d Brigade arrived in December 1965, and was sent to the Central Highlands; the bulk of the division arrived in March 1966, and was sent to III Corps, where it was based at **Cu Chi** throughout the period it was in Vietnam. It operated mostly in the area north of Saigon, though some units did get down to the northern part of the Mekong Delta, southwest of Saigon. (The 3d Brigade remained in the Highlands, and in August 1967 it was reassigned to the 4th Infantry Division; the 4th gave the 25th Division its own 3d Brigade in exchange.)

The 25th Division was a major participant in Operation *Cedar Falls*, an attack on the **Iron Triangle** in January 1967, and Operation *Junction City*, an attack on War Zone C from February to May 1967. It participated in the Cambodian Incursion of 1970. The bulk of the division left Vietnam by December 1970, but its 2d Brigade remained until April 1971.

*The 101st Airborne Division* ("Screaming Eagles") sent its 1st Brigade to Vietnam in July 1965, but the bulk of the division did not arrive until November 1967. The brigades of this division were often more widely scattered than was usual for American divisions in Vietnam. The main body of the division went initially to III Corps just north of Saigon, but in March 1968 moved north to I Corps. The 1st Brigade had been operating mostly in II Corps before the rest of the divison arrived. The 3d Brigade was sent to Dak To in mid-1968, and then to III Corps in August 1968.

The division's helicopters were actively involved in *Lam Son 719*, the 1971 incursion into **Laos**, although American troops were not allowed into Laos on the ground. Elements of the division participated in Operation *Jefferson Glenn* (September 1970 to October 1971) in **Thua Thien** province, in cooperation with the 1st **ARVN** Division. This was the last operation in which U.S. ground troops conducted major offensive actions. Eventually the 101st was the last United States division in Vietnam. The bulk of its strength was pulled out in December 1971 and January 1972; division headquarters did not pull out until March 1972.

The U.S. **Marines** divided their divisions into regiments, instead of into brigades like the Army.

*The 1st Marine Division* was based at Chu Lai from February to November 1966, then shifted to **Danang**, where it remained until the division's withdrawal from Vietnam in April 1971.

*The 3d Marine Division* was based at Danang from May 1965 to October 1966, when it moved to **Phu Bai** just southeast of **Hue**. In March 1968 it moved to Quang Tri, and in June to **Dong Ha**, where it remained almost until the division's withdrawal from Vietnam in November 1969.

**DO CAO TRI** (1929–1971). **ARVN** lieutenant general. Born in **Bien Hoa** province, he completed an officer training course in Vietnam in 1947, then a course at Infantry School in Avour, France, in 1948. Tri commanded the Airborne Group from 1954 to 1956, and the III **Military Region** from 1956 to 1958, then went to the U.S. Army Command and General Staff College, in Leavenworth, Kansas. As a colonel commanding the ARVN 1st Division he was sent to **Hue** to put down the **Buddhist** uprising in June 1963, which he did with great firmness. As a reward he was promoted to brigadier general in July, and given command of **I Corps** in August. But a few months later, he joined the plot that overthrew **Ngo Dinh Diem**. He was shifted from I Corps to **II Corps** in December 1963; he was removed from that position in September 1964, with Buddhist hostility apparently a factor.

Tri was an aggressive and able combat commander, but sometimes lacking in tact, and reputed to be quite corrupt. General **William Westmoreland**, who respected Tri's abilities, tried repeatedly to have him given another important military command; Tri was finally brought back from a 1967–1968 exile as ambassador to South **Korea** and given command of **III Corps** in 1968. As commander of III Corps, he advocated extending the ground war into **Cambodia** to disrupt Communist base areas there. In 1970, his forces started to cross into sections of Cambodia on April 14; the more famous **Cambodian Incursion** by U.S. troops did not begin until May 1. And while U.S. troops had pulled out of Cambodia by the end of June, General Tri kept ARVN forces fighting in Cambodia on a substantial scale until his death in a **helicopter** crash on February 23, 1971.

**DOGS.** The scout dogs used by U.S. **Army** and **Marine** forces in Vietnam were typically either German shepherds, or mixed breeds with a substantial component of German shepherd ancestry. They were important for their ability to smell or hear enemy forces, and sometimes (depending on the training of the dog) also to smell **mines** and **booby traps**. They did not generally function as attack dogs. The sentry dogs that the U.S. **Air Force** used to guard air bases *were* attack dogs.

U.S. **advisers** helped the **ARVN** begin a scout dog program in 1962, but the first U.S. Marine scout dog platoons did not arrive in Vietnam until February 1966, and the first U.S. Army scout dog unit did not arrive until June 1966.

**DOMINO THEORY.** The domino theory stated that if Vietnam fell to the Communists, a substantial number of other countries, some of them not bordering on Vietnam, would quickly fall also. The breadth of the theory varied. What might be considered an average version said that if Vietnam fell, so would **Cambodia, Laos, Thailand**, Burma, Malaysia, and Indonesia, but the **Philippines** might still be saved. Minimalist versions said that only the fall of countries as far as Thailand would be inevitable, and there would be a chance of saving Malaysia and Indonesia. Maximalist versions said that if Vietnam were lost, not only Asia but the Pacific Ocean would fall under Communist domination, and American defenses would have to be pulled back to San Francisco. Dwight Eisenhower was the first to use the image of dominoes as a way of expressing the theory, in a presidential press conference on April 7, 1954, but this was simply a new and slightly more extreme way of phrasing an already existing idea.

Two patterns of thought buttressed the theory. One was the legacy of Munich. Policy makers remembered 1938, when Britain and France had neglected an opportunity to try to stop Hitler while he was still comparatively weak. They probably could have stopped Hitler in Czechoslovakia, but didn't; they then were unable to stop him in Poland, Belgium, or France. By analogy, it was argued that if the Communists were not stopped in Vietnam, it would be impossible to stop them in Thailand, Burma, and perhaps far beyond.

The other pattern of thought was an extreme vagueness about the identity of the Communists who would take the countries the fall of which was predicted. Many statements of the domino theory would have been grossly implausible if the prediction had specified which Communists were going to take the predicted areas; vagueness on this point allowed the theory more plausibility.

**DONG HA.** The northernmost significant town in **South Vietnam**, on the south bank of the Cam Lo River (which flows into the Cua Viet) in northern **Quang Tri** province, about 20 kilometers south of the **Demilitarized Zone**. It was a minor port. It was the base for the U.S. 3d **Marine Division** from June 1968 to late 1969.

Destruction of the bridge at Dong Ha by U.S. Marine **advisers** on April 2, 1972, during the **Easter Offensive**, blocked **PAVN tanks** coming south along **Route 1**. But Dong Ha fell on April 28 as PAVN forces attacked from the west and southwest as well as from the north.

**DONG SI NGUYEN,** Dong Sy Nguyen, a.k.a. Nguyen Huu Vu, Nguyen Van Dong (1923– ). **PAVN** general. Born in Quang Binh province of northern **Trung Bo**, he joined the Communist Party in 1939. In the early part of the First Indochina War he served in Quang Binh, and was conspicuous even by Communist standards for his hostility to **Catholics**; later he served in **Laos** and in the Dien Bien Phu campaign. He became the political officer for **Military Region** 4 early in 1965. He commanded **Group 559**, which operated the **Ho Chi Minh Trail**, from January 1967 to 1975. After the war he was a member of the Communist Party Central Committee from 1976 to 1991, and an alternate member (1982–1986) and then full member (1986–1991) of the Politburo. He published a book on the Ho Chi Minh Trail, *Duong xuyen Truong son*, in 1999.

**DOUMER BRIDGE.** The Paul Doumer Bridge (Long Bien Bridge) in **Hanoi**, carrying both road and railway traffic across the Red River, originally built by the French before World War I, was a key point in the North Vietnamese transportation system, but **Lyndon Johnson** was reluctant to authorize bombing of targets in Hanoi. When **Harrison Salisbury** visited Hanoi in December 1966, he saw bomb damage that seemed to reflect an effort to hit the bridge, but U.S. records indicate the bridge was not bombed until August 11, 1967. It was hit again on October 25, and twice in December. The first three raids had closed the bridge for moderate periods; the raid of December 19 damaged it so severely that it was not even partially back in use until June 1968, and not fully repaired until 1969. During the periods when the bridge was out of service from bomb damage, the Vietnamese got people and cargoes across the river by means of ferries, and a pontoon bridge that was only used at night (during daylight the bridge was dismantled and the pontoons were concealed). U.S. aircraft made a night attack on the pontoon bridge on February 23, 1968.

The Doumer Bridge was heavily damaged by U.S. smart bombs (*see* **bombs**) on the first day of Operation *Linebacker*, May 10, 1972, and again on May 11 or 12. It had not yet been put back into service when it was bombed again on September 10. Smart bombs had given the United States the ability to keep the bridge out of operation indefinitely.

**DRAFT.** *See* SELECTIVE SERVICE SYSTEM.

**DRINAN, ROBERT FREDERICK** (1920– ). Priest, congressman. Born in Boston, he graduated from Boston College in 1942 and entered the Society of Jesus the same year. He was ordained a **Catholic** priest in 1953. He was dean of the Boston College Law School when elected, as an anti-war candidate, to the U.S. House of Representatives in 1970; he served five terms. In July 1973, Drinan proposed that President **Richard Nixon** be impeached for having bombed **Cambodia** secretly and lied to the **Congress** about the bombing. He was the author of *Vietnam and Armageddon* (1970).

**DRUGS.** The "Golden Triangle" in the northern parts of **Laos, Thailand,** and Burma produced much of the world's **opium,** the source from which morphine and heroin are derived. Several countries of Southeast Asia also produced marijuana. Shipment of the drugs into Vietnam was comparatively easy, and indeed was often assisted by local government officials, who were profiting from the traffic. American servicemen in Vietnam, therefore, could obtain marijuana and heroin of far higher quality than that usually available in the United States, for a fraction of the American prices. Two factors converged to create a dramatic increase in drug use among American servicemen in Vietnam in the late 1960s. First, there was a cultural shift in the United States, which greatly increased the proportion of young people who regarded drug use as acceptable. Second, there was a serious decline in the general level of morale and discipline in the American forces in Vietnam during the late stages of the war, which in many units, though by no means all, compromised the ability of the command to control drug use.

Some unit commanders retained the ability to forbid drug use by their men, and in many combat units the obvious fact that for a man to use drugs in combat situations would imperil the other men of the unit led the men to police one another, reducing the need for discipline to be imposed from above. But drug use became widespread in many rear area units, and in some combat units.

**DU QUOC DONG** (?– ). **ARVN** general. A **Nung** from **North Vietnam**, he became commander of the ARVN **Airborne Division** in late 1964. This was an elite force, but General Dong is not generally said to have been a very good general. Politically he was a supporter of **Nguyen Van Thieu** against **Nguyen Cao Ky**. He has been criticized for slack performance in *Lam Son 719*, the incursion into **Laos** in 1971. His forces managed to retake **Quang Tri** in 1972, after a prolonged struggle, but he was removed from the Airborne Division, and made commander of the Capital Military District, in November 1972. In February 1973, he was appointed the chief ARVN representative on the Joint Military Commission established to implement the **Paris Peace Agreement**. After that he commanded the Non-Commissioned Officer School at **Nha Trang**. He was made commander of **III Corps** at the end of October 1974, but was relieved of that command in February 1975.

**DUONG VAN MINH,** often called "Big Minh" (1916–2001). **ARVN** general. A **Buddhist** from a wealthy family, Minh was probably born in **Long An** province (some sources say in the **Mekong Delta** town of My Tho). He joined the French colonial forces in 1940. He underwent military training in **France** around the time of his transfer, in 1952, to the **Vietnamese National Army**. He was a colonel commanding the **Saigon-Cholon** garrison of the VNA when the **Sect** Crisis of 1955 broke out. Minh proved himself very effective against the **Binh Xuyen** and **Hoa Hao** during the months that followed, and was well rewarded for this;

by the late 1950s, he was a major general, and commander of the ARVN's Field Command Headquarters. He was highly regarded by the Americans, but President **Ngo Dinh Diem** eventually came to distrust him, and in December 1962 Minh was removed from his troop command, becoming simply an "adviser" to President Diem.

General Minh was one of the leaders of the **coup** that overthrew Diem on November 1, 1963, and appears to have been the one who ordered the execution of Diem and his brother **Ngo Dinh Nhu** on November 2. Following the coup Minh was promoted to lieutenant general and became chairman of the Executive Committee of the Revolutionary Council, and president of the Provisional Government of the **Republic of Vietnam**. This was not a one-man government; he shared power with Major Generals Le Van Kim and **Tran Van Don**.

The triumvirate of Generals Minh, Kim, and Don was overthrown in a second coup on January 30, 1964. Minh served as nominal chief of state, with no real power, for most of 1964. By the end of the year he was actually gaining some power, but in December he was arrested in a coup conducted jointly by **Nguyen Khanh** and the "**Young Turks.**" Minh then left the country, and lived in **Thailand** for several years. He attempted to return to be a candidate in the presidential **election** of 1967, and was popular enough so that he could have been a serious candidate, but he was barred from entering Vietnam. **Nguyen Van Thieu**, who won the election, finally permitted Minh to return in October 1968. General Minh was briefly a candidate in the presidential election of 1971, but dropped out of the race, stating that the election was being rigged.

In April 1975, as **PAVN** troops closed in on Saigon, President Thieu resigned his office and left Vietnam. General Minh became president of the Republic of Vietnam on April 28; he formally announced the surrender of his government to the Communists on April 30. He was finally permitted to emigrate to France in 1983.

**DUST OFF.** The evacuation of wounded men by **helicopter.** *See* **medical evacuation**.

**DUSTER.** M-42A1 light tracked vehicle, mounting two 40-mm cannon. Originally designed as **anti-aircraft** weapons, the Dusters were used in Vietnam as ground combat vehicles. The United States sent two battalions of Dusters to Vietnam in November 1966, and a third in 1967. They are said to have fired more than 4,000,000 40-mm shells before being pulled out of Vietnam in 1971.

*Note:* the term "Duster" was also sometimes applied to a truck with four .50-caliber **machine guns** on it, used to escort convoys on the roads (see photograph 4).


## - E -


*EAGLE PULL,* Operation. The evacuation of Americans, and some people of other nationalities, from **Phnom Penh**. The preliminary stages, conducted by fixed-wing aircraft, began on April 4, 1975. The last stage was carried out by **helicopter** on the morning of April 12.

**EASTER OFFENSIVE,** 1972. A large coordinated offensive, carried out mostly by **PAVN** troops, on several fronts in **South Vietnam**; it began a few days before Easter.

Attacks straight across the **Demilitarized Zone** (DMZ) into **Quang Tri** province on March 30, led by **tanks**, achieved considerable surprise and at first were stunningly successful. They captured many **artillery** pieces at the fire bases immediately south of the DMZ. The forces of the **Republic of Vietnam** (RVN) held **Dong Ha** (on the south bank of the Cam Lo River about 20 kilometers below the DMZ) until April 28, delaying the PAVN forces advancing directly down **Route 1**, but other PAVN forces were threatening Dong Ha, Quang Tri City, and **Hue** (in **Thua Thien** province) from the west and southwest. RVN forces lost Dong Ha on April 28, and withdrew from Quang Tri City on May 1, but were able to hold Hue.

The offensive in **Kontum** province in the **Central Highlands**, by two PAVN divisions (the 2d and 320th) and several independent regiments under General **Hoang Minh Thao**, is also listed in Communist histories as having begun on March 30, but it got off to a more gradual start than the fighting in Quang Tri. This portion of the Easter Offensive came as no surprise; U.S. and **ARVN** commanders had expected and prepared for it, and at first the defenders did well; casualties were high among the PAVN forces that almost but not quite overran Fire Base Delta on April 3. But Delta fell on April 21, and the ARVN 22d Division headquarters at Tan Canh, and nearby **Dak To**, were overrun on April 24; both the use of **Sagger** anti-tank missiles to knock out ARVN tanks and the use of T-54 tanks by the PAVN came as surprises to the defenders. The ARVN 22d Division collapsed at Tan Canh and Dak To—more than 200 vehicles and 30 artillery pieces were abandoned—but the PAVN spent almost three weeks reorganizing and preparing before following up this victory with a serious push against the town of Kontum. By that time the ARVN 23d Division had been brought north from **Ban Me Thuot**, the ARVN forces had been given additional training for fighting tanks, and the Americans were ready to provide more air support, notably **B-52** strikes and **helicopters** firing the **TOW** anti-tank missile. The PAVN push against Kontum came close to success (PAVN forces actually got into the town on May 25–27), but in the end failed with heavy casualties.

Attacks by **Viet Cong** and PAVN forces in Binh Long province, on the Cambodian border in northern **III Corps**, began on April 2 and also achieved considerable surprise. They overran Loc Ninh on April 7 and then besieged An Loc, the province capital. The PAVN suffered heavy casualties, many of them from air strikes, both at An Loc—the PAVN held portions of the town until June 12—and to the south where the PAVN was trying to block ARVN relief forces.

Attacks by the 3d PAVN Division in Hoai An district of coastal **Binh Dinh** province began on April 9. The district fell on April 19, and two other districts did so in the next two weeks.

By May 1, General **Creighton Abrams**, commander of **Military Assistance Command, Vietnam**, was becoming very pessimistic; he reported that most of the ARVN's top leaders were losing their will to fight, and that both Hue and Kontum might fall. But the slow, methodical advance of the PAVN forces allowed time for ARVN forces to reorganize and brace themselves for further combat after defeats, and for the United States to bring massive air power to bear. The PAVN advances were stopped, and an ARVN counteroffensive was beginning by June.

**EB-66.** A variant of the B-66 Destroyer bomber, modified for electronic warfare, informally called the Soowie. It was used in Southeast Asia in two variants. The EB-66B and an improved version, the EB-66E, carried powerful **radar** jamming equipment; they could protect other aircraft from being locked onto by the radar that guided **surface-to-air missiles** and the largest **anti-aircraft artillery**. The EB-66C was an electronic **intelligence** aircraft that could locate and analyze enemy radar installations.

**EC-121.** Various military versions of the Lockheed Constellation airliner, carrying **radar** or sometimes other electronic equipment. Several EC-121D radar planes were sent to Vietnam in 1965. These aircraft, under the code name *Big Eye* (changed to *College Eye* in March 1967) remained well outside **North Vietnam** (some out to sea and others over **Laos**) but could scan the air over North Vietnam, both watching for **MiGs** and guiding the movements of U.S. aircraft. EC-121R *Batcat* aircraft orbited over Laos to pick up signals from the *Igloo White* electronic sensors that monitored traffic on the **Ho Chi Minh Trail**.

**ELECTIONS, in Laos**. Elections for a National Assembly of 39 members were held on December 25, 1955. The **Pathet Lao** (Laotian Communists) refused to participate. The National Assembly was expanded to 59 members through elections on May 4, 1958, which chose 20 new members, and a replacement for one old member who had died. This was the first Laotian election in which women could vote. Of the 21 seats at stake, the **Neo Lao Hak Sat** (the overt political representative of the Pathet Lao) won nine, and a Left-leaning neutralist party, the Santiphab (Peace) Party, took four. Elections for all 59 seats were held in April 1960. Some of the most popular Neo Lao Hak Sat politicians were unable to run because they were in jail, others because educational qualifications had been established for candidacy, which made them ineligible. These factors, plus fraud in the counting of votes, led to a massive victory for rightist candidates.

Elections were held in July 1965, January 1967, and January 1972 only in areas controlled by the Royal Laotian Government. The main victors were rightists in 1965, supporters of **Souvanna Phouma** in 1967, and rightists in 1972.

**ELECTIONS, in South Vietnam**. The **Geneva Accords of 1954** had called for an election to be held in 1956, throughout Vietnam, supervised by the **International Control Commission**. **Ngo Dinh Diem** had refused to sign the accords, and in July 1955 he announced his refusal even to discuss holding the 1956 elections.

On October 23, 1955, Diem held a referendum in South Vietnam, asking the people to choose between him and Chief of State Bao Dai. It was officially announced that Diem had won 98.2 percent of the votes. Diem then became president, and the State of Vietnam became the **Republic of Vietnam**. Diem was re-elected in 1961, defeating two little-known opponents with an officially reported total of 89 percent of the votes.

A Constituent Assembly was elected in September 1966; it had completed a new constitution for the Republic of Vietnam by March 1967. It created a strong presidency, and a National Assembly made up of a Senate (upper house) and a House of Representatives (lower house).

**Nguyen Van Thieu** won election as president on September 3, 1967, with **Nguyen Cao Ky** as his running mate. The Armed Forces Council and the United States had applied heavy pressure for Ky and Thieu, who were political rivals, to run together rather than opposing one another. There were 10 civilian candidates for president, all comparatively weak; former general **Duong Van Minh**, by far the most prominent challenger to the Thieu-Ky ticket, was not permitted to run. The campaign activities of the candidates were tightly restricted, preventing any single civilian candidate from emerging as a clear leader of the opposition to Thieu and Ky. Thieu had hoped that under these conditions he could obtain a respectable vote, perhaps on the order of 50 percent. He was shocked when the vote began to come in, and there apparently was some last-minute falsification of the count, but even so his official tally was only 35 percent of the votes. Division of the votes against him among 10 candidates made this more than adequate for victory. **Truong Dinh Dzu**, who had said that if elected he would ask for a cessation of U.S. bombing of **North Vietnam** and try to initiate peace talks, got 17 percent of the vote. **Phan Khac Suu** was third with 11 percent, and **Tran Van Huong** fourth with 10 percent. (Dzu was imprisoned for his views the following year.)

Elections for the Senate were also held in September 1967. Candidates were required to run in slates of 10, rather than singly. The six slates getting the most votes—one headed by retired Major General **Tran Van Don**, one from the Revolutionary Dai Viet Party, one a coalition of the **Hoa Hao** and **Cao Dai**, and three that were predominantly **Catholic**—were elected. The militant **Buddhists** led by **Thich Tri Quang** were not permitted to run a slate of candidates. Elections for the House of Representatives were held on October 22, 1967.

Nguyen Van Thieu ran unopposed in the presidential election of 1971, with Tran Van Huong as his vice-presidential candidate. Nguyen Cao Ky and Duong Van Minh had dropped out of the race, saying that the election was being rigged.

Another election for the Senate was held in 1970, and for the House of Representatives in 1971. In these, as in the elections of 1967, some candidates had been barred from running, but there was a lively competition among those permitted to run. In the Senate elections of August 6, 1973, however, the field was much narrower; a decree that went into effect in March had eased the way for Thieu's Democracy Party by dissolving most of the other parties.

Elections for hamlet and village officials were abolished by Ngo

Dinh Diem in 1956, restored by Premier Nguyen Cao Ky in 1966, and abolished again under Nguyen Van Thieu in August 1972.

**ELECTIONS,** in the United States. The presidential election of 1964 was the first in which Vietnam was an issue. The Republican Party nominated **Barry Goldwater**, an extreme conservative, who advocated expanding the war by bombing **North Vietnam**. Democratic President **Lyndon Johnson** ran as the peace candidate, concealing the fact that he was expecting to begin bombing North Vietnam soon after the election. Johnson won overwhelmingly.

Senator **Eugene McCarthy** announced on November 30, 1967, that he would run for president in the 1968 election, fighting President Johnson for the Democratic Party's nomination. McCarthy was opposed to the Vietnam War; this was his only major issue. In the Democratic Party's New Hampshire primary on March 12, 1968, McCarthy did not win, but he came close enough (42.2 percent of the vote to President Johnson's 49.4 percent) for the result to count as a stunning demonstration of Johnson's political vulnerability. The Republican Party's primary was occurring at the same time, and with no Republican running as a strong anti-war candidate, thousands of Republicans who wanted to vote against the war wrote in McCarthy's name on their ballots. If the write-in votes on Republican ballots were included, the vote for McCarthy in New Hampshire came within a fraction of a percent, 230 votes, of equalling that for Johnson. **Robert Kennedy**, younger brother of the assassinated President **John Kennedy**, declared his own candidacy on March 16.

President Johnson's announcement on March 31 that he would not run for re-election left McCarthy and Kennedy the only major candidates in the later primaries. Both opposed the war, but they disliked one another, and the hostility between their followers persisted after Robert Kennedy was assassinated on June 5. At the Democratic Convention in August, Vice President **Hubert Humphrey** (whose name had not been on the ballot in most of the state primaries) won the Democratic nomination. The convention otherwise was a disaster for Humphrey. The **anti-war movement** was by 1968 growing more raucous and less committed to peaceful and legal forms of protest than it had been in the early years of the war. Chicago Mayor Richard Daley was the host of the convention. He and most of his police were conservative and hawkish on the war; they reacted very strongly to provocation. The result has often been described as a "police riot"; the police were beating not only stone-throwing protesters but peaceful ones in the streets near the convention hall, and sometimes bystanders whom they mistakenly thought to be anti-war protesters. Disputes between pro- and anti-war forces inside the convention hall were also bitter, and left the Democratic Party too divided to give full support to Humphrey.

**Richard Nixon**, the Republican nominee, had a much more united party behind him. He said he had a plan to end the Vietnam War, but did not say what this plan was. Many people summarized this by saying Nixon had claimed to have a "secret plan," but Nixon had not used that phrase.

George Wallace, who had become famous as an opponent of racial integration while he was governor of Alabama, ran as a candidate of the American Independent Party. Wallace's running mate was General **Curtis LeMay**, former **Air Force** chief of staff, famous for his suggestion that North Vietnam be "bombed back to the Stone Age."

Nixon seemed far ahead at first. The gap narrowed after Humphrey shifted to a more anti-war stance, and in November Nixon won a narrow victory, getting 43.4 percent of the vote, to 42.7 percent for Humphrey and 13.5 percent for Wallace.

In 1972, the Democrats nominated Senator **George McGovern**, an extreme opponent of the Vietnam War. His views were so far to the Left, on both foreign and domestic issues, that he would have had little chance even without the further handicap of chosing a vice-presidential candidate, Senator Thomas Eagleton, who was soon forced to withdraw from the race after revelation that he had several times been under psychiatric treatment for "nervous exhaustion." President Nixon's re-election campaign was further helped by **Henry Kissinger**'s "peace is at hand" statement on October 26. Nixon won overwhelmingly on November 7, with 60.7 percent of the vote to 37.5 percent for McGovern. Burglars sent by Nixon's campaign organization to search files and plant electronic bugging devices in Democratic Party offices in Washington, D.C., had been arrested on June 17, 1972, but this attracted little attention at the time. Only after the election did investigation of the burglary lead to revelation of a wide pattern of illegalities, in what became known as the Watergate scandal, which forced Nixon's resignation as president.

**ELLSBERG, DANIEL** (1931– ). Born in Chicago, Illinois, he graduated from Harvard *summa cum laude*, majoring in economics, in 1952. He joined the **Marines** in 1954, and was very successful as a company commander. He returned to Harvard in 1957, went to the Rand Corporation in 1959, and then in August 1964 began working in the Pentagon, under Assistant Secretary of Defense for International Security Affairs John McNaughton.

In 1965, he inquired about returning to the Marine Corps, hoping to be given command of a company in Vietnam. When this proposal was rejected, he went to Vietnam as a civilian, on the staff of **Edward Lansdale**. He quickly came under the influence of **John Paul Vann**, who persuaded him that the key to the war was in winning the villages, rather than in the massed application of American firepower, and taught him the habit of travelling around the countryside by road, seeing the situation on the ground, instead of flying by **helicopter**. Ellsberg was at this point still a hawk, dedicated to achieving victory in Vietnam.

Ellsberg had to leave Vietnam when he caught hepatitis; he returned to the Rand Corporation in May 1967. He soon became one of the more than 30 scholars who worked on the Defense Department history of the Vietnam War that later became known as the **Pentagon Papers**. In 1969, after this history was completed, Ellsberg read the whole thing (he had been involved in writing only one section). This turned him decisively against the war; he became convinced that the United States should never have gone into Vietnam, and should get out. He felt that others should have the opportunity to see the information that had convinced him of the wrongness of the war. After failing to interest Senator **William Fulbright** in making the study public, he gave **Neil Sheehan**, of *The New York Times*, large portions of the study. The newspaper began publishing excerpts from and summaries of this material on June 13, 1971. When the goverment obtained an injunction temporarily halting publication in *The New York Times*, Ellsberg gave portions of the Pentagon Papers to *The Washington Post* and several other newspapers.

When the Supreme Court rejected the government's attempt to forbid newspapers from publishing the Pentagon Papers, it allowed the possibility of criminal penalties for those who gave classified documents to the papers. Ellsberg and another Rand Corporation employee were brought to trial in Los Angeles. But on May 11, 1973, the judge dismissed all charges, citing a pattern of "gross misconduct" by the government, including the fact that the White House "plumbers," who by this time had attained fame through the Watergate burglary, had burglarized the office of Ellsberg's psychiatrist, hoping to find evidence against Ellsberg in the psychiatrist's file on him.

The fact that Ellsberg was under indictment had not deterred him from leaking a further substantial body of classified information in the spring of 1972, this one more recent: National Security Study Memorandum 1, a summary of the views of various agencies on many key questions about the war, drawn up shortly after **Richard Nixon** became president in 1969. He published a memoir *Secrets* in 2002.

**ENCLAVE STRATEGY.** When U.S. ground troops were first committed to **South Vietnam** in 1965, there was for a brief period a theory that they should primarily be used to hold enclaves around major towns and air bases, mostly along the coast, but should leave the bulk of the ground fighting in the interior of South Vietnam to the Army of the Republic of Vietnam (**ARVN**). Advocates of the enclave strategy within the government, of whom Ambassador **Maxwell Taylor** was probably the most important, felt that bombing of **North Vietnam** was a more appropriate way to apply American military power than putting troops into the ground war in South Vietnam. General **William Westmoreland** argued strongly against this policy, and in retrospect Westmoreland's victory in the dispute, embodied in President **Lyndon Johnson**'s decision of July 1965 giving Westmoreland the authority to use his troops anywhere in South Vietnam, appears to have been inevitable.

*ENHANCE,* Project, 1972. The United States increased weapons shipments to the **Republic of Vietnam** (RVN) beginning in May 1972 under Project *Enhance*, both to replace weapons lost as a result of the Communists' **Easter Offensive** and to allow expansion and strengthening of RVN forces. The weapons delivered included 39 175-mm **artillery** pieces; 120 M48 **tanks**; 32 UH-1H and 37 CH-47 **helicopters**; 48 A-37 attack aircraft; 23 AC-119K fixed-wing **gunships**; photo-**reconnaissance**, electronic reconnaissance, and transport planes; plus numerous other items.

*ENHANCE PLUS,* Project, 1972. In October 1972, the **Paris negotiations** produced what appeared to be an almost final draft of a peace agreement. It stated that the levels of weaponry of armed forces in **South Vietnam** could not be increased after the agreement went into effect; weapons could be brought into South Vietnam, on either side, only to replace weapons worn out or damaged after the peace went into effect. The United States immediately launched Project *Enhance Plus*, to raise the baseline by expanding the **Republic of Vietnam** Armed Forces, especially the **Vietnamese Air Force** (VNAF), before the agreement went into effect. Deliveries to South Vietnam began on October 23 and were completed on December 12; most deliveries were by sea but some were by air. There are some inconsistencies in the figures, but the equipment delivered apparently included at least 277 UH-1H **helicopters**; 28 A-1 **Skyraider** propeller-drive attack aircraft; 90 A-37 jet attack aircraft; 116 F-5A fighters; 72 M48A3 **tanks**; 117 M-113 **armored personnel carriers**; 44 105-mm howitzers; 12 155-mm howitzers; 1,726 trucks; and other materiel. There were also upgrades of some aircraft; the VNAF was given **C-130** transport planes and O-2 observation planes, while returning to the United States its C-47, C-119K, and C-123 transport planes, and O-1 observation planes.

By the end of *Enhance Plus* the VNAF had about 2,075 aircraft, including helicopters. This made it the fourth largest air force in the world. The number of aircraft provided, however, had surpassed what the VNAF was capable of handling, and many of them went into storage on arrival in Vietnam. It was hoped that the capabilities of the VNAF would expand to a point at which it would be able to handle all these aircraft, but this did not occur.

## -F-

**F-4 PHANTOM** (see photograph 14). The McDonnell Douglas F-4 fighter-bomber, with a crew of two, first flew in 1958 as a U.S. **Navy** aircraft; the **Air Force** began procuring Phantoms in 1963. The Phantom was very effective in air-to-air combat, and Phantoms were often sent as **Combat Air Patrol** when **F-105 Thunderchiefs** struck targets in **North Vietnam**. The F-105s would hit the targets, and the more maneuverable Phantoms would defend against enemy **MiGs**. Phantoms wanting to lure MiGs into air-to-air combat sometimes used flight patterns and radio call signs designed to create the impression that they were the more vulnerable F-105s. The first successful use of this tactic was on July 10, 1965; the most famous was Operation *Bolo*, on January 2, 1967, in which the United States claimed seven MiGs shot down for no loss of U.S. aircraft.

Phantoms also were often used directly to attack ground targets, with **bombs**, **napalm**, and **rockets**.

**F-104 STARFIGHTER.** A fighter that saw only rather limited use in the war, flying from Danang in 1965, and from Udorn in **Thailand** beginning in the summer of 1966, on missions over **North Vietnam** and **Laos**.

**F-105 THUNDERCHIEF** ("Thud"). The Republic F-105, nominally a fighter, functioned in Vietnam primarily as a bomber. It was large and heavy for a fighter plane, and not very maneuverable, but quite fast. It had an internal M61A1 **Vulcan** cannon, and could carry a substantial bomb load. It had originally been designed with an internal bomb bay, but in Southeast Asia it typically carried an extra fuel tank in that space, and carried its **bombs** under the wings. The first F-105 unit sent to Southeast Asia arrived at Korat, in **Thailand**, on August 9, 1964, and began flying missions over **Laos** within a week. F-105s did much of the bombing of **North Vietnam** during Operation *Rolling Thunder*, 1965–1968. The only bases from which the F-105 normally flew during the war were Korat (from August 1964 onward) and Takhli (from February 1965 onward).

Because the F-105 was considered less qualified for air combat than the **F-4 Phantom**, it had more opportunities for air combat; North Vietnamese **MiGs** tended to avoid the F-4s and seek out the F-105s. The result was that a substantial proportion of the MiGs shot down were hit by the F-105s.

**F-111.** The General Dynamics F-111 ("Aardvark") two-seat fighter-bomber was a subject of considerable controversy. Many of its problems arose from the way the designers tried to fit so many capabilities into it. To enable it to fly long-range bombing missions, they made it larger and far heavier than other fighter aircraft. It had swing wings—its wings stuck out to the sides for maximum lift at low speeds, but then pivoted to a swept-back position for reduced drag at high speeds. It had a terrain-following radar that was supposed to let it fly on autopilot at low altitudes, with the autopilot lifting and lowering the plane to avoid hills and obstacles.

Six F-111s were sent to Takhli, in **Thailand**, and began combat operations in March 1968. They bombed targets in **North Vietnam**, flying alone, at low altitude at night; the defenders were seldom aware an F-111 was in the area until it was too late for ground fire to be effective. Three of the six planes crashed, one through mechanical failure and the other two for unknown reasons, in the first month of combat operations. The remaining three were withdrawn from Southeast Asia later in 1968.

F-111s were again sent to Thailand in September 1972. Again there were some mysterious crashes, but the aircraft successfully hit many targets in North Vietnam, and also had a significant impact on the fighting in northern **Laos**.

***FARM GATE.*** On October 11, 1961, without waiting for the **Taylor-Rostow Mission** to make its recommendations for expansion of the U.S. role in Vietnam, President **John Kennedy** ordered an **Air Commando** detachment from the 4400th Combat Crew Training Squadron sent to **South Vietnam**, under the code name *Farm Gate*. The mission initially was supposed to be training the **Vietnamese Air Force** (VNAF), but on December 6, the **Joint Chiefs of Staff** authorized *Farm Gate* pilots to fly combat missions as long as there was always a Vietnamese aboard the aircraft for training. The old, propeller-driven **B-26s** and **T-28s** had VNAF markings, and were the sort of aircraft that plausibly could have been flown by the VNAF.

In February and March 1963, General **Curtis LeMay** asked permission to acknowledge openly that *Farm Gate* was a U.S. **Air Force** unit, and put U.S. markings on the planes. The fact that U.S. pilots were flying combat missions was becoming widely known, and indeed had begun to be mentioned in the press. LeMay's request was rejected, apparently because of resistance from the State Department. Early in 1964, the Joint Chiefs of Staff recommended that *Farm Gate* be given B-57 **Canberra** jets, to enable it to bomb **North Vietnam**. This proposal also was rejected.

**FAST-MOVER.** Common term for U.S. jet fighter-bombers.

**I FIELD FORCE, VIETNAM.** The U.S. military command for **II Corps** from March 1966 to April 1971. Its headquarters was at **Nha Trang**.

**II FIELD FORCE, VIETNAM.** The U.S. **Army** command for **III Corps**, from March 1966 to May 1971. Its headquarters was initially at **Bien Hoa**, then moved in 1967 a very short distance to the east, to a location that is sometimes considered to have been part of the **Long Binh** base, sometimes considered a separate facility north of the Long Binh base.

**FINAL COLLAPSE** of the **Republic of Vietnam** (RVN), 1975. The campaign that ended the war in **South Vietnam** was conducted primarily by the North Vietnamese forces of the People's Army of Vietnam (**PAVN**); General **Van Tien Dung** was in command. Its first major success was the capture of **Ban Me Thuot**, in the **Central Highlands**, which was attacked on March 10 and fell on March 12. RVN President **Nguyen Van Thieu** decided that his forces were over-extended, and that he should abandon some provinces to strengthen his defenses in more vital ones. On March 14, he ordered the abandonment of most of what he still held in the Central Highlands. The forces retreating from **Pleiku** and **Kontum** toward the coast lost organization and cohesion; those which reached the coast were so demoralized that most of them were militarily useless.

Thieu also decided on March 12 to bring most of the elite **Airborne Division** south from **I Corps** to the **Saigon** area. This left too little in I Corps to hold all provinces, and orders were issued on March 14 for the RVN **Marines** to pull southward out of **Quang Tri** province; PAVN forces occupied Quang Tri City without a fight on March 19.

At the time the attack against Ban Me Thuot began on March 10, the PAVN had still been planning on only modest territorial gains from the campaign; the final conquest of South Vietnam was expected probably to take until 1976. But the possibility of a much more rapid conclusion had been considered. The disintegration of the **ARVN** forces in the Central Highlands persuaded the Politburo that an opportunity existed to finish the war within a matter of weeks; the order to attempt this reached General Van Tien Dung on March 24.

The popular image of a PAVN juggernaught rolling down South Vietnam from north to south is not really accurate; forces coming from the west, out of the Central Highlands, took most of the coast of central Vietnam without waiting for the arrival of the units that advanced south along the coast directly from North Vietnam. The province capitals of Quang Ngai and Quang Tin fell on March 24; this helped trigger panic among the defenders of **Hue** and **Danang**, farther north. Hue fell on March 26, and Danang on March 30, to attackers coming from north, west, and southwest. **Qui Nhon**, 270 kilometers south of Danang, fell on the morning of April 1. **Nha Trang**, 175 kilometers south of Qui Nhon, was abandoned that afternoon; Communist forces occupied it on April 2, and **Cam Ranh** to its south on April 3. The ARVN abandoned some province capitals when no Communist forces were near enough to occupy them promptly. Only at **Xuan Loc**, less than 75 kilometers east of Saigon, did ARVN forces hold long and firmly enough, from April 9 to 20, to cause serious delay for the PAVN forces.

The causes of the collapse were numerous. Reductions in U.S. aid were certainly among them, but were not so crippling as has sometimes been suggested. The growing strength of PAVN **anti-aircraft** defenses in South Vietnam was probably more important than reductions in the flow of air munitions and aviation fuel from the United States, in stripping the RVN of many of the advantages of air superiority. The official figures on stocks of ground ammunition (though their accuracy is questionable) indicate that there were still 121,000 tons in stock in February 1975, supplemented each month by continuing shipments from the United States. The precipitous decline in stocks after February was caused more by Communist capture of ammunition stockpiles, as the ARVN collapsed, than by combat expenditures. Cuts in aid from the United States had reduced the ARVN to levels of ammunition supply near equality with the levels of the Communist forces, not to levels far below those of the Communist forces. The ARVN, however, had been structured and trained to depend on overwhelming superiority in firepower and supplies; it could not adjust to losing this superiority. Incidents in which senior ARVN officers abandoned their commands and fled also contributed to the disintegration.

PAVN troops took **Bien Hoa** during the night of April 28–29, and closed **Tan Son Nhut** (Saigon's airport) by **artillery** and **rocket** bombardment on the morning of April 29. **Duong Van Minh**, who had replaced Nguyen Van Thieu as president of the Republic of Vietnam, announced the surrender of his government over the radio on the morning of April 30, as PAVN forces entered Saigon without resistance.

**FIRST OBSERVATION GROUP.** A special operations unit established in February 1956. It was nominally part of the **Republic of Vietnam** Armed Forces (RVNAF), but was separated from normal RVNAF command channels; actual control was exercised from the Presidential Palace by the Presidential Liaison Office (later renamed Presidential Survey Office). Its initial mission was to prepare to conduct **guerrilla warfare** in the area just south of the **Demilitarized Zone**, in the event that a North Vietnamese invasion overran this area. It was later used for covert operations into **Laos** and **North Vietnam** and, starting in 1960, for combat operations within South Vietnam against the **Viet Cong**, which soon became its main activity. In mid-1961 its personnel strength was reported as 340, with 10 U.S. **advisers** (nine from the **Central Intelligence Agency**, one from the **Military Assistance Advisory Group**). Plans at that time called for it to be greatly expanded, and for its use on combat operations against the Viet Cong to be curtailed so it would be more available for operations into North Vietnam and Laos.

It went through several name changes in the early 1960s, finally becoming the Vietnamese **Special Forces**.

**FISHHOOK.** The American nickname for an area of **Cambodia** projecting into **South Vietnam**, between **Tay Ninh** and Binh Long provinces. The **PAVN** established Base Area 352 in the Fishhook, and Base Area 353 just west of it, taking advantage of restrictions on U.S. combat actions against Cambodian territory. The **Trung uong cuc mien Nam** (COSVN), the Communist headquarters for the southern half of South Vietnam, had a large portion of its facilities in Base Area 353 in the late 1960s. The United States secretly bombed Base Areas 352 and 353 in Operation *Menu* in 1969 and 1970. The U.S. 11th Armored **Cavalry**, elements of the 101st Airborne **Division**, and **ARVN** forces went into this area at the beginning of May 1970, in the **Cambodian Incursion**. They found massive Communist supply caches, but not the Trung uong cuc mien Nam, which had evacuated to a location considerably farther north in Cambodia in late March.

***FLAMING DART,*** Operation. In January 1965, the military situation in **South Vietnam** had become so bad that U.S. leaders decided they had to begin bombing **North Vietnam**. They decided to send a *Desoto* **Patrol**, a **reconnaissance** patrol of two U.S. **Navy** destroyers, into the Gulf of Tonkin off the coast of North Vietnam, in the hope that the North Vietnamese would attack it and that this would provide an occasion for U.S. retaliatory air strikes. Plans were prepared, under the code name *Flaming Dart*, for the air strikes that would be flown if the North Vietnamese took the bait. The *Desoto* Patrol was cancelled at the last minute, but in the early morning of February 7, the very day the *Desoto* Patrol had been scheduled to begin, the **Viet Cong** attacked military facilities at **Pleiku**, killing nine American servicemen, wounding 104, and destroying 11 aircraft. The *Flaming Dart* air strikes were flown, officially announced as retaliation for this incident, on the afternoon of February 7 and on February 8.

On February 10, Viet Cong forces attacked facilities at **Qui Nhon**, killing 23 U.S. and seven Vietnamese personnel. *Flaming Dart II* hit targets in North Vietnam the following day, this time officially announced not as specific retaliation for the incident at Qui Nhon, but as general retaliation for the ongoing pattern of Communist activities in South Vietnam. This set a precedent for future strikes not following directly after conspicuous incidents in the South, which would occur under the name *Rolling Thunder* beginning in early March.

**FLECHETTES.** Small metal darts, resembling nails, used as an antipersonnel weapon. A **rocket** or a shell fired against troops would burst open in the air, releasing hundreds or thousands of flechettes (the 152-mm "Beehive" round used by the Sheridan light **tank** in the late stages of the war released about 9,900 flechettes) that would strike the target area in a lethal spray.

**FONDA, JANE** (1937– ). Actress. Born in New York, daughter of actor Henry Fonda, she was beginning by 1960 to achieve success in Hollywood for herself. In the late 1960s, she became increasingly involved in radical leftist politics, especially the **anti-war movement**.

While in **North Vietnam** in July 1972, Jane Fonda made a series of broadcasts over Radio Hanoi, some of them directly addressed to American servicemen. Her statements reflected a total commitment to Hanoi's viewpoint on the Vietnam War; she said at one point that in Vietnam the United States was "committing the most heinous crimes I think have ever been committed." She also allowed herself to be photographed sitting in the gunner's seat of an **anti-aircraft** gun.

There were many calls for Jane Fonda to be imprisoned, but the government could not find a good legal basis for such an action. Members of the Committee on Internal Security of the House of Representatives, enraged, tried to pass a law giving the president the authority to forbid Americans to travel to countries whose armed forces were engaged in hostilities with the United States. Anyone travelling without permission to a country the president had so designated could be fined up to $10,000, or imprisoned for up to 10 years, or both. The Justice Department endorsed the proposed law, though its spokesman said a law allowing the president to forbid travel even to countries not engaged in hostilities with the United States would have been preferable. The supporters of the proposed law were not willing to wait the length of time required to get it to a vote under normal procedures, so they used a special procedure by which it could be brought to a vote immediately, but would require a two-thirds vote to pass. A majority of the House of Representatives voted for the bill (230 to 140) on October 2, 1972, but this fell short of the required two-thirds.

In 1973, Jane Fonda married Tom Hayden, who had been one of the leaders of the anti-war movement. In July 1988, she broadcast an apology for some of her actions, on the ABC television show *20/20*. She said "I am proud of most of what I did and I am very sorry for some of what I did." The particular things for which she said she was sorry were the incident in which she was filmed sitting in the seat of an anti-aircraft gun, and her statement early in 1973 that she believed U.S. **prisoners of war** returning from captivity were lying about torture by the North Vietnamese.

**FOO GAS** or **FU GAS** (from the French *fougasse*). A large metal drum containing **napalm** or some impromptu substitute, with an explosive charge at the bottom, buried in a slanted position with the top approximately level with the ground. The explosive charge was wired to be detonated on command, spraying burning napalm over a wide area in front of the device. These devices were included in the defenses of many American positions in Vietnam.

*FOOTBOY.* Overall code name applied to a variety of covert operations against **North Vietnam** carried out by **SOG**, many of which had their own code names. *Plowman* was the general name for the maritime components of *Footboy*, including *Loki*, *Mint*, and *Cado*; *Midriff* was the general name for the airborne components, including *Timberwork* and *STRATA*. *Footboy* was designed to collect **intelligence**, impede the **infiltration** of men and supplies from North to **South Vietnam**, foment dissatisfaction among the population of North Vietnam, and create the impression that a movement of opposition to the **Democratic Republic of Vietnam** (DRV) existed within the population. This last objective—psychological warfare designed to convince the DRV leaders that they were in danger of losing control of their population—was increasing in relative priority by 1968 (*see* **Forae**).

*FORAE.* "Diversionary" operations designed to convince the **Democratic Republic of Vietnam** (DRV) of the existence of imaginary threats within **North Vietnam**. Components of *Forae* included *Oodles* (designed to create the illusion of a widespread anti-Communist organization called the "Sacred Sword Patriotic League," primarily in the western part of North Vietnam); *Borden* (designed to create the illusion of an agent network specifically within the **PAVN**); and *Urgency* (to create the illusion of an agent net in coastal areas). *Forae* as a whole was a component of *Footboy*. *Oodles* was based essentially on spurious radio messages, meant to be intercepted, addressed to fictitious agents. *Borden* and *Urgency* used human assets, North Vietnamese who were captured, indoctrinated as agents or pseudo-agents, and then sent back into North Vietnam. There were also cases in which a block of ice would be parachuted into North Vietnam. The ice would melt after reaching the ground, leaving the parachute to be found with the harness empty. It was hoped that the North Vietnamese would waste time hunting the imaginary parachutists.

*Forae* operations were greatly expanded during 1968, but after November 1, 1968, *Urgency* ceased and *Borden* was redirected from North

Vietnam to areas of Communist operations in **Laos**, **Cambodia**, and **South Vietnam**.

**FORD, GERALD RUDOLPH** (1913– ). President of the United States. Born in Omaha, Nebraska, Ford grew up in Michigan, attended the University of Michigan, and then got a law degree from Yale in 1941. He served in the **Navy** during World War II. He was elected to the U.S. House of Representatives (as a Republican from Michigan) in 1948, and served until 1973. He supported military spending, tended to oppose social welfare programs, and was lukewarm on civil rights. He became House minority leader in 1965. He criticized **Lyndon Johnson** for not prosecuting the Vietnam War vigorously enough; he particularly suggested using **mines** to close **Haiphong** harbor. After 1969, he strongly supported **Richard Nixon**'s conduct of the war.

President Nixon chose Ford to become vice president in 1973, replacing **Spiro Agnew**, who had resigned as a result of prosecution for bribery. Nixon resigned on August 9, 1974, as a result of the Watergate scandal, and Ford became president. On September 8, Ford granted Nixon a pardon, blocking any prosecution for crimes Nixon had committed while president. Ford denied that this was the result of a deal, but suspicions that Ford might have promised to give Nixon safety from prosecution, in return for Nixon's giving Ford the presidency, compromised Ford's authority.

The levels of U.S. aid for the **Republic of Vietnam** (RVN) and for **Cambodia** had been falling since 1973. Nixon and Ford had been unable to persuade the **Congress** to maintain higher levels. During the final Communist offensives in **South Vietnam** and Cambodia in 1975, Ford asked for supplemental appropriations. The first time he asked, in January, he did not treat this as an emergency request; he was still following the longstanding U.S. policy of exaggerating the strength of the RVN to make it seem more worthy of U.S. support. The second time he asked, in April, he acknowledged that there was an emergency and that the RVN might be about to fall. The Congress did not believe the extra money would make any difference, and refused both requests.

Democrat Jimmy Carter defeated Ford, by a narrow margin, in the presidential election of 1976.

**FORRESTAL, MICHAEL VINCENT** (1927–1989). Government official. Born in New York, he obtained an LL.B. from Harvard Law School in 1953. Forrestal had been an assistant to **W. Averell Harriman** when Harriman was running the Marshall Plan, 1948–1950, and it was

Harriman who arranged for Forrestal to be hired by **John Kennedy**'s administration when Harriman was negotiating a settlement of the war in **Laos**. Forrestal became a member of the National Security Council staff in January 1962, and served as liaison between Harriman and President Kennedy. Forrestal is said to have started out as a cold warrior, but there was little indication of this in his actions regarding Vietnam.

During 1962, Forrestal urged restraint in the use of **herbicides** for crop destruction. He expressed dissatisfaction with the government of **Ngo Dinh Diem** and, toward the end of the year, became increasingly pessimistic about the war as a whole; he urged more U.S. pressure on Diem to reform. During 1963, Forrestal became very much a voice against Diem; he supported the sending of the famous cable of August 24, 1963, written primarily by Harriman and **Roger Hilsman**, authorizing Ambassador **Henry Cabot Lodge**, in **Saigon**, to encourage a **coup** against Diem.

In July 1964, Forrestal transferred to the State Department, where he became the secretary of state's special assistant for Vietnam affairs, and chairman of the interagency Vietnam Coordinating Committee (formerly the "Sullivan Committee"). He appears to have had doubts about the war during this last period of his involvement, but he did not express these doubts forcefully, and he does not seem to have tried very hard to have an impact on the debates over possible escalation of the war. In January 1965 he retired from the government, and returned to the private practice of law.

**FORWARD AIR CONTROLLER** (FAC). In Vietnam the Forward Air Controller, the man who directed air strikes to their targets, was usually in a small aircraft, though he could be on the ground near the target area. Early in the war, FACs often flew single-engine propeller-driven Cessna aircraft, the O-1 Bird Dog and the O-2 Skymaster. These planes were very vulnerable to ground fire. The Rockwell **OV-10 Bronco** (see photograph 12), a twin-engine turboprop aircraft, carried more high-tech equipment than the O-1 or O-2, and was less at risk from ground fire, since it could still fly with one of its engines knocked out. In the later stages of the war "Fast FACs," **F-4 Phantoms**, were sometimes used in high-risk areas; they were less effective (the FAC had a much harder time spotting targets from a fast-moving F-4), but they were less at risk in hostile environments.

U.S. **Air Force** FACs began operating over northern **Laos** in 1964, and over the **Ho Chi Minh Trail** in southern Laos as part of the *Tiger Hound* Task Force late in 1965. FACs also began operating over the southernmost part of **North Vietnam**, just north of the **Demilitarized Zone**, in 1966 under Operation *Tally Ho*.

The United States assigned large cargo planes to loiter in the air at night over sections of enemy territory where there were no **anti-aircraft** guns large enough to reach the altitudes they used, searching with starlight scopes for enemy activity, dropping flares when targets were found, and directing strike aircraft in against the targets. C-123s did this over Laos under the name *Candlestick*; **C-130**s did it over Laos and parts of North Vietnam under the names *Blind Bat* and *Lamplighter*.

**FORWARD AIR GUIDES.** American or indigenous personnel who directed air strikes. A Forward Air Guide might be in an aircraft piloted by an American **Forward Air Controller**, or on the ground with an infantry unit.

**FRAGGING.** As morale and discipline in U.S. units deteriorated in the late stages of the Vietnam War (*see* **drugs**, **combat refusal**), the frequency of armed attacks by soldiers against their superiors increased. The term "fragging" came from the most common method, chosen because of its anonymity: rolling a fregmentation grenade into the target's tent at night. This was not usually fatal; indeed the fragger sometimes put a grenade into a tent when the target was not there, to intimidate rather than injure.

The official statistics on the subject are incomplete, unreliable, and often misunderstood. U.S. **Army** figures indicate that during the worst years, 1970 and 1971, incidents averaged about one per day. In one sense, these figures may understate the problem; they probably omit fraggings in **Marine** units, and there were fraggings in Army units that either were never reported, or were incorrectly reported as enemy action. But the figures can also convey an exaggerated impression. They have sometimes been interpreted as meaning that officers and non-commissioned officers (NCOs) were being killed at a rate of about one per day. In reality the number of deaths was a small fraction of the number of incidents, and not all of the targets were officers or NCOs. A significant number of attacks by U.S. enlisted men against other enlisted men were included in the Army's figures, and even a few attacks against Vietnamese.

**FRANCE.** The French had repeatedly promised to grant independence to the State of Vietnam, but they had not yet really done so when the **Geneva Accords** ended the First Indochina War in 1954. They released their control over the State of Vietnam and the **Vietnamese National Army** gradually in late 1954 and early 1955. They pulled their last military forces from **North Vietnam** in May 1955, and from **South Vietnam** in 1956. They tried to maintain cultural links with both North and South Vietnam, but it was only in the South that they had significant investments (since those in the North had been confiscated by the Communist government there), and it was only in the South that they had an ambassador.

French President Charles de Gaulle advised **John Kennedy** not to get involved in the Vietnam War, and in 1963 he began publicly urging a negotiated settlement of the war, leading to some sort of neutral status for Vietnam. During the massive escalation of U.S. military efforts from 1965 to 1968, de Gaulle was publicly critical. Premier **Nguyen Cao Ky** reacted to the lack of French support for the anti-Communist struggle in Vietnam by breaking off diplomatic relations with France in 1965, and for the next several years France seemed more sympathetic to **Hanoi** than to **Saigon**. France and the **Democratic Republic of Vietnam** (DRV) upgraded their representatives in one another's capitals from economic missions to "general delegations" in 1966. The DRV would have liked to exchange ambassadors with France, but the French were unwilling to go that far.

The French hosted the **Paris negotiations** from 1968 to 1973, and during this period tried to maintain a strict neutral stance on the war, in their capacity as hosts. In 1973, after the conclusion of the negotiations, the French decided to establish full diplomatic relations, at the ambassadorial level, both with Saigon and with Hanoi.

**FREE FIRE ZONE.** The U.S., **ARVN**, and allied forces in **South Vietnam**, not having a common language and not having a unified command structure controlling all forces, needed procedures to hold down the frequency with which they fired on one another, or on civilians. The rules of engagement for U.S. units defined the circumstances under which they could decide for themselves to fire, and the circumstances under which they were required first to check with a higher-level U.S. commander, with an official of the **Republic of Vietnam** (RVN) who was supposed to know the locations of RVN military personnel and civilians, or with both. The rules of engagement varied from time to time and from area to area. Troops who were fired upon were almost always allowed to fire back with their own weapons, immediately and without checking with anyone. But beyond this, the rules varied according to circumstances. Firing without consultation of higher authority was more likely to be acceptable with weapons like rifles and machine guns, which allowed the men firing to see what they were shooting at, than with **artillery** firing at a distance. Artillery fire was more likely to be acceptable if it was "observed" (if there was someone in a position to see the target area, and verify that the shells were falling where they were supposed to). Fire without consutation was most acceptable in unpopulated areas, and least acceptable in densely populated areas.

A "Free Fire Zone" was an area in which there were not supposed to be civilians or RVN personnel, where the RVN had granted blanket advance approval for the use of firepower, so even unobserved artillery fire could be used without consultation. After negative publicity about the term, it was changed to "Specified Strike Zone." **Military Assistance Command, Vietnam**, ordered that the term "Free Fire Zone" was no longer to be used under any circumstances, but it continued to be used unofficially to some extent.

**FREEDOM DEAL**, Operation. The official name for bombing of **Cambodia** by U.S. fighter-bombers from July 1970 onward. Such bombing had been occurring under other names (*see* Operation *Patio*) since late April. Until February 1971, there was a public pretense that *Freedom Deal* air strikes were occurring only in a limited area of northeastern Cambodia. The fact that about 44 percent of the strikes were outside the announced area was concealed by a double reporting system somewhat similar to the one that had been used for Operation *Menu* earlier.

**FREEDOM TRAIN**, Operation. A campaign of U.S. air strikes against **North Vietnam**, begun on April 6, 1972, in response to the **Easter Offensive**. The strikes were mostly south of the 20th parallel. The most important extension of *Freedom Train* north of the 20th parallel was on April 16, when a substantial force of **B-52**s and fighter-bombers hit fuel storage and other targets in the **Hanoi-Haiphong** area. The **Soviet Union** protested damage to four Soviet ships in Haiphong.

**FREQUENT WIND**, Operation. The **helicopter** evacuation from **Saigon** of Americans, along with a considerable number of Vietnamese, begun on April 29, 1975, after **PAVN artillery** and **rocket** fire closed **Tan Son Nhut** airport to fixed-wing aircraft. The original plan had been to conduct almost all the helicopter evacuation from Tan Son Nhut, but in the event, many Vietnamese were flown from the U.S. Embassy compound in the middle of Saigon. Ambassador **Graham Martin** had delayed ordering *Frequent Wind*, hoping that fixed-wing flights could be resumed, but once helicopter evacuation began, Martin tried to keep it going as long as possible to get out as many Vietnamese as possible. It extended into the early morning hours of April 30, when Martin's superiors ordered it halted, despite Martin's objection that there were still hundreds of Vietnamese at the embassy awaiting flights.

**FRONT** (*chien truong*), Communist territorial unit. The Vietnamese Communist leadership sometimes called **North Vietnam** Front A, **South Vietnam** Front B, **Laos** Front C, and **Cambodia** Front D (later K). These terms, however, are seldom used; the term "Front" is most often encountered in references to the subdivisions of Front B.

The B2 Front within South Vietnam corresponded to **III Corps, IV Corps**, and the southern seven (after late 1963, five) provinces of **II Corps** in the territorial units used by the United States and the **Republic of Vietnam** (RVN) during the late stages of the war. Units within the B2 Front were **Military Region** (*Quan khu*) 6 (Ninh Thuan, Binh Thuan, Quang Duc, Tuyen Duc, and Lam Dong provinces, and up to late 1963, also Dac Lac and Khanh Hoa, in the RVN's II Corps); Military Region 7 (eastern **Nam Bo**); Military Region 8 (central Nam Bo); Military Region 9 (western Nam Bo); and the **Saigon-Gia Dinh** Military Region.

Originally, the B1 Front covered **I Corps** and half of II Corps in the U.S.-RVN system, and it expanded farther southward in late 1963 by the absorption of Dac Lac (Darlac) and Khanh Hoa provinces, but in May 1964, the **Central Highlands** were detached from it to form the B3 Front. The provinces of **Quang Tri** and **Thua Thien** were detached from the B1 Front in April 1966 to make the B4 Front (the **Tri-Thien** Military Region), and two months later, the northern part of Quang Tri province acquired separate status as the B5 Front. The B1 Front from 1966 onward was just the coastal provinces from **Quang Nam** to Khanh Hoa.

**FULBRIGHT, J. WILLIAM** (1905–1995). U.S. Senator. Born in Fayetteville, Arkansas, he graduated from the University of Arkansas at age 19, majoring in history. He studied at Oxford as a Rhodes scholar, took a law degree at George Washington University, and became president of the University of Arkansas at age 34. Fulbright was elected to the U.S. House of Representatives in 1942, and to the Senate in 1944. An internationalist, he urged the creation of a stronger **United Nations** than the one actually created at the end of World War II, and sponsored the creation of what became the Fulbright Program for international educational and scholarly exchanges.

Fulbright was at first a cold warrior, but he soon decided that the Cold War was being carried to excess, and by the time he became chairman of the Senate Foreign Relations Committee in 1959, he was an advocate of reducing East-West tensions. Fulbright helped persuade the Senate to pass the **Tonkin Gulf Resolution** in 1964—which he realized was in theory a blank check that could be used to authorize a major war in Vietnam—because he had been assured that President **Lyndon Johnson** would not use it for such a purpose. At that time he supported Johnson, but by January 1965 he was beginning to worry that Johnson might launch a major escalation of the war without real consultation of the **Congress**. Later that year the U.S. intervention in the Dominican Republic, and the dramatic escalation of the Vietnam War, turned Fulbright against Johnson. He made the Foreign Relations Committee the strongest institutional base within the U.S. government for opposition to the Vietnam War.

Fulbright was defeated when running for re-election in 1974. He was the author of *The Arrogance of Power* (1966), *The Pentagon Propaganda Machine* (1970), and *The Crippled Giant* (1972).

**FULRO** (Front Unifié de Lutte des Races Opprimées, United Struggle Front of the Oppressed Races). An organization primarily of **Montagnards**, formed in 1964 to fight for autonomy for the Montagnards, later joined by some **Chams** and **Khmers**. It was derived to some extent from the **Bajaraka Movement**. It quickly developed considerable strength among troops of the **Civilian Irregular Defense Groups** (CIDG), many of whom bitterly resented efforts to place CIDG units under the control of the Vietnamese **Special Forces**. Several CIDG units in the area of **Ban Me Thuot** rebelled in September 1964. FULRO was also behind more widely scattered uprisings among CIDG units in December 1965. Some members of FULRO eventually were able to work out a cooperative relationship with the **Republic of Vietnam** (RVN), based on common hostility to the Communists; some continued to infiltrate CIDG units against the wishes of the RVN; some withdrew into **Cambodia**.

Following the end of the war, FULRO continued to resist the Com-

munist government. It was reported that FULRO forces even briefly
seized the town of Cheo Reo in April 1978.

## -G-

*GAME WARDEN,* Operation. The United States used small vessels,
mainly **PBRs** belonging to the U.S. **Navy's River Patrol Force** (Task
Force 116, officially established December 18, 1965), and **helicopters,** to patrol rivers and canals in **South Vietnam**. PBRs began to
arrive in March 1966; operations began in the **Rung Sat** Special Zone
in April, and were extended to parts of the **Mekong Delta** in May. **Air
Cushion Vehicles** were also tried, and although they could go places
where even the shallow-draft PBRs could not, they proved unsatisfactory in other ways and were sent north to **I Corps** in 1968.

**GENEVA ACCORDS OF 1954.** The First Indochina War was ended by
negotiations that began on May 8, 1954, in Geneva, Switzerland, among
representatives—in most cases the foreign ministers—of **France**, the
**Democratic Republic of Vietnam** (DRV, which later became the government of **North Vietnam**), the **Soviet Union, China, Great Britain,** the United States, the State of Vietnam (which later became the
**Republic of Vietnam,** the government of **South Vietnam**), **Laos,** and
**Cambodia**. On the night of July 20–21, the conference completed the
Geneva Accords. These included separate peace agreements for Vietnam, Cambodia, and Laos (signed by French, DRV, and Cambodian
officers), and an unsigned declaration of the conference. There were
also unilateral declarations by several governments.

An International Commission for Supervision and Control, usually
called simply the **International Control Commission** (ICC), for which
neutral **India,** anti-Communist **Canada,** and Communist Poland each
supplied one-third of the personnel and India furnished the chairman,
was set up to supervise implementation of the accords. Nominally
there were three ICCs, one each for Vietnam, Laos, and Cambodia, but
the three had the same composition and cooperated with one another.

Vietnam was to be divided at the 17th parallel, the North to be governed by the DRV and the South by the French Union, until 1956. A
**Demilitarized Zone** (DMZ) was established between North and South.
The DRV got slightly more than half the population of Vietnam, but
less territory and population than it controlled at the time the agreement was signed. The authorities in each zone were forbidden to take

any reprisals against people in their zones who had supported the other side in the recent war. The two zones were to be reunified following internationally supervised **elections** in 1956; it was assumed that the Communist leaders of the DRV would win such elections.

All DRV (Viet Minh) armed forces were to leave the South and all French Union forces to leave the North within 300 days—by May 18, 1955. The withdrawal of anti-Communist military forces from the North was almost complete, though a few units of non-Vietnamese tribal forces in the highlands, and a few Vietnamese who had been trained and equipped by the United States to conduct guerrilla resistance against the Communists, were still in North Vietnam when the last French troops pulled out of **Haiphong**. It is usually estimated that 5,000 to 10,000 Viet Minh troops remained in the South.

During this 300-day period, civilians could also move from one zone to the other if they chose. It is usually estimated that almost 900,000 civilians, mostly **Catholic**, moved from North to South before the deadline. Catholic leaders, with some help from the United States, conducted a vigorous propaganda campaign urging northern Catholics to go south, and the U.S. **Navy** provided much of the transportation. Communist leaders told their followers in the South that there was no need to go north, since the two parts of Vietnam would be reunited under Communist leadership in 1956. The International Control Commission recorded only 2,598 civilians as having gone from South to North before the May 18 deadline, though there are suggestions that as many as 40,000 civilians may have gone north with the Viet Minh armed forces, without having been counted in the ICC figures for civilians. The ICC extended the deadline for movement of civilians from May 18 to July 20; during this extension 1,671 additional civilians moved from South to North, and 4,797 from North to South.

The Laotian and Cambodian governments associated with the French Union were left in control of their respective countries, except for two provinces of northeast Laos where the **Pathet Lao** (Laotian Communists) were to concentrate their forces pending a political settlement.

The accords forbade Vietnam, Laos, and Cambodia to participate in military alliances; this is why none of them became members of the **Southeast Asia Treaty Organization** (SEATO) when that body was established in September 1954. The Accords also limited the introduction of foreign troops, and weapons, into these countries. As large portions of the Geneva Accords collapsed over the following years, the restriction on foreign troops eventually was among the few parts of the accords that continued to be taken seriously, with at least a pretense of compliance and enforcement. The United States exceeded the limit of 342 military **advisers** for South Vietnam beginning in 1956, but pretended for several years that the extra personnel were not there as advisers (*see* **Temporary Equipment Recovery Mission**). When the United States began sending military advisers to Laos in 1959, they went through the motions of pretending to retire from the U.S. **Army**, so they could be regarded officially as civilians (*see* *Hotfoot*).

The Soviet Union and China wanted a reduction in world tensions. They pressed the DRV to sign the Geneva Accords in 1954, giving up substantial territory in the short run, in the expectation of getting it back, and more, when Vietnam was reunified in 1956. The DRV, not sure that reunification would actually occur on schedule, submitted reluctantly to this pressure. A number of authors have stated that the DRV was actually certain that reunification would not occur as promised, but the evidence for this assertion seems weak.

The widespread belief that the United States pledged not to violate the accords arises from misreading of a U.S. declaration of July 21, 1954. The United States hoped to prevent the reunification of Vietnam called for by the accords, but was not sure of its ability to do so. Years later, after reunification had indeed been blocked, the United States began claiming that the Geneva Accords had said South Vietnam was to be an independent country.

Premier **Ngo Dinh Diem** of the State of Vietnam protested the accords, but he had little power in 1954; his representative at Geneva was unable to influence the text of the accords, and it was not obvious that Diem would have the ability to block their implementation. In early 1955, however, Diem attained effective control of South Vietnam, and in July of that year he declared his refusal to discuss with the DRV the holding of the 1956 elections. He endorsed national unity—indeed he treated the division of Vietnam as a crime perpetrated by the Communists—but rejected the procedures established by the accords for achieving reunification.

**GENEVA ACCORDS OF 1962**, in regard to **Laos**. An international conference to settle the war in Laos opened in Geneva, Switzerland, on May 16, 1961. The Geneva Accords—a Declaration on the Neutrality of Laos, and a Protocol primarily concerned with the removal of all non-Laotian military and paramilitary personnel from the country—

were finally signed on July 23, 1962. They had essentially been negotiated between the United States and the **Soviet Union**; **China** and the **Democratic Republic of Vietnam** (DRV) assented to the accords unwillingly. The accords gave international sanction to the Second Coalition Government, which had been formed on June 23. This was headed by Prince **Souvanna Phouma**, leader of the "neutralist" forces, and included representatives both of the **Pathet Lao** (Laotian Communist movement) and the rightists.

The Geneva Accords decreed that all involvement of outside military forces in Laos was to end; the **International Control Commission** that had originally been created to supervise the **Geneva Accords of 1954** was to check compliance. These terms, if actually implemented, would have constituted a triumph for the United States; withdrawal of the People's Army of Vietnam (**PAVN**) from Laos would have meant closing down the **Ho Chi Minh Trail**, the route by which men and equipment went from **North Vietnam** through eastern Laos to **South Vietnam**. The DRV signed the agreement but did not then withdraw PAVN forces from Laos. The contrast between DRV violation of the accords and nearly complete compliance on the anti-Communist side (though some small paramilitary units from **Thailand** remained in Laos in violation of the accords) was one factor pushing Souvanna Phouma into alliance with the United States during the following year.

**W. Averell Harriman**, the chief American representative at the conference, told his superiors in November 1961 that Georgi M. Pushkin, a deputy foreign minister who was the chief Soviet representative, had promised the Soviet Union would be responsible for ensuring compliance with the agreement by the DRV, and that traffic from North to South Vietnam along the Ho Chi Minh Trail would be halted when the agreement went into effect. The Soviet Union may indeed have tried to get the DRV to obey the accords. The friendship that had existed between Moscow and Hanoi in 1962 had evaporated by 1964, and it seems possible that arguments over DRV violation of the agreement the Soviets had negotiated could have contributed to the decline in the relationship.

The Americans obtained two major benefits from the 1962 accords. One was that they ended direct Soviet involvement in Laos. The other was that they began the process by which Souvanna Phouma and his neutralist followers, who had considerable influence, became allied with the United States. The right-wing seizure of power in December 1960 had pushed Souvanna into an alliance with the Communists; the

1962 agreement allowed him to return to a neutral posture. The end of Soviet involvement in Laos made the neutralists turn toward the United States as a source of foreign aid. By early 1963, neutralists and Pathet Lao were competing for power within the framework of the coalition government established in 1962, and their troops were occasionally shooting at one another. At the beginning of April 1963, the Pathet Lao members of the cabinet left Vientiane, and on April 10 President **John Kennedy** ordered a covert resumption of U.S. military aid both to Souvanna's troops and to **Hmong** forces.

The price the United States paid for these benefits was restraining U.S. military actions in Laos, keeping them within the limits that Souvanna Phouma would accept. These limits eventually became quite broad for air operations—the U.S. **bomb** tonnage on Laos (*see* **air war**) was considerably greater than the combined total of the tonnages the United States dropped on Germany and Japan during World War II—but there were never large operations by U.S. ground troops in Laos.

**GIA DINH.** The province that surrounded the city of **Saigon**. The province capital, also called Gia Dinh, was effectively a suburb of Saigon, on the north side of the city. In the 1960s, Gia Dinh province was extended southward to the sea, absorbing the **Rung Sat**, which had been the southern part of **Bien Hoa** province.

**GOLDWATER, BARRY M.** (1909–1998). U.S. Senator. Born in Phoenix, Arizona, he graduated in 1928 from Staunton Military Academy in Virginia, and was commissioned a second lieutenant in the U.S. **Army** in 1930. He became president of his family's department-store chain in 1937. During World War II he rose to the rank of colonel in the Army Air Forces. Following the war he became commander of the Arizona Air National Guard.

Goldwater's political career began with his election to the Phoenix City Council in 1949. In 1952, he was elected as a Republican to the United States Senate. He continued to serve in the **Air Force** Reserve, from which he finally retired as a major general in 1967. He was very conservative, and stridently anti-Communist in foreign affairs.

Senator Goldwater won the Republican nomination for president in 1964, in a triumph of the right wing of the party, based largely in the South and West, over the more moderate Republican establishment strongest in the Northeast. During the campaign, Goldwater said the loss of **South Vietnam** would lead to the loss of all of Southeast Asia (*see* **domino theory**). He advocated stronger military action, including bombing of **North Vietnam**. In informal conversations, he suggested that even low-yield nuclear weapons might be used against the supply lines supporting the **Viet Cong**, and that perhaps the United States should have used nuclear weapons in Vietnam in 1954. Such statements made it easy for **Lyndon Johnson** to persuade most of the public that Goldwater was irresponsible and dangerous; Johnson won overwhelmingly in November.

Having run for president rather than for another term in the Senate in 1964, Goldwater was out of the Senate until elected to it once again in 1968. He remained a strong supporter of military action in Vietnam. When the United States resumed large-scale bombing of North Vietnam in April 1972, Goldwater replied to fears that Soviet ships in **Haiphong** harbor might be hit by saying in the Senate on April 19 "I hope we hit them all." In January 1973, however, Goldwater helped President **Richard Nixon** pressure President **Nguyen Van Thieu** into signing the **Paris Peace Agreement**.

Goldwater's last major accomplishment, just before he left the Senate, was the Goldwater-Nichols Act of 1986. This restructuring of the U.S. military command system, which strengthened the chairman of the **Joint Chiefs of Staff**, is generally considered to have been successful in improving cooperation between the armed services. Goldwater wrote his memoirs twice, first *With No Apologies* (1979) and then *Goldwater* (1988).

**GRAVEL MINE.** The gravel mine (XM-121 and perhaps other models) was a small explosive device that usually looked like a rock (one variant looked like dog feces). It was designed to be dropped in a frozen state from small aircraft (fighter-bombers or **helicopters**). Once scattered on the ground the mines soon thawed and armed themselves; they would then detonate if touched. The Communist forces in areas where they were used devised systems for warning troops of their presence, and detonating them harmlessly, which reduced their effectiveness below the level that could justify the considerable cost to the United States of dropping them in a refrigerated state from small aircraft. Most of the available stock (1,200 tons) of XM-121 mines were then disposed of in June and July 1969 through Project *Commando Scarf*, which dropped them in Southern **Laos** from **C-130** transport aircraft, which could deliver them at a much lower cost per ton than helicopters or fighter-bombers could.

Gravel mines continued to be used in special circumstances. In 1972, for example, a U.S. pilot who had been downed in enemy territory was protected from capture by the dropping of a belt of gravel mines surrounding his position. **PAVN** troops attempted to clear paths through the mines, but the United States was able to drop additional mines as fast as the earlier ones were cleared, and prevent any path from being cleared all the way through the mine field.

Some gravel mines, called "sterilizing," were designed to disarm themselves again and become harmless a set period after being dropped. Others were designed to remain dangerous for an indefinite period.

**GREAT BRITAIN.** Britain had been one of the two co-chairs of the Geneva Conference of 1954, and it was always assumed that the same would occur if the conference were to be called back into session. This gave Britain a peripheral role in Vietnamese events, and may explain why the British kept a low-level diplomatic representative, a consul general, in **Hanoi** even while their American allies were bombing **North Vietnam**.

In September 1961, Britain established a small advisory mission in **Saigon**, nominally civilian, helping the **Republic of Vietnam** (RVN) in **police** and **counterinsurgency** techniques. It was headed by **Robert G. K. Thompson**, who had participated in the suppression of the Communist insurgency in Malaya in the 1950s. The initial announcement said the mission was to consist of four or five officers; by late 1964, it had grown to seven. When **Lyndon Johnson** asked Britain in December 1964 to send a token military force to **South Vietnam**, the British declined.

Britain did provide verbal backing for U.S. actions in Vietnam, while privately trying to restrain the United States, as when Prime Minister Harold Wilson in early 1966 advised President Johnson not to authorize bombing of fuel storage facilities in Hanoi and **Haiphong**. Britain also decided not to cut off all trade with North Vietnam; the frequent presence in Haiphong of freighters from Hong Kong, flying the British flag, was one of the factors inhibiting President Johnson from bombing the port. There was dispute as to whether injuries to crewmen of the freighter *Dartford* during a U.S. air strike on April 25, 1967 were caused by U.S. weapons or by North Vietnamese anti-aircraft shells.

**GREENE, WALLACE** (1907–2003). U.S. **Marine** general. Born in Waterbury, Vermont, he graduated from Annapolis in 1930, joined the Marine Corps, and saw considerable combat in the Pacific Theater during

World War II. He was commandant of the Marine Corps from January 1964 to January 1968. He was an advocate of escalation. In the autumn of 1964, he thought the United States should begin systematic bombing of **North Vietnam**, as soon as possible. By mid-1965, with the bombing begun, he was telling President **Lyndon Johnson** that it should be expanded, and that the United States should put 500,000 men into Vietnam.

By early 1966, he was advocating a major change in U.S. policy, shifting the focus in **South Vietnam** from combat against enemy military forces to **pacification**—establishing control over the densely populated areas, and winning the loyalty of the peasants there.

**GRENADE LAUNCHER.** The single-shot M79 grenade launcher ("duper," "blooper," "blooker") was an effective and well-liked weapon. It opened with a hinge at the breech so that a shell could be loaded into it. It fired a variety of rounds, including high explosive, **white phosphorus** (incendiary), and shotgun. The rounds were 40-mm in diameter, and bullet-shaped. The effective range was 375 meters.

Rapid-fire automatic grenade launchers, also 40-mm, were most commonly used as armament for **helicopters**.

**GROUP 559.** This **PAVN** unit, also called the Truong Son troops, was responsible for creating and operating the **Ho Chi Minh Trail**, the route by which men, weapons, and supplies were sent from **North Vietnam** through southeastern **Laos** to **South Vietnam**. It was established on May 19, 1959, and began operations immediately. It was commanded by Vo Bam from its origin to 1965, by Phan Trong Tue from April to December 1965, by **Hoang Van Thai** (not the **Hoang Van Thai** who had been PAVN chief of staff during the First Indochina War, but another general of the same name) from December 1965 to 1967, and by **Dong Si Nguyen** from 1967 to 1975. It is said to have carried more than 1,000,000 tons of cargo, of which more than 500,000 tons were delivered to South Vietnam.

**GROUP 759.** This was the unit that shipped weapons and ammunition from **North Vietnam** to **South Vietnam** by sea, in substantial steel-hulled trawlers. A preliminary organization—a group of staff officers assigned to study the feasibility of such operations—was set up in July 1959; Group 759 was established as an operational unit on October 23, 1961. The first success, in which the ship *Phuong Dong 1* delivered 28 tons of cargo to **Ca Mau** (the southernmost tip of South Vietnam, presumably chosen because it was the place where the **Republic**

**of Vietnam** would least expect to find North Vietnamese vessels approaching the coast), was in September or October of 1962. By February 1963, there had been three more deliveries, of about 30 tons each, to the same area. Vessels with capacities of 50 to 60 tons made numerous deliveries during 1963; vessels with capacities up to 100 tons came into use before the end of 1964. Group 759 was redesignated Group 125 on January 24, 1964. By February 1965, a total of almost 5,000 tons had been delivered in 88 voyages, mostly to **Nam Bo**.

Security was excellent for more than two years. Many senior U.S. naval officers refused to believe the rumors that the **Viet Cong** were receiving significant munitions shipments by sea until Vessel 143 was spotted by aircraft and sunk at Vung Ro, on the coast of Phu Yen province, on February 16, 1965. After this incident, the United States and the Republic of Vietnam greatly expanded their efforts to patrol the coast of South Vietnam (*see* Operation *Market Time*). Group 125 continued its efforts to deliver munitions to South Vietnam, but these efforts became far more difficult and dangerous.

**GUAM.** The largest island (541 square kilometers, 209 square miles) of the Marianas, in the western Pacific, Guam became an American possession after the Spanish-American War of 1898. In February 1965, as the United States was considering a great expansion of air operations in Vietnam, the U.S. **Air Force** sent 30 **B-52** bombers, and 30 KC-135 tankers, to Andersen Air Force Base on Guam. The B-52s began bombing targets in **South Vietnam** in June 1965, and later also bombed other areas of Indochina. On a visit to Guam in 1969, President **Richard Nixon** proclaimed what was briefly called the Guam Doctrine before being renamed the **Nixon Doctrine**.

**GUERRILLA WARFARE.** In a very unequal confrontation, in which one side has so much greater military strength that its opponent would have no chance in a direct confrontation between the main forces of the two sides, the weaker side may choose to use guerrilla warfare, splitting up into small groups, which try to evade battles they cannot win. If the terrain of an area does not provide natural concealment, the guerrillas may dig **tunnels** in which to hide, or simply depend on being indistinguishable from ordinary civilians when not carrying their weapons. The stronger force that the guerrillas are fighting almost always needs to disperse at least some of its personnel in small units—to guard supply lines, to maintain control of the population, and to hunt the guerrillas. The guerrillas can fight these small units in ambushes and surprise attacks, or can harass them with sniper fire, **booby traps**, etc.

In areas with a substantial population, its attitude is crucial. The stronger force can obliterate the guerrillas if it can find them; for them to avoid being found will be difficult or impossible in an area where large numbers of civilians dislike them. In jungles where the population is so sparse that guerrillas can go weeks at a time without seeing a civilian, the attitude of the population is less important.

During the Vietnam War it was common for guerrillas and government troops to coexist within a village for extended periods. During daylight, when government troops could see what was going on well enough to derive full advantage from their superior weaponry, the guerrillas had to remain hidden to avoid destruction, so the government was able to control the village. At night the guerrilas could be more active. If the government troops were too nervous about the risks of ambush to move around much at night, the guerrillas could control most of the village. What was sometimes called the "change of government" occurred twice a day in such villages, at dawn and dusk.

**GUNSHIPS,** fixed-wing. The need for fighter planes to be fast and highly maneuverable seriously restricts the weight and bulk of the guns and ammunition that can be fitted into them; this limits their ability to strafe ground targets. A cargo plane, with **machine guns** in the cargo bay firing sideways, is not subject to these restrictions and can place much heavier fire on ground targets.

The United States began giving serious consideration to this idea in 1963. In December 1964, combat tests began in Vietnam of an aircraft initially designated the FC-47: an old C-47 cargo plane, with six 7.62-mm **miniguns** each capable of firing either 3,000 or 6,000 rounds per minute, all pointed to the same side of the aircraft. The tests were successful, and more C-47s were converted in the following months, with varying armaments. Three miniguns per plane eventually became standard. The plane was redesignated the AC-47 late in 1965. It was officially called the "Spooky," unofficially "Puff the Magic Dragon." The U.S. **Air Force** (USAF) stopped operating AC-47s in Southeast Asia toward the end of 1969; most of the aircraft were turned over to the **Vietnamese Air Force** and the Royal Laotian Air Force. The AC-47 had had an impact on the war far out of proportion to its numbers—only 53 were built—and very low cost.

Toward the end of 1966, modified AC-47s with added armor and fire extinguishers were being sent to Nakhon Phanom in **Thailand**, to be used for operations in **Laos**, where the danger of ground fire was too great for the unarmored AC-47s used for missions in **South Vietnam**.

The AC-130 Spectre was a larger and much more modern aircraft. It carried four 7.62-mm miniguns, and also four 20-mm **Vulcan** cannons. The Vulcan used the same basic Gatling-gun design as the minigun: six barrels rotating at high speed around a common axis. Early Vulcans could fire 2,500 rounds (usually high-explosive incendiary, sometimes armor-piercing incendiary) per minute. Later models fired up to 6,000 rounds per minute. The AC-130 also carried more equipment than the AC-47 for detecting targets at night: a side-looking **radar**, an infrared device that could detect the engines of trucks by their heat, and a starlight scope that could amplify images in dim light. Initial combat tests from September to December 1967 were highly successful, but there was resistance to the AC-130 design from people who felt that the Air Force needed its limited number of **C-130** aircraft for transport purposes, and could not afford to convert any significant number of them to gunships. Arguments over this issue, and problems with the infrared gear and other equipment, delayed the program; in late 1968 and early 1969 only four were in action, based at Ubon in Thailand, and mainly devoted to hunting trucks on the **Ho Chi Minh Trail**.

Some AC-130 aircraft were given heavier weapons, both to make their fire more destructive and to enable them to fire from a greater distance and thus reduce their exposure to **anti-aircraft** fire. The Surprise Package variant of the AC-130A, carrying two 40-mm Bofors cannon originally designed as anti-aircraft guns, plus two 20-mm guns, underwent its first combat trial in December 1969; the 40-mm cannon became standard equipment for the AC-130 during 1970. The Pave Aegis variant of the AC-130E, introduced around the beginning of 1972, had a 105-mm cannon as well as one 40-mm and two smaller guns.

The AC-130 also came to be equipped with a laser target designator, to guide a smart bomb (*see* **bombs**) to its target. The first combat use of this system was on February 1, 1971; the bomb was dropped by an **F-4 Phantom**.

The AC-119, based on the old C-119 "Flying Boxcar" transport plane, was slower than the AC-130 and had less armor and much less powerful guns, but it was cheaper; it eventually replaced the AC-47 as the USAF gunship for use inside South Vietnam, and was also used to a significant extent in **Cambodia** and Laos. The AC-119G Shadow, equipped with four 7.62-mm miniguns, began to arrive in Vietnam in the last week of 1968, and began combat trials early in 1969. The

AC-119K Stinger, with four miniguns and two 20-mm cannon, began to arrive in South Vietnam in November 1969 and began combat trials the same month.

**GUNSHIPS,** helicopter. In 1962, the United States began using UH-1A and UH-1B **helicopters** in **South Vietnam**, armed with .30-caliber **machine guns** and 2.75-inch **rockets**, to attack ground targets and to escort transport helicopters. They were less heavily armed than fixed-wing fighter-bombers, but were more maneuverable, and could fly low and slow in a way fixed-wing aircraft could not. This was crucial not only for spotting concealed enemies, but for placing fire on ground targets with great precision, particularly useful when providing close air support to friendly ground forces. The helicopter gunships used up to 1967 were made simply by taking a body designed for a transport helicopter, and mounting weapons on it. The UH-34 helicopters that the **Marines** converted into gunships, and began trying in Vietnam at the end of 1964, worked out badly, but all of those derived from various models of the UH-1 (UH-1E gunships were arriving at **Danang** by May 1965) were quite successful.

The AH-1G Cobra, a helicopter designed as a gunship rather than a converted cargo helicopter, entered combat in October 1967. It had a narrow fuselage, making it a smaller target for ground fire. It was also faster, more heavily armored, and much more heavily armed than previous helicopter gunships. It proved enormously successful.

## -H-

**HAIG, ALEXANDER MEIGS, JR.** (1924– ). U.S. **Army** general. Born in Philadelphia, he graduated from West Point in 1947. He soon showed himself a superb staff officer, serving as an aide to General Edward Almond in the Korean War. He earned an M.A. in International Relations at Georgetown University in 1961, and served in various staff positions at the Pentagon from 1962 to 1965, ending as an assistant to Deputy Secretary of Defense Cyrus Vance. Haig commanded first a battalion and then a brigade of the 1st Infantry **Division** in Vietnam, 1966–1967.

In 1969, Haig became the military assistant to **Henry Kissinger**, President **Richard Nixon**'s national security adviser. In 1970, he was promoted to Kissinger's deputy. Much of the president's information about defense and foreign policy matters came through Haig. Nixon began sending Haig on missions to Vietnam, at first primarily to survey the situation there, in 1970. In late 1972 and early 1973, these missions became more important; Haig was one of the principal emissaries Nixon used while persuading President **Nguyen Van Thieu** to sign the **Paris Peace Agreement**. The value Nixon place on Haig's services was reflected in his rank; he rose from colonel to four-star general during his four years serving under Kissinger in the White House.

Haig's views on the Vietnam War were hawkish. In 1969, he strongly advocated the covert U.S. bombing of **Cambodia**, Operation *Menu*. During the negotiations for a settlement of the war, he urged Nixon not to accept a total pullout of U.S. forces from Vietnam; he wanted the United States to maintain a military presence there indefinitely, as it had done in Korea. In October 1972, he became more conciliatory, accepting the draft agreement Kissinger had worked out with **Le Duc Tho**, but when the negotiations stalemated again in December, Haig urged Nixon to initiate a massive new bombing campaign against **North Vietnam**, Operation *Linebacker II*.

In January 1973 he went briefly to the Pentagon as deputy chief of staff of the Army, but within months he returned to the White House to replace H. R. Haldeman, Nixon's chief of staff, who had resigned as a result of the spreading Watergate scandal. Haig played a major role in the Nixon administration's efforts to deal with the scandal. After Nixon's resignation as president in 1974, Haig returned to active service, and served as supreme allied commander of the North Atlantic Treaty Organization from 1974 to 1978. He was secretary of state from 1981 to 1982. His memoir *Inner Circles* was published in 1992.

**HAIPHONG.** The principal seaport of **North Vietnam**, located in the **Red River Delta**, about 90 kilometers southeast of **Hanoi**. The harbor suffers from silting. Continuous dredging was required during the war to keep the entrance deep enough so that vessels with drafts up to about eight meters could enter and leave at high tide. Larger vessels had to offload their cargoes to lighters outside the mouth of the harbor.

Most imports to North Vietnam came through Haiphong, but there was disagreement among U.S. **intelligence** agencies as to whether weapons in particular did so. The **Central Intelligence Agency** and the Defense Intelligence Agency believed that the **Soviet Union** and **China** made a point of routing weapons shipments by land, across the border from China, instead of by sea through Haiphong. It seems possible the Chinese and Soviets felt that the United States would be less likely to close Haiphong by bombing if there were not substantial weapons shipments entering North Vietnam through the port.

The U.S. military repeatedly requested permission to close Haiphong. These requests usually specified that the port was to be bombed or closed by naval **mines**; permission to do these things was always denied until 1972. Permission to impede use of the port by destroying the dredge that kept it from silting closed would have been easier to obtain, but the military was reluctant to ask for this, probably feeling that if it obtained permission to close the port gradually by silting, this would eliminate any possibility of obtaining permission to close it quickly by bombing or mining.

President **Lyndon Johnson** was very hesitant to bomb or mine Haiphong; he feared the repercussions if Soviet, Chinese, or British flag ships were damaged or sunk. The military finally persuaded him to allow destruction of the handling and storage facilities for gasoline and other fuels, on June 29, 1966. Bombing of other targets in the city, but still not the docks, occurred sporadically until 1968, then stopped for four years. (On November 21, 1970, the United States staged a fake bombing raid on Haiphong—the planes dropped flares, not bombs—to distract North Vietnamese air defenses during an attempted rescue of **prisoners of war** from **Son Tay**.)

On April 16, 1972, U.S. **B-52** bombers made a substantial raid against Haiphong. Ships in the port were not specifically targeted, but the bombers were not as careful about avoiding accidental hits on ships as U.S. aircraft had been between 1966 and 1968. They hit four Soviet ships, one of which may have been sunk. Haiphong was bombed again in Operation *Linebacker* from May to October 1972, and in Operation *Linebacker II* in December. More important was the use of mines dropped into the harbor by aircraft; these effectively closed the port from May 11, 1972, until early 1973. Under the **Paris Peace Agreement** of January 1973, the United States was required to help clear the mines.

**HALBERSTAM, DAVID** (1934– ). Journalist. Born in New York City, he graduated from Harvard in 1955, and worked as a reporter in West Point, Mississippi, and Nashville, Tennessee, before being hired by *The New York Times* in 1960. He was assigned first to Washington, D.C., then for a year to the Congo, before being sent to Vietnam in September 1962.

Halberstam quickly became one of the reporters most loathed by top U.S. officials in Vietnam. U.S. **Army** officers (Lieutenant Colonel **John Paul Vann** and others) in the field as **advisers** to the **ARVN** were telling Halberstam the war was being very seriously mishandled. He could also see serious problems with the political behavior of **Ngo Dinh Diem**'s government. The stories Halberstam wrote placed him sharply in conflict with the optimistic General **Paul Harkins**, commander of the U.S. **Military Assistance Command, Vietnam**, and Ambassador **Frederick Nolting**.

It was not that Halberstam opposed the war effort. He strongly believed that **South Vietnam** must be saved from Communism, and that U.S. military personnel should be in Vietnam helping in this struggle. But when he saw political and military problems that were interfering with the conduct of the war, he resisted the pressure he was getting from Harkins and Nolting to ignore those problems and write as if everything were going well. Reporters like Halberstam played a significant role in undermining American faith in President Diem during 1963. In October 1963, President **John Kennedy** asked Arthur Sulzberger, publisher of *The New York Times*, to pull Halberstam out of Vietnam. Although Sulzberger did not do so at that time, Halberstam did leave Vietnam early in 1964. He and **Malcolm Browne** of the Associated Press shared the Pulitzer Prize in 1964 for their 1963 reporting on Vietnam. Halberstam's account of what he had seen in Vietnam, *The Making of a Quagmire*, published in 1965, took the same attitude as the reports written while he had been in Vietnam; he said it was very important that the United States defeat the Communists in Vietnam, both for the sake of the Vietnamese and because Vietnam was "truly vital to U.S. interests." But he did not think an American victory was likely.

In January 1965, *The New York Times* send him to Poland. Before the end of the year, the Communist government there had expelled him for his critical reporting. Soon afterward he left *The New York Times*; he began devoting himself to long-term projects, instead of the day-to-day work of a reporter. In 1972, he published *The Best and the Brightest*, a very influential, best-selling history of U.S. policy toward Vietnam during the administrations of John Kennedy and **Lyndon Johnson**, based on much interviewing of former officials. By this time he had come to doubt the fundamental wisdom of U.S. involvement in Vietnam, not just the details of the way it was being handled.

**HAM RONG** (Dragon's Jaw) Bridge. The Ham Rong road and rail bridge, across the Ma River (Song Ma) in Thanh Hoa province of northern **Trung Bo**, was completed in 1964. It lay on **Route 1**, the main route from **Hanoi** and **Haiphong** to the southern **panhandle** of **North Vietnam**, and to the **Ho Chi Minh Trail** and **South Vietnam**. It was heavily defended against air attack, and heavily attacked by U.S. aircraft. The first raid, on April 3, 1965, damaged but did not destroy it, at the cost of two planes shot down by ground fire. One more was downed by ground fire, and two by **MiG** fighters, during a restrike the following day. Many other raids followed, but the bridge proved frustratingly strong; probably it had been deliberately designed to withstand bombing. One of the first combat trials of the new Walleye smart bomb (*see* **bombs**), on March 12, 1967, scored three direct hits but failed to knock it down. After a 44-plane raid on January 28, 1968, first bad weather and then a **bombing halt** ended attacks for more than four years.

On April 27, 1972, the bridge was damaged again with Walleyes. By this time, however, the United States had far more powerful smart bombs. On May 13, the fourth day of Operation *Linebacker*, these large smart bombs finally managed to drop a span of the Ham Rong Bridge, and it was further bombed during the following months.

**"HAMBURGER HILL"** (Hill 937, Dong Ap Bia). A mountain in the northern part of the **A Shau Valley**, in western **Thua Thien** province near the Laotian border. The 3/187 Battalion of the U.S. 101st **Airborne Division** began the attack on it on May 11, 1969, as part of Operation *Apache Snow*. Two battalions of the **PAVN** 29th Regiment, well dug in with underground bunkers and **tunnels**, held out until May 20 against an attacking force that grew to four battalions (three U.S. and one **ARVN**), with heavy air and **artillery** support. Official reports indicated 56 American and five ARVN soldiers died in the battle, against more than 600 PAVN dead. A figure of 70 U.S. dead and 372 wounded may include casualties U.S. troops suffered on May 10 near Dong Ap Bia, before the battle specifically for that mountain began on May 11.

American doctrine at the time was that the presence of a strong PAVN force on the mountain constituted an adequate reason to attack it. On May 19, however, a report appeared in many American newspapers that contained complaints by U.S. soldiers about being required to charge up the mountain against strong PAVN defenses, and on May 20, Senator Edward Kennedy denounced the action in the Senate as "senseless and irresponsible." The controversy that followed appears to have influenced President **Richard Nixon** to order U.S. troops to make a greater effort to avoid casualties—in other words, not to attack such fortified PAVN positions—soon afterward.

U.S. forces held Dong Ap Bia briefly, in the hope that the PAVN would try to take it back, leading to another battle in which the PAVN would suffer further casualties. This did not occur, and U.S. forces were pulled off the mountain on June 5. The PAVN promptly reoccupied it, and when the U.S. command chose not to assault it again, critics cited this as further evidence that the assault in May had been pointless.

**HAMLET EVALUATION SYSTEM** (HES). A system initiated during 1967, in which each hamlet in **South Vietnam** was rated on a scale of six categories. Few hamlets were given the extreme ratings of A (securely under government control) or V (Communist controlled); most were in the intermediate categories B, C, D, and E. The number of hamlets in each HES rating was used as a measure of the success of **pacification**, and indeed of the war as a whole. Good ratings improved the career prospects of officals responsible for the hamlets in question; this sometimes led to bias in the ratings.

**HANOI.** Capital of the **Democratic Republic of Vietnam** (DRV), located in the **Red River Delta**, about 95 kilometers from the sea. Under the name Thang Long, the city had been the traditional capital of Vietnam up to the late 18th century. Hanoi was not a major industrial center; its importance during the Second Indochina War was as a transportation nexus (both road and rail traffic crossed the Red River by the **Doumer Bridge** in Hanoi), an administrative center, and a symbol.

The question of bombing Hanoi was a contentious one through much of the war. The U.S. **Air Force**, dominated by doctrines of strategic bombing, urged attacks on targets in Hanoi. President **Lyndon Johnson** was very reluctant; he feared the possible reactions of **China**, the **Soviet Union**, and public opinion in the West, and he may have felt (some of his advisers are known to have felt) that once targets were destroyed, the United States would no longer be able to threaten to destroy them. President Johnson initially defined a restricted zone, a circular area with a radius of 30 nautical miles (55.56 kilometers) measured from the center of the city, in which air strikes could be flown only with his specific permission. The degree of his willingness to grant such permission fluctuated. Sometimes there was a smaller circle within the large one, inside which air strikes were completely prohibited.

The first air strikes within five nautical miles of the city center were in June and August 1966. The next strikes in this area, in the first half of December, were considerably heavier. The DRV, wishing to publicize this intensification of the bombing, invited **Harrison Salisbury** of *The New York Times* to come to Vietnam late in December. Salisbury's reports from Hanoi caused considerable controversy. The restrictions on bombing were futher loosened in 1967. In May and June there were numerous raids on the edges of Hanoi, and a few against targets such as the electric power plant and the waterworks, well inside the city. Beginning in August there were occasional attacks on the Doumer Bridge, very close to the city center.

U.S. bombing of the Hanoi area was terminated in April 1968 (*see* **bombing halts**), and did not resume until April 1972. Even then it was on a much more limited scale than most people realize. Operation *Linebacker II*, the so-called "Christmas bombing" of December 1972, hit many targets on the edges of Hanoi but did little damage to the city center.

**HARASSMENT AND INTERDICTION** (H&I). **Artillery** units, when they did not have information about the locations of enemy units, would fire (usually at night) at routes along which enemy units were known sometimes to move, and at areas where enemy units might be found, in the hope that a lucky shot would inflict some casualties on the enemy. The Army of the Republic of Vietnam (**ARVN**) was making frequent use of this practice at least as early as 1962; the United States did it on a larger scale after 1965.

**HARKINS, PAUL D.** (1904–1984). U.S. **Army** general. Born in Massachusetts, he graduated from the U.S. Military Academy at West Point in 1929. By the late stages of World War II he was deputy chief of staff of the Third Army under George Patton. He was for many years closely associated with **Maxwell Taylor**, and Taylor's influence was probably the reason Harkins was appointed the first commander of **Military Assistance Command, Vietnam** (MACV), when that command was established in February 1962. His background was conventional; he had no experience in, nor had he shown an interest in, **guerrilla** or counterguerrilla operations.

As commander of MACV, Harkins considered it his duty to support President **Ngo Dinh Diem** of the **Republic of Vietnam**, and to say that Diem's war against the **Viet Cong** was going well. He placed pressure on **intelligence** officers to hold down their estimates of Viet Cong strength. He blocked efforts by military **advisers**, attached to **ARVN** units, to report serious problems with the war effort, some of them directly traceable to President Diem; the reports MACV sent to Washington spoke of progress and success. Some of the advisers, most conspicuously **John Paul Vann**, became so frustrated they began telling to reporters like **Malcolm Browne, David Halberstam**, and **Neil Sheehan** the things they were unable to get into the official reports. This led to conflict between Harkins and these reporters, especially after the Battle of **Ap Bac**, which Harkins praised as an ARVN victory.

High officials in Washington were divided. Some doubted Harkins's optimistic reports, but others, including Maxwell Taylor, Secretary of Defense **Robert McNamara**, and General **Victor Krulak**, endorsed the optimism. It was only toward the end of 1963, around the time of the **coup** (which Harkins opposed) that overthrew Ngo Dinh Diem, that most top U.S. officials recognized the war had been going considerably worse than Harkins had been saying.

General **William Westmoreland** replaced Harkins as commander of MACV in June 1964, and Harkins retired from the Army before the end of the year.

**HARRIMAN, W[ILLIAM] AVERELL** (1891–1986). Politician and diplomat. Son of railroad tycoon and "robber baron" Edward H. Harriman, Averell Harriman graduated from Yale in 1913. He had a very diversified career, serving among other things as U.S. ambassador to the Soviet Union, 1943–1946; secretary of commerce, 1946–1948; and governor of New York, 1955–1958. Harriman was an ambassador at large from February to November 1961; while in this position he became involved in negotiations for the neutralization of **Laos**. He continued this work as assistant secretary of state for Far Eastern affairs from November 1961 to April 1963; he headed the U.S. delegation in Geneva that negotiated the **Geneva Accords of 1962** in regard to Laos. Harriman was under secretary of state for political affairs from April 1963 to March 1965, after which he once again became ambassador at large, a job in which he looked for possible ways of negotiating a settlement of the Vietnam War without, at first, having much power or backing.

Harriman opposed U.S. aid to the French war effort in Vietnam in the late 1940s, but by 1954 he had become a strong advocate of U.S. military intervention in Vietnam. By the 1960s, he was becoming ambivalent again. Harriman was one of the most important of the officials who advocated U.S. support for a **coup** against **Ngo Dinh Diem** in 1963; he and **Roger Hilsman** were the principal authors of the cable of August 24, 1963, that authorized Ambassador **Henry Cabot Lodge** to signal to **ARVN** officers that the United States might not object to a coup.

Under **Lyndon Johnson** Harriman opposed escalation of the war, being very doubtful about the possibility of an American military victory, but he also opposed the idea of a quick American withdrawal. He wanted a negotiated settlement, and a precipitous withdrawal would have left the United States no leverage with which to negotiate. He sometimes may have exaggerated his support for military action, in public, in order to retain his status as a member of the foreign policy team. When President Johnson assembled the **"Wise Men"** and consulted them about Vietnam in November 1967, Harriman said little, but acquiesced in the general expression of support for American policy in the war.

Harriman was chosen as the U.S. representative when the **Paris negotiations** began in May 1968. By the summer and fall of 1968, Harriman was urging President Johnson to halt all bombing of **North Vietnam** without waiting for any clear commitment to a quid pro quo from **Hanoi**, simply relying on the threat that the bombing could be resumed if Hanoi took advantage of the halt by increasing support for the combat in the South. He was replaced in Paris by Henry Cabot Lodge in January 1969.

**HATCHET TEAMS.** Combat units, larger than **Spike Teams**, made up of indigenous personnel (at first mostly **Nung**, later mostly **Montagnards**) under American leadership, used for raids across the border into **Laos**. They were controlled by **SOG**.

**HAU NGHIA.** A province just west of **Saigon**, bordering on the "**Parrot's Beak**" of **Cambodia**, created by **Ngo Dinh Diem** in 1963 out of portions of **Long An**, **Tay Ninh**, and Binh Duong provinces. It was a very insecure area in 1963, in mid-1965 it was the most Communist-controlled of the provinces immediately around Saigon, and it was still insecure in the early 1970s. Diem picked a minor hamlet to become the province capital; he renamed it Khiem Cuong, but many people continued to call it by its previous name of Bau Trai.

**HÉBERT, F[ELIX] EDWARD** (1901–1979). Congressman, Democrat of Louisiana. Born in New Orleans, Louisiana, he graduated from Tulane University and became a journalist, rising to city editor of the

*New Orleans States.* Hébert served in the U.S. House of Representatives from 1941 to 1976. His power was especially great after he became chairman of the House Armed Services Committee in 1971. He was a supporter of the U.S. military, and of the Vietnam War, feeling that **Lyndon Johnson** should have escalated the war much more rapidly than he did after the **Tonkin Gulf incidents** of 1964. His subcommittee of the Armed Services Committee conducted the only major congressional investigation of the **My Lai Massacre**. While Hébert and the subcommittee criticized the **Army**'s coverup of the massacre, they sympathized with some of the American personnel involved in the massacre. Hébert derailed the prosecution of at least one of them, Sergeant David Mitchell. Several of the people scheduled to be witnesses against Mitchell had testified before the subcommittee. Hébert refused to release transcripts of their testimony, and the judge at Mitchell's trial ruled that they could not testify against Mitchell at the trial if transcripts of their previous testimony before the subcommittee were not made available.

Hébert published a memoir, *Last of the Titans*, in 1976, his last year in **Congress**.

**HELICOPTER.** A rotary-wing aircraft; it is held in the air by the lifting power of one or two airfoils rotating in a horizontal plane. It is less stable in flight than a fixed-wing aircraft, but it can hover. United States helicopter designations usually begin with two letters, the first of which refers to the purpose of the helicopter (most often A for Attack, C for Cargo, O for Observation, or U for Utility) and the second of which is H for Helicopter. The first letter is often omitted; thus a CH-21 can simply be called an H-21.

The H-21 Shawnee had a rotor at either end of a long fuselage, the shape of which inspired the nickname "Flying Banana." The first U.S. **Army** helicopter companies in Vietnam, which arrived on December 11 and began operations on December 23, 1961, used the H-21.

The HUS-1, redesignated the UH-34D in November 1962, was a single-engine helicopter, built by Sikorsky, capable of carrying eight to 12 men loaded for combat (see photograph 9). The U.S. Army called it the Choctaw and the **Marines** called it the Sea Horse. The first Marine Corps squadron of Sea Horses arrived in Vietnam in April 1962 (*see Shufly*).

The UH-1 Iroquois, or "Huey," was the prototypical American helicopter in Vietnam. It was a tough, reliable aircraft, smaller than the

Shawnee and Choctaw and far more maneuverable, making it less vulnerable to ground fire. It was used very successfully for transporting troops and cargo, for **medical evacuation**, and as a **gunship**. Early models began to arrive in Vietnam in 1962.

The CH-37 Mohave, or "Deuce," saw limited use by Marine units in Vietnam; it could lift heavy loads but was not used for the purpose for which it had originally been designed, delivering troops into combat.

The CH-46 Sea Knight began to arrive in Vietnam, in Marine units, in March 1966. As originally designed it was supposed to be able to deliver 25 troops into combat, but the addition of armor and **machine guns** reduced the number to about 15.

The CH-47 Chinook, with a rotor at either end, was used mostly as a cargo carrier (see photograph 10). The early models, which arrived in Vietnam in 1965, had a payload of about 7,000 pounds when operating in the highlands, 8,000 pounds in the denser air of lower altitudes near the coast. The Chinook had enough lifting capacity to hoist a 105-mm howitzer, making it possible to create an **artillery** fire base on almost any clear hilltop, and navigation systems good enough to allow it to deliver ammunition and supplies to American units in darkness or bad weather.

The H-53 Sea Stallion was a very large, very powerful helicopter originally designed for the U.S. Marines, who wanted to be able to deliver a substantial number of Marines into battle in combat gear aboard a single aircraft; in Vietnam the standard load was reduced to 33 Marines late in 1970, but loads of 38 Marines had been common earlier, and much larger numbers of Asian troops were often carried. But the first CH-53s to arrive in Vietnam, at the beginning of 1967, were assigned the job of picking up smaller helicopters that had been shot down, to bring them back to U.S. bases for possible repair. Use of CH-53s as bombers (Operation *Thrashlight*), each helicopter dropping 8,000 pounds of **napalm** in 55-gallon drums, began in late May and early June 1970.

The **Air Force** operated some H-53s from Nakhon Phanom in **Thailand**. Some of these were CH-53s used for various special operations, mostly in **Laos** (inserting patrols and special units into enemy territory, carrying supplies to various military and paramilitary forces, etc.). These were armed with two 7.62-mm **miniguns**, and came equipped with titanium armor, but often flew with much of the armor removed to allow them to carry more men and cargo. Others were HH-53 "Jolly

Green Giants" used to rescue U.S. pilots who had been shot down in Laos or **North Vietnam** (*see* **search and rescue**). These were armed with three 7.62-mm miniguns, and had titanium armor.

The CH-54 Tarhe ("Sky Crane" or "Flying Crane") had no cargo compartment; its loads were either slung underneath, or carried in a detachable pod. It could lift up to 20,700 pounds; this allowed it to deliver 155-mm howitzers to hilltop fire bases. It began to arrive in Vietnam at the beginning of 1966.

Most observation helicopters, used to scout for enemy forces, were very small and light. The OH-13 Sioux was arriving in Vietnam with U.S. Army units not later than 1965. The OH-6 Cayuse, commonly called the "Loach," began to arrive in 1967 and was the most widely used observation helicopter in Vietnam. Only a few OH-23 Raven helicopters served in Vietnam. The OH-58 Kiowa, built by Bell Aircraft, was larger and more heavily armed than most observation helicopters; it began to arrive in 1969.

Several systems were devised by which a helicopter could pick men up from the ground even if there was no open space large enough for it to land. For pickups in areas that were actually covered with trees, a jungle penetrator had to be used. This was a steel cylinder, heavy enough so that when it was lowered on a cable from a hovering helicopter through the branches of jungle trees, it would not be stopped by the branches but would go down to the ground. Three one-man seats folded out of the bottom of the cylinder. If there was an opening in the trees, just not one wide enough to land a helicopter, a metal net might be lowered, which men could grab, but this was heavy enough to be a problem for the helicopter. A single rope, with loops attached to it at 10-foot intervals, worked very well to pick up teams of men wearing harnesses designed to allow each man to attach himself quickly and firmly to one of the loops. *See also* AIRMOBILE; GUNSHIP.

**HELICOPTER VALLEY.** American nickname for the Ngan Valley in **Quang Tri** province just south of the **Demilitarized Zone** (DMZ), in which numerous **helicopters** were shot down. The name was coined after four helicopters crashed there on July 15, 1966, during Operation *Hastings*, but the valley remained a danger spot for helicopters long after this.

**HELMS, RICHARD MCGARRAH** (1913–2002). Director of central intelligence. Born in St. Davids, Pennsylvania, he graduated from Williams College in 1935, and worked as a journalist. He became a naval officer in 1942, and joined the Office of Strategic Services (OSS) in 1943. He helped to organize the **Central Intelligence Agency** (CIA) in 1947. During his career at the CIA, he focused more on operations than on **intelligence** analysis.

Helms was deputy director for plans at the CIA from 1962 to 1965, deputy director of central intelligence from April 1965 to June 1966, and director of central intelligence, succeeding **William Raborn**, from June 1966 to February 1973. At the urging of President **Lyndon Johnson**, Helms began in 1966 various programs (*see* **Central Intelligence Agency**) to investigate dissidents within the United States, including the **anti-war movement**, in violation of the CIA's charter.

The views on Vietnam that Helms presented to other agencies, and to the president, generally reflected the consensus of his subordinates at the CIA; he was less inclined to bend intelligence reporting to fit a political agenda than **John McCone** had been. The most controversial issue was Operation *Rolling Thunder*. The CIA did not feel that the bombing of **North Vietnam** was a success, and from late 1966 onward the CIA seldom expressed much optimism that even a significant expansion of the bombing would achieve decisive results. These estimates annoyed some senior military officers enough so that Helms seems to have felt he could not afford to offend them in other ways. In 1966 and 1967, CIA analysts noticed that there were far more Communist personnel in **South Vietnam** than showed in the figures compiled by military intelligence agencies (*see* **Order of Battle Dispute**). In September 1967, Helms ordered his subordinates not to push for higher figures than the military was willing to accept.

**Richard Nixon**, as president, did not seem to have great trust in the CIA or in Helms. The CIA increasingly delivered raw intelligence data to the White House, so the staff there could make their own intelligence estimates instead of relying on the CIA's. Helms supported the **Cambodian Incursion** in 1970.

President Nixon decided late in 1972 to remove Helms as director of central intelligence, replacing him with James Schlesinger. Helms believed the reason for his dismissal was that he had not cooperated as fully as Nixon wished in the cover-up of the Watergate affair. Helms left the CIA in 1973 to become U.S. ambassador to Iran, where he served until 1977.

**HERBICIDES.** The United States began spraying herbicides from modified C-123 aircraft in **South Vietnam** in January 1962, under Operation *Ranch Hand.* Most spraying missions were intended to kill trees and brush to deprive Communist forces of cover, especially along the sides of roads, and along riverbanks. There was also some spraying to destroy crops in Communist-controlled areas. Large fixed-wing aircraft did most of the spraying, but **helicopters** and hand-held sprayers on the ground were sometimes used, particularly to clear brush around U.S. bases.

The program started out on a small scale, with about 5,700 acres sprayed in 1962, but grew rapidly and continuously until more than 1,500,000 acres were sprayed in 1967, the peak year. The scale of spraying remained very large in 1968 and 1969, but declined sharply in 1970. By late in that year spraying of trees and brush essentially ceased, and only a small amount of crop destruction continued. U.S. herbicide spraying ended in 1971, though the **Republic of Vietnam** continued some spraying. Estimates of the total quantity of herbicides used range from 17.7 million gallons to 19.1 million gallons.

The herbicides used are commonly known by the colors with which the U.S. labelled the drums holding them. More than half of all the herbicide sprayed was Agent Orange. Its active ingredients were esters of 2,4-D (2,4-dichlorophenoxyacetic acid) and 2,4,5-T (2,4,5-trichlorophenoxyacetic acid). Agents Pink, Green, and Purple were also based on 2,4-D and/or 2,4,5-T. Agent White used a mixture of ingredients, based on 2,4-D and picloram; Agent Blue was based on cacodylic acid.

2,4-D and 2,4,5-T were generally accepted as harmless to humans, but during the 1960s increasing worries were expressed about very toxic chemicals known as dioxins, which had not been included deliberately in any herbicides, but which were found in Agent Orange as contaminants, by-products of the manufacturing process. Arguments over the health hazards of the dioxins in Agent Orange were a major factor leading to the termination of Operation *Ranch Hand.* After the end of the war, the U.S. government long resisted claims, by many Vietnam veterans with cancers and other health problems, that these problems had been caused by Agent Orange.

**HILSMAN, ROGER** (1919– ). Born in Waco, Texas, Hilsman graduated from West Point in 1943, was wounded fighting behind Japanese lines in Burma in Merrill's Marauders, and then joined the Office of Strategic Services. He took a Ph.D. in International Relations at Yale University in 1951, and taught at Princeton from 1953 to 1956. He then went to work for the Legislative Reference Service at the Library of Congress (which does research on questions asked by the **Congress**), as head of the Foreign Affairs Division. It may have been there that he caught the eye of then-Senator **John F. Kennedy**; when Kennedy became president in 1961, he promptly appointed Hilsman director of the Bureau of Intelligence and Research (INR) at the State Department, where Hilsman served from February 1961 to April 1963. He felt U.S. policy in Vietnam should be based more on a political effort to win the allegiance of the peasants than on military action against the **Viet Cong**; he was an early advocate of **strategic hamlets**. By the end of 1962, he was becoming very pessimistic about the war, and very critical of President **Ngo Dinh Diem** of the **Republic of Vietnam** (**RVN**).

In April 1963, he became assistant secretary of state for Far Eastern affairs. Hilsman was one of the most important of the officials who advocated U.S. support for the idea of a **coup** against Ngo Dinh Diem in 1963; he and **W. Averell Harriman** were the principal authors of the cable of August 24, 1963, that authorized Ambassador **Henry Cabot Lodge** to signal to **ARVN** officers that the United States would not object to a coup.

President Kennedy encouraged Hilsman to report his doubts about the way the war was being conducted, even when Secretary of State **Dean Rusk** urged Hilsman not to rock the boat. (Long afterward, Hilsman became one of the principal advocates of the theory that Kennedy would have abandoned the war had he remained in office.) After Kennedy's assassination, Hilsman's influence declined, and he resigned from the State Department in February 1964. He became a professor at Columbia University in New York, and began writing a book, *To Move a Nation: The Politics of Foreign Policy in the Administration of John F. Kennedy*, published in 1967.

**HMONG.** The Hmong (the alternate name "Meo" is sometimes considered derogatory) were a people of the higher mountain areas in northern **Laos**. They practiced swidden ("slash-and-burn") agriculture, with **opium** as a cash crop. The Communist forces attempted to recruit the Hmong, but had very limited success; far larger numbers, led mainly by Touby Lyfoung (1919–1978) and **Vang Pao**, fought on the anti-Communist side. The "Secret Army" commanded by Vang Pao and supported by the **Central Intelligence Agency** was made up mostly of Hmong; it was the strongest ground force fighting against the **Pathet**

**Lao** and the People's Army of Vietnam (**PAVN**) in Laos from the mid-1960s through the early 1970s. It was based in the area south of the **Plain of Jars**, initially at Padong and later at **Long Cheng**. Following the end of the Second Indochina War in 1975, many Hmong fled Laos; some of those who remained continued armed resistance against the Communist government.

**HO BO WOODS.** A forested area, notorious as a **Viet Cong** stronghold, in **III Corps** about 15 kilometers north of **Cu Chi** and just west of the **Iron Triangle**. The first serious U.S. attack on it occurred during Operation *Crimp*, in January 1966.

**HO CHI MINH,** original name Nguyen Tat Thanh, a.k.a. Nguyen Ai Quoc and many other aliases (1890–1969). The man who was to found the Vietnamese Communist movement was born in Nghe An province of northern **Trung Bo**, son of a Confucian scholar. He attended the Quoc Hoc (National Academy) in **Hue**, and then in 1911 he left Vietnam as a cook's apprentice on an ocean liner. By the end of World War I he was in Paris, where he began using the name Nguyen Ai Quoc (Nguyen the Patriot) and joined the French Socialist Party. He presented a petition to the Paris Peace Conference requesting greater freedom for Vietnam, but was ignored. In 1920, he became a founding member of the French Communist Party. He later said that what had first led him to Communism was that the Communists seemed to be the only organized group offering to help countries like Vietnam attain independence.

He went to the **Soviet Union** for the first time in 1923. In November 1924, he arrived at Canton, in South **China**, as an agent of the Communist International (Comintern), assigned to develop a Communist movement in Vietnam. For many years he did this work at long distance; for him to have tried to do it on Vietnamese soil would have meant almost certain death at the hands of the French. (He was actually tried in absentia, and sentenced to death, in 1929.) He founded a proto-Communist organization, the Revolutionary Youth League of Vietnam (the Thanh Nien) in 1925, and presided over the founding of the Indochinese Communist Party (ICP) in 1930. He had held a relatively high rank in the Comintern's Bureau of the East in the 1920s, but by the early 1930s, he was less trusted. The Comintern suspected that he was too much a nationalist to be a good Communist.

He was arrested by the British police in Hong Kong in mid-1931, and held for a year and a half. In 1934 he returned to Moscow, where he worked for the Comintern, and studied, but had no significant influence on the ICP. He went to China in 1938, and in 1940 he re-established contact with the ICP organization inside Vietnam. At the end of that year, travelling under the new pseudonym of Ho Chi Minh, he returned to Vietnam for the first time since 1911. By May 1941, when the ICP Central Committee met at Pac Bo in extreme northern Vietnam, he had regained his position as leader of Vietnamese Communism. The meeting decided that the struggle for national independence must be made the highest priority, and that class struggle (which, according to Marxist doctrine, was supposed to be the heart of the revolution) would have to take second place. This meeting endorsed the creation of the Viet Nam Doc Lap Dong Minh (League for the Independence of Vietnam), commonly called the Viet Minh, a nationalist organization under Communist leadership.

Ho worked during World War II in northern Vietnam and southern China, promoting the development of the Viet Minh political organization and the first beginnings of a military force in Vietnam, while talking in China with non-Communist Vietnamese exile groups, Chinese authorities (who jailed him for more than a year), and the U.S.military. Ho cooperated eagerly with the Americans, providing intelligence about the Japanese in Indochina and rescuing downed American pilots, and won some American military aid in return.

In 1945, when Japan surrendered, Ho proclaimed the **Democratic Republic of Vietnam** (DRV) as an independent nation. In the opening paragraph of his Declaration of Independence he quoted from the American Declaration of Independence; he was doing everything he could think of to develop a relationship with the United States strong enough to give him some leverage when the French returned. But once the war against Japan was over, the United States wanted nothing further to do with him.

The French were returning before the end of September 1945. Ho tried desperately through most of 1946 to avoid a war against a nation so much more powerful than Vietnam—to negotiate some compromise allowing Vietnam partial independence along the lines of the British Commonwealth—but no compromise was possible; the French were determined to have more control over Vietnam than the Vietnamese were willing to grant. There was fighting in some areas even while the negotiations went on, and all-out war broke out in December 1946.

Ho Chi Minh led the DRV through the war against the French until 1954, then for a few years in peace, then in the war against the **Repub-**

**lic of Vietnam** and the United States until his death in 1969. His position as head of the Communist Party, renamed the **Lao Dong** (Workers') Party in 1951, was unquestioned. But he did not have the domination that the head of the Communist Party usually had in a Communist country; he presided over a collective leadership. In the late 1950s, his influence over domestic policy declined. He retained a major voice on diplomacy, and on strategy in the struggle for **South Vietnam**, until his health began to deteriorate seriously around 1965. His level of activity diminished gradually until his death in 1969.

**HO CHI MINH CITY.** At the end of the war in 1975, **Saigon**, which had been the capital of the **Republic of Vietnam**, was renamed Ho Chi Minh City. The name Saigon continued to be widely used, however. The city had swollen to a huge size during the 1960s, some migrants driven by the way military operations were devastating the countryside, others attracted by the prosperity American spending created in the city. The new Communist rulers made some effort during 1975 to shift people from the city back to the countryside, but this program was gradual and limited in scale; there was nothing like the sudden total evacuation that the **Khmer Rouge** enforced on **Phnom Penh** in April 1975. In 1976, the population of Ho Chi Minh City was 3,604,000.

**HO CHI MINH TRAIL.** The major land route by which men, weapons, and supplies were moved from **North Vietnam** to **South Vietnam**. It ran through the Truong Son (Annamese Cordillera), the mountain range along the border between Vietnam and the "**panhandle**" of southern **Laos**. The trail was established by **Group 559**, named for the date of its creation (May 1959). Initially it ran down the eastern side of the Truong Son, crossing the **Demilitarized Zone** (DMZ) directly and remaining within Vietnam. In 1961, it shifted to the west, detouring through Laos to bypass the DMZ. It was not a single trail, but rather a network.

For the first few years, it was a network of footpaths only, better suited to movement of troops than to the transportation of bulky cargoes. More than 40,000 men are said to have come down it by the end of 1963. There were of course no neatly defined dates for the shifts from foot traffic to bicycles (see photograph 16) and then to trucks, allowing larger quantities of munitions and supplies to be moved along it. Some portions of the trail were upgraded before others. But the key date for the decision to upgrade large sections of the trail to make them usable by trucks appears to have been 1964. Cargo being transported down the trail usually crossed from North Vietnam into Laos through the Nape Pass, the Mu Gia Pass, or the Ban Karai Pass, about 220, 115, and 55 kilometers, respectively, northwest of the DMZ. Troops coming down the trail often used crossing points closer to the DMZ. Construction of a gasoline pipeline running along the trail, allowing much more use of motor vehicles than had previously been possible, began in June 1968. The final link to create a continuous system of pipelines running from the Chinese border south as far as **Military Region 7** (in **III Corps**, by the territorial units the United States used) was completed in December 1972.

From 1965 to 1973, the United States used air power—mainly **B-52** bombers, fighter-bombers, and fixed-wing **gunships**—on a massive scale to try to block the flow of men and munitions down the trail. **Anti-aircraft** defenses expanded steadily; by 1972, **surface-to-air missiles** were seriously limiting the ability of the United States to use gunships over some crucial sections of the trail. On the ground, the United States sent only small teams under **SOG** to harass the trail (*see* Operations *Shining Brass, Prairie Fire*). *Lam Son 719*, an **ARVN** effort to block the trail in 1971, had U.S. air support but not U.S. troops or even **advisers** on the ground in Laos.

Figures on cargo have been inconsistent. A total figure of 1,500,000 tons had been given as the amount of cargo transported on the trail, but it has also been suggested that only a little more than 500,000 tons was actually delivered to destinations in South Vietnam.

**HO TAN QUYEN** (1927–1963). Commander of the **Vietnamese Navy** from 1959 to 1963. He was loyal to **Ngo Dinh Diem**, and was killed by one of his subordinates during the **coup** that overthrew Diem.

**HOA HAO.** The Hoa Hao **Buddhist** sect was founded in 1939 by a visionary named Huynh Phu So. It drew on the millenarian and secret-society traditions within Buddhism. Its center was in the western part of the **Mekong Delta**, near the Cambodian border. It began to acquire political and military power in the 1940s. In 1947, when the Hoa Hao were at war simultaneously against the French and the Viet Minh, the Viet Minh killed Huynh Phu So. In 1949, the Hoa Hao allied with the French. By 1954, they had no effective overall leader, but several Hoa Hao generals had substantial armies, and controlled significant areas.

Early in 1955, the Hoa Hao joined with the **Binh Xuyen** gangster organization and elements of the **Cao Dai** religious sect in a very serious challenge to Premier **Ngo Dinh Diem** (*see* Sects). By May 1955 it was plain that Diem was winning, but some Hoa Hao forces continued resistance. The last important Hoa Hao general at large, Ba Cut, was not captured until April 13, 1956; he was executed three months later. The Hoa Hao, with very strong grudges against both Diem and the Communists, faced difficult choices in the following years. Some joined the **Viet Cong**, but not many (the record has been confused by the way Viet Cong units that were not Hoa Hao sometimes masqueraded as Hoa Hao in the late 1950s). Hoa Hao Battalion 104 tried to fight both Diem and the Communists until 1962, when the growing military power of both the Viet Cong and the **ARVN** forced it to flee to **Cambodia**. Hoa Hao were rallying to the **Republic of Vietnam** in substantial numbers within a few months after Ngo Dinh Diem's overthrow in 1963, and from this point onward, the Hoa Hao became a strongly progovernment force. By the end of 1964, Hoa Hao were serving in **Civilian Irregular Defense Group** (CIDG) companies in An Giang, Kien Phong, and Kien Tuong provinces.

Early in 1975, however, when it became apparent the ARVN might be on the point of collapse, the Hoa Hao attempted once more to create independent armed forces, so they would not be dependent on the ARVN for protection against the Communists. President **Nguyen Van Thieu** refused to tolerate independent Hoa Hao forces; he ordered the Hoa Hao militia dissolved, and his efforts to disarm them led to clashes in several provinces of the Mekong Delta.

**HOANG MINH THAO** (probably 1921– ; some sources say 1919– ). **PAVN** general. He was born in Thai Binh province of the **Red River Delta**. He commanded the PAVN 304th Division from 1950 to 1953. During the Second Indochina War he was regarded as one of the best PAVN generals. He was first deputy commander, then commander of the B3 **Front**, the PAVN command for the **Central Highlands**, from late 1966 to 1974; he directed the attack on **Kontum** in the **Easter Offensive** of 1972. In August 1974, he was made deputy commander of **Military Region** 5 (the coastal provinces of Central Vietnam). He was briefly brought back to the Central Highlands to command the final Communist offensive there in March 1975, but on the completion of that campaign, returned immediately to MR5 to resume his responsibilities there, and take command of the forces assigned to seize **Cam Ranh**.

**HOANG VAN THAI,** original name Hoang Van Xiem, a.k.a. Muoi Khang, Tam Thanh (1915–1986). **PAVN** general. Born in Thai Binh province in the **Red River Delta**, he joined the Indochinese Communist Party in 1938. He became a friend of **Vo Nguyen Giap** in late 1944, when he was a member of the armed propaganda unit that was to become the nucleus for the PAVN. He became the first PAVN chief of staff in 1945. He was demoted to deputy chief of staff when **Van Tien Dung** became chief of staff (probably 1953, though there are sources giving dates of 1954 and 1957), but he remained very influential. In 1966, he was briefly made commander of **Military Region** 5 (the coastal provinces of Central Vietnam). From 1967 to 1973, he served at the **Trung uong cuc mien Nam** (COSVN), officially commander of the People's Liberation Army of South Vietnam. He served again as PAVN deputy chief of staff from 1974 to 1981.

**HOANG VAN THAI,** original name Huynh Duc Tui (1920– ). **PAVN** general. Born in **Quang Nam** province, he joined the Communist Party in 1945, and was one of the leaders of the Viet Minh siezure of power in Quang Binh province. He commanded **Group 559** from the end of 1965 to 1967. In 1969, he became deputy commander of the **Tri-Thien Military Region**, and it seems he held that position (sometimes combined with others) until 1974. In 1974, when the 2d Army Corps (*see* **PAVN**) was organized, initially based in **Thua Thien**, he became its first commander. *Note:* see p. 181 for another **Hoang Van Thai.**

**HOTFOOT.** A military training group, made up of U.S. **Army Special Forces** personnel "sheepdipped" to become nominal civilians and forbidden to wear military uniforms, was sent to **Laos** in July 1959 to train the Royal Lao Army. The first *Hotfoot* group, commanded by Lieutenant Colonel Arthur "Bull" Simons, served a six-month tour; a second group came in early 1960. The name was changed from *Hotfoot* to *Monkhood* in late 1960, and then to *White Star* when the United States decided to announce openly that there were U.S. military **advisers** in Laos, in the spring of 1961.

**HRE.** A **Montagnard** group, speaking a language in the Mon-Khmer group, living in a mountainous area inland from the city of Quang Ngai in southern **I Corps**. They are sometimes considered a subgroup of the **Sedang**.

**HUE.** A city on the Perfume River (Song Huong) in **Thua Thien** province of **I Corps**, Hue had been the capital of Vietnam under the Nguyen Dynasty, from 1802 until the French conquest. Many of the leaders of modern Vietnam, including **Ngo Dinh Diem, Ho Chi Minh, Pham**

**Van Dong**, and **Vo Nguyen Giap**, were educated at the Quoc Hoc (National Academy) in Hue. In 1968, Hue had a population of about 140,000; by 1975 it was perhaps slightly over 200,000.

The crisis that led to the overthrow of Ngo Dinh Diem began with a **Buddhist** demonstration in Hue on May 8, 1963. Hue was again a center for Buddhist opposition to the government from March to May 1966.

**PAVN** and **Viet Cong** units occupied Hue on the morning of January 31, 1968, in the **Tet Offensive**. They held the city as a whole for several days, and portions of it until February 24. They arrested government officials and others they regarded as enemies early in the occupation; many of these were executed, in what became known as the Hue Massacre as mass graves were discovered over the following months. By late 1969, it was reported that about 2,800 bodies had been found, though there is dispute as to whether all of these were actually victims of the massacre. PAVN General **Tran Van Quang** was reprimanded by his superiors for the massacre, but not severely punished.

In March 1975, **Republic of Vietnam** (RVN) **Marines** were pulled out of **Quang Tri** province, to the north of Thua Thien, to reinforce the defenses of Hue. This backfired; the occupation of the capital of Quang Tri by PAVN forces on March 20 triggered a panic in Hue. By March 21, civilians and **ARVN** soldiers were beginning to flee southward from Hue toward **Danang**. The ARVN decided on March 24 to abandon Hue, and the PAVN occupied the city without significant opposition March 26; by this time most of the population had left.

**HUEY.** Nickname for the UH-1 **helicopter**.

**HUMPHREY, HUBERT HORATIO** (1911–1978). U.S. senator, vice president. Born in Wallace, South Dakota, he graduated from the University of Minnesota in 1939 and then took an M.A. in political science at Louisiana State University. He was elected mayor of Minneapolis, Minnesota in 1945, and then elected to the United States Senate as a Democrat in 1948. He served in the Senate from 1949 to 1964. Humphrey was very liberal but also strongly anti-Communist, not only in foreign policy but domestically; in 1954 he proposed legislation to outlaw the Communist Party and impose criminal penalties on its members. In the early 1960s, he was very effective in helping Presidents **John Kennedy** and **Lyndon Johnson** get their programs through the Senate; he was floor manager for the Civil Rights Act of 1964. He was elected vice president, as Lyndon Johnson's running mate, in November 1964.

In February 1965, Vice President Humphrey argued against the *Flaming Dart* air strikes, and followed this with a memo to President Johnson generally opposing escalation of the war in Vietnam. Johnson excluded him from foreign policy decision making for a year thereafter. But early in 1966, Humphrey became a vigorous advocate of the war, which he said was going well; he strongly attacked critics of the war.

President Johnson announced in March 1968 that he would not run in the presidential election that year, and Humphrey won the Democratic Party's nomination in August. The nominating convention in Chicago, however, proved a disaster for him. The conflicts between supporters and opponents of the war in the convention hall, and the more violent ones between anti-war protesters and the Chicago police outside, made a poor backdrop for Humphrey's nomination.

Humphrey was still vice president; he could not easily go against President Johnson. Yet Johnson's Vietnam policies were terribly unpopular, and in the early part of the campaign, when Humphrey endorsed them, he lagged far behind Republican candidate **Richard Nixon** in the polls. When he began talking in September about beginning to withdraw U.S. troops from Vietnam in 1969, President Johnson was offended. On September 30, Humphrey said he would halt the bombing of North Vietnam. Following this the gap between Humphrey and Nixon narrowed rapidly, and Humphrey lost the election by only a very small margin (*see* **elections**).

Humphrey was elected to the Senate once again in 1970; he served until his death in 1978.

**HUYNH TAN PHAT** (1913–1989). Born in My Tho in the **Mekong Delta**, he probably joined the Indochinese Communist Party in 1936, though a date of 1940 has also been cited. When he participated in the organizing work that led in 1960 to the foundation of the **National Liberation Front** (NLF), he was a **Saigon** architect and was pretending to be a non-Communist. He was general secretary of the NLF from 1964 to 1966, and president of the **Provisional Revolutionary Government** (PRG) from 1969 to 1976. After the reunification of Vietnam, he became one of the deputy premiers (there were seven) of the Socialist Republic of Vietnam.

**HUYNH VAN CAO** (1927– ). **ARVN** general. Born to a **Catholic**

family probably in **Hue** (though some sources say **Quang Tri** province), he attended the Lycée Pellerin in Hue. He joined a French-sponsored regional militia in 1946, and became an officer on graduation from a military academy in Hue in 1949 or 1950. He commanded a platoon 1950–1951, a company 1951–1952, and a battalion 1953–1954. Cao became chief of **Ngo Dinh Diem**'s personal military staff 1955–1957, and then commanded the ARVN 13th Infantry Division 1957–1958. He was sent for training in 1958 to the U.S. Army's Command and General Staff College, in Fort Leavenworth, Kansas, and then from 1959 to 1962 he commanded the 7th Division, a crucial unit because it was in the northern part of the **Mekong Delta**, close enough to **Saigon** to be part of Diem's defense against possible **coups**. In December 1962, Cao was promoted to brigadier general and given command of the newly created **IV Corps**. Cao's conspicuous loyalty to Diem was the main reason he had been given this position, and he lost it after Diem's overthrow. From 1965 to 1966 he was director of the General Political Warfare Department under the Joint General Staff. He was not a man greedy either for money or for power; he avoided involvement in the factional struggles for power in the mid-1960s.

General Cao accepted command of **I Corps** on May 16, 1966, during the **Buddhist** uprising there, when more influential ARVN generals did not want the job. He firmly resisted pressure from **Nguyen Ngoc Loan** to attack a Buddhist pagoda in **Danang**. He was removed from command of I Corps at the end of May. In July, a military court convicted him of supporting the Buddhists and ordered him retired from the ARVN, though it allowed him to keep his pension. In 1967, the predominantly Catholic Troi Viet (Vietnamese Sun) slate of candidates, which he headed, won election to the Senate (*see* **elections**). In the 1970 senatorial election he again headed a slate, and again won. He was first deputy chairman of the Senate 1970–1971.

## - I -

**IA DRANG VALLEY.** On October 19, 1965, the 33d and 320th Regiments of the People's Army of Vietnam (**PAVN**) attacked the **Special Forces** camp at Plei Me, in the **Central Highlands** south of **Pleiku**. PAVN forces had been in **South Vietnam** for almost a year, but they had been taking a considerable time getting adjusted to the area; this was one of the first offensive actions they had taken. After the attack on Plei Me had been beaten off, General **William Westmoreland** ordered the 1st **Cavalry Division (Airmobile)** to pursue the retreating PAVN forces and destroy as many of them as possible, taking advantage of the tremendous mobility that **helicopters** gave the division. The 1st Cavalry Division inflicted especially severe losses on the PAVN 33d Regiment as it retreated toward the Ia Drang Valley, southwest of Pleiku near the Cambodian border. In that valley, however, the Americans encountered more opposition.

The most famous action of the Ia Drang Valley campaign began on November 14, when elements of the 1/7 Cavalry Battalion were airlifted into a clearing that the Americans designated Landing Zone X-Ray (see photograph 2). Much of the PAVN 66th Regiment was on a hill overlooking the landing zone, and attacked immediately. American reinforcements arrived only slowly, and the position seemed for a while in serious danger of being overrun, but effective combat performance by the U.S. troops, combined with plentiful air and **artillery** support, enabled them to hold their perimeter and inflict very heavy casualties on their attackers.

After the battle at X-Ray was over, the 2/7 Cavalry Battalion was ordered to march from there to another clearing slightly more than three kilometers north of X-Ray, designated Landing Zone Albany. As they arrived at Albany in the early afternoon of November 17, they were caught in a surprise attack by one battalion of the 66th PAVN Regiment and one battalion (understrength because of losses in the previous weeks' fighting) of the 33d. The U.S. troops were strung out in march formation, with many of the officers away from their units, conferring with one another at the head of the column. Portions of the 2/7 were overrun; total American losses at the Battle of Landing Zone Albany were 155 killed and 124 wounded.

The American command was very satisfied with the Battle of the Ia Drang overall. American casualties had been substantial, but PAVN casualties had been far higher.

***IGLOO WHITE*** (originally *Muscle Shoals*). A program under which the movements of Communist personnel and vehicles were detected by electronic **sensors**. The sensors were usually dropped from aircraft. A spike going into the ground held them upright; the portions above ground level looked like small bushes. Various types of sensors detected sounds, smells, or vibrations in the ground. Information broadcast by the sensors would be picked up by an **EC-121R** *Batcat* aircraft, which would relay it to the Infiltration Surveillance Center at Nakhon Phanom, in **Thailand**. *Igloo White* sensors began to be dropped in **Laos** late in 1967. They had a considerable impact on the fighting for **Khe Sanh** in 1968. Adequate attention, however, was not always paid to the data from such sensors. Sensor signals indicating much movement in the vicinity of the **Demilitarized Zone** (DMZ) should have provided warning of the attack across the DMZ into **Quang Tri** Province in the **Easter Offensive** of 1972, but this information was essentially ignored and the attack came as a surprise.

**INCAPACITATING AGENTS.** Non-lethal chemicals that render an enemy unable to fight, or unable to fight effectively. The U.S. made massive use of **CS**, sometimes called "super tear gas," and somewhat more limited use of Adamsite (DM), 10-chloro-5,10-dihydrophenarsazine.

**INDIA.** A neutral country at a time in the Cold War when few such existed, India was chosen in 1954 as the balancing element on the **International Control Commission** (ICC) set up under the **Geneva Accords**, standing between Communist Poland and anti-Communist **Canada**. The border conflict between India and **China** that culminated in the border war of late 1962 shifted India to an anti-Communist stance, which affected Indian behavior in Vietnam, but by this time the ICC had become so irrelevant that the **Republic of Vietnam** (RVN) did not profit much from India's shift in attitude. By 1966, India was becoming more favorable to the **Democratic Republic of Vietnam** (DRV) once more; Prime Minister Indira Gandhi repeatedly called for a halt to U.S. bombing of **North Vietnam**.

U.S. support for Pakistan in its 1971 war with India may have been a factor pushing India farther in sympathy for the Communist side in Vietnam. In 1972, India announced the establishment of full diplomatic relations with the DRV, but not with the RVN, and high Indian officials made public comments bitterly critical of U.S. policy in Vietnam.

**INFILTRATION,** of Communist forces and supplies into **South Vietnam**. Communist military personnel were sent into South Vietnam primarily by land, along the **Ho Chi Minh Trail**. From 1959 to 1964, those sent were almost all natives of South Vietnam, who had gone north in 1954 or 1955, and were being sent back to the South. Significant numbers of northerners began to be sent south to be spread out as individuals, among units made up primarily of southerners, around the middle of 1964. The first **PAVN** regiments made up predominantly of northerners that remained together as units once in the South began to arrive in

December 1964; there is some information suggesting that units of company or battalion size may have arrived significantly earlier.

Weapons, ammunition, and supplies were sent both by land and by sea. Some went down the Ho Chi Minh Trail, although until about 1964, deliveries by this route were limited primarily to what the soldiers coming down the trail carried for their own use. Some were delivered to the South Vietnamese coast by substantial cargo vessels of **Group 759** beginning in September 1962. Some were carried on civilian cargo vessels that sailed openly into ports in **Cambodia** (though the fact that they carried munitions was secret), and the cargoes were then smuggled across Cambodia to be delivered to Communist forces along the South Vietnamese border (*see* **Sihanouk Trail**).

**INFRASTRUCTURE.** There were large areas of **South Vietnam** where the **Viet Cong** had a functioning government structure, with some degree of control over the population. Americans referred to Communist political and administrative organizations in such areas as the Viet Cong Infrastructure (VCI). There were political organizers, tax collectors, local administrative personnel, and heavily armed police units with a considerable combat capability. In some areas the infrastructure competed for power with the government apparatus of the **Republic of Vietnam** (RVN); many villages were administered predominantly by the RVN in daylight, and by the VCI at night. In other areas RVN authority was at times eliminated, and the VCI was the only functioning government.

The RVN managed to destroy most of the VCI in the middle and late 1950s, but it regained strength dramatically in the 1960s. The *Phoenix* **Program**, begun in 1967 and 1968, was supposed to coordinate U.S. and RVN attacks on the VCI. This program, and the weakening of the Viet Cong military forces that had previously provided support and protection, led to a dramatic weakening of the VCI by 1971. It was not, however, so nearly eliminated as some authors have suggested.

**INTELLIGENCE.** The United States relied more on high-tech means of gathering intelligence information than on the recruitment of human agents in Vietnam. The National Security Agency, the Army Security Agency, and the Naval Security Group obtained signals intelligence (SIGINT) by monitoring enemy radio traffic. Aircraft with radio direction-finding gear circled over the jungles, locating enemy radio transmitters for attack. Other aircraft took photographs, used side-looking airborne **radar**, starlight scopes, and infrared vision devices to spot enemy forces in the dark, used "people-sniffer" **sensors** to detect them by their odors, or monitored sensors on the ground that detected the vibrations of footsteps or vehicular movements. Captured documents, interrogation of prisoners, and the reports of **Long-Range Patrol** units also provided valuable information.

The **Central Intelligence Agency** (CIA) had a significant number of intelligence officers in Vietnam, but the number of Military Intelligence personnel there was far larger. The effectiveness of Military Intelligence was compromised by the system of the one-year **tour**. Intelligence officers who were in Vietnam for only a year seldom acquired a deep knowledge of the culture or of the areas where they served, especially since the military seldom thought it worth the investment of time and effort to teach a man to speak Vietnamese fluently before putting him in an intelligence job in Vietnam that he was expected to hold for only a year. The problem was accentuated when an intelligence job was filled not with an intelligence officer on a one-year tour, but with an infantry officer who was put in the position for a few weeks while his superiors waited for a vacancy to open up in a combat unit.

In the later stages of the war, the *Phoenix* **Program** established in every province and every district a center for coordination of intelligence from various sources and organizations, and for interrogation of prisoners.

There were sometimes disputes between U.S. intelligence agencies, and accusations that the intelligence estimates some of them furnished to policy makers were subject to political bias. The CIA tended to be more pessimistic about the war than the various military intelligence agencies (*see* **Central Intelligence Agency, Order of Battle Dispute**). The Bureau of Intelligence and Research (INR), the State Department's own intelligence agency, was more pessimistic about the war in Vietnam than the CIA and much more so than the military intelligence agencies. This seriously annoyed the **Joint Chiefs of Staff** and Secretary of Defense **Robert McNamara**.

The **Republic of Vietnam** (RVN) also had a variety of intelligence agencies, military and civilian. They had a greater ability to recruit or place agents within Communist organizations, but they were also much more vulnerable to penetration by Communist agents than the U.S. agencies were. **Ngo Dinh Nhu** and the Social and Political Research Department coordinated intelligence agencies up to 1963; later in the war the Central Intelligence Office provided some coordination.

The Communists relied much more on direct gathering of intelligence by human personnel. They had very extensive networks of agents within government-controlled areas, ranging from ordinary citizens to high government officials. Employees of the Americans, both on U.S. military bases and elsewhere, included many Communist agents. **Reconnaissance** teams on foot did much of the work that the U.S. and the RVN did with aircraft. The only high-tech means of intelligence gathering that the Communists are known to have used to an important degree was signals intelligence.

The identities of a number of important Communist agents within the government are known. Most of them were or at least pretended to be **Catholic**; the Catholic Church in Vietnam was strongly anti-Communist, so Catholicism was a perfect cover for a Communist agent.

—Colonel **Pham Ngoc Thao**, an **ARVN** officer, played an important role in the **Strategic Hamlet** program, and in 1963 and 1964 was heavily involved in the plotting of various potential military **coups**. The CIA was aware there were rumors he was a Communist agent, and speculated uneasily what would happen if one of his plots actually succeeded, and he gained control of the government of **South Vietnam**.

—Vu Ngoc Nha, from Thai Binh province in the **Red River Delta**, joined the Communist Party in 1949 and was sent south in 1955, pretending to be one of the anti-Communist Catholics fleeing from the Communist victory in the North. He ran a Communist intelligence network in the South until he was caught and imprisoned. But after **Ngo Dinh Diem** was overthrown and killed, Nha was released from prison; Communist agents were able to destroy the records indicating that he had been identified as a spy. He was then able to resume his espionage career, not only running a network of agents, but himself becoming an influential friend and adviser to President **Nguyen Van Thieu**. He was arrested for a second time in 1969, as a result of an investigation initiated by the CIA.

—**Nguyen Huu Hanh**, an ARVN colonel, was appointed in 1967 as head of the 44th Special Tactical Zone, in charge of ARVN efforts to block infiltration from **Cambodia** into **IV Corps**; it is likely that in this position he was able to assist the **Viet Cong** forces in preparing for the **Tet Offensive** of 1968. During the last hours before the fall of **Saigon**, on April 30, 1975, he was the senior ARVN officer, and thus acting commander, at Joint General Staff Headquarters in Saigon.

**INTERNATIONAL COMMISSION OF CONTROL AND SUPERVI-SION** (ICCS). This body was established under the **Paris Peace Agreement** of 1973, to monitor compliance with the agreement and investigate violations. It originally was made up of equal numbers of personnel from Communist Hungary and Poland, and anti-Communist **Canada** and Indonesia. No neutrals were included. The ICCS was totally helpless right from the start; it did not have even the limited effectiveness of the **International Control Commission**, which had tried to enforce the **Geneva Accords of 1954**. Both sides were violating the Paris agreement much more flagrantly in 1973 than either side had violated the Geneva Accords in 1954, and the ICCS could not take any formal action, not even the issuance of a statement denouncing the violations, unless its members, Communist and anti-Communist, could agree unanimously on the action in question.

The greatest danger facing the ICCS was travelling by **helicopter** over Communist-held areas. The Communist forces had for so long been able to assume that all aircraft were hostile that some of them, still subject to air attack by forces of the **Republic of Vietnam**, were slow to learn that the clearly marked ICCS helicopters were not to be fired upon. On April 7, 1973, an ICCS helicopter wandered out of its designated safe flight corridor in **Quang Tri** province and was shot down by a **surface-to-air missile**; all who were aboard died. Several other ICCS helicopters were fired upon, though with less disastrous results, when not seriously out of their flight corridors. Two Canadian officers of the ICCS were detained, accused of being American spies, while trying to move through a Communist-held area on the ground on June 30. They were held until mid-July.

Canada had begun threatening to withdraw from the ICCS as early as March 1973; External Affairs Minister Mitchell Sharp said "Canadians should not take part in a charade." Canada did formally withdraw on July 31, and was eventually replaced by Iran.

**INTERNATIONAL CONTROL COMMISSION** (ICC). Formally called the International Commission for Supervision and Control in Vietnam, this body was set up to enforce the **Geneva Accords of 1954**. Communist Poland, anti-Communist **Canada**, and neutral **India** each supplied one-third of the personnel; India supplied the chairman. ICCs with the same composition were set up to supervise the implementation of the accords in **Laos** and in **Cambodia**.

The ICC was never able to make the Communist and anti-Communist forces in Vietnam obey any clause of the accords that they were determined to violate, but for a while both sides tried to remain at least partially in compliance with the accords, hoping to avoid being accused by the ICC of flagrant violation. By the 1960s, the ICC's only important role was as a facilitator of communication. J. Blair Seaborn, who became the chief Canadian representative on the ICC in mid-1964, served during the following months as a private intermediary for communication between Washington and **Hanoi**. Even after systematic bombing of **North Vietnam** began in 1965, there was an ICC aircraft that continued to make semi-regular flights (sometimes cancelled when U.S. bombing was unusually heavy) from **Phnom Penh** and Vientiane to Hanoi, bringing people and supplies to the ICC office there. This was Hanoi's only direct air link with the non-Communist world, and was the usual means of transport for Western journalists and others visiting North Vietnam.

**INTERNATIONAL VOLUNTARY SERVICES** (IVS). A private non-profit organization (though much of its funding came from the U.S. government), IVS was established in 1953 to assist education and economic development in Third World nations. It may have provided some of the inspiration for the U.S. Peace Corps. Originally an American organization, it grew to include volunteers from a variety of nations. IVS began to send volunteers to **South Vietnam** in 1957, and Vietnam became a major focus for the organization; there were about 80 IVS volunteers there at the beginning of 1969.

As the struggle in South Vietnam intensified, some members of IVS supported U.S. policy. An IVS volunteer near **Ban Me Thuot** in the **Central Highlands**, who felt that a new paramilitary force was needed to fight the Communists in the area, talked with an officer of the **Central Intelligence Agency** (CIA) in 1961, and after the two of them had come up with a plan for the CIA to provide arms for a force recruited from among the local villages, resigned from IVS to work for the CIA winning the agreement of village elders and putting the plan into effect. The force he helped create became the nucleus for the **Civilian Irregular Defense Groups**.

Other IVS volunteers became hostile to U.S. policy, feeling that U.S. military operations were devastating Vietnam. Don Luce, who arrived in 1958 to work in agricultural development, and was director of IVS for South Vietnam from 1961 to 1967, became so distressed that he resigned from IVS in 1967 so as to be able to speak publicly against U.S.

policy. He became an influential opponent of the war, responsible for example for publicizing the **"tiger cages"** in the prison on **Poulo Condore** island in 1970.

***IRON HAND.*** American bombing missions, beginning in August 1965, attacking **surface-to-air missile** launch sites in **North Vietnam**. *See also WILD WEASEL.*

**IRON TRIANGLE.** An old Communist base area, dating back to the First Indochina War, lying mostly in the southern part of Binh Duong province. Its borders were approximately defined on the southwest by the Saigon River, on the east by the Thi Tinh River, and on the north by a line running from Ben Suc east to Ben Cat. The southern tip of the Iron Triangle was only about 20 kilometers from the northern edge of **Saigon**. It contained the headquarters for the **Viet Cong**'s Saigon-**Gia Dinh** Military Region. The 173d **Airborne** Brigade launched the first major U.S. attack on the Iron Triangle on October 8, 1965, but this achieved only modest success.

The considerably larger Operation *Cedar Falls* began on January 8, 1967. Its goals were to destroy Viet Cong forces and facilities in and near the Iron Triangle to the extent that they could be found; to remove all civilians (mostly the inhabitants of Ben Suc and three smaller villages on the north edge of the Triangle, a total of about 6,000 people), so the area could become a **free fire zone**; and to strip off concealment from crucial areas by using bulldozers (including the very large **Rome Plows**) to obliterate the villages that had been evacuated, and also 11 square kilometers of jungle—not only crucial areas, but also strips that were simply cut through the jungle, so that enemy troops moving through the area in the future would be in danger of being seen while crossing the cleared strips. Official totals for the operation showed almost 750 Viet Cong killed, many prisoners taken, and 3,700 tons of rice captured. The Iron Triangle was seriously weakened as a Communist base, but not eliminated.

# - J -

**JAPAN.** The United States had many military facilities in Japan. The most important of these were on the island of **Okinawa**, which had been under direct American administration since World War II. Only the bases on Okinawa were used for launching direct combat missions against targets in Vietnam. But various facilities on the main islands of Japan, such as the shipyards at Sasebo and Yokosuka, were extremely important to the war.

Politically, the Japanese public was not very sympathetic to the American war effort in Vietnam. The ability of the United States to continue using Japanese bases to support a war effort of which most of the Japanese public disapproved was due partly to the fact that the Japanese government was dominated by men who were politically conservative, and more sympathetic with U.S. policy than the Japanese public as a whole, and partly to the fact that the war was economically profitable for Japan. U.S. bases and military personnel in Japan, and U.S. purchases of equipment and supplies from Japan, pumped money into the Japanese economy. Also, the U.S. government was generous in trade dealings with Japan, allowing Japanese manufacturers to compete with American manufacturers on more favorable terms than would have been likely to be tolerated under normal circumstances, as a sort of quid pro quo for the Japanese government's support of U.S. policy in Vietnam.

Japan did a lot of trade with South Vietnam, but also a little with the North. Japanese merchant ships were occasionally seen visiting **Haiphong** in the late 1960s, though not in the early 1970s.

In September 1973, Japan and the **Democratic Republic of Vietnam** (DRV) reached an agreement for the establishment of diplomatic relations, but Japan did not withdraw diplomatic recognition from the **Republic of Vietnam** (RVN), and it was the RVN, not the DRV, that got significant Japanese aid ($54.6 million) in 1974. As a result of Japan's decision to remain friendlier to the RVN than to the DRV, the September 1973 agreement did not lead to the actual opening of a Japanese embassy in **Hanoi** until after the war had ended in 1975.

**JARAI,** Gia Rai. A **Montagnard** group speaking a Malayo-Polynesian language. Their territory stretches from the Darlac Plateau of the **Central Highlands**, around **Pleiku**, west into **Cambodia**. Many Jarai served in the **Civilian Irregular Defense Groups**, but some were also among the early recruits to **Khmer Rouge** armed forces in Ratanakiri province of Cambodia between 1968 and 1970.

**JOHNSON, HAROLD KEITH** (1912–1983). U.S. **Army** general. Born in Bowesmont, North Dakota, he graduated from West Point in 1933. A survivor of the Bataan "death march" of 1942, he remained a prisoner of the Japanese until 1945. As a regimental commander in the 1st

**Cavalry** Division in Korea 1950–1951, he objected to scorched-earth policies under which U.S. troops, when retreating, were to burn villages and blow up bridges. He was also less enthusiastic than many generals about air support and massive use of heavy weapons. He succeeded **Earle Wheeler** as U.S. Army chief of staff on July 3, 1964.

In March 1965, President **Lyndon Johnson** sent General Johnson to Vietnam with instructions to come up with ideas for the war, and the general, with some hesitation, returned recommending a **division** of U.S. troops be sent into the **Central Highlands**. The 1st Cavalry Division (**Airmobile**) was sent that summer.

General Johnson was the member of the **Joint Chiefs of Staff** who pushed the president hardest, in 1965, to mobilize the **Reserves**. There is a widely believed story that at the end of July, after the president's decision not to mobilize the Reserves or declare a national emergency, General Johnson actually got into a car and had the driver take him to the White House where he intended to resign in protest; he changed his mind only when he reached the White House gate. It is also said that in August 1967, he urged his colleagues on the Joint Chiefs to resign en masse in protest against the way President Johnson and Secretary of Defense **Robert McNamara** were running the war.

General Johnson was briefly acting chairman of the Joint Chiefs of Staff in September 1967, while General Earle Wheeler was recovering from a mild heart attack. He was Army chief of staff until July 1968, when he retired from the Army.

**JOHNSON, LYNDON BAINES** (1908–1973).  President of the United States.  Born in Stonewall, Texas, he graduated from Southwest Texas State Teachers College in 1930.  He was elected to the U.S. House of Representatives as a Democrat, and a strong supporter of the New Deal, in 1937.  When World War II broke out, he (like a few others) joined the military without resigning from Congress.  When told he would have to choose, Johnson resigned his commission as a naval officer in mid-1942 to remain in Congress.

In 1948, he won election to the U.S. Senate, and then rose to great power in it faster than was usual in that seniority-conscious body.  He became majority leader in 1955.  He was superbly skilled in legislative maneuvering, knowing what inducements or pressures could get a senator to vote the way he wanted.

He tried for the Democratic nomination in the presidential race of 1960, but was defeated by **John F. Kennedy**, who then offered him the vice-presidential nomination. They barely won against **Richard Nixon** and **Henry Cabot Lodge**. Johnson was unhappy as vice president. He did not fit into the group around Kennedy, made up mostly of younger men who had graduated from elite universities.

Vice President Johnson was probably exaggerating, striking a strong Cold War stance because he thought it was expected of him, when in 1961 he called **Ngo Dinh Diem** the "Winston Churchill of Southeast Asia," and said the United States must either draw the line against the Communists in Vietnam and **Thailand**, or else pull its defenses back to San Francisco. But he was clearly sincere in 1963 when he argued the United States should continue supporting Diem, rather than throw U.S. support to the officers of the Army of the Republic of Vietnam (**ARVN**) who were plotting the **coup** that overthrew Diem.

The assassination of John Kennedy on November 22, 1963, made Johnson president. His concerns were primarily domestic; he was much less interested in foreign affairs than Kennedy had been. Johnson wanted strong civil rights legislation, a tax cut to stimulate the economy, and what he called the "Great Society," a package of programs in education, health, and the "War on Poverty." To make these things possible he cut spending on the military. Kennedy had always devoted over 46 percent of the federal budget to the military; Johnson managed to cut this to under 42 percent in fiscal year 1965 (July 1964 to June 1965).

Johnson feared, however, right from the beginning, that the war in Vietnam might expand to a scale that would drain money from his domestic programs. Top officials through most of 1963 had been comparatively optimistic about the war. They thought it could be won by the ARVN with a moderate amount of American weaponry and money, and little enough direct American participation in combat that this participation could be kept quiet, and a public pretense maintained that the Americans were there only as **advisers**. In the last weeks of Kennedy's life, they had begun to acknowledge that the struggle against the **Viet Cong** guerrillas had not been going as well as the reports had been saying; within weeks after Kennedy's death they were realizing that the war was going very badly. The men Kennedy had chosen for the top positions in foreign affairs and defense—Secretary of State **Dean Rusk**, Secretary of Defense **Robert McNamara**, Chairman of the **Joint Chiefs of Staff Maxwell Taylor**, Director of Central Intelligence **John McCone**, and Special Assistant for National Security Affairs **McGeorge Bundy**—all urged Johnson to stand firm in Vietnam, and expand the war if necessary rather than allow the guerrillas to win.

It was plain to Johnson that if he allowed the Communists to win in Vietnam he would be widely seen as having betrayed Kennedy's policies, and he believed this would be a political disaster. It is also likely that he had some genuine belief in the **domino theory**, which said that an American pullout from Vietnam would trigger a chain reaction in which many other countries would quickly fall to Communism.

In January 1964, Johnson approved *OPLAN 34A*, a program of covert attacks against **North Vietnam**, but these were pinpricks not really expected to have much effect; *OPLAN 34A* was what Johnson and his advisers did so they would be able to tell one another they were doing *something*, while they tried to make up their minds to do something big enough to matter. Contingency planning for a serious bombing campaign against North Vietnam went on for most of 1964, but Johnson did not want to put such plans into effect at all, and he especially did not want to do so before the 1964 presidential **election**. The Republican Party nominated **Barry Goldwater**, a very conservative and stridently anti-Communist senator who advocated strong action in Vietnam. Johnson ran as the man of peace, and portrayed Goldwater as trigger-happy and unstable, and likely to get the United States into an unnecessary war.

In the first of the **Tonkin Gulf incidents**, on August 2, 1964, a U.S. destroyer exchanged fire with three torpedo boats off the coast of North Vietnam. On August 4, in a very confused night incident much farther from the coast, two destroyers mistakenly reported they were being attacked by torpedo boats. Johnson bombed North Vietnam in retaliation on August 5, which allowed him to look tough, refuting Goldwater's charges that his Vietnam policy was weak and fearful. The **Congress** passed almost unanimously on August 7 the **Tonkin Gulf Resolution**, giving Johnson authority to use whatever force might be necessary in Vietnam; the Johnson administration found this most convenient the following year.

Johnson would have won the election without these incidents, but probably not by the wide margin—he got over 61 percent of the popular vote—that he achieved in November 1964. The incidents left less pleasant legacies. Johnson's discovery a few days after the retaliatory air strikes that there probably had not been any attack on the destroyers on August 4 may have undermined his faith in the military. And when some members of the Congress, the press, and the public realized a few years later that much of what they had been told about the incidents had been false, this certainly undermined their faith in Johnson.

The guerrillas continued to grow stronger in **South Vietnam**, and by early 1965 the Johnson administration was simply waiting for an appropriate incident to trigger more U.S. air strikes against North Vietnam. Guerrillas shelled the **helicopter** base at **Pleiku** on February 7, destroying several aircraft and killing several Americans, and Johnson once again bombed in retaliation. In March he began Operation *Rolling Thunder*, an extended bombing of North Vietnam no longer tied to specific incidents, and sent **Marine** battalions to guard the air base at **Danang**. By the end of 1965, there were 184,000 U.S. military personnel in South Vietnam, and more were coming fast as the war expanded. Many who had supported Johnson as the peace candidate in the 1964 election were shocked. Many American military leaders, on the other hand, were shocked by the restraints he imposed on expansion of the war outside South Vietnam, and by the gradual, low-key approach he adopted even in regard to South Vietnam.

Johnson remembered how General Douglas MacArthur had assured President Harry Truman in 1950 that the United States could invade North Korea, in retaliation for the North Korean attack on South Korea, without provoking a war with **China**. He distrusted assurances from his generals in 1965 that they could bomb **Hanoi** and **Haiphong** without provoking a war with China and/or the **Soviet Union**. He allowed them a comparatively free choice of targets in the southern part of North Vietnam, but tightly limited bombing in the northern part, at first entirely prohibiting bombing near Hanoi and Haiphong. He allowed heavy bombing of the areas of **Laos** where the Vietnamese Communist forces had bases and supply lines, but not of the areas of **Cambodia** where they had much smaller bases. He forbade significant ground operations by U.S. troops into North Vietnam, Laos, or Cambodia.

Johnson took the United States to war in 1965 by small steps, making a deliberate effort to ensure that the increase in military activities from one week to the next was never enough to imply a dramatic change in policy, or to trigger a major national discussion of where the policy was going. The longer he could keep the Congress from realizing how big and expensive the war was going to become, the more components of his Great Society he could get the Congress to pass. He did not ask for a declaration of war, and he dismayed military leaders by his decision in July 1965 not to proclaim a national emergency or mobilize the **Reserves**.

Johnson did not want to inspire a war psychology among the American people. Doing so would have made it hard to maintain the limits on U.S. action against North Vietnam, which he considered necessary to avoid a disastrous war with China or the Soviet Union, but he also felt this would be unhealthy for American society. There was a significant **anti-war movement** even in 1965; Johnson did not want the majority who supported his policies to decide the anti-war protesters were traitors, and rise up and smite them, because he felt such polarization would poison national life. Some of the protesters reciprocated his courtesy; others chanted "Hey, hey, LBJ, how many kids did you kill today?" Most of the American public had supported Johnson's decisions in 1965, expecting a relatively quick and cheap victory. As the war became steadily larger and more expensive without producing victory, support declined and the anti-war movement grew.

The Communist forces in South Vietnam grew stronger from 1965 to 1967, despite the efforts of increasing numbers of American ground troops, and the enormous amount of air power applied against them. Johnson was whipsawed in a rancorous debate. Most of his top military officers said he must loosen restrictions on actions outside South Vietnam; what they mainly wanted was permission to bomb much more freely in the northern half of North Vietnam, and to **mine** Haiphong harbor. Many of Johnson's civilian advisers told him that such measures would not win the war any more than past measures had, and might trigger a disastrous Chinese or Soviet intervention. Some of them urged him to halt the bombing of North Vietnam, rather than expand it. Johnson loosened the restrictions gradually, watching for Soviet and Chinese reactions. He allowed bombing of fuel storage facilities on the outskirts of Hanoi in June 1966, and of considerable numbers of targets on the outskirts and some near the center of the city in 1967.

By late 1967, in an effort to shore up public support for the war, military spokesmen were saying that the Communists were weakening and that victory in the war might be approaching. The **Tet Offensive** that began at the end of January 1968 came as a stunning shock. For four consecutive months—February, March, April, and May 1968— the number of Americans killed in action each month was larger that it had ever been in any month of the war before the Tet Offensive. In the end the Communists were defeated with heavy losses, but they would not have been able to make the effort if they had been as weak, before the offensive, as U.S. spokesmen had been saying. The effect on the overall pattern of U.S. public opinion was less than has often been suggested; public support for the war had been declining for two years, and the Tet Offensive did not greatly accelerate the decline. The effect on elite opinion was much greater. Tet turned many very influential people, including **Clark Clifford**, just coming into office as Johnson's new secretary of defense, against the war.

General **Earle Wheeler** (chairman of the Joint Chiefs of Staff) and General **William Westmoreland** (commander of U.S. forces in South Vietnam) asked Johnson to mobilize the Reserves, so that substantial reinforcements, perhaps as many as 206,000 men, could be sent to Vietnam. Instead, Johnson announced on March 31, 1968, that he would make a major effort to reach a negotiated settlement of the war; that he was halting the bombing of the northern part of North Vietnam to aid the peace process; and that he would not be a candidate in the 1968 presidential election. On October 31, he expanded the **bombing halt** to cover all of North Vietnam.

**Eugene McCarthy**, running as an opponent of the Vietnam War, came close to defeating Johnson in the Democratic primary for the state of New Hampshire on March 12, and **Robert Kennedy**, brother of the slain president, entered the race also as an anti-war candidate on March 16. The prospect of having to fight simply to obtain his party's nomination in the 1968 election was one reason Johnson withdrew from the race on March 31.

After leaving the presidency in January 1969, Johnson returned to his ranch in Texas. He published his memoirs, *The Vantage Point*, in 1971 and died in 1973.

**JOINT CHIEFS OF STAFF.** The highest military body in the United States is the Joint Chiefs of Staff, made up of the top officers of the four armed services—the **Army** chief of staff, the **Air Force** chief of staff, the chief of naval operations, and the commandant of the **Marine Corps**—plus the chairman of the Joint Chiefs of Staff (CJCS).

The strongest intervention of the Joint Chiefs in the policy process was during the administration of **Lyndon Johnson**. They endorsed the **domino theory**, stating that if South Vietnam were lost, the rest of Southeast Asia would fall to Communism, and they urged the president to escalate the war by bombing **North Vietnam**. Once the bombing began, they protested Johnson's limitations on air strikes in the **Hanoi** and **Haiphong** areas.

# -K-

**KENNEDY, JOHN FITZGERALD** (1917–1963). President of the United States. He was born in Brookline, Massachusetts. His father Joseph Kennedy, a wealthy and powerful Irish **Catholic**, was able to promote his sons' careers very effectively.

John Kennedy joined the **Navy** in 1941, and was decorated for heroism as commander of a torpedo boat in combat in the Solomon Islands in 1943. With his father's support he was elected to the U.S. House of Representatives in 1946. Although a member of the Democratic Party, he criticized President Harry Truman in 1949 for not having tried hard enough to prevent the Communists from winning control of **China**. He was elected to the U.S. Senate in 1952.

During the 1950s, John Kennedy showed more interest in Vietnam than most American politicians. In 1951, and again in 1953, he went to Vietnam. He did not just accept the official briefings given by the French Army, but made a serious effort to talk with people unofficially, who told him that the situation was much worse than the official briefings said it was. In the mid-1950s he became a strong supporter of President **Ngo Dinh Diem** of the **Republic of Vietnam** (RVN).

He won election as president of the United States in 1960, despite religious suspicions (he was the first Catholic ever to become president). He first defeated **Lyndon Johnson** for the Democratic Party's nomination, and then defeated Republican **Richard Nixon** by a tiny margin in the general election. Both Kennedy and Nixon had favored a strongly anti-Communist foreign policy. Kennedy came into office with an image of youthful vigor and glamour; his serious health problems (he had Addison's disease) were carefully concealed.

Under President Dwight Eisenhower, American defense had been based mainly on nuclear weapons, under the doctrine of "massive retaliation" for any attack. Kennedy continued the buildup of nuclear forces, but he also rebuilt conventional forces, to give the United States the ability to fight smaller wars under the doctrine (particularly championed by General **Maxwell Taylor**) of "flexible response." The active-duty strength of the armed forces rose by slightly more than 200,000 under Kennedy; most of the increase was in the **Army**. Kennedy particularly promoted unconventional forces; the Navy **SEAL**s and the **Air Commandos** were created during his administration, and the Army **Special Forces** were considerably expanded.

Before leaving office, Eisenhower had begun preparations for an invasion of Cuba, using Cuban exiles trained and equipped by the **Central Intelligence Agency** (CIA), to overthrow Fidel Castro. The operation was carried out under Kennedy in April 1961. Cuban exile pilots began to bomb airfields in Cuba shortly before the invasion force landed at the Bay of Pigs. A cover story, designed to conceal the fact that the United States had supplied the **B-26** bombers used in the air strikes, collapsed immediately after the United States had presented it to the **United Nations**. After this embarrassment, Kennedy cancelled further air strikes. The invasion, which would have had little chance of success even with the originally planned number of air strikes, had none after they were cut short. Kennedy came out of this experience with less faith in very thin cover stories, and in the CIA as a manager of military operations (*see* **National Security Action Memorandum 57,** *Switchback*).

Dwight D. Eisenhower, leaving office as president in 1961, told Kennedy that the crisis point in Asia would be **Laos**, where an American-supported right-wing regime under General **Phoumi Nosavan** was fighting a coalition of neutralist and Laotian Communist (**Pathet Lao**) forces, supported by the **Democratic Republic of Vietnam** (DRV) and the **Soviet Union**. Kennedy authorized the U.S. military **advisers** in Laos, who until then had been **sheepdipped** (disguised as civilians), to put on U.S. Army uniforms; he seriously considered putting substantial ground troop units into Laos; and he authorized covert air strikes using B-26s flown by sheepdipped **Air Force** pilots, scheduled to begin in April under Project *Mill Pond*. But after the Bay of Pigs fiasco, Kennedy cancelled the *Mill Pond* air strikes, and worked to negotiate a compromise settlement at a conference in Geneva, Switzerland. The **Geneva Accords of 1962** did not end the problem in Laos—their nominal terms were so favorable to the United States that the DRV never came close to obeying the agreement—but the level of crisis in Laos decreased; Vietnam became the main flash point in the area.

The problem in **South Vietnam** seemed less dramatic at first, because the **Viet Cong** guerrillas there did not have North Vietnamese troops aiding them, or a direct supply line from the Soviet Union, the way the Pathet Lao had in Laos in 1961. But the guerrillas were growing stronger and gaining influence nonetheless. In October 1961, Kennedy sent Maxwell Taylor and **Walt Rostow** to investigate the situation. They recommended a substantial increase in American involvement, including several thousand ground troops. Kennedy rejected the idea of sending ground troops, but accepted the rest of the recommendations. He increased weapons shipments to South Vietnam, sent more military advisers, including Special Forces troops who directly led **Civilian Irregular Defense Group** (CIDG) troops in combat, and put American pilots into combat, flying Army and Marine **helicopters** and the fixed-wing aircraft of the *Farm Gate* force. This commitment of Americans to combat was not announced, however; a public pretense was maintained that American military personnel were in Vietnam only as advisers.

For much of 1962, the Army of the Republic of Vietnam (**ARVN**), with increased firepower and American air support, seemed to be doing well. The Viet Cong, however, began forming larger and better armed units, and toward the end of the year President Ngo Dinh Diem's interference in the conduct of the war became increasingly disastrous. By the beginning of 1963, some U.S. military officers and civilian officials were growing deeply pessimistic about the war. Others, including U.S. Ambassador **Frederick Nolting** and General **Paul Harkins**, commander of **Military Assistance Command, Vietnam** (MACV), remained optimistic and reported that the war was being won under President Diem's capable leadership. When optimist **Victor Krulak** and pessimist Joseph Mendenhall returned from Vietnam late in 1963, their reports differed so sharply that Kennedy asked whether they had visited the same country. Kennedy does not seem to have committed himself strongly either to the optimists or to the pessimists.

In May 1963, a crisis broke out pitting the **Catholic** President Diem against **Buddhist** leaders. This persuaded some American officials that Diem had become such a liability the war could not be won under his leadership, and that the United States should encourage ARVN officers to stage a **coup** and overthrow him. Others felt that the United States should not betray an ally, and that there was no reason to believe a coup would put a leader in power who would be better able to conduct the war than Diem had been. Kennedy was very ambivalent, but he hesitantly went along with those of his subordinates (the most important of whom were **Henry Cabot Lodge**, who had replaced Nolting as U.S. ambassador in Saigon, and some officials in the State Department) who wanted to encourage the coup. Kennedy's hesitation appears to have been caused by a mixture of genuine qualms about betraying Diem and a desire for deniability. Kennedy was shocked when the coup led to Diem's death on November 2, 1963.

Kennedy was killed in Dallas, Texas, on November 22, 1963. The official investigation concluded that a single assassin, Lee Harvey

Oswald, had committed the crime. A wide variety of theories, mostly involving large conspiracies, have been proposed as alternatives.

Several years later, some of Kennedy's subordinates began to say that had he lived, he would have withdrawn U.S. forces from Vietnam, probably in 1965, rather than massively escalating the war. What shows clearly in the records is that during 1963, when the optimists were reporting that the war against the Viet Cong was being won, President Kennedy ordered that plans be drawn up for U.S. military personnel to be withdrawn from Vietnam when the war had been sufficiently won so they were no longer needed. During the last weeks of Kennedy's life it was becoming apparent that the war had not been going as well as the optimists had been saying, but Kennedy was killed before he had had time to react to this development. It seems unlikely that he had made up his mind whether he would pull out of Vietnam or go in deeper, if the Viet Cong continued to grow stronger.

**KENNEDY, ROBERT FRANCIS** (1925–1968). Politician. The younger brother of **John F. Kennedy**, he was born in Brookline, Massachusetts, son of Joseph Kennedy, a wealthy Irish **Catholic** who served as U.S. ambassador to Great Britain in the late 1930s. Robert Kennedy dropped out of an officer training program at Harvard in 1944 to enlist as a seaman in the **Navy**, because he wanted to get quickly into active military service, but the destroyer to which he was assigned did not see combat. He graduated from Harvard in 1947, and from the University of Virginia Law School in 1950. Robert Kennedy worked briefly as a lawyer for the Justice Department, then in 1952 managed the campaign of his brother John Kennedy for the U.S. Senate; the campaign was successful. He worked as assistant counsel to Senator Joseph McCarthy's Senate Permanent Committee on Investigations, but later opposed some of the more extreme actions of the committee.

Robert Kennedy managed his brother's successful campaign for the presidency in 1960, and became attorney general in 1961. He was a very influential adviser on subjects other than law, including foreign affairs. He strongly endorsed the Vietnam War.

Robert Kennedy and **Lyndon Johnson** disliked one another. After John Kennedy was assassinated and Johnson became president in November 1963, Robert Kennedy remained attorney general for less than a year, then resigned to run for the U.S. Senate in New York.

When Kennedy took his seat in the Senate at the beginning of 1965, he was still a supporter of the Vietnam War. By early 1966, he was becoming ambivalent about it, but his view had not really shifted very far. He said the United States could not accept defeat in Vietnam; if the only way to avoid withdrawing in defeat was to fight through to victory, even at the risk of widening the war, then the United States would have to take that risk. He said it might be possible to negotiate a compromise settlement, but the terms of which he was thinking in 1966 called for something close to a **Viet Cong** surrender; his belief that such a settlement would be desirable did not represent a very radical position.

On March 2, 1967, he went much further; he said that in order to create a climate for **negotiations**, the United States should halt bombing of **North Vietnam**, and maintain that halt for what would presumably be prolonged negotiations, without demanding that the **infiltration** of personnel from North Vietnam to the battlefields of **South Vietnam** cease; the United States would demand only that the Communists not take advantage of the bombing halt to increase the rate of infiltration substantially, or expand the war in the South. And his comments about what sort of peace the negotiators should be trying to achieve, during the **bombing halt**, suggested a much more genuine offer to share power with the Communists in South Vietnam, not the near-surrender of the Viet Cong he had hoped for the previous year. This was a radical deviation from U.S. policy, but it was not really an anti-war position. Kennedy was still talking about the war as something the United States was doing *for* the people of South Vietnam, and saying that the United States must not abandon them even if this meant continuing the war; he was only considering the possibility there might be a way to end the war without abandoning them.

Soon, however, he began publicly questioning the fundamental morality of the war, discussing it as something the United States was doing *to* South Vietnam, perhaps against the wishes of the people of South Vietnam, because of a fear (which he clearly thought unfounded) that pulling out of Vietnam would direly imperil American security. He said in a televised interview on November 26, 1967, "we're going in there and we're killing South Vietnamese, we're killing children, we're killing innocent people because we don't want to have the war fought on American soil, or because they're 12,000 miles away and they might get to be 11,000 miles away." This was a seriously anti-war position.

Another Democratic senator opposed to the war, **Eugene McCarthy**, declared himself a candidate for president in the 1968 **election**. Many of Kennedy's followers urged him to do the same; he was more power-ful than McCarthy and would have a better chance of wresting the Democratic Party's nomination from President Johnson. Kennedy re-sisted this pressure until the New Hampshire primary election on March 12, 1968, which showed how vulnerable Johnson had become; Johnson got only 49.4 percent of the Democratic votes, to 42.2 percent for McCarthy. Kennedy declared his candidacy on March 16. He seemed to have a good chance of winning the Democratic Party nomination, but he was shot on June 4 by a young Palestinian named Sirhan B. Sirhan, who hated him for supporting Israel. He died on June 6.

**KENT STATE.** The **Cambodian Incursion** of 1970 sparked **anti-war** pro-tests on many college campuses; some of these turned violent. At Kent State University, in Kent, Ohio, the Reserve Officer Training Corps (ROTC) building was burned down. The governor of Ohio sent Na-tional Guard troops onto the campus to restore order on May 4. Fol-lowing a confrontation with rock-throwing students, the guardsmen opened fire, killing four students and wounding nine. This led to a huge outburst of protest, not only by students but by faculty, at educa-tional institutions across the country. More than 500 colleges closed down for varying lengths of time. ROTC buildings were attacked by arson or bombs on 30 campuses.

**KERRY, JOHN FORBES** (1943– ). **Anti-war movement** leader, U.S. senator. Born in Denver, Colorado, he graduated from Yale in 1966. He served in the U.S. **Navy** 1966–1969, winning the Silver Star and three Purple Hearts in Vietnam. He was the national coordinator of **Vietnam Veterans Against the War**, 1970–1971. He was elected to the U.S. Senate, as a Democrat from Massachusetts, in 1984. He served as chairman of the Senate Select Committee on POW-MIA Affairs, 1991–1992. He became a candidate for president of the United States in 2004. He is the author of *The New Soldier* (1971).

**KHE SANH.** A village in a valley in northwestern **Quang Tri**, about 10 kilometers from the border of **Laos** and 23 kilometers south of the **Demilitarized Zone** (DMZ). The United States first sent a **Special Forces** A-team to establish a **Civilian Irregular Defense Group** (CIDG) camp there in July 1962; a crude airstrip was constructed around September. Over the following years, Khe Sanh was used as a base for a variety of **reconnaissance** units, including **SOG** teams crossing the border into Laos. In September 1966, General **William Westmoreland** decided to improve the airstrip there and install a **Marine** garrison. In

December, the Special Forces and their CIDG troops moved from Khe Sanh southwest to **Lang Vei**, closer to the Laotian border. On April 24, 1967, bloody fighting began in the hills surrounding the valley; **PAVN** troops had apparently spent an extended period building fortified positions on these hills before the Marines discovered them, and despite heavy air and **artillery** support, the Marines lost 155 men killed and 425 wounded attacking these bunker complexes.

In late 1967, PAVN troops began to gather again in the Khe Sanh area, and the Marine garrison there was reinforced. Large-scale shelling of the base began on January 21, 1968. During the following weeks, as Khe Sanh was besieged by a strong PAVN force, many people (including President **Lyndon Johnson**) worried that the Battle of Dien Bien Phu was being repeated. The United States, however, had enormously more air power in 1968 than France had had in 1954, so the air support that could be given to a surrounded force was far more effective. American cargo planes were able to continue landing at Khe Sanh to deliver cargoes; Viet Minh gunners had been able to stop French cargo planes from landing at Dien Bien Phu. And the American bombing of the PAVN forces surrounding Khe Sanh, Operation *Niagara*, which began on January 22, placed a huge bomb tonnage on them and inflicted severe casualties. Also, there were U.S. positions close enough to Khe Sanh—Camp Carroll and the Rockpile, about 19 and 25 kilometers to the northeast, respectively—to provide supporting fire with 175-mm artillery pieces.

Operation *Pegasus*, in which the 1st **Cavalry Division (Airmobile)**, together with some Marine and **ARVN** units, broke the siege of Khe Sanh by reopening **Route 9** from Ca Lu to Khe Sanh, began on April 1 and was successfully completed on April 15.

General Westmoreland had seemed inclined to hold Khe Sanh indefinitely, but on June 12, 1968, one day after replacing Westmoreland as commander of U.S. forces in Vietnam, **Creighton Abrams** ordered U.S. troops withdrawn from Khe Sanh. They were out by July 6.

Khe Sanh was reoccupied on January 31, 1971, in Operation *Dewey Canyon II*, and the airstrip re-opened, to provide support for *Lam Son 719*, the ARVN incursion into Laos.

**KHMER.** The majority ethnic group of **Cambodia**. They are Theravada **Buddhist**. They are related by language, but not really by culture, to some **Montagnard** tribes of **South Vietnam**, and to the **Lao Theung** of **Laos**. Some Khmer, the **Khmer Krom**, live in **South Vietnam**.

**KHMER KROM.** The **Khmer** minority in **South Vietnam**. Many of them were recruited into units of the **Civilian Irregular Defense Groups** (CIDG), serving under the leadership of U.S. **Special Forces** troops. **Son Ngoc Thanh**, a Khmer Krom who had been a major figure in **Cambodia** in the 1950s, and was by the 1960s leading a group called the **Khmer Serei**, hostile to Prince **Norodom Sihanouk**'s government in Cambodia, helped the United States recruit CIDG troops among the Khmer Krom, and was helped by the United States and the **Republic of Vietnam** (RVN) to recruit followers for himself among them. In 1970, the United States, the RVN, and Son Ngoc Thanh cooperated to arrange the transfer of many Khmer Krom, mostly CIDG troops, from South Vietnam to the government army under **Lon Nol** in Cambodia. They were among the best troops available to Lon Nol for the next several years.

**KHMER ROUGE** (Red **Khmer**). An informal term for the Communist movement in **Cambodia**. The Indochinese Communist Party (ICP) was in the 1940s an essentially Vietnamese organization, but it had a few Khmer members. In 1951, the Vietnamese Communist leaders decided it was no longer appropriate to have a single Communist Party for all three countries of Indochina. They established the **Lao Dong** (Workers') Party for Vietnam. Their Khmer comrades, still very much under Vietnamese influence, established the Khmer People's Revolutionary Party (KPRP). Many future leaders of the Khmer Rouge, however, were at this time not in the jungles waging guerrilla war against the French, but in France as students, picking up radical ideas from French left-wing politics.

By 1954, the KPRP may have had about 2,000 members. This was not enough strength to give the party any real leverage at the Geneva Conference (*see* **Geneva Accords of 1954**), and it was sacrificed by the stronger Communist powers. The Vietnamese Communists agreed to pull their forces out of Cambodia without obtaining in return any power-sharing role, or real protection from government repression, for their Cambodian comrades. Many Khmer Communists went into exile in Vietnam; others tried to keep the party going in Cambodia. The Communists established a public political party, the Pracheachon, which contested elections in 1955 and 1958, but it was not permitted to campaign freely; indeed it was so persecuted and harassed that its existence seemed pointless, and it disappeared in 1962.

The KPRP renamed itself the Khmer Workers' Party on September

30, 1960, and the Communist Party of Kampuchea in 1966. Saloth Sar (the future **Pol Pot**) became head of the party in 1963. The party, which was very small and very secret, did not announce publicly its various changes in name. It concealed itself behind the euphemistic terms "revolutionary organization" (*angkar padevat*) or "higher organization" (*angkar loeu*) until 1977.

In January 1968, the Khmer Rouge decided to launch an armed struggle against the government. This was a very small guerrilla struggle by a small force, and the Vietnamese Communists did not at first try to turn it into a big one. It seems the Khmer Rouge did not feel strong enough even to make much of a protest against the paucity of the assistance given them by the **Democratic Republic of Vietnam** (DRV).

The **coup** that overthrew Prince **Norodom Sihanouk** in March 1970 changed the situation dramatically. Sihanouk allied himself with the Khmer Rouge and the DRV against the new government of **Lon Nol**. Khmer Communists who had been living in **Hanoi** for years returned to Cambodia. **PAVN** troops began fighting alongside the Khmer Rouge against government forces. DRV and Chinese aid, while still not generous, was far larger than before. The great prestige of Prince Sihanouk aided enormously in the recruitment of Khmer Rouge forces within Cambodia, and also gave them international recognition. This alliance, however, was an uneasy one from the beginning. By late 1971, the Khmer Rouge were growing strong enough no longer to need to pretend friendship for those they distrusted; they reduced their use of Sihanouk's name and portrait, and began to purge the Hanoi-trained Khmer Communists.

The PAVN, which had been doing most of the fighting on the Communist side in Cambodia, withdrew the bulk of its forces in late 1972, leaving the Khmer Rouge to take the predominant role in the war there. Tension between the Khmer Rouge and the PAVN increased greatly at about this time; there were some shooting incidents between their forces. The Khmer Rouge also became ideologically more extreme, showing more clearly the behavior patterns that were to lead to the mass slaughters of 1975–1978.

During the last years of the war, the Khmer Rouge pushed their effort to take **Phnom Penh** regardless of the cost to anyone. They sacrificed thousands of their own troops in an offensive in mid-1973, during the last stage of the American bombing of Cambodia. In late 1973 and early 1974, they began bombarding the city with **rockets** and **artillery**; the victims were mostly the refugees who had swollen the city to huge size. In 1975 they cut off most of the city's food supplies, and starvation set in.

The Khmer Rouge finally took Phnom Penh on April 17, 1975, ending the war. They then imposed on Cambodia, which they called Kampuchea, a regime of unspeakable horror. Partly this was deliberate killing based on ideology—they attacked the upper class, the Westernized middle class, the **Buddhist** monks, and so on. Partly it was ethnic hatred, directed against the **Cham** minority, and those of the Vietnamese minority who had not already been driven out of Cambodia under Lon Nol. Partly it was starvation brought on by mismanaged schemes to build an agrarian socialist utopia. In the period of less than four years before the Khmer Rouge were driven from power by a Vietnamese invasion in late 1978 and early 1979, more than a tenth of the total population of Cambodia—by some estimates, more than a fifth—is believed to have died.

**KHMER SEREI** (Free **Khmer**). After the end of the First Indochina War in 1954, **Son Ngoc Thanh**, who had had little success in trying to create a non-Communist guerrilla resistance to the French in **Cambodia** despite his personal popularity in the country, led his followers to the vicinity of the Thai-Cambodian border, where they began calling themselves the Khmer Serei. They were supported by **Thailand**, and to some extent by the **Republic of Vietnam** (RVN), with U.S. acquiescence. In the early 1960s, Prince **Norodom Sihanouk** was infuriated by Khmer Serei radio broadcasts attacking him and his family, coming from transmitters in both **South Vietnam** and Thailand. The Khmer Serei became involved in the Vietnam War during the 1960s; Son Ngoc Thanh helped recruit **Khmer Krom** troops for the **Civilian Irregular Defense Groups** (CIDG).

Around 1969, there was a rapprochement between the Khmer Serei and Prince Sihanouk, who wanted to be able to bring pressure against the Vietnamese Communist armed forces in Cambodia. Some of the Khmer Serei units that had been fighting in South Vietnam went into Cambodia to support Sihanouk at this time; they later supported **Lon Nol**.

**KING, MARTIN LUTHER, JR.** (1929–1968). Born in Atlanta, Georgia, King graduated from Morehouse College in 1948. He became pastor of a Baptist Church in Montgomery, Alabama, in 1954, while still working toward his Ph.D. in theology at Boston University; he was awarded the degree in 1955.

At the end of 1955, he became leader of a campaign by blacks in Montgomery to end racial segregation on the city buses, and quickly became famous. In 1957, he helped found the Southern Christian Leadership Conference, of which he was president until his death. In 1960, he helped organize the Student Nonviolent Coordinating Committee. King preached a doctrine of strict nonviolence, strongly influenced by the writings of Mohandas Gandhi. He felt that when civil rights demonstrators were attacked by mobs or by local police, they should not defend themselves; their enemies would eventually become ashamed of beating and clubbing people who did not fight back, and would stop. Demonstrators should violate immoral laws, sitting down for example in facilities forbidden to blacks by local ordinances, but should then allow themselves to be arrested and jailed without resistance. King's stress on nonviolence had a strong influence on the overall tone of the civil rights movement well into the 1960s. By 1963, when King gave his famous "I Have a Dream" speech to a massive demonstration he had organized in Washington, D.C., he was a major national leader. In 1964, he was awarded the Nobel Prize for Peace.

Beginning in mid-July 1965, King began to urge greater efforts to achieve a negotiated settlement of the Vietnam War. Any war would have violated his principles, and this war was diverting money that might otherwise have been used to improve the lives of poor people, many of whom were black, in the United States. Also, he objected to the fact that the proportion of blacks among the U.S. **Army** troops dying in Vietnam in 1965 and 1966 was far higher than the proportion of blacks in the U.S. population (*see* **racial tension**). On April 13, 1966, he said that the war was "degenerating into a sordid military adventure." Early in 1967, he began to denounce the war much more frequently, and in stronger language; at an Easter rally he called it "a blasphemy against all that America stands for." Such statements worsened his relations with the federal government, which were already shaky (J. Edgar Hoover, head of the Federal Bureau of Investigation, hated King and had long been trying to discredit him).

King appeared to doubt that the war in Vietnam was truly the struggle against Communism that the U.S. government said it was. False accusations of Communism had often been made against King and other leaders of the civil rights movement in the American South; he seemed to believe that the U.S. government's accusations that the **Viet Cong** were Communist might also be false, or at least exaggerated.

By the middle and late 1960s, King was shifting his emphasis from racial integration to alleviation of the poverty of many black people. He was in Memphis, Tennessee, to support a strike by sanitation workers when he was assassinated on April 3, 1968. King's death triggered widespread race riots.

**KISSINGER, HENRY ALFRED** (1923– ). U.S. government official. Born in Fuerth, Germany, he immigrated to the United States in 1938 and became a citizen in 1943. He was drafted into the Army in 1943 and went into military intelligence. He served until 1946, and then went to Harvard University. He graduated *summa cum laude* in 1950, and remained for his M.A. (1952) and Ph.D. (1954). Kissinger joined the faculty at Harvard as a lecturer in the Department of Government in 1957, and by 1962 had become a full professor. He was director of Harvard's Defense Studies Program from 1959 to 1969, and during these years he began splitting his time between Harvard and Washington, D.C., where he served as a consultant to the State Department and other agencies.

After **Richard Nixon** was elected president in 1968, Kissinger became Nixon's special assistant for national security affairs (often called national security adviser), and soon acquired extraordinary power. Nixon, who distrusted the bureaucracy of the federal government, dealt with the Departments of State and Defense, and the **Central Intelligence Agency**, through Kissinger and the National Security Council staff of which Kissinger was head. Nixon shifted into Kissinger's office much of the power that had formerly been exercised by the secretary of state, and some of what had formerly been exercised by the secretary of defense.

Kissinger's focus was on great-power diplomacy. He saw the relationship between the United States and the **Soviet Union** as the central issue in world affairs, and he advocated "linkage" of problems in different areas of the world. By 1969, **China** and the Soviet Union had become bitterly hostile to one another. Kissinger and Nixon set out to improve U.S. relations with both under the policy called détente, hoping to use each of them as leverage in relations with the other, and both of them as leverage against the **Democratic Republic of Vietnam** (DRV). The United States, and Kissinger and Nixon as individuals, had long been deeply hostile to China. Kissinger's secret visit to China in July 1971, and Nixon's very public visit in February 1972, marked a stunning reversal in policy.

Kissinger and Nixon were unusually secretive in their conduct of foreign policy, though Nixon was more obsessive about this than Kissinger. In Nixon, the secretiveness went with hatred of the American media, and an avoidance of contact with journalists. Kissinger, however, maintained good relations with journalists.

Kissinger was determined to avoid a humiliating defeat in Vietnam, which he felt would damage American credibility in other areas of the world. But he apparently did not believe that the United States could achieve victory there; he placed his hopes in a compromise settlement. Unfortunately, preoccupied with the Soviet Union and China, he had not learned enough about the policies and views of either Communist or anti-Communist Vietnamese to understand the obstacles to such a compromise.

The official **Paris negotiations** produced little result. Private conversations between Kissinger and **Le Duc Tho**, one of the most powerful leaders of the **Lao Dong Party**, began on February 21, 1970, and continued intermittently thereafter. The fact that these private negotiations were occurring was at first kept strictly secret, but was revealed to the public in January 1972. In October 1972, Kissinger and Le Duc Tho completed an agreement, and Kissinger announced to the press on October 26, "peace is at hand." President **Nguyen Van Thieu** of the **Republic of Vietnam**, however, objected violently to the agreement, which he felt likely to lead to Communist conquest of **South Vietnam**. Kissinger went back to Paris in November and asked Le Duc Tho for extensive changes in the October draft. The climate of the negotiations deteriorated (there is a widely believed myth that the DRV even broke off the negotiations), and in December Nixon ordered *Linebacker II*, a major bombing campaign in the northern half of **North Vietnam**. In January 1973, Kissinger and Le Duc Tho signed the **Paris Peace Agreement**, only slightly modified from the October 1972 draft. Substantial portions of it were not implemented, however, and the war continued. (Kissinger later said that one of the things he liked about the agreement was that there seemed little danger its provisions for resolving the political future of South Vietnam would actually be put into effect.) In October 1973, Kissinger and Le Duc Tho were jointly awarded the Nobel Prize for Peace, for having negotiated the Paris Peace Agreement.

President Nixon announced in August 1973 that Kissinger would replace **William Rogers** as secretary of state, and he was confirmed by the Senate and took office in September. He continued in that office for the remainder of the Nixon administration (until August 1974), and through the administration of **Gerald Ford** (until January 1977). For more than two years, until November 1975, he remained national security adviser. In 1974 and 1975, he tried without success to persuade the **Congress** to maintain high levels of U.S. aid for the Republic of Vietnam.

After his retirement from the government, he wrote his memoirs in three large volumes, published in 1979, 1982, and 1999.

**KIT CARSON SCOUTS.** Former **Viet Cong** or **PAVN** soldiers who had switched sides, and were used as scouts by U.S. and **ARVN** forces. A single Kit Carson Scout was often attached to an American **Long-Range Patrol** (LRP) team; in other contexts they operated in groups.

**KOHO.** A **Montagnard** tribe, speaking a language of the Mon-Khmer group, living in the southern part of the **Central Highlands**, southwest of **Dalat**. Subgroups include the Maa, Sre, and Lat.

**KOMER, ROBERT** "Blowtorch" (1922–2000). Born in Chicago, he graduated *magna cum laude* from Harvard in 1942, then served in Army intelligence on the Italian front. After World War II, he earned a master's degree in Business Administration at Harvard, then in 1947 joined the **Central Intelligence Agency**, where he worked in the Office of National Estimates until 1960. Komer moved to the National Security Council (NSC) staff after **John Kennedy** became president. Up until 1966, he had never worked particularly on Asia; his specialties had been Western Europe, the **Soviet Union**, the Middle East, and Africa. But in the spring of 1966, his assignment at the NSC was switched from handling Middle Eastern and African affairs to handling **pacification** in Vietnam. As he set himself to learn about Vietnam, Komer was influenced among others by **Daniel Ellsberg** and **John Paul Vann**.

In May 1967, Komer was sent to Vietnam to head a new organization, **Civil Operations and Revolutionary Development Support** (CORDS), which would unify all American military and civilian pacification efforts in a single organization. CORDS was under **Military Assistance Command, Vietnam** (MACV); as head of CORDS Komer was a deputy commander of MACV, and he was also given the rank of ambassador.

Komer's very optimistic, statistics-laden 1967 reports about progress in the war became somewhat embarrassing when the **Tet Offensive** came along early in 1968. He left Vietnam in November 1968 to become very briefly ambassador to Turkey. He worked for the Rand

Corporation from 1969 to 1977, then went to the Defense Department. While at Rand, he wrote *Bureaucracy Does Its Thing: Institutional Constraints on U.S.-GVN Performance in Vietnam* (1972), which criticized "overmilitarization" of U.S. policy in Vietnam.

**KONG LE** (1934– ). Born in Savannakhet province, southern **Laos**, a member of a **Lao Theung** (sometimes called Kha) ethnic group. He joined the Royal Lao Army in 1952, and proved an outstanding officer; in 1958 he became executive officer (he often served as acting commander) of the 2d Parachute Battalion. By 1959, he had helped to make this the best battalion in the army. The battalion, under Kong Le's acting command, provided the military force for the bloodless **coup** of December 25, 1959, that brought the rightist **Phoumi Nosavan** to power. But on August 9, 1960, Captain Kong Le carried out another coup and placed the neutralist Prince **Souvanna Phouma** in power.

In December 1960, Phoumi Nosavan's forces, with U.S. and Thai assistance, drove Kong Le and Souvanna Phouma from Vientiane. They retreated to the **Plain of Jars**, where they allied with the **Pathet Lao** and the **PAVN**, and began to get military aid from the **Soviet Union**. When the Second Coalition Government was formed in June 1962, Souvanna Phouma returned to Vientiane as prime minister. Soviet and PAVN support for Kong Le's forces ceased, and before the end of 1962 he was turning to the United States for aid. During the following years, however, he was weakened both by the defection of some of his forces to the Communists, and by the hostility of the rightists in Vientiane. His resignation as commander of the neutralist armed forces was announced in November 1966, and he fled Laos in 1967. Those of his forces that had not defected to the Communists were absorbed into the rightist-dominated Royal Lao Army.

After the Pathet Lao victory of 1975, Kong Le tried to inspire resistance against the Communist government of Laos; in the early 1980s he cooperated with the government of **China** in organizing guerrilla groups to be infiltrated into Laos to try to overthrow the Pathet Lao government there.

**KONTUM.** The town of Kontum was about 40 kilometers north of **Pleiku** in the **Central Highlands**. It was the capital of Kontum province, the northernmost province of **II Corps**. The people of the province were mostly **Montagnards**, including **Bahnar**, **Jarai**, and **Sedang**. The Studies and Observations Group (**SOG**) established a regional headquarters—Command and Control, Central (CCC)—at Kontum in 1968.

The province was the scene of heavy fighting from 1967 onward, especially in the area around **Dak To** and **Ben Het**, near the **tri-border** where **Laos, Cambodia,** and **South Vietnam** came together. Thirty percent of the American combat deaths in II Corps from 1967 to 1972 occurred in Kontum. The town of Kontum was one of the places attacked in the early morning hours of January 30, 1968, 24 hours ahead of schedule, in the **Tet Offensive**. The province was one of the main theaters of fighting in the **Easter Offensive** of 1972; Dak To was overrun by **PAVN** forces, and the town of Kontum was very nearly overrun. The portions of the province that **ARVN** forces still held in mid-March 1975 were abandoned as part of the overall ARVN withdrawal from the Central Highlands (*see* **final collapse**).

**KOREA,** South. As early as November 1963, the Republic of Korea (ROK) offered to send troops to Vietnam if the United States wanted them, but the offer was not accepted at that time. The first significant ROK force sent to Vietnam, a 2,000-man military engineering group (the "Dove Unit"), arrived in March 1965 and was stationed at **Bien Hoa**. The ROK soon added two combat divisions: the Capital Division (also called the Tiger Division), which arrived in late 1965 and early 1966, and the 9th ROK Infantry Division (White Horse Division), which arrived in 1966 and 1967. They operated mostly in the coastal provinces of **II Corps**. The number of ROK troops in Vietnam reached 45,000 late in 1967, and from that point remained relatively stable, in the range of 45,000 to 50,000, until the beginning of 1972. The ROK forces did not withdraw nearly as fast as the Americans did in the late stages of the war. At the end of 1972, when the United States was down to 24,200 military personnel in South Vietnam, the ROK forces still numbered over 36,000. ROK losses in Vietnam are reported as 5,077 dead and 10,962 wounded.

The Korean troops in Vietnam had a fearsome reputation; they were said to be very effective in combat, but also inclined to kill civilians on comparatively little provocation. By early 1972, however, the Koreans, stationed in the lowland areas of II Corps roughly from **Nha Trang** to **Qui Nhon**, had become much less aggressive, wanting to avoid casualties.

The United States provided massive financial aid to Korea in return for the services of Korean troops, and the war provided economic benefits to South Korea even beyond the direct aid. About 20,000 Korean civilians worked in South Vietnam, at wages far higher than those prevailing in Korea; these people brought considerable wealth back to Korea with them when they returned. Also, the war stimulated the Korean economy by providing a market for exports.

**KRULAK, VICTOR HAROLD** "Brute" (1913– ). U.S. **Marine** general. Born in Denver, Colorado, he graduated from the U.S. Naval Academy at Annapolis in 1934 and went into the Marine Corps. He was stationed in China from 1937 to 1939. He helped to develop the front-ramp landing craft for amphibious operations. During World War II, he commanded a battalion in combat on Choiseul, and later he was operations officer of the 6th Marine Division during the fighting on **Okinawa**.

**John Kennedy**, who knew and liked Krulak, picked him in 1962 to become the first **special assistant for counterinsurgency and special activities** (SACSA), under the **Joint Chiefs of Staff**. During 1963, he said the United States should continue backing **Ngo Dinh Diem**, and not encourage a **coup** against Diem. When doubts arose about the validity of General **Paul Harkins**'s very optimistic reports on the progress of the war, Krulak was one of the strongest voices supporting Harkins. When he and Joseph Mendenhall of the State Department went out together to investigate the state of the war in September 1963, the contrast in their reports—Krulak's saying the war effort was succeeding splendidly and Mendenhall's saying it was failing—was so striking that President Kennedy asked whether they had visited the same country. By the end of the year it was becoming clear that Mendenhall had been correct and Krulak wrong, but Krulak did not suffer for this; early in 1964 he was promoted to lieutenant general and made commander, Fleet Marine Force, Pacific. One of his last actions as SACSA, in January 1964, was to help write the final version of *OPLAN 34A*, a program of covert actions against **North Vietnam** that President **Lyndon Johnson** approved in that month.

By late 1965 and early 1966, Krulak was becoming an advocate of two major changes in U.S. policy. One was to change the focus in South Vietnam from combat against enemy military forces to **pacification**—establishing control over the densely populated areas, and winning the loyalty of the peasants there. Many of the Communists' main-force units were in the thinly populated hills and jungles near the Laotian and Cambodian borders. Krulak said sending U.S. troops after them in such areas would not accomplish enough to justify the casualties it cost. The other policy change he advocated was to be much more aggressive in bombing the northern half of North Vietnam, which the Johnson administration was limiting out of a fear of reactions from the **Soviet Union** and **China**.

Krulak retired from the Marine Corps in 1968, and became vice president of the Copley Newspaper Group. He is the author of *First to Fight: An Inside View of the U.S. Marine Corps* (1984).

# - L -

**LAIRD, MELVIN R.** (1922– ). Secretary of defense. Born in Omaha, Nebraska, he graduated from Carlton College in 1942, and served aboard a destroyer in the Pacific during World War II. Laird was elected to the U.S. House of Representatives from Wisconsin as a Republican in 1952, and served for 16 years. In 1965, he was a conspicuous leader of the group in **Congress** that said that if the United States committed ground troops in Vietnam, there should not be a limited war, but a drive for total victory. But in September 1968, Representative Laird predicted that the United States would withdraw a substantial portion of its military personnel—about 90,000 men—from **South Vietnam** in the first half of 1969.

In January 1969, Laird became secretary of defense. He endorsed the secret U.S. bombing of **Cambodia** initiated in 1969 (Operation *Menu*), and argued that the United States should announce this bombing openly. On other issues, however, he soon became a voice of military restraint. He urged a rapid pullout of U.S. forces from Vietnam, and opposed the **Cambodian Incursion** of 1970. He supported *Lam Son 719*, the 1971 incursion into **Laos**, but opposed the decision to place **mines** in **Haiphong** in May 1972, and opposed *Linebacker II* in December. In November 1972, Laird announced he would resign as secretary of defense as of January 1973.

*LAM SON.* Name for an extended series of operations by the **ARVN** 1st Infantry Division, numbered in sequence. Often in joint American-Vietnamese operations, the U.S. component would have an American name and the Vietnamese component would be a numbered *Lam Son* operation. Thus the first substantial ground raid into the **Demilitarized Zone**, in May 1967, was *Lam Son 54* for the ARVN and Operations *Hickory* and *Beau Charger* for the U.S. **Marines**. The drive to reopen **Route 9** and relieve the siege of **Khe Sanh**, in April 1968, was *Lam Son 207* for the ARVN and Operation *Pegasus* for the United States. The raid into the **A Shau** Valley soon afterward was *Lam Son*

*216* for the ARVN and Operation *Delaware* for the United States.

**LAM SON 719,** Operation, 1971. An effort by the Army of the Republic of Vietnam (**ARVN**), with U.S. support, to cut the **Ho Chi Minh Trail** in southern **Laos**. Some ARVN forces were to go into Laos by **helicopter**; others were to move along **Route 9** by ground, going as far west as **Tchepone**. The United States assisted by opening Route 9 as far as the Laotian border; providing **artillery** support, from the Vietnamese side of the border, for ARVN units in Laos; and providing a great deal of air support—not just strikes by fixed-wing aircraft and helicopter **gunships**, but also many of the transport helicopters that put ARVN troops into landing zones in Laos. The United States also tried to draw off North Vietnamese attention and forces by making spurious preparations for a landing by U.S. **Marines** (a raid, not a real invasion) on the North Vietnamese coast. U.S. personnel did not, however, get directly into the ground fighting in Laos, even as **advisers**. General **Creighton Abrams**, Commander of **Military Assistance Command, Vietnam**, had urged this operation on the ARVN.

U.S. troops began the opening of the portion of Route 9 that lay within **South Vietnam** on January 30, 1971, as part of Operation *Dewey Canyon II*. The ARVN move into Laos began on the morning of February 8. Despite bad weather which interfered with both ground and air operations, the ARVN forces reached Ban Dong (a.k.a. A Luoi), about 20 kilometers inside Laos, by the end of February 10, but there the advance halted. ARVN forces spread out to some extent north and south of Ban Dong, and in the areas between Ban Dong and the Vietnamese border, but President **Nguyen Van Thieu** ordered them not to proceed westward toward Tchepone. During the following weeks General Abrams urged the ARVN to push onward and indeed to throw more forces into the operation, but ARVN leaders were more cautious.

The fighting was heavy. **PAVN** forces on the ground attacked the ARVN very aggressively, accepting heavy casualties in their determination to drive back the ARVN offensive. PAVN **anti-aircraft** defenses proved shockingly effective. Officially, the United States acknowledged 103 helicopters destroyed and 614 damaged; General William Momyer, commander of the U.S. 7th Air Force, believed the number destroyed had been closer to 200.

On March 6, ARVN troops were airlifted into the Tchepone area, but they did not remain long, and did not spread out enough to do serious damage to PAVN supply dumps in the area. Their main purpose appears to have been to allow the ARVN to say it had reached Tchepone. On March 9, President Thieu, on the advice of his senior commanders, ordered the ARVN to withdraw from Laos. The ARVN forces, under heavy PAVN attack, had a great deal of difficulty getting out of Laos; most of the forces that managed to get out had done so by March 25. Photos of troops clinging to the skids of helicopters got wide distribution, and created an impression that the ARVN had been badly defeated.

**LAND REFORM.** During the French colonial period, most of the land in the **Mekong Delta** in extreme southern Vietnam, and significant amounts of land in many other areas of Vietnam, had been farmed by tenants. The possibility of a land reform that would distribute landlord land to peasants was a major political issue from the 1940s into the 1970s.

During most of the First Indochina War, Viet Minh policy was to take land from landlords and give it to peasants (or achieve an equivalent result less formally by reducing rent to near-zero levels) only in the case of landlords closely associated with the French. The result was very substantial land transfers in the Mekong Delta, where large absentee landlords owned most of the land and many of them were French citizens, but less impressive results elsewhere.

In 1953, the Communists began testing a more radical land reform campaign in small areas, and by 1956 this had spread through all ethnically Vietnamese areas of **North Vietnam**. It became more extreme as it spread, both economically, with far more people being classified as "landlords" than actually met the official definition of the term, and politically, with an increasingly frenzied search for landlords and landlord agents within the Viet Minh village leadership. Thousands of people were executed (though not the hundreds of thousands later claimed by some anti-Communist propagandists). In mid-1956, the Communist leaders realized how disastrously they were attacking their own political base; they initiated a correction of errors in which Viet Minh village leaders who had been falsely accused of being enemy agents were rehabilitated, and people who had been wrongly classified as landlords had part of their confiscated land returned to them. Repairing the damage that land reform had done to Communist political power in North Vietnam was a daunting task, absorbing the energies of Communist leaders for more than a year; this was probably an important part of the reason there was so little Communist pressure on **Ngo Dinh Diem**'s government in the South from 1956 to 1958.

When Ngo Dinh Diem began to consolidate his control of **South Vietnam** in 1955, his first approach to the land problem was to reverse the effects of the Viet Minh's land distribution, and reaffirm ownership by the original landlords of land that the Viet Minh had transferred to peasants during the First Indochina War. Ordinance No. 2, of January 8, 1955, regulated the terms of tenancy, required landlord and tenant to sign a written tenancy contract, and stated that the rents were to be between 15 percent and 25 percent of the crop. Many landlords ignored the 25 percent limit in the following years.

Ordinance No. 57, of October 22, 1956, was Diem's land reform law. It stated that no landlord could own more than 100 hectares of rice-growing land (1 hectare = 2.47 acres), plus in some cases 15 additional hectares for the maintenance of his family's ancestral cult, and 30 additional hectares if the landlord farmed the land directly (using hired labor) rather than letting it out to tenants. Landlords were to be paid for the land an amount equal to about half its current market value; one-tenth of the payment was given to the landlords immediately, and nine-tenths was in bonds maturing over a period of 12 years. Peasants were to pay for the land they were getting, in installments for six years. Approximately 700,000 hectares, almost all of which were in the Mekong Delta, should have been redistributed if this law had been carried out as it was written. Statistics on what actually did happen are confusing and contradictory, but the amount of land that actually ended up in peasant hands seems to have been far less than the law decreed, and some of the recipients—it is unclear how many—were apparently refugees from the North rather than local tenant farmers. It is plain that the impact of this land reform, overall, was far from adequate to satisfy peasant desires.

When **guerrilla warfare** began around 1960, the **National Liberation Front** (NLF) offered peasants a more generous land reform program than the government did, offering to do a far more thorough job of stripping the landlords of their land, and giving it to the peasants free instead of requiring payment. This was one of the most important bases of the NLF's appeal to the peasants in the early 1960s, especially in the Mekong Delta but also in other areas. The NLF land reform, which affected landlords owning much less than 100 hectares, had an impact in areas where there were no landlords owning enough land to be affected by Diem's Ordinance No. 57.

On March 26, 1970, the government of **Nguyen Van Thieu** issued Law No. 003/70, commonly known as the Land-to-the-Tiller Program.

This was not only far more thorough in theory than Diem's program had been, taking rented land even from quite small landlords; it was implemented far more seriously. For the first time the government was really competing with the Communists in offering land to the peasants. By the time the war ended in 1975, the combined effect of the NLF's land reform and Thieu's had reduced tenancy to negligible levels in South Vietnam.

**LANG VEI.** A **Civilian Irregular Defense Group** (CIDG) camp, run by **Special Forces** Detachment A-101, on **Route 9**, southwest of **Khe Sanh**. It was established on December 21, 1966. It was heavily damaged and almost overrun by a **PAVN** attack (assisted by Communist agents among the CIDG troops in the camp) early on the morning of May 4, 1967. It was rebuilt on a new location, about a kilometer west of the old one, and less than two kilometers from the Laotian border. **Helicopters** brought in the materials for heavy fortifications, stronger than were usual for CIDG camps. But it was overrun by a PAVN force with PT-76 light **tanks** on the night of February 6–7, 1968.

**LANSDALE, EDWARD GEARY** (1908–1987). Born in Detroit, Michigan, he attended the University of California at Los Angeles 1927–1931, but did not graduate. He then became an advertising executive.

Lansdale began active military service in 1943, as an Army intelligence officer. In 1947 he shifted to the Air Force, where he remained an officer until he was retired in 1963. But his real career was defined more by other positions he held. He had joined the Office for Strategic Services (OSS) as a civilian in 1942, and he worked more for the OSS than for the Army until 1945. At the end of 1949, the Air Force assigned him to the Office of Policy Coordination (OPC), a covert operations agency that was nominally part of the **Central Intelligence Agency** (CIA), but actually autonomous. The OPC was integrated into the CIA in the early 1950s, but Lansdale himself retained considerable autonomy during his years with the CIA.

Lansdale served in the **Philippines** in the late 1940s as an Army officer. In 1950 he went there again, both working directly on the struggle against the Communist-led Hukbalahap guerrillas and working to make the Philippine political system more democratic. Lansdale, like Defense Minister Ramón Magsaysay, preferred to use psychological warfare and social and economic programs, rather than massive military force, in the struggle against the guerrillas. Lansdale left the Philippines at the beginning of 1954, shortly after helping Magsaysay win election as president.

The CIA sent him to Vietnam on June 1, 1954. He headed the Saigon Military Mission (SMM), organizing psychological warfare and sabotage against the Communists in **North Vietnam**. The SMM planted rumors in North Vietnam to discredit the Communists; one of these, for example, stated that the Viet Minh had brought Chinese troops into the country, who were abusing the people. The SMM also sabotaged the railroads in North Vietnam and the engines of city buses in **Hanoi**, and trained some Vietnamese in **guerrilla warfare** techniques, infiltrating them into North Vietnam just before the final pullout of the French in 1955, to establish an underground organization there.

Lansdale also became an adviser to **Ngo Dinh Diem**. He supported Diem during the sect crisis of early 1955 (*see* **sects**), when Ambassador **J. Lawton Collins** wanted to abandon Diem. Lansdale provided U.S. funds to Diem (according to plausible rumor, about $10 million, coming from the CIA), which were used to buy the support of key sect generals, who rallied to Diem in late 1954 and early 1955.

By 1956, Diem's autocratic tendencies and the influence of **Ngo Dinh Nhu** were beginning to disturb Lansdale. He urged senior officials in Washington to press Diem to make political reforms, but this advice was rejected. Lansdale left Vietnam, and left the CIA, at the beginning of 1957. Later that year he became deputy assistant secretary of defense for special operations. In this position he had an extraordinary amount of power, for an Air Force colonel (brigadier general after 1960).

Early in the administration of **John Kennedy**, Lansdale tried to gain a major role in shaping U.S. policy toward Vietnam, but powerful people in the Departments of State and Defense blocked him. He had gone on an inspection mission to Vietnam in January 1961, and returned recommending a major increase in U.S. support for Diem. In May 1961, he became assistant secretary of defense for special operations. He accompanied the **Taylor-Rostow Mission** to Vietnam in October, but had little influence on its recommendations, and he was largely excluded from Vietnam policy making thereafter. His opposition to plans for a **coup** against Ngo Dinh Diem in 1963 had no impact, and he was retired both from the Air Force and from his position in the Defense Department. He then got a job with the Food for Peace program.

He finally got another long-term assignment to **Saigon** in 1965, when he went there as an assistant to Ambassador **Henry Cabot Lodge**. His job, rather vaguely defined, was to be Lodge's liaison with the agencies of the **Republic of Vietnam** that handled pacification. He argued that the United States should place more emphasis on **pacification** and less on the use of massive military force, and should not be so eager to do things for the Vietnamese that they could do for themselves. He had little power or influence; he left Vietnam, and ended his career with the U.S. government, in 1968.

Lansdale's autobiography, *In the Midst of Wars* (1972), covers only the years up to 1956. Lansdale has to varying degrees inspired several fictional characters. In *The Quiet American*, by Graham Greene (1955), the ignorant and naive Alden Pyle is not really based on Lansdale, but is a composite containing elements of Lansdale. In *The Ugly American*, by William Lederer and Eugene Burdick (1958), the competent and effective Colonel Edwin Hillandale is unmistakably Lansdale. In the Oliver Stone film *JFK* (1991), "General Y," who is shown managing the assassination of President Kennedy, is clearly supposed to be Lansdale.

**LAO.** The dominant ethnic group in **Laos**, making up about half the national population. The Lao live mostly on the lowlands near the border with **Thailand**, and are related by language and culture to the Thai. They grow rice in irrigated fields, and are Theravada (Hinayana) **Buddhists**.

**LAO DONG PARTY** (Workers' Party). The name used by the Communist Party in Vietnam from 1951 to 1976. It was successor to the Indochinese Communist Party, founded in 1930.

**Ho Chi Minh**, the founder of the party, had a special status in it until his death in 1969. The administrative head of the party was its general secretary (1951–1960) or first secretary (1960–1976). This position was held by **Truong Chinh** from 1951 to 1956, by Ho Chi Minh from 1956 to 1957, and by **Le Duan** probably from 1957 to 1986 (though his appointment was not formally announced until 1960). Only after Ho's death did Le Duan's position as first secretary make him clearly the top leader of the party.

Party congresses were held very seldom. The First Congress had been in 1935. The Second Congress established the Lao Dong Party in 1951. The Third Congress, in 1960, announced publicly the decision (reached the previous year) to promote the overthrow of **Ngo Dinh Diem** in **South Vietnam**. The Fourth Congress, in 1976, renamed the party the Communist Party of Vietnam, and celebrated the unification of Vietnam.

The Politburo (Bo chinh tri) was the supreme leadership group of the party. The Central Committee (Ban chap hanh truong uong) was a broader group. Important decisions were usually taken at a numbered plenum of the Central Committee. The numbering system for plenums started over with the number one after each party congress. Thus the 15th Plenum in 1959, which decided to launch a guerrilla war in South Vietnam, was the 15th since the party congress of 1951. The 9th Plenum in 1963, which decided to increase North Vietnamese support for that guerrilla war, was the 9th since the party congress of 1960.

The party leaders best known in the West, such as Ho Chi Minh, **Pham Van Dong**, and **Vo Nguyen Giap**, were educated and cosmopolitan enough to be able to communicate easily with Westerners. Men like Le Duan, **Le Duc Tho**, and **Pham Hung**, shaped more by French colonial prisons than by schools, were less conspicuous to foreigners but very powerful within the party.

The People's Revolutionary Party was formally established in 1962, nominally a separate Communist party for South Vietnam, but this was a propaganda ploy; the Lao Dong Party remained in reality the Communist party for all Vietnam, North and South.

**LAO THEUNG.** Collective term (the alternate name Kha is sometimes considered derogatory) for a number of ethnic groups, making up about one-third of the population of **Laos**. They live in the hills, but not in the highest mountains; they speak languages of the Mon-Khmer group.

The United States began to recruit paramilitary units of Lao Theung in southern Laos—the Bolovens Plateau and the area of Saravane—late in 1961 under Operation *Pincushion*. The United States hoped to use these units to attack the **Ho Chi Minh Trail**. The **Central Intelligence Agency** (CIA) sponsored the program; **Special Forces** personnel in Laos as part of *White Star* handled the training. But the Laotian government did not like the idea of Lao Theung paramilitary units outside its control. The U.S. **Military Assistance Advisory Group**, apparently sharing the negative attitude of the Lao government, was imposing restraints on the program even before the **Geneva Accords of 1962** led to the withdrawal of the *White Star* teams from Laos and the termination of the program.

By the mid-1960s the CIA was recruiting small teams of Lao Theung to serve as watchers along the Ho Chi Minh Trail. A U.S. proposal to establish a substantial Lao Theung paramilitary force for harassment of the Ho Chi Minh Trail was dropped in 1967 after the Laotian government made it clear that it would want to control any such force itself and not allow the United States to control it.

**LAOS.** Nation bordered by **China** to the north, Burma and **Thailand** to the west, **Cambodia** to the south, and Vietnam to the east. The area is 236,800 square kilometers, or 91,428 square miles. The population was probably somewhat over 2,000,000 in 1965; the 1985 census showed a population of 3,584,803. The most densely settled areas, inhabited by the **Lao**, are in the valley of the **Mekong River**, which for much of its length forms the western border of the country, separating Laos from Thailand. Most of the land area of Laos is much more thinly settled hills and forests, inhabited by a variety of peoples. The **Lao Theung** (who are not similar by language or culture to the lowland Lao) live at moderate elevations and make up about one-third of the population. Of the smaller groups living at the highest elevations, the **Hmong** played the most important role in the Second Indochina War; many Hmong fought in the "Secret Army" sponsored by the U.S. **Central Intelligence Agency** (CIA).

The modern nation was essentially a creation of French colonialism, which in the late 19th century combined the territories of the ethnically Lao kingdoms of Luang Prabang, Xieng Khouang, and Champassak with those of various highland tribes to make Laos, which in turn became part of French Indochina. There were two capitals. The actual government was in Vientiane, just across the Mekong River from Thailand. The king, a purely ceremonial figure, lived in Luang Prabang about 210 kilometers to the north.

During the First Indochina War there was some fighting in Laos, pitting forces of the Viet Minh and of the Laotian Communist movement known as the **Pathet Lao** against those of France and the Kingdom of Laos (to which by the late stages of the war the French had conceded something closer to actual independence than they had to the State of Vietnam), but the scale of combat remained small. The **Geneva Accords of 1954** temporarily divided Laos, giving control of most of the country to the government of the Kingdom of Laos but allocating two provinces in the Northeast, **Sam Neua** and **Phong Saly**, temporarily to the Pathet Lao. These two provinces were reintegrated with the rest of Laos in 1958, but following the outbreak of war in 1959, they again came under Communist control.

A three-way division in Laotian politics emerged in the mid-1950s. The Pathet Lao, under Communist leadership, were closely associated with the **Democratic Republic of Vietnam** (DRV) and had bases in the

Northeast near the Vietnamese border. The rightists, closely associated with the governments of Thailand and the United States, had bases of support in the South near the Thai border; the United States hoped by bolstering rightist political and military power to make Laos an anti-Communist bastion. The neutralists thought that Laos, a small and weak country surrounded by larger and far more powerful Communist and anti-Communist states, would have a better chance of survival as a neutral than as an ally of one side against the other.

The neutralist Prince **Souvanna Phouma** was prime minister when the Geneva Accords ended the First Indochina War in 1954. He was replaced by a rightist government in October 1954, but came back into office in March 1956, and in 1957 he managed to create the First Coalition Government; cabinet positions were shared between representatives of the Pathet Lao, the rightists, and the neutralists. The United States disapproved, however, and a cutoff of U.S. foreign aid in 1958 forced Souvanna to resign. War between the rightist government of Phoui Sananikone and the Pathet Lao began on a small scale in 1959, and U.S. military **advisers**, disguised as civilians, arrived to begin training the Royal Lao Army under Project *Hotfoot*.

A military **coup** organized by **Kong Le** brought Souvanna Phouma briefly back to power in 1960, but by the end of the year, the forces of the rightist **Phoumi Nosavan**, with Thai and U.S. aid, had retaken the capital. Kong Le's neutralist forces retreated northeastward, allied with the Pathet Lao and the DRV, and soon were getting military aid from the **Soviet Union**. President **John Kennedy** authorized covert U.S. air strikes, scheduled to begin on April 17, 1961, but these were cancelled at the last minute (*see Mill Pond*).

An international conference convened in Geneva, Switzerland, in 1961, to negotiate a settlement of the war; the real bargaining was done mainly by representatives of the United States and the Soviet Union. The **Geneva Accords of 1962** made Souvanna Phouma prime minister once more, as head of the Second Coalition Government. By this time the United States was much more willing to tolerate a neutral Laos than it had been in the 1950s, and the *White Star* military advisers were pulled out in compliance with the accords. The DRV however had become less willing to accept a neutral Laos, because the **Ho Chi Minh Trail**, passing through the eastern part of southern Laos, had become an important route by which the DRV supported the **Viet Cong** guerrillas in **South Vietnam**. The refusal of the DRV to pull all **PAVN** forces out of Laos pushed Souvanna Phouma toward an alliance with the

United States. The Second Coalition Government effectively ceased to function, and the Pathet Lao representatives left Vientiane, in 1963. Over the years that followed, the neutralist Prime Minister Souvanna Phouma was de facto allied with the United States against the Communists, and what had been a separate neutralist army was absorbed into the rightist-dominated Royal Lao Army.

The alliance with Souvanna Phouma proved frustrating for the United States. He eventually allowed the Americans almost unrestricted air action against the Communist forces on Laotian territory—the United States dropped more tons of **bombs** on Laos than it had dropped in the whole of the European Theater during World War II—but he had restricted American air action at first, and he never agreed to large-scale use of U.S. ground troops. He feared that if he removed all restrictions on American action, this might provoke the DRV into making an all-out effort to overthrow his government. The Royal Lao Army proved of little value in combat; the Americans got around this problem by creating the "Secret Army" of Hmong tribesmen, operating under the control of the CIA with a nominal affiliation to Souvanna's government in Vientiane, and also by bringing troops of the Thai Army into Laos.

There were really two wars in Laos. One was the war of ground combat in northern Laos, especially around the **Plain of Jars**, where PAVN and Pathet Lao forces usually advanced during the winter dry season, and were driven back during the summer rainy season. The other was along the Ho Chi Minh Trail in southern Laos, where the United States bombed PAVN forces on a huge scale, but hardly ever sent in more than tiny covert operations (*see* **Prairie Fire**, **Shining Brass**, **SOG**) on the ground.

The biggest incursions by U.S. ground troops into Laos were in 1969, and were modest in scope. Elements of the 2/9 **Marines** crossed into Laos in February 1969—at first just a few men without permission from **Military Assistance Command, Vietnam**, later three companies with permission from MACV—as part of Operation *Dewey Canyon*, attacking a PAVN base area that straddled the border between Laos and **Quang Tri** province of South Vietnam. There was a much larger incursion by troops of the Army of the Republic of Vietnam (**ARVN**) in the spring of 1971, called *Lam Son 719*. The United States also sometimes got around the prohibition on ground operations into Laos by changing the maps. U.S. Army maps in the early 1960s had shown the southern part of the **A Shau** Valley, including the spot where the United States later built the A Shau **Special Forces** Camp, as being in Laos.

Later maps defined these areas as falling within South Vietnam.

As direct American involvement in Indochina and U.S. aid for anti-Communist forces there shrank, the level of fighting in most areas of Laos declined. Negotiations between Souvanna Phouma and the Pathet Lao led to a cease-fire on February 21, 1973. An agreement on the formation of a Third Coalition Government was signed on September 14, 1973, and it took office on April 5, 1974. Small-scale fighting between Pathet Lao and Royal Lao Army forces occurred in several areas in the first half of 1975, but the final seizure of power by the Pathet Lao in August was bloodless. They proclaimed the Lao People's Democratic Republic on December 2, 1975.

**LAVELLE, JOHN DANIEL** (1916–1979). U.S. **Air Force** general. Born in Cleveland, Ohio, Lavelle graduated from John Carroll University in 1938, joined the Army in 1940, and went into the Air Corps. He supervised the program to drop **sensors** along the **Ho Chi Minh Trail** (see *Igloo White*), then became commander of the Seventh Air Force, the Air Force command for Southeast Asia, in mid-1971.

Frustrated by the policy that forbade bombing of targets in **North Vietnam** except in retaliation for North Vietnamese attacks on U.S. **reconnaissance** aircraft, Lavelle began having pilots make false reports of such attacks, in order to be able to bomb in retaliation for the imaginary incidents. He was relieved of his command in 1972 and forced to retire from the Air Force. At first Lavelle took full personal responsibility for the bombing incidents. But in testimony on September 12, 1972, before the Senate Armed Services Committee, he said he had had permission for some of the missions from General **Creighton Abrams** (commander of **Military Assistance Command, Vietnam**) and Admiral **Thomas Moorer** (Chairman of the **Joint Chiefs of Staff**). Abrams denied this the following day. Lavelle then signed a statement, "It seemed clear to me that higher authorities had recommended, encouraged and commended an extremely liberal policy, well beyond the literal language of the rules of engagement."

**LE DUAN,** a.k.a. Anh Ba (Brother Number Three) or just Ba (1907–1986). Born in **Quang Tri** province, he began revolutionary activities in 1928, and was a founding member of the Indochinese Communist Party in 1930. Le Duan was imprisoned 1931–1936 and 1940–1945; it was as a prisoner on **Poulo Condore** that he got most of his education. In 1946, largely due to **Le Duc Tho**'s backing, he was given responsibility for leading the resistance against the French in **Nam Bo** (the southern third of Vietnam), as secretary first of the Nam Bo Regional Committee, later of the **Trung uong cuc mien Nam** (COSVN). After the **Geneva Accords of 1954** he remained in **South Vietnam** as a leader of the Communist organizations in Nam Bo until 1957. In August 1956 he wrote "The Revolutionary Line in the South," arguing that **Ngo Dinh Diem** would have to be overthrown by revolution. This is generally regarded as among the most important Communist policy statements of the period, though the policy it advocated was not adopted by the party until 1959.

Le Duan, Le Duc Tho, and **Pham Hung**, who had worked together in the South, were close allies in **Hanoi** from the late 1950s onward. They eventually became very hostile to **Vo Nguyen Giap**, and they did not much care for Premier **Pham Van Dong** either. The power of this faction was shown when Le Duan became the administrative head of the **Lao Dong Party** shortly after arriving in Hanoi from the South. **Truong Chinh** had been general secretary of the Lao Dong Party until dismissed in late 1956 as a result of his errors in the **land reform** campaign. **Ho Chi Minh** replaced Truong Chinh as general secretary in 1956. Le Duan took over much of the actual work of this job after his arrival in Hanoi in 1957. His formal promotion to the position, renamed first secretary, was announced in September 1960. The title was shifted back to general secretary when the party was renamed the Communist Party of Vietnam in 1976. Le Duan held the office until his death in 1986.

Le Duan was primarily responsible for the decision of the 15th Plenum, in 1959, to initiate **guerrilla warfare** in South Vietnam. He also played a major role in aligning the DRV on the Chinese side in the Sino-Soviet dispute (*see* **China**) during the next few years. When Ho Chi Minh's health was failing in the mid-1960s, Le Duan became more and more clearly the leader of the Lao Dong Party, leaving nobody in a position to contest the succession when Ho finally died in 1969. He does not seem to have taken conspicuously extreme positions on war policy from the mid-1960s onward.

**LE DUC ANH** (1920– ). **PAVN** general. Born near **Hue**, he joined the Indochinese Communist Party in 1938, and served in the PAVN from 1945 onward. From 1948 to 1950 he was chief of staff successively to **Military Regions** 7 and 8, and to the **Saigon-Cholon** Special Region. In 1951, he became deputy chief of staff for **Nam Bo**. He went north after the **Geneva Accords**, and in 1963 became deputy chief of the PAVN General Staff. Shortly afterward Anh returned to **South Vietnam**, serv-

ing from 1964 to 1968 first as chief of staff and then as deputy commander of the People's Liberation Army of South Vietnam. He was one
of the commanders (along with **Tran Van Tra** and Mai Chi Tho) of the
command that was responsible for attacking Saigon from the north
during the **Tet Offensive** of 1968. From 1969 to 1974, he commanded
Military Region 9, the southernmost section of South Vietnam. In 1973,
Anh and **Vo Van Kiet**, as commanders of Military Region 9, were very
aggressive in combat operations against the **ARVN** following the **Paris
Peace Agreement**, ignoring the policy coming from **Hanoi** that called
for a greater degree of compliance with the agreement. During the last
months of the war he was again deputy commander of the People's
Liberation Army of South Vietnam, and during the fall of Saigon he
commanded the forces attacking from the southwest.

Anh commanded PAVN forces in **Cambodia** from 1981 to 1987. He
was minister of defense of the Socialist Republic of Vietnam from 1987
to 1991, and president from 1992 to 1997. He was a member of the
Politburo from 1982 to 1997.

**LE DUC THO,** original name Phan Dinh Khai, a.k.a. Sau, Sau Bua, Sau Tho
(1910–1990). Communist party leader. He was born in Nam Dinh province, in **Bac Bo**, and was a founding member of the Indochinese Communist Party in 1930. He was not an intellectual; he was shaped by the
time he spent in colonial prisons in the 1930s, rather than by formal
schooling.

Tho was sent south to take control of the Communist Party organization in **Nam Bo** (the southern third of Vietnam) in 1946. He
promoted **Le Duan**, and also worked with **Pham Hung**. In the late
1950s, these three men, all members of the **Lao Dong Party** Politburo,
became an extremely powerful faction in **Hanoi**. The witch-hunts searching for "**Revisionists**" in the People's Army of Vietnam (**PAVN**) in the
1960s appear to have been motivated partly by the hostility of this
faction to **Vo Nguyen Giap**.

Tho was sent as the Politburo's representative to **South Vietnam** in
February 1968; he apparently delivered a decision of the Politburo that
the forces in South Vietnam were to continue attacking, instead of
letting the **Tet Offensive** be a relatively brief episode. He later became
nominally an "adviser," actually the chief negotiator, of the delegation
of the **Democratic Republic of Vietnam** (DRV) at the **Paris negotiations**. The **Paris Peace Agreement** of January 27, 1973, was primarily
negotiated between Le Duc Tho and **Henry Kissinger**. When Tho and

Kissinger were jointly awarded the Nobel Prize for Peace for having negotiated the accords, Tho declined, explaining that the accords had not actually brought peace.

When the Politburo decided on March 25, 1975, to attempt to complete the conquest of South Vietnam immediately (*see* **final collapse**), Le Duc Tho was sent south to convey the decision to the military commanders there personally, and help to supervise its implementation. He worked with Pham Hung and **Van Tien Dung** to supervise the final campaign against **Saigon**.

Tho resigned from the Politburo in 1986, but remained very powerful until his death in 1990.

**LE KHA PHIEU** (1931– ). **PAVN** political officer, later Communist Party general secretary. Born in Thanh Hoa province, Le Kha Phieu joined the Indochinese Communist Party in 1949, and the PAVN in 1950. By 1954 he was political officer of a company. From 1961 to 1967 he held mostly staff positions in the 304th Division, but commanded a regiment in the division for part of that time. In 1967 he was sent to the **Tri-Thien Front**, where he served as a political officer and staff officer for the rest of the war. He served with the Vietnamese forces in **Cambodia** from 1984 to 1988. Phieu became a member of the Communist Party Central Committee at the Seventh Congress in 1991, and was the party's general secretary from 1997 to 2001.

**LE NGUYEN KHANG** (1931–1996). Vietnamese **Marine Corps** (VNMC) general. Born in **Son Tay** province, **Bac Bo**, a **Buddhist**, he graduated from high school in Hanoi in 1951, and from a reserve officer training school in Nam Dinh in 1952. He then served in the 3d River Force Detachment in the war against the Viet Minh.

Khang became commander of the Headquarters Company, Marine Group, **Republic of Vietnam** (RVN) in 1956, and of the VNMC 2d Battalion in 1957. In 1958 he became the first Vietnamese Marine to graduate from the U.S. **Marines'** Amphibious Warfare School at Quantico, and he spoke fluent English by the time he became commandant of the VNMC in 1960.

In December 1963, the generals who had overthrown **Ngo Dinh Diem** decided that Khang was too closely associated with Diem; they removed him from command of the VNMC (replacing him with Lieutenant Colonel Nguyen Ba Lien, who had been assistant commandant and chief of staff), gave him a courtesy promotion to colonel, and sent him to the Philippines.

In February 1964, Khang was re-appointed head of the VNMC, which at that time was a brigade of four battalions; before the end of the year he had been promoted first to brigadier and then to major general. He was one of the **"Young Turks"** who made **Nguyen Cao Ky** premier in 1965. He retained command of the Marines (expanded to become the Marine Division in 1968) while serving as commander of the Capital Military District from June 1965 to June 1966, and of **III Corps** from June 1966 to August 1968. Khang was generally regarded as one of the best combat generals the RVN had. Politically, he was a supporter of Nguyen Cao Ky against **Nguyen Van Thieu**. His talents allowed him to retain his division command for a while after Thieu defeated Ky, but he finally was removed from command of the Marines in 1972. He became inspector general of the Republic of Vietnam Armed Forces.

*LEAPING LENA,* Project. In late June 1964, the United States parachuted five eight-man teams of Vietnamese **Special Forces** personnel into southern **Laos**, around **Tchepone**, to reconnoiter the **Ho Chi Minh Trail**. **PAVN** forces reacted vigorously, and soon killed or captured all but four of the 40 men who had been sent in.

The name *Leaping Lena* also appears to have been used for a program of long-range **reconnaissance** patrols in **South Vietnam**, made up mostly of **Montagnards** or members of the Vietnamese Special Forces, trained by men of the U.S. **Army Special Forces**. It was begun on May 15, 1964, under the control of the **Central Intelligence Agency**, but control was almost immediately transferred to the U.S. military. It later became Project *Delta* (*see* **Special Forces**, U.S.).

**LEMAY, CURTIS EMERSON** (1906–1990). U.S. **Air Force** general. Born in Columbus, Ohio, LeMay became an officer in the U.S. Army Air Corps in 1930. As commander of the 20th Bomber Group, he presided over the fire-bombing of Japanese cities in 1945. He commanded the Strategic Air Command from 1948 to 1961, and was Air Force chief of staff from 1961 until his retirement in 1965. LeMay was a strident cold warrior; some historians who have examined his actions in the 1950s suspect he actually wanted to provoke a nuclear war with the **Soviet Union**. In the early 1960s, he was the most conspicuous advocate, on the **Joint Chiefs of Staff**, of the overt commitment of U.S. military forces to combat in Vietnam. His suggestion that the U.S. bomb **North Vietnam** "back to the Stone Age" epitomized his conception of the proper way to handle the war. He was the vice-presidential candidate—running mate to George Wallace—of the American Independent Party in the **election** of 1968. During this campaign he aroused controversy by saying that in Vietnam the United States should "use anything we could dream up, including nuclear weapons."

**LIEN DOI NGUOI NHAI** (LDNN), literally "Frogman Unit." The **Republic of Vietnam** (RVN) equivalent of the U.S. **Navy's SEAL** teams. The first Vietnamese personnel were sent to Taiwan for training in 1960. Early in 1961 arrangements were made for the government of the **Republic of China** to send instructors to Vietnam, to conduct training in underwater operations at **Danang** and **Vung Tau**. The LDNN was formally established in July 1961; the successful students from the group sent to Taiwan in 1960 formed its nucleus. After the U.S. Navy established the SEALs in 1962, American SEALs began to train some LDNN units. The quality and nature of LDNN units varied widely; by 1964, some of them at least were becoming pretty good general-purpose commandos, suitable for missions into enemy territory on land as well as for work in the water.

**LIGHT ANTI-TANK WEAPON** (LAW), also called Light Anti-tank Assault Weapon (LAAW), M72. A small shoulder-fired **rocket**, 66-mm in diameter, weighing 1.25 kilograms and fired from a 1.25-kilogram launcher, used by U.S. troops. It was a single-shot weapon; the launcher was discarded after the rocket had been fired. The effective range was about 250 meters. The warhead was smaller than that of the Communists' shoulder-fired weapon, the **RPG**.

**LIMA SITE** (LS). In large areas of **Laos**, the anti-Communist war effort was organized around bases supplied by air, called Lima Sites and assigned numbers. Most had airstrips, which even if short and bumpy could accommodate a sufficiently capable fixed-wing aircraft such as the **Pilatus Porter**. A few could be supplied only by **helicopter**. The most important was **Long Cheng**, the base for the **Hmong** "Secret Army." It was designated LS 20A, often called 20 Alternate or just "Alternate."

Lima Site 85 was an important adjunct to the U.S. **air war** in northern Indochina. The vital portion of this facility was at the peak of Phou Pha Thi (Phu Pha Thi), a precipitous mountain, sacred to the **Hmong**, in **Sam Neua** province of northeast **Laos**, 34 kilometers from the Vietnamese border. The mountain, a nearly vertical cliff on one side and very steep on the others, provided no room for even the smallest airstrip, though **helicopters** could land on it. There was a small airstrip in the valley below. A TACAN (tactical air navigation) system was installed on the peak in 1966. In June 1967, installation of a much more sophisticated TSQ-81 *Combat Skyspot* bomb control radar (*see* **radar**) began; this facility, called *Commando Club*, became operational in November 1967. *Commando Club* allowed aircraft to drop **bombs** with acceptable accuracy over large portions of Laos and **North Vietnam** in darkness or bad weather; it is said to have controlled 23 percent of all air strikes against North Vietnam in January 1968. Without the assistance of such a fixed radar site, aircraft would have needed to operate at lower altitudes, where they would be more vulnerable to **anti-aircraft artillery**, in order to bomb accurately. The area of coverage of LS 85 included **Hanoi**. The U.S. **Air Force** personnel manning the site had been "**sheepdipped**"—disguised as civilian employees of the Lockheed Corporation. Indigenous troops provided military protection for the site.

Early in 1968, troops of the **PAVN** 316th Division began closing in on LS 85. It became obvious that the site would eventually become untenable, but the Americans believed that the terrain would provide such advantages to the defending forces that the attackers would have to fight their way up the mountain gradually, allowing time for the site to be evacuated by air before it could be stormed. On the night of March 10–11 1968, however, the PAVN sent 20 **sappers** (said to have been Hmong) up the cliff, which had been unguarded because it was assumed to be impassable. They took the site by surprise at about 3:00 a.m., and overran it. The situation was confused enough that at dawn, U.S. helicopters were able to come in and rescue eight of the 19 U.S. personnel who had been at the site at the time of the attack; the remainder were listed as missing, presumed dead.

The Hmong forces of General **Vang Pao** suffered heavy casualties in unsuccessful efforts to recapture the mountain later in 1968.

***LINEBACKER,*** Operation, May–October 1972. A major U.S. air campaign against **North Vietnam**; it followed the smaller Operation *Freedom Train*, which had begun on April 6, 1972.

On May 9, 1972, U.S. aircraft dropped **mines** into the mouths of North Vietnamese ports in Operation *Pocket Money*. On May 10, the first day of *Linebacker*, U.S. planes attacked key bridges in the **Hanoi** and **Haiphong** areas, including the **Doumer Bridge**, with smart **bombs**, and also bombed railroad yards, fuel storage, and other targets. Other aircraft attacked **radar** sites and **anti-aircraft artillery** to protect the bombing planes. This coordinated attack on high-value targets was celebrated as the antithesis of the gradual escalation that had typified Operation *Rolling Thunder* from 1965 to 1968.

*Linebacker* ended on October 23, but this did not end U.S. bombing of North Vietnam; bombing continued south of the 20th parallel.

***LINEBACKER II,*** Operation, 1972. The **Paris negotiations** seemed close to success in October 1972, and U.S. bombing of the northern part of **North Vietnam** was halted. But the negotiations stalled amid mutual recriminations in December; there is a widespread though false story that the **Democratic Republic of Vietnam** (DRV) had even walked out of the peace talks. The DRV began evacuating the civilian population of **Hanoi** in anticipation of possible heavy bombing. President **Richard Nixon** indeed ordered a major bombing campaign, *Linebacker II*, which ran from December 18 to 24, stopped for one day on Christmas, and then resumed from December 26 to 29. During the 11 days of bombing, **B-52**s dropped 15,237 tons of **bombs** on North Vietnam, almost all north of the 20th parallel and mostly in the area of Hanoi. Fighter-bombers dropped about 5,000 tons. These tonnages exceeded the usual levels of U.S. bombing, but not by a huge margin. The reason the damage done was far greater than usual was that *Linebacker II* went for much more important targets than U.S. bombing of North Vietnam usually had done. The fear of aircraft losses that had previously kept B-52s out of the areas of heaviest air defenses was completely discarded, and the fears of international repercussions that had inhibited bombing in the Hanoi and **Haiphong** areas were largely discarded.

The U.S. military said 15 B-52s had been lost and nine damaged, and denied rumors that some of the damaged ones were beyond repair. The number of smaller airplanes lost was variously given as 11 or 13.

*Linebacker II* inspired a worldwide storm of outrage, based on a serious misunderstanding of its nature. Most people got the impression that it was an extraordinarily ruthless campaign, pounding cities in the style of World War II. All of America's major allies were bitterly critical. The U.S. government made little effort to explain that while the Hanoi *area* was being heavily bombed, almost all the bombs were directed at military targets on the outskirts; the city center was little damaged.

The Vietnamese have released a variety of figures on the casualties. Preliminary data released immediately after the bombing, before there had been time to do a thorough search for bodies under the rubble, indicated that 1,318 civilians had been killed in Hanoi and 305 in Haiphong. Later figures, indicating that either 2,027 or 2,196 people had been killed in Hanoi, included civilian bodies discovered after the preliminary figures were released, but they may also have included military casualties. A figure of 2,368 dead for North Vietnam as a whole was probably a final total for civilian dead only.

*Linebacker II* left both sides eager for a settlement. Nixon needed peace to counter the widespread belief that he had engaged in a mass slaughter of civilians, and the DRV needed an opportunity to rebuild transport systems, power plants, and many military facilities. The **Paris Peace Agreement** was signed on January 27, 1973; it was similar in most ways to the agreement that had almost been signed in October 1972.

**LODGE, HENRY CABOT, JR.** (1902–1985). Born in Nahant, Massachusetts, to a politically powerful family, he was elected to the U.S. Senate in 1936. He resigned to enter the Army during World War II. Lodge was elected again to the Senate in 1946, but was defeated by **John Kennedy** in 1952; he served as U.S. ambassador to the United Nations 1953–1960. He was the vice-presidential candidate of the Republican Party in 1960. John Kennedy asked Lodge in June 1963 to become U.S. ambassador to South Vietnam. Lodge arrived in **Saigon** in August, and almost immediately began to urge U.S. support for a **coup** against **Ngo Dinh Diem**. He resigned as ambassador in June 1964 and tried to win the Republican nomination for president, but then served as ambassador in Saigon again from August 1965 to 1967. Lodge regarded a victory in Vietnam as vital for the United States, and by early 1966 he was urging a massive expansion in U.S. bombing of **North Vietnam**. He headed the American delegation at the **Paris peace negotiations** from January to November 1969. His memoir *The Storm Has Many Eyes* was published in 1973.

**LOGISTICS.** The United States established four major logistics centers for military forces in Vietnam. From north to south, these were **Danang**, in **Quang Nam** province of **I Corps**; **Qui Nhon**, in northern **II Corps**; **Cam Ranh**, in southern II Corps; and **Long Binh**, just northeast of **Saigon**. Supplies arrived in Vietnam primarily by sea, but a substantial amount came by air. Within **South Vietnam** they were distributed by trucks, boats, fixed-wing transport aircraft, and **helicopters**.

Communist forces in South Vietnam had to make do with much lower levels of supply. Some of their needs were supplied within South Vietnam; the remainder arrived by three major routes, the relative importance of which varied with time. Delivery by sea to the coast of

South Vietnam (*see* **Group 759**) was most important in the early 1960s. Delivery by sea through the port of **Sihanoukville** in **Cambodia** was very important in the mid to late 1960s. The **Ho Chi Minh Trail** through **Laos** was also very important from the mid-1960s onward, and Communist logistics came to rely overwhelmingly on this route in the 1970s. Distribution within South Vietnam in the early days of the war was mostly by human porters, bicycles (see photograph 16), and small boats. Trucks were increasingly used in some areas in the later stages.

**LON NOL** (1913–1985). Cambodian marshal. Born in Prey Veng province of **Cambodia**, he was educated at the Lycée Chasseloup-Laubat in **Saigon**, and then became a provincial civil servant in Cambodia. He was one of the founders of the Khmer Renovation Party in 1947, and became its dominant figure. The party was allied with Prince **Norodom Sihanouk** from 1951 onward, and was formally dissolved, in deference to Sihanouk's Sangkum, in May 1955. By the beginning of 1950, and probably earlier, Lon Nol was chief of the Cambodian National Police. He was chief of staff of the Cambodian Armed Forces from August 1955 onward, and intermittently served concurrently as minister of defense. He was not very competent in running the Army; he was better at supervising the security police.

Lon Nol became prime minister in 1966; Sihanouk almost immediately began to distrust him, and removed him from control of the Army. He resigned as prime minister in 1967 on grounds of ill health, and went to France for six months for medical treatment. He again became minister of defense in May 1968, and prime minister in August 1969.

Lon Nol and Prince Sisowath Sirik Matak overthrew Sihanouk in a bloodless **coup** on March 18, 1970, and Nol was the dominant figure of the Cambodian government for most of the next five years. He spent two months in the United States recovering from a stroke early in 1971, and after his return officially resigned his positions as prime minister, defense minister, and Army chief of staff, but he promptly took the new title of marshal. He was named head of state on March 10, 1973, and president a few days later.

Lon Nol was not very capable either as a military manager—the officer corps he built up was riddled with corruption—or as a combat commander. He was quite superstitious, and encouraged his soldiers to carry magical amulets to protect them from enemy bullets. He left Cambodia (claiming to be going abroad for medical treatment) on April 1, 1975, as **Khmer Rouge** forces were about to take **Phnom Penh**.

**LONG AN.** The province of Long An was created in 1957, by the amalgamation of Tan An with part of what had been the province of **Cholon**. Initially, it stretched all the way from the South China Sea to the border of **Cambodia**. In 1961 or 1962, however, the **Rung Sat**, the southern part of the province near the sea, was detached from it. In 1963, the part bordering on Cambodia was combined with portions of **Tay Ninh** and Binh Duong to form the new province of **Hau Nghia**.

Even after being reduced in size, Long An remained highly important. The main roads from **Saigon** into the **Mekong Delta** passed through Long An: **Route 4** leading to **Can Tho** and the heart of the delta, and Route 5 to Go Cong. Long An was a **Viet Cong** stronghold for many years; it was the base for many of the forces that attacked the Saigon area in 1968.

**LONG BINH.** Northeast of **Saigon** in **Bien Hoa** province, Long Binh became the largest military base in Vietnam, said to have had 43,000 U.S. personnel at one point. It was one of the four great centers of American **logistics** in **South Vietnam**. Its ammunition supply depot, by far the largest in Vietnam, was a prime target for Communist **sappers**. There were three successful attacks on the depot in 1966, one in 1967, two in 1968, and one in 1969. The headquarters for U.S. Army, Vietnam (USARV), was on the northern edge of the Long Binh base.

Long Binh Jail (LBJ) was the main U.S. **Army** detention facility in Vietnam. Conditions became notorious; the LBJ was overcrowded by 1968, and seriously overcrowded by 1969. Many prisoners were housed in steel shipping containers.

**LONG CHENG** (Long Tieng, Long Chieng). A valley in **Laos**, south of the **Plain of Jars**. It was chosen in 1962 by Colonel **Vang Pao**, leader of a **Hmong** force sponsored by the **Central Intelligence Agency**, as the base for his forces. As Vang Pao's "Secret Army" expanded to 30,000 men, Long Cheng became a major center of the war in Laos. It was designated **Lima Site** 20A, often called 20 Alternate or just "Alternate." Offensives by Communist forces, mostly **PAVN**, several times came close to taking Long Cheng—a PAVN offensive of January 1972 was barely stopped in very heavy fighting. In May 1975, however, as the resistance to Communist rule collapsed in Laos, Long Cheng was abandoned without a fight as PAVN and **Pathet Lao** forces approached.

**LONG-RANGE PATROL** or **LONG-RANGE RECONNAISSANCE PATROL** (LRP or LRRP, both pronounced "lurp"). When U.S. **Army divisions** began to arrive in Vietnam, they found that they needed re-

**connaissance** personnel capable of moving unobtrusively through the jungle to locate Communist units and facilities. At first, divisions made their own arrangements, but the need for standardization soon became apparent. The **Recondo School** at **Nha Trang** was expanded to allow it to train a substantial proportion (though not all) of the personnel of the various LRP companies. A reorganization at the beginning of 1969 made the LRP companies **Ranger** companies and made them all formally parts of a single regiment, the 75th Infantry (Ranger). The LRP company of the 1st Infantry Division, for example, had up to that time been Company F of the 52nd Infantry; it was renamed Company I of the 75th Infantry.

**LONG TAU RIVER.** Flowing in a southerly direction through the **Rung Sat** swamps, this is the main channel by which ocean-going ships can reach **Saigon**. Coming from the South China Sea, ships go up the Long Tau River to reach the **Nha Be** River, which in turn leads to the Saigon River and Saigon.

**LONG THANH,** Camp. The U.S. **Army Special Forces** began training Vietnamese **airborne** and **Ranger** forces at Long Thanh, in **Bien Hoa** province 22 kilometers east of **Saigon**, in 1961. In 1963, the **Central Intelligence Agency** began training Vietnamese teams there to be airdropped into **North Vietnam**; **SOG** began training personnel for *Shining Brass* operations into **Laos** there in 1965. Late in 1968, Camp Long Thanh was made the overall training center for SOG, and the training of cross-border personnel, previously done at the three command and control centers, was shifted there.

**LY TONG BA** (1931– ). **ARVN** general. Born the son of a landlord in Long Xuyen province, in the southern part of the **Mekong Delta**, Ba got officer training in **Hue** in 1950, and by 1954 was commanding a platoon of armored cars fighting on the side of the French against the Viet Minh. He later got a year's training (1957–1958) at the U.S. Army's Armor School in Fort Knox.

As a captain in 1962, commanding a company of M-113 **armored personnel carriers** in the northern part of the Mekong Delta, he was aggressive and effective in combat. But at the Battle of **Ap Bac**, on January 2, 1963, his unit did very poorly.

Ba was province chief for Binh Duong from 1966 to 1968. In January 1972, he was given command of the 23d ARVN Division at **Ban Me Thuot**. The 23d Division was moved north from Ban Me Thuot to defend **Kontum** after the collapse of the 22d Division north of Kontum on April 24, 1972. The close relationship between Ba and **John Paul Vann** contributed to the successful defense of Kontum against the **PAVN** attack beginning on May 14. Ba commanded the 25th ARVN Division, northwest of **Saigon**, from 1973 to 1975.

## - M -

**M-16 RIFLE.** In the late 1950s, Eugene Stoner, working for the Armalite Corporation, designed a rifle called the AR-15 or simply the Armalite. It fired a small (5.56-mm) bullet, much lighter than the 7.62-mm bullet of the M-14 rifle, standard for U.S. military forces at the time. The rifle itself was also much lighter than the M-14. In the early 1960s, there was increasing interest in the AR-15 as a weapon for use in Vietnam. Its great advantage was that the light weight of the rifle, and of the ammunition, made it practical for an infantryman to carry far more rounds into battle. The high velocity of the bullets ensured adequate lethality at short and medium ranges. The bullets lost accuracy and killing power at very long ranges, but this was almost irrelevant to the sort of combat occurring in Vietnam. The AR-15 had considerably less recoil than the M-14, and thus was far more accurate in full automatic fire. It was extremely reliable. The only defect of the AR-15 that was significant under Vietnam combat conditions was that the light bullet was easily deflected when passing through brush.

AR-15s may have been supplied to the **Sea Swallows** as early as 1960; some were issued to the **ARVN** on an experimental basis in 1962. The results were excellent. The **Special Forces** obtained permission to use the AR-15 as their standard rifle in 1963. There was increasing pressure on the U.S. **Army** to adopt the weapon.

What was sent to Vietnam in large numbers beginning in 1966 was a version modified by the Army, called the M-16A1. As a rifle the M-16A1 was slightly inferior to the AR-15, but not by a great margin. The real problem was that the ammunition sent with it used a propellant substantially different from that for which the rifle had been designed, and it turned what had been a very reliable weapon into an unreliable one, prone to jam in combat. There were outraged protests from the troops. Gradually the rifle was modified to make it more compatible with the ammunition, reducing the tendency to jam, but the M-16A1 still was not as reliable as the AR-15 had been.

**MACHINE GUNS.** The standard American machine gun, the M60, fired

7.62-mm ammunition. Its bore was the same size as the older .30-caliber, but the ammunition was not interchangeable because the cartridges were shorter. It was widely used both in infantry units (see photograph 3) and as a weapon for the door gunners of **helicopters**. It had an effective range of about 1,000 meters. The 7.62-mm **minigun** had a much higher rate of fire than the M60, but weighed too much to be easily carried by infantry units. The .50-caliber machine gun, firing a much heavier projectile with an effective range of about 1,450 meters, was mounted on many vehicles. The M-55 Quad 50 was a mount, shielded on the front, holding four .50-caliber machine guns that all fired together. This was normally mounted on the bed of a truck (see photograph 4), to add firepower to truck convoys.

**Viet Cong** soldiers were able to shoot down helicopters firing at very short ranges in the battle of **Ap Bac** in January 1963, with machine guns that were probably 7.62-mm or .30-caliber. The arrival soon afterward of .50-caliber machine guns and similar Soviet-bloc weapons gave the Viet Cong a much better capability against helicopters.

**MANSFIELD, MIKE** (Michael Joseph) (1903–2001). U.S. Senator. Born in New York City, he worked as a mining engineer and a history professor before entering politics as a Democrat. He represented Montana in the U.S. House of Representatives from 1943 to 1953, and in the Senate from 1953 to 1977. He was Senate majority leader from 1961 to 1977. From December 1963 through early 1965, Mansfield privately urged President **Lyndon Johnson** to seek a negotiated compromise on the war. When Johnson met with 16 key senators on August 4, 1964, to discuss his decision to bomb **North Vietnam** in retaliation for the second **Tonkin Gulf incident**, Mansfield was the only one who opposed the bombing. He did not, however, bring public pressure to bear on the president up through 1965; he supported Johnson's decisions in public even while arguing against them in private. When he became a public advocate of a negotiated settlement, in Johnson's last years and the early part of **Richard Nixon**'s administration, he still tried to do this in a way that would not set him against the president. Only in 1970, in response to the **Cambodian Incursion**, did Mansfield become a strong opponent of the war. He did not run for re-election in 1976. He was U.S. ambassador to Japan 1977–1988.

**MARBLE MOUNTAIN.** A small but steep and conspicuous mountain at the base (the south end) of the **Tien Sha Peninsula**, on the coast of the South China Sea about seven kilometers southeast of **Danang**.

Marble Mountain Air Facility, a little to the north of Marble Moutain itself, was completed in August 1965; by this time the main Danang airfield was severely crowded, and there was a need for another base to which U.S. **Marine helicopters** could be moved. A **Viet Cong** raiding party of about 90 men, supported by 60-mm **mortar** fire, made a well-planned attack on the facility on the night of October 27–28, 1965, destroying 19 helicopters and damaging 35 others.

**MARINE CORPS,** U.S. The United States Marine Corps (USMC) is in most ways a separate service, but remains to some extent an affiliate of the **Navy.** Its highest officer is the commandant. General David L. Shoup became commandant in January 1960, General **Wallace M. Greene** in January 1964, General Leonard F. Chapman in January 1968, and General Robert E. Cushman in January 1972.

USMC Lieutenant Colonel Victor Croizat arrived in Vietnam on August 2, 1954. He worked for several months helping to organize the flow of refugees from North to South, and then early in 1955 became the first U.S. **adviser** to the newly organized Vietnamese **Marine Corps.** A few other USMC advisers were added soon after that.

The first U.S. Marine unit to join directly in combat operations in Vietnam was Task Unit *Shufly*, a **helicopter** squadron, which arrived in April 1962. Initially it was stationed at Soc Trang in the **Mekong Delta**; in September 1962, it moved north to **Danang.** During 1964, without public notice, the Marine Corps began sending small ground troop units to guard facilities in the area: a reinforced company to guard the airfield at Danang, a detachment of about 80 men to guard a radio listening post on Tiger Tooth Mountain northeast of Danang, and possibly smaller detachments elsewhere.

In March 1965, President **Lyndon Johnson** decided to send two battalions of Marines to guard the airfield at Danang. Battalion Landing Team 3/9, which had been sitting on ships off the coast near Danang since early February, began landing on a beach just northwest of the city on the morning of March 8. The 1/3 Battalion was flown in from Okinawa; it began arriving at Danang Air Base early that afternoon. The arrival of these units, unlike the smaller ones that had been guarding Danang since the previous year, was announced to the press.

In May, the Third Marine Amphibious Force (III MAF) was established, based at Danang. By the end of the year, the theoretical strength of the III MAF was 39,989 officers and men, of whom 23,369 were in the 3d Marine **Division** and 9,605 were in the 1st Marine Aircraft Wing.

Most of the rest were support personnel of various sorts. The 1st Marine Division arrived in 1966, and was also placed under III MAF. The Marines were at first the only large U.S. ground force in **I Corps**. Even when U.S. **Army** units began to arrive in I Corps, they were at first placed under the command of III MAF.

The leaders of the U.S. Marine Corps tended to advocate a different strategy for the war than those of the Army, based less on combat against Communist military forces, and more on **pacification**: efforts to establish control in the villages and win the allegiance of the peasants. By early 1966, Generals **Victor Krulak** (commander, Fleet Marine Force, Pacific) and Wallace Greene (commandant of the Marine Corps) were advocating a strategy based on pacification, and Major General Lewis Walt (commander, III MAF, 1965–1967) was implementing it by, among other things, the **Combined Action Platoons**. Walt was criticized by **William Westmoreland** and the Army generals dominating **Military Assistance Command, Vietnam**, who felt that the Marines should be spending less time establishing control in the populated areas along the coast, and more time hunting enemy main-force units in the hills and mountains of the interior.

The emphasis shifted in the second half of 1966. Elements of the **PAVN** 324B Division began appearing just south of the **Demilitarized Zone** (DMZ) in June and July. Westmoreland ordered Marine units north into the area to fight them, in operations like *Hastings* (July 7 to August 2) and *Prairie* (beginning August 3). In September, Westmoreland told the Marines to establish a base at **Khe Sanh**, at the northwest corner of **South Vietnam** only 10 kilometers from the Laotian border. As more Marines were committed to the hills of the extreme northern section of I Corps, fighting the PAVN, fewer were available for the populated areas along the coast. General Krulak protested that the PAVN troops were coming across the DMZ simply as a diversion, wanting to lure the Marines away from more important tasks, but Westmoreland did not believe there was any task more important than fighting the PAVN, so if the area just south of the DMZ was where the PAVN chose to fight, that was where he would send the Marines to fight them.

The headquarters of the 3d Marine Division was moved north from Danang to **Hue** in October 1966, and the division soon had a string of bases across northern Quang Tri province. Gio Linh and Con Thien, at the eastern end of the string, were very close to the DMZ. Cam Lo, Camp Carroll, the "Rockpile," Ca Lu, and Khe Sanh were further south.

The Marines did not abandon their efforts in the lowlands along the coast, but their main effort was devoted to the struggle against the PAVN in extreme northern I Corps for the next several years. The siege of Khe Sanh in early 1968 was their most famous battle.

Increasing numbers of Army troops had been sent into I Corps, both to replace the Marines in coastal areas from which they had withdrawn, and to join them in the fighting in the hills. These Army units were placed under III MAF as the overall U.S. headquarters for I Corps. By early 1968 III MAF was becoming a joint headquarters, with an Army general serving for part of that year as a deputy commander of III MAF.

When the United States began pulling troops out of Vietnam in 1969 under President **Richard Nixon**'s policy of **Vietnamization**, the Marines were pulled out of I Corps faster than the Army troops were; the 3d Marine Division was gone before the end of the year. Marine combat activity focused increasingly on a single province, **Quang Nam**. It no longer made much sense for III MAF to be the overall headquarters for U.S. forces in I Corps, and in March 1970 it turned that responsibility over to an Army headquarters, XXIV Corps. The 1st Marine Division and the III MAF headquarters withdrew from Vietnam in the first half of 1971.

There were 14,821 Marines who died in the Vietnam War. Of these 13,073 died as a result of hostile action, and 1,748 from other causes. The ratio of deaths to number of men in Vietnam, the ratio of enlisted to officer deaths, and the ratio of deaths from hostile action to those from other causes, were all higher for the Marine Corps than for the U.S. Army, Navy, or **Air Force**.

The Marine Corps had traditionally been made up of volunteers, but about 44,000 men were drafted into the Corps during the Vietnam War. Of the Marines who died in Vietnam, 683 (4.6 percent) were draftees.

**MARINE CORPS,** Vietnamese. On October 13, 1954, Premier **Ngo Dinh Diem** proclaimed the creation of the Vietnamese Marine Corps (VNMC). The bulk of its initial personnel, about 2,400 men, were troops who had been serving in riverine forces, under French command, in the **Red River Delta** of **North Vietnam**. After moving south following the **Geneva Accords**, they served very effectively in combat against **Hoa Hao** and **Binh Xuyen** forces in 1955 and into the early part of 1956. They formally became the Marine Group in 1956, and the Marine Brigade in 1962. **Le Nguyen Khang**, who became commander of the Marines in 1960, was sent into exile in the **Philippines** after the **coup** that overthrew Ngo Dinh Diem in 1963. Lieutenant Colonel Nguyen Ba Lien replaced him.

By early 1964, the Marine Brigade, which had four battalions and a nominal strength of 6,109 men, was suffering from low morale and a high desertion rate. In February Colonel Khang was recalled from the Philippines, promoted to brigadier general, and given command of the Marine Brigade; he was able to improve it substantially. The process of creating a fifth battalion began in mid-1964; this battalion became ready for combat in June 1965. But on December 31, 1964, the 4th Battalion was devastated in the Battle of **Binh Gia**, and ceased to be combat effective for about three months. Expansion continued in later years; the Marine Division was formally established in 1968. It had an official strength of 12,471 by mid-1970, and 17,681 by mid-1972.

From the mid-1960s onward, the Marines were an important elite force, more effective and more aggressive in combat than most **ARVN** units. But relations with the ARVN were not always good. Marine Brigade 147, in **Laos** in March 1971 as part of Operation *Lam Son 719*, had great difficulty obtaining **artillery** or air support from the ARVN general commanding the operation.

In 1972, Marine units put up a stubborn resistance to the **PAVN Easter Offensive**, first at the western end of the defense line south of the **Demilitarized Zone**, and later on the line north of **Hue** where the offensive was stopped. The Marine Division was a major participant in the counteroffensive that began on June 28 to retake **Quang Tri** City, and most of the division remained in the area thereafter. Withdrawal of the Marines from Quang Tri province to strengthen the defenses of Hue and **Danang** in March 1975, which allowed the PAVN to take Quang Tri City without a fight on March 19, was one of the events triggering the **final collapse** of the **Republic of Vietnam**.

*MARKET TIME*, Operation. In the early 1960s, there was disagreement within the U.S. government as to whether the Communist forces were bringing significant amounts of munitions into **South Vietnam** by sea. Patrols along the coast were not finding signs of significant **infiltration**. (Significant shipments had in fact begun in 1962; *see* **Group 759**.)

The argument was settled on February 16, 1965, when a 100-ton steel-hulled trawler loaded with munitions was spotted from the air in Vung Ro Bay, on the coast of Phu Yen province in **II Corps**, and sunk.

The United States decided to supplement the patrol forces of the **Vietnamese Navy** (VNN) with U.S. **Navy** forces. The cooperative effort was designated *Market Time* as of March 24, 1965.

U.S. ocean-going naval vessels patrolled up to 40 nautical miles from the coast, and the VNN's Sea Force somewhat closer in; the VNN's Coastal Force (composed, at least at this time, mostly of wooden junks) and U.S. Navy **Swift Boats** patrolled in immediate proximity to the coast. Patrol aircraft and U.S. **Coast Guard** vessels also participated. During the first weeks of the program the VNN did not allow U.S. vessels actually to stop and search local vessels, only to report suspicious vessels so that VNN patrol boats could come and search them. This cumbersome procedure ended, and U.S. vessels were authorized to stop and search vessels in Vietnamese waters, as of May 12, 1965.

The *Market Time* patrol area at first included some of the larger rivers in the **Mekong Delta**, but river patrols did not become significantly effective until after they became a separate operation, *Game Warden*.

For more than a year after the Vung Ro incident, *Market Time* found no further large infiltration vessels, though it did capture numerous small wooden-hulled junks transporting Communist personnel, weapons, and supplies from one point to another along the South Vietnamese coast. Finally, a second steel-hulled infiltration trawler was sunk near the southern tip of South Vietnam on May 10, 1966, and a third was caught on the night of June 20–21, at the mouth of the Co Chien River (one of the branches of the **Mekong River**), about 110 kilometers south of Saigon. Sinkings of infiltration trawlers peaked in early 1968 in the aftermath of the **Tet Offensive**. The last known sinking was on the morning of April 11, 1971, off the **Ca Mau** Peninsula.

**MARTIN, GRAHAM ANDERSON** (1912–1990). Diplomat. Born in Mars Hill, North Carolina, Martin joined the Foreign Service in 1947, and served as U.S. ambassador to **Thailand** from July 1963 to July 1967. He pushed, successfully, for a substantial increase in U.S. aid to Thailand. In 1969 he became U.S. ambassador to Italy; it is said that he chose to involve himself directly, when he could have avoided doing so, in the **Central Intelligence Agency**'s provision of subsidies to the Christian Democratic Party.

Martin was appointed U.S. ambassador to the **Republic of Vietnam** (RVN) in 1973. He was a strong supporter of President **Nguyen Van Thieu**, and of U.S. aid to **South Vietnam**. He came into considerable conflict with the press; he was claiming that Thieu's government was strong and had a good chance of winning its struggle against the Communists, while many in the press were reporting much more pessimistically.

During the **final collapse** of the RVN in 1975, Martin continued to be optimistic, saying that the situation was still salvageable after this had become obviously false. He was determined not to do anything that would imply the United States was giving up hope of preventing a Communist victory, since he was afraid this would cause panic in the **ARVN**. To have begun large-scale evacuation of those Vietnamese who had worked for the United States in ways that would make them likely targets of Communist retaliation, or to have taken vigorous action to destroy the files that listed the Vietnamese who had served as **intelligence** agents on the anti-Communist side, would have implied that the United States was giving up hope. Martin finally authorized evacuation in late April. When **PAVN** artillery fire closed **Tan Son Nhut** airport to fixed-wing aircraft on April 29, Martin delayed for several hours ordering the beginning of a **helicopter** evacuation, Operation *Frequent Wind*, hoping that fixed-wing flights could somehow be resumed. But once *Frequent Wind* began, Martin lobbied his superiors to keep it going as long as possible, to evacuate not only the Americans in **Saigon** but also as many as possible of the Vietnamese considered most at risk. Martin's superiors halted the helicopter airlift over his objections in the early morning of April 30, a few hours before PAVN troops entered Saigon.

**MARY ANN,** Fire Support Base. A base used by the 196th Light Infantry Brigade of the 23d Infantry **Division** (Americal), in Quang Tin province of southern **I Corps**. In the early morning hours of March 28, 1971, the 2d Company of the **PAVN** 409th **Sapper** Battalion hit the base with a surprise attack. The complacency and poor discipline that were becoming widespread in American units by this time were conspicuously present at Mary Ann—the physical defenses had not been well maintained, few men were on guard, and those few were not alert—so the attack was far more successful than was usual in attacks on fire support bases. Thirty-one U.S. soldiers were killed and 82 wounded.

*MASHER,* Operation. A major operation, aimed at Communist forces in the coastal plains and nearby areas of **Binh Dinh** province (northern **II Corps**), was called *Masher* when it began on January 24, 1966. **Lyndon Johnson** did not like the name, so it was renamed *White Wing* on February 4. **Korean** troops moved north from their base at **Qui Nhon**, at the southeast corner of Binh Dinh. The 1st **Cavalry Division (Airmobile)** was airlifted into the northeastern part of the province, starting in the **Bong Son Plain** and working up into the An Lao Valley. A U.S. **Marine** amphibious landing, Operation *Double Eagle*, in the southern part of Quang Ngai province beginning on January 28, was to block escape of Communist forces northward. The 1st Cavalry encountered heavy combat at the beginning of the operation, but after that, enemy forces mostly evaded combat. *White Wing* ended on March 6.

*MAYAGUEZ.* On May 12, 1975, the SS *Mayaguez*, an American container vessel going from Hong Kong to **Thailand**, was passing near an island belonging to **Cambodia** and was seized by a gunboat of the **Khmer Rouge** government that had completed its seizure of power in that country the previous month. The ship was taken to the island of Koh Tang (closer to the mainland than the island near which the ship had been seized); the crew were taken from there to the port of Kompong Som on the mainland. The United States, believing that some or all of the crew might still be held on Koh Tang, landed a **Marine** force there by **helicopter** on the morning of May 15. The United States also bombed targets on the mainland. The crew of the *Mayaguez* were released (sent out by boat from Kompong Som) later that morning, but the Marines on Koh Tang spent all day fighting the large, well-armed, and well-led Khmer Rouge garrison on the island, which inflicted significant losses on the U.S. forces. Fifteen Americans were killed, three missing, and 50 wounded; four helicopters were destroyed and numerous others seriously damaged. The Marines were finally extracted, with considerable difficulty, around nightfall.

**MCCARTHY, EUGENE JOSEPH** (1916– ). U.S. senator. Born in Watkins, Minnesota, he graduated from St. John's University in 1935, and served in the Army during World War II. He was elected to the U.S. House of Representatives in 1948, and served until he was elected to the Senate in 1958, where he served until 1971.

McCarthy began moderate criticism of the Vietnam War in 1966, and much more forceful criticism in 1967. He announced on November 30, 1967, that he would run for president in the 1968 **election**; opposition to the war was his only major issue. His campaign relied heavily on college students with no previous political experience, who carefully distanced themselves from popular stereotypes of scruffy antiwar protesters under the slogan "Neat and Clean for Gene." In the

Democratic Party's New Hampshire primary on March 12, 1968, McCarthy got almost as many votes (42.2 percent) as incumbent President **Lyndon Johnson** did (49.4 percent). **Robert Kennedy** declared his own candidacy on March 16.

President Johnson's announcement on March 31 that he would not run for re-election left McCarthy and Kennedy the only major candidates in the later primaries. They became bitterly hostile to one another, despite the fact that both were against the war. After Robert Kennedy was assassinated on June 5, McCarthy did not win over many of Kennedy's supporters, and indeed did not seem to be trying very hard to do so. At the Democratic Convention, Vice President **Hubert Humphrey** won the Democratic nomination; McCarthy did not give Humphrey even a lukewarm endorsement until October 29, just before the election.

McCarthy resigned from the Senate Foreign Relations Committee in 1969, and then chose not to run for re-election to the Senate in 1970. He is the author of *The Year of the People* (1969).

**MCCONE, JOHN ALEX** (1902–1991). Director of central intelligence. Born in San Francisco, he graduated from the University of California in 1922, then became a worker in a steel mill, and rose to become an executive first in the steel business, then in construction of petroleum refineries and power plants, then in a firm that built ships and planes.

McCone was deputy secretary of defense for part of 1948, and became under secretary of the **Air Force** in 1950. He was strongly anti-Communist, and endorsed a massive buildup of U.S. nuclear weapons. He left government in 1951, but returned to serve as chairman of the Atomic Energy Commission from 1958 to 1961. Although McCone was a conservative Republican, President **John Kennedy** made him director of central intelligence—head of the **Central Intelligence Agency** (CIA)—in November 1961.

McCone was an optimist about the Vietnam War up to 1963, and he put pressure on his subordinates to report that the war was going well, or at least not report that it was going badly. McCone urged that the United States remain allied with **Ngo Dinh Diem**, and not encourage a **coup** against Diem, in 1963; he argued that there was no leader in sight as a plausible replacement for Diem. After the coup, he became pessimistic. During the arguments over escalation of the Vietnam War in 1964 and early 1965, he said that the half measures under consideration would be too little and too late. He said the United States should either make a massive intervention, in particular bombing **North Vietnam** much more heavily than was in fact done in the early stages of Operation *Rolling Thunder*, or not escalate the war at all. It was the first alternative, a massive bombing campaign, that he wanted. McCone continued endorsing the **domino theory** even after his analysts at the Office of National Estimates had disavowed it in late 1964. He was not, however, enthusiastic about committing U.S. ground troops to **South Vietnam**. He left the CIA and the government in April 1965.

**MCGARR, LIONEL CHARLES** (1904–1988). U.S. **Army** general. He was born in Yuma, Arizona, and graduated from West Point in 1928. In World War II he served initially in North Africa, and later commanded the 30th Infantry Regiment in Italy, France, and Germany. He was assigned to the Intelligence Division of the Army General Staff in 1947. He went to Korea in 1952 as deputy commander of the 2d Infantry Division.

Major General McGarr was commandant of the Command and General Staff College (CGSC), at Fort Leavenworth, Kansas, from July 1956 to August 1960. The Vietnamese officers who came to the CGSC as students during this period included **Do Cao Tri, Huynh Van Cao, Nguyen Huu Hanh**, and **Nguyen Van Thieu**. An article that McGarr wrote on the need for doctrinal flexibility in the Army, including doctrine for limited wars, was published in the CGSC monthly *Military Review* in September 1959, and suggests his attitudes at the time. He made only brief references to "unconventional warfare," and did not mention **guerrilla warfare** or **counterinsurgency** at all. His concern was that the Army incorporate new high-tech weapons into its doctrine as quickly as possible; he urged the development of "smaller . . . tactical nuclear weapons for use in limited war."

Lieutenant General McGarr was commander of the **Military Assistance Advisory Group** (MAAG) in Vietnam from August 1960 to February 1962. He urged that the **Civil Guard** and **Self-Defense Corps** be placed under command of the regular Army of the Republic of Vietnam **(ARVN)** to make it easier to upgrade them, allowing them to take more responsibility for local security and free ARVN units for offensive operations. President **Ngo Dinh Diem** rejected this advice.

McGarr was a bit more inclined than either his predecessor (**Samuel Williams**) or his successor (**Paul Harkins**) to accept the idea that special counterinsurgency techniques, not just conventional tactics, might be needed to deal with the Communist threat in Vietnam. One should not, however, overestimate the difference; McGarr's main focus was on the use of military force, and he was sometimes naively optimistic about the ability of regular troops to locate guerrillas in their jungle redoubts. In 1961, he began to recommend that American combat troops be sent to Vietnam. Although **Maxwell Taylor** and **Walt Rostow** supported this idea after they had talked with McGarr during their October 1961 mission to Vietnam, President **John Kennedy** rejected it. McGarr retired from the Army shortly after leaving command of MAAG in 1962.

**MCGOVERN, GEORGE S.** (1922–  ).  U.S. Senator.  Born in Avon, South Dakota, he won the Distinguished Flying Cross as a bomber pilot in World War II, then returned to school, earning a B.A. at Dakota Wesleyan University in 1945 and a Ph.D. in history at Northwestern University in 1953.  He served in the U.S. House of Representatives from 1957 to 1961 and in the Senate from 1963 to 1980.  McGovern was strongly opposed to the Vietnam War; he was a sponsor of several bills and amendments to restrict or end the war, including the Vietnam Disengagement Act of 1969, which if passed would have required that all U.S. military personnel be withdrawn from Vietnam by December 1, 1970.  He was the Democratic Party candidate in the presidential **election** of 1972, opposing the war and favoring very liberal policies domestically, and was defeated overwhelmingly; McGovern got only 37.5 percent of the popular vote and 17 electoral votes, to 60.7 percent of the popular vote and 520 electoral votes for **Richard Nixon**.

**MCNAMARA, ROBERT STRANGE** (1916–  ).  Secretary of defense. Born in San Francisco, he graduated from the University of California in 1937, and then got a master's degree in Business Administration from Harvard in 1939.  He was at first rejected for military service for poor vision, but his work for the Army Air Corps on statistical analysis of operations and planning led to his becoming an officer, and he rose to lieutenant colonel before the end of World War II.  He and some other officers of similar skills (later to be nicknamed the "whiz kids") joined the Ford Motor Corporation after the war, and McNamara rose to become president of the corporation late in 1960.  Within weeks, the newly elected President **John Kennedy** appointed McNamara secretary of defense.

The typical secretary of defense of the 1950s had been a corporate executive without much background in either government or the military, and had not intruded much in the activities of the armed services.

McNamara brought civilian systems analysts into the Pentagon with him, and they intruded deeply into the services' decisions, sometimes rejecting proposed weapons systems as wasteful and unnecessary, and trying to force the services to purchase more of their equipment in common for greater efficiency, instead of having each service choose and purchase its own. He was bitterly resented for this by many senior officers even before the management of the Vietnam War became an issue.

During the Kennedy administration, McNamara was an optimist on Vietnam. He approved of the military effort being made there, he accepted overly optimistic reports from **Saigon** about how well that effort was going, and he quashed those who tried to raise doubts. His love for briefings filled with statistics was famous, but he would accept such briefings only if the numbers added up to a favorable conclusion.

At the end of 1963, McNamara finally acknowledged that the policies of the time were failing. He told the National Security Council on May 24, 1964, that the situation was "going to hell" and that nothing the United States was then doing could win the war. He urged U.S. attacks on **North Vietnam** as the only way of rescuing the situation in the South.

Having urged a wider war, McNamara began to doubt that policy soon after the escalation began. By 1966, perhaps even in late 1965, he was losing faith that the war could be won at acceptable cost. It was too late for him to halt the escalation, but he did act to slow it; he and President **Lyndon Johnson** restricted U.S. bombing of the northern half of North Vietnam, to the great frustration of the **Joint Chiefs of Staff**. In public he pretended to believe the policy was working, but in 1967, he began suggesting to President Johnson that the United States begin to de-escalate the war. Faced with McNamara's growing doubts, President Johnson no longer wanted him as secretary of defense; McNamara became president of the World Bank (formally the International Bank for Reconstruction and Development) early in 1968.

McNamara was not proud of the role he had played in the war, and for more than a decade he refused to discuss it in public. General **William Westmoreland**'s libel suit against CBS Television (*see* **Order of Battle Dispute**), in which McNamara was called as a witness and for the first time discussed publicly the disillusionment he had felt about the war during his last months as secretary of defense, began the process of breaking his silence. Finally in 1995 he published a memoir, *In Retrospect*, in which he acknowledged that his decisions on Vietnam had been made without proper analysis of the situation and the likely consequences.

**MEDICAL EVACUATION** (MEDEVAC, "Dust Off"). One reason the ratio of killed to wounded was so low among the American **casualties** in Vietnam was that **helicopters** could pick up wounded men from the battlefield and deliver them to hospitals fast enough so that many men survived wounds that would have been fatal in previous wars. MEDEVAC was also sometimes available to **ARVN** personnel and civilian casualties.

**MEKONG DELTA.** The land south and west of **Saigon** was created by silt laid down by the **Mekong River**, which splits into a number of branches as it flows through this flat and swampy area. The Vietnamese have lived in the Mekong Delta for only a few centuries, and in the 20th century the population density there was still not nearly as great as in the coastal areas farther north, which had been Vietnamese far longer. The relatively large amount of farmland per person reduced the pressure on people in the Mekong Delta to work as hard as they possibly could to avoid starvation; other Vietnamese stereotyped them as lazy. Large farms, leading to large crops per person, also made it far more practical to extract substantial rents from tenant farmers without driving them into starvation. Tenancy was far more prevalant in the Mekong Delta than in any other part of Vietnam, so **land reform** programs, both those of the Communists and those of the **Republic of Vietnam**, were more important there.

Combat was left to locals more in the Mekong Delta than in any other area of **South Vietnam**; there were fewer North Vietnamese troops on the Communist side, and fewer Americans on the anti-Communist side. The first significant operation by U.S. ground troops there was Operation *Deckhouse V*, a brief foray into Kien Hoa province by the U.S. **Marines'** Special Landing Force, January 6–15, 1967. The U.S. 9th Infantry **Division** operated on a substantial scale in the delta from 1967 to 1969. American efforts to achieve control of the waterways occurred under Operation *Game Warden* beginning in 1966, and *SEALORDS* beginning in 1968. The **Mobile Riverine Force**, in which the 2d Brigade of the 9th Infantry Division worked together with a U.S. **Navy** force from February 1967 to August 1969, was quite effective. The United States reported that North Vietnamese troops were beginning to be added to **Viet Cong** units in the delta during 1968, but the first identification of a **PAVN** regiment in the delta did not occur until after mid-1969, when U.S. forces were already beginning to pull out.

**MEKONG RIVER.** The Mekong originates in southwest **China** and flows southward, forming the border between **Thailand** and **Laos** for much of its length. Vientiane (the capital of Laos) and **Phnom Penh** (the capital of **Cambodia**) are both on the Mekong. At Phnom Penh, it splits into the Mekong and the Bassac. It further subdivides while flowing across the **Mekong Delta** of **South Vietnam** to reach the South China Sea.

The Mekong is a major transport artery. Small ocean-going vessels can go up it as far as Phnom Penh, and there have been extended periods when imports entered Cambodia primarily by the Mekong, rather than arriving by coastal ports.

In the early 1970s, as **Khmer Rouge** forces cut more and more roads in Cambodia, the Mekong became the lifeline of the government in Phnom Penh. Convoys of vessels, with heavily armed escorts, faced increasing opposition getting up the river. The last convoy to reach Phnom Penh was in late January 1975. The strength of the Khmer Rouge forces on the banks, and the number of Chinese-made **mines** in the water, was too great after that, and Phnom Penh received only the much smaller quantity of supplies that could be brought in by air.

*MENU*, Operation. Up until 1969, the United States had taken hardly any military action against Vietnamese Communist base areas, often called "**sanctuaries**," in a number of areas of **Cambodia** just across the border from **South Vietnam**. In 1969, President **Richard Nixon** decided to begin bombing these base areas using **B-52**s. Operation *Menu* began early in the morning of March 18, 1969, with the bombing of Base Area 353, which the Americans code-named *Breakfast*, on the eastern edge of the **Fishhook**, north across the Cambodian border from **War Zone C**. It had been chosen because the United States believed it contained the **Trung uong cuc mien Nam** (COSVN), the Communist headquarters for the southern half of South Vietnam. Over the following months, other base areas north and east of *Breakfast* were bombed under the code names *Lunch, Snack, Dinner, Dessert,* and *Supper*.

President Nixon, who wished to maintain a pretense that the United States was respecting Cambodian neutrality even though the **PAVN** did not, was determined to keep *Menu* absolutely secret—to prevent the press, the **Congress**, and even most of the U.S. military from learning that the U.S. **Air Force** was bombing targets in Cambodia. After every mission, false reports were filed, indicating that the **bombs** had fallen on targets in South Vietnam. Journalist William Beecher learned of the bombing, and published an article about it in *The New York Times* on May 9, 1969, but this attracted no public attention; *Menu* was still essentially a secret when it ended, having dropped 108,823 tons of bombs, in late May of 1970. The secret *Menu* missions overlapped by a few weeks the openly announced U.S. bombing of Cambodia that had begun early in May. From that point onward, B-52 bombing of Cambodia was conducted openly under Operation *Arc Light*. The bombing that had occurred under *Menu* was finally revealed in hearings of the Senate Armed Services Committee in 1973. Some people such as Representative **Robert Drinan** were outraged over the falsification of reports that had kept the operation secret up to that time, and said President Nixon should be impeached for this.

The double reporting system of *Menu*, in which reports giving false target locations were widely distributed in the U.S. Air Force, while reports giving the actual locations were given to only a few people with a "need to know," was later copied in modified form for Operations *Patio* and *Freedom Deal* in Cambodia, and for Operation *Good Look* in the **Plain of Jars** in **Laos**.

**MICHELIN RUBBER PLANTATION.** A large plantation, owned by a French corporation, in **III Corps** about 30 kilometers east of **Tay Ninh** City. American soldiers were startled by the ability of this plantation to continue functioning while the war raged around it, and assumed that the owners were paying off the Communists.

**MICHIGAN STATE UNIVERSITY GROUP** (MSUG). In May 1955, Michigan State University signed a contract with the United States Operations Mission in Vietnam to provide police and public administration specialists to train government personnel in **South Vietnam**. What might have been the most important program of the MSUG was training of the **Civil Guard**; what weapons and equipment the United States provided for the Civil Guard were funneled through the MSUG until 1959. The effort was crippled, however, by disputes over the proper nature of the Civil Guard. The MSUG, and Ambassador Elbridge Durbrow, believed the Civil Guard should be a **police** organization, and should be given only light weapons appropriate for small-scale counterguerrilla operations. **Ngo Dinh Diem**, however, believed it should be essentially a military organization, and should be armed and trained for military combat on a substantial scale. For several years, the dispute prevented much weaponry or equipment of any sort from reaching the Civil Guard. In 1959, when the United States decided to endorse an essentially military concept of the Civil Guard, the MSUG withdrew from its training role.

**MIG.** A series of fighter planes, named after the Soviet aircraft design team of Mikoyan and Gurevich. Both Soviet-made MiGs and Chinese copies are referred to as MiGs. The MiGs used by the **Democratic Republic of Vietnam** (DRV) were typically armed with cannon (23-mm or 30-mm) and/or short-range Atoll heat-seeking **missiles**.

The MiG-17, sometimes called *Fresco* by the Americans, was a small, short-range fighter. It was not very fast but could turn more tightly than the American fighters. Some of those used by the DRV were made in **China**, under the designation Shenyang J-5. When the United States launched its first air strikes against **North Vietnam**, Operation *Pierce Arrow*, on August 5, 1964, after the **Tonkin Gulf incidents**, there were no MiGs in North Vietnam, but a group of DRV pilots were being trained in southern China to fly MiG-17s. They flew back to Vietnam in their MiGs on August 6. The first success against U.S. aircraft was on April 4, 1965, when two MiG-17s shot down two **F-105**s near the **Ham Rong** Bridge in Thanh Hoa province. The first U.S. success against the MiGs was on June 17, when two **F-4B Phantoms** shot down two MiG-17s.

The MiG-19, sometimes called *Farmer* by the Americans, was not quite so maneuverable but considerably faster. The DRV only acquired a few MiG-19s during the war, some or all of which were made in China under the designation Shenyang J-6.

The MiG-21, sometimes called *Fishbed* by the Americans, began to arrive in late 1965 and became available for combat in February 1966. It was faster than the MiG-17 but less maneuverable, and also gave its pilot a much more restricted field of vision. The MiG-21 was the main DRV fighter in the late stages of the war.

**MILITARY ASSISTANCE ADVISORY GROUP** (MAAG), **Laos.** Up until 1961, the United States kept its military advisory effort in Laos covert, to avoid the appearance of violating the **Geneva Accords of 1954**. U.S. military **advisers** did not use their military ranks or wear uniforms, and the "Programs Evaluation Office" (PEO) was also nominally civilian. On April 14, 1961, the **Joint Chiefs of Staff** authorized

U.S. military personnel in Laos to wear their uniforms, and lifted all restrictions on their participation in combat (*see White Star*). On April 19, the PEO formally became the Military Assistance Advisory Group, Laos. The MAAG was pulled out of Laos in October 1962, under the terms of the **Geneva Accords of 1962**.

**MILITARY ASSISTANCE ADVISORY GROUP** (MAAG), Vietnam. The United States first established the Military Assistance Advisory Group for Indochina, based in **Saigon**, in 1950, but it did not become seriously involved in advising and training the **Vietnamese National Army** (later Army of the Republic of Vietnam or **ARVN**) until 1955. That year it was split; separate MAAGs were established for Vietnam and for **Cambodia**.

Lieutenant General **John O'Daniel** took command of the MAAG in Saigon in April 1954; he supported **Ngo Dinh Diem** very firmly during the **Sect** Crisis of early 1955, when some other U.S. officials were thinking of abandoning Diem. Lieutenant General **Samuel T. Williams** took command in October 1955. In the late 1950s he shaped the ARVN as a conventional force, trained and organized for combat against a large-scale invasion from the North, rather than against guerrillas within **South Vietnam**. The MAAG was hampered in this period by the **Geneva Accords of 1954**. Under the accords as they were originally understood, the number of U.S. military personnel in Vietnam was not to exceed 342. In order to evade this limitation, the United States pretended that personnel of the **Temporary Equipment Recovery Mission** (TERM) were not involved in the advisory effort and that the 342 limit therefore did not apply to them. By 1959, the actual total of U.S. personnel had reached 736, of whom 342 were openly assigned to MAAG, 350 were with TERM, and the remainder were concealed under another subterfuge. In 1960, the Geneva Accords were reinterpreted in a way that lifted the limit from 342 to 685. TERM ceased to exist, and the nominal strength of MAAG in late 1960 and early 1961 was 685. The new limit seems to have been evaded as the old one had been; the true total of U.S. military **advisers** in Vietnam at the beginning of 1961 was probably about 900.

Lieutenant General **Lionel C. McGarr** replaced Williams as commander of MAAG on August 31, 1960. During 1961, as the war in Vietnam expanded, the U.S. pretense of compliance with the personnel limits of the Geneva Accords was abandoned, and there were about 3,200 U.S. military personnel in Vietnam by the end of the year. On

January 20, 1962, the Commander in Chief, Pacific (CINCPAC) autho- rized all MAAG advisers to accompany into combat the Vietnamese units they were advising. **Military Assistance Command, Vietnam**, was established in February 1962 and immediately overshadowed MAAG, which was formally abolished in May 1964.

**MILITARY ASSISTANCE COMMAND, VIETNAM** (MACV). The U.S. military command for South Vietnam, established on February 8, 1962. From May 1962 to June 1965 the commander of MACV served concur- rently as commander of Military Assistance Command, **Thailand**. MACV was headed by General **Paul Harkins** from its establishment to June 1964, by **William Westmoreland** until July 1968, by **Creighton Abrams** until June 1972, and by **Frederick Weyand** until it was dis- banded on March 29, 1973. It was housed in rather unsatisfactory quarters in the city of **Saigon** until the summer of 1967, when it moved to a large facility (nicknamed "Pentagon East") at **Tan Son Nhut** Air Base, on the northwest edge of the city.

The structure of command has often been criticized. The commander of MACV was the closest thing the United States had to a theater com- mander in Indochina, but he did not control all important U.S. military activities in the theater; considerable portions of the bombing of **North Vietnam** and **Laos** were outside his control, and even in **South Viet- nam** the **B-52** bombers that did much of the bombing were not under his command. MACV could recommend B-52 strikes, but command over them was retained by higher authorities in Washington.

On the other hand, when massive escalation of the war began in 1965, General Westmoreland chose to keep in his own hands the com- mand of U.S. **Army**, Vietnam (USARV), instead of naming a subordinate to be commander of USARV. The time that generals Westmoreland and Abrams devoted to direct control of U.S. ground units, as commanders of USARV, reduced the attention they could give to broader policy issues as commanders of MACV.

**MILITARY REGION** (*quan khu*, MR). Shortly after the **Geneva Accords of 1954**, the State of Vietnam divided **South Vietnam** into three military regions, numbered (in order from north to south) 2, 4, and 1. MR 1, covering **Nam Bo**, was by far the largest and most important. Later in the 1950s, the **Republic of Vietnam** (RVN) revised this to create military regions numbered, from north to south, 2, 3, 4, 1, and 5, with the Capital Military Region a separate unit between 1 and 5. Dur- ing the 1960s the number was reduced to four, numbered in order from north to south, and they corresponded to the **corps tactical zones**: MR 1 was the area usually called **I Corps**, and so on.

The Communists used two systems of numbered military regions within **South Vietnam**. The one most often encountered was derived from one developed during the First Indochina War, and did not use the numbers 1 through 4 because those were in the North. MR 5 (the B1 **Front**) was by far the largest; when first established in 1961, it reached from the **Demilitarized Zone** (DMZ) as far south as Phu Yen province (covering what readers in the West think of as I Corps and the northern half of **II Corps**). In late 1963, it was expanded further by the addition of Dac Lac (Darlac) and Khanh Hoa. But the **Central Highlands** were made separate from MR 5 in May 1964 (becoming the B3 Front), leaving only the coastal provinces. Then the two northernmost provinces, **Quang Tri** and **Thua Thien**, were removed in April 1966 to form the **Tri-Thien Military Region** (B4 Front).

MR 6 was originally the southern half of what readers in the West think of as II Corps. Two of its provinces, Lam Dong and Quang Duc, were combined with Phuoc Long from MR 7 to create Region 10 at the end of 1961. MR 6 absorbed Region 10 in October 1963, but at the same time two provinces, Dac Lac (Darlac) and Khanh Hoa, were transferred to MR 5; this left six provinces (Ninh Thuan, Binh Thuan, Quang Duc, Phuoc Long, Tuyen Duc, and Lam Dong) in MR 6. Region 10 was re-created in 1966—this time taking Quang Duc and Phuoc Long from MR 6, and Binh Long from MR 7—but dissolved for a second time in 1971.

MR 7 was eastern Nam Bo, MR 8 was central Nam Bo, and MR 9 was western Nam Bo. The **Saigon-Gia Dinh** Military Region was separate, between MR 7 and MR 8.

Military regions 6, 7, 8, and 9 together constituted the B2 Front.

There was an alternate numbering scheme in which the Communists did use the numbers 1 through 4 for military regions in South Vietnam. In this scheme, eastern Nam Bo was MR 1, central Nam Bo was MR 2, western Nam Bo was MR 3, and the Saigon-Gia Dinh Military Region was MR 4. This was the scheme under which these military regions were initially established on February 15, 1962.

*MILL POND*, Project. Four **B-26** bombers belonging to the **Central Intelligence Agency** (CIA) were sent to Takhli, in **Thailand**, at the end of 1960. Other B-26s contributed by the **Air Force** arrived early in 1961. President **John Kennedy** approved a plan for them to conduct air strikes against Communist forces in **Laos**, scheduled to begin on April 17. The planes would carry no markings. Some of the pilots worked for the CIA proprietary firm **Air America**; the rest were **sheepdipped** Air Force officers, who had gone through a pretense of resigning from the Air Force. Only hours before the air strikes would have begun, the president cancelled the mission. A CIA-sponsored air strike against Cuba on April 15, using B-26s flown by Cuban exile pilots, had turned into a public relations disaster; the cover story designed to conceal the degree of U.S. involvement in it had collapsed within hours. Kennedy apparently decided he could not carry out a covert air strike in Laos two days later, using the same model of bomber but with even more direct U.S. involvement than there had been in the Cuban operation, and not have the truth about it come out.

**MINES,** land. Both sides in the war made extensive use of land mines: explosive devices buried in the ground. Those used by U.S. and allied forces were typically small, designed to be triggered by the weight of an individual stepping on them. There was far more diversity in the mines used by Communist forces. Some were anti-personnel mines like the ones the Americans used; indeed some were American mines, dug up from where U.S. or **ARVN** soldiers had buried them, and moved to other locations. Some were far larger, capable of destroying trucks and **armored personnel carriers**. These could either be triggered by the weight of vehicles passing over them, or they could be command-detonated (triggered by an individual watching from some place of concealment). There were many roads that were regularly checked by American minesweeping teams every morning, to remove mines buried by Communist forces during the preceding night. *See also* CLAYMORE MINE; GRAVEL MINES.

**MINES,** naval. The United States had considered mining North Vietnamese ports at least as early as 1964, and the **Joint Chiefs of Staff** repeatedly asked the president for permission to do this in later years. Permission to mine the major ports used by ocean-going vessels from foreign countries was always denied until 1972. In early 1967, the United States did begin mining smaller ports and waterways, where only North Vietnamese vessels were expected to be imperiled. On January 4, 1968, an American pilot sent to drop mines a few miles upriver from **Haiphong** made a navigation error and dropped them directly into Haiphong harbor, where they damaged a Soviet freighter.

On May 8, 1972, President **Richard Nixon** announced that the major

North Vietnamese ports were being mined. Operation *Pocket Money*, the dropping of the mines by aircraft from U.S. aircraft carriers, began exactly at the time the president spoke, but this was the morning of May 9 in Vietnam. The mines were set not to activate themselves and become dangrous for three days, to allow ships in port when the mining began an opportunity to leave safely. Only five ships left before the deadline; 31 remained and were trapped until 1973. Mark 52 mines weighing 1,000 pounds (of which 650 pounds was explosive), detonated by the magnetic field of the hulls of steel ships, were dropped in Haiphong. Mark 36 Destructors weighing 500 pounds (of which 192 pounds was explosive), detonated either by magnetism or by the engine noise of vessels, were dropped both in Haiphong and in other areas.

The mining completely closed all important North Vietnamese ports to shipping. Chinese ships continued to deliver a small quantity of supplies to North Vietnam, anchoring off the coast and offloading cargo into small vessels—lighters—which carried it to shore. This process was laborious, and for the Vietnamese it was dangerous, since while the Chinese ships were off-limits to U.S. air attack, the lighters were not.

Under the **Paris Peace Agreement** of January 1973, the United States was required to help clear the mines it had dropped in North Vietnamese waters. The mine clearance was designated Operation *End Sweep*. It began on February 6, 1973, was temporarily halted on April 17, resumed on June 18, and was completed on July 18, 1973.

Communist forces used mines in harbors in **South Vietnam** and along inland waterways, most importantly the **Long Tau River** leading from the sea to the port of **Saigon**. Some of these mines had been supplied by the **Soviet Union**, but most were locally manufactured, containers filled with explosives and placed in the water with a wire leading to shore, so an observer could command-detonate them when an appropriate vessel was close enough. The United States sent 57-foot wooden-hulled minesweeping boats to **Danang** in October 1965. These and other minesweeping vessels were later used in the major harbors in South Vietnam, and along some rivers and canals.

Mines supplied to the **Khmer Rouge** by **China** played an important role in closing the **Mekong River** early in 1975 to the boats that had previously brought food, ammunition, and other supplies to **Phnom Penh**.

**MINIGUN.** A 7.62-mm **machine gun** built on the Gatling Gun design, with six parallel barrels, which rotated around a common axis when the weapon was fired. After each barrel fired, the rotation carried it to the position where the spent shell was extracted, then to the position where a new shell was loaded, then back to firing position. The minigun weighed too much to be easily carried by infantry in the field. It was often mounted on aircraft, especially **gunships**. The **Air Force** version fired 3,000 rounds per minute on its slow setting, 6,000 on its fast setting. The **Army** version fired 2,000 or 4,000 rounds per minute.

**MISSILES.** The primary weapon of U.S. fighters against North Vietnamese **MiGs** was the Air Intercept Missile (AIM). The AIM-9 Sidewinder was a short-range, heat-seeking missile. The AIM-7 Sparrow was a radar-guided missile, with a considerably longer range. The K-13 Atoll was a missile similar to the Sidewinder, made in the **Soviet Union**, used by fighters of the **Democratic Republic of Vietnam**. *See also* ROCKETS; SURFACE-TO-AIR MISSILES; *WILD WEASEL.*

**MISSING IN ACTION** (MIA). During the Vietnam War, the term "Missing in Action" was reserved for men whose fate was unknown. There was a separate category for those believed definitely to be dead, "Killed in Action/Body Not Recovered" (KIA/BNR). After the return of **prisoners of war** in 1973, the United States had 1,392 men listed as MIA and 1,113 listed as KIA/BNR.

Since that time, the recovery and identification of remains has resulted in removal of some names from both lists. But the two have also been amalgamated in common usage; all missing Americans are now customarily described as MIA, even those known for certain to have been killed in action, as long as no body has been recovered. This is the reason for the relatively large figures given for the number of Americans missing in action from the Vietnam War—1,849 (1,815 military, 34 civilian) as of September 2004.

**MNONG.** A **Montagnard** group, speaking a Mon-Khmer language, living in the southern portion of the **Central Highlands**, between **Ban Me Thuot** and **Dalat**.

**MOBILE RIVERINE FORCE.** A force combining the 2d Brigade of the U.S. 9th Infantry **Division** with the U.S. **Navy**'s Riverine Assault Force (Task Force 117), formally established on February 28, 1967, to conduct warfare along the waterways of the **Mekong Delta**. Its base was at Dong Tam, in Dinh Tuong province. It was inspired to some the *dinassauts* used by the French in the First Indochina War. It proved quite effective. Movement by water, sometimes in boats with silent motors, gave flexibility to infantry operations.

Firepower was provided by armored vessels. The monitor was a 60-foot vessel, with a speed of eight knots, carrying .50-caliber, 20-mm and 40-mm guns, and an 81-mm **mortar**. Some monitors known as "Zippos" also carried flamethrowers. Late in 1967, the 50-foot Assault Support Patrol Boat (ASPB) was added; it was much faster (16 knots), and much less noisy because its engine exhaust was vented under water. It carried an 81-mm mortar and 20-mm and smaller guns and was armored not only above the waterline but below it, so it could be used as a minesweeper. 105-mm howitzers mounted on barges gave the force mobile fire bases.

In the last months of the force's existence, river patrol boats (**PBR**s) were occasionally transported by CH-54 Tarhe **helicopters**, to appear suddenly in areas they could not have reached so quickly, or could not have reached at all, by water. The Mobile Riverine Force was formally deactivated on August 25, 1969; both its **Army** and Navy components had been chosen to be among the first units to leave Vietnam when President **Richard Nixon** began withdrawing U.S. forces.

**MONTAGNARDS** (French for "people of the mountains"). A variety of tribes, inhabiting the highland areas of Vietnam (*see* **Bahnar**, **Bru**, **Cor**, **Hre**, **Jarai**, **Koho**, **Mnong**, **Raglai**, **Rhadé**, and **Sedang**). In the mid-1960s there were estimated to be more than 700,000 Montagnards in **South Vietnam**. They were only about 5 percent of the total population, but the areas they inhabited were a much larger proportion of the total territory of South Vietnam. They did not traditionally get along well with the Vietnamese. In the 1950s and early 1960s, the Communists tried harder than the **Republic of Vietnam** (RVN) did to overcome this animosity, and won the allegiance of some Montagnards. But beginning in late 1961, the United States began forming alliances with the Montagnards, and not suffering from the disadvantage of being Vietnamese, the Americans quickly won large numbers of Montagnard supporters. Tens of thousands of Montagnards enlisted to fight under American leadership, mostly in the **Civilian Irregular Defense Groups** (CIDG), but also in the **Trailwatchers**, the **Mountain Scouts**, **SOG**, and other organizations.

Relations between the Americans and the Montagnards were complicated by the fact that the United States was allied with the RVN, and persistently tried to place Vietnamese officers over the Montagnard troops of the CIDG. The worst problem occurred in September 1964, when several CIDG units near **Ban Me Thuot** mutinied, killing 36 of the Vietnamese **Special Forces** personnel the Americans had tried to place over them.

Montagnards established the **Bajaraka Movement** in 1957 and **FULRO** in 1964 to give an organized voice to their demands.

**MOORER, THOMAS HINMAN** (1912–2004). U.S. admiral. Born in Mount Willing, Alabama, he graduated from Annapolis in 1933 and became a naval aviator. He survived having his plane shot down by a Japanese fighter in 1942. Moorer was commander of the Seventh Fleet, October 1962–1964; commander in chief, U.S. Pacific Fleet, 1964–1965; chief of naval operations, 1967–1970; and chairman of the **Joint Chiefs of Staff**, 1970–1974.

Admiral Moorer was, for the most part, a hawk on Vietnam. He advocated mining the harbors of **North Vietnam**. Early in 1970, Moorer argued for a slowdown in the withdrawal of U.S. forces from **South Vietnam**. He supported the **Cambodian Incursion**. In 1972 during the **Easter Offensive**, he was the most vigorous proponent, within the upper levels of the U.S. government, of closing **Haiphong** harbor by dropping **mines** there. After the war, he said that **Lyndon Johnson** should have sent ground forces into North Vietnam in the 1960s to overthrow the Communist government there.

**MORSE, WAYNE LYMAN** (1900–1974). U.S. Senator. Born in Madison, Wisconsin, he was dean of the Law School at the University of Oregon before being elected as a Republican to the U.S. Senate in 1944. He won re-election as a Republican in 1950, but left the party in 1952, and in 1956 and 1962 he was re-elected to the Senate as a Democrat. He was an early and vocal critic of the Vietnam War; he was one of only two senators to vote against the **Tonkin Gulf Resolution** in 1964. He was defeated when running for re-election in 1968.

**MORTAR.** When a normal **artillery** piece is fired, great pressure is developed inside the barrel, to accelerate the shell to a high velocity and thus achieve long range. The barrel must be thick (and therefore heavy) in order to be strong enough to contain this pressure safely; the powerful recoil requires that the carriage and the recoil absorption mechanism be strong (and therefore heavy).

The principle behind the mortar is that if a very low muzzle velocity can be accepted, then the pressure inside the barrel can be far lower, so a thinner and lighter barrel will be adequate. Low muzzle velocity also makes for a low recoil. The weapon is normally fired at a high angle, so the shell follows a high, arching trajectory. Since the shell goes upward the recoil is downward, and is usually absorbed simply by a base plate resting on the ground. The result is that a weapon that can fire an explosive shell of substantial size is so light that soldiers can carry it on their backs. Most mortars have smooth bores in which the shells slide freely, which makes loading and firing them very simple: shells are dropped in from the muzzle, and impact against a firing pin at the bottom of the barrel causes them to fire.

60-mm mortars were more important for Communist forces, in the early stages of the war, than they ever were for U.S. forces. The American M19 60-mm mortar weighed 45.2 pounds and had an effective range of 2,000 meters; similar weapons were made in the **Soviet Union** and **China**.

The American M29 81-mm mortar weighed 115 pounds and had an effective range that varied from 2,300 to 3,650 meters, depending upon the type of ammunition fired. Communist forces obtained some of these and also used the equivalent Soviet weapon, an 82-mm mortar, weighing 123 pounds and with a maximum range of 3,040 meters. The difference of 1-mm meant that captured American shells could be fired from the Soviet weapon, but not the other way around.

The 81-mm and 82-mm mortars were extremely important to Communist forces, because they were the largest weapons that could readily be carried through the jungle, with no single piece too heavy to be carried by a single man. Communist forces occasionally used 120-mm mortars, weighing about 600 pounds, with a maximum range of 5,700 meters. U.S. forces used the M30 4.2-inch (107-mm) mortar, weighing 330 pounds and with a maximum range of 4,020 meters.

Many American bases had counter-mortar **radar** that could track mortar shells in flight, allowing immediate counterfire with artillery against locations from which mortar shells had been fired.

**MOUNTAIN SCOUTS.** The Mountain Scouts (Mountain Commandos) were **Montagnards** trained to operate in small teams in the jungle, in a program initiated by the **Central Intelligence Agency** (CIA). At the end of 1962, U.S. **Army Special Forces** were training Mountain Scouts for **I Corps** at Hoa Cam, in the **Danang** area, and training those for **II Corps** at Plei Yt, in **Pleiku** province. Control of the program was transferred from the CIA to the U.S. military in 1963.

**MY LAI MASSACRE.** An incident in the village of Son My, mainly in the hamlet (a subunit of the village) known as My Lai 4, in Quang Ngai province of **I Corps**, on March 16, 1968. A U.S. infantry company (C Company, Task Force Barker, 11th Infantry Brigade, 23d Infantry Division), and especially the company's 1st Platoon, commanded by Lieutenant **William Calley**, killed several hundred peasants.

Several background factors had caused problems for these troops. The brigade had been sent to Vietnam prematurely, before finishing its scheduled training in Hawaii. Then during its first months in Vietnam, officers encouraged in the soldiers an attitude of hostility and contempt toward all Vietnamese. C Company had been suffering casualties from **mines** and **booby traps** during the weeks preceding the massacre. The men, apparently unaware of how many such devices had been planted in the area by friendly forces, blamed the **Viet Cong** and local peasants for the casualties.

C Company was sent into the village on the morning of March 16 expecting to find an enemy military unit there, the Viet Cong 48th Local Force Battalion. The information they had been given was incorrect; no enemy unit was present. Three guerrillas who were in the village fled when they heard the **helicopters** approaching, and were killed outside the village by gunfire from helicopters, but by the time C Company entered the village, no armed enemies were there. The killing began while the American troops were searching the village for guerrillas, but it continued after they had realized that no guerrillas seemed to be present. Many peasants were gathered together, held under guard in the open for several minutes, and then gunned down. The Criminal Investigation Division of the U.S. Army later estimated that 347 peasants were killed in My Lai 4, but some of the killing by C Company occurred in the adjoining hamlet of of Binh Tay, and these would not have been included in the 347. The U.S. troops also raped women, burned down homes, and killed livestock.

The incident was officially reported as a battle against Viet Cong troops, and at first the reports were accepted, despite the number of people who had heard a helicopter pilot, Warrant Officer Hugh Thompson, protesting the massacre over his radio and trying to stop it. The cover-up was finally broken by Ronald Ridenour, a soldier who had heard of the massacre from friends, and protested it vigorously enough to trigger an investigation in 1969. Formal charges were filed against Lieutenant Calley on September 5, 1969, and a military court eventually convicted him of the murder of 22 civilians. He was sentenced to life at hard labor, but this sentence was repeatedly reduced; what he actually served was about three years' house arrest in the apartment where he had been living before his conviction, and about five months' actual imprisonment.

The **Army**'s investigators had recommended charges against many officers and men, both for the massacre and for its cover-up, but most never came to trial. Three officers and two sergeants were tried and acquitted; only Calley was convicted.

## - N -

**NAM BO,** also called Nam Ky, Nam Phan, or Cochinchina. The southernmost of the three major administrative divisions of Vietnam from the early 19th century to 1954. *Note:* in this dictionary the term **South Vietnam** will be reserved for the southern of the two halves into which Vietnam was divided from 1954 to 1975, an area much larger than Nam Bo, but some authors, especially Vietnamese, call Nam Bo "South Vietnam."

The Vietnamese have occupied Nam Bo only in recent centuries, and in the 20th century, the ratio of population to good agricultural land has still been lower there than in **Trung Bo** and **Bac Bo**. This is why Nam Bo has been more prosperous than the other regions, leading other Vietnamese to stereotype its people as lazy. Nam Bo was the first region of Vietnam conquered by the French in the 19th century, and it was the one most deeply influenced by the French economically and culturally. Ownership of rice-growing land by large absentee landlords, some of them French citizens, was far more prevalent in Nam Bo (especially in the **Mekong Delta**) than in other regions.

**NAPALM.** Gasoline (or sometimes other flammable liquids such as kerosene), mixed with thickening agents to form a gel, and developed as a military incendiary during World War II. The name "napalm" was based on the original thickening agents, naphthenic and palmitic acids, but the name remained when the formula changed. Napalm-B, a mixture of polystyrene plastic, benzene, and gasoline, was considerably better than the original product. Some units that did not have access to the industrially produced standard formulas made their own, mixing gasoline with whatever thickening agents were available.

Napalm was typically dropped from fighter-bombers in thin-walled canisters that allowed the gel to splash over a wide area upon impact.

A BLU-27 napalm canister weighed 750 pounds and would spread blobs of burning gel over an area about 210 feet long by 70 feet wide. The burning gel stuck to objects and people, instead of flowing off as liquid gasoline would have done. It burned with a very hot flame.

Larger quantities could be delivered, with less precision, by dumping 55-gallon drums out the hatch of a cargo plane. **Korean** units developed the technique, adopted in 1970 by the U.S. **Marines**, of dropping it in 55-gallon drums from **helicopters**; this was very accurate, and in dense jungle, where the thin-walled canisters dropped by fighter-bombers would have wasted much of their napalm in the treetops, the 55-gallon drums would fall to ground level before scattering their load.

Napalm was used in air strikes in **South Vietnam** from very early in the 1960s, but there were political inhibitions on its use in **Laos** for a while.

**NASTY BOAT.** A fast patrol boat 88 feet long, diesel powered, built in Norway. The U.S. **Navy** sent six Nasty Boats to the **Danang** area early in 1964, to be used by **SOG** for *OPLAN 34A* raids against **North Vietnam**. These were nominally transferred to the **Vietnamese Navy** late in 1964. Though they carried no torpedoes, U.S. personnel sometimes called them PT boats, because of all the U.S. naval vessels with which they were familiar, the PT boat (torpedo boat) was the one that most closely resembled the Nasty.

**NATIONAL LIBERATION FRONT** (NLF). The National Front for the Liberation of South Vietnam (Mat tran dan toc giai phong Mien nam Viet nam), commonly called the National Liberation Front, was formally established on December 20, 1960, as the official leadership organization for the **guerrilla war** then already under way. It presented itself as a coalition of South Vietnamese Communists and non-Communists, an organization controlled neither by the **Democratic Republic of Vietnam** (DRV) nor by Communists. Its president, **Nguyen Huu Tho**, was a **Saigon** attorney without a known record of membership in the Communist Party. It was superseded by the **Provisional Revolutionary Government** (PRG) in 1969.

During the war, those in the United States and other Western countries who sympathized with the guerrillas in **South Vietnam** usually called them the NLF, sometimes the People's Liberation Armed Forces (PLAF), accepting in whole or in part the claims the NLF made that it was an independent organization not dominated by Communists. Supporters of the U.S. war effort against the guerrillas usually thought of the NLF as a sham, a puppet controlled by North Vietnamese, and called the guerrillas the **Viet Cong**. They have often said in recent years that the true situation was revealed at the end of the war, when the Communists united North and South to form the Socialist Republic of Vietnam, and its leaders were all North Vietnamese; they have said that none of the leaders of the NLF had any important role in the post-war government. Each of these viewpoints was mistaken in important respects.

It is plain in retrospect that the people in the NLF who had real power were the Communists, and that the top leaders of the Communist Party were in **Hanoi**. The nominal independence of the NLF had been a public relations ploy. The real Communist power structure behind the mask of the NLF, however, had been one in which South Vietnamese Communists—some of them in the NLF structure in South Vietnam, and some in Hanoi—had a great deal of real power. The argument that no South Vietnamese were in leading positions after the end of the war is simply false. **Le Duan**, head of the **Lao Dong** (Communist) Party in Hanoi when the war ended in 1975, had been born in South Vietnam, and he brought two southerners who had been NLF leaders, **Vo Chi Cong** and **Vo Van Kiet**, into the highest leadership of the Communist party. Eventually, Vo Van Kiet became prime minister of the Socialist Republic of Vietnam. Nguyen Huu Tho, who had been president of the NLF, became one of the two vice presidents of the Socialist Republic of Vietnam (and briefly acting president 1980–1981). Other NLF leaders given important positions in Hanoi after the war included **Huynh Tan Phat, Nguyen Thi Binh, Nguyen Thi Dinh**, and Nguyen Van Hieu (1922–1991), NLF general secretary 1961–1963, who served as minister of culture 1976–1986.

**NATIONAL SECURITY ACTION MEMORANDUM 57** (NSAM 57). On June 28, 1961, President **John Kennedy** directed that any paramilitary operation that required the use of substantial military manpower or equipment should fall under the control of the Defense Department, not the **Central Intelligence Agency**. (For the eventual effects of this order in Indochina, *see* **Civilian Irregular Defense Groups, SOG**, and Operation *Switchback*.)

**NAVAL GUNFIRE SUPPORT.** Warships of the U.S. **Navy** (and sometimes **Australia**) provided an important supplement to shore-based **artillery** for shelling targets in **South Vietnam**, and also could shell **North Vietnam**. The workhorses of naval gunfire support were destroyers armed with 5-inch guns (guns firing shells five inches in diameter). The first use of such gunfire was by the destroyer *Henry W. Tucker* against a target in **II Corps** on May 16, 1965. When the 5-inch/38-caliber guns of older destroyers were firing standard shells (weighing 54 pounds of which 14.75 pounds was actual explosive), they had a range of 17,306 yards. In the later stages of the war they occasionally fired Rocket Assisted Projectiles, with a range of 28,000 yards. The 5-inch/54-caliber guns of newer destroyers fired 70-pound shells (18.25 pounds of explosive) to a range of 25,909 yards. A few cruisers, with larger guns, were also used.

In 1968, the *Iowa*-class World War II battleship *New Jersey* (BB 62) was reactivated, to provide an even more powerful source of gunfire. The battleship's nine 16-inch guns fired shells weighing 2,750 pounds, at ranges up to 24 miles. The secondary battery of 5-inch guns added substantially to the battleship's capabilities at shorter ranges. The *New Jersey* arrived off the coast of northern **I Corps** on September 28, 1968. The timing was poor. While the gunfire of the *New Jersey* was useful for destroying targets in South Vietnam, there were few such targets that the United States could not attack well enough by other, cheaper methods. It was attacks on targets in North Vietnam that most called for the very powerful guns and virtual immunity to counterfire of the *New Jersey*, enough so to have pushed the U.S. government to the expense of bringing the battleship out of mothballs and sending her across the Pacific. But all naval shelling of North Vietnam was terminated by President **Lyndon Johnson** as of November 1, 1968, in an effort to assist the **Paris negotiations**; it did not resume until 1972. In March 1969, the *New Jersey* left Vietnamese waters. At that time, this was regarded simply as the end of a tour, and there were plans for the ship to return to Vietnam after a few months in the United States, but in August 1969, it was announced that the battleship was to be decommissioned once more. She had fired over 3,000 16-inch shells, and almost 11,000 5-inch shells. *See also* Operation *SEA DRAGON*.

**NAVY,** U.S. (USN). The most conspicuous contribution of the U.S. Navy was the use of aircraft from carriers, which bombed **North Vietnam** and provided air support for ground forces in **South Vietnam** (*see* **air war**). But Navy ships also shelled targets in both North and South Vietnam (*see* **naval gunfire support,** Operation *Sea Dragon*). The Navy patrolled off the coast to block **infiltration** by sea from North Vietnam (*see* Operation *Market Time*). It was a major participant in the war on the inland waterways of South Vietnam, especially in the **Mekong Delta** (*see* Operation *Game Warden*, **Mobile Riverine Force, River Patrol Force,** and *SEALORDS*). Navy **SEALs** conducted small-unit operations in the Mekong Delta and the **Rung Sat**, and various covert operations elsewhere.

The highest military officer in the U.S. Navy was the Chief of Naval Operations (CNO). Admiral George W. Anderson became CNO in August 1961; Admiral David L. McDonald in August 1963; Admiral **Thomas H. Moorer** in August 1967; Admiral **Elmo R. Zumwalt** in July 1970; and Admiral James L. Holloway in July 1974.

**NEAK LUONG.** A town on the **Mekong River,** in Prey Veng province of **Cambodia.** Vehicles travelling from **Saigon** to **Phnom Penh** by **Route 1** crossed the Mekong by ferry at Neak Luong. It became a major base in May 1970 for **ARVN** forces operating in Cambodia. A ground beacon used as a reference point to allow **B-52** bombers to locate their targets was placed there probably early in 1973. On August 6, 1973, a B-52 accidentally targeted its **bombs** directly on the beacon, killing 137 people in the town. **Khmer Rouge** forces took the town on April 1, 1975.

**NEGOTIATIONS.** During the early stages of the escalation of the war, many U.S. officials opposed the idea of peace negotiations, because they did not believe talks could lead to an acceptable settlement (one giving anti-Communist forces complete control of **South Vietnam**) unless preceded by great improvements in the military situation on the ground.

As the size and cost of the war increased, Americans seeking a way out of it increasingly came to favor negotiations. Some of them, including some high officials, seemed to attribute an almost magical power to negotiations, neglecting to ask themselves what U.S. and Communist representatives would say to one another if and when they did meet. When the **Paris negotiations** finally did begin in 1968, they produced no result for years.

**NEO LAO HAK SAT** (Lao Patriotic Front). An overt political party, established early in 1956, the public representative of the **Pathet Lao** Communist movement in **Laos.** Its greatest electoral success was in the national **elections** of 1958, in which it took nine of the 21 seats at stake.

**NEUTRALISM.** Neutrality was more discussed than practiced during the Vietnam War. The **Geneva Accords of 1954** had said that Vietnam, **Laos**, and **Cambodia** were all to be neutral. The most important effects of this were that the **Republic of Vietnam** (RVN) did not become a member of the **Southeast Asia Treaty Organization**, and that U.S. military **advisers** in Laos had to be disguised as civilians up to 1961.

In Laos, the faction headed by **Souvanna Phouma** was referred to as the Neutralists, not because they always were neutral, but because they were trying to create a neutral Laos. Souvanna was actually neutral as prime minister from 1956 to 1958, but was forced from office by U.S. pressure; during Dwight Eisenhower's administration the United States disapproved of neutralism. Souvanna and the Neutralists were allied with the Communists from 1960 to 1962. **John Kennedy** was more favorable to neutralism, and accepted the **Geneva Accords of 1962**, after which Souvanna and the Neutralists ended their alliance with the Communists and became de facto allies of the United States.

The RVN regarded advocacy of neutralism as a disguised way of supporting the Communists, and forbade it for that reason. This was one of the crimes for which **Truong Dinh Dzu** was imprisoned in 1968.

**NEW ZEALAND.** The first personnel New Zealand committed to the War in Vietnam, a platoon of engineers and a medical team, arrived in July 1964. A battery of 105-mm howitzers arrived in July 1965, initially attached to the U.S. 173d **Airborne** Brigade, later to the **Australian** forces. Some infantry arrived in May 1967, but total numbers always remained very modest. During the period of greatest commitment, from late 1967 to early 1970, the number of New Zealand military personnel was about 520 to 550; they were concentrated mainly in Phuoc Tuy province, on the coast east of **Saigon**. The last company of the Royal New Zealand Infantry departed in December 1971. New Zealand paid the financial costs of its force in Vietnam, rather than taking U.S. aid for the purpose. New Zealand's main motives for sending a force were fear of Communism and a desire to consolidate its alliance with the United States.

**NGO DINH CAN** (1913–1964). Born in the area of **Hue**. In the 1950s, his brother **Ngo Dinh Diem** (president of the **Republic of Vietnam**, 1955–63) gave Can a great deal of power in the provinces of central Vietnam, which he ruled as a semi-autonomous fiefdom from his home in Hue. By 1963, however, Diem and another brother, **Ngo Dinh Nhu**, were cutting down Can's power. After the **coup** that overthrew Diem in 1963, Can appealed to American officials for protection, but this was not provided; he was executed in May 1964.

**NGO DINH DIEM** (1901–1963). President of the **Republic of Vietnam**. Born probably in the area of **Hue**, he was the son of Ngo Dinh Kha, a mandarin from a family that had been **Catholic** for many generations. Diem graduated in 1921 from the School for Law and Administration in **Hanoi**. He served in several posts in rural areas of Annam (**Trung Bo**), and in 1929 became governor of Phan Thiet province. In 1933 he became minister of the interior for Annam, but he found that he did not have the authority to make the reforms he wanted, and resigned after about two months, denouncing the subservience of Emperor Bao Dai to the French. For the next 21 years he held no official positions and did not have much involvement with any political party either, but the prestige he had won from his official career, and especially from the way it had ended, was enough to win him offers of high positions under the Japanese in 1945 and under Bao Dai in 1949.

Diem left Vietnam in August 1950. From early 1951 to May 1953, he lived in Catholic seminaries in the United States; he made useful contacts with people such as Senators **John Kennedy** and **Mike Mansfield**. In May 1953, he went to Europe, going first to Paris and eventually to a Benedictine monastery in Belgium. He finally became premier (under Bao Dai as chief of state) of the State of Vietnam, also taking the offices of minister of defense and minister of the interior, on June 16, 1954. He protested the **Geneva Accords** of July 20–21, 1954, but at that time he had so little power that it was not obvious his hostility to the accords would prevent them from being implemented.

On September 10, 1954, Diem attempted to dismiss the chief of staff of the **Vietnamese National Army**, General Nguyen Van Hinh. This attempt failed at first; the officers whom Diem tried to appoint as replacements for General Hinh refused to accept the position. General Hinh continued to function as chief of staff for more than two additional months; he told U.S. Ambassador Donald Heath that he was seriously considering a military coup against Diem. Hinh finally gave up his post and left Vietnam on November 19, bowing to the combined pressure of Diem, Chief of State Bao Dai, and the United States. Only at this point did Diem acquire effective control of the Vietnamese National Army.

His next major problem was what were known as the **Sects**: the **Binh Xuyen** gangster organization and the **Hoa Hao** and **Cao Dai** religious sects, all of which had substantial armies in or near Diem's capital, **Saigon**. Diem defeated or won over most of the major sect leaders in 1955; by early May he had attained military control of Saigon, and in the following months his forces established effective control of most of South Vietnam. In July, he formally announced his refusal even to discuss the **elections** that, under the Geneva Accords, were supposed to be held in 1956 to reunify **North** and **South Vietnam**.

Diem replaced Bao Dai as chief of state in a referendum on October 23, 1955, in which it was officially announced that Diem had won 98.2 percent of the votes. The State of Vietnam became the Republic of Vietnam on October 26; a constitution enacted in 1956 formalized Diem's position as president. He was re-elected president in 1961, with 89 percent of the votes by the official count.

Diem's government was based to a considerable extent on his family; the two most powerful men in South Vietnam, after Diem, were his younger brothers **Ngo Dinh Nhu** and **Ngo Dinh Can**. Nhu was far more attuned to politics than Diem, and had stayed active in Vietnam while Diem was in exile in the United States and Europe. Without Nhu's lobbying, Diem might not have become premier in 1954. Nhu had responsibility for the **police**, the **Can Lao Party**, **intelligence** operations, and various paramilitary organizations. Can ran the northernmost provinces of South Vietnam on a semi-autonomous basis, though in the last years of Diem's rule, Diem and Nhu reduced Can's power. Finally there were Nhu's relatives by marriage: his wife's father Tran Van Chuong (ambassador to the United States for almost the whole of Diem's rule) and his wife's uncle Tran Van Do (foreign minister 1954–1955).

The North Vietnamese, most of them Catholic, who came south in late 1954 and early 1955 under the terms of the Geneva Accords, also provided vital support for Diem's regime. Diem's elder brother **Ngo Dinh Thuc**, bishop of Vinh Long and later archbishop of Hue, helped to mobilize the Catholic support for the government.

The State of Vietnam in 1954 was basically a French puppet government; its officials had been motivated to join it more often by a desire for wealth than by dedication to the national welfare. Diem did not have the talent for inspiring loyalty that would have been required to turn this government into an effective tool for his rule. **Corruption** remained widespread. After a military **coup** led by **Nguyen Chanh Thi** almost overthrew Diem in November 1960, his worries about the loyalty of the Army of the Republic of Vietnam (**ARVN**) became especially acute. He picked officers for key commands as much by personal loyalty as by competence. He weakened the **Civil Guard** by his efforts to keep it separate from the regular ARVN forces, so he could balance one against the other. Finally, in the early 1960s, it appears he came to believe that the ARVN would be unhappy, and thus be more inclined to carry out a coup against him, if it suffered serious casualties. By 1963, he was crippling military operations against the **Viet Cong** by his determination to avoid battles in which the ARVN might suffer serious casualties.

Diem was able to destroy most of the Communist organization in South Vietnam between 1955 and 1958, while the southern Communists' hands were tied by orders from the North. The **Lao Dong Party** leaders in **Hanoi** forbade their followers in the South to use large-scale violence, and narrowly restricted their use even of small-scale violence and assassinations; this left them terribly vulnerable to Diem's army and police. In 1959, however, the Lao Dong Party 15th Plenum authorized the beginning of a **guerrilla war** in South Vietnam, and this was in full swing by 1960.

The U.S. government supported Diem strongly in public. In private, some officials were offended by his inability to inspire broad support within South Vietnam, by the police-state methods that his brother Nhu used to keep him in power, by the inefficiency of his government (caused partly by Diem's tendency to lose himself in minutiae, and partly by his deliberate policy of playing his subordinates against one another), or by his lack of responsiveness to American advice. During the **Buddhist** Crisis of 1963 Diem's status as a Catholic ruler of a country in which the Catholics were a small minority became a massive liability. At this point Diem's critics in the U.S. government, led by **W. Averell Harriman**, **Roger Hilsman**, and from August 1963 onward even more by Ambassador **Henry Cabot Lodge** in Saigon, were able to push the U.S. government into supporting, rather hesitantly, a coup against Diem. Hesitant support was all that was necessary; a startling number of senior officers in the ARVN were eager to overthrow Diem, once they were told the United States would not object (*see* **coups**). The plotters struck about noon on November 1, 1963. Diem and Nhu escaped the Presidential Palace, but surrendered the following day, and were both promptly shot on orders of General **Duong Van Minh**.

**NGO DINH NHU** (1910–1963). A younger brother of **Ngo Dinh Diem**

(president of the **Republic of Vietnam**, 1955–63), he was probably born in **Hue**. He began political activity as a student in France in the 1930s. After his return to Vietnam, he worked as an archivist.

By 1953 he was becoming important in **Saigon** politics, organizing a **Catholic** labor movement, building support for his brother Diem, and establishing ties with the **Central Intelligence Agency** (CIA). After Diem became premier of the State of Vietnam in 1954, Nhu was his principal political adviser and political organizer. He did not take a position in the cabinet, but was far more powerful than any cabinet minister. Diem tended to lose himself in administrative detail; Nhu was the one who had a feel for politics, and he took responsibility for many activities having strong political implications. He ran the **Can Lao Party**, a major bulwark of Diem's rule. He supervised a variety of **intelligence**, security, **police**, and paramilitary organizations. He coordinated with the CIA on many of its activities in and near **South Vietnam**.

Many Americans blamed Nhu for the dictatorial character of Diem's government. American calls for Diem to get rid of Nhu were intensified after Nhu's **Special Forces** raided **Buddhist** pagodas on August 21, 1963, and after Nhu put out feelers for negotiations with the Communist leaders in **Hanoi**. But even if Diem had believed he could survive without Nhu's political and organizational talents, he would have been far too proud to submit to American demands that he discard his brother. American hostility to Nhu was one of the reasons Washington backed the military **coup** of November 1, 1963. Diem and Nhu were killed together on November 2.

Nhu's wife Tran Le Xuan had been been influential in promoting legislation outlawing divorce, dancing, prostitution, and other activities she considered immoral. Madame Nhu shared her husband's unpopularity with Americans, many of whom were offended by her enthusiasm for the public suicides by fire of Buddhist monks in 1963, and her offer to provide gasoline. She was travelling abroad at the time of the coup; she eventually settled in Italy.

**NGO DINH THUC** (1897–1984). **Catholic** archbishop. The elder brother of **Ngo Dinh Diem** (president of the **Republic of Vietnam**, 1955–63), he was born in the area of **Hue**, and was ordained a priest in 1925. He was bishop of Vinh Long from 1938 to 1961; he was archbishop of Hue, and head of the Catholic hierarchy in Vietnam, from 1961 to 1963. Archbishop Thuc was not sensitive to the feelings of the

**Buddhist** majority. He made a bad mistake in urging local authorities in Hue to enforce the often ignored law that only the flag of the **Republic of Vietnam** could be displayed in public places, when the Buddhists were displaying Buddhist flags in celebration of Buddha's birthday in May 1963. This led to a Buddhist protest demonstration on May 8, which ended with eight or nine people killed. The deaths were usually attributed to **ARVN** troops attacking the crowd, though there is dispute over the actual responsibility. Outrage against the government initiated the train of events that led to the fall of Ngo Dinh Diem in November of that year.

Archbishop Thuc was persuaded to go on a prolonged visit to Rome in September 1963; he lived in exile for the rest of his life. In 1976, he began consecrating people as Catholic bishops on his own authority. The Vatican was offended by this practice, and even more so by the behavior of some of the individuals Thuc had elevated. The first of these, Clemente Dominguez Gomez, whom Archbishop Thuc ordained as a priest in December 1975 and then consecrated as a bishop in January 1976, proclaimed himself pope about two years later. Archbishop Thuc was twice excommunicated by the Vatican, but twice forgiven.

**NGO QUANG TRUONG** (1929– ). **ARVN** general. He was born in Kien Hoa province of the **Mekong Delta**. Often said to have been the ARVN's best general, he became commander of the ARVN 1st Infantry Division in June 1966. His troops were heavily involved in the fighting in **Hue** during the **Tet Offensive** of 1968. He was a strong supporter of the U.S. **Marines' Combined Action Platoon** (CAP) program. In August 1970, Truong was shifted southward to command **IV Corps**, where he also did well. During the **Easter Offensive** of 1972, he was sent north to replace Hoang Xuan Lam as commander of **I Corps**, and he remained in command there from May 1972 until the Communist victory of 1975.

**NGUYEN CAO KY** (1930– ). General and prime minister. Born in **Son Tay** province west of **Hanoi**, he graduated from a secondary school in Hanoi in 1948, and joined the **Vietnamese National Army** in 1950. He graduated from the Reserve Officer School at Nam Dinh in 1952, and then spent several years being trained as a pilot in Morocco, France, and Algeria. By the time he returned to Vietnam, the First Indochina War was over. Ky became commander of the 1st Transport Squadron of the **Vietnamese Air Force** (VNAF) in 1955. He attended the Air Command and Staff College in the United States in 1958, then became the deputy chief of staff for operations of the VNAF in 1959. He became commander of the 1st Transport Group on March 1, 1960. Soon afterward he began flying transport planes on covert operations, controlled by the **Central Intelligence Agency**, to drop agents into **North Vietnam**.

When the **coup** against **Ngo Dinh Diem** began on November 1, 1963, Colonel Ky arrested the commander of the VNAF, who was a Diem supporter, and threw the VNAF to the side of the coup. As his reward, he became acting commander of the VNAF on December 16, 1963. In July 1964, he publicly urged that the war be escalated with bombing not only of **North Vietnam** but even of **China**. Ky was formally commander of the VNAF from August 12, 1964, to November 1967. He continued at least occasional participation in combat, most conspicuously flying the lead VNAF plane in the *Flaming Dart* air strikes against North Vietnam in February 1965.

Ky, with the threat of bombing by the VNAF, was able to block a coup that almost overthew **Nguyen Khanh** in September 1964. In the aftermath, he and other officers who came to be called the "**Young Turks**" became increasingly powerful. They worked in partnership with Khanh for a while, then in February 1965 forced Khanh into exile and became unmistakably the strongest force in **Saigon**. They allowed the civilian Premier **Phan Huy Quat** to remain in office until June 1965, at which point Ky became premier himself; he held that office until September 1967.

During his years as premier, he and fellow Young Turk **Nguyen Van Thieu** increasingly became rivals for power. When Ky submitted to pressure from fellow generals and the United States not to run against Thieu in the presidential **election** of 1967, instead accepting the position of vice president and allowing Thieu to become president, this did not at first seem a decisive victory for Thieu. Ky's power was based not on what office he held but on the network of high officers who were loyal to him, including General **Nguyen Ngoc Loan** (the very powerful commander of the National **Police**) and **Le Nguyen Khang** (the commander of the **Marine Corps**). These remained Ky's men, not Thieu's, even when Thieu became president. During Ky's years as vice president (1967–1971), however, Thieu was able to whittle down his power very seriously. Ky was briefly a candidate against Thieu for president in the election of 1971, but dropped out of the race, saying the election was being rigged.

Thereafter he had no official position, but he retained his rank of marshal, his house at **Tan Son Nhut** Air Base, and the use of aircraft to fly around the country visiting other bases.

On March 27, 1975, Ky launched the National Salvation Committee in an effort to displace Thieu as leader of the **Republic of Vietnam**. He was supported by former Foreign Minister Tran Van Do, labor leader Tran Quoc Buu, and the anti-**corruption** crusader, Father Tran Huu Thanh. He left Vietnam by **helicopter** a few hours before the fall of Saigon at the end of April, and later settled in the United States. He is the author of *Twenty Years and Twenty Days* (1976).

**NGUYEN CHANH THI** (1923– ). **ARVN** general. Born in Hue, he became a soldier under the French in 1940. In 1956 he was given command of the **Airborne** Group of the Army of the Republic of Vietnam, which became the **Airborne Brigade** in 1959. Colonel Thi led the brigade in an unsuccessful **coup** against **Ngo Dinh Diem** in November 1960. He became commander of **I Corps** in 1965; he was removed from this position in March 1966 because he had aligned himself with radical **Buddhist** elements led by **Thich Tri Quang**. News of his dismissal was followed by massive Buddhist demonstrations, and General Thi's troops seized **Danang** and **Hue**. Premier **Nguyen Cao Ky** assigned Colonel **Nguyen Ngoc Loan** to supervise the suppression of this rebellion, which Loan did very effectively; the government regained control of Danang in May and of Hue in June. General Thi was exiled to the United States. He attempted to return to Vietnam on February 23, 1972, but was refused entry. He published a memoir, *Viet nam: mot troi tam su*, in 1987.

**NGUYEN CHI THANH**, a.k.a. Truong Son (1914–1967). **PAVN** general. Born in **Thua Thien** province, he began revolutionary activity at the age of 17, and became secretary of the Thua Thien Province Committee of the Indochinese Communist Party in 1938. Thanh came from a poor peasant family and had little formal schooling, but self-education and attending study groups while in French prisons had brought him up to a reasonable educational level. From 1945 to 1950, he held various positions in **Trung Bo**; from 1950 to 1961 he was head of the PAVN's General Political Directorate. He became a member of the Politburo in 1950 or 1951.

In the early 1960s, Thanh was the Politburo member particularly responsible for supervising the struggle in the South, but also had responsibilities regarding agriculture in the North. In 1964, he was sent south to become secretary of the **Trung uong cuc mien Nam** (COSVN), effectively commander of the Communist forces in the southern half of **South Vietnam**. He held this position until his death on July 6, 1967. Thanh took a very aggressive approach to the war. He believed it was necessary to keep military pressure on the American forces, fighting frequent battles pitting substantial American and Communist units against one another, even at the cost of substantial Communist casualties. The Americans were in an unfamiliar environment; Thanh did not want to allow them to adjust to it and become comfortable operating in it. He opposed those like **Truong Chinh** who would have preferred to hold down the intensity of combat, gearing Communist efforts to a very protracted struggle. Thanh also firmly opposed efforts to settle the war through **negotiations**; indeed he was probably the strongest opponent of negotiations within the Communist leadership.

The **Tet Offensive** of 1968 was originally Thanh's idea—another example of his very aggressive approach to the war—but he died while the planning for it was at an early stage. There are a variety of stories on the circumstances of his death. The version supported by the strongest evidence indicates that he died suddenly of a heart attack while attending strategy meetings in **Hanoi**, but there is also serious evidence supporting the belief of many Americans that he was actually killed by American **bombs** in the South. Finally, some people suspect that he died in Hanoi not of natural causes but as a victim of assassination by factional opponents within the Communist leadership.

**NGUYEN HUU HANH** (1926– ). Brigadier general, a Communist agent within the **ARVN**. Born in My Tho province of the **Mekong Delta**, he was a **Catholic**. He attended the Command and General Staff College at Fort Leavenworth, Kansas, 1958–1959, and the Advanced Intelligence School at Fort Holabird, Maryland, in 1962. In 1967, as a colonel in the ARVN 21st Division, he was appointed head of the 44th Special Tactical Zone, in charge of ARVN efforts to block **infiltration** from **Cambodia** into **IV Corps**; it is likely that in this position he was able to assist the **Viet Cong** forces in preparing for the **Tet Offensive** of 1968. During the last hours before the fall of **Saigon**, on April 30, 1975, he was the senior ARVN officer, and thus acting commander, at Joint General Staff Headquarters in Saigon. He broadcast an order for all ARVN troops to lay down their arms. He later became a member of the Fatherland Front for Ho Chi Minh City.

**NGUYEN HUU THO** (1910–1996). Born in **Cholon**, he obtained a law degree in France, returned to Vietnam, and practiced law for many

years. He became a member of the revolutionary movement, but is not
known to have joined the Communist Party. Tho was imprisoned by
the French from 1950 until 1952 for his role in leading a demonstration in **Saigon** against U.S. support of the French.

He later led demonstrations in the Saigon area calling for compliance with the **Geneva Accords of 1954**. There are sharply conflicting
versions of what happened to him as a result. It is generally believed
that he spent years in prison or under house arrest, and only escaped at
the end of 1961. But some anti-Communist sources have said he spent
this period not as a prisoner in the South but in **North Vietnam**, and
came south in 1961. In 1962, Tho became chairman of the **National
Liberation Front** (NLF). When the **Provisional Revolutionary Government** was established in June 1969, he became chairman of its
Council of Government Advisers.

In retrospect, it appears that Tho was largely a figurehead as nominal head of the NLF, a non-Communist chosen to create the impression
that the NLF as a whole was not a Communist organization. But he
continued to enjoy high nominal rank even after the need for this façade
had ended. He became one of the two vice presidents of the Socialist
Republic of Vietnam in 1976, and served briefly as acting president
1980–1981.

**NGUYEN KHANH** (1927– ). **ARVN** general and prime minister. Born
in Tra Vinh (later renamed Vinh Binh) province, in the **Mekong Delta**,
he graduated from the French Army's Airborne School at Pau in 1949,
and soon became commander of a company of paratroopers in the **Vietnamese National Army**. He became chief of staff to **Duong Van Minh**
in 1955.

General Khanh was chief of staff of the General Staff, **Republic of
Vietnam** Armed Forces (RVNAF), from 1960 to 1962. He became
commander of **II Corps** in December 1962. He supported the **coup**
that overthrew **Ngo Dinh Diem** in November 1963, though II Corps
was too far north for his troops to play a direct role. In late November
1963, he was moved to **I Corps**, even farther north, but he had enough
influence over the generals with troops close to **Saigon** to be able to
organize a coup of his own in January 1964, overthrowing the group of
generals led by Duong Van Minh who had taken power in November
1963. Khanh charged them with **neutralism**. He formally became
premier on February 8. In late May he began urging on the United
States, in private, the need for attacks on **North Vietnam**, which he

said would raise morale and strengthen unity in the South. In July, he began making such calls very publicly and protesting the lack of U.S. enthusiasm for attacks on the North.

Khanh proclaimed a state of emergency on August 7, with press censorship and a prohibition of mass meetings. On August 16, he issued a new constitution, usually called the Vung Tau Charter, under which he would have become president, with considerably more power than he had had as premier. This led to explosive protests by students and radical **Buddhists**, and he had to back down. After some complex maneuvers he resigned as premier on October 30, while retaining real power as commander in chief of the RVNAF, and from December 18 onward, chairman of the Armed Forces Council.

By the end of 1964, Khanh was on very hostile terms with U.S. Ambassador **Maxwell Taylor**, and indeed publicly asked that the United States recall Taylor, for excessive meddling in Vietnamese internal affairs. When he installed **Phan Huy Quat** as premier in February 1965, he was hoping at first to retain real control of the government as chairman of the Armed Forces Council, but within days the generals known as the **"Young Turks"** had removed him from that position, and sent him out of the country as an "ambassador at large." After the war, Khanh settled in France.

**NGUYEN NGOC LOAN** (1930–1998). General. Born in **Hue** to a middle-class family, he studied pharmacy at the University of Hue. He joined the **Vietnamese National Army** in 1951, and quickly entered an officer training school, where he was a classmate of **Nguyen Cao Ky**. He served briefly in Vietnam, then was sent to Morocco to be trained as a pilot. Loan returned to Vietnam in 1955, and for the next 10 years served in the **Vietnamese Air Force** (VNAF). At some point during this decade he went to the United States for further training, so by the time he became a prominent figure in the late 1960s, he spoke good English.

Although his duties were increasingly administrative, with an emphasis on **intelligence** and security, Loan remained a pilot long enough to fly as wingman to his old friend Ky, by that time commander of the VNAF, in the *Flaming Dart* air strikes against **North Vietnam** in February 1965. But when Ky emerged in June 1965 as prime minister of the **Republic of Vietnam**, he made Loan a colonel and gave him control of military intelligence and security. In April 1966 Loan was made, in addition, director general of the National **Police**. He had enormous power, and was trusted with vital tasks like supervising the suppression of the rebellion by radical **Buddhists** and General **Nguyen Chanh Thi** in **Danang** and Hue early in 1966. When Ky in 1967 consented to become vice president, with **Nguyen Van Thieu** as president, one of the reasons Ky expected still to have a great deal of power was that he was counting on Loan's continued support.

On February 1, 1968, during the **Tet Offensive**, a **Viet Cong** officer in civilian clothing was captured by police in **Cholon**, the Chinese section of **Saigon**. General Loan walked up to the prisoner, whose arms were bound, and shot him through the head. An Associated Press photographer caught the execution in a still photo, and an NBC-TV crew recorded it with a movie camera. The images caused a worldwide sensation.

General Loan initially explained his action by saying that the Viet Cong had killed a lot of Vietnamese, and Americans. A story emerged years later that this particular Viet Cong had been believed to have killed the family of a subordinate (and personal friend) of Loan.

General Loan suffered severe wounds during fighting in the Saigon area in May 1968. He was sent for treatment first to **Australia** and then to the United States. President Thieu, who was consolidating his own power and reducing Nguyen Cao Ky's, found Loan's absence from Vietnam convenient, and arranged to have it prolonged even after Loan was out of the hospital. When Loan finally returned to Vietnam, he was given a job supposedly involving long-range planning, in which he had no real power. Loan escaped from Vietnam in 1975 and went to the United States, where he operated a pizza restaurant in Virginia.

**NGUYEN THI BINH** (1927– ). Born near **Saigon**, she became involved in revolutionary activities as a student; in March 1950 she led a student demonstration in Saigon against U.S. support for the French. She was imprisoned from 1951 to 1954. In the early 1960s, she became a member of the Central Committee of the **National Liberation Front** (NLF) and vice president of the South Vietnam Women's Union for Liberation. Binh was often sent abroad to represent the NLF, and in 1969, she became minister of foreign affairs of the **Provisional Revolutionary Government** (PRG). In that capacity she represented the PRG at the **Paris negotiations**. After the war, Binh was a member of the Communist Party Central Committee until 1986, and minister of education 1976–1987. She was vice president of the Socialist Republic of Vietnam 1992–1993.

**NGUYEN THI DINH** (1920–1992). Born in **Ben Tre** province (eastern **Mekong Delta**), she became involved with the Communist movement in the late 1930s, and was imprisoned by the French from 1940 to 1943. She was one of the leaders in the Viet Minh seizure of power in Ben Tre in 1945. In January 1960, Dinh led the **Viet Cong** uprising in Ben Tre. In 1964, she became a member of the Presidium of the **National Liberation Front** (NLF) Central Committee. In 1965, she became chairwoman of the South Vietnam Women's Liberation Association and deputy commander of the South Vietnam Liberation Armed Forces. After the war, Dinh was a member of the Central Committee of the Communist Party of Vietnam, and had more than trivial influence as president of the Vietnam Women's Association. She was the author of *No Other Road to Take: Memoir of Mrs. Nguyen Thi Dinh* (1976).

**NGUYEN VAN LINH,** original name Nguyen Van Cuc, a.k.a. Muoi Cuc (1915–1998). He was born in Hung Yen province near **Hanoi,** probably in 1915 (some sources say 1913), but he was brought up in the South. He was imprisoned for revolutionary activities 1930–1936 and 1941–1945; he served under **Le Duan** in **Nam Bo** (the southern third of Vietnam) during the First Indochina War. Linh became a member of the **Lao Dong Party** Central Committee in 1960. He replaced Le Duan as head (secretary) of the Nam Bo Regional Committee at the end of 1957; this body was upgraded to become the **Trung uong cuc mien Nam** (COSVN) in 1961. Linh remained head until 1964, and then served as deputy head, under **Nguyen Chi Thanh** from 1964 to 1967 and under **Pham Hung** from 1967 to the end of the war. He became head of the party committee of **Ho Chi Minh City,** and a member of the Politburo, in 1976. He lost both these positions (in 1978 and 1982 respectively), reportedly because of his opposition to socialist transformation of the South, but then regained them, and in December 1986 he was named general secretary of the Communist Party. In this position he pushed the policy of *Doi moi* ("renovation"), allowing more freedom for private enterprise. He retired due to ill health in 1991.

**NGUYEN VAN THIEU** (1924–2001). President of the **Republic of Vietnam**. Born in Ninh Thuan province of southern **Trung Bo**, probably in 1924, though many sources say 1923. He was in the first class of the National Military Academy at **Dalat** in 1948. He then completed a course at the Infantry School in Coëtquidan, France, in 1949. Thieu attended the U.S. Army Command and General Staff College, in

Fort Leavenworth, Kansas, in 1957. His wife converted him to the **Catholic** faith, and he joined the **Can Lao Party** in 1962. He commanded the **ARVN** 21st Infantry Division in 1959, the 1st Infantry Division 1960–1962, and the 5th Infantry Division 1962–1964. In this last position, Thieu provided many of the troops for the **coup** that overthrew President **Ngo Dinh Diem** on November 1, 1963. But he also supported the coup of January 1964, in which **Nguyen Khanh** overthrew the generals who had taken power in the previous coup. He became commander of **IV Corps** in September 1964, a deputy premier in January 1965, and defense minister (while remaining a deputy premier) in February. Thieu was chairman of the National Leadership Committee and head of state 1965–1967, though initially he seemed to be second to **Nguyen Cao Ky** among the "**Young Turks**," the group of officers who had displaced Nguyen Khanh.

In 1967, when both the United States and crucial ARVN generals were determined that Thieu and Ky should cooperate rather than run against one another in the presidential **election**, Thieu was able to arrange that he be the candidate for president, and Ky the candidate for vice president. They won, though with an embarrassingly small vote. At first Vice President Ky was Thieu's near-equal, but before long Thieu trimmed Ky's power and established himself very firmly as ruler of the Republic of Vietnam. It is generally believed that he became very wealthy during his years as president.

For the most part Thieu was a consensus figure; his power was based on maintaining the support both of a coalition of Vietnamese officers and of the United States. Many things went well for him for several years. The Communist forces in **South Vietnam** suffered heavy casualties in the **Tet Offensive** early in 1968, and in the heavy fighting that followed that offensive. The *Phoenix* **Program** also weakened the Communists. Thieu's government finally initiated an effective **land reform** program, competing with the Communists for peasant loyalties, though it is unclear to what extent this was Thieu's personal initiative. American aid allowed him to increase the size of his armed forces, and especially their weaponry, very dramatically. His big worry was the withdrawal of U.S. forces beginning in mid-1969. In 1971, General **Creighton Abrams**, commander of **Military Assistance Command, Vietnam**, found Thieu's caution in *Lam Son 719*, an incursion into **Laos** in which ARVN units had U.S. air support but were not accompanied by U.S. troops on the ground, very frustrating.

Several of Thieu's predecessors in power in Saigon, including Ngo

Dinh Diem, **Duong Van Minh**, and Nguyen Khanh, had been willing to consider negotiating some kind of compromise with the Communists. Thieu was adamant in his opposition to any compromise, and especially to anything implying recognition of the **National Liberation Front** (NLF) and later the **Provisional Revolutionary Government** (PRG) as entities having any power in South Vietnam. This eventually put him into conflict with his American allies. His refusal even to attend peace talks if an NLF delegation were officially involved delayed the beginning of formal talks in the **Paris negotiations** until the beginning of 1969. In October 1972, when he was shown the draft peace agreement that **Henry Kissinger** had negotiated with **Le Duc Tho**, Thieu was horrified by many aspects of it, including its recognition of Communist areas of control in South Vietnam, and by its calling for a withdrawal of U.S. but not of **PAVN** forces from South Vietnam. He demanded massive modifications in it, but failed to obtain them. In January 1973, President **Richard Nixon** forced him to sign the **Paris Peace Agreement**, only slightly modified from the October draft, by blunt threats that if Thieu did not sign, the United States would pull out of Vietnam and cut off all military aid.

During the first months after the agreement was signed, Thieu put his forces on the offensive, and they were able to take significant territory from the Communists. But by late 1973, the Communist forces in South Vietnam were growing stronger, and U.S. aid to the ARVN was shrinking. Thieu's forces were increasingly on the defensive. In 1975, faced with a major Communist (primarily PAVN) offensive, they disintegrated (*see* **final collapse**). Thieu resigned as president and went to Taiwan, then to Britain, and eventually to the United States.

**NGUYEN VIET THANH** (1931–1970) **ARVN** general. Born in **Long An** province, Thanh was educated at the Lycée Chasseloup-Laubat in **Saigon**. He graduated from the military academy at **Dalat** in 1951, and became an officer in the **Vietnamese National Army**. In the middle or late 1950s, he had further military training in the United States. As a major, he became Long An province chief in October 1961, when the province was largely under **Viet Cong** control. He launched a vigorous military campaign against the Viet Cong, but was also conspicuously honest, and concerned for the welfare of the people. He significantly extended government control in the province, before he was dismissed in June 1963 as a penalty for his refusal to rig the 1963 **elections** to the National Assembly. He commanded the 7th Division from 1965 to 1968, and was sometimes said to be the most competent and least corrupt division commander in the ARVN. He became commander of **IV Corps** in July 1968, and occupied that position until his death in a **helicopter** crash May 2, 1970, during the **Cambodian Incursion**.

**NGUYEN XUAN OANH,** sometimes called "Jack Owen" by Americans (1921–2003). He was born in Phu Lang Thuong, **North Vietnam**, a **Buddhist**. He attended the Lycée Albert Sarraut in **Hanoi**, then went to Japan from 1940 to 1949, and earned a bachelor's degree in economics from Kyoto Imperial University. Oanh earned a Ph.D. in economics in 1954 at Harvard University, and then taught at various institutions in the United States, including Harvard, from 1955 to 1960. He worked for the International Monetary Fund in Washington from 1960 to 1963.

Oanh was governor of the National Bank of Vietnam from January 1963 to August 1965. He was minister of finance and vice minister for economy of the **Republic of Vietnam** from February to November 1964. He soon also became deputy premier, and there were brief periods (August 29 to September 3, 1964, and January 28 to mid-February 1965) when he was acting premier. He then became president of the National Institute of Economic Development in **Saigon**.

After the end of the war, Oanh spent about a year under house arrest, but then began to win acceptance from the Communist government. By the late 1980s, he was a member of the National Assembly and was playing an important role in shaping the economic policies of the Socialist Republic of Vietnam.

**NHA BE.** The Nha Be River is one section of the shipping channel by which ocean-going ships can reach **Saigon**. Coming from the South China Sea, ships proceed northward through the **Rung Sat** swamps on the **Long Tau River**, then follow the Nha Be River to the Saigon River and Saigon.

Nha Be, on the west bank of the river, was a base for military forces (especially those engaged in operations in the Rung Sat), and also the site of the huge Shell Oil Terminal, a major point of import and storage for petroleum products. An attack by Communist **sappers** on December 3, 1973, which destroyed 35 million liters of fuel at Nha Be, was a major blow to fuel supplies in **South Vietnam**.

**NHA TRANG.** A town on the coast of **South Vietnam** in Khanh Hoa province, **II Corps**, north of **Cam Ranh**. It had a major air base and the **ARVN** Non-Commissioned Officer (NCO) School. It was the main center of U.S. **Army Special Forces** in Vietnam from 1957 onward, and the headquarters of the Fifth Special Forces Group was formally established there in October 1964. The Special Forces **reconnaissance** school in Nha Trang was expanded to become the **Recondo School** in 1966.

**NIXON, RICHARD MILHOUS** (1913–1994). President of the United States. Born in Yorba Linda, California, he graduated from Whittier College in 1934 and from Duke University Law School in 1937. He served in the Navy during World War II. Elected to the U.S. House of Representatives as a Republican in 1946, he became a member of the Committee on Un-American Activities, and achieved national fame with his accusations that Alger Hiss had been a Communist agent in the State Department. He was elected to the Senate in 1950, and then elected vice president in 1952. In 1954, he urged President Dwight Eisenhower to commit U.S. air power in Vietnam on the side of the French; he later described Eisenhower's decision not to intervene in the Battle of Dien Bien Phu as a "critical mistake."

Nixon was the Republican nominee for president in 1960; he lost to **John Kennedy** by a tiny margin. When he ran again in 1968, he was vague about his views on the Vietnam War. His critics later said he had claimed to have a "secret plan," but he had not actually made such a claim. He won a narrow victory in the three-way race (*see* **elections**).

Nixon distrusted the bureaucracy, and shifted power from the major departments of government into the White House. His special assistant for national security affairs (usually called national security adviser), **Henry Kissinger**, was the man Nixon used to control foreign policy; Secretary of State **William P. Rogers** was reduced to a secondary role. Nixon had far less direct contact with officials in the executive departments of government than previous presidents had had; much of his communication with them was filtered through Kissinger, **Alexander Haig**, and other members of the White House staff.

The biggest foreign policy initiative of Nixon's first term was his opening of friendly relations with **China**. This surprised many people, since Nixon had long been a strident anti-Communist not only in domestic politics but in foreign affairs, bitterly hostile to China. In 1964, he had urged bombing **North Vietnam**, said that the actual liberation of North Vietnam from Communist rule should be made a goal of the war, and strongly hinted that the United States should extend the Vietnam War even beyond North Vietnam into China, commenting that the United States should have extended American bombing in the Korean War beyond North Korea into China. But by 1969, he was beginning to think of how a friendly relationship with China would increase his leverage not only against the Vietnamese Communists but against the **Soviet Union**. After cautious feelers from both sides, Nixon sent Kissinger on an extremely secret trip to Beijing in 1971, and then went himself, with huge publicity, in 1972.

When Nixon became president, the American public was disenchanted with the war in Vietnam. Most thought it had been a mistake for the United States to get into the war. Many wanted to pull out; others (including some who felt it had been a mistake to go in) thought the United States should escalate the war and win it. Combat in **South Vietnam** was intense. The United States was bombing South Vietnam and **Laos** very heavily, but not North Vietnam or **Cambodia**.

In mid-1969, Nixon announced that he would begin pulling U.S. troops out of South Vietnam and strengthening the Army of the Republic of Vietnam (**ARVN**) so that it could take a greater share of the fighting, in a program called **Vietnamization** of the war. At the same time, he announced that he had ordered U.S. military commanders in South Vietnam to hold U.S. casualties to a minimum; this meant being less aggressive in launching ground attacks against enemy forces.

For the next three years, Nixon walked an unsteady tightrope. The strength of the Communist forces in South Vietnam had peaked at about the beginning of 1968; by mid-1969 they had been significantly weakened. But the price that had been paid to achieve this was more than the American **Congress** and public were willing to continue paying. Nixon could maintain even minimally adequate public support for the war only by reducing the burden the war placed on American society. In the first half of 1969, the announced figures for American deaths in combat averaged 1,057 per month, almost as high as the rate (1,216) for the year 1968. In the second half of 1969, after Nixon's June order for less agressiveness in combat, the average was only 512 per month. It was 224 per month for the second half of 1970, and 46 per month for the second half of 1971. The number of men being drafted each month declined gradually at first, then suddenly dropped to near-zero levels in mid-1971. The danger, for Nixon, was that the pullouts might weaken the anti-Communist forces so much that the Communists would regain the military edge. When the Communist forces launched the massive **Easter Offensive** in the spring of 1972, the withdrawal of American personnel continued even while the ARVN was fighting for survival. Delaying the withdrawal, even for a few months in an emergency, would have been more of a political risk than Nixon was willing to take.

Nixon thought of politics very much in terms of personal hostilities. He had first become famous through attacks on prominent liberals, and he continued to think in such terms after becoming president. This applied especially to the media; Nixon was disliked by many journalists, he tended to think he was disliked even more than he was, and he strongly reciprocated the hostility, real and imagined. He avoided contact with journalists, neglecting opportunities to put his own spin on media coverage of his administration, and he assigned Vice President **Spiro Agnew** to lead a public attack on the media.

The controversy over the Vietnam War would have made this a time of conflict regardless of who was president. **Lyndon Johnson** had been by inclination a conciliator; he had not tried to whip up public hatred against anti-war protesters. Nixon had fewer compunctions, and was faced with a much more raucous and violent set of protesters, but by the time he was president the unpopularity of the war limited the extent to which the public would support a crackdown on the **anti-war movement**, even when that movement used tactics that offended most Americans.

In their eagerness to find evidence that the anti-war movement was getting secret support and direction from foreign governments, and to identify and/or discredit the government officials who leaked to the press embarrassing secrets about the war, Nixon and some of those around him at the White House began pushing the limits of the law. When the Federal Bureau of Investigation (FBI) resisted pressure to use burglary, wiretapping, and electronic bugging as investigative tools, the White House urged the **Central Intelligence Agency** to expand its investigations of the anti-war movement. The White House also began to take a more direct role: after **Daniel Ellsberg** was arrested for leaking the massive collection of documents on the Vietnam War known as the **Pentagon Papers** to *The New York Times*, the burglars who broke into the office of his psychiatrist, looking for evidence against Ellsberg, were working directly for the White House. These men were nicknamed the "plumbers" because they were supposed to fix leaks. The activities of the "plumbers" eventually triggered the Watergate scandal, which forced Nixon to resign as president.

Nixon felt he needed to do more to cut off the Communist forces in South Vietnam from outside support, both because his troop withdrawals were reducing his ability to bring direct pressure on them in South Vietnam, and because they were becoming more dependant on outside support; the proportion of North Vietnamese troops among the Communist forces in South Vietnam, and the proportion of their supplies that came from external sources, were both far higher in 1970 than they had been a few years earlier. The People's Army of Vietnam (**PAVN**) used a very extensive network of bases and supply routes in eastern Laos to support its operations in South Vietnam, and also provided massive assistance to the **Pathet Lao** (Laotian Communist) forces fighting for control of Laos. Lyndon Johnson had bombed PAVN forces in Laos very heavily, but made only small covert attacks on them with ground forces. PAVN and **Viet Cong** forces had a smaller string of bases in eastern Cambodia, and they had an understanding with the Cambodian government of Prince **Norodom Sihanouk** under which they used these bases to support their war effort but did not support the tiny **Khmer Rouge** (the Cambodian Communist movement). Lyndon Johnson had grudgingly tolerated this understanding; it prevented PAVN and Viet Cong forces from extending themselves into any substantial portion of Cambodia, at the cost of allowing them to use their bases almost unmolested for their war effort in South Vietnam.

Nixon decided he could not accept such handicaps to his war effort in South Vietnam. He began secret bombing of PAVN and Viet Cong bases in Cambodia (Operation *Menu*) in March 1969, and then on April 30, 1970, announced the **Cambodian Incursion**, using not only air power but substantial U.S. and ARVN ground forces. There was an explosion of outrage from the anti-war movement at this extension of the U.S. war effort to another country. National Guardsmen sent onto the campus of **Kent State** University in Ohio to try to restore order killed four students. The deaths at Kent State provoked an even larger explosion of outrage. Hundreds of colleges across the country were closed down by student and faculty strikes, and at the end of the year, both houses of Congress passed legislation making it illegal for United States ground troops to be sent into either Laos or Cambodia, and forbidding even U.S. military **advisers** on the ground in Cambodia (*see* **Congress**, **Frank Church**, and **John Sherman Cooper**).

The incursion into Cambodia had done much damage to Communist bases there, though it failed to find the Communist headquarters, the **Trung uong cuc mien Nam** (COSVN), which had been one of Nixon's major announced goals for the operation. When ARVN troops launched an incursion into Laos in February 1971, attempting to cut the **Ho Chi Minh Trail**, Nixon was able to give them air and **helicopter** support, and **artillery** fire from American firebases in South Vietnam, but U.S. ground troop units did not cross the border with them. This operation, *Lam Son 719*, was far less successful than the Cambodian Incursion.

Lyndon Johnson had halted U.S. bombing of North Vietnam in 1968 in an effort to get peace talks going. Nixon had for the most part continued the **bombing halt**, but the talks had gone nowhere for years. Occasional air strikes increased in frequency late in 1971 (*see* **John D. Lavelle, protective reaction, *Proud Deep Alpha***). When Communist (mostly PAVN) forces launched the **Easter Offensive** in April 1972, President Nixon resumed systematic bombing of North Vietnam with Operation *Freedom Train*, which began on April 6, and then expanded it massively with Operation *Linebacker*, which began on May 10. He also closed the major seaports of North Vietnam with **mines**, something Johnson had never been willing to risk. Nixon had been improving relations with both China and the Soviet Union, and he gambled, successfully, that they would not react violently against what he was doing to North Vietnam.

Soon afterward, talks between Kissinger and **Lao Dong Party** Politburo member **Le Duc Tho** finally reached a breakthrough in Paris. They completed a draft peace agreement in October. When the draft was presented to President **Nguyen Van Thieu** of the **Republic of Vietnam**, however, Thieu was horrified; the agreement, which called for a withdrawal of American but not of PAVN troops from South Vietnam, seemed to Thieu likely to lead to Communist victory in South Vietnam. Kissinger announced publicly, "Peace is at hand" on October 26, but the United States at Thieu's urging asked for major alterations in the agreement, and by December the negotiations once more seemed deadlocked. Nixon at this point ordered a dramatic escalation of the U.S. bombing of North Vietnam, Operation *Linebacker II*, which led to a storm of outrage not only in the United States but throughout the world; almost everyone was under the impression that this was a ruthless attack on North Vietnamese cities (especially **Hanoi**) comparable to the U.S. bombing of German and Japanese cities during World War II. Nixon made little effort to explain to the public, in the United States or abroad, how little damage had actually been done to the city of Hanoi.

In January 1973, Kissinger and Le Duc Tho completed their negotiations, and the **Paris Peace Agreement** was signed on January 27. It closely resembled the draft of the previous October. President Thieu was still horrified at it, but Nixon persuaded him to sign, using a mixture of promises of future support if he signed, and threats the United States would cut off military aid if he did not.

At this time, Nixon seemed in a strong position domestically. The Democratic nominee in the 1972 election had been **George McGovern**, very liberal and anti-war, indeed so much so as to be outside the American mainstream. Nixon had won the election overwhelmingly, with 60.8 percent of the vote. On June 17, 1972, however, five employees of Nixon's campaign organization had been caught burglarizing the Democratic Party headquarters in the Watergate Building in Washington, searching the files and planting electronic listening devices. Up to the time of the election the impact of this was limited, but during 1973, evidence emerged that important subordinates of the president had ordered the burglary and that Nixon himself had been heavily involved in covering it up. This triggered investigations that revealed other scandals. Nixon resigned as president on August 9, 1974. His successor, **Gerald Ford**, granted him a pardon in September, preventing him from being brought to trial.

Long before his actual resignation, the Watergate scandal had eroded Nixon's power, leaving him little leverage with Congress. Had this not happened, Nixon probably would have been able to get somewhat larger appropriations for military aid to South Vietnam during the period following the Paris Agreement. The United States had trained the ARVN to fight in a style demanding lavish supplies; by 1974 the U.S. Congress was no longer providing them.

Nixon was the author of numerous books, including his memoirs *RN* (1978) and *No More Vietnams* (1985).

**NIXON DOCTRINE.** On July 25, 1969, during a trip around the world, President **Richard Nixon** held a press conference on the island of **Guam** at which he announced that the United States in the future would be less inclined to supply U.S. troops to defend Asian nations under attack, though it would continue to supply equipment and financial aid, to help Asian nations defend themselves when under attack. This was at first called the Guam Doctrine but was quickly renamed the Nixon Doctrine. It was the theory behind Nixon's policy of **Vietnamization**.

**NOLTING, FREDERICK ERNEST** "Fritz" (1911–1989). Diplomat. Born in Richmond, Virginia, Nolting served in the Navy during World War II, then joined the Foreign Service in 1946, specializing in European affairs. He was politically conservative. He had no significant background in Asia when President **John Kennedy** chose him to become U.S. ambassador to **South Vietnam** early in 1961.

Nolting's predecessor, Elbridge Durbrow, had by 1960 become very critical of **Ngo Dinh Diem**, and had been suggesting that Diem dismiss his brother **Ngo Dinh Nhu**. Nolting was more conciliatory; he did not press Diem for reforms, and he tried to block reports critical of Diem's performance. He and General **Paul Harkins**, commander from February 1962 onward of the U.S. **Military Assistance Command, Vietnam**, had considerable success blocking reports critical of Diem from going to Washington in government channels, but they had more trouble with the press. Reporters like Homer Bigart and **David Halberstam** of *The New York Times*, **Malcolm Browne** of the Associated Press, and François Sully of *Newsweek* were aware that Diem was far less popular in South Vietnam than Nolting was reporting, and U.S. military officers in the field as **advisers** to the Army of the Republic of Vietnam (**ARVN**) were telling the journalists that the war against the Communists was going far less well than Harkins was reporting it was. Nolting's pressure on the press to avoid publishing negative reports led to bitter hostility.

The **Buddhist** crisis that broke out in May 1963 stripped all credibility from Nolting's praise of Diem's political skills; he left Vietnam on August 15, 1963, to be replaced by **Henry Cabot Lodge**. It was not so obvious at that date, though it would be a few months later, that Nolting's and Harkins's optimism about the progress of the war in the countryside had been equally unfounded.

Back in Washington late in 1963, Nolting argued against U.S. support for the **coup** that overthrew Ngo Dinh Diem. He retired from government service in 1964. His memoir *From Trust to Tragedy* was published in 1988.

**NORODOM SIHANOUK** (1922– ). King and prince. He was born in **Phnom Penh**, but was educated at the Lycée Chasseloup-Laubat in **Saigon**. The French picked him in 1941 to be king of **Cambodia**, apparently believing he would be a pliable puppet, but he was able to win genuine independence from France in 1953. Once Viet Minh forces had withdrawn from Cambodia under the **Geneva Accords of 1954**, he had effective control of the country. In March 1955, King Sihanouk, feeling it would be easier to exercise real power if he had fewer ceremonial burdens, abdicated the throne; from this point onward he was referred to as Prince Sihanouk. His father became the king.

From 1955 to 1963, he accepted military aid from the United States, but in the 1960s he became more closely aligned with the **Democratic Republic of Vietnam** (DRV). He permitted **Viet Cong** and **PAVN** forces to use base areas inside Cambodia (*see* **sanctuaries**). But he firmly suppressed the Cambodian Communist movement known as the **Khmer Rouge**. (For more on his policies, *see* **Cambodia**.)

In 1970, Sihanouk was overthrown in a bloodless coup led by **Lon Nol**. He promptly allied himself not only with the DRV and **China** but with the Khmer Rouge, formerly his deadly enemies. In this alliance Sihanouk was a helpless puppet of his Communist partners. The Khmer Rouge found his prestige a valuable asset both within Cambodia and in the international community. Sihanouk was in China when the Khmer Rouge won control of Cambodia in 1975. He returned to his homeland in 1976 and was essentially a prisoner until 1979, when he went into exile again. He spent years in China and North Korea before a settlement sponsored by the United Nations brought him back to Cambodia in late 1991. He became king again in 1993, but abdicated in 2004.

**NORTH VIETNAM.** The northern of the two sections into which Vietnam was divided following the **Geneva Accords of 1954**. It was ruled by the **Democratic Republic of Vietnam** from then until the two halves of Vietnam were formally reunited in 1976. It had an area of 158,750 square kilometers (61,293 square miles). Estimates of the population varied, but it seems likely that the lower estimates, suggesting a population of around 18.25 million in 1966, were more accurate.

There was heavy bombing and some shelling of North Vietnam (*see* **air war**, **naval gunfire support,** Operation **Sea Dragon,**), but hardly any ground combat there during the Vietnam War. The two known operations in which the United States deliberately put American soldiers on the ground there lasted only a few hours each: the 1970 raid on **Son Tay**, attempting to rescue **prisoners of war**, and a mission on October 16, 1966, by a **Spike team** of **Nung** led by three Americans, attempting to locate and rescue a downed pilot in Thanh Hoa province. Cases in which the United States sent non-U.S. personnel on raids into North Vietnam were more numerous (*see* ***OPLAN 34A***, **SOG**), but these raids were small and accomplished little.

*Note*: the term "North Vietnam" is used by some authors, especially Vietnamese, to refer to **Bac Bo** (Bac Ky, Tonkin), the northernmost of the three sections into which Vietnam had been divided during the

French colonial period.

**NUI BA DEN** (Black Virgin Mountain). A conical mountain 986 meters high, in **Tay Ninh** province only about 10 kilometers northwest of Tay Ninh City. It was the site of several temples and overlooked a very wide area of comparatively flat land. The United States established a position at its peak in 1964, with radio relay and radar equipment, visual observers, and eventually searchlights for night illumination of the surrounding area. But Communist forces occupied the slopes below for the duration of the war; the ravines and caves of the slopes provided so many positions of concealment and defense that the casualties that would have been suffered, in any U.S. effort to search out and destroy all the Communist forces on the slopes, were felt to be too high for the job to be justified. Communist forces took the peak of Nui Ba Den on January 6, 1975.

**NUNG.** An ethnic minority of extreme northern Vietnam and southern **China**, belonging to the Tai language group. Considerable numbers of Nung have migrated from China to Vietnam since the 16th century. In Vietnam they are found mostly in Cao Bang and Lang Son provinces. About 15,000 Nung, mostly soldiers of a French Union Forces division, went south in 1954–1955 following the **Geneva Accords**. They constituted the core of the **ARVN** 5th Infantry Division until it was "Vietnamized" in the 1960s. Their military reputation was formidable; many worked in elite units under U.S. leadership during the Vietnam War, and as hired guards for various facilities.

The most prominent Nung in **South Vietnam** were General Vong A Sang, who had joined the French Army in the 1930s, was a division commander in the ARVN before his retirement in 1957, and was elected to the Senate in 1967; and General **Du Quoc Dong**, who commanded the ARVN **Airborne Division** from late 1964 to late 1972, then commanded the Capital Military District, and briefly (October 1974 to January 1975) **III Corps**.

A cover story sometimes used for personnel from the **Republic of China**, serving in Vietnam in various covert capacities, was to pretend that they were Nung. This may help to explain the belief of many Americans that the Nung were Chinese; several accounts of the war by Americans contain references to "Chinese Nung."

# - O -

**O'DANIEL, JOHN WILSON** "Iron Mike" (1894–1975). Born in Newark, Delaware, he graduated from the University of Delaware in 1917. During World War I he joined the Army as a private, but by the time he entered combat he was an officer. He saw extensive combat in World War II, commanding the 3d Infantry Division from February 1944 onward.

Twice in 1953, the United States sent O'Daniel to investigate the situation in Vietnam. He commanded the **Military Assistance Advisory Group** from April 1954 to October 1955. General O'Daniel supported **Ngo Dinh Diem** very firmly during the **Sect** Crisis of 1955, when many other American officials were thinking of abandoning Diem. After his return to the United States, O'Daniel became National Chairman of the **American Friends of Vietnam** (AFV), an organization dedicated to strengthening U.S. support for the **Republic of Vietnam**. In the last years of Diem's rule, when most other leaders of the AFV decided that Diem had become a liability to the anti-Communist struggle in Vietnam, O'Daniel again stayed firmly loyal to Diem; his influence delayed the AFV taking an organizational stand hostile to Diem. O'Daniel resigned as national chairman, disgusted with the attitude of most of those in the organization, in September 1963.

**OFFICE OF CIVIL OPERATIONS** (OCO). An organization established in November 1966 to provide unified control over the **pacification** programs in Vietnam of the **Central Intelligence Agency**, Agency for International Development, and United States Information Agency. It was initially headed by Deputy Ambassador William Porter. It was superseded in 1967 by **Civil Operations and Revolutionary Development Support** (CORDS).

**OKINAWA.** The largest (1,286 square kilometers or 497 square miles) of the Ryukyu Islands, between **Japan** and Taiwan. The Ryukyu Islands are part of Japan, but Okinawa was occupied and administered by the United States from late in World War II up to 1972. It was one of the major hubs for U.S. military forces in Asia. When U.S. **Marine** or U.S. **Army Special Forces** units were sent to Vietnam, they often came from Okinawa, rather than directly from the United States. Kadena Air Base, on Okinawa, was used by **B-52** aircraft bombing targets in Vietnam and **Laos**.

**ONTOS.** A lightly armored, tracked vehicle, mounting six 106-mm **recoil-less rifles**, plus one .30-caliber **machine gun** and four .50-caliber spotting rifles. Nominally an anti-**tank** weapon, the Ontos was used by the U.S. **Marines** in Vietnam initially in infantry support and convoy escort duties. But its high vulnerability to **mines** was a problem in these functions, and it was eventually restricted mainly to base defense.

**OPIUM.** The sap of the opium poppy contains the narcotic drug morphine. Opium has traditionally been used in Asia both as a medicine and as an addictive drug—raw opium, the dried sap of the plant, was smoked in opium pipes. In modern times, it has been possible to separate the morphine from the dried sap, giving a drug that can be injected by hypodermic needle; this is more powerful, whether as a medicine to relieve pain or as an addictive drug, than raw opium. The morphine can be modified chemically to produce heroin, more potent still.

Opium production in Southeast Asia occurred mainly in the "Golden Triangle," in the northern portions of **Laos**, **Thailand**, and Burma. It was the primary cash crop in many of the highland areas. There is no evidence to support the image in numerous novels and films of the **Central Intelligence Agency** as an institution, or CIA officers as individuals, growing wealthy from participation in the opium trade. But the CIA did ally itself with people involved in the trade, tolerating and occasionally assisting their opium trade in return for their assistance for U.S. military, political, and intelligence goals. An alternate approach, sometimes used when the CIA wanted to prevent opium from reaching the market but could not afford to offend the producers, was to buy it at fair market prices and then destroy it.

***OPLAN 34A.*** During 1963, senior U.S. military leaders began to advocate a program for covert paramilitary harassment of **North Vietnam**. The **Central Intelligence Agency** (CIA) had been running such a program but was thinking of cutting it back because it was not producing worthwhile results. Military leaders, however, felt that by expanding such operations to a much larger scale, they could make them effective. Operations Plan (*OPLAN*) *34A* was drawn up in December 1963, a graduated plan of covert military pressures against North Vietnam, building up from very minor covert raids to fairly serious bombing. The plan was then trimmed down to eliminate the riskier elements, and the version President **Lyndon Johnson** approved on January 16, 1964, while bigger than the CIA's program, was too small to have more than symbolic significance. It was something U.S. leaders did so they would be able to tell themselves they were doing *something* to North Vietnam, while they tried to make up their minds to do something big enough to matter. A military organization, **SOG**, was established on January 24 to take over the operations from the CIA.

The personnel who went on the missions were not American— they were Vietnamese, other Asians, and a few Europeans—but the United States controlled the operations. Between January and July 1964, more than 60 men were air-dropped into North Vietnam; they were promptly killed or captured and accomplished nothing. For maritime operations, SOG brought in **Nasty Boats**, larger and faster than the vessels the CIA had been using, so that a heavily armed party of 20 or 30 men could be landed on the North Vietnamese coast to blow up a bridge or some other facility. Maritime raiding parties suffered some losses, but not the 100 percent casualty rate of the air-dropped teams, and the maritime raiders often succeeded in destroying their targets.

The only important result of *OPLAN 34A* was to arouse the North Vietnamese. On August 2, 1964, near an island that had recently been hit by an *OPLAN 34A* raid, North Vietnamese Navy vessels attacked the U.S. **Navy** destroyer *Maddox*, beginning the **Tonkin Gulf incidents**.

The Vietnamese sent on missions to the North were promised that if they were captured, their families would continue to get their pay as long as they were prisoners. So many were captured, however, that SOG began to save money by declaring them dead and terminating the payments to their families. They remained in prison in North Vietnam for years after the end of the Vietnam War. In the early 1990s, some of the survivors who had finally been released and who went to the United States sued the U.S. government, asking for their back pay.

**ORDER OF BATTLE DISPUTE.** One of the tasks facing **intelligence** officers at **Military Assistance Command, Vietnam** (MACV), and to a lesser extent those at some other agencies, was to compile an Order of Battle for the Communist forces in **South Vietnam**—a list of the forces the Communists had. MACV's first such list was issued in 1962, but for several years the strength of **Viet Cong** forces as listed in MACV Order of Battle reports lagged behind the actual strength. The main problem was lack of personnel; not until 1965 did MACV come close to having enough intelligence officers to be able to collect and analyze the data on the growing Viet Cong forces. At times there was pressure from senior officers determined to paint an optimistic picture of the war, who resisted increases in estimates of the strength of enemy forces.

When the United States began pouring ground troops into Vietnam in 1965, there was nothing approaching a complete list of the enemy forces those troops were to fight. As intelligence improved during 1966, the figures for the Communists' regular combat units came to be reasonably accurate. MACV's monthly Order of Battle reports also, however, contained figures for three other categories: (1) the support services that provided medical care, communications, and the "logistical tail" of the combat units; (2) the **infrastructure**—the people who governed and taxed the areas of South Vietnam that were to some extent under Communist rule; and (3) "irregulars"—local guerrillas and two types of village militia, with little capability for open combat but a very large membership: the "self-defense" militia in Communist-controlled villages and the "secret self-defense" militia in government-controlled villages. Nobody knew how many people were in any of these categories, but the unfounded estimates for them in each month's Order of Battle Report would generally be repeated, to the last digit, in the next month's report.

By early 1967, U.S. intelligence officers, mostly in military intelligence in Vietnam, but to some extent also at the headquarters of the **Central Intelligence Agency** (CIA) in the United States, had compiled enough information to make realistic estimates possible for all categories. This created a major problem. The new estimates, especially for the support personnel and irregulars, were far higher than the old ones. The U.S. government was trying to persuade **Congress** and the public that the war was being won; a dramatic increase in the estimate of Communist personnel in South Vietnam would not have helped.

There followed a series of acrimonious conferences at which the CIA argued for comparatively high estimates of Communist personnel and MACV intelligence argued for much lower estimates. In September 1967, an agreement was worked out under which the definitions used in compiling the estimates were drastically changed. U.S. intelligence simply stopped estimating the number of people in the self-defense and secret self-defense militia. Estimates for the infrastructure continued to be compiled but were no longer included in the Order of Battle. Having dropped these categories, MACV accepted higher estimates of some others (though not as high as CIA estimates) without any increase in the overall total.

The issue became a major public controversy in the 1980s through the efforts of **Samuel Adams**, a CIA analyst of Order of Battle issues, who believed that the MACV estimates had been grossly dishonest, and that the underestimation of Communist strength had dangerously reduced American readiness for the **Tet Offensive** early in 1968. After Adams's charges had been presented in a major documentary on CBS Television in 1982, General **William Westmoreland** sued for libel, but he dropped his suit after several officers who had been in MACV intelligence, including two very senior ones, testified as witnesses for CBS.

*OREGON*, Task Force. In 1966, the **Marines** who were the main U.S. force in **I Corps** began to shift northward toward the **Demilitarized Zone**; this left a shortage of U.S. troops in the southern part of I Corps. The United States wanted to put a U.S. **Army division** into the area. No whole division was available, so the interim solution was to put together a division-sized force, Task Force *Oregon*, from brigades borrowed from several divisions. It was based at **Chu Lai**. It used a different style of fighting than had been used by the Marines, involving more destruction of Vietnamese villages. This led to controversy when a detailed description of *Oregon*'s operations, by Jonathan Schell, was published in the *New Yorker* magazine on March 9 and 16, 1968. Task Force *Oregon* was used as the basis for the creation of the 23d Infantry Division (Americal) in September 1967.

**OV-10 BRONCO.** A twin-engine, propeller-driven aircraft. The Broncos used for patrolling waterways as part of *SEALORDS* were heavily armed, with 5-inch Zuni **rockets**, 2.75-inch rockets, **machine guns**, and 20-mm cannon. Broncos used as **Forward Air Controllers** (FACs) were less heavily armed (see photograph 12). Modified Broncos known as Pave Nails, based at Nakhon Phanom in **Thailand** during the late stages of the war, were equipped with a LORAN electronic navigation system, a night vision device, and a laser target designator to provide guidance for smart bombs (*see* **bombs**).

## - P -

**PACIFIC ARCHITECTS AND ENGINEERS** (PA&E). A corporation that had contracts with the U.S. military to maintain many American bases in Vietnam.

**PACIFICATION.** Efforts to establish government control in the villages of **South Vietnam**. Pacification programs operated along two major tracks. One was to win the friendship and loyalty of the peasants by providing concrete benefits to them, somewhat supplemented by propaganda. Village schools, village dispensaries, Medical Civic Action Program (MEDCAP) visits to villages by U.S. military medical personnel, and assistance in improving crop yields through improved seed varieties, fertilizer, and pesticides, all helped to improve village life. The other track was to establish control of the villages and kill, capture, or drive away Communist military forces and political cadres.

The **Strategic Hamlet** program, begun in 1962, was in theory supposed to work on both tracks, but in practice it was overwhelmingly oriented to establishing contol; there was little effort to provide economic benefits to the peasants. The program had been discredited by 1964.

The **People's Action Teams**, sponsored by the **Central Intelligence Agency** (CIA), began going out to the villages to conduct pacification in 1964. These were modified in 1966 to become the **Revolutionary Development** Cadres, later renamed Rural Development Cadres.

The **Office of Civil Operations** was established in November 1966 to provide unified control over the pacification efforts of the three U.S. civilian agencies involved: the CIA, Agency for International Development, and United States Information Agency. In 1967, all U.S. pacification programs, civilian and military, were placed under **Civil Operations and Revolutionary Development Support** (CORDS), later renamed Civil Operations and Rural Development Support. The head of CORDS was always a civilian, but most CORDS officers were military, and CORDS was under **Military Assistance Command, Vietnam,** in the chain of command.

The *Phoenix* **Program**, established in 1967 and 1968, assisted pacification by attacking the Communist **infrastructure** in the countryside.

The greatest successes of pacification were between 1969 and 1971. The substantial resources devoted to the effort, and the weakness of **Viet Cong** military forces following the very heavy fighting of 1968, allowed a greater extension of goverment control in the countryside than had been seen since the late 1950s. By 1972, however, the American withdrawal from Vietnam had greatly reduced both the resources directly devoted to pacification and the military forces available to support and protect Rural Development Cadres; the progress of pacification ended, and began to be reversed.

**PANHANDLE.** Laos and **North Vietnam** each have a relatively broad area in the north, with a much narrower extension to the south. In each case, the Americans called the narrower southern extension the "panhandle." American bombing of both Laos and North Vietnam was heaviest in the panhandles of those countries; the panhandles were closer to the battlefields of **South Vietnam**, and also bombing there seemed less risky because they were farther from **China**. The major towns in the panhandle of North Vietnam were essentially destroyed during Operation *Rolling Thunder*.

**PARIS NEGOTIATIONS.** On March 31, 1968, President **Lyndon Johnson** announced he was halting the bombing of the northern part of **North Vietnam**, and he asked for peace talks. The **Democratic Republic of Vietnam** (DRV) accepted on April 3. Preliminary talks began in Paris on May 13, **W. Averell Harriman** representing the United States and **Xuan Thuy** representing the DRV. Talking in public, under the eyes of the world, both sides were intransigent. Private talks, in which it was hoped actual negotiation and compromise would be easier to achieve, began on June 26. **Le Duc Tho**, a Politburo member and one of the most powerful men in **Hanoi**, joined the private talks on September 8 as a "special adviser" to Xuan Thuy.

On October 26, the DRV accepted an American proposal that representatives of the **Republic of Vietnam** (RVN) and the **National Liberation Front** (NLF) be brought into the negotiations. On October 31, President Johnson announced he was halting all U.S. bombing, shelling, and mining of North Vietnam. But little progress toward an actual peace settlement resulted.

Agreement that the RVN and the NLF should be brought into the talks led to a prolonged dispute about how they should be included. The DRV wanted the conference table to reflect the presence of four delegations: U.S., RVN, DRV, and NLF. The United States and RVN, not wanting the NLF to have the status of a separate delegation at the talks, wanted a two-sided conference table with a joint U.S.-RVN delegation on one side, and a joint DRV-NLF delegation on the other. Agreement was finally reached in January 1969 on an ambiguous table setup, which could be interpreted either way, and full-scale formal negotiations began. These led nowhere; the real negotiations, when they finally occurred, were not conducted by the nominal heads of delegations at the conference table that had been so long disputed, but by Le Duc Tho and President **Richard Nixon**'s national security adviser,

**Henry Kissinger**. They met privately for the first time on February 21, 1970.

The essential problem was that the struggle for control of **South Vietnam**, between the Communist forces and those of the Republic of Vietnam, could not be compromised. President **Nguyen Van Thieu** was determined to achieve the total elimination of all Communist political and military organizations in South Vietnam, because he knew the Communists were just as determined to eliminate the RVN and bring South Vietnam under Communist rule. A peace agreement might be a disguised surrender by one side, creating conditions guaranteeing that the other would, within a moderate period, achieve total control of South Vietnam. Or it might define the rules under which the two sides would continue their struggle to eliminate one another. Or it might be empty words, promises that the two sides made but did not keep. What it could not be was a genuine compromise under which the two sides actually ended their efforts to achieve total domination of South Vietnam. This reality was not well understood in the United States. Many Americans, including some senior officials, would have been willing to accept a solution under which power in South Vietnam would be shared, and did not understand how impossible this was.

Initially, the DRV representatives argued for a settlement centering on a clear resolution of the struggle for control of South Vietnam; it would remove President Thieu from power. The United States proposed a settlement limited to military issues, the withdrawal of U.S. and PAVN military forces from South Vietnam, and the release of **prisoners of war**; it would not specify how Thieu and the NLF would then settle their differences.

After prolonged stalemate, Kissinger and Le Duc Tho worked out a deal in October 1972. The United States gave up its demand for symmetry in the resolution of military issues; U.S. military forces were to withdraw from South Vietnam, but nothing was said about a PAVN withdrawal. The DRV gave up its demand for a clear resolution of the struggle for South Vietnam; the agreement specified procedures by which the fate of South Vietnam was to be determined, but these procedures were so impractical they seemed designed to fail. By October 11, the issues still in dispute were so small it seemed obvious they would be resolved; Kissinger and Le Duc Tho even agreed on a date for the formal signature of the agreement. The DRV concluded that the fundamental shape of the agreement was so favorable that it would be foolish to delay the completion and signing of the document by quibbling about details; on October 20, the DRV accepted the American version of all sections of the draft agreement that were still in dispute.

When Kissinger showed the draft to President Thieu in **Saigon**, however, Thieu's evaluation of it was the same as **Hanoi**'s: this was an agreement likely to lead to complete Communist victory in South Vietnam. He rejected it utterly. Kissinger and Nixon then asked the DRV for extensive revisions in the draft. The DRV felt it had been doublecrossed, and the tone of the negotiations in Paris deteriorated seriously. By December they were deadlocked. Nixon responded by ordering a massive new bombing campaign, Operation *Linebacker II*, directed at the northern half of North Vietnam, particularly the area around Hanoi, from December 18 to 29. There is a myth that the DRV had actually walked out of the Paris negotiations, thereby providing the provocation for *Linebacker II*, but this is unfounded. The talks were still going on, though unproductively, and DRV Vice Foreign Minister Nguyen Co Thach bitterly protested the renewed bombing during the negotiating sessions of December 20 and December 23. *Then* the DRV walked out.

The negotiations resumed in January. Both sides were in a conciliatory mood, and by January 13 they had agreed on a text not very different from the October 1972 draft. Thieu still objected vigorously, since it still looked to him like a blueprint for Communist victory, but Nixon persuaded him to sign by threatening that all U.S. military aid would be cut off if he did not. The agreement was formally signed on January 27, 1973. *See also* NEGOTIATIONS; PARIS PEACE AGREEMENT.

**PARIS PEACE AGREEMENT,** January 27, 1973. The "Agreement on Ending the War and Restoring Peace in Viet Nam" and several protocols going into detail on certain issues were signed in Paris on January 27, 1973, in two slightly different versions. One was signed only by the United States and the **Democratic Republic of Vietnam** (DRV). The other was signed by all four of the parties that had participated in the **Paris negotiations**: the United States, the DRV, the **Republic of Vietnam** (RVN), and the **Provisional Revolutionary Government** (PRG). The agreement signed only by the United States and the DRV listed the four parties by name twice—once in the preamble and again in the last article. The version signed by all four parties does not contain such a list; President **Nguyen Van Thieu** of the RVN was so determined not to recognize the existence of the PRG that he refused to sign an agreement that mentioned the PRG by name. In the body of both versions of the agreement, the rights and obligations of the PRG are described in euphemistic language about "the parties" (the U.S., DRV, RVN, and PRG) or "the two South Vietnamese parties" (the RVN and PRG).

There was to be a cease-fire in place at 8:00 a.m. **Saigon** time, January 28, 1973, after which each side would control the territory it had controlled at that time. All military forces of the United States and of U.S. allies such as South **Korea** were to pull out of Vietnam, taking their weapons and munitions with them. The United States was to dismantle its military bases in **South Vietnam**, removing or destroying military equipment so as to make the bases "unusable for military purposes." The agreement said nothing about a pullout of the **PAVN** forces that were in South Vietnam, but it forbade the introduction of additional military personnel into South Vietnam. No weapons, munitions, or other war materiel could be brought into South Vietnam by either side except as replacement on a one-for-one basis, under international supervision, of items that had been destroyed, damaged, worn out, or used up after the cease-fire.

The **Demilitarized Zone** (DMZ) separating **North Vietnam** from South Vietnam was to be respected by both sides. All foreign military actions in **Laos** and **Cambodia** were to cease, and foreign military forces, armaments, and munitions were to be excluded from Laos and Cambodia. These two items, combined, meant that to the extent that the agreement permitted resupply of the Communist forces in South Vietnam, that resupply could not occur either across the DMZ or along the **Ho Chi Minh Trail**; it could occur only by sea.

On the relationship between North and South Vietnam, the agreement was flatly self-contradictory. Article 1 indicated that North and South Vietnam were one country; Article 15 called for the reunification of North and South. Article 9, however, guaranteed the South Vietnamese people the right to decide for themselves the political future of South Vietnam, and Article 18 referred to "the principle of respect for the sovereignty of South Viet Nam." The clauses of the agreement that described the procedures that were supposed to lead to free elections in South Vietnam were vague and seemed clearly incapable of being put into practice.

All **prisoners of war** were to be released within 60 days. The two sides were to assist one another in determining the fate of military personnel **missing in action**. In strangely convoluted language, the agreement said that the release of all civilian detainees was a "question" that both South Vietnamese parties were to "do their utmost" to "resolve" within 90 days.

In Article 21, the United States promised to "contribute to healing the wounds of war and to postwar reconstruction of the Democratic Republic of Vietnam and throughout Indochina." President **Richard Nixon** had indicated informally that the United States would provide $3.25 billion in postwar economic aid for Vietnam, but no specific figure was included in the formal peace agreement.

An **International Commission of Control and Supervision** (ICCS) was to be established to supervise the implementation of the agreement. It was composed at first of equal numbers of representatives from two Communist countries, Hungary and Poland, plus two anti-Communist countries, **Canada** and Indonesia.

**PARROT'S BEAK.** A part of Svay Rieng province of **Cambodia** that projected deep into **South Vietnam**, between **Hau Nghia** province of **III Corps** and Kien Tuong province of **IV Corps**, with its tip about 50 kilometers east of **Saigon**. Communist Base Area 367 in the Parrot's Beak was among the first targets of **ARVN** forces in the **Cambodian Incursion** that began on April 30, 1970.

**PATHET LAO.** The Communist movement of **Laos**. From 1956 onward, the Pathet Lao was represented in electoral politics by the **Neo Lao Hak Sat**, a mass political party. The Lao People's Party (the formal name of the Communist party from 1955 to 1972) formed its inner guiding core. Prince **Souphanouvong** was the nominal head of the Pathet Lao; Kaysone Phomvihan (1920–1992) was the real leader.

The **Geneva Accords of 1954** allocated the two northeastern provinces of **Sam Neua** and **Phong Saly** to the Pathet Lao as a temporary regrouping zone. The Pathet Lao joined in the First Coalition Government in 1957, and the two provinces were re-integrated into Laos in 1958. The Pathet Lao did very well in **elections** for the National Assembly in May 1958, taking nine of the 21 seats at stake. Despite this, the Pathet Lao hesitated to take the final step in integrating into the mainstream of Laotian politics, integrating their two battalions of troops into the Royal Lao Army. They became even more reluctant to give up this independent military force after the neutralist **Souvanna Phouma** was replaced as prime minister by the anti-Communist Phoui Sananikone in August 1958. Faced with an ultimatum from government forces in May 1959, the 1st Pathet Lao Battalion surrendered, but the 2d managed to escape, fleeing to the northeast, on the night of May 18. Prince Souphanouvong and other Pathet Lao leaders who were in the Laotian capital, Vientiane, were arrested.

Some of the personnel of the 1st Battalion escaped in August 1959. Souphanouvong and the other Pathet Lao leaders imprisoned in Vientiane escaped in turn on the night of May 23, 1960, assisted by some of their guards (who went with them).

In the war that began on a small scale when troops of the 2d Pathet Lao Battalion began overrunning government outposts in Sam Neua in July 1959, the Pathet Lao had assistance from **North Vietnam**; indeed as the war went on, the People's Army of Vietnam (**PAVN**) began putting significant units of North Vietnamese troops into Laos, to assist the Pathet Lao, years before it began putting them into **South Vietnam**.

The creation of the Second Coalition Government in June 1962 brought Pathet Lao representatives back to Vientiane, but the second never worked as well as the first had. Warfare pitting Pathet Lao and PAVN forces against the American-supported government of Souvanna Phouma began in 1963, and the Pathet Lao representatives left Vientiane again. During the years of warfare that followed, the main burden of combat in Laos was carried by the PAVN; Pathet Lao forces, while not insignificant, played a secondary role. Pathet Lao representatives returned to Vientiane with the formation of the Third Coalition Government in April 1974. The Pathet Lao seized full control of the country in August 1975.

*PATIO*, Operation. A secret campaign of bombing by U.S. fighter-bombers in northeastern **Cambodia**, begun on April 24, 1970, as a supplement to Operation *Menu*. The scale was very small; 156 sorties dropped 263 tons of munitions. Most targets were within 18 miles of the border of **South Vietnam**. *Patio*, like *Menu*, was concealed through a double reporting system. The pilots were under orders to report, when debriefed after their missions, that their targets had been in South Vietnam (except for the mission of May 14, 1970, which was reported as having been in southern **Laos**). The **Forward Air Controller** (FAC) who guided the strike aircraft to their targets would report separately to **SOG**, giving the actual location of the target in Cambodia.

The United States began large-scale, publicly announced bombing of Cambodia at the beginning of May, but the small-scale secret *Patio* missions continued until May 14.

**PAVN.** The Viet Minh forces created during World War II, which became the army of the **Democratic Republic of Vietnam** (DRV) in 1945, were named the People's Army of Vietnam (PAVN) in 1950. The founder of the PAVN, and its commander in its early years, was **Vo Nguyen Giap**. By the 1960s, however, Giap's power was being seriously reduced by the hostility of **Le Duan** and **Le Duc Tho**. Giap was minister of defense, and **Van Tien Dung** was PAVN chief of staff, throughout the Vietnam War.

Until 1954, the PAVN had operated and recruited throughout Vietnam. When **North Vietnam** and **South Vietnam** were separated under the **Geneva Accords of 1954**, the PAVN units in the South, made up mostly of southerners, were required to regroup to North Vietnam. Some people soon began to call the PAVN the North Vietnamese Army (NVA). In 1959, PAVN soldiers who had been born in the South began being taken out of PAVN units in the North, and sent down the **Ho Chi Minh Trail** to join **Viet Cong** units in the South. When PAVN regiments were first sent south late in 1964, remaining together as units to fight in the South, they were composed primarily of North Vietnamese. Some of these units took in southerners after they arrived in the South.

In the first years after PAVN units began to arrive in the South, their numbers remained modest; the Viet Cong remained the primary Communist force in most areas. PAVN units were more important in the extreme northern and western parts of South Vietnam, near the **Demilitarized Zone** and the borders of **Laos** and **Cambodia**. A surge in the number of PAVN troops moving south in late 1967, and massive Viet Cong losses in 1968, left the PAVN as the main Communist combat force in South Vietnam after 1968. The **Easter Offensive** of 1972, and the campaign that brought the **final collapse** of the **Republic of Vietnam** in 1975, were primarily conducted by North Vietnamese troops in PAVN units.

The PAVN was the main Communist force in Laos from quite early in the war there up to the end, and in Cambodia from before large-scale warfare broke out there in 1970, up to late 1972.

Until 1973, the largest military unit in the PAVN was the division (*su doan*). Above the division level, the PAVN was organized in territorially defined commands: **fronts** or **military regions**. As the end of the war approached, the PAVN began to the prepare for the possibility of a mobile campaign that would cut across the existing boundaries between fronts. The 1st Army Corps (*quan doan*), containing three infantry divisions, a **tank** brigade, and various other units, was established in North Vietnam in October 1973, and sent to the South in March 1975. Other army corps were established in South Vietnam—the 2d in **Thua Thien** in May 1974, the 3d in the **Central Highlands** in March 1975, and the 4th, probably not far north of **Saigon**, in July 1974. All four army corps converged on Saigon in April 1975, in just the sort of mobile campaign for which they had been created.

**PBR** (Patrol Boat, River). A fast, maneuverable vessel with a fiberglass hull 31 feet long, driven by a Jaccuzi water jet rather than a propeller. It carried a crew of four. The usual weapons were .50-caliber **machine guns**, plus 7.62-mm machine guns and/or 40-mm **grenade launchers**. The initial model, which began to arrive in Vietnam in March 1966, could do 25 knots; the Mark II, which began to arrive at the end of 1966, could do 29 knots. Keeping the PBR light enough to attain these speeds precluded heavy armor, but there was a small quantity of ceramic armor in key locations. The PBR was the mainstay of the **River Patrol Force**, which began operations in the **Mekong Delta** and the **Rung Sat** in 1966 under Operation *Game Warden*.

**PENTAGON PAPERS.** When Secretary of Defense **Robert McNamara** decided the Vietnam War had been a mistake, he ordered a historical study of how it had happened. More than 30 authors produced a narrative accompanied by the original texts of many documents. Formally titled *United States-Vietnam Relations, 1945–1967*, it is usually called the "Pentagon Papers."

Dr. **Daniel Ellsberg** had been one of the authors. After the project was completed, he studied the whole manuscript carefully; it convinced him that the American involvement in Vietnam had been fundamentally wrong, and should be ended immediately. Late in 1969, he began photocopying large sections of the Pentagon Papers. After failing to persuade several U.S. senators to make this material public, he delivered it to **Neil Sheehan** of *The New York Times* in March 1971.

On June 13, 1971, the newspaper began publishing a series of 10 articles, each accompanied by the texts of key documents. The articles were not abridged versions of the corresponding sections of the narrative that had been written in the Department of Defense; they were written by Sheehan and others at *The New York Times*, using information from both the narrative and the documents in the Defense Department version.

On June 15, the Justice Department asked for an injunction to block this series. A judge in New York halted publication for a few days, during which time Ellsberg gave sections of the Pentagon Papers to *The Washington Post*. The case went immediately to the Supreme Court, which on June 30 ruled, by a vote of six to three, that the government could not forbid publication.

Before the end of 1971, two sets of selections from the Pentagon Papers much more complete than any newspaper could have published had appeared in book form: one published by the Government Printing Office after formal declassification, and the other released by Senator Mike Gravel of Alaska and published by Beacon Press. Between them these contained essentially all of the narrative history, except for the sections dealing with **negotiations** to end the war; those sections were published only in 1983. Many of the source documents that had been appendices to the original Pentagon Papers were included in various versions published in 1971, but many others remained unreleased.

**PEOPLE'S ACTION TEAMS** (PATs). Armed teams of about 40 Vietnamese, formed under the sponsorship of the **Central Intelligence Agency** (CIA), designed to attack the Communist **infrastructure**, recruited in the districts where they were to serve but sent for training to a center at **Vung Tau**. The program was derived from a highly effective experiment in Quang Ngai province in the spring of 1964, in which the teams both fought the **Viet Cong** and tried to assist, and indoctrinate, the peasants. Peer de Silva, the CIA station chief in Saigon, learned of the program soon after its establishment and decided to spread it. Before the end of 1964, the CIA had established a camp at Vung Tau to train teams for the whole of **South Vietnam**; about 16,000 people had graduated from this training by the beginning of 1966.

The PATs were transferred from CIA to military control in 1966. In 1966 and 1967, the 40-man PATs were replaced by 59-man **Revolutionary Development** (RD) Cadre teams. The RD Cadres got less training than the PATs, and are generally considered to have had lower average levels of morale and discipline.

**PGM** (Motor Gunboat; the acronym may have originated from "Patrol Gunboat, Medium"). U.S. **Navy** designation for small combat vessels, about the size of a large torpedo boat, but slower and without torpedoes. The Swatow Boats in the navy of the **Democratic Republic of Vietnam** were classified by the United States as PGMs.

**PHAM HUNG,** original name Pham Van Thien, a.k.a. Bay Cuong (1912–1988). Born in Vinh Long province, in the **Mekong Delta**, he had little education. He began revolutionary activities in 1928–1929, and was arrested by the French in 1931. Hung was initially sentenced to death; the sentence was commuted, but he was imprisoned (mostly on **Poulo Condore**) from 1931 to 1945. He became secretary of the **Nam Bo** Provisional Regional Committee in 1946. He became a member of the **Lao Dong Party** Central Committee in 1951, and by 1952 he was deputy secretary of the **Trung uong cuc mien Nam** (COSVN), the Communist command for Nam Bo. After the **Geneva Accords of 1954**, Hung became the chief **PAVN** delegate to the **International Control Commission** in Saigon. In 1956, he became a member of the Politburo, and head of the Central Reunification Committee. In 1958, he became deputy premier of the **Democratic Republic of Vietnam**. He was factionally aligned with **Le Duan** and **Le Duc Tho**, with whom he had worked in the South, against **Vo Nguyen Giap**.

Hung held mostly economic posts in the early to mid-1960s, but in 1967 he replaced **Nguyen Chi Thanh** as head of the Trung uong cuc mien Nam, commander of the Communist effort in the southern half of **South Vietnam**. He held that position until the end of the war in 1975. Hung became minister of the interior of the Socialist Republic of Vietnam (controlling the security forces) in 1980, and replaced **Pham Van Dong** as premier in 1987.

**PHAM NGOC THAO** (1922–1965). **ARVN** colonel and Communist agent. Born in **Saigon**, he joined the Viet Minh not later than 1945. By the end of the First Indochina War he was an officer, perhaps a battalion commander, in the Viet Minh. After the **Geneva Accords**, Thao pretended to break with the Communists, stressing his identity as a **Catholic**. If he did not already have a personal friendship with **Ngo Dinh Thuc**, Bishop of Vinh Long and brother of **Ngo Dinh Diem**, he established one at this point. Bishop Thuc helped him win acceptance in Saigon despite his Viet Minh background. Thao worked briefly in the National Bank in 1956, and then in military and paramilitary positions. He commanded **police** units in Vinh Long and Binh Duong provinces, and was sent for training in the United States. He was province chief for Kien Hoa province in 1962, and attracted attention by the way he ran the **Strategic Hamlet** program there. In late 1962 or early 1963, **Ngo Dinh Nhu** made him special inspector for the Strategic Hamlet program.

During 1963, when it became apparent there was a real chance that Ngo Dinh Diem might be overthrown by an ARVN military **coup**, Colonel Thao became very aggressively involved in plotting such a coup. After plots of which he was a major leader had failed to gather adequate support, he became a minor participant in the plot that actually did overthrow Diem on November 1. He was then sent to the United States for another course of officer education. Thao returned to Vietnam in mid-1964 and became press attaché to Premier **Nguyen Khanh**. He was briefly sent again to the United States, then recalled to Vietnam at the end of 1964. He promptly assembled a group of ARVN officers to stage a coup. They were able to seize key positions in Saigon on February 19, 1965, but not to hold them for long. Presumably Colonel Thao was willing to take the risk of a coup that had little chance of success because even an unsuccessful plot could serve Communist purposes by increasing the level of confusion and suspicion in the ARVN. He went underground to avoid arrest, but continued plotting. A planned coup in which he was heavily involved was broken up by the arrest of about 40 military and civilian officials May 20–21. Thao was caught and killed, probably at the initiative of **Nguyen Van Thieu**, in July 1965.

**PHAM VAN DONG** (1906–2000). Prime minister of the **Democratic Republic of Vietnam** (DRV). Born in Quang Ngai province of southern **Trung Bo**, he attended the Quoc Hoc (National Academy) in **Hue**. Dong was an intellectual, the son of a mandarin who had held a high position in the court of Emperor Duy Tan. He joined the Revolutionary Youth League (a precursor to the Indochinese Communist Party) in 1925, and received some military training at Chiang Kai-shek's Whampoa Academy in China. In 1929 he returned to Vietnam and became one of the leaders of the Revolutionary Youth League in **Nam Bo**. He served a long prison term on **Poulo Condore** in the early to mid-1930s. Dong did some of the preparatory work for the foundation of the Viet Minh in 1941, and when the DRV was founded in 1945, he became minister of finance. He became foreign minister in 1954, and in that capacity represented the DRV at the Geneva Conference of 1954. In 1955, Dong became prime minister of the DRV, remaining foreign minister until 1961. He remained a Politburo member until 1986 and premier until 1987.

There have been recent suggestions that during his years as premier he was not really as powerful as he sometimes seemed to foreigners. Dong did much of the work of running the civilian administration of the DRV (and from 1976 to 1987 of the Socialist Republic of Vietnam), but he did not get on well with the faction centering on **Le Duan** and **Le Duc Tho**, who had enormous power in the Communist Party and did not much care for intellectuals.

**PHAN HUY QUAT** (1909–1979). Doctor, prime minister of the **Republic of Vietnam** (RVN). Born in Ha Tinh province, northern **Trung Bo**, he completed medical training in **Hanoi** in 1936, and taught at the Hanoi School of Medicine from 1936 to 1945. He served as chief of staff in the government of Tran Trong Kim, established by the Japanese as a nominally independent government of Vietnam during the last months of World War II. Quat was a member of the Dai Viet Party. He became minister of education of the State of Vietnam in 1949, and was minister of national defense very briefly in 1950, and again from June 1953 to June 1954.

Quat became a member of the "Caravelle Group" of politicians, who issued a denunciation of **Ngo Dinh Diem**'s government in April 1960. He became RVN foreign minister in February 1964. He was prime minister from February 16 to June 11, 1965. The United States did not genuinely consult him about, and indeed barely gave him advance notice of, major steps it was taking to escalate the war during this period. His position was so weak he did not feel able to protest this very much. Dr. Quat remained in Vietnam after the end of the war, and died in prison.

**PHAN KHAC SUU** (1905–1970). Born in **Can Tho** in the **Mekong Delta**, he eventually converted to the **Cao Dai** sect. He trained as an agricultural engineer in France. He joined the Viet Nam Quoc Dan Dang, a nationalist group, and was imprisoned from 1940 to 1945 on **Poulo Condore**. Suu became minister of agriculture, social welfare, and labor of the State of Vietnam in 1949, and resigned after five months. He became minister of agriculture and director general of land in **Ngo Dinh Diem**'s government in 1954, but later resigned in protest against Diem's dictatorship. He was elected to the National Assembly in 1959. Suu was imprisoned after the attempted **coup** of November 1960 (though there is dispute as to whether he had actually had any involvement in the plot). He was released and given a ceremonial post as president of the National Supreme Council at the end of 1963, after Diem's overthrow. He was head of state of the **Republic of Vietnam** from 1964 to 1965, and president of the Constituent Assembly from 1966 to 1967. Suu ran for president in the **election** of 1967, coming in third.

**PHILIPPINES.** Aid from the Philippines for **Ngo Dinh Diem**'s government began in 1954, arranged to a considerable extent by **Edward Lansdale** of the **Central Intelligence Agency** (CIA). Operation Brotherhood, run by the Junior Chambers of Commerce International with quiet CIA encouragement, sent Filipino medical personnel to Vietnam. The Freedom Company, much more closely associated with and subsidized by the CIA, was a "non-profit" corporation established in 1954 to send Filipinos with military backgrounds to other Asian countries, especially Vietnam, for various unconventional operations. Some of its personnel were members of the Philippines Army "sheepdipped" to become nominal civilians. Among other things, Freedom Company personnel trained Ngo Dinh Diem's Presidential Guard, and helped write the Constitution of the **Republic of Vietnam**. Later the CIA connection weakened (though it did not disappear) and the Freedom Company was renamed the Eastern Construction Company, under which name it provided personnel and performed services on a commercial basis in Vietnam. By 1961, its personnel in Vietnam and **Laos** (of whom there were about 500 at that time) were mostly working in military **logistics**.

Overt involvement of the government of the Philippines in the Vietnam War began on a very small scale in 1964, when two military surgical teams and a psychological warfare detachment, adding up to about 40 people, went to **South Vietnam**. Negotiations began in 1964 for a much larger program, the Philippine Civic Action Group (PHILCAG), but PHILCAG, containing engineering construction units, medical personnel, and some combat troops for security, did not begin to arrive until September 1966. It was sent to **Tay Ninh** province, where it built roads and a large refugee camp, worked in **pacification**, and performed various other tasks. The number of Philippine military personnel in South Vietnam, almost all members of PHILCAG, averaged slightly more than 2,000 from late 1966 through early 1968, and was still over 1,500 at the end of 1968.

There was a public pretense that the Philippines was paying for PHILCAG; American subsidies were carefully concealed. President Ferdinand Marcos's decision to withdraw PHILCAG from Vietnam at the end of 1969, which brought the number of Filipino government personnel abruptly down to fewer than 200, seems to have been prompted partly by embarrassment after hearings of a U.S. Senate Foreign Relations Committee subcommittee revealed the extent of U.S. payments to the Philippines for PHILCAG..

**PHNOM PENH.** The capital of **Cambodia**, located on the **Mekong River** about 70 kilometers upstream from the Vietnamese border. Its population in 1970 was on the order of 500,000. Refugees from other towns and from the countryside had swollen the population to about 3 million by the time the war ended in 1975, although it was not really a place of safety; the **Khmer Rouge** bombarded the city intermittently with **rockets** beginning in December 1973, and with 105-mm **artillery** fire beginning early in 1974. Hunger was a worse threat. At the end of January 1975 the Khmer Rouge were able to close the Mekong River to the boats that had brought food from **South Vietnam** to Phnom Penh, and the amount of rice that could be brought in by air was not adequate.

All Americans except a few journalists left Phnom Penh on April 12, 1975, in Operation *Eagle Pull*. The Khmer Rouge took the city on April 17, and immediately ordered the entire population out to the countryside.

*PHOENIX* **PROGRAM.** During the Vietnam War, **Viet Cong** power in **South Vietnam** was based not only on military forces, but on the administrative organizations and networks of political cadres that the Americans called the Viet Cong **infrastructure**. These organizations were the local government in many areas. The United States and the **Republic of Vietnam** (RVN) had been trying to destroy the infrastructure since the mid-1950s, before the war even began.

The Infrastructure Coordination and Exploitation (ICEX) Program was established in 1967; at the end of that year it was renamed *Phoenix* (*Phung Hoang*). Its goal was to improve coordination among the many U.S. and RVN bodies working to destroy the infrastructure, including RVN **police** forces; RVN province chiefs and district chiefs, and their troops; and the **Provincial Reconnaissance Units** (PRUs), small teams of Vietnamese often trained and led by U.S. Navy **SEAL**s, capable of raiding deep into Communist-ruled areas. Each province and each district had an American *Phoenix* adviser and a Province Intelligence and Operations Coordinating Center (PIOCC) or District Intelligence and Operations Coordinating Center (DIOCC), where information from various sources was amassed and prisoners and suspects were interrogated. The **Central Intelligence Agency** (CIA), which had created the PRUs, was heavily involved in establishing and running the *Phoenix* Program; the *Phoenix* Directorate was always headed by a CIA officer.

Implementation of the concept was delayed by the **Tet Offensive** early in 1968, but soon it was inflicting serious losses on Communist organizations, and it continued to do so until the program was crippled by the U.S. withdrawal from South Vietnam in the 1970s. The way it worked varied widely from area to area. Hardly anywhere did it function the way it was supposed to, with all the relevant organizations working in concert. But if one or two of those organizations operated effectively, significant results could be achieved.

Stories that *Phoenix* was a program of assassination and torture began to cause scandal in the United States in the early 1970s. There had in fact been assassinations, especially by the PRUs, though the number had not been as large as has sometimes been suggested; at first large numbers of Communists killed had been a mark of success instead of a political liability, and some officers had exaggerated the number of kills in an effort to make the program look good. The number of people captured alive had been greater than the number killed. Some of these had been brutally tortured, some had been interrogated without torture (this sometimes produced more reliable information), and some had not been interrogated at all. There had been **corruption**; some jailers could be bribed to release Communist prisoners, and some people not really suspected of being Communists were arrested simply so their families would have to pay bribes to win their release. Few valid generalizations can be made about the program; there was too much variation.

The original system was heavily dependent on American personnel, but most of these were withdrawn, as part of the overall U.S. withdrawal from Vietnam, in 1971 and 1972. Responsibility for controlling the program was therefore transferred to the Vietnamese National Police in 1972.

**PHONG SALY.** The northernmost province of **Laos**, bordering **North Vietnam** to the northeast and **China** to the northwest. It was designated as a regrouping zone for **Pathet Lao** (Communist) troops under the **Geneva Accords of 1954**, and reintegrated with the rest of Laos in 1958, but following the resumption of civil warfare in 1959, began to fall back under Communist control. The Pathet Lao finally regained control of the province capital on January 1, 1961.

**PHOUMI NOSAVAN** (1920–1985). Rightist leader in **Laos**. Born in Savannakhet, he served in the colonial administration, but he became a leader of the Lao Issara and worked against the French, cooperating with the Viet Minh, in the late 1940s. In 1950, Phoumi switched back and joined the Lao National Army (renamed Royal Lao Army in 1953), allied with the French. He became chief of the General Staff in 1955. In 1958, he became a leader of the **Committee for Defense of National Interests**, a group of mostly young, right-wing officers and officials. He was the principal organizer of the **coup** that brought this group to power at the end of 1959. This coup made Phoumi the most powerful man in the government, and he was promoted from colonel to brigadier general, but he chose to take only the office of minister of defense, not prime minister. When a coup organized by **Kong Le** brought the neutralists to power in August 1960, Phoumi retreated to Savannakhet in the south, and before the end of the year his forces, with assistance from **Thailand** and from the **Central Intelligence Agency**, moved north and drove the neutralists from power. Phoumi was again the real head of the government from December 1960 until 1962, though he made Prince **Boun Oum** prime minister, and contented himself with the titles of deputy prime minister and minister of defense.

Under Phoumi's leadership the Laotian government aligned itself more openly with the United States than it ever had before. A **Military Assistance Advisory Group** for Laos was formally established in April 1961, and military **advisers** in U.S. uniform trained the Royal Lao Army; up to this time all such advisers had been disguised as civilians.

Phoumi opposed the negotiations that began in Geneva, Switzerland, in 1961, to create a coalition government for Laos combining Communist, rightist, and neutralist forces. But after rightist troops suffered a humiliating defeat at Nam Tha in northern Laos in May 1962, Phoumi reluctantly accepted the **Geneva Accords of 1962**; he became deputy prime minister and minister of finance in the Second Coalition Government, headed by neutralist Prince **Souvanna Phouma**.

The events of 1962 had stripped Phoumi of part of his power. He lost most of the rest of it in 1964 and 1965, in a struggle with fellow rightist Kouprasith Abhay. He went into exile in Thailand.

**PHU BAI.** By 1964, there was a small U.S. facility at Phu Bai in **Thua Thien** province, on **Route 1** about 12 kilometers southeast of **Hue**, used for intercepting enemy radio communications. In March 1965, the U.S. **Marines** began to establish a somewhat larger base there. By the end of that year the Marines had a **helicopter** squadron and a reinforced battalion there, close to 2,000 officers and men all told. The 3d Marine **Division** had its headquarters there from October 1966 to March

1968. From February 1968 to March 1970, the headquarters for U.S. military forces in **Quang Tri** and Thua Thien provinces was at Phu Bai. It was called MACV (**Military Assistance Command, Vietnam**) Forward from February to March 1968; Provisional Corps, Vietnam, from March to August; and XXIV Corps thereafter (*see* **I Corps**).

**PILATUS PORTER** (PC-6). A single-engine, propeller-driven aircraft capable of landing and taking off on very short, very rough airstrips, and thus ideal for **Air America**'s deliveries of men and supplies to remote outposts in **Laos**. The Pilatus Porter was much simpler and safer to fly than the Helio Courier, which had previously been used. It was occasionally used as a **Forward Air Controller** during the early stages of the the U.S. bombing campaign in Laos.

**PLAIN OF JARS.** A plateau in northern **Laos**, dotted with huge stone jars believed to be about 2,000 years old. Its most important center is Xieng Khouang, about 170 kilometers northeast of Vientiane. The Plain of Jars was taken by one side, then retaken by the other, over and over during the war.

Bombing in the Plain of Jars was narrowly restricted for several years. Bombing by fighter-bombers increased in March 1969 under Operation *Raindance*. Bombing in this area by **B-52**s began on February 17, 1970, under Operation *Good Look*. Until April 1972, the fact that the United States was using B-52s to bomb this area was extremely secret, and *Good Look* used a double reporting system based on that devised for Operation *Menu* in **Cambodia**. The reports given broad distribution in the U.S. **Air Force** falsely described the targets as having been in southern Laos (or occasionally in **South Vietnam** or Cambodia).

**PLAIN OF REEDS.** An extensive area of marshland, west of **Saigon** on the border between **South Vietnam** and **Cambodia**, covering substantial areas of Kien Tuong, **Hau Nghia**, **Long An**, and Dinh Tuong provinces. It was a **Viet Cong** stronghold.

**PLEIKU,** Play Cu. The town of Pleiku, capital of the province that the **Republic of Vietnam** called Pleiku and the Communists called Gia Lai, was one of the major centers of the **Central Highlands**. An attack by a **Viet Cong sapper** company in the early morning of February 7, 1965, against Camp Holloway, a **helicopter** base at Pleiku, killed nine American servicemen, wounded 104, and destroyed 11 aircraft. This triggered Operation *Flaming Dart*, an air strike against **North Viet-**

**nam**. Several U.S. infantry brigades were later based at Pleiku.

***PLOWMAN***. Attacks mounted by sea, usually (perhaps always) using **Nasty Boats**, by **SOG** against the coast of **North Vietnam**. The name *Plowman* was in use by 1967; the operations had been going on before this code name came to be applied to them. *Plowman* was halted on November 1, 1968. *Cado* was a component of *Plowman* that involved actual landing of commando teams on shore. *Loki* and *Mint* were targeted at small craft along the coast of North Vietnam. Fishermen seized from their boats along the coast were taken to an island off **Danang** where they were interrogated and indoctrinated before being returned to the North. SOG seemed to have only limited hope that they would actually become agents in the North as a result of their indoctrination. The main goal apparently was to cause confusion by getting officials in the North to worry about the possibility that fishermen might become U.S. agents.

**POL POT**, original name Saloth Sar (1925–1998). Cambodian Communist leader. He was born in 1925 in Kompong Thom province; the date of 1928 given in some sources originated during his student days, when he falsified his age to extend his eligibility for the government scholarship under which he studied in France from 1949 to 1952. While in France he was converted to Communism. He was one of the founders, in 1960, of the Khmer Workers' Party (the guiding core of what was to become the **Khmer Rouge**), and soon became its head. But he also held a respectable job, teaching history, geography, French literature, and civics at a private school in **Phnom Penh** from 1956 to 1963. Pol Pot went into the jungle in 1963, though he did not initiate genuine guerrilla activity until 1968. His forces remained relatively small until 1970, when an alliance with **China**, the **Democratic Republic of Vietnam**, and Prince **Norodom Sihanouk** allowed them to expand dramatically (*see* **Cambodia, Khmer Rouge**).

Khmer Rouge forces took Phnom Penh on April 17, 1975. They imposed on Cambodia a regime of unparalleled severity. The death toll from mass executions, illness, and starvation between then and the end of 1978 is generally believed to have been more than a million people. In the early stages, there were factional divisions among the leaders, but Pol Pot's group, the most brutal in its treatment of the population, soon eliminated the other factions.

The Vietnamese invasion launched on December 25, 1978, drove Pol Pot from power, but he led a guerrilla struggle for years thereafter, with foreign assistance (mostly Chinese) reaching him through **Thailand**. His reputation as the man most responsible for the horrors of 1975 to 1978 made him a diplomatic liability, and he formally resigned as commander of the Khmer Rouge armed forces in 1985 in an effort to make the Khmer Rouge more respectable, but he retained actual leadership.

In 1997, Pol Pot ordered the death of his subordinate Son Sen, and Son Sen's whole family. Other Khmer Rouge leaders came to distrust him. They arrested him, staged a show trial in July 1997, and then held him under house arrest until his death, said to have been by heart attack.

**POLICE.** The Vietnamese National Police, aside from their regular law enforcement duties, were heavily involved in efforts to suppress the Communists, and in controlling non-Communist opponents of the **Republic of Vietnam**. Police Field Forces were in effect combat troops. They were one component of the *Phoenix* **Program**, and in 1972 were given control of the program.

National Police strength expanded gradually from 52,000 at the end of 1965 to 88,000 at the end of 1970. As more of **South Vietnam** became secure enough so police units could operate there, they began to expand more rapidly, reaching 121,000 by the end of 1972.

In the early 1960s, the **Central Intelligence Agency** was the main U.S. provider of advice and support to the National Police. By the late stages of the war, the Office of Public Safety, within the Agency for International Development (AID), which was responsible for assistance to civil police organizations in foreign countries, was playing a conspicuous role. It brought foreign police officials to the United States for training, and sent advisers abroad. This relatively small organization concentrated a large portion of its resources on Vietnam; in January 1973, the number of public safety advisers in Vietnam—133—was almost as large as its total for the rest of the world.

U.S. **Army** Military Police (MP) units helped to maintain order among U.S. troops (there was an MP company attached to each **division**), but also had a significant combat role. Some MP units, for example, escorted trucks on roads in the **Central Highlands** where there was a danger of Communist ambushes.

**POPULAR FORCES** (PF). Local defense units in the **Republic of Vietnam**, operating at the village level, with less armament and training than regular **ARVN** forces. They had been called the **Self-Defense**

**Corps** until 1964. They were often lumped together with the **Regional Forces** (RF) as the RF/PF or "Ruff-Puffs." In **I Corps**, some PF platoons worked together with U.S. **Marines** in the **Combined Action Platoons**. The Popular Forces had an official strength of 164,284 in mid-1968, and 234,681 in mid-1972.

**POULO CONDORE** (Con Son). An island about 15 kilometers long, located about 83 kilometers southeast of the Vietnamese coast, off the mouths of the **Mekong River**. Its isolation made it suitable for use as a prison island. The French imprisoned many Communists there, including **Le Duan, Le Duc Tho, Nguyen Chi Thanh, Nguyen Van Linh, Pham Hung, Pham Van Dong**, and **Tran Van Tra**, and also one future leader of the **Republic of Vietnam** (RVN), **Phan Khac Suu**. After 1955, it became an RVN prison. Publicity about mistreatment of prisoners there caused a scandal in July 1970 (*see* "**tiger cages**").

*PRAIRIE FIRE,* Operation, 1967–1971. **SOG** sent small **reconnaissance** teams composed of Americans and either **Montagnards** or **Nung** into eastern **Laos** (the area of the **Ho Chi Minh Trail**). These operations had been called *Shining Brass* from 1965 to March 1967. Targets located by the small reconnaissance teams were sometimes attacked by larger **Hatchet Teams**; the largest operations by Hatchet Teams were in 1970 (*see Tailwind*). Prime Minister **Souvanna Phouma** of Laos had not been told about the program, and William Sullivan, the U.S. ambassador to Laos, considered it clear Souvanna Phouma would not approve if told. General **William Westmoreland**'s desire to expand *Prairie Fire* led to friction with Sullivan during 1967. Teams that got into trouble in Laos could obtain support from U.S. fixed-wing aircraft and **helicopter gunships**, unlike the teams sent into **Cambodia** under Operation *Daniel Boone*.

"Prairie Fire" was also the code used to call for an emergency rescue effort if a small reconnaissance team, of the sort described above, were detected by powerful enemy forces and seemed in danger of being wiped out.

Americans were no longer to enter Laos as part of reconnaissance teams after February 8, 1971. In early April, the shift of *Prairie Fire* to Vietnamese control led to its being renamed *Phu Dong*.

## PRESIDENT'S FOREIGN INTELLIGENCE ADVISORY BOARD
(PFIAB). When **John Kennedy** became president, the President's Board of Consultants on Foreign Intelligence Activities was moribund

and Kennedy decided to abolish it. After the Bay of Pigs fiasco, however, he saw a need for an external watchdog on the **intelligence** community. He renamed the body the President's Foreign Intelligence Advisory Board and greatly strengthened it. James R. Killian, Jr., president of the Massachusetts Institute of Technology, chaired the board until 1963; **Clark Clifford** from 1963 until he left to become secretary of defense in 1968; and **Maxwell Taylor** from 1968 to 1969.

PFIAB had far more influence than such boards usually do. Some of its members had both expertise and prestige in military matters and foreign affairs. Perhaps more important, some others had great expertise in science and technology, and were able to give PFIAB a significant voice in the development of high-tech intelligence-gathering devices.

PFIAB also had remarkable access to information. In August 1964, for example, during the **Tonkin Gulf incidents**, members of PFIAB looked directly at raw information, such as intercepted North Vietnamese radio messages, and apparently understood what they were seeing better than some senior military officers who looked at the same information. They also were able to get from a senior **Central Intelligence Agency** (CIA) official a more candid evaluation of the incidents than was appearing in the CIA's official reports. PFIAB may well have been President Johnson's best source of information on Tonkin Gulf.

**PRISONERS OF WAR** (POWs). Under international law, the procedures for handling prisoners of war, as codified by the Geneva Convention of 1949, are supposed to apply in large armed conflicts either between nations or within a nation, whether or not there has been a declaration of war. These procedures, however, were sometimes violated on both sides in the Vietnam War. Prisoners were sometimes abused, tortured, or killed.

Communist personnel captured by U.S. forces in **South Vietnam**, or at sea off the coast of South Vietnam, were normally handed over to the custody of the **Republic of Vietnam** (RVN). A small number of naval officers and men of the **Democratic Republic of Vietnam** (DRV), captured at sea off the coast of North Vietnam in 1966, were kept in U.S. custody at **Danang** until the United States released them to North Vietnam in 1967 and 1968.

The Hoa Lo Prison in **Hanoi**, commonly called the "Hanoi Hilton," became the most famous POW facility in Vietnam, but many American POWs were held elsewhere in North Vietnam, and smaller numbers in

South Vietnam and **Laos**. After the unsuccessful U.S. effort to rescue POWs at **Son Tay** in 1970, some of the smaller facilities were closed, as POWs were transferred to larger facilities easier to guard against rescue attempts.

Both sides occasionally released small numbers of prisoners, sometimes with much publicity, during the war.

Under the **Paris Peace Agreement** of January 27, 1973, all prisoners of war on both sides were supposed to be released within 60 days. The 591 U.S. military personnel who were released by the DRV during these 60 days had mostly been captured in North or South Vietnam, but 10 of them had been captured in Laos. Some American civilians who had been captured by the Communist forces, and some European civilians, were released along with the American POWs. Two U.S. pilots whose planes had strayed into Chinese airspace during the war, and had been shot down, were released by the Chinese. One U.S. Marine—Robert Garwood, who had been captured late in 1965 in South Vietnam, had soon begun to collaborate with his captors, and by the early 1970s was being treated by the Communists as a defector rather than a prisoner—was not included in the 1973 release of POWs. He finally returned to the United States in 1979 and was tried and convicted as a defector.

Much larger numbers of Vietnamese POWs were released after the Paris Agreement—26,880 Communist personnel released by the RVN, and 5,336 RVN personnel released by Communists. These releases, on both sides, stretched on beyond the 60-day deadline.

There has been continuing controversy, in the United States, as to whether there were American prisoners still in captivity in Vietnam or Laos after the 1973 releases of prisoners; *see* **missing in action**.

**PROTECTIVE REACTION.** President **Lyndon Johnson** ordered a **bombing halt** for **North Vietnam** as of November 1, 1968, and this remained in effect until 1972. The United States continued to fly **reconnaissance** aircraft over North Vietnam, however, and considered itself entitled to protect them by retaliating if **anti-aircraft artillery** or **surface-to-air missiles** attacked them, or if **radar** tracked the aircraft in ways that suggested to the Americans that an attack might be about to occur. The number of protective reaction air strikes increased substantially in 1970 and 1971, and the way the United States used the system became increasingly flexible. From 1970 onward, sites in North Vietnam could be attacked for threatening U.S. aircraft over Laos, not just reconnaissance aircraft over North Vietnam, and air strikes were flown not just against anti-aircraft units but against other targets nearby. Late in 1971, **Air Force** officers began falsifying reports to justify "protective reaction" air strikes when there had not actually been an attack against the reconnaissance aircraft (*see* **John D. Lavelle**).

***PROUD DEEP ALPHA,*** Operation. A series of air strikes from December 26 to 30, 1971, attacking storage sites, truck parks, **surface-to-air missile** sites, and other targets in the southern part of **North Vietnam**. There were more than 1,000 sorties, dropping almost a thousand tons of **bombs**; these were the heaviest air strikes against North Vietnam since 1968.

**PROVINCIAL RECONNAISSANCE UNITS** (PRUs). Relatively small elite units, sponsored by the **Central Intelligence Agency**, used for military and paramilitary activities. The original name was **Counter-Terror Teams**; this was changed to Provincial Reconnaissance Units in 1966. The PRUs were an important, and often very effective, part of the ***Phoenix* Program**. Accusations that the *Phoenix* Program was an assassination campaign usually refer to the activities of the PRUs. They were often trained and led by U.S. **Navy SEAL**s. In 1969 they were placed under, though not at first really integrated into, the Vietnamese National **Police**.

**PROVISIONAL REVOLUTIONARY GOVERNMENT** (PRG). In June 1969, Communist leaders elevated the formal status of the revolutionary movement in **South Vietnam** by proclaiming the establishment of the Provisional Revolutionary Government of the Republic of South Vietnam; it largely superseded the **National Liberation Front** (NLF), previously the highest formal organization of the movement. The major motive was probably the need to elevate the formal status of the NLF representatives at the **Paris negotiations**.

　　**Huynh Tan Phat** was president of the PRG; other prominent leaders included Minister of National Defense **Tran Nam Trung**, and Minister of Foreign Affairs **Nguyen Thi Binh**, who represented the PRG in Paris.

# - Q -

**QUANG NAM.** Third to the northernmost province of **South Vietnam**, in **I Corps**. Under the French, Quang Nam province had been very large. The **Republic of Vietnam** split it in two, the northern half keeping the name Quang Nam and the southern half becoming Quang Tin province. The Communist forces continued for a while to treat these as a single province, Quang Nam.

Quang Nam's most important city was **Danang**, the main **logistic** center for I Corps and the headquarters for U.S. **Marines** in Vietnam. Major facilities included the huge Danang Air Base, and **Marble Mountain** Air Facility just to the southeast of Danang. Quang Nam was the scene of very heavy fighting, and was second only to **Quang Tri** in the number of American combat deaths from 1967 onward.

**QUANG TRI.** The northernmost province of **South Vietnam**, Quang Tri had actually been split when North and South Vietnam were separated in 1954 (the section of Quang Tri that lay north of the **Demilitarized Zone** [DMZ] was called the Vinh Linh Zone). The major centers were Quang Tri City (the province capital) and **Dong Ha**, both of which were on **Route 1**, the main north-south road near the coast. **Route 9** ran westward from Dong Ha across the northern part of the province, through **Khe Sanh** to **Laos**.

For the **Republic of Vietnam** (RVN), Quang Tri was part of **I Corps**. For the Communists it was initially part of **Military Region 5** (the B1 **Front**). In 1966, the People's Army of Vietnam (**PAVN**) decided to begin fighting a more conventional style of combat against U.S. forces in certain upland areas, both to inflict casualties and erode American political will, and to draw American attention and resources away from the populated lowlands. Quang Tri was an ideal area to implement this policy. It had the shortest supply lines to **North Vietnam**, which would be important because a more conventional style of conflict required more ammunition for PAVN troops, and it had very rough terrain and generally rainy weather, which to some extent reduced the advantages of American firepower and air power. Quang Tri and its neighbor **Thua Thien** were separated from Military Region 5 to become the **Tri-Thien Military Region** (B4 Front) in April 1966. Substantial PAVN forces began crossing the DMZ into northern Quang Tri in June 1966; the U.S. **Marines** responded with Operation *Hastings* in July. Heavy fighting went on for years. The Marines developed a string of bases across northern Quang Tri south of the DMZ. Roughly in order from east to west, these included: Gio Linh and Con Thien; Cam Lo and Camp Carroll; the "Rockpile" and Ca Lu; and finally Khe Sanh. Between 1967 and 1972, more Americans died in combat in Quang Tri than in any other province of South Vietnam.

PAVN forces attacking southward from the DMZ into Quang Tri in the **Easter Offensive** of 1972 overran the northernmost bases in the province very quickly, then were delayed for several weeks, took Quang Tri City on May 1, and completed their conquest of the province on May 3. An RVN counteroffensive later in the year retook Quang Tri City, but did not regain the lost bases in the northern part of the province.

**QUE SON VALLEY** (Nui Loc Son Basin). This was a heavily populated valley extending a considerable distance inland from the coast on the border between **Quang Nam** and Quang Tin provinces, in **I Corps**. The Que Son Mountains lay to the north of the valley. The first major U.S. effort to drive the **Viet Cong** out of the Que Son Valley, and thus deprive them of an important source of food for their forces, was Operation *Harvest Moon* in December 1965, involving several U.S. **Marine** battalions and several **ARVN** battalions. Fighting continued in the area for years.

**QUI NHON.** The capital of **Binh Dinh** province, in northern **II Corps**. Qui Nhon was chosen as the main U.S. **logistic** center for the northern half of II Corps; it was a seaport, and **Route 19** ran west from Qui Nhon to **Pleiku** in the **Central Highlands**. In 1965, the Capital Divison of the Republic of **Korea** (ROK) established its base at Qui Nhon.

**QUYNH LUU UPRISING,** November 2–14, 1956. **Catholic** peasants rioted in Quynh Luu district of Nghe An province, in northern **Trung Bo**. The crisis over the excesses of **land reform** had exacerbated pre-existing tensions pitting Catholics in the area against local officials of the **Democratic Republic of Vietnam**, who in late 1954 and early 1955 had prevented the departure of many Catholics who wanted to move to **South Vietnam** under the provisions of the **Geneva Accords**. Estimates of the number of people killed in the suppression of these riots vary widely; the lowest figures indicate fewer than a dozen deaths, while the highest indicate thousands.

## - R -

**RABORN, WILLIAM FRANCIS** (1905–1990). U.S. Admiral, director of central intelligence. Born in Decatur, Texas, Raborn graduated from the U.S. Naval Academy at Annapolis in 1928. He eventually became a specialist in guided missile systems; he was particularly important in the development of the Polaris submarine-launched missile. He retired from the **Navy** as a vice admiral in 1963.

In April 1965, Raborn became director of central intelligence. Not having had previous experience in the **Central Intelligence Agency**, he is generally said to have been a weak director. He generally favored expansion of the **air war** against **North Vietnam**, but also encouraged the idea of **bombing halts**, as a possible route to peace **negotiations**. He also seems to have believed that the war needed to be won on the ground in the villages of **South Vietnam**, not just by bombing the North. He retired from government once again, returning to private industry, in June 1966.

**RACIAL TENSION.** The U.S. armed forces no longer practiced formal racial segregation by the time of the Vietnam War, but racial tension and some racial discrimination persisted. There were accusations that the men being put in harm's way in Vietnam were disproportionately black.

Figures for the war as a whole show that 12.5 percent of the Americans who died in Vietnam were black. Of those killed by hostile action, 12.3 percent were black. These averages conceal substantial variations between different ranks, different years, and different services. Few blacks reached officer rank in this era; 14.2 percent of the enlisted men who died were black, but only 1.9 percent of the officers. In the **Army** 13.1 percent of those killed by hostile action were black; the average for the **Air Force, Navy**, and **Marines** was slightly less than 11 percent. Most important, black deaths in the Army occurred disproportionately in 1965 and 1966, when blacks were over-represented in the sort of Army infantry units that suffered heavy casualties in Vietnam. In 1966, 9 percent of the men in the U.S. armed forces as a whole were black, and 11 percent of the men in Vietnam were black, but 16 percent of the U.S. military personnel killed by hostile action were black, 20.8 percent of the Army personel killed by hostile action were black, and about 23 percent of the Army enlisted personnel killed by hostile action were black. Protests by **Martin Luther King Jr.** and others, over the high black casualty levels of 1965–1966, were one factor causing the Army to make a deliberate effort to reduce the concentration of blacks in combat infantry units.

About 11 percent of the U.S. population was black. Those who argue that the number of blacks who died in the war was not disproportionately large often say that the proportion of blacks among males of military age was higher than among the population as a whole; a figure of 13.5 percent is sometimes given. This figure is incorrect; its origin is unclear. The 1970 census found that 11.0 percent of American males aged 18 to 25 were black, and the census figures make it clear that this percentage was rising; less than 11 percent of the males of military age had been black during the years of peak U.S. participation in combat in Vietnam, 1966 through 1969.

In the late 1960s, the "Black Power" movement and a general decline in morale and discipline raised the potential for racial problems within the U.S. military units in Vietnam. Black and white personnel fought side by side in combat units, but their social lives in base camps were often racially segregated. Sometimes they fought one another. Violence between black and white personnel, ranging from individual fights and robberies to racial riots, were becoming a serious problem among U.S. troops in **I Corps** by the end of 1968; race riots were occurring at a rate of about one per month in I Corps in the second quarter of 1969.

The worst racial violence in the Navy did not occur until 1972; there was a race riot aboard the aircraft carrier *Kitty Hawk* beginning on October 12, 1972, and lasting until the following morning.

**RADAR.** Radar equipment, mostly (perhaps all) imported from the **Soviet Union**, was an important part of the air defense system of **North Vietnam**. **Surface-to-air missiles** and the fire of all large-caliber **antiaircraft artillery** and some medium-caliber (57-mm) weapons were guided by radar. The U.S. aircraft assigned to attack radar installations, especially the radar the Americans called *Fan Song*, which guided surface-to-air missiles, were designated *Wild Weasel*. Beginning in about 1972, Communist forces in some parts of **South Vietnam** also began to use radar.

The United States began to send *Skyspot* (sometimes called *Combat Skyspot*) radar systems to South Vietnam in April 1966. These allowed ground controllers to control a bombing mission, instructing the pilot how to adjust his course, altitude, and speed, and telling him when to drop his **bombs**. Using *Skyspot*, pilots could achieve reasonable accuracy bombing targets they could not see, whether because of night and heavy cloud or simply because the targets were not conspicuous from the air. Given the potential for error, bombing by *Skyspot* was seldom done within 1,000 yards of friendly ground troops. The system was soon controlling most **B-52** strikes in South Vietnam, and a substantial fraction of the strikes by fighter-bombers. A *Skyspot* radar at **Lima Site 85** in northeast **Laos** became operational in November 1967. It was able to control bombing missions over large areas of Laos, and as far into North Vietnam as the city of **Hanoi**, though bombing of such distant targets was not very accurate. It was in use for only a few months, however; PAVN forces overran the site on March 11, 1968.

U.S. aircraft used Doppler radar to detect vehicles at night, mainly along the **Ho Chi Minh Trail** in Laos. Side-Looking Airborne Radar (SLAR) was far more satisfactory than the forward-looking Doppler radar used by some B-57 **Canberra** bombers beginning in 1970.

U.S. forces also used radar on the ground in South Vietnam. The AN/MPQ-4 counter-**mortar** radar was a relatively old design dating from about 1950, but it still had significant ability to track mortar shells in flight; the Americans could quickly determine the location from which they were being shelled and order immediate counterfire with **artillery** on that location. The main disadvantage of this radar was its narrow field of observation; it could detect mortar shells only if it was pointed in the correct direction. The Communists could observe the direction in which the antennas of these radars were pointed, and make mortar attacks from some other direction. The Americans countered by mounting screens that hid the radar antennas, preventing Communist observers from seeing which way they were pointed. In mid-1969, it was estimated that when one of these radars was operating properly, it had a 43 percent chance of determining the firing point of a mortar attack; this was a high enough probability to make it a significant tool for base defense, but not high enough to please the American forces.

The AN/TPS-25 Ground Surveillance Radar was more satisfactory. It was a Doppler radar, which could distinguish moving objects such as vehicles and walking men from stationary ones such as trees by the fact that the radar echoes from moving objects would not come back to the radar set with exactly the same wavelength as those from stationary ones. It was widely used to spot targets for artillery fire at night. Under ideal conditions its range could be as great as fifteen miles, but most detections of targets were at ranges of eight miles or less, and it lost its effectiveness in the rain. It required line of sight; while it could distinguish the echoes of men moving among bushes, even if most of the radar bounce came from the bushes, it could not detect anything on the far side of a dense tree line.

A few AN/TPS-58 (RATAC) radars were brought to Vietnam in the later stages of the war. These were basically similar to the AN/TPS-25, but with a greater range and a wider field of view.

There was also a more portable radar with a much shorter range—about one hundred meters early in the war, several hundred later on. It was small enough so that standard procedure was to take it down every morning and not set it up again until after dark, so that Communist forces would not have the opportunity to see where it was located and which way it was pointed.

**RAGLAI.** A **Montagnard** group, speaking a Malayo-Polynesian language, and living in two areas of **South Vietnam**, one inland from **Nha Trang** and the other inland from Phan Rang and south of **Dalat**.

**RANGER.** In the early stages of the Vietnam War, the term "Ranger" in the U.S. **Army** normally designated an individual rather than a unit; a Ranger was a man who had completed the very demanding Ranger training course at Fort Benning, Georgia.

At the beginning of 1969, the various **Long-Range Patrol** (LRP) companies of the U.S. Army in Vietnam were formally made Ranger companies; the 75th Infantry (Ranger) was made their parent regiment. Membership in one of these units did not imply graduation from the Ranger course.

The Army of the Republic of Vietnam (**ARVN**) began to organize Ranger companies in 1960. By 1965, these companies had all been gathered into Ranger battalions. They had less heavy weaponry than regular ARVN units. Some were elite units, but some suffered from low morale, either because senior officers were more interested in using them as personal guards than in giving them a real combat capability, or because they had been thrown into situations where their lack of heavy weapons had subjected them to crippling losses. When the **Civilian Irregular Defense Groups** were amalgamated into the ARVN, it was as Ranger units.

**RAVEN.** Forward Air Controllers (FACs) of the U.S. **Air Force** 56th Special Operations Wing controlled air strikes in large parts of **Laos** from 1966 onward with the radio call sign Raven. Nominally based at Udorn in **Thailand**, they usually flew from forward bases in Laos. They flew single-engine propeller-drive aircraft, usually Cessna O-1s. They did *not* fly the OH-23 Raven **helicopter**.

**RAYE, MARTHA** "Maggie," born Margaret Teresa Yvonne Reed (1916–

1994). Singer and actress. Born in Butte, Montana, she worked as an entertainer from early childhood, but her career did not take off until she was about 20. In her late teens, earning too little to live on as a singer in the evenings, she took a second job, working days as a nurse's aide in a hospital.

Martha Raye was perhaps the most loved of the Hollywood entertainers who toured **South Vietnam** performing for U.S. forces during the war. She came often, and visited small, remote, and sometimes dangerous outposts. In areas where the combat had been intense, she sometimes dropped her role as an entertainer and went to work as a nurse in surgery, so competently that many thought she must have had substantial medical training. She had a particular bond with the U.S. **Army Special Forces**, and after her death it was the Special Forces who buried her, with full military honors, in the post cemetery at Fort Bragg, North Carolina.

**RAYMOND MORRISON-KNUDSEN - BROWN & ROOT, JONES** (RMK-BRJ). A giant conglomerate created by four major American construction firms—Raymond International, Morrison-Knudsen, Brown & Root, and J. A. Jones—to build bases for the U.S. military in Vietnam. By mid-1966, RMK-BRJ had about 50,000 Vietnamese employees. Brown & Root had been strongly connected with **Lyndon Johnson** since the 1930s.

**RECOILLESS RIFLE.** When a normal **artillery** piece fires a shell, the barrel is pushed strongly to the rear, in accord with Newton's Third Law. When a recoilless rifle is fired, a blast of propellant gases is directed to the rear; the force that sends the shell in one direction is balanced by the force that sends this blast of gases in the opposite direction, and the gun does not recoil. This allows the gun to do without the heavy structures needed to absorb the recoil of a conventional cannon. Recoilless rifles also have a relatively low muzzle velocity; this allows the barrel to be kept comparatively light. The result is a gun with a relatively short range, usually used on targets within line of sight of the gunner, that is far lighter and more portable than conventional artillery. The American M40A1 106-mm recoilless rifle, for example, weighed only 114 kilograms. (For comparison, the M102 105-mm howitzer weighed more than 1.5 tons. It is true that the projectile of the 105-mm howitzer was much heavier than that of the 106-mm recoilless rifle.) Care was needed in the use of these weapons; the blast of propellant gases could injure or kill people standing behind a recoilless rifle when it was fired.

The United States used recoilless rifles in Vietnam ranging from the M18, a 57-mm weapon weighing 20.15 kilograms and firing a 1.25-kilogram projectile with a maximum range of 4,000 meters but an effective range of only 450 meters, up to the M40A1, a 106-mm, 114-kilogram weapon firing a 7.71-kilogram projectile with a maximum range of 6,000 to 9,000 meters. Single recoilless rifles were often mounted on vehicles of various sorts. The **Ontos** was a tracked vehicle with six 106-mm recoilless rifles mounted on it.

The forces staging covert raids by sea against the coast of **North Vietnam** during 1964 (*see OPLAN 34A*) sometimes used 57-mm recoilless rifles. When they tried 106-mm recoilless rifles, they found that the backblast of propellant gases did too much damage to their vessels when the weapons were fired.

The **Viet Cong** began using 57-mm recoilless rifles (some the American-made M18, some the almost identical Chinese-made Type 36), light enough to be easily carried through the jungle by guerrillas, to a significant extent in 1963. They were used mainly against vehicles.

**RECONDO SCHOOL.** A school at **Nha Trang**, operated by the U.S. **Army Special Forces**, which taught **reconnaissance** techniques. It was originally established in 1964 to train personnel for Project *Delta*. It began accepting students from the 1st Brigade of the 101st **Airborne Division** in September 1965. In September 1966, it officially became the MACV **(Military Assistance Command, Vietnam)** Recondo School, training personnel for **Long-Range Patrol** and other American and allied units. It was closed on December 19, 1970.

**RECONNAISSANCE.** RF-101 "Voodoo" reconnaissance aircraft, equipped for aerial photography, began to fly missions from **Thailand** in 1961. They were used very widely for a while, but after one was shot down by a **MiG**-21 in September 1967, reconnaissance over the most dangerous portions of **North Vietnam** was assigned to RF-4Cs. The RF-101s were shifted to **Tan Son Nhut** in **South Vietnam**; they continued to fly missions over the less dangerous parts of Indochina until 1970. The RB-57 (*see* **Canberra**) was also used widely in Indochina. For very high altitude aerial photography of North Vietnam, the United States used the **U-2** in the early years of the war, the much faster (and thus less vulnerable to **surface-to-air missiles**) A-12 in 1967 and 1968, and the SR-71 from 1968 onward. The United States also used unmanned drones (*see Buffalo Hunter*) for low-altitude photography.

The observation aircraft used by **Forward Air Controllers** also did a great deal of aerial reconnaissance by visual scanning. Most of these were propeller-driven: the single-engine O-1 Bird Dog and O-2 Skymaster, and the twin-engine **OV-10 Bronco** (see photograph 12).

The Communist forces did their reconnaissance on the ground, rather than by air. Since Vietnamese civilians worked on many American military bases, it was sometimes possible for Communist forces to prepare for an attack not just by having scouts examine the perimeter from the outside, but by having agents walk around inside the base, noting the layout and pacing off distances. The United States also did a lot of reconnaissance on the ground, using both American and Asian personnel. *See DANIEL BOONE; LEAPING LENA;* LONG-RANGE PATROL; *PRAIRIE FIRE;* ROADRUNNERS; *SHINING BRASS;* SPECIAL FORCES; SPIKE TEAMS.

**RED RIVER DELTA.** The relatively flat, open area where the Red River spreads out and flows to the sea through numerous branches has most of the population of **North Vietnam**, though its area is only about 15,000 square kilometers. Its most important cities are **Hanoi**, **Haiphong**, and Nam Dinh.

**REGIONAL FORCES** (RF). Troops of the **Republic of Vietnam** (RVN) organized at the province level, less heavily armed than the regular **ARVN** units. Their official strength was 197,917 in mid-1968, and 294,571 in mid-1972. They had been called the **Civil Guard** until 1964. They were often lumped together with the **Popular Forces** (PF) as the RF/PF or "Ruff-Puffs." In 1970 and 1971, mostly or entirely in **Quang Nam** province, some RF troops served with U.S. **Marines** in the **Combined Action Platoons** (CAPs).

By the late stages of the war, the RF/PF made up most of the ground combat manpower of the RVN; actual combat troops made up a larger percentage of total manpower in the RF/PF than in the regular ARVN. In January 1973, there were somewhere between 192,000 and 229,000 ground combat troops in regular ARVN units, and somewhere between 497,000 and 519,000 in the RF/PF.

**REPUBLIC OF CHINA** (ROC), often called Nationalist China. When the Chinese Communist Party under Mao Zedong (Mao Tse-tung) won control of **China** in 1949, the previous government, under Chiang Kai-shek, was able to hold onto the island of Taiwan. There it continued to claim that it was the legitimate government of all of China. With the vigorous assistance of the United States, it was able to persuade most non-Communist countries, and the **United Nations**, to accept this theory until the early 1970s.

Chiang Kai-shek was eager to assist the struggle against Communism in Vietnam. The very low official figures for ROC military personnel in **South Vietnam** (the maximum number has been reported as 31) represent the overt personnel of the Republic of China Military Assistance Advisory Group, established in October 1964. It provided advisers in political warfare stationed in all four **corps tactical zones**, at the Political Warfare College in **Dalat**, and in **Saigon**. There were also medical teams, and technical advisers working in agriculture and in the electrical power system. These overt personnel were the tip of the iceberg; military personnel in Vietnam covertly were more numerous and more important. When the **Republic of Vietnam** decided to train some soldiers for underwater operations in what eventually became the **Lien Doi Nguoi Nhai**, it got scuba instructors from Taiwan. When the U.S. **Central Intelligence Agency** (CIA) began parachuting paramilitary teams into **North Vietnam** during the administration of **John Kennedy**, Chinese pilots from Taiwan flew some of the planes. In 1964, Chinese nationals from the ROC arrived in **Danang** to serve as captains of **Swift Boats** for *OPLAN 34A* raids against North Vietnam. In mid-1964, the CIA estimated that there were "several hundred military and paramilitary personnel" from the ROC in South Vietnam, and there were plans to increase the number.

The ROC repeatedly offered to send regular troops to South Vietnam, but the United States thought this would be unwise, and indeed the United States tried to restrain the Republic of Vietnam from bringing in too many covert personnel. Probably the closest the ROC came to putting regular combat troops into Vietnam was its dispatch in 1961, 1964, and perhaps other years, of reinforcements for the **Sea Swallows**, a paramilitary organization run by a Chinese Catholic priest.

**REPUBLIC OF VIETNAM** (RVN). Often called the Government of Vietnam (GVN) or **South Vietnam**, the RVN had its capital at **Saigon**. In its early years it claimed to be the legitimate government of all Vietnam; it did not regard North and South Vietnam as separate nations. It was derived from the State of Vietnam; the change in name was proclaimed on October 26, 1955. **Ngo Dinh Diem**, who had been premier of the State of Vietnam, was president of the RVN until his overthrow on November 1, 1963. A triumvirate of Major Generals **Duong Van Minh**, Le Van Kim, and **Tran Van Don** ruled until a second **coup** on

January 30, 1964, brought **Nguyen Khanh** to power. Khanh gave nominal power to civilian premiers **Tran Van Huong** (November 1964 to January 1965) and **Phan Huy Quat** (February–June 1965). A group led by Generals **Nguyen Cao Ky** and **Nguyen Van Thieu** stripped Khanh of his position of backstage domination in February 1965. In June 1965, Ky replaced Quat as premier. In September 1967, Thieu was elected president and Ky vice president. At first they were near-equals, but Thieu soon trimmed back Ky's power, and dominated the Republic of Vietnam until his resignation on April 21, 1975. Tran Van Huong became president for a week, and then Duong Van Minh for two days, before the fall of Saigon to the Communists on April 30.

**RESERVES.** In July 1965, Secretary of Defense **Robert McNamara** and the **Joint Chiefs of Staff** (especially **Army** Chief of Staff **Harold Johnson**) strongly urged President **Lyndon Johnson** to proclaim a national emergency and mobilize the Reserves, to provide adequate manpower for serious fighting in Vietnam without excessively drawing down U.S. strength elsewhere. They thought they had persuaded him, but on July 26 he decided not to do this. The results included not just a strain on military manpower in sheer quantititative terms, but also an eventual degradation in quality. The Reserves included many men with years of experience in the military; not mobilizing them forced a greater reliance on new recruits and draftees. The shortage of experienced non-commissioned officers in infantry units would become a serious problem. The lack of an official national emergency meant that men would continue to leave military units as their terms of enlistment expired. The 1st **Cavalry Division (Airmobile)**, for example, had been preparing to go to Vietnam and training in the newly developed tactics of airmobility. Many of the men, however, were approaching the end of their enlistments, and the lack of a declared national emergency meant that they were rotated out of the division, and replacements brought in who had not participated in that training, just before the division left the United States for Vietnam in August 1965.

The Joint Chiefs repeated their request for mobilization of the Reserves at intervals thereafter. The last major effort was in early 1968, when General **Earle Wheeler**, chairman of the Joint Chiefs of Staff, went to Vietnam to evaluate the results of the **Tet Offensive**. He reported on his return that General **William Westmoreland**, commander of U.S. forces in **South Vietnam**, needed 206,000 more men; he recommended mobilizing the Reserves to make this manpower available.

Most historians accept Westmoreland's claim that Wheeler was seriously exaggerating Westmoreland's needs, and that what Wheeler actually had in mind was that this gloomy picture could be used as leverage to get the Reserves mobilized, and then when most of the men proved not to be needed for Vietnam after all, Wheeler would be able to use them to replenish forces in other areas of the world, which had been weakened as the United States tried to fight a war in Vietnam without mobilization. If this was what Wheeler had in mind, it did not work; President Johnson sent about 32,000 more men to Vietnam during the following months, but mobilized fewer than that number from the Reserves and National Guard, so the manpower shortage in areas other than Vietnam became worse rather than better. The secretary of defense announced on April 11 that 24,500 reservists and national guardsmen were being mobilized, about 10,000 of whom would be included among the reinforcements being sent to Vietnam. The units sent to Vietnam included two battalions of **artillery** and one of combat engineers, but only a single company of infantry, Company D of the 151st Infantry, a **long-range patrol** unit that served in **III Corps** from December 1968 to November 1969.

**REVISIONISTS.** In Marxism, the term "Revisionist" has traditionally been applied to those who stripped Marxism of its revolutionary content and worked for peaceful reform. During the Sino-Soviet split (*see* **China**), when leaders of the **Soviet Union** were promoting a doctrine of peaceful coexistence between Communism and capitalism, the Chinese denounced them as Revisionists. When the Soviet Union tried to restrain the actions of the **Democratic Republic of Vietnam** (DRV) in **South Vietnam** and **Laos**, the DRV joined Chinese denunciations of Soviet Revisionism.

In 1964, DRV security personnel began searching for Revisionists within **North Vietnam**. Suspects, including **PAVN** officers, were interrogated and arrested; some were imprisoned for years without trial. This turned into a witch-hunt. It may have been, at least in part, an effort by the faction led by **Le Duan** and **Le Duc Tho** to weaken the influence of **Vo Nguyen Giap**.

In the United States, "revisionists" are simply people who challenge traditional interpretations of history. The term can be either a compliment or an insult, depending on whether the person speaking accepts or rejects the traditional interpretations.

**REVOLUTIONARY DEVELOPMENT** (RD, renamed Rural Development as of January 1, 1970). The **Republic of Vietnam** (RVN) established the Ministry of Revolutionary Development in 1965 to control its **pacification** programs. Revolutionary Development Cadres in teams of 59, trained at **Vung Tau**, became in 1966 the centerpiece of RVN pacification efforts. There were 27,000 RD Cadres by the end of 1966; the number increased to 46,000 by the end of 1968, but then declined to 21,000 by the end of 1972. The Revolutionary Development (later Rural Development) Cadres are generally considered not to have been as well motivated or as effective as the **People's Action Teams** from which they had been derived.

**RHADÉ.** A **Montagnard** group, sometimes (especially since the war) called the Ede, speaking a Malayo-Polynesian language and living in an area stretching from the Darlac Plateau of the **Central Highlands**, west into **Cambodia**. Rhadé near **Ban Me Thuot**, in Darlac province, were the first Montagnards to be organized in 1961 into what became the **Civilian Irregular Defense Groups**.

**RHEAULT, ROBERT B.** (1925– ). U.S. **Army** colonel. Born in Dedham, Massachusetts, he graduated from West Point in 1946, and joined the **Special Forces** in 1960. He served one tour in Vietnam ending in late 1964, served in the office of the **Special Assistant for Counterinsurgency and Special Activities** (SACSA) under the **Joint Chiefs of Staff**, supervising **SOG**'s covert operations into **Laos**, and finally was made commander of the 5th Special Forces Group, in Vietnam, in May 1969.

He lost this job and his career almost immediately. Officers and men at **Nha Trang** had concluded that a Vietnamese named Thai Khac Chuyen, who had been recruited as an **intelligence** agent for Project *Gamma* (an intelligence operation run by Special Forces Detachment B-57, gathering information on Communist operations in **Cambodia**), was a double agent, a Communist who had infiltrated the project. Special Forces personnel interrogated Chuyen at length, then (with Rheault's approval) killed Chuyen and dumped his body into the South China Sea on the night of June 20, 1969. Within days, General **Creighton Abrams**, commander of **Military Assistance Command, Vietnam**, had heard of the matter from the **Central Intelligence Agency** (CIA). Abrams had his chief of staff ask Rheault about it, and Rheault said Chuyen was not dead, but on an intelligence mission in Cambodia. It is widely believed in the Special Forces that Abrams disliked the Special Forces, and would have taken drastic action against them if Rheault had told the truth. In any case, he took drastic action upon deciding Rheault had lied. Rheault and seven of his subordinates were arrested for murder in late July. The case, however, was not tried. On instructions from President **Richard Nixon**, the CIA refused to allow its personnel to testify, on grounds that this would compromise secret intelligence operations, and it was ruled that the defendants could not be given a fair trial if they could not call CIA personnel as witnesses. The Army announced on September 29, 1969, that the charges were being dismissed.

**RIPCORD,** Fire Support Base. This base in western **Thua Thien** province was established by the U.S. 101st **Airborne Division** in April 1970, with the intent that it be used by that division and the **ARVN** 1st Division to launch attacks into the **A Shau** and Da Krong Valleys in the summer of 1970. But **PAVN** forces brought heavy pressure against it, and Ripcord was evacuated on July 23; several **artillery** pieces were abandoned in the process. Some of the worst damage to Ripcord had occurred when PAVN anti-aircraft fire hit CH-47 **helicopters**, which crashed into the base and exploded on July 18 and July 23.

**RIVER PATROL FORCE.** The U.S. **Navy**'s Task Force 116 was established on December 18, 1965, to patrol rivers and waterways in **South Vietnam**, especially in the **Mekong Delta**. It was equipped with large numbers of **PBR**s (31-foot river patrol boats). *See also* Operation *GAME WARDEN.*

**RIVERS, L[UCIUS] MENDEL** (1905–1970). U.S. Representative, Democrat of South Carolina. Born in Gumville, South Carolina, he was elected to the U.S. House of Representatives in 1940, and immediately became a member of the Naval Affairs Committee, which was later merged into the Armed Services Committee. He was chairman of the Armed Services Committee from 1965 until his death in 1970. He supported a strong military, and championed higher pay for the military. He was a strong opponent of civil rights for blacks.

Rivers endorsed the **domino theory** and urged that the Vietnam War be fought through to victory. In 1965, he said the conduct of the war should be left to the military, with less interference from civilians such as Secretary of Defense **Robert McNamara**, and said it was "folly" for the United States not to be bombing targets in the cities of **Hanoi** and **Haiphong**. He urged strong measures against war protesters, whom he called "traitors," and against draft resisters.

When he got a letter from a soldier informing him of the **My Lai**

**Massacre**, he asked the **Army** to investigate, but he later criticized the Army's effort to prosecute those involved. He headed a brief investigation by a subcommittee of the Armed Services Committee, and then announced he had found "no evidence sufficient to convict anyone of any massacres." Asked whether he was whitewashing what had happened, he said "I am not in that business, but neither am I in the business of trying to cater to some people who want to gut the military and destroy it during this time when we should be backing them up." (*The New York Times*, December 13, 1969.) He assigned **F. Edward Hébert** to head a further investigation by a smaller special subcommittee; Hébert was not as opposed as Rivers was to any prosecutions in the case, but he did seriously impede the prosecution of at least one defendant. Rivers also had been influential in the decision not to bring **Special Forces** Colonel **Robert Rheault** to trial in another murder case.

When **Richard Nixon**'s administration in 1969 began Operation *Menu*, the secret bombing of **Cambodia**, Rivers was one of the few members of **Congress**, expected to approve of the operation, who were briefed about it.

**ROADRUNNERS.** Small **reconnaissance** teams, typically made up of four men each, all indigenous (usually **Montagnards**), used to conduct reconnaissance along Communist trail networks. They were under the operational control of U.S. Army **Special Forces** through Projects *Delta*, *Omega*, and *Sigma*.

The term "Roadrunner" was also used for heavily armed U.S. task forces sent along roads to prove that U.S. forces were capable of travelling on those roads, regardless of enemy effort to block them.

**ROCKET RIDGE.** A series of ridges west of, and parallel to, the section of **Route 14** that runs north from **Kontum** to **Dak To**. The United States built a string of firebases along the ridge line, at which the Communists fired large numbers of 122-mm **rockets**; this led to the name. By 1972, the firebases had been handed over to the **ARVN**. **PAVN** attacks against Rocket Ridge as part of the **Easter Offensive** began in late March 1972.

**ROCKETS.** U.S. **helicopter gunships** and a variety of fixed-wing aircraft carried pods of Folding-Fin Aerial Rockets, 2.75 inches in diameter, for use against ground targets. Fixed-wing aircraft sometimes carried the 5-inch diameter Zuni rocket. These were not guided after being fired; they were simply supposed to fly in a straight line. Statistics on the total number used in the war are not available, but

U.S. aircraft fired millions of 2.75-inch rockets, and tens of thousands of Zunis.

Communist forces used several models of ground-to-ground rockets in **South Vietnam** and **Cambodia**. These were not nearly as accurate as **mortars**, but had a much longer range; they were the best long-range weapons available to Communist forces in the areas where they did not have proper field **artillery** (most of South Vietnam up to about 1972). The rockets could be fired from a comparatively light launch tube, or even fired without a launch tube with a lesser degree of accuracy. The rocket could be laid on a sloping earth ramp, or its tail could rest on the ground while the front was supported at the proper angle by a framework of wooden sticks or bamboo, tied together with string (see photograph 17).

The first model used was the Soviet 140-mm rocket, 1.1 meter long, weighing 40.8 kilograms (of which 4.1 kilograms were the TNT explosive of the warhead), fired from a 10-kilogram launch tube with a range of 10,000 meters. The first use of this weapon was an attack on **Danang** Air Base on February 27, 1967. Many of the rockets malfunctioned, but 12 Americans were killed.

The Soviet 122-mm rocket was more powerful. It was 1.9 meters long, weighed 46.2 kilograms (of which 6.6 kilograms were the explosive of the warhead), and had a range of 11,000 or 12,000 meters. The launch tube was comparatively heavy, 54.9 kilograms including a tripod. The first known use was on March 6, 1967, against Camp Carroll in northern **Quang Tri**, but U.S. forces did not recognize the long-range capabilities of the weapon until a massive attack on Danang Air Base in the early morning hours of July 15, 1967, in which about 50 rockets killed eight Americans and wounded 176, destroyed 10 aircraft and damaged 40, and destroyed 13 barracks and a bomb dump. For years thereafter, it was the 122-mm rocket's range that determined the areas where U.S. forces conducted systematic air and ground patrolling, trying to spot rocket teams before they could set up and fire rockets at major targets. U.S. personnel referred to the "rocket belts" around Danang, **Bien Hoa**, and **Tan Son Nhut**, and the "rocket pocket" west of **Chu Lai**. From 1968 onward, rockets were sometimes fired not just at military bases, but also at the center of **Saigon**.

The Chinese 107-mm rocket was a less powerful weapon, 0.83 meters long, weighing 19 kilograms, with a range of 8,000 meters. If launch tubes were used, they tended to be multiple launchers; a two-tube launcher weighed 22.2 kilograms, and a 12-tube launcher weighed 248.8

kilograms. The first use in South Vietnam was in February 1967. Toward the end of the war the **Khmer Rouge** fired many 107-mm rockets against **Phnom Penh**. *See also* LIGHT ANTI-TANK WEAPON, MISSILES, RPG, SAGGER, SURFACE-TO-AIR MISSILE, TOW, *WILD WEASEL*.

**ROGERS, WILLIAM PIERCE** (1913–2001). Secretary of state. Born in Norfolk, New York, he graduated from Colgate University in 1934, then from Cornell Law School in 1937, and became an assistant district attorney, under Thomas E. Dewey, in New York. As a naval officer in World War II, he was aboard the aircraft carrier *Intrepid* during the invasion of Okinawa. He was a close associate of **Richard Nixon** from the late 1940s, when he encouraged Nixon to pursue accusations against Alger Hiss, onward. He served as deputy attorney general of the United States from 1953 to 1957, and attorney general from 1957 to 1961, but then left both government and politics for eight years, becoming a senior partner in a major law firm.

After Nixon was elected president in 1968, he chose Rogers as his secretary of state. Rogers had little experience in foreign affairs; the choice seems to have reflected Nixon's desire to run foreign policy from the White House, giving to his national security adviser, **Henry Kissinger**, much of the role normally performed by the secretary of state. As Kissinger later put it, Nixon excluded Rogers and the State Department "relentlessly, and at times humiliatingly, from key decisions." Rogers functioned competently as secretary of state but kept a low profile, not protesting the extent to which foreign policy decisions were being made elsewhere.

Rogers advocated improved relations with **China**, and strongly endorsed the withdrawal of U.S. troops from Vietnam and **Vietnamization** of the war there. He opposed the U.S. covert bombing of Communist bases in **Cambodia**, Operation *Menu*, which began in 1969; the **Cambodian Incursion** of 1970; and the 1971 incursion into Laos, *Lam Son 719*. He resigned in September 1973 and returned to the private practice of law. In 1986, he chaired the committee that investigated the explosion of the space shuttle *Challenger*.

**ROLLING THUNDER,** Operation. A program of sustained bombing of **North Vietnam**, authorized by President **Lyndon Johnson** on February 13, 1965, initially scheduled to begin on February 20, but twice postponed; the first air strikes were flown on March 2 against a storage facility at Xom Bang, not far north of the **Demilitarized Zone** (DMZ).

*Rolling Thunder* at first was narrowly limited both in scale and in the range of targets permitted. President Johnson feared that if pushed too far the program might trigger entry into the war by **China** or the **Soviet Union**, and to the great frustration of the **Joint Chiefs of Staff**, he increased the range of permitted targets only by small increments, watching for Chinese and Soviet reactions at each step. From 40,554 tons of **bombs** delivered in 1965, the program grew to 128,904 tons in 1966, and 246,328 tons in 1967. The modest decline to 227,331 tons for 1968 masked sharp fluctuations; tonnage dropped to low levels from January to March, shot up above 1967 levels from April to October, and fell to near zero for the months of November and December, which are not usually considered part of *Rolling Thunder* (see below). The missions were flown at first entirely by fighter-bombers, from bases in **South Vietnam** and **Thailand** and from aircraft carriers off the coast. **B-52**s began to participate in April 1966; by the time *Rolling Thunder* ended, B-52s had delivered about 10 percent of the bomb tonnage.

At first, President Johnson approved bombing only against specific targets, but by the middle of 1965 he was approving "armed reconnaissance" missions, in which aircraft were assigned to search an area and bomb targets such as trucks on the roads, wherever they found them. Armed reconnaissance occurred mainly in the southern **panhandle** of North Vietnam, stretching about 350 kilometers from the DMZ to the 20th parallel. The U.S. military at first had high hopes that bombing could cut the flow of men and supplies down the panhandle, but this failed; the North Vietnamese proved able to keep the roads open. The president kept tighter control over bombing of the northern part of North Vietnam. **Hanoi**, **Haiphong**, and the area immediately adjoining the Chinese border were the most sensitive.

Senior military officers stressed the importance of hitting fuel storage facilities in the Hanoi and Haiphong areas, to cripple the North Vietnamese transportation system. Major facilities near Hanoi and in Haiphong were hit beginning on June 29, 1966. There was little effect; the North Vietnamese dispersed their fuel so that not enough of it was in any one place for the United States to achieve crippling results by bombing. The **Doumer Bridge**, crossing the Red River near the center of Hanoi, was finally bombed for the first time in August 1967.

Bombing of the launch sites for **surface-to-air missiles** (SAMs) was not permitted until July 27, 1965. Although a minor airfield in the southern panhandle was bombed as early as April 24, 1965, the most important military air bases farther north remained off limits, to the frustration of the Joint Chiefs of Staff, until 1967. One key air base, Phuc Yen, was not bombed until October 25, 1967. By this time, President Johnson had given permission to bomb most of the targets that he had previously rejected.

*Rolling Thunder* had been interrupted by occasional **bombing halts**. The "partial bombing halt" of April to October 1968 restricted the bombing to south of the 19th parallel (see photograph 15), but during this period the quantity of bombs dropped increased to higher levels than had ever been seen before. *Rolling Thunder* is generally considered to have ended on November 1, 1968, when President Johnson halted bombing of North Vietnam, but some sources treat the occasional air strikes that occurred between then and April 1972 (*see* **protective reaction**, ***Proud Deep Alpha***) as having been part of *Rolling Thunder*.

**ROME PLOW.** A very large and powerful bulldozer, built by the Rome Caterpillar Company, of Rome, Georgia. The blade had a sharp, protruding lower edge that could cut through trees as thick as three feet in diameter. There was a spike on one side of the blade that could be used to split trees too large simply to be cut with the blade. Rome Plows were used to destroy jungle and enemy fortifications.

**ROSTOW, WALT WHITMAN** (1916–2003). Government official. Born in New York City, he graduated from Yale in 1936, went to Oxford on a Rhodes scholarship, then returned to Yale and completed his Ph.D. in 1940. He served in the Office of Strategic Services during World War II. He taught at Massachusetts Institute of Technology (MIT) from 1950 to 1960.

Rostow became a foreign policy adviser to Senator **John Kennedy** in 1958, and when Kennedy became president in 1961, Rostow became a deputy to **McGeorge Bundy**, Kennedy's special assistant for national security affairs. He was a hawk on Vietnam; as early as 1961 he was suggesting attacks against **North Vietnam**, and officials in the Kennedy administration sometimes jokingly referred to the idea of attacking the North as "Rostow's Plan Six." In October 1961, Rostow and General **Maxwell Taylor** went on a mission to **Saigon** and returned recommending that thousands of U.S. ground troops be sent to Vietnam (*see* **Taylor-Rostow Mission**).

Toward the end of 1961, Rostow was transferred to the State Department, where he became head of the Policy Planning Council; for the next several years he had little direct impact on Vietnam policy. But in 1964, he again began arguing vigorously that the United States must bring direct military pressure to bear on North Vietnam, in order to end external support for the insurgency in **South Vietnam**.

On March 31, 1966, President **Lyndon B. Johnson** (LBJ) brought Rostow back to the White House to replace Bundy as his special assistant for national security affairs. During 1966, he urged widening the bombing of North Vietnam, but during 1967 he became more willing to narrow it.

The end of Johnson's presidency in January 1969 ended Rostow's job at the White House. He was unable to return to teaching at MIT, or at a similar school in the Northeast; there was too much bitterness at such institutions over the role Rostow had played in the war. He got a job at the University of Texas. He did not, like some other top officials of the Kennedy and Johnson adminstrations, change his mind about the rightness of the war and the **domino theory**. In an oral history interview for the LBJ Presidential Library, on March 21, 1969, he said: "There's nobody in Asia who doesn't understand that if we pull out of Vietnam, we'd have to pull out of all of Asia, the place would fall."

**ROUTE 1.** The main road linking the most important cities of Vietnam and **Cambodia**. It ran from **Hanoi** south to Thanh Hoa, then along the coast of central Vietnam to Phan Thiet, turned east away from the coast through **Xuan Loc** and **Bien Hoa** to reach **Saigon**, then ran northeast through **Cu Chi** and Go Dau Ha, crossed into Cambodia, continued to **Neak Luong** where vehicles had to cross the **Mekong River** by ferry, then ran on to **Phnom Penh**.

**ROUTE 4.** The main road linking **Saigon** with the **Mekong Delta**, running from Saigon southwest to **Can Tho**, southeast to Soc Trang, and southwest again through Bac Lieu to **Ca Mau**.

**ROUTE 9.** The east-west road just south of the **Demilitarized Zone**. It ran across northern **Quang Tri** province from **Dong Ha** west to near the "Rockpile," turned south to Ca Lu, then turned west again, passing just south of **Khe Sanh**, through **Lang Vei**, across the border into **Laos**, and through **Tchepone** to Savannakhet on the **Mekong River**. PAVN forces seized Tchepone in May 1961, but did not take the sections of the road immediately adjoining the Vietnamese border until January 1968. The following month, PAVN **tanks** coming along the road attacked Lang Vei. Route 9 was the main axis of advance for **ARVN** forces in *Lam Son 719*, the 1971 incursion into Laos.

**ROUTE 13.** The road that ran north from **Saigon** through Ben Cat, Lai

Khe, An Loc, and Loc Ninh before crossing into **Cambodia**.

**ROUTE 14.** The major north-south road through the **Central Highlands** of **South Vietnam**. From Chon Thanh on **Route 13** in Binh Long province it ran northeast to **Ban Me Thuot**, then northward through **Pleiku, Kontum**, and **Dak To**, and finally turned eastward in **Quang Nam** province to meet **Route 1**, the coastal highway, not far south of **Danang**.

**ROUTE 19.** The road running from the port of **Qui Nhon**, on the coast in northern **II Corps**, westward to An Khe and **Pleiku** in the **Central Highlands**. It was a major supply route for U.S. forces in the Central Highlands. The road passes through the An Khe Pass just before reaching An Khe, and through the Mang Yang Pass about two-thirds of the way from An Khe to Pleiku.

**ROUTE PACKAGES** (Packs). During *Rolling Thunder*, the United States divided **North Vietnam** into six sections for purposes of air operations. Route Packs I, II, III, and IV covered (in that order from south to north) the southern **panhandle** of North Vietnam. Route Pack V was the Northwest, and VI was the Northeast. Route Pack VI was later subdivided into VI-A and VI-B. As of April 1966, the U.S. **Navy** was given control of air operations in Route Packs II, III, IV, and VI-B; the **Air Force** was given control of Route Packs V and VI-A; and **Military Assistance Command, Vietnam**, was given control of operations in Route Pack I.

**RPG.** A shoulder-launched anti-**tank** weapon, developed in the **Soviet Union**, to some extent inspired by the German *Panzerfaust* of World War II. The initials RPG originally stood for the Russian *Ruchnoy Protivotankovy Granatomet* (light anti-tank grenade launcher), but English-language works often treat the letters as an abbreviation for rocket-propelled grenade. The RPG-2 (which the **PAVN** called the B-40) fired a projectile weighing 1.6 or 1.8 kilograms, with an effective range of 150 meters. The RPG-7 (which the PAVN called the B-41) fired a projectile weighing 2.2 or 2.5 kilograms, with an effective range of 300 meters. These projectiles, with substantial shaped-charge warheads, could be fired from small, light launchers (weighing 2.75 kilograms for the RPG-2 and 5 or 6.4 kilograms for the RPG-7) because the warhead did not need to fit inside the 40-mm diameter launch tube. Only a shaft with fins, attached to the rear of the warhead, went inside the launch tube. The PAVN obtained RPGs from the Soviet Union and

**China** and used them frequently against vehicles, sometimes against other targets.

**RUBBER PLANTATIONS.** The French had established many rubber plantations in Vietnam during the colonial period, mostly in the area that became **III Corps** during the Vietnam War. Many of these were still in operation during the 1960s; Americans assumed, no doubt correctly, that many of the plantations were paying taxes to the **Viet Cong** as the price of being permitted to function. The most famous were the large **Michelin Rubber Plantation** about 30 kilometers east of **Tay Ninh** City, and the somewhat smaller Filhol Plantation, in **Cu Chi** District just to the northeast of the main base of the U.S. 25th Infantry **Division**. U.S. policy was to try to avoid damage to rubber plantations, and the United States paid compensation to the plantation owners for every rubber tree destroyed.

**RUNG SAT** ("Forest of Death" or "Forest of Assassins"), also known as Rung Sac. The swampy jungle area between **Saigon** and the sea. The **Long Tau River**, the channel by which ocean-going ships reach Saigon, passes through the Rung Sat. Communist forces used the Rung Sat as a place of refuge, and also attacked shipping passing through the area. In December 1962, the **Republic of Vietnam** (RVN) created the Rung Sat Special Zone (Dac Khu Rung Sat), in which a **Vietnamese Navy** officer was in charge of the war effort. The Communists did not establish their own Rung Sat Special Zone until April 1966.

The U.S. **Navy** began assisting in the struggle to keep the shipping channel open in August 1964; the first joint operation there by U.S. Navy and **Marine** forces, Operation *Jackstay*, was in March 1966. In April 1966, the 1/18 Battalion, of the 1st Infantry **Division**, became the first regular U.S. **Army** unit to enter the struggle for the Rung Sat during Operation *Lexington III*. In January 1967, units of the 9th Infantry Division replaced them. These became part of the **Mobile Riverine Force**, a cooperative effort between the U.S. Army and Navy, that began trying out its tactics in the Rung Sat in February 1967 and later applied them in other areas.

U.S. Navy **SEALs**, operating at first by themselves, later sometimes with **Provincial Reconnaissance Units**, also fought effectively in the Rung Sat.

Overall, the efforts of U.S. and RVN forces in the Rung Sat were comparatively successful. Communist forces managed to sink only one U.S. merchant ship passing through the Rung Sat, the freighter

*Baton Rouge Victory* on August 23, 1966.

**RUSK, DEAN** (1909–1994). Secretary of state. Born in Cherokee County, Georgia, he graduated from Davidson College, went to Oxford on a Rhodes scholarship, and in 1934 began teaching political science at Mills College, in California. He served in the Army during World War II. He joined the State Department in 1946, and in 1950 became assistant secretary of state for Far Eastern affairs. He was strongly anti-Communist, and particularly hostile to Mao Zedong's new government in **China**.

Rusk became president of the Rockefeller Foundation in 1952, but returned to government when President **John Kennedy** made him secretary of state in 1961; he held the office until 1969.

Rusk supported escalation of the war; he believed that what the United States was fighting in Vietnam was Chinese expansion, and that negotiations would be useless or worse until military success had given the United States a position of strength from which to negotiate. Some observers commented it was odd that the secretary of state seemed more inclined to rely on military force, and less interested in the possibility of a diplomatic solution, than the secretary of defense. When General **Earle Wheeler** proposed in February 1968 that Johnson send 206,000 more troops to Vietnam, Rusk supported the idea. He was, however, sensitive about the danger of provoking direct Chinese intervention in the war.

In 1969, after leaving the State Department, Rusk became a professor of international law at the University of Georgia.

**RUSSELL, RICHARD BREVARD** (1897–1971). U.S. senator. Born in Winder, Georgia, he was elected to the Georgia Assembly in 1921 and as governor of Georgia in 1930. He was elected to the U.S. Senate in 1932, and served there from 1933 until his death. He supported the New Deal, but after World War II generally opposed further social welfare programs. He strongly opposed efforts to extend the civil rights of blacks.

He was chairman of the Senate Armed Services Committee 1951–1953 and 1955–1969. He advocated a strong military. He was very doubtful about getting the United States heavily involved in Vietnam, but once this decision had been made, he said the war should be pushed through to victory, and in particular he repeatedly urged a considerable intensification of the bombing of **North Vietnam**.

In 1969, he stepped down from the chairmanship (while remaining an influential member) of the Armed Services Committee to become chairman of the Appropriations Committee. When **Richard Nixon** began Operation *Menu* (the secret bombing of **Cambodia**) in that year, Russell was one of the few members of the Senate, expected to approve of the operation, who were briefed about it. He also was one of the few Democratic senators who supported the **Cambodian Incursion** of 1970.

## - S -

**SAGGER MISSILE** (AT3). This wire-guided anti-**tank rocket**, made in the **Soviet Union**, was effective in destroying tanks, but its flight was slow enough to allow the possibility that counterfire directed at the point from which it had been fired could injure or startle the person operating the guidance mechanism, and thus prevent the missile from being steered all the way to the target. The Sagger was introduced into combat in **South Vietnam** at widely separated locations on April 23, 1972, during the **Easter Offensive**, and came as a severe shock to the **ARVN**. West of **Dong Ha** in **Quang Tri** province, Saggers destroyed eight ARVN vehicles that day. At Tan Canh, the headquarters of the ARVN 22d Division in the **Central Highlands**, they knocked out seven tanks and the division command bunker, clearing the way for the **PAVN** to overrun Tan Canh the following morning.

**SAIGON.** Capital of the **Republic of Vietnam** (RVN), on the Saigon River slightly more than 40 kilometers from the sea. Saigon is a major seaport; the river is deep enough to allow ocean-going vessels of substantial size to dock there. Before the war, Saigon had been an attractive city of moderate size. During the war, the population ballooned, some people driven in from the countryside by the war, others attracted by the economic opportunities offered by American spending in Saigon. There were about 1.4 million people in "greater metropolitan Saigon" in 1962; there were 3.5 to 4 million by 1968. **Cholon**, where the ethnic Chinese were concentrated, was on the south side of the city; **Tan Son Nhut** Air Base, which housed **Military Assistance Command, Vietnam**, from 1967 onward, was on the northwest side.

The **Viet Cong** made occasional attacks on targets in Saigon early in the war, the most spectacular being the sinking of the small aircraft carrier *Card* while the ship was docked in Saigon in 1964, delivering a shipment of aircraft. The first large-scale Communist attack on Saigon was in the **Tet Offensive** of 1968. Sporadic **rocket** fire against the city began not long afterward.

In April 1975, during the **final collapse** of the RVN, it became apparent that Saigon would fall to the approaching Communist forces. The final **helicopter** evacuation of Americans and some Vietnamese from Saigon, Operation *Frequent Wind*, began on April 29, after **PAVN** rocket and **artillery** fire had closed **Tan Son Nhut** Airport to fixed-wing aircraft. *Frequent Wind* was terminated early on April 30, and PAVN forces entered the city without resistance later that morning. The new rulers promptly renamed Saigon **Ho Chi Minh City**. There were not the mass executions that many had feared, but RVN government officials and military personnel were taken to re-education camps.

**SALISBURY, HARRISON EVANS** (1908–1993). Journalist. Born in Minneapolis, Minnesota, he attended the University of Minnesota. He was a reporter for United Press from 1930 to 1948. He joined *The New York Times* in 1949, and won the Pulitzer Prize in 1955 for the reporting he had done while *The New York Times'* bureau chief in Moscow from 1949 to 1954. He was assistant managing editor of *The New York Times* from 1964 to 1972.

During 1966, Salisbury tried repeatedly to get permission to go to **North Vietnam**. The **Democratic Republic of Vietnam** finally gave him permission in December; he arrived in North Vietnam on December 23 and stayed into January 1967. Most of his time was spent in **Hanoi**, which had begun to be hit, though not heavily, by U.S. bombing under Operation *Rolling Thunder*. He made one trip south as far as Nam Dinh, which had been more heavily bombed than Hanoi, but did not visit the most heavily bombed towns still farther to the south. The articles he wrote, which were published in *The New York Times* beginning on December 25, 1966, said that the U.S. bombing was not achieving its goal of blocking the movement of military supplies in North Vietnam, but was hitting many civilians in its unsuccessful effort to block the movement of supplies.

These articles provoked an immediate storm of controversy, which has never completely ended. Salisbury's detractors said he was serving as a mouthpiece for Communist propaganda. They said that in an extreme case, Salisbury's discussion of a U.S. bombing raid that had occurred in Nam Dinh during the previous April was not as he claimed based on what he was told when he visited Nam Dinh, but simply cribbed from a Communist propaganda pamphlet.

Salisbury's defenders have pointed out that Salisbury's article differed from the pamphlet not only in language but in its facts, enough to make the charge that the article had been copied from the pamphlet blatantly absurd. More generally, Salisbury's defenders say that his descriptions of the effects of the bombing appear in retrospect to have been quite accurate—far more accurate than most of the descriptions that had appeared in the American press during the preceding months, which were based primarily on statements by U.S. military officers.

The Pulitzer Prize jury voted to give Salisbury a Pulitzer Prize for his reporting from Hanoi, but the Pulitzer Prize advisory board overruled the jury by a 5-4 vote.

**SAM NEUA.** Name both of a province (also known as Houaphan) in northeastern **Laos**, bordering on **North Vietnam**, and of the province capital. Sam Neua was temporarily assigned to the **Pathet Lao** (the Laotian Communist movment) under the **Geneva Accords of 1954**. It was reintegrated with the rest of Laos in 1958, but following the outbreak of warfare in 1959, much of the province once again came under Pathet Lao control. During the Second Indochina War, the headquarters of the **Pathet Lao** was at Vieng Say, in Sam Neua province. The karst terrain provided numerous caves, which were useful for protection against air attack.

**SANCTUARIES.** From 1961 onward, support from **North Vietnam** for the Communist forces in the South came through **Laos** along the **Ho Chi Minh Trail**. This was later supplemented by the **Sihanouk Trail** across **Cambodia**. **Viet Cong** and **PAVN** forces used bases in Laos and Cambodia to support their activities in **South Vietnam**. But **Lyndon Johnson**, wanting to limit the spread of the war into Laos and Cambodia, restricted U.S. military action against these bases, which therefore came to be called Communist "sanctuaries." This outraged many in the U.S. military. Their frustration was increased by public statements of U.S. policy that pretended the restrictions were tighter than they really were.

The publicly stated policy was that the U.S. military was permitted to hit Communist units in Cambodia only if those units had fired across the border at U.S. forces in Vietnam. There were hardly any announced cases of this during the Johnson administration. Actual policy allowed covert missions into Cambodia from 1967 onward (*see **Daniel Boone***), but these were very small and very secret.

The publicly announced policy of respect for Laotian neutrality hid covert operations on the ground there that were kept relatively small (*see* Operations ***Prairie Fire***, ***Shining Brass***), though not as small as those in Cambodia. But U.S. bombing of the "sanctuaries" in Laos was persistent, very heavy, and not in any genuine sense secret.

By the time **Richard Nixon** became president in 1969, the Communist bases in Cambodia were becoming larger and more important to the Communist war effort. U.S. bombing and shelling of Communist units in Cambodia that had fired across the border into South Vietnam became somewhat more common; there were five announced cases between July 1969 and March 1970. Much more important was a substantial secret bombing campaign, Operation *Menu*, begun in March 1969. Finally, on April 30, 1970, President Nixon announced the **Cambodian Incursion**. U.S. troops fought Communist forces in Cambodia for the next two months, and **ARVN** troops did so for several years. But the only large-scale incursion of ground forces from South Vietnam into Laos, *Lam Son 719* in 1971, was relatively brief and was an ARVN operation without U.S. participation on the ground.

North Vietnam is also often described as having been a sanctuary for PAVN forces. North Vietnam was free of significant ground attack throughout the war. Large-scale bombing and shelling of North Vietnam occurred only from 1965 to 1968, and 1972 to early 1973.

**SAPPERS.** In normal military terminology a "sapper" is a military engineer, but in the Vietnam War the term was applied to the special task (*dac cong*) units of the **PAVN** and the **Viet Cong**. Sapper units sometimes led the way in large-scale night attacks on U.S. units; the most skilled of them had an impressive ability to worm their way in complete silence through barbed wire entanglements. Some sappers worked underwater, placing explosive devices against the sides of American ships in various harbors. Their most famous success was the sinking of the small U.S. aircraft carrier *Card* on May 2, 1964; the ship had docked in **Saigon** to deliver a shipment of aircraft.

*SEA DRAGON*, Operation. Attacks by U.S. (or sometimes Australian) naval gunfire against targets along the coast of **North Vietnam**, begun on October 25, 1966. At first the operation was limited to a short stretch of coast immediately north of the 17th parallel, and the targets were mainly boats along the coast; the only targets on land that could be hit were coastal **artillery** batteries and **radar** stations that threatened the *Sea Dragon* vessels. The area was extended north to the 18th parallel almost immediately. The area was extended to the 20th parallel, and attacks on a variety of land targets including trucks on the coastal roads were authorized, on February 27, 1967. The limit was moved southward again to the 19th parallel in April 1968, and *Sea Dragon* was terminated at the end of October. *See also* NAVAL GUNFIRE SUPPORT.

**SEA SWALLOWS.** Father Yuan Lo Wha, a Catholic priest from **China**, usually referred to in Vietnam as Nguyen Lac Hoa, Nguyen Loc Hoa, or just "Father Hoa," became commander of a significant paramilitary force in the southernmost part of the **Mekong Delta** around the time the Vietnam War was beginning. He had been a priest in South China in the 1930s, had joined the armed forces of the **Republic of China** (ROC) in 1939, and is said to have risen to the rank of lieutenant colonel before returning to the priesthood around 1949. Following the Communist victory of 1949 in China, he got several hundred of his parishioners out of China to Vietnam and then to **Cambodia**. In 1959, he brought his followers to Binh Hung, in the **Ca Mau** Peninsula, the southernmost tip of **South Vietnam**. He soon established a paramilitary force called the Sea Swallows, conspicuously effective against the **Viet Cong** in the area; arms and supplies were provided both by the **Republic of Vietnam** and by the U.S. **Central Intelligence Agency**. By late 1962, the United States estimated his force at 1,560 men. The Sea Swallows expanded through recruiting within Vietnam and also through the arrival of a significant number of ROC troops sent from Taiwan to reinforce Father Hoa.

**SEAL** (Sea, Air, Land) Teams, U.S. **Navy**. An elite force for special operations, established as a result of President **John Kennedy**'s enthusiasm for unconventional warfare. SEAL Team 1 was formally established on the West Coast of the United States, and SEAL Team 2 on the East Coast, on January 1, 1962; they were derived from the previously existing Underwater Demolition Teams (UDT). Men from both Team 1 and Team 2 participated in the Vietnam War.

The SEALs combined the scuba training of the Underwater Demolition Teams with great expertise at stealthy movement, and combat, on land. They usually operated in or near the water, but could be assigned a wide variety of missions: locating and destroying enemy ammunition stockpiles, rescuing a pilot who had been shot down in an area where Communist forces were so strong that it was not possible simply to pick the pilot up by **helicopter**, abducting Communist officers or officials for interrogation, and so forth. Study of this subject is complicated by the substantial numbers of men who have falsely claimed to have served as SEALs in Vietnam, and have invented sometimes extravagant stories of their exploits. The greatest concentrations of SEAL operations were in the **Rung Sat** and the **Mekong Delta**, and these are the areas for which the most complete and reliable information is available.

In 1962, SEALs were sent to **Danang**, where for the next several years they trained various Asians, not only Vietnamese belonging to the **Lien Doi Nguoi Nhai** (LDNN, the Vietnamese equivalent of the SEALs) but also **Nung** and others, for **Central Intelligence Agency** (CIA) covert operations against **North Vietnam**. This program became part of *OPLAN 34A* in 1964, and control of it was transferred from the CIA to **SOG** at that time. SEALs were also assigned to train and lead **Provincial Reconnaissance Units** (PRUs), which played an important role in the *Phoenix* **Program**, in the later stages of the war.

*SEALORDS* (Southeast Asia Lake, Ocean, River, and Delta Strategy). A program initiated in October 1968, designed to establish control of waterways along the border between **South Vietnam** and **Cambodia**, from the Gulf of Siam to **Tay Ninh** province. It was designed to cut supply lines by which Communist forces in South Vietnam were supported from Cambodia; there were canals running parallel to the border for much of its length. Patrols by boats and aircraft (both **helicopters** and heavily armed **OV-10 Bronco** twin-engine propeller planes) were supplemented in some areas by the planting of electronic **sensors**. Operations *Market Time* and *Game Warden*, and the Riverine Assault Force (the Navy component of the **Mobile Riverine Force**), were cut back so forces could be transferred to *SEALORDS*.

During 1969, *SEALORDS* was expanded to waterways not close to the Cambodian border: in broader areas of the **Mekong Delta**, in sections of **III Corps** north of **Saigon**, and in **Quang Nam** province in **I Corps**.

**SEARCH AND RESCUE** (SAR). Rescue of personnel from downed aircraft. Almost always **helicopters** made the actual pickup of the downed personnel. Early in 1965, SAR for pilots shot down in **Laos** was performed by U.S. **Air Force** HH-43B Husky helicopters based at Nakhon Phanom in **Thailand** (handicapped by their small size and short range, though the range could be extended by carrying extra fuel in 55-gallon drums in the cabin) and by larger H-34 Choctaw helicopters flown by **Air America**, the proprietary airline controlled by the **Central Intelligence Agency**. Before the end of the year, two versions of the H-3—

first the CH-3C, and later the HH-3E that was to become famous as the "Jolly Green Giant"—were available to perform SAR for pilots shot down over Laos and some parts of **North Vietnam**. In 1967, the much larger HH-53B, which eventually came to be called the "Super Jolly Green Giant," began to become available.

Fixed-wing aircraft tried to keep enemy ground forces away while the helicopters were attempting to pick up the downed personnel. A-1 **Skyraiders** were the best in this role, since their fuel endurance enabled them to remain for hours in an area where a pilot had gone down, but other aircraft might assist if available.

Overall coordination for the rescue mission might be provided by an HU-16 Albatross amphibious plane, or an SC-54 (later called HC-54) Rescuemaster in the earliest part of the war, or by an HC-130 Hercules, equipped to provide air-to-air refueling for some helicopters, after about the beginning of 1966.

**SECTS.** The **Hoa Hao** and **Cao Dai** religious sects, and the **Binh Xuyen** gangster organization, were collectively known as "the sects." They had substantial armed forces, most of which were allied with the French in 1954.

**Ngo Dinh Diem**'s efforts to centralize power in **South Vietnam** threatened the power and autonomy of the sects. By March 1955, it was plain that this was leading toward a crisis, and it was not obvious that Diem had the power to defeat the sects; their armed strength was considerable, and the Binh Xuyen controlled the **Saigon** police force. On March 29, Diem fired the chief of the National **Police**, a Binh Xuyen leader named Lai Van Sang. That night, Binh Xuyen troops attacked forces of the **Vietnamese National Army** at several locations in the city, and shelled the Presidential Palace. The following day, the French, who still had substantial military forces in the area, imposed a truce.

From April 28 to May 2, Diem's forces fought and decisively defeated the Binh Xuyen in the Saigon area. This gave Diem an advantage that he pressed vigorously during the following months in operations against the remaining dissident sect units. The Hoa Hao maintained a serious resistance to Diem's forces the longest. Hoa Hao General Tran Van Soai finally rallied to the government on February 12, 1956. Hoa Hao General Ba Cut was captured by government forces on April 13, and was executed in July.

The Communists did not intervene when Diem made his move against the sects in the spring of 1955. In October, by which time Binh Xuyen and Cao Dai resistance to Diem had almost ceased and the Hoa Hao had been seriously weakened, the **Lao Dong Party** Central Committee issued a directive to Communists in the South stating that the sects, like the Dai Viet Party in **Quang Tri** province and the Viet Nam Quoc Dan Dang in **Quang Nam** province, were resisting Diem, but were doing so strictly in their own interests; in the past they had been strongly anti-Communist. The Communists should try to win over the rank-and-file of such organizations on the basis of common hostility to Diem, and perhaps to some extent their middle-level leadership, but should make no effort to win over their top leaders. It is likely that all of the Binh Xuyen and Cao Dai units that had not surrendered to Diem or been destroyed came under Communist control. Some Hoa Hao units that refused to join with the Communists managed to survive until the early 1960s.

Personnel from the sects made up a substantial fraction of **Viet Cong** military strength up to 1963, but their alliance with the Communists had been based more on shared hostility to Diem than on genuine compatibility. Many of them, especially the Hoa Hao, left the Viet Cong after Diem's death. The Hoa Hao areas in particular soon became anti-Communist bastions.

**SEDANG.** A **Montagnard** group, speaking a language of the Mon-Khmer group, living mostly in the area northwest of the town of **Kontum**. The **Cor** and **Hre** are sometimes considered subgroups of the Sedang. The Sedang appear to have been more under Communist influence than most Montagnards at the time the Vietnam War began.

**SELECTIVE SERVICE SYSTEM.** The United States had had a system of military conscription during the years before the Vietnam War began, but the number of conscripts needed each year, to maintain the military at peacetime levels, had been small enough so that the Selective Service System had the luxury not only of exempting from military service those considered physically or mentally unfit, but also encouraging young men to devote themselves to activities the government approved of, such as college study or work in certain occupations, by rewarding them with deferment or exemption from conscription. This was called "manpower channeling."

Each community had a draft board made up of local citizens. Administration by local boards led to variations in the way the rules set by the Selective Service System were applied in practice. Some draft boards punished troublemakers, including anti-war protesters and men with criminal records, by drafting them; others deliberately avoided drafting such people, believing they would make poor soldiers. Some draft boards were far more willing to defer students with poor academic records or those with minor medical conditions, or to grant conscientious objector status, than others. Some found excuses to defer the sons of people influential in their communities.

| Fiscal Year | Inductions during Fiscal Year | Active-Duty Personnel at End of Fiscal Year |
| --- | --- | --- |
| 1960 | 90,549 | 2,476,435 |
| 1961 | 61,070 | 2,483,771 |
| 1962 | 157,465 | 2,807,819 |
| 1963 | 71,744 | 2,697,689 |
| 1964 | 150,808 | 2,685,161 |
| 1965 | 103,328 | 2,653,142 |
| 1966 | 343,481 | 3,092,000 |
| 1967 | 298,559 | 3,377,000 |
| 1968 | 341,404 | 3,547,000 |
| 1969 | 262,646 | 3,459,432 |
| 1970 | 203,707 | 3,066,000 |
| 1971 | 153,631 | 2,715,000 |
| 1972 | 25,273 | 2,323,000 |
| 1973 | 35,527 | 2,253,000 |

During fiscal years 1960 to 1964, the average number of men inducted into the armed forces had been about 106,000 per year. During fiscal year 1965 (July 1964 through June 1965), despite the growing prospect of a serious U.S. involvement in Vietnam, the number of inductions was slightly below this average; the U.S. military was not expanding but shrinking slightly. **Marine** battalions were landed at **Danang** in March 1965; not until September 1965 did the number of men drafted rise above the levels of the early 1960s.

During fiscal years 1966, 1967, and 1968, the armed forces expanded substantially. Large numbers of men were drafted in order to accomplish this expansion, but the loopholes that allowed many young men to avoid military service remained open. Rather than draft large numbers of college students, the government decided late in 1966 to lower its standards, and begin taking into the military 100,000 men per year (some by enlistment, others by induction) who would previously have been considered unsuitable for military service because of low education, low intelligence, or physical unfitness. This "Project 100,000" became a source of considerable controversy. In 1967 and 1968, the government cut back on draft deferments for graduate students.

A draft lottery system was announced in 1969: a random drawing of birthdays was made a major factor in deciding which young men were to be drafted. The first drawing, held on December 1, 1969, determined the lottery numbers of all young men who had been born between 1944 and 1950. All the days of the year were assigned numbers, from 1 to 366, on the basis of the order in which they had been drawn from a large barrel. Draft boards were instructed to choose, from among the men eligible for the draft, first those with birthday number 1, then those with birthday number 2, and so on. How far along the sequence the draft board got before filling its quota varied from one community to another. Nobody with a birthday number above 195 was drafted. Those with numbers below 100 were seriously at risk in almost any community.

The lottery numbers for men born during 1951 were determined by a drawing held on July 1, 1970; the drawing for men born during 1952 was held on August 4, 1971.

In each year beginning with 1970, there was a "pool" of men who were eligible to be drafted that year. If a man did not get a deferment, he would be in the pool for the year during which he had his 20th birthday. The men who were in the pool for each year would be subject to being drafted during that year and perhaps during the first three months of the following year, but if they were not drafted by March 31 of the following year, they were permanently safe; they could not be put into the pool for any later year. A man who got a deferment (to go to college, for example) would be a member of the pool for the year in which he graduated, or otherwise lost his deferment.

It was not necessary to have spent a whole year in the pool, only the last part of it. A man who lost or renounced his deferment even in December of a given year became a member of the pool for that year, and was eligible for induction only through March of the following year.

What had much more impact than any changes in the way young men were chosen for the draft was the shrinking total number of inductions. President **Richard Nixon** was not only pulling U.S. military personnel out of Vietnam, but reducing the overall size of the U.S. Armed

Forces, to such an extent that after the middle of 1971 there was hardly any need for a draft. Only 10,640 men were drafted in the second half of 1971. Nobody at all was drafted in the first quarter of 1972, and only 14,633 in the second quarter. Even of this small number of draftees, furthermore, hardly any were sent to Vietnam; in late June 1972, it was estimated that out of the approximately 50,000 U.S. military personnel in Vietnam, less than a tenth—about 4,000—were draftees. The announcement on June 28, 1972, that draftees would no longer be sent to Vietnam (unless they volunteered to go) thus came as an anticlimax.

The draft lottery had been a response to perceptions that the draft had been falling primarily on those who did not have the wealth or education to avoid it. Some of the loopholes that had formerly allowed young men to avoid the draft were eliminated or seriously narrowed, but not all were closed. Having a good lawyer or a good draft counselor still greatly improved a man's chances of attaining conscientious objector status, being found unfit for medical reasons, or simply postponing induction indefinitely through a series of appeals. When the lottery system was first introduced, students could still get deferments for four years of college.

A revision of the Selective Service law that went into effect in December 1971 was aimed at eliminating college student deferments, but it was implemented in a way that undermined this purpose; it led to the drafting of hardly any students.

The last regular inductions, of men taken from the pool, occurred on December 29, 1972, but there were a few hundred inductions of a nonstandard sort during the first half of 1973. The men involved had violated the Selective Service law in their efforts to avoid induction in previous years, and were still subject to prosecution for their past violations; they agreed to accept induction in lieu of prosecution. No inductions of any sort occurred after June 1973.

There were very few draftees among the first U.S. units sent to Vietnam. Less than 1 percent of the Americans killed in action (KIA) from 1961 to 1964 were draftees, and only 16 percent in 1965. The proportion rose to a peak of 43 percent in 1970, then dropped back to 6 percent in 1972. The average for the whole war was 34 percent.

Draftees served mostly as Army enlisted men, though about 44,000 served in the Marines, about 3,000 served in the **Navy**, and a tiny number were promoted and became officers. Draftees made up 54 percent of the Army enlisted men KIA. In 1969, the peak year, 62 percent of the Army enlisted men KIA and 69 percent of the Army enlisted infantrymen KIA were draftees.

**SELF-DEFENSE CORPS** (Dan Ve). A paramilitary organization of the **Republic of Vietnam**, whose units were organized at the village level. In the late 1950s, the Self-Defense Corps was not under the Joint General Staff of the Republic of Vietnam Armed Forces, and it got little support from either the regular **ARVN** or the United States.

In 1962, the U.S. military finally began handing out large quantities of reasonably modern rifles and automatic weapons to the Self-Defense Corps. This proved a disaster; much of the Self-Defense Corps was scattered across the countryside in outposts so small that the **Viet Cong** could easily overrun them. The weapons placed in these outposts, vulnerable to capture, were a major factor in the massive expansion of Viet Cong military power that began in late 1962.

In September 1962, the Self-Defense Corps had a strength of 65,000. It was renamed the **Popular Forces** in 1964 and brought under the Joint General Staff.

**SENSORS.** The United States used a variety of devices for sensing enemy forces:

Vibration sensors could detect human footsteps and moving vehicles by picking up vibrations in the ground (*see Igloo White*).

A "people sniffer," a device capable of detecting certain strong smells, could be dangled beneath a **helicopter** flying low over the jungle, or could be planted in the jungle, reporting detections by radio like a vibration sensor.

Infrared sensors, usually carried by aircraft, could detect warm objects, such as people and the engines of vehicles, by the infrared radiation they emitted.

Starlight scopes could amplify light in the visible wavelengths; they were used both on the ground and in aircraft.

Doppler **radar** was used by ground installations for detecting enemy troops, and aboard aircraft for detecting vehicles.

**SHARP, ULYSSES S. G.** (1906–2001). Admiral. Born in Chinook, Montana, he graduated from Annapolis in 1927. He became commander of the U.S. Pacific Fleet in September 1963, and commander in chief, Pacific (CINCPAC), commanding all U.S. military forces (not just the **Navy**) in the Pacific Area in June 1964; he held this position until July 1968.

During 1964, Sharp advocated U.S. bombing of **North Vietnam**, and after that bombing began in 1965, he consistently urged that the scale be increased and the range of targets broadened. His urgent request in late February 1965 that **Marine** battalions be sent to **Danang** also helped start a major escalation of the ground war in **South Vietnam**, and he encouraged large increases in the U.S. ground troop commitment during the months that followed. For a while in 1966, Admiral Sharp supported Marine Corps generals in endorsing a strategy based more on **pacification** than on major military combat, but he did not persist in this.

After Sharp retired from the Navy in 1968, he became a consultant to an aerospace firm. He also wrote a book about the Vietnam War, *Strategy for Defeat* (1978).

**SHEEHAN, NEIL** (1936– ). Journalist. Born in Holyoke, Massachusetts, he graduated from Harvard in 1958. He was the chief **Saigon** correspondent for United Press International (UPI) from 1962 to 1964. He was one of the journalists who were pessimistic about the conduct of the war and about the government of **Ngo Dinh Diem**, defying the optimism of General **Paul Harkins** and Ambassador **Frederick Nolting**. From 1964 to 1972, he worked for *The New York Times*. When **Daniel Ellsberg** gave large portions of the **Pentagon Papers** to *The New York Times* in 1971, Sheehan was one of the people who edited the collection, and wrote articles based on it for publication in the newspaper. His biography of **John Paul Vann**, *A Bright Shining Lie* (1989), won the Pulitzer Prize and the National Book Award.

**SHEEPDIP.** When the personnel needed for certain operations in **Laos** and Vietnam (and probably other countries) were such that revelation of their identities would lead to diplomatic or political repercussions, they were sometimes provided with more innocuous, false identities. Thai military personnel who had been provided documentation identifying them as Laotians, and U.S. and Filipino military personnel who had been provided documentation identifying them as civilians, were said to have been "sheepdipped."

*SHINING BRASS*. Ground operations sent by **SOG** from **South Vietnam** into **Laos**, typically by small **reconnaissance** teams made up of Americans and **Nung** or **Montagnards**, beginning in October 1965. At first the U.S. ambassador to Laos, **William Sullivan**, imposed very tight restrictions both on the area of operations and on the use of **helicopters**. The Laotian government had not been informed of the operations and Sullivan was convinced it would disapprove of them, perhaps very strongly, if it learned of them. The area of operations was expanded in 1966, the restrictions on helicopters were eased, and the teams increasingly engaged in active harassment of enemy forces, not just unobtrusive reconnaissance, but the United States continued to conceal the program from the Laotian government. Casualties were heavy, but the value of the information produced was considerable, especially after the teams began to plant wiretaps, late in 1966, on the telephone lines that linked **PAVN** units along the **Ho Chi Minh Trail**. The name was changed from *Shining Brass* to *Prairie Fire* in March 1967.

**SHUFLY.** A U.S. **Marine Corps** medium **helicopter** squadron, and some supporting elements, were sent to **South Vietnam** in April 1962. The squadron had 24 HUS-1 Sea Horse helicopters. This was a single-engine helicopter built by Sikorsky, capable of transporting eight to 12 soldiers loaded for combat. The squadron also had three single-engine Cessna OE-1 observation aircraft, and one R4D transport aircraft. Task Unit *Shufly* was based at Soc Trang in the **Mekong Delta**, and operated in what was at that time **III Corps**. The designation *Shufly* remained constant when the original squadron left and another replaced it, in a rotation based on a policy of having helicopter crews serve only four-month tours in the war zone, presumably to give as many crews as possible the benefit of combat experience. *Shufly* moved north to **Danang**, in **I Corps**, in September 1962.

**SIHANOUK TRAIL.** An American term for the routes (in fact simply the ordinary roads of **Cambodia**) by which equipment and munitions, arriving at the port of **Sihanoukville**, were hauled across Cambodia on trucks to be delivered to **Viet Cong** and **PAVN** forces near the border of **South Vietnam**. Such shipments may have begun in 1964. Most of the areas through which they passed were under the control of the Cambodian government, not of Communist forces. The government, and individual officers of the Cambodian Army, were paid generously to allow trucks owned by private firms to haul these cargoes through their territories, or sometimes to transport the cargoes in Cambodian Army vehicles.

*Note*: a few sources also apply this term to the section of the **Ho Chi Minh Trail** that extended southward from **Laos** across the northeast part of Cambodia.

**SIHANOUKVILLE** (Kompong Som). The only deepwater seaport of **Cambodia**, located on the southwest coast. Cargoes brought to Sihanoukville by ocean-going freighters may have become a major source of military materiel for the Communist forces in **South Vietnam** as early as 1964. There was debate within the U.S. government about the extent to which Communist forces were obtaining supplies and munitions through Sihanoukville; the **Central Intelligence Agency** tended to downplay Sihanoukville. The fact that such use had occurred on a massive scale was not universally understood until 1970, by which time it had largely stopped.

**SKYRAIDER.** The Skyraider ("Spad") was a large single-engine fighter-bomber, used by the U.S. **Navy** starting shortly after World War II. It proved ideal for Vietnam. A propeller-driven aircraft, it was slower than the jets, which gave the pilot a better chance of identifying targets accurately on the ground. It carried a heavy bomb load, and could loiter in the air in the combat zone much longer than jet fighter-bombers. It served under a variety of designations: the AD-5 and A1-E (see photograph 11) were two-seat models, while the AD-6 and the A1-H were single-seaters.

The United States began giving Skyraiders to the **Vietnamese Air Force** in 1960; they were being flown by U.S. pilots over Vietnam and **Laos** by 1964.

**SOG** (initially "Special Operations Group"; name changed late in 1964 to "Studies and Observations Group" because the original name revealed too clearly the nature of the organization). A covert operations group, it was formally established on January 24, 1964. It is often called MACSOG or MACV-SOG to indicate that it was under the authority of **Military Assistance Command, Vietnam** (MACV), though in fact MACV had only partial control; SOG had a direct relationship with the **Special Assistant for Counterinsurgency and Special Activities** (SACSA) in the Pentagon. It was given control of covert operations that had formerly been controlled by the **Central Intelligence Agency** (CIA). There may have been some friction between the CIA and SOG; it is said that the CIA refused to furnish a deputy commander for SOG in 1965. The **Republic of Vietnam** established the **Special Exploitation Service** in 1964 as a counterpart to SOG; this was later renamed the Strategic Technical Service early in 1965, and the Strategic Technical Directorate (STD) late in 1967.

SOG was commanded by U.S. **Army** colonels, usually members of the **Special Forces**. Colonel Clyde Russell became the first commander of SOG on January 1964. Colonel Donald Blackburn, who had served as a leader of guerrillas in the Philippines during World War II, took over in June 1965. Colonel John Singlaub, who had been parachuted behind German lines in France in 1944 by the Office for Strategic Services, took command in April 1966. Colonel Stephen E. Cavanaugh, who had served as a paratrooper in the Pacific Theater in World War II, and had served a tour in Vietnam training **ARVN** forces in 1961, arrived in September 1968. Colonel John F. Sadler, who had served in the same paratroop unit as Cavanaugh in World War II, and had served in **Laos** with *White Star*, became the last commander of SOG in December 1970.

SOG ran covert operations against **North Vietnam** (*see Footboy, Forae, OPLAN 34A, Plowman, STRATA, Timberwork*), Laos (*see* **Hatchet Teams**, *Prairie Fire*, *Shining Brass*, **Spike Teams**), and **Cambodia** (*see Daniel Boone*).

SOG headquarters was in **Saigon**, but the organization used bases scattered throughout **South Vietnam** and, from 1966 onward, at Nakhon Phanom in **Thailand**. There was a major training center at Camp **Long Thanh** in **Bien Hoa** province. From 1968 onward, there were three sub-headquarters: Command and Control, North (CCN), at **Danang**, Command and Control, Central (CCC), at **Kontum**, and Command and Control, South (CCS), at **Ban Me Thuot**.

When SOG was formally disbanded in 1972, some of its functions were taken over by the "STD Advisory Team 158," and others were transferred to Thailand.

**SON NGOC THANH** (1908–1977). Son of a **Khmer** father and a Sino-Vietnamese mother, he was born in Tra Vinh Province of **South Vietnam**. Thanh's parents were prosperous landowners, and were able to send him to school in France. He returned to Vietnam in 1933, and obtained a job in the colonial civil service. Soon afterward he moved to **Phnom Penh**, where he became secretary of the Buddhist Institute and also worked for a newspaper. In May 1945 he became King **Norodom Sihanouk**'s minister of foreign affairs, and then in August became prime minister. The French arrested him on October 15, as a first step in re-establishing their control of **Cambodia**.

Sihanouk persuaded the French to allow Thanh to return to Cambodia in October 1951; he received a huge public welcome. But in March 1952, he went into the jungle and joined a guerrilla group with support from **Thailand**. In September 1954, Thanh offered to rally to Sihanouk's government, but was rebuffed. He withdrew to the vicinity of the Cambodian-Thai border, where by 1955 he had about 2,000 men calling themselves **Khmer Serei** (Free Khmer), supported by Thailand and the **Republic of Vietnam** (RVN).

In the 1960s, Thanh cooperated with the RVN and the U.S. **Central**

**Intelligence Agency** in recruiting **Khmer Krom** (ethnic Khmer in South Vietnam) to fight in the Vietnam War, mostly in the **Civilian Irregular Defense Groups** (CIDG). Around 1969, Thanh had a rapprochement with Sihanouk; he sent several hundred of his Khmer Serei troops back to Cambodia, where Sihanouk hoped to use them to bring pressure against the Vietnamese Communist forces there. After Sihanouk's overthrow in 1970, Thanh himself returned to Cambodia. For a few months in 1972, he held the impressive-sounding position of "first minister" in **Lon Nol**'s government, but had little actual power. He then retired and returned to South Vietnam.

**SON TAY.** The town of Son Tay, capital of Son Tay province, was about 40 kilometers northwest of **Hanoi**. A prison near the town, which had housed American **prisoners of war**, was the target of a rescue mission, Operation *Kingpin,* in the early morning hours of November 21, 1970. The rescue force commanded by **Special Forces** Colonel Arthur "Bull" Simons took the prison, but found no prisoners there.

**SOUPHANOUVONG** (Suphanuvong), Prince (1909–1995). Born in Luang Prabang, **Laos**, younger half-brother of **Souvanna Phouma**, he studied civil engineering in Paris, and from 1938 to 1945 worked as an engineer for the French colonial administration in central Vietnam and in Laos. In 1945, Souphanouvong went to **Hanoi**, where he reached an agreement with the Communist leaders of the newly proclaimed **Democratic Republic of Vietnam**. He then went to Laos, where he became one of the leaders of the Lao Issara resistance against the French, at first in Laos, later in exile in **Thailand**. Most of the Lao Issara leaders became uneasy about their alliance with the Viet Minh, and switched sides to ally with the French in 1949. Souphanouvong remained closely allied with the Viet Minh, and emerged as one of the top leaders of the **Pathet Lao**, the Laotian Communist movement, in the late stages of the First Indochina War. In 1955, he was one of the founders of the Lao People's Party, which from that point onward was the guiding core of the Pathet Lao.

In 1957, Souphanouvong represented the Pathet Lao in the negotiations that brought them into the First Coalition Government. He himself became minister of planning, reconstruction, and town planning, and performed capably in that office. He became very popular in Vientiane, the capital of Laos, and was elected to the National Assembly in 1958 as a representative of Vientiane. When the Pathet Lao refused to accept integration of their armed forces into the Royal Lao

Army in 1959, Souphanouvong and the other Pathet Lao leaders who were in Vientiane as members of the coalition government were arrested. They escaped in May 1960.

Souphanouvong helped to negotiate the creation of the Second Coalition Government, one of the cornerstones of the **Geneva Accords of 1962**, and he returned to Vientiane to become deputy prime minister and minister of economy and planning. This second coalition was much less successful than the first; Souphanouvong and the other Pathet Lao representatives left for **Sam Neua**, the Pathet Lao base in the Northeast, in April 1963.

Souphanouvong remained the nominal leader of the Pathet Lao (in reality he seems to have been number three) through the end of the Second Indochina War. In 1972 and 1973, he helped to negotiate the Third Coalition Government, and there was little fighting in Laos after it took office in April 1974. The Pathet Lao seized power in the second half of 1975, and in December 1975, Souphanouvong officially became president of the Lao People's Democratic Republic. He ceased to perform the duties of this office due to ill health in 1986, but did not formally resign until 1991.

**SOUTH VIETNAM.** The southern of the two halves into which Vietnam was divided after the **Geneva Accords of 1954**; it was ruled by the **Republic of Vietnam** from 1955 to 1975. It had an area of 173,809 square kilometers (67,108 square miles). Its population was estimated at 17 million in 1966.

*Note:* the term "South Vietnam" is also used by some authors, especially Vietnamese, to refer to **Nam Bo** (Nam Ky, Cochinchina), the southernmost of the three sections into which Vietnam had been divided during the French colonial period.

**SOUTHEAST ASIA TREATY ORGANIZATION** (SEATO). Military alliance established by the Southeast Asia Mutual Defense Treaty, sometimes known as the Manila Pact, signed in Manila on September 8, 1954. The members were **Australia, France, Great Britain, New Zealand**, Pakistan, the **Philippines, Thailand**, and the United States. **Cambodia, Laos**, and the **Republic of Vietnam** did not sign the treaty, but were designated as "protocol states," to be protected by SEATO as if they were members.

SEATO was never a strong organization; not all its members were really convinced Southeast Asia was vital to their security. The treaty did not clearly commit them to *fight* if a member or protocol state were the victim of aggression, only to act to meet the common danger in accordance with their constitutional processes, which meant in effect that they would fight only if their respective parliaments or equivalent bodies felt that fighting was a good idea. In the 1960s, the United States was able to persuade some of the members of SEATO to participate in the Vietnam War, but not all of them, and SEATO as an organization did not play a significant role in the war.

**SOUVANNA PHOUMA** (Suvanna Phuma), Prince (1901–1984). Born in Luang Prabang, **Laos**, he studied engineering in France, then returned to Laos, and worked from 1940 to 1945 as an engineer for the Department of Public Works of the colonial government. At the end of World War II, he supported the effort of the Lao Issara to prevent a return of French colonial control. In 1949, along with most other Lao Issara leaders, he reached an accommodation with France. He became minister of public works in the Royal Lao Government, still at that time controlled by the French. In November 1951, he became prime minister; in October 1953, he reached an agreement with France under which Laos obtained a much greater degree of independence than before. He was forced from office in October 1954 by rightists who opposed his policy of making Laos neutral in the Cold War.

For the next 20 years, there were three main power blocks in Laotian politics—the rightists, the neutralists, and the **Pathet Lao** (Laotian Communist movement). Souvanna Phouma was leader of the neutralists, though at times forced by circumstances to ally himself with either the Pathet Lao or the rightists.

Souvanna became prime minister again in March 1956. In August, he reached an agreement to form the First Coalition Government, including rightists, neutralists, and the Pathet Lao. Opposition by the rightists and the United States delayed implementation until late 1957, and in 1958 the United States cut off aid to Laos, which forced Souvanna to resign as prime minister in July, allowing the rightist Phoui Sananikone to take power. Souvanna became ambassador to France. War between the rightists and the Pathet Lao began in 1959.

In August 1960, a military **coup** led by **Kong Le** made Souvanna prime minister once again, but in December, troops of the rightist general **Phoumi Nosavan** moving up from the South took the capital, Vientiane. The neutralist forces of Souvanna Phouma and Kong Le retreated eastward from Vientiane to the **Plain of Jars**, where they allied with the Pathet Lao and the **Democratic Republic of Vietnam**

(DRV) and soon were getting a modest quantity of Soviet military aid.

Peace negotiations in Geneva, Switzerland, began in mid-1961. Souvanna Phouma became prime minister of the Second Coalition Government in June 1962, and his position was given international endorsement by the **Geneva Accords** of July 23, 1962. These agreements allowed Souvanna to shift back to a neutral posture, ending his alliance with the Communists. Within months, he was shifting farther; he remained in theory a "neutralist" prime minister, but became de facto an ally of the rightists and the United States against the Pathet Lao and the DRV. He still tried, however, to limit escalation of the war in Laos.

After American participation in the war had ended, Souvanna in April 1974 once again brought Pathet Lao representatives into his cabinet in the Third Coalition Government. The Pathet Lao seizure of full power in Laos in August 1975 was essentially bloodless. Souvanna remained nominally prime minister until December, and even after that remained in Laos; he was given the title of supreme adviser to the Pathet Lao government.

**SOVIET UNION** (Union of Soviet Socialist Republics, USSR). In the early years of the world Communist movement, the Soviet Union was its inspiration and headquarters, and exercised a great deal of control over Communist parties in other countries. **Ho Chi Minh**, for example, had instructions and funds from the Soviet Union when he began to lay the groundwork, in 1925, for the establishment of a Communist party for Vietnam. And when the Soviets came to suspect Ho Chi Minh of nationalist tendencies, in the 1930s, he was removed from control of the Vietnamese Communist movement for several years. During World War II, however, the Soviets were too busy with their war against Germany to pay attention to Vietnam, and they never regained the degree of influence they had had over Vietnamese Communism before 1939.

Between 1950 and 1954, the Soviet Union provided some aid, via **China**, to the **Democratic Republic of Vietnam** (DRV) in its war against the French. In 1954 the Soviets and Chinese, who believed they would benefit from a general reduction in international tensions, pressed the DRV, which was winning the war and controlled most of Vietnam, to sign the **Geneva Accords**. Vietnam was split approximately in half, which meant the DRV was giving up huge amounts of territory in the South, on a promise that the country would be reunified in 1956. When the reunification did not occur in 1956, the Soviet Union, following its doctrine of "peaceful coexistence," urged the Vietnamese Communist leaders not to resume armed struggle in the South, but to rely on peaceful political means to carry out the revolution there. When peaceful political struggle proved a disastrous failure, the Vietnamese Communists decided in the first half of 1959 to shift back to armed struggle. The Soviet Union gave at least grudging consent to this decision, but urged that North Vietnamese support for the renewed **guerrilla war** in the South be kept as small as possible, and also be carefully concealed.

For a while the Soviets took a more vigorous role in **Laos**, but soon they began to see the war there, like the one in South Vietnam, more as a danger than as an opportunity. The **Geneva Accords of 1962** on Laos, negotiated essentially between the United States and the Soviet Union, called for Laos to be neutralized and all foreign military personnel pulled out. The DRV was horrified; withdrawal of DRV military personnel from Laos would have closed down the **Ho Chi Minh Trail**, the network of paths by which personnel and equipment were sent from **North Vietnam** via Laos to the guerrilla forces in **South Vietnam**. What outcome the Soviet negotiators expected to materialize from this agreement is very unclear.

Relations between Moscow and **Hanoi** deteriorated dramatically during the next two years. DRV leaders committed to reunification of Vietnam resented Soviet advice that they minimize the scale of the guerrilla warfare in South Vietnam and minimize North Vietnamese support for it. If there was Soviet pressure for the DRV actually to obey the 1962 accord on Laos, which the DRV was violating flagrantly, that pressure would presumably have been resented also.

The Ninth Plenum of the **Lao Dong Party**, in December 1963, decided on a substantial escalation of the war in the South, and of North Vietnamese support for it. This led to the lowest ebb in relations between Hanoi and Moscow, in the first half of 1964. Those in North Vietnam who opposed the decisions of the Ninth Plenum were accused of being **"Revisionists,"** in other words supporters of the Soviet Union's doctrine of peaceful coexistence, and were subject to arrest. Two "Revisionist" army officers sought political asylum in the Soviet Union. Soviet aid to the DRV had fallen to near-zero levels; DRV officials abandoned even a pretense of courtesy toward the Soviet ambassador, and suggested that the Soviet military advisers still in North Vietnam were no longer serving a useful function and should perhaps go home.

In the second half of 1964, however, the Soviets decided that they could not afford to be completely without influence in Hanoi, and they began to consider a resumption of significant levels of military aid. Soviet Premier Alexi Kosygin was in Hanoi discussing military aid when the Americans flew the *Flaming Dart* air strikes in February 1965; Kosygin's anger that the Americans had chosen to bomb North Vietnam while he was there may have strengthened his determination to support the DRV.

Some of the weapons the Soviets provided, the DRV could have obtained from China, but there was other materiel, particularly for air defense, that was beyond Chinese capabilities. Only the Soviet Union could provide **radar**-guided **surface-to-air missiles** (SAMs) and sophisticated fighter aircraft like the **MiG**-21. The Soviets also provided technical personnel; the first SAM to down a U.S. aircraft, on July 24, 1965, was fired by a Soviet crew.

The Soviet aid program was also valuable for the restraining effect it had on American actions. There was a period of several months when **Lyndon Johnson**, fearful of the consequences of killing Soviet personnel in North Vietnam, including the technicians helping to build SAM launch sites, forbade U.S. aircraft to attack the sites while they were under construction. Waiting until the sites had been finished before attacking them made the attacks much more dangerous for U.S. aircraft. Fear of hitting Soviet ships also inhibited U.S. air strikes against North Vietnamese harbors, although this factor did not absolutely control U.S. behavior, as was illustrated when the Soviet freighter *Turkestan* was strafed by an American plane in the port of Cam Pha in June 1967.

The Soviet Union did not want a direct Soviet-American conflict any more than Lyndon Johnson did. The Soviets made it easier for President Johnson to resist pressure from U.S. military leaders to attack Soviet ships in North Vietnamese harbors by avoiding the use of ships to transport weapons; most of the weapons shipments went overland across China, despite the serious problems caused by the Sino-Soviet dispute and the Cultural Revolution (*see under* **China**), while the ships arriving in North Vietnamese harbors carried food, fuel, and supplies. The Americans did not react against the Soviet Union when planes bombing North Vietnam were shot down by Soviet-made SAMs, but the Soviets preferred not to find out how the United States would react if a large number of Americans were killed all at once by a missile hit on an American ship off the coast of North Vietnam, so they did not send the sort of anti-ship missiles that might have enabled the DRV to defend its coast effectively against shelling by U.S. naval warships.

The Soviets remained eager to see the war de-escalated, and urged

Hanoi to open **negotiations** with the United States. Relations between Moscow and Hanoi, which had improved substantially in 1965 with Moscow's decision to provide substantial military aid, improved further when the leaders in Hanoi decided, between 1966 and 1968, that the Soviet belief in the utility of negotiations with the United States was correct.

After **Richard Nixon** became president of the United States in 1969, he hoped that his policy of détente with the Soviet Union could help him to negotiate a favorable settlement in Vietnam. But he was unable to persuade the Soviets to resume putting the sort of pressure on the DRV to make concessions that they had applied between 1954 and 1964. And the Soviet Union continued to provide the DRV with substantial quantities of weaponry, not as much as the United States had provided to the RVN, but enough to enable the DRV to win the war in 1975.

**SPECIAL ASSISTANT FOR COUNTERINSURGENCY AND SPECIAL ACTIVITIES** (SACSA). A position under the **Joint Chiefs of Staff**, established in January 1962. The importance of the SACSA increased in 1963 when what had been a competing position, the assistant secretary of defense for special operations (*see* **Edward Lansdale**), was abolished and the SACSA took over most of its powers. Despite the title, the SACSA was often an officer with a rather conventional approach to warfare, not a specialist in **pacification** and **counterinsurgency**. The first SACSA, **Marine** Major General **Victor Krulak**, was later to become an advocate of pacification as an alternative to large-unit combat in Vietnam, but was not yet conspicuously one while SACSA. He was replaced early in 1964 by U.S. **Air Force** (USAF) Brigadier General Rollen Anthis, who as commander of USAF forces in Vietnam in 1962 and 1963 had been an advocate of conventional firepower; his reaction to the presence of guerrillas in a village had often been to bomb the village. **Army** Major General William Peers had a real background in special operations; he had served with the Office of Strategic Services in World War II, and later for several years with the the **Central Intelligence Agency**. He became SACSA in 1966, but in 1967 was replaced by the more conventional Army Major General William Depuy, who had been a very aggressive commander of the 1st Infantry **Division** in Vietnam 1966–1967. Depuy was probably the most powerful SACSA, having considerable influence over the conventional aspects of the Vietnam War, not just the special operations. His successor, Army Brigadier General Donald D. Blackburn, who like Peers had much background in special operations (he had commanded **SOG** 1965–1966), developed the plan for the effort to rescue American **prisoners of war** from **Son Tay** in November 1970. He was replaced by USAF Brigadier General Leroy J. Manor soon after that operation.

**SPECIAL EXPLOITATION SERVICE** (sometimes called Strategic Exploitation Service). A Vietnamese organization, created in 1964 to act in partnership with the newly established U.S. Special Operations Group (**SOG**) in covert operations both within and beyond the borders of **South Vietnam**. It was renamed Strategic Technical Service on January 5, 1965, and then Strategic Technical Directorate (STD) on November 1, 1967.

**SPECIAL FORCES,** U.S. In the late 1950s and early 1960s the U.S. **Army** activated several Special Forces Groups charged with unconventional operations, based on **Okinawa** and at Fort Bragg in North Carolina. They were expected to work behind enemy lines in conventional-war situations. In Indochina, in the 1960s, their main mission was training and leading indigenous forces in an unconventional war.

The Special Forces were not always liked or trusted by the conventional generals who dominated the Army. But after they caught President **John Kennedy**'s eye and imagination late in 1961, they were given substantially more resources, and permission to wear their headgear of choice, the green beret, previously forbidden by the Army. General **William Westmoreland**, U.S. commander in Vietnam from 1964 to 1968, was somewhat more friendly to the Special Forces than his successor, **Creighton Abrams**.

When the United States decided to send military **advisers** disguised as civilians to **Laos** to train the Royal Lao Army in mid-1959, Special Forces personnel were picked for the work (*see Hotfoot*). In April 1961, these men were allowed to begin operating openly, wearing military uniform, under the new designation *White Star*. Their number increased to more than 400 by mid-1962. Some trained the regular forces of the Royal Lao Army; others trained paramilitary groups, under **Central Intelligence Agency** (CIA) sponsorship, made up of **Hmong** and **Lao Theung** tribesmen. They were pulled out of Laos in September and October 1962, as a result of the **Geneva Accords** of July 1962.

Men from the 1st Special Forces Group were sent to Vietnam in 1957, to train men of the **First Observation Group** at the Commando Training Center at **Nha Trang**. Thirty Special Forces personnel were sent to

Vietnam in 1960 as part of the U.S. advisory effort for the **ARVN**. What was to become their biggest mission in Vietnam, however, opened up late in 1961, when the Special Forces began to provide men to the CIA to train and lead **Montagnard** forces, in what became the **Civilian Irregular Defense Groups** (CIDG).

The standard operational unit of the Special Forces in Vietnam was the A detachment or A-team, normally consisting of a captain, a lieutenant, and 10 sergeants. An A detachment usually trained and led (either by itself or in cooperation with Vietnamese **Special Forces**) a force of several hundred indigenous personnel. Above them was a structure of B and C detachments; in theory a B detachment controlled four A detachments, and a C detachment controlled three B detachments. Many Special Forces personnel in Vietnam, however, worked outside this standard structure.

In the early 1960s, the Special Forces in **South Vietnam** were working mostly on CIA-controlled projects such as the CIDG, the **Mountain Scouts**, the **Trailwatchers**, and local militias in **Catholic** villages led by their priests under the "Fighting Fathers" program. A decision was made in July 1962 to transfer control of these projects and their Special Forces personnel from the CIA to the U.S. military; the biggest part of this, the transfer of the CIDG, began in September 1962 and was completed on July 1, 1963 (see *Switchback*). By February 1963, a provisional Special Forces headquarters at Nha Trang, in the military chain of command under **Military Assistance Command, Vietnam** (MACV), was in operational control of the Special Forces A detachments in South Vietnam. It remained provisional until the spring of 1964. Finally on October 1, 1964, the 5th Special Forces Group (**Airborne**) was assigned to Vietnam, with headquarters at Nha Trang. Over the next seven months, personnel of other Special Forces Groups that had been working in Vietnam were phased out, and the 5th became responsible for all Special Forces activities there. The assigned strength of the 5th Special Forces Group surpassed 2,000 early in 1966, and reached 2,745 in January 1967.

The commander of Special Forces, Vietnam, from September 1962 to November 1963, was Colonel George C. Morton. His role associated him with **Ngo Dinh Nhu**, who controlled paramilitary programs of the **Republic of Vietnam**, and the Vietnamese Special Forces. Colonel Morton was abruptly pulled out of Vietnam after the **coup** that overthrew Nhu and his brother **Ngo Dinh Diem**. He was replaced by Colonel Theodore Leonard, an infantry officer with no previous Special

Forces experience, who remained until September 1964.

The 5th Special Forces Group was commanded by Colonel John H. Spears from October 1964 to July 1965; by Colonel William A. McKean (like Leonard, lacking previous Special Forces experience) from July 1965 to June 1966; by Colonel Francis J. Kelly from June 1966 to June 1967; by Colonel Jonathan F. Ladd from June 1967 to June 1968; by Colonel Harold R. Aaron from June 1968 to May 1969; by Colonel **Robert B. Rheault** from May 1969 until his removal in July 1969 after the killing of a suspected double agent by Special Forces personnel at Nha Trang; by Colonel Alexander Lemberes (another officer lacking Special Forces experience) from July to August 1969; and by Colonel Michael D. Healy from August 1969 until the group's official withdrawal from Vietnam in March 1971.

Aside from regular CIDG units, Special Forces personnel worked in a variety of other situations. Many of them were assigned to **SOG**. Others were in projects such as the following:

—Mobile Strike Forces or MIKE Forces, more heavily armed and given better combat training than was given to the ordinary strike forces of the CIDG camps. They were formed during the last quarter of 1965; each was led by an A detachment and had three companies of slightly less than 200 men each. The MIKE Forces were at first completely under U.S. Special Forces control; until December 1966 there was not even a pretense of Vietnamese Special Forces command.

—Mobile guerrilla forces, similar to MIKE Forces but intended to be sent into areas of total enemy control to remain for one to two months, doing **reconnaissance**, and conducting the same sorts of military activities that **Viet Cong** guerrillas conducted in government-held areas—ambushes, surprise attacks on camps small enough to be vulnerable, and general harassment—but had the options not open to Viet Cong guerrillas of obtaining air support and aerial resupply. These remained under exclusively American command. Their operations, which began in 1966 and ended in 1968, were in most cases given the code name *Blackjack*, followed by a number in which the first digit designated the **corps tactical zone**. Thus when the predominantly **Khmer** mobile guerrilla force for **III Corps** began regular operations in January 1967, its missions were designated *Blackjack-31*, *-32*, *-33*, and so on.

—Project *Delta* (Detachment B-52, based at Nha Trang), which became operational at the end of 1964, used reconnaissance teams typically made up of two U.S. Special Forces men and a small group of Vietnamese (the standard was initially eight, later reduced to four). At

first the small teams were supposed to limit themselves to reconnaissance; later they were authorized to attack enemy forces if they found
targets within their capabilities. *Delta* was deactivated on June 30,
1970.

—Projects *Omega* (Detachment B-50, based at Nha Trang and operating in **II Corps**) and *Sigma* (B-56, with headquarters at Ho Ngoc Tau
in **Gia Dinh** province, and operating in **III Corps**) had **Roadrunner**
teams of four indigenous personnel each to conduct reconnaissance
on enemy trail networks, and reconnaissance teams like those of Project
*Delta*, of two U.S. Special Forces and four indigenous personnel. Each
project had three MIKE Force reaction companies, to rescue small teams
in trouble, to attack targets discovered by the small teams, or for large
reconnaissance missions.

—The MACV **Recondo School** at Nha Trang, operated by Special
Forces, taught reconnaissance techniques not just to Special Forces
but to the reconnaissance personnel of other American and allied units
in Vietnam. The Recondo School as such was officially established in
September 1966, but it was derived from a school that had been created
by Project *Delta* in 1964 to train its reconnaissance personnel, which
had begun accepting students from the 1st Brigade of the 101st Airborne **Division** in September 1965.

The first known Special Forces mission into **North Vietnam** was on
October 16, 1966, when a **Spike Team** of **Nung** led by three Special
Forces sergeants were landed by helicopter in Thanh Hoa province, in
an unsuccessful effort to rescue a downed U.S. pilot. The **Son Tay**
rescue mission in 1970 was much larger.

**SPECIAL FORCES,** Vietnamese. The Luc Luong Dac Biet (LLDB) were
formally established in 1963, derived from the **First Observation Group**.
They were not really controlled by the **ARVN**; their commander, Colonel Le Quang Tung (a **Catholic** from **Hue**), reported to **Ngo Dinh Nhu** in
the Presidential Palace.

The LLDB were primarily a palace guard, kept mainly in the **Saigon**
area and used more for political purposes than for combat against the
Communists. Their most famous operation was a brutal raid on **Buddhist** pagodas in Saigon in August 1963. The United States repeatedly
demanded that President **Ngo Dinh Diem** shift them back to military
operations, and finally announced a cutoff of U.S. funding for them.
The ARVN generals who overthrew Ngo Dinh Diem in November 1963
were determined to bring the LLDB under effective ARVN command

(they started by executing Colonel Tung), and put them to military tasks.

Efforts to put LLDB personnel into **Civilian Irregular Defense Groups** (CIDG), in the hope that they could eventually replace the U.S. **Army Special Forces** that had initially led CIDG units, had begun to some extent as early as 1962. These efforts were accelerated in 1964. Many of the **Montagnard** CIDG troops, however, despised the LLDB; a number of CIDG units rebelled, killing their LLDB leaders, in September 1964.

There was a substantial improvement in the quality of the LLDB in 1966 and 1967. This made it possible for the first time during 1967 to give Vietnamese LLDB officers actual (as distinguished from nominal) command of Montagnard CIDG camps with some degree of success; up to then most camps with Vietnamese commanders had been under the de facto command of the U.S. Special Forces **"advisers"** to the camp commanders.

**SPECIAL WAR.** Term used in Communist writings to describe **John Kennedy**'s strategy in **South Vietnam**, of providing support and assistance to the **ARVN**, including some combat participation by U.S. personnel (especially pilots), but having the war fought primarily by ARVN rather than U.S. forces.

*SPEEDY EXPRESS*, Operation, December 1, 1968 to May 31, 1969. An effort by the U.S. 9th Infantry **Division** to destroy **Viet Cong** forces, centering on the **Mekong Delta** province of Kien Hoa. It used massive firepower and caused considerable civilian casualties.

**SPIKE TEAMS.** Small teams, controlled by **SOG**, composed mostly of indigenous personnel (usually **Montagnards**) but with American leaders, sent on **reconnaissance** missions into **Laos** to observe, and sometimes actively disrupt, enemy activities. Their activities were part of Operation *Prairie Fire*.

**STALEY MISSION.** On June 16, 1961, Dr. Eugene Staley, research director of the Stanford Research Institute, led a team to Vietnam formally called the Special Financial Group, to evaluate the scale of efforts that should be made in Vietnam, and how those efforts should be financed. The team returned to the United States in mid-July, and recommended a substantial expansion of the **ARVN**.

*STARLITE*, Operation. The first major offensive operation by U.S. **Marines** in South Vietnam, August 18–24, 1965. The Marines were trying to trap and destroy the 1st **Viet Cong** Regiment, on the coast in the northern part of Quang Ngai province, about 15 to 20 kilometers southeast of **Chu Lai**. Some of the Marines landed on the coast by amphibious assault; others landed by **helicopter** to block the escape of Viet Cong forces inland. Forty-five Marines were killed and 203 wounded during the operation; the United States reported 614 Viet Cong bodies had been counted, and believed that the actual number of Viet Cong killed had been even larger.

***STEEL TIGER.*** Program of U.S. air strikes against targets along the **Ho Chi Minh Trail**, in southern **Laos**, begun in April 1965.

**STENNIS, JOHN CORNELIUS** (1901–1995). Senator, Democrat of Mississippi. Born in Kemper County, Mississippi, he earned an LL.B. at the University of Virginia Law School in 1928. He served as a state legislator, a prosecutor, and a judge before being elected to the U.S. Senate in 1947, where he remained through 1988. During the Vietnam War, he was extremely powerful as a member of the Appropriations Committee and the Armed Services Committee, even before he became chairman of the Armed Services Committee in 1969. Stennis had not wanted the United States to put large forces into Vietnam, but once they were there he became a strong supporter of the war. His intervention in the policy process was perhaps most conspicuous in August 1967, when he presided over hearings of the Preparedness Investigating Subcommittee of the Armed Services Committee, which gave a forum for senior military leaders to protest **Lyndon Johnson**'s restrictions on the bombing of **North Vietnam**. The subcommittee endorsed the protests of the military leaders, and these hearings were a significant factor in the loosening of the restrictions that occurred shortly afterward; most of the targets that had been off limits in August had been bombed by October. When **Richard Nixon** began Operation *Menu*, the secret bombing of **Cambodia**, Stennis was one of the few members of the Senate, expected to approve of the operation, who were briefed about it.

***STRATA*** (Short-Term Roadwatch and Target Acquisition) teams. Small teams normally between five and 15 men, controlled by **SOG**, infiltrated by air (usually H-3 **helicopter**) into **North Vietnam** starting in September 1967. The *STRATA* teams were made up of indigenous personnel, trained and controlled by SOG. They were typically expected to remain in North Vietnam for only 15 to 30 days. They accomplished little, but most of them at least returned safely, unlike the men SOG had sent into

North Vietnam for long-term operations (*see OPLAN 34A, Timberwork*).

*STRATA* operations were ordered terminated as of November 1, 1968; the teams that had been trained for them were shifted to operations in **Laos** (*Prairie Fire*) and **Cambodia** (*Daniel Boone*).

**STRATEGIC HAMLETS** (*ap chien luoc*). In 1961, the head of the British Advisory Mission in Vietnam, Sir **Robert Thompson**, proposed a strategy for establishing control in the villages, derived from the "New Villages" that the British had used while suppressing a Communist insurgency in Malaya. Peasant homes in many South Vietnamese villages, especially in the **Mekong Delta**, were scattered. Thompson proposed that the peasants be gathered into compact communities, which could be surrounded by barbed wire and simple fortifications to make them defensible. The government would provide enough services such as agricultural development, improved education, and medical care, to compensate the peasants for this, and indoctrinate them in loyalty to the government. **Police** would search out Communist agents in the strategic hamlets. With military forces in the area adequate to prevent the **Viet Cong** from launching the kind of large attacks that could break through their simple defenses, genuine security could be created, and peasants would be reasonably safe from retaliation if they chose to support the government. The program was to spread on the "oil spot" principle, starting in a limited number of locations and then spreading outward. Newly established strategic hamlets on the edges of the spreading "oil spot" would have the support of the older ones nearby. With a lot of careful work, Thompson proposed that villages that had been bases of Viet Cong power could be made bases of resistance against the Viet Cong. He quickly obtained the support of U.S. Ambassador **Frederick Nolting** and officials of **John Kennedy**'s administration in Washington. President **Ngo Dinh Diem**, who had already been considering similar proposals from some Vietnamese officials, approved the program on March 19, 1962, and made his brother **Ngo Dinh Nhu** head of it.

The first major trial of the concept, Operation *Sunrise*, began on March 22, 1962. The conditions were not optimal. The location, the Ben Cat area in Binh Duong province, on the eastern edge of the guerrillas' **War Zone D**, had been proposed by General **Lionel McGarr** not because it was relatively secure but because it was so insecure he was looking for some way of remedying the situation. The locations chosen involved uprooting virtually all the peasants from their original homes, and the government was not generous in compensating the peasants for the destruction of their former homes.

Diem and Nhu became very enthusiastic and decided on a rapid and massive extension of the program, ignoring Thompson's ideas about slow and methodical development. Before the end of 1962, government officials claimed that more than 4 million peasants were in strategic hamlets. Such rapid construction stretched funds very thin. Peasant resentment over forcible relocation was accentuated by the fact that their new homes were in most cases far less desirable than their old ones had been. Also, simultaneous construction of so many reduced the government's ability to provide them with security. But despite these serious weaknesses, the program did cause significant problems for the Viet Cong by increasing government control over the peasantry.

The military junta that seized power in November 1963 disliked the strategic hamlet program because it had been to a large extent a personal project of Ngo Dinh Nhu, and perhaps also to some extent because it was seen as having been oppressive and unpopular. The Viet Cong were able to break up far more strategic hamlets after Diem's overthrow than before it. This was when the program became a disaster for the government, since breakup of the hamlets destroyed the benefits they had brought the government, in increased control, but did not eliminate the peasants' resentment of the way the government had forced them into strategic hamlets. The collapse of the strategic hamlets happened fastest in **III Corps**, with **IV Corps** close behind. Those that still survived were renamed new life hamlets in mid 1964.

The strategic hamlets should not be confused with agrovilles (*ap tru mat*). The agroville program, initiated in 1959 and abandoned in 1961, had called for larger units, and was never implemented on the massive scale of the strategic hamlet program.

**STUDENTS FOR A DEMOCRATIC SOCIETY** (SDS). In 1960, the Student League for Industrial Democracy was renamed the Students for a Democratic Society. For several years it was concerned mostly with the civil rights movement; it was small and drew little attention. It expanded dramatically after it became the main forum for opposition to the Vietnam War on many college campuses. SDS was the primary sponsor of the first really large protest demonstration against the war, held in Washington, D.C., on April 17, 1965 (*see* **anti-war movement**). SDS was at first remarkably successful in avoiding the sectarian squabbling so common among left-wing political movements. The radical minorities within it, including members of the Communist Party of the USA, the Progressive Labor Party (PL, a Maoist organization), and the Socialist Workers Party (followers of Leon Trotsky), refrained for several years either from trying to seize control of the organization or from tearing it apart in struggles with one another. The focus of the organization was on peaceful protest; it offered to debate supporters of the war, rather than trying to shout them down.

Eventually, however, radicalization of the anti-war movement undermined both the commitment of the organization as a whole to peaceful protest tactics, and the willingness of its internal factions to get along. The national organization of SDS was effectively destroyed in June 1969, when its last national convention witnessed a power struggle between the Progressive Labor Party and the group that came to be known as the Weathermen. Some SDS chapters at individual campuses continued to function. The Weathermen, after abandoing SDS, turned to bombs as tools of political protest.

**SULLIVAN, WILLIAM HEALY** (1922– ). Diplomat. Born in Cranston, Rhode Island, he graduated from Brown University, joined the Navy during World War II, and served aboard a destroyer. Following the war he joined the Foreign Service. Sullivan became an assistant to **W. Averell Harriman** when Harriman was assistant secretary of state for Far Eastern affairs; in that capacity he was deeply involved in U.S. policy toward **Laos**, during the Geneva Conference of 1961–1962 on Laos. When Harriman became under secretary of state for political affairs in April 1963, Sullivan became Harriman's special assistant in that office. In February 1964, he became the secretary of state's special assistant for Vietnamese affairs and head of the interagency Vietnam Coordinating Committee (the "Sullivan Committee"). In July 1964, he went to **Saigon** as an assistant to U.S. Ambassador **Maxwell Taylor**; he remained until the end of November. He then went to Vientiane, to replace Leonard Unger as U.S. ambassador to **Laos**; he held that position until 1969. Sullivan had more control over U.S. military operations in Laos than the U.S. ambassador in Saigon had over operations in **South Vietnam**. He accepted some U.S. ground operations in Laos (*see Prairie Fire, Shining Brass*), carried out without permission of the Laotian government, but annoyed the U.S. military by his requirement that they be kept sufficiently small and unobtrusive that it would not be obvious to the Laotian government that they were occurring.

He returned to the State Department in 1969, and was once again placed in charge of matters relating to Indochina. In practice, he worked as much under **Henry Kissinger** as he did in the State Department, on matters including the **Paris negotiations**. He served as U.S. ambassador to the Philippines from 1973 to 1976, and to Iran from 1977 to 1979. His memoir *Obbligato* was published in 1984.

**SURFACE-TO-AIR MISSILE** (SAM). A **rocket** designed to be fired from the ground against aircraft.

Early in 1965, the **Soviet Union** began to supply the Dvina missile to the DRV. This was a relatively large two-stage rocket, with a solid-fuel booster and a liquid-fuel final stage. Approximate specifications (subject to some variation between models): length 10.7 meters, warhead 130 kilograms, range 40 to 50 kilometers, ceiling 18,000 meters. It was referred to in American sources usually as the SA-2 or SAM-2, sometimes as the Guideline.

The Dvina did not itself track its target; instead a **radar** on the ground, of the type the United States called *Fan Song*, tracked both the rocket and the target aircraft, and furnished data to a control unit also on the ground, which steered the rocket by radio. The percentage of hits achieved by Dvina rockets was relatively low; a pilot who saw the rocket coming could usually dodge it successfully, and pilots usually had some warning that missiles were in the air—they saw the conspicuous takeoff of the missile, they got warning from detection devices in their aircraft that the *Fan Song* was tracking them, or they got warnings by radio from other pilots. The Americans also sometimes could jam either the *Fan Song* radar or the radio signals that steered the missile to the target.

The first success by a Dvina over **North Vietnam** was the downing of an **F-4C Phantom** on July 24, 1965. The U.S. military, which had been asking President **Lyndon Johnson** for permission to bomb the SAM launching sites, construction of which had been observed by U.S. **reconnaissance**, got that permission after this incident. The first air strikes against SAM launch sites were flown on July 27. American aircraft assigned to attack the launch sites and guidance radars later came to be called *Iron Hand* and *Wild Weasel*.

The Dvina was designed to hit aircraft at relatively high altitudes. American aircraft in areas where there were SAMs usually stayed at lower altitudes, to be less vulnerable to the missiles, but this made them more vulnerable to fire from **anti-aircraft artillery**. When SAMs were fired, dodging them involved diving still lower. **B-52** high-altitude bombers usually stayed away from the sections of North Vietnam defended by missiles; not until November 1972 was a B-52 shot down by a SAM.

In 1967, some Dvinas began to be guided optically, rather than by the *Fan Song* radar, depriving the American pilots of the warning they had been getting when a *Fan Song* locked onto a plane.

The fact that the Dvina was the only important SAM threat to aircraft over North Vietnam allowed American pilots to use standardized procedures for avoiding SAMs. The Soviet Union could have made the air defenses of the DRV more effective by providing a greater variety of SAMs, such that a single avoidance technique would not be appropriate for all, but this did not happen for a long time if at all. According to some sources, the S-125 Neva, also called the SA-3 or Goa, effective at lower altitudes than the Dvina, finally entered service in North Vietnam in late 1972.

A few Dvinas began to be used in **Laos**, to defend the **Ho Chi Minh Trail** against air attack, in March 1971. They became a serious threat, forcing the United States to restrict the operations of fixed-wing **gunships** in crucial areas of Laos, in 1972. Dvinas were first fired at aircraft over the northernmost portion of **South Vietnam**, some from launch sites in North Vietnam or in the **Demilitarized Zone**, some apparently from sites inside South Vietnam, during the **Easter Offensive** in 1972.

The Strela, which the U.S. called the SA-7 or Grail, was a shoulder-launched missile that steered itself to the target, using an infrared sensor to home in on the engine heat of an aircraft. Its very short range—3,500 meters—did not allow much effectiveness against jet aircraft, since the missile would normally have to overtake the target from the rear, and it could not often overtake a jet before running out of fuel. The Strela was much more effective against **helicopters**. Its greatest effect on fixed-wing air operations was that it forced the relatively slow aircraft used by most **Forward Air Controllers** (FACs) to shift to higher altitudes for safety, which greatly reduced the FACs' ability to spot targets on the ground. Its first impact on the war was in Laos during *Lam Son 719*, the **ARVN** effort to cut the Ho Chi Minh Trail in 1971. The Strela did not appear in South Vietnam until the Easter Offensive of 1972; the first downing of a helicopter by a Strela in South Vietnam occurred on May 2, 1972, and the first downing of a jet occurred on May 26. A modified version with a somewhat greater range was introduced toward the end of the war.

The United States deployed a few Hawk surface-to-air missiles to

South Vietnam beginning in late 1964, in case the North Vietnamese attempted air attacks against U.S. bases in South Vietnam. Two Hawk missile battalions were sent in September 1965. The missiles were never used; they were withdrawn in 1968 and 1969.

**SWIFT BOAT.** A 50-foot aluminum-hulled vessel, displacing 19 tons, with diesel engines and a maximum speed of 28 knots. The first Swift Boats had been built as civilian craft, used for moving men and cargoes to and from oil rigs in the Gulf of Mexico. In the early 1960s, the **Central Intelligence Agency** purchased several for use in covert operations against Cuba, and in 1963 sent three of them to **Danang** for use against **North Vietnam**. Before the middle of 1964, however, Swifts were increasingly being replaced in these operations by **Nasty Boats**, which were larger and faster than the Swifts (*see OPLAN 34A*).

In 1965, the U.S. **Navy** began procuring a modified version, still called the Swift informally while formally designated PCF (Patrol Craft, Fast), for use in more conventional operations along the coasts and inland waterways of **South Vietnam**; these began to arrive in October 1965. Standard armament was three .50-caliber **machine guns** and an 81-mm **mortar**.

***SWITCHBACK***, Operation. Following the failure of the **Central Intelligence Agency** (CIA)'s April 1961 invasion of Cuba at the Bay of Pigs, President **John Kennedy** issued **National Security Action Memorandum 57**, which directed that paramilitary activities that had begun under CIA control should be handed over to the military if they grew to a large size. On July 23, 1962, Secretary of Defense **Robert McNamara** decided that some of the CIA programs in Vietnam had grown large enough so that this policy should be applied to them. By far the most important such program, the **Civilian Irregular Defense Groups** (CIDG), was transferred under Operation *Switchback*; this was completed by July 1963.

The CIA's program (begun in June 1962) to put small teams called **Trailwatchers** along the borders of **South Vietnam**, to check on **infiltration** of Communist forces across the borders, was transferred to the U.S. **Special Forces** in October 1963, and amalgamated with the CIDG program in November. The CIA handover to the military of control of covert operations against **North Vietnam** did not occur until **SOG** was established in January 1964.

# - T -

**T-28 TROJAN.** Originally built as a trainer, this single-engine propeller-driven aircraft was simple to fly and not likely to arouse the press interest that modern jets might have caused if seen in Third World countries. It was used, especially in the early stages of the war, to bomb and strafe Communist forces in **South Vietnam** (*see Farm Gate*) and **Laos**. It continued to be flown in combat over Laos, by U.S. **Air Commando** pilots, even after the more modern jets had entered the war on a large scale. It was the main strike aircraft of the Royal Lao Air Force (RLAF) in the mid-1960s, flown sometimes by Laotian pilots, sometimes by "**sheepdipped**" Thais pretending to be Laotians.

In September 1963, an RLAF pilot defected to the **Democratic Republic of Vietnam** (DRV) flying a T-28; this became the DRV's first operational fighter, and it is said to have scored the first air combat success of the DRV, shooting down a C-123 transport plane that had been sent on a covert operation over **North Vietnam**, probably by **SOG**, on the night of February 15–16, 1964.

*TAILWIND*, Operation. On September 11, 1970, **SOG** landed a **hatchet team** of 16 Americans and 110 **Montagnards** by **helicopter** in an area of southern **Laos** much farther from the Vietnamese border than SOG teams usually operated (*see Prairie Fire*). They remained in the area for several days, in combat against numerically superior **PAVN** forces, surviving (with heavy casualties) only with considerable assistance from air support. Just before their extraction by helicopter, they overran a headquarters for one section of the **Ho Chi Minh Trail**, and captured a large quantity of documents that later proved very valuable. Their operation also diverted PAVN forces away from combat against a **Hmong** force operating in another section of southern Laos.

Allegations broadcast on June 7, 1998, that Sarin nerve gas had been used in the operation, and that killing Americans who had defected to the Communist forces had been among its goals, are generally believed to have been false.

**TAM CHAU, Thich,** original name Doan Van Hoanh (1921– ). Born in Ninh Binh province of **Bac Bo**, he became a **Buddhist** monk, and founded the Vietnam Unified Buddhist Order, combining Mahayana and Theravada Buddhism. He was one of the leaders of the radical Buddhists against **Ngo Dinh Diem** in 1963, and was jailed for 74 days beginning August 20, 1963. In 1966, he shifted to a more moderate stance, and was bitterly criticized by more radical Buddhists associated with Thich **Tri Quang**. By 1967, he was considered a supporter of **Nguyen Cao Ky**.

**TAN SON NHUT.** The airfield of **Saigon**, on the northwest side of the city. It was an important military base, but also was Saigon's international airport, used by commercial airliners. Several important headquarters were at Tan Son Nhut, including those of the **Vietnamese Air Force** (VNAF) and the U.S. Seventh Air Force. The headquarters of U.S. Army, Vietnam (USARV), was there until mid-1967. After mid-1967 **Military Assistance Command, Vietnam**, was at Tan Son Nhut, in a large facility sometimes called "Pentagon East."

As **PAVN** forces approached Saigon in April 1975, Tan Son Nhut continued to function until April 28, with cargoes of U.S. military aid arriving, and both Vietnamese and foreigners flying out to safety. PAVN **artillery** and **rocket** fire finally closed the airport to fixed-wing aircraft early on the morning of April 29, but it continued to be used for evacuation of Americans by **helicopter** as part of Operation *Frequent Wind*.

**TANKS.** The primary tank of U.S. forces in Vietnam was the M48A3 Patton, with a combat weight of 52 tons, carrying a 90-mm main gun and varying numbers of **machine guns**. It proved highly effective; it could fire explosive shells, canister, or "Beehive" rounds (which released large numbers of **flechettes**).

In 1969, the M551 Sheridan began to arrive. It had a bigger gun than the Patton, 152-mm, but its armor was so thin that even the term "light tank," often applied to it, was questionable. Officially it was an "Armored Reconnaissance Airborne Assault Vehicle."

The **ARVN** had inherited a few World War II-era M24 Chaffee light tanks from the French. The United States began supplying M41A3 Walker Bulldog light tanks to the ARVN in January 1965. In the second half of 1971, as the last U.S. armored units withdrew from Vietnam, it became obvious that the ARVN would need main battle tanks, and the U.S. began providing M48A3 tanks. Far more M48A3 tanks arrived in 1972 under Projects *Enhance* and *Enhance Plus*.

The first **PAVN** tank to appear on the battlefields of **South Vietnam** was the Soviet-built PT-76 light amphibious tank; its weight of under 16 tons allowed it to float, and its speed in the water was substantial, but its low-velocity 76-mm gun and very thin armor made it vulnerable in combat. The PAVN also used the Chinese Type 63, with a hull very similar to that of the PT-76 (as a result it was often mistaken for the PT-76 on the battlefield) but an 85-mm gun; the PAVN called this the PT-85 or K63-85. The heavier PAVN tanks were the Soviet-built T-54, weighing 40 tons and with a 100-mm gun, and a Chinese copy of the T-54 called the T-59.

PT-76 tanks of Battalion 198, 203d PAVN Regiment, first appeared in South Vietnam at the beginning of 1968, moving along **Route 9** eastward from **Laos** into **Quang Tri** province. They helped overrun **Lang Vei** on February 7.

The only direct combat between U.S. and PAVN tanks was on the night of March 3–4, 1969, when PAVN PT-76 tanks attacked **Ben Het** and were soundly defeated by the much more powerful U.S. M48A3s.

The PAVN threw considerable numbers of tanks into combat in both **I Corps** and **II Corps** during the **Easter Offensive**, which began at the end of March 1972.

**TAY NINH.** Tay Ninh City, about 80 kilometers northwest of **Saigon**, was the headquarters of the **Cao Dai** religious sect, and the capital of Tay Ninh province, which occupied the northwest corner of **III Corps**, and was bordered on the north and west by **Cambodia**. The most conspicuous terrain feature was **Nui Ba Den**, a conical mountain about 10 kilometers northwest of Tay Ninh City. The province was somewhat reduced in size in 1963, when its southern edge was incorporated into the newly created province of **Hau Nghia**.

Tay Ninh was among the first provinces where the **Viet Cong** formed substantial military units, and was the scene of the first really ambitious Viet Cong military operation, on the night of January 26, 1960, when four companies overran an **ARVN** regimental base camp at Trang Sup, seven kilometers from Tay Ninh City. The Communists' **War Zone C** occupied roughly the northern half of the province; the meeting that officially founded the **National Liberation Front** in December 1960 was held there, and the **Trung uong cuc mien Nam** (COSVN), the Communist headquarters for the southern half of **South Vietnam**, was there from 1961 to 1966. Heavy combat between U.S. and Communist forces in War Zone C began in 1966, and continued for years. The number of Americans killed in combat in Tay Ninh province between 1967 and 1972 was higher than in any other province of III Corps, indeed higher than in any province outside **I Corps**. The modest number of military personnel that the **Philippines** sent to Vietnam were assigned mostly to Tay Ninh province.

**TAYLOR, MAXWELL DAVENPORT** (1901–1987). General, ambassador. Born in Keytesville, Missouri, he graduated from West Point in 1922. He was in Asia 1935–1939, studying Japanese in Tokyo and briefly serving as an assistant military attaché in China. Taylor commanded the 101st Airborne Division in the European Theater 1944–1945. He commanded Eighth Army in Korea during the last months of the Korean War, and remained in Asia until 1955. He served as U.S. **Army** chief of staff from 1955 to July 1, 1959, during which time he was an advocate of "flexible response" against the Eisenhower administration's doctrine of "massive retaliation." Taylor was somewhat more favorable to paramilitary operations and **counterinsurgency** than most of his peers, but only somewhat. His support had been crucial to the creation of the 10th **Special Forces** Group in 1952, but for most of his years as Army chief of staff he was not particularly supportive of Special Forces or special operations. Only toward the end of his tenure in that position did he resume advocacy of special operations.

Taylor retired from the Army in 1959, but President **John Kennedy** began using him in 1961 for various special jobs involving military affairs. In late 1961, Taylor headed the **Taylor-Rostow Mission** to study the situation in **South Vietnam**, and returned recommending a larger U.S. role in the war there, including some ground troop units. He chaired a number of important committees, including the National Security Council (NSC) Special Group (Counter-Insurgency) established in January 1962 to oversee U.S. policy toward Vietnam, **Laos**, and **Thailand**.

In 1962, Kennedy recalled Taylor to active service and made him chairman of the **Joint Chiefs of Staff**. In this office he supported the new concept of **airmobility**, and the Special Forces. During 1963, when doubts began to grow about whether the war in South Vietnam was really going as well as General **Paul Harkins** reported it was, Taylor strongly supported Harkins's views. Taylor's faith in Harkins's reports, which greatly exaggerated the effectiveness of **Ngo Dinh Diem**'s war against the **Viet Cong**, was probably part of the reason Taylor opposed U.S. support of the **coup** that overthrew Diem in November 1963. In mid-1964, President **Lyndon Johnson** picked Taylor to succeed **Henry Cabot Lodge** as U.S. ambassador to South Vietnam.

As ambassador, Taylor repeatedly urged bombing **North Vietnam** in retaliation for various incidents (the **Tonkin Gulf incidents** of

August 2 and 4, and various Viet Cong attacks in South Vietnam). What he was proposing, however, was more a matter of "tit-for-tat" raids than the larger and more systematic bombing campaign that the Joint Chiefs of Staff were urging at the time. He no longer favored the introduction of U.S. ground troops into Vietnam.

Taylor resigned as ambassador at the end of July 1965 (Lodge arrived in August to replace him). He became special consultant to President Johnson on September 17, 1965. He became once again a member of the **President's Foreign Intelligence Advisory Board** in 1965, and served as chairman 1968–1969. Taylor also was one of the **"Wise Men"** whom Johnson consulted periodically about Vietnam; he was one of the few members of this group who continued to support the war in Vietnam when the majority turned against it and advised Johnson to find a way out of it, in 1968 after the **Tet Offensive**. He was president of the Institute for Defense Analyses from 1966 to 1969. His memoir *Swords and Plowshares* was published in 1972; his other books include *The Uncertain Trumpet* (1959) and *Responsibility and Response* (1967).

**TAYLOR-ROSTOW MISSION.** In October 1961, President **John Kennedy** sent General **Maxwell Taylor** to investigate the situation in **South Vietnam**, accompanied by **Walt Rostow** (a senior member of the National Security Council staff in the White House) and others. For some reason this is often called the Rostow-Taylor Mission, as if Rostow had been its most important member. Their report, presented to Kennedy on November 3, said the United States faced a Communist effort to seize all of Southeast Asia. It recommended reforms in the government of President **Ngo Dinh Diem**; more U.S. **advisers**, but also U.S. administrators to be inserted into Diem's government; more weapons, including considerable quantities for the **Civil Guard** and **Self-Defense Corps**; funding for civic action programs in the villages; U.S. **helicopter** units; an **Air Commando** unit (which Kennedy had already ordered to Vietnam before getting the report—*see Farm Gate*); and a substantial task force of U.S. ground troops, perhaps 8,000 men. The report urged that the Americans become partners of the Vietnamese, not just advisers; "show them how the job might be done," not just tell them. President Diem refused to make the suggested reforms, and both Diem and Kennedy rejected the idea of sending U.S. ground troops, but most of the rest of the recommendations were accepted. The idea of ground troops having been rejected, the fact that such a recommendation had been made was concealed, and the public was given the impression that the Taylor-Rostow mission had recommended against sending ground troops.

**TCHEPONE** (Xepon, Sepon). A small town in southern **Laos**, about 35 kilometers west of the Vietnamese border, significant only as a station on the **Ho Chi Minh Trail**. It was close to the point where Route 92, which ran northwest to southeast through Laos and had become part of the Ho Chi Minh Trail, met **Route 9**, running east to **Khe Sanh**. PAVN forces held Tchepone from May 1961 onward; it eventually became notorious among U.S. pilots for the strength of its **anti-aircraft** defenses. Tchepone was the farthest point reached by **ARVN** forces during *Lam Son 719*, the 1971 incursion into Laos, but they pulled out again almost immediately, not staying long enough to destroy many of the PAVN supply stockpiles in the vicinity.

**TEMPORARY EQUIPMENT RECOVERY MISSION** (TERM). Under the **Geneva Accords of 1954**, as they were originally understood, the United States was allowed only 342 military **advisers** in **South Vietnam**. As a way of getting around this limitation, the United States announced that an additional 350 military personnel were being sent to Vietnam, beginning in June 1956, simply to recover U.S. military hardware that had been sent to Vietnam as aid to the French during the First Indochina War. This cover story was spurious; TERM devoted more of its energies to training the **ARVN** than to recovery of equipment. It was absorbed by the **Military Assistance Advisory Group** in 1960.

**TERRITORIAL FORCES.** Collective term for the the paramilitary forces of the **Republic of Vietnam**. The most important were the **Regional Forces**, the **Popular Forces**, and the National **Police**, but the **Revolutionary Development** (later Rural Development) Cadres were also included.

**TET.** The lunar new year, Tet, is the most important holiday in Vietnamese culture—more important than any single holiday in American or British culture. Its date falls sometimes in late January, sometimes in February by the Western calendar. During the Vietnam War, it became customary for there to be a cease-fire for Tet; many soldiers on both sides went home to celebrate the holiday with their families. The cease-fire was not the result of a negotiated agreement; each side separately declared a unilateral cease-fire, and the beginning and ending times announced by the two sides did not always match.

**TET OFFENSIVE.** In 1968, as usual, each side in the war announced a cease-fire for **Tet**. The Communists, however, launched an all-out attack on cities, towns, and military bases, while many **ARVN** officers and men were away from their units, celebrating the holiday with their families. General **Nguyen Chi Thanh** seems to have originated the plan, but he died in July 1967 before the details had been worked out.

It is not entirely clear to what extent this extraordinary gamble was based on hopes it could achieve its maximum goals—causing a real collapse of the **Republic of Vietnam**, and drawing the population of the cities into a "general uprising"—and to what extent it was based on a reasonable assurance of achieving more modest disruptions of the U.S. and ARVN war effort, and of U.S. public support for the war.

At the end of October 1967, Communist forces initiated large-scale fighting in the areas of Song Be and Loc Ninh, near the Cambodian border in northern **III Corps**. They did the same in early November at **Dak To**, in northern **II Corps** near the Vietnam-**Laos-Cambodia tri-border**. They began gathering around **Khe Sanh** in **Quang Tri** province, and launched heavy attacks beginning on the night of January 20, 1968. They were trying to draw American troops and attention out to these remote areas, to clear the way for the planned surprise attacks on cities and towns.

Coordination was poor. The attacks were supposed to begin simultaneously, during the early morning hours of January 31, but **Danang, Qui Nhon, Nha Trang, Pleiku, Ban Me Thuot**, and **Kontum** were attacked prematurely, in the early morning of January 30. In an effort to preserve surprise, the Communist command delayed informing some units of the plan until shortly before the offensive began. In some cases the time allowed was too short, and units fought without adequate preparation, or did not attack on schedule because they had not reached their assigned positions in time.

The offensive achieved partial surprise. The United States had received indications a major offensive was impending, but did not know exactly when, and did not realize the scope of the Communist plan. The fact that U.S. military **intelligence** was underestimating the strength of the forces the Communists had available in **South Vietnam** (*see* **Order of Battle Dispute**) contributed to the surprise. Some local commands, however, were prepared. The most important was **II Field Force**, the U.S. **Army** command for **III Corps**. General **Frederick**

**Weyand** listened to warnings from the Army Security Agency detachment attached to his headquarters, based on analysis of enemy radio communications, and pulled troops back from the border areas toward **Saigon**. The attack on Saigon during the early hours of January 31 achieved considerable surprise, but General Weyand had forces nearby to send to the rescue.

The Communist forces were expelled from most cities and towns within a few days; only in **Hue** did they hold out until late February. But they pressed the offensive in the countryside for four months; not until June did the level of combat, and the rate of casualties in the U.S. forces, subside to the levels that had prevailed before Tet. In Communist histories the Tet Offensive is treated simply as the first stage of the 1968 General Offensive. The second stage was launched in early May; Americans refer to this as "Mini-Tet," but the actual number of Americans killed in action in May 1968 was the largest for any month of the Vietnam War. The third stage was launched in mid-August.

Militarily the Tet Offensive was a defeat for the Communists, especially for the southerners in the **Viet Cong**. Attacking so persistently against forces having superior firepower, they suffered very heavy casualties. Their military gains—temporary disruption of **pacification** in the countryside, and some territorial gains their weakened forces could not hold for long—were not worth this cost.

Politically the offensive may well have been a Communist victory. Before the Tet Offensive, **Military Assistance Command, Vietnam**, had been saying the Communist forces were seriously weakened. The way they were able to make the attacks of January 30 and 31, and then sustain for four months afterward a level of combat beyond anything previously seen in the war, undermined to some extent the American public's faith that the war was being won, and it very seriously undermined the faith of the American elite, including President **Lyndon Johnson** and his top advisers (*see* **Wise Men**). Repelling the offensive involved much American use of air strikes and **artillery** in South Vietnamese towns and cities, which horrified some Americans. Finally, there was the incident in which the commander of the Vietnamese National **Police**, General **Nguyen Ngoc Loan**, was photographed executing a prisoner.

**THAILAND.** Thailand, to the west of **Laos** and **Cambodia**, is a large (514,000 square kilometers; 198,456 square miles) and prosperous nation by the standards of Southeast Asia. Its capital is Bangkok. Its dominant ethnic group, the Thai, are Theravada **Buddhists**. They are related in language and culture to various Tai ethnic groups in neighboring countries, including the **Lao** of Laos and the **Nung** of **North Vietnam** and southern **China**.

Thailand is a constitutional monarchy. Actual power during most of the Vietnam War was in the hands of generals: Sarit Thanarat from 1957 to 1963, and Thanom Kittikachorn from 1963 to 1973. They successfully suppressed a low-level Communist insurgency that broke out in northeastern Thailand in the 1960s, preventing it from becoming a serious threat. And they helped in a variety of ways the American efforts to suppress Communism in Laos, Cambodia, and Vietnam.

Thailand's most important involvement in the Vietnam War was as a base for U.S. **Air Force** (USAF) operations over Vietnam, Laos, and (late in the war) Cambodia. Until 1967, Thailand forbade public announcement of the fact that Vietnam was being bombed from Thai bases. The number of U.S. military personnel in Thailand peaked at about 49,000 in 1969. The number had dropped to 32,000 by mid-1971, as the war seemed to be winding down, then increased again to 45,000 in 1972, as the United States expanded the **air war** in response to the **Easter Offensive**. The United States used a number of air bases in Thailand:

—Don Muang, also the main civilian airfield for Bangkok, became in April 1961 the base for the first USAF combat aircraft to be stationed in Thailand, some F-102 Delta Daggers. Four RF-101 Voodoo **reconnaissance** planes were added, under the code name *Able Mabel*, in November 1961. These began flying photographic missions over Laos and **South Vietnam** the same month. During the main part of the Vietnam War, however, few U.S. combat aircraft were stationed at Don Muang.

—Korat, a moderate distance northeast of Bangkok, began to have USAF personnel in April 1962. Korat became one of the two main bases for **F-105 Thunderchiefs**.

—Nakhon Phanom (NKP), in northeastern Thailand near the border of Laos, was built by U.S. personnel in 1963. **SOG** began to use it as an operational base in 1966. Nakhon Phanom was a major base for covert military operations in Laos, and was also one of the bases for the **helicopters** and A-1 **Skyraiders** used for **search and rescue** (SAR) of downed pilots. The Infiltration Surveillance Center where data gathered by *Igloo White* **sensors** was compiled and analyzed was also at Nakhon Phanom. When **Military Assistance Command, Vietnam,** was closed down in 1973, some of its functions were shifted to the **United States Support Activities Group** at Nakhon Phanom.

—Takhli, a moderate distance north of Bangkok, became a base for **Central Intelligence Agency B-26** bombers as early as late 1960. These planes were almost used for air strikes against targets in Laos in April 1961, cancelled at the last minute (*see* Project *Mill Pond*). Takhli was a base for USAF F-100 Super Sabres by 1962; it became a base for F-105 Thunderchiefs, and EB-66 electronic warfare aircraft, in 1965. It was essentially closed by the end of 1970. It was reactivated in 1972, when the United States began moving aircraft back into Southeast Asia in response to the 1972 **Easter Offensive** in South Vietnam.

—U Tapao, southeast of Bangkok on the coast, became an important base for **B-52** bombers in 1967.

—Ubon was near the point where Thailand, Laos, and Cambodia come together. The first USAF personnel arrived there in 1961. By 1965, Ubon was home to substantial numbers of **F-4 Phantoms**.

—Udorn was in northeast Thailand only about 48 kilometers from Vientiane, the capital of Laos. From 1963 onward, Udorn was the base from which the United States managed much of its covert paramilitary effort in Laos. By 1966, Udorn also housed numerous RF-101 and RF-4C reconnaissance aircraft, F-104 Starfighters, and A-1E Skyraiders.

—Nam Thong, between Korat and Udorn in northeastern Thailand, became a base for U.S. **Marine Corps** F-4 and A-6 jets when these were pulled out of South Vietnam in 1972. They began flying combat missions on June 17, 1972.

There were occasional attacks by small groups of Communist **sappers** against the air bases the United States used in Thailand. The first such attack was against Udorn, on July 26, 1968. Sappers damaged three aircraft, killed one American and one Thai guard, and wounded three other Americans; three of the attackers were killed. Two aircraft were damaged at Ubon on July 28, 1969; three B-52s were damaged at U-Tapao on January 10, 1972. Attacks against Ubon on January 12, 1970, and on June 4, 1972, were unsuccessful.

Thailand also provided some military forces to fight in Vietnam. A 16-man contingent of the Royal Thai Air Force arrived in South Vietnam in September 1964, and a 200-man naval group arrived in December 1966. The first Thai ground troop unit, the Royal Thai Army Volunteer Regiment (the "Queen's Cobras"), arrived in September 1967 and was stationed in **Bien Hoa** province. The number of Thai military

Infantry Division for the last stage of the war in Europe. He commanded the 187th **Airborne** Regimental Combat Team in Korea, 1952–1953, and was at Fort Bragg, commanding the XVIII Airborne Corps, at the end of 1963 when the decision was made to send him to Vietnam to become deputy commander of **Military Assistance Command, Vietnam** (MACV). He served as deputy commander from January to June 1964, and then replaced **Paul Harkins** as commander. It was probably intended right from the beginning that he would step up to commander of MACV after a few months as Harkins's deputy.

Westmoreland favored a conventional style of warfare, using large units and massive firepower, though at first he doubted **tanks** would be useful in Vietnam. He preferred to fight conventionally organized **PAVN** units in the hills and jungles, rather than fighting **Viet Cong** guerrillas in the villages. When he did send troops into the villages, it was usually on sweeps; the U.S. troops would go through the villages attacking the Communists they could find there, and then move on, perhaps having to do the same thing a few months later after the Communists had reoccupied the village. He questioned the **Marines'** policy in **I Corps** of stationing troops in villages for extended periods in an effort to keep the Communists out of them (*see* **Combined Action Platoons**).

In public and in reports to Washington, he usually took an upbeat approach, stressing the progress that was being made in the war. When his **intelligence** officers told him in May 1967 that Communist personnel strength in **South Vietnam** was larger than had previously been reported, he refused to accept the figures. Instead the definitions were changed a few months later—MACV intelligence simply stopped counting the Viet Cong's low-level village militia, in which Westmoreland had never been interested anyway—and the total figure for Communist strength shrank instead of expanding (*see* **Order of Battle Dispute**). Press briefings about declining Communist capabilities late in 1967 made the **Tet Offensive** of January 1968, and the very heavy combat that lasted for months after Tet, more shocking to the public.

Westmoreland was chief of staff of the U.S. Army from July 1968 until his retirement from the Army in June 1972. In 1982, he sued the CBS television network over a documentary charging that intelligence figures on Communist strength in South Vietnam in 1967 had been deliberately falsified, but he dropped the suit partway through the trial.

**WEYAND, FREDERICK CARLTON** (1916– ). U.S. **Army** general. Born in Arbuckle, California, he was commissioned into the Army in

1938 through the Reserve Officer Training Corps (ROTC) at the University of California, Berkeley. He served in the militarily irrelevant Coast Artillery during the early part of World War II. Weyand then transferred to Intelligence, and served in the China-Burma-India Theater. In 1949 he transferred again to Infantry, and achieved his first conspicuous success in the military in 1951, commanding a battalion in combat in Korea.

He was commander of the 25th Infantry **Division** from January 1964 to March 1967. General Weyand was an early advocate of the use of armored vehicles in Vietnam. He was determined to bring the 25th Division's **tank** battalion when the division was deployed to Vietnam at the beginning of 1966, despite suggestions from a number of senior officers that the tanks would better be left in the United States. But he also came to some extent under the influence of **John Paul Vann**, who advocated **pacification** of the villages as an alternative to the massive use of American firepower.

Major General Weyand became deputy commander in March 1967, and commander in July, of **II Field Force**, the U.S. Army command for **III Corps**; he held this position until August 1968. In January 1968, taking the possibility of major Communist attacks on **Saigon** during the upcoming **Tet** holiday more seriously that some other U.S. commanders did, he persuaded General **William Westmoreland**, commander of **Military Assistance Command, Vietnam** (MACV), to let him shift troops closer to Saigon to meet this threat. Had this not happened, the outcome of the **Tet Offensive** might have been significantly different in that area.

General Weyand returned to the United States in August 1968; in 1969 he became the military adviser to the American delegation at the **Paris negotiations**. He became deputy commander of MACV in April 1970, and commander from June 1972 until the formal dissolution of MACV on March 29, 1973. In 1973, he became vice chief of staff of the U.S. Army; he was chief of staff from October 1974 until his retirement from the Army in October 1976. He was the first officer not a graduate of West Point ever to have become chief of staff.

At the end of March 1975, General Weyand was sent to inspect the situation in **South Vietnam**. His conclusion, reached early in April, a few days after the fall of **Hue** and **Danang** (*see* **final collapse**), was that the situation was still salvageable; he recommended $722 million in additional military aid for South Vietnam, which the **Congress** refused to grant.

**WHEELER, EARLE GILMORE** (1908–1975). U.S. **Army** general. Born in the District of Columbia, he graduated from West Point in 1932. An infantry officer, Wheeler was chief of staff of the 63d Division from 1944 to 1945. The division was in combat for several months in the European Theater in 1945, but some critics later said that Wheeler himself had never experienced combat. He was commander of the 2d Armored Division 1958–1959, director of the Joint Staff 1960–62, and Army chief of staff from October 1962 to July 1964. In 1963 and 1964, he advocated escalating the Vietnam War with attacks on **North Vietnam**.

Wheeler succeeded **Maxwell Taylor** as chairman of the **Joint Chiefs of Staff** (CJCS) on July 3, 1964. He suffered his first heart attack in early September 1967, but was able to remain CJCS until his retirement in 1970.

Wheeler is usually considered to have been a weak CJCS, who had less influence on the White House than Taylor had had. After major escalation of the Vietnam War began in 1965, Wheeler and other senior officers were shocked at President **Lyndon Johnson**'s decision not to mobilize the **Reserves** to provide a proper manpower base for the escalation, and by the restrictions on combat operations outside **South Vietnam** imposed by President Johnson and Secretary of Defense **Robert McNamara**. Many officers were disappointed that Wheeler did not protest more vigorously over these issues. There is a widely believed story that in August 1967 he decided that all of the Joint Chiefs should resign in protest, but that he changed his mind.

In February 1968, Wheeler went to Vietnam to evaluate the results of the **Tet Offensive**. He returned with a recommendation that he and General **William Westmoreland**, commander of U.S. forces in Vietnam, had worked out, that the Reserves should be mobilized so that the manpower would be available to send substantial reinforcements, perhaps as many as 206,000 men, to Vietnam. Most historians accept Westmoreland's claim that Wheeler was pressing him to pretend he needed reinforcements more than he really did, and that what Wheeler actually had in mind was that a request from Westmoreland could be used as leverage to get the Reserves mobilized, and then when most of the men proved not to be needed for Vietnam after all, Wheeler would use them to strengthen forces in other areas of the world, which had been weakened as the United States tried to fight a war in Vietnam without mobilization. If this was what Wheeler had in mind, it did not work. The request leaked to the press and caused considerable excitement, further undermining public faith in the military's claims that the Tet Offensive had been a major American victory that had seriously weakened Communist forces in South Vietnam. President Johnson mobilized only a few small reserve units, and sent only very modest reinforcements to Vietnam.

In mid-1969, General Wheeler tried unsuccessfully to persuade the new president, **Richard Nixon,** to delay his plans for pulling U.S. combat forces out of South Vietnam under Nixon's policy of **Vietnamization** of the war. He strongly endorsed the **Cambodian Incursion** of 1970.

**WHITE PHOSPHORUS** (WP, "Willie Pete"). An incendiary, the fire of which is very difficult to extinguish effectively, since white phosphorus will spontaneously re-ignite whenever it comes into contact with air. Delivered by **rockets** or 40-mm grenades, it was used as an anti-personnel weapon, and as a marker (since it made very conspicuous white smoke) placed on targets for air strikes.

*WHITE STAR*, Project. When the United States decided in April 1961 to make overt the fact that it was providing military aid in **Laos** to the Royal Lao Army, and to allow U.S. **Army Special Forces** teams advising and training Lao troops to wear military uniforms, the designation of the teams was changed from *Monkhood* to *White Star*. The number of *White Star* personnel increased to more than 400 by mid-1962. Some trained the regular forces of the Royal Lao Army; others trained irregular forces of **Hmong** and **Lao Theung** tribesmen under the auspices of the **Central Intelligence Agency**. They were withdrawn from Laos in September and October 1962, under the terms of the **Geneva Accords** of July 23, 1962.

*WILD WEASEL.* When the **Democratic Republic of Vietnam** (DRV) began using **radar**-guided **surface-to-air missiles** (SAMs) against U.S. aircraft in 1965, the United States decided that certain aircraft should be specifically assigned to deal with SAM launch sites and guidance radars; these aircraft were code-named *Wild Weasel*. They had crews of two: one pilot and one Electronic Warfare Officer. The first *Wild Weasels*, F-100 Super Sabres, began combat service in December 1965. At that time, what was distinctive about them was not their weapons but the electronic equipment used to locate SAM radars and to tell when a launch was occurring, and the training of the crews. The *Wild Weasels* did not at first have weapons suitable for destroying the targets they had located; that would be done by another aircraft, code-named *Iron Hand*, an **F-105** or **F-4**. Only in April 1966 did the

AGM-45 Shrike Anti-Radar Missile (ARM) become available, which would be carried by the *Wild Weasel*. This was a 10-foot, 400-pound missile carrying a 145-pound warhead, which could home in on radars. A larger missile with a much longer range, the General Dynamics AGM-78 Standard ARM, began use in March 1968.

The principal defect of the F-100 was its low speed; it was phased out of *Wild Weasel* service in 1966, replaced by the much faster F-105 Thunderchief (in a modified version, the F-105G, with two seats). F-4 Phantoms were also later brought into the *Wild Weasel* program.

**WILLIAMS, SAMUEL T.** "Hanging Sam" (1897–1984). U.S. **Army** general. Born in Denton, Texas, Williams joined the Texas Militia in 1916, and commanded a company in combat in France in the last stage of World War I. He was an assistant commander of the 90th Division in the D-Day invasion of Normandy in World War II. He took command of the 25th Division in mid-1952 in Korea, and later briefly became de facto commander (nominally deputy commander) of a Korean corps in combat in 1953.

Williams succeeded **John W. O'Daniel** as commander of the **Military Assistance Advisory Group** (MAAG) for Indochina, on October 24, 1955. It was renamed Military Assistance Advisory Group, Vietnam, one week later as a result of the establishment of a separate MAAG for **Cambodia**. General Williams, who served in this position until August 1960, encouraged the Army of the Republic of Vietnam (**ARVN**) to develop as an essentially conventional force; he did not take **guerrilla warfare** very seriously. He retired from the Army on August 31, 1960, at the end of his service in Vietnam.

**WISE MEN.** A group of informal advisers to the president, made up of long-term members of the Washington establishment. The membership fluctuated. In 1965, President **Lyndon Johnson** consulted them about Vietnam and they recommended a strong U.S. commitment. In November 1967, when Johnson consulted them again on Vietnam, those involved were **Dean Acheson, George Ball**, Omar Bradley, **McGeorge Bundy, Clark Clifford**, Arthur Dean, Douglas Dillon, Abe Fortas, **Henry Cabot Lodge**, Robert Murphy, and **Maxwell Taylor**. **W. Averell Harriman** was a semi-member, marginal in status because he was also working in the State Department at the time (by tradition, the Wise Men were former but not current members of the government). The Wise Men said, almost unanimously, that President Johnson's policy was fundamentally sound. Only George Ball spoke against the war.

This unity of view was, however, to some extent artificial; three former members of the group had not been invited to the 1967 meeting because they had turned against the war.

Clark Clifford, however, turned against the war soon after becoming secretary of defense on March 1, 1968. He reconvened the Wise Men, with Cyrus Vance and Matthew Ridgway added to the group, later that month. They were briefed again, and when they reported to the president on March 26, the majority opinion was that the war was not being won and that the United States should prepare to disengage from Vietnam. This stark shift in the opinions of leading members of the foreign policy establishment was crucial in shaping President Johnson's decisions, announced in a televised speech on March 31, to withdraw from the 1968 presidential race and to halt bombing of the northern part of **North Vietnam**.

**WOMEN.** The only woman who took an important public leadership role in the **Republic of Vietnam** (RVN) was Tran Le Xuan, generally known as Madame Nhu, wife of **Ngo Dinh Nhu**. As the sister-in-law of the unmarried President **Ngo Dinh Diem**, she was the closest thing the RVN had to a first lady; she was also a member of the National Assembly. The wives of a number of senior RVN officials and military officers are believed to have had considerable power in private, handling their husbands' business and financial affairs.

On the Communist side, there were women in high public leadership roles in **South Vietnam**, though not in **North Vietnam**. **Nguyen Thi Binh** was foreign minister of the **Provisional Revolutionary Government** (PRG), and represented the PRG at the **Paris negotiations**. **Nguyen Thi Dinh** was the leader of the **Ben Tre** Uprising in 1960, and later, at least nominally, deputy commander of the People's Liberation Armed Forces. There were considerable numbers of women in paramilitary units—militia units in the North, militia and guerrilla units in the South. Women also served as **anti-aircraft** gunners in the North.

The Republic of Vietnam Armed Forces (RVNAF) included a women's corps, but it drew little attention, and its members apparently did not become involved in combat to the extent that occurred in the Communist forces.

The war took so many men away for military service that women became a majority of the civilian labor force in large areas of North Vietnam and South Vietnam. In the case of the thousands of women who served in the work crews that kept roads open under U.S. bombing, in North Vietnam and along the **Ho Chi Minh Trail** in **Laos**, labor took on many of the characteristics and risks usually associated with military service.

The United States military sent women to Vietnam mainly as military nurses. Lieutenant Sharon Lane, an **Army** nurse killed in a **rocket** attack on **Chu Lai** on June 8, 1969, was the only woman in the U.S. military killed by hostile action in the war; seven other U.S. military nurses died from causes other than hostile action. Aside from the nurses, the U.S. military also had some women in Vietnam in administrative and clerical positions, and serving as **advisers** to the women's corps of the RVNAF.

American civilian women worked in Vietnam in many roles. The ones who are most famous, because they are mentioned in the reminiscences of the soldiers, are the ones who provided entertainment and other morale-boosting services for the troops. These included the "Donut Dollies" of the Red Cross. Civilian women working for U.S. Army Special Services ran service clubs and libraries for soldiers. The United Services Organization (USO) ran centers where homesick soldiers could get a milk shake and read a magazine; the USO also organized shows by travelling performers. There were entertainers who came as individuals, such as **Martha Raye**. But there were also American women in less conspicuous roles, as missionaries, journalists, administrators, and so forth.

## - X -

**XUAN LOC.** Capital of Long Khanh province in **III Corps**, on **Route 1** between **Bien Hoa** and Phan Thiet. During the **final collapse** of the **Republic of Vietnam** in 1975, the **ARVN** 18th Division, an airborne brigade, and some other units held Xuan Loc under attack by several **PAVN** divisions from April 9 to April 20. This stubborn defense against superior forces, ending with a well-organized retreat during the night of April 20–21, was the best performance by any ARVN force in the last stage of the war.

**XUAN THUY,** original name Nguyen Trong Nham (1912–1985). Born in Ha Dong province near **Hanoi**, he began revolutionary activities in 1926 and was imprisoned by the French in Son La from 1939 to 1945. He became a member of the **Lao Dong Party** Central Committee in 1951. He became a specialist in foreign affairs, particularly relations with left-wing organizations and governments. Thuy was foreign minister of the **Democratic Republic of Vietnam** (DRV) from April 1963 to April 1965. In 1968, he became head of the DRV delegation at the **Paris negotiations**, though **Le Duc Tho**, nominally an "adviser" to the delegation, later became its real head.

## - Y -

**Y BIH ALEO** (1901–?). Born in Darlac province, a member of the **Rhadé** tribe, he was an officer in a civil guard unit under the French, but joined the Viet Minh in 1945. He was captured by the French in 1946 and imprisoned for several years.

He headed the Darlac delegation at the meeting that founded the **Bajaraka Movement** in May 1958. In 1961, he became vice chairman of the Central Committee Presidium of the **National Liberation Front** (NLF), and in 1962 he was elected chairman of the NLF's minorities committee. When the **Provisional Revolutionary Government** was established in 1969, he was a member of its Advisory Council. After the war, he became a member of the Presidium of the Vietnam Fatherland Front.

**YANKEE STATION.** A point off the coast of Vietnam where the United States usually kept one or more aircraft carriers, available for air strikes against targets in **North Vietnam**, **Laos**, and the northern part of **South Vietnam**, beginning in 1964. Initially it was at about the latitude of **Danang**; it was shifted north to latitude 17 degrees 30 minutes in 1966.

*YANKEE TEAM.* In May 1964, the U.S. began photographic **reconnaissance** flights over **Laos** under the code name *Yankee Team*, conducted by **Air Force** RF-101 jets based in **South Vietnam** and **Navy** RF-8A jets flying from aircraft carriers at **Yankee Station**. Soon the reconnaissance aircraft began to be escorted by fighters, some of which were based in **Thailand**. One of the reconnaissance planes was shot down by ground fire on June 6, 1964, and one of the escorts on June 7. The first overt U.S. air strikes in Laos were flown in response to these incidents.

**"YOUNG TURKS."** A faction of officers whose most important leaders were Generals **Nguyen Cao Ky** and **Nguyen Van Thieu**. Other members included Generals **Cao Van Vien**, **Le Nguyen Khang**, Nguyen Bao Tri, **Nguyen Chanh Thi**, Nguyen Duc Thang, and Nguyen Huu

Co, and also Admiral **Chung Tan Cang**. They increasingly controlled the Armed Forces of the **Republic of Vietnam** beginning in September 1964, when some of them (particularly Nguyen Cao Ky) blocked an attempted **coup** against **Nguyen Khanh**. They forced Khanh into exile themselves in February 1965. They then split into factions headed by Nguyen Cao Ky and Nguyen Van Thieu. Thieu's faction triumphed in 1967 and 1968, and dominated the Republic of Vietnam until 1975.

## - Z -

**ZUMWALT, ELMO R., JR.** (1920–2000). Admiral. Born in San Francisco, he graduated from the U.S. Naval Academy at Annapolis in 1942. He served aboard destroyers in the Pacific Theater during World War II. From 1962 to 1965, he worked under Paul Nitze in the Pentagon. He, like Nitze, doubted the desirability of a commitment of U.S. ground forces to Vietnam, feeling this would divert U.S. military resources from more important needs elsewhere in the world.

Zumwalt was commander, U.S. Naval Forces Vietnam, from 1968 to 1970, commanding the forces patrolling the South Vietnamese coast as part of Operation *Market Time*, and those operating on the rivers and canals in operations like *Game Warden* and *SEALORDS*, including the **River Patrol Force** and the **Navy** component of the **Mobile Riverine Force**. He pushed these U.S. activities vigorously and competently, but he was also enthusiastic about handing over activities to the Vietnamese as fast as possible, even before President **Richard Nixon**'s announcement of **Vietnamization** as U.S. policy in 1969.

Zumwalt was chief of naval operations from 1970 to 1974. He launched a series of reforms designed to improve conditions for the Navy's enlisted men, and to relax regulations in matters like permitted hair styles. After his retirement, he published a memoir, *On Watch* (1976). His son Elmo R. Zumwalt III, who had served as a naval officer in the Mekong Delta 1968–1970, died August 13, 1988, of cancer; there is suspicion that the use of Agent Orange in the area, authorized by the father, was the ultimate cause of the son's death.

# Bibliography

Adams, Sam. *War of Numbers: An Intelligence Memoir*. South Royalton, Vt.: Steerforth Press, 1994.

Allen, George W. *None So Blind: A Personal Account of the Intelligence Failure in Vietnam*. Chicago: Ivan R. Dee, 2001.

Andradé, Dale. *Trial by Fire: The 1972 Easter Offensive, America's Last Vietnam Battle*. New York: Hippocrene, 1995.

Asselin, Pierre. *A Bitter Peace: Washington, Hanoi, and the Making of the Paris Agreement*. Chapel Hill: University of North Carolina Press, 2002.

Ball, George. *The Past Has Another Pattern*. New York: Norton, 1982.

Baskir, Lawrence M., and William A. Strauss. *Chance and Circumstance: The Draft, the War, and the Vietnam Generation*. New York: Vintage, 1978.

Bergerud, Eric M. *Red Thunder, Tropic Lightning: The World of a Combat Division in Vietnam*. Boulder, Colo.: Westview, 1993.

Bilton, Michael, and Kevin Sim. *Four Hours in My Lai*. New York: Viking, 1992.

Blackburn, Robert M. *Mercenaries and Lyndon Johnson's "More Flags": The Hiring of Korean, Filipino, and Thai Soldiers in the Vietnam War*. Jefferson, N.C.: McFarland, 1994.

Braestrup, Peter. *Big Story: How the American Press and Television Reported and Interpreted the Crisis of Tet 1968 in Vietnam and Washington*. 2 vols. Boulder, Colo.: Westview, 1977.

Brigham, Robert K. *Guerrilla Diplomacy: The NLF's Foreign Relations and the Viet Nam War*. Ithaca, N.Y.: Cornell University Press, 1999.

Browne, Malcolm. *The New Face of War*. Indianapolis, Ind.: Bobbs-Merrill, 1965.

Buckingham, William A., Jr. *Operation Ranch Hand: The Air Force and*

*Herbicides in Southeast Asia, 1961–1971*. Washington, D.C.: Office of Air Force History, 1982.

Bui Diem, with David Chanoff. *In the Jaws of History*. Boston: Houghton Mifflin, 1987.

Bui Tin. *Following Ho Chi Minh: The Memoirs of a North Vietnamese Colonel*. Honolulu: University of Hawaii Press, 1995.

Buttinger, Joseph. *Vietnam: A Dragon Embattled*. 2 vols. New York: Praeger, 1967.

Catton, Philip E. *Diem's Final Failure: Prelude to America's War in Vietnam*. Lawrence: University Press of Kansas, 2002.

Chandler, David P. *The Tragedy of Cambodian History: Politics, War, and Revolution since 1945*. New Haven, Conn.: Yale University Press, 1991.

Chen Jian. *Mao's China and the Cold War*. Chapel Hill: University of North Carolina Press, 2001.

Chinnery, Philip D. *Vietnam: The Helicopter War*. Annapolis, Md.: Naval Institute Press, 1991.

Clodfelter, Mark. *The Limits of Air Power: The American Bombing of North Vietnam*. New York: The Free Press, 1989.

Colby, William, with James McCargar. *Lost Victory*. Chicago and New York: Contemporary Books, 1989.

Conboy, Kenneth J., and Dale Andradé. *Spies and Commandos: How America Lost the Secret War in North Vietnam*. Lawrence: University Press of Kansas, 2000.

Conboy, Kenneth, with James Morrison. *Shadow War: The CIA's Secret War in Laos*. Boulder, Colo.: Paladin Press, 1995.

Croizat, Victor J. *The Brown Water Navy: The River and Coastal War in Indo-China and Vietnam, 1948–1972*. Dorset, United Kingdom: Blandford Press, 1984.

Corfield, Justin, and Laura Summers. *Historical Dictionary of Cambodia*. Lanham, Md.: Scarecrow Press, 2003.

Dawson, Allan. *55 Days: The Fall of South Vietnam*. Englewood Cliffs, N.J.: Prentice Hall, 1977.

Deac, Wilfred P. *Road to the Killing Fields: The Cambodian War of 1970–75*. College Station: Texas A & M University Press, 1997.

Dillard, Walter Scott. *Sixty Days to Peace: Implementing the Paris Peace*

*Accords, Vietnam 1973*. Washington, D.C.: National Defense University, 1982.

Duiker, William J. *Historical Dictionary of Vietnam*. 2d. ed. Lanham, Md.: Scarecrow Press, 1998.

_____. *Ho Chi Minh*. New York: Hyperion, 2000.

_____. *Sacred War: Nationalism and Revolution in a Divided Vietnam*. New York: McGraw-Hill, 1995.

Edwards, Peter, general editor. *The Official History of Australia's Involvement in Southeast Asian Conflicts, 1948–1975*. 8 vols. projected. St. Leonards, Australia: Allen & Unwin, 1992– .

Elliott, David. *The Vietnamese War: Revolution and Social Change in the Mekong Delta*. 2 vols. Armonk, N.Y.: M. E. Sharpe, 2003.

Ellsberg, Daniel. *Secrets: A Memoir of Vietnam and the Pentagon Papers*. New York: Viking, 2002.

Ford, Harold P. *CIA and the Vietnam Policymakers: Three Episodes, 1962–1968*. Langley, Va.: Center for the Study of Intelligence, 1998.

Fulton, William B. *Riverine Operations, 1966–1969*. Vietnam Studies. Washington, D.C.: U.S. Department of the Army, 1985.

Gaiduk, Ilya. *The Soviet Union and the Vietnam War*. Chicago: Ivan R. Dee, 1996.

Gelb, Leslie H., with Richard K. Betts. *The Irony of Vietnam: The System Worked*. Washington, D.C.: The Brookings Institution, 1979.

Gibbons, William C. *The U.S. Government and the Vietnam War: Executive and Legislative Roles and Relationships,* 4 vols. Washington, D.C.: Government Printing Office, 1984, 1984, 1988, 1994. Reprinted Princeton: Princeton University Press, 1986, 1986, 1989, 1995.

Glasser, Jeffrey D. *The Secret Vietnam War: The United States Air Force in Thailand, 1961–1975*. Jefferson, N.C.: McFarland, 1995.

Goldstein, Joseph, Burke Marshall, and Jack Schwartz. *The My Lai Massacre and Its Cover-up: Beyond the Reach of Law? The Peers Commission Report with a Supplement and Introductory Essay on the Limits of Law*. New York: The Free Press, 1976.

Gwin, Larry. *Baptism: A Vietnam Memoir*. New York: Ivy Books, 1999.

Halberstam, David. *The Making of a Quagmire*. New York: Random House, 1964. Rev. ed. New York: Knopf, 1988.

Hallin, Daniel C. *The "Uncensored War": The Media and Vietnam.* New York: Oxford University Press, 1986.

Hammer, Ellen J. *A Death in November: America in Vietnam, 1963.* New York: E. P. Dutton, 1987.

Hemingway, Al. *Our War Was Different: Marine Combined Action Platoons in Vietnam.* Annapolis, Md.: Naval Institute Press, 1994.

Hickey, Gerald C. *Free in the Forest: Ethnohistory of the Vietnamese Central Highlands, 1954–1976.* New Haven, Conn.: Yale University Press, 1982.

_____. *Shattered World: Adaptation and Survival among Vietnam's Highland Peoples during the Vietnam War.* Philadelphia: University of Pennsylvania Press, 1993.

_____. *Window on a War: An Anthropologist in the Vietnam Conflict.* Lubbock: Texas Tech University Press, 2002.

Hilsman, Roger. *To Move a Nation.* New York: Doubleday, 1967.

Hunt, Richard A. *Pacification: The American Struggle for Vietnam's Hearts and Minds.* Boulder, Colo.: Westview, 1995.

Isaacs, Arnold. *Without Honor: Defeat in Vietnam and Cambodia.* Baltimore, Md.: Johns Hopkins University Press, 1983.

Jamieson, Neil L. *Understanding Vietnam.* Berkeley: University of California Press, 1993.

Johnson, Lyndon. *The Vantage Point.* New York: Popular Library, 1971.

Kahin, George M. *Intervention: How America Became Involved in Vietnam.* New York: Knopf, 1986.

Kaiser, David. *American Tragedy: Kennedy, Johnson, and the Origins of the Vietnam War.* Cambridge, Mass.: Harvard University Press, 2000.

Karnow, Stanley. *Vietnam: A History.* New York: Viking, 1983.

Kelly, Francis J. *U.S. Army Special Forces, 1961–1971.* Vietnam Studies. Washington, D.C.: U.S. Department of the Army, 1985.

Kimball, Jeffrey. *Nixon's Vietnam War.* Lawrence: University Press of Kansas, 1998.

Kissinger, Henry. *White House Years.* Boston: Little, Brown, 1979.

Krepinevich, Andrew F., Jr. *The Army in Vietnam.* Baltimore, Md.: Johns Hopkins University Press, 1986.

LeGro, William E. *Vietnam from Cease-Fire to Capitulation*. Washington, D.C.: Center of Military History, 1981.

Levinson, Jeffrey L. *Alpha Strike Vietnam: The Navy's Air War, 1964 to 1973*. Novato, Calif.: Presidio, 1989.

Logevall, Fredrik. *Choosing War: The Lost Chance for Peace and the Escalation of War in Vietnam*. Berkeley: University of California Press, 1999.

Mangold, Tom, and John Penycate. *The Tunnels of Cu Chi: The Untold Story of Vietnam*. New York: Random House, 1985.

Metzner, Edward P. *More than a Soldier's War: Pacification in Vietnam*. College Station: Texas A & M University Press, 1995.

Michel, Marshall. *Clashes: Air Combat over North Vietnam, 1965–1972*. Annapolis, Md.: Naval Institute Press, 1997.

Moïse, Edwin E. *Land Reform in China and North Vietnam: Consolidating the Revolution at the Village Level*. Chapel Hill: University of North Carolina Press, 1983.

_____. *Tonkin Gulf and the Escalation of the Vietnam War*. Chapel Hill: University of North Carolina Press, 1996.

Moore, Harold G., and Joseph L. Galloway. *We Were Soldiers Once . . . and Young*. New York: Random House, 1992.

Nalty, Bernard C. *Air War over South Vietnam, 1968–1975*. Washington, D.C.: Air Force History and Museums Program, 2000.

Newman, John M. *JFK and Vietnam: Deception, Intrigue, and the Struggle for Power*. New York: Warner, 1992.

Nguyen Tien Hung and Jerrold Schecter. *The Palace File*. New York: Harper & Row, 1986.

Oberdorfer, Don. *Tet*. New York: Doubleday, 1971.

*The Pentagon Papers: The Defense Department History of United States Decisionmaking on Vietnam*. 5 vols. Boston: Beacon, 1971–1972.

Plaster, John L. *SOG: The Secret Wars of America's Commandos in Vietnam*. New York: Simon & Schuster, 1997.

Prados, John. *The Blood Road: The Ho Chi Minh Trail and the Vietnam War*. New York: Wiley, 1999.

Prados, John, and Ray W. Stubbe. *Valley of Decision: The Siege of Khe Sanh*. Boston: Houghton Mifflin, 1991.

Pribbenow, Merle L., trans. *Victory in Vietnam: The Official History of the People's Army of Vietnam, 1954–1975*. Lawrence: University Press of Kansas, 2002.

Prochnau, William. *Once Upon a Distant War*. New York: Random House, 1995.

Quincy, Keith. *Harvesting Pa Chay's Wheat: The Hmong and America's Secret War in Laos*. Seattle: University of Washington Press, 2000.

Race, Jeffrey. *War Comes to Long An*. Berkeley: University of California Press, 1972.

Robbins, Christopher. *Air America*. New York: Putnam, 1979.

Rochester, Stuart I., and Frederick Kiley. *Honor Bound: American Prisoners of War in Southeast Asia, 1961–1973*. Annapolis, Md.: Naval Institute Press, 1999.

Rudenstine, David. *The Day the Presses Stopped: A History of the Pentagon Papers Case*. Berkeley: University of California Press, 1996.

Schell, Jonathan. *The Military Half: An Account of Destruction in Quang Ngai and Quang Tin*. New York: Knopf, 1968.

_____. *The Village of Ben Suc*. New York: Knopf, 1967.

Schoenebaum, Eleanora, and Nelson Lichtenstein, eds. *Political Profiles*. 5 vols. New York: Facts on File, 1976–1979.

Schreadley, R. L. *From the Rivers to the Sea: The U.S. Navy in Vietnam*. Annapolis, Md.: Naval Institute Press, 1992.

Shaplen, Robert. *The Lost Revolution: The U.S. in Vietnam, 1946–1966*, rev. ed. New York: Harper Colophon, 1966.

Shawcross, William. *Sideshow: Kissinger, Nixon, and the Destruction of Cambodia*. New York: Simon & Schuster, 1979.

Sheehan, Neil. *A Bright Shining Lie: John Paul Vann and America in Vietnam*. New York: Random House, 1988.

Snepp, Frank. *Decent Interval*. New York: Random House, 1977.

Sobel, Lester A., Stanley Millet, and Edward W. Knappman, eds. *South Vietnam: U.S.-Communist Confrontation in Southeast Asia*. 7 vols. New York: Facts on File, 1966–1973.

Sorley, Lewis. *A Better War: The Unexamined Victories and the Final Tragedy of America's Last Years in Vietnam*. New York: Harcourt Brace, 1999.

Spector, Ronald. *After Tet: The Bloodiest Year in Vietnam*. New York: The Free Press, 1993.

Stanton, Shelby L. *Vietnam Order of Battle*. New York: Exeter, 1986.

Starry, Donn A. *Mounted Combat in Vietnam*. Vietnam Studies. Washington, D.C.: U.S. Department of the Army, 1978.

Stuart-Fox, Martin, and Mary Kooyman. *Historical Dictionary of Laos*. 2d ed. Lanham, Md.: Scarecrow, 2001.

Terry, Wallace. *Bloods: An Oral History of the Vietnam War by Black Veterans*. New York: Random House, 1984.

Thayer, Carlyle. *War by Other Means: National Liberation and Revolution in Viet-Nam, 1954–60*. Cambridge, Mass.: Unwin Hyman, 1989.

Thayer, Thomas C. *War without Fronts: The American Experience in Vietnam*. Boulder, Colo.: Westview, 1985.

Thompson, Wayne. *To Hanoi and Back: The U.S. Air Force and North Vietnam, 1966–1973*. Washington, D.C.: Smithsonian Institution Press, 2000.

Tolson, John J. *Airmobility: 1961–1971*. Vietnam Studies. Washington, D.C.: U.S. Department of the Army, 1973.

Trest, Warren A. *Air Commando One: Heinie Aderholt and America's Secret Wars*. Washington, D.C.: Smithsonian Institution Press, 2000.

Trullinger, James. *Village at War*. New York: Longman, 1980.

Turley, Gerald H. *The Easter Offensive*. Novato, Calif.: Presidio, 1985.

Turley, William S. *The Second Indochina War: A Short Political and Military History, 1954–1975*. Boulder, Colo.: Westview, 1986.

U.S. Air Force. *The United States Air Force in Southeast Asia*. Washington, D.C.: Office of Air Force History, 1981– .
    Ballard, Jack S. *Development and Employment of Fixed-Wing Gunships, 1962–1972* (1982).
    Bowers, Ray L. *Tactical Airlift* (1983).
    Futrell, Robert F., and Martin Blumenson. *The Advisory Years to 1965* (1981).
    Schlight, John. *The War in South Vietnam: The Years of the Offensive, 1965–1968* (1988).
    Van Staaveren, Jacob. *Interdiction in Southern Laos, 1960–1968* (1993).

U.S. Army. *The United States Army in Vietnam*. Washington, D.C.: Center of Military History, 1983– .

  Carland, John M. *Combat Operations: Stemming the Tide, May 1965 to October 1966* (2000).

  Clarke, Jeffrey J. *Advice and Support: The Final Years, 1965–1973* (1988).

  Hammond, William M. *Public Affairs: The Military and the Media, 1962–1968* (1988).

  Hammond, William M. *Public Affairs: The Military and the Media 1968–1973* (1996).

  MacGarrigle, George L. *Combat Operations: Taking the Offensive, October 1966 to October 1967* (1998).

  Spector, Ronald. *Advice and Support: The Early Years, 1941–1960* (1983).

U.S. Department of Defense. *United States–Vietnam Relations, 1945–1967: A Study Prepared by the Department of Defense*. 12 vols. Washington, D.C.: Government Printing Office, 1971.

U.S. Department of State. *Foreign Relations of the United States*. Washington, D.C.: Government Printing Office, various dates. The 11 volumes for Vietnam 1961–1968, and the volume for Laos 1964–1968, are on the Internet at http://www.state.gov/r/pa/ho/frus/c1716.htm

U.S. Marine Corps. *U.S. Marines in Vietnam*. 9 vols. Washington, D.C.: History and Museums Division, Headquarters, U.S. Marine Corps, 1977–1997.

Van Staaveren, Jacob. *Gradual Failure: The Air War over North Vietnam, 1965–1966*. Washington, D.C.: Air Force History and Museums Program, 2002.

Warner, Roger. *Back Fire: The CIA's Secret War in Laos and Its Link to the War in Vietnam*. New York: Simon & Schuster, 1995.

Westmoreland, William. *A Soldier Reports*. New York: Doubleday, 1976.

Zaroulis, Nancy, and Gerald Sullivan. *Who Spoke Up? American Protest against the War in Vietnam, 1963–1975*. New York: Doubleday, 1984.

Zhai, Qiang. *China and the Vietnam Wars, 1950–1975*. Chapel Hill: University of North Carolina Press, 2000.

The author has placed a more complete bibliography on the Internet at http://www.clemson.edu/~eemoise/bibliography.html

# Name Index

Page numbers in bold type indicate an entry on the person in question.

Killian, James, 324
Kim, Le Van, 110, 336, 404
Kim, Tran Trong, 315
King, Martin Luther, xxxviii, 34–35, **210–12,** 329
Kinh, Tran Thuc *see* Tran Van Quang
Kinnard, Harry, 32
Kissinger, Henry, xliii–xlv, 87, 133, 162–63, **212–14,** 231–32, 287, 289–90, 293, 305–6, 343, 382
Komer, Robert, 92, 107, **214–15,** 415
Kong Le, xxviii, xxxi, 109, **215,** 227, 319, 368, 395
Kosygin, Alexi, 371
Kouprasith Abhay (Kupasit Aphai), 109, 319
Krepinevich, Andrew, 8
Krulak, Victor, 98, 169, 203, **217–18,** 244, 372
Ky, Nguyen Cao *see* Nguyen Cao Ky
Kyle, Wood, 424

Ladd, Jonathan, 375
Lai Van Sang, 356
Laird, Melvin, **218,** 421
Lam, Hoang Xuan, 278
Lam Van Phat, xxxiii, 110
Lane, Sharon, 433
Lansdale, Edward, 81, 134, **222–24,** 316
Lavelle, John, **229**
Le Duan, xxvi, 6, 117, 224–25, **229–30,** 231, 270, 285, 310, 313, 314, 323, 338, 408, 413, 422
Le Duc Anh, **230–31,** 406, 413, 423
Le Duc Tho, xliii–xlv, 213, 225, 229–30, **231–32,** 293, 304–5, 310, 313, 315, 323, 338, 413, 422, 434
Le Kha Phieu, **232**
Le Nguyen Khang, **232–33,** 245–46, 279, 421, 434
Le Quang Luong, 31
Le Quang Tung, 376–77
Le Van Kim, 110, 336, 404

Le Van Vien, 54
Lederer, Willliam, 224
LeMay, Curtis, 27, 133, 138, **233–34**
Lemberes, Alexander, 375
Leonard, Theodore, 374
Lien, Nguyen Ba, 232, 246
Linh, Nguyen Van, xlix, **285,** 323, 408
Loan, Nguyen Ngoc, 61, 185, 279, 280, **283–84,** 392
Lodge, Henry Cabot, xxx, 32, 48, 82, 110, 170, 203, 223, **237,** 276, 431
Lon Nol, xl, xlvi, 68, 70, 108, 208, 209–10, **238,** 296, 366
Luce, Don, 192–93, 397
Luong, Le Quang, 31
Luong, Tran *see* Tran Nam Trung
Ly Tong Ba, **240–41**

MacArthur, Douglas, 198
Magsaysay, Ramón, 222
Mai Chi Tho, 231, 406
Man, Chu Huy, **89,** 421
Manor, Leroy, 373
Mansfield, Mike, 32, 99, 100, **242,** 274
Mao Zedong, 83, 335
Marcos, Ferdinand, 316
Martin, Graham, 116, 149, **247–48**
McAlister, Elizabeth, 52
McCarthy, Eugene, 132, 200, 205–6, **249–50**
McCone, John, 174, 196, **250–51**
McConnell, John P., 27
McDonald, David, 272
McGarr, Lionel, **251–52,** 258, 379
McGovern, George, 100, 133, **252,** 294
McKean, William, 375
McNamara, Robert, 49, 55, 62, 100, 169, 189, 195–96, **252–54,** 311, 337, 340, 384, 429
McNaughton, John, 134
Mendenhall, Joseph, 203, 217
Minh, Duong Van *see* Duong Van Minh
Minh Tam *see* Ton That Dinh
Mitchell, David, 171

Momyer, William, 219
Moorer, Thomas, 229, **265,** 272
Morse, Wayne, **265,** 400
Morton, George, 374
Muoi Cuc *see* Nguyen Van Linh
Muoi, Do, 423
Muoi Khang *see* Hoang Van Thai
  (Hoang Van Xiem)
Murphy, Robert, 431
Murray, John, 115

Nam, Anh *see* Truong Chinh
Nam Cong *see* Vo Chi Cong
Nam Nga *see* Tran Nam Trung
Ngo Dinh Can, 78, **273–74,** 275
Ngo Dinh Diem, xxv–xxviii, xxx, 2, 4–
  5, 15–16, 31, 44, 48, 54, 60, 71, 74,
  75, 77–78, 81, 91, 97, 109–10, 127,
  130–32, 145, 153, 168–70, 176,
  180–81, 185, 196, 201, 203, 217,
  221, 223, 232, 237, 245–46, 251,
  256, 258, 273, **274–76,** 277–80, 282,
  286–87, 295, 298, 313, 315–16, 336,
  356–57, 362, 376, 379–80, 388, 389,
  397, 403, 404, 407, 414, 416–17, 421
Ngo Dinh Nhu, xxx, 60, 67, 71, 78, 81,
  127, 189, 223, 250, 273, 275, **276–
  77,** 295, 313, 374, 376, 379–80
Ngo Dinh Thuc, 60, 78, 275, **277–78,**
  313
Ngo Dzu, 415
Ngo Quang Truong, 98, **278**
Nguyen Ai Quoc *see* Ho Chi Minh
Nguyen Ba Lien, 232, 246
Nguyen Bao Tri, 434
Nguyen Cao Ky, xxxiv, 44–45, 61, 110,
  126, 131–32, 147, 233, **278–80,**
  283–84, 286, 337, 386, 404, 434–35
Nguyen Chan *see* Tran Van Tra
Nguyen Chanh Thi, xxviii, xxxv, 31, 44,
  61, 109, 275, **280,** 284, 434
Nguyen Chi Thanh, **280–81,** 285, 323,
  391, 408, 409, 422
Nguyen Co Thach, 306

Nguyen, Dong Si, **124,** 158
Nguyen Duc Thang, 434
Nguyen Huu Co, 434–35
Nguyen Huu Hanh, 190, 251, **281**
Nguyen Huu Tho, 269–70, **281–82**
Nguyen Huu Vu *see* Dong Si Nguyen
Nguyen Khanh, xxxi–xxxiii, 44, 60,
  110–11, 127, 279, **282–83,** 286–87,
  314, 337, 397, 403, 404, 405, 407,
  435
Nguyen Lac Hoa, Nguyen Loc Hoa,
  354
Nguyen Ngoc Loan, 61, 185, 279, 280,
  **283–84,** 392
Nguyen Tat Thanh *see* Ho Chi Minh
Nguyen Thi Binh, 270, **284,** 326, 432
Nguyen Thi Dinh, 51, 270, **285,** 432
Nguyen Trong Nham *see* Xuan Thuy
Nguyen, Tu *see* Tran Van Tra
Nguyen Van Cuc *see* Nguyen Van Linh
Nguyen Van Dieu, 38
Nguyen Van Dong *see* Dong Si Nguyen
Nguyen Van Hieu, 270
Nguyen Van Hinh, xxv, 274, 403
Nguyen Van Linh, xlix, **285,** 323, 408
Nguyen Van Thieu, xxxiv, xxxvii,
  xxxix, xlii–xlvii, 31, 44–45, 68, 70,
  78–79, 110, 126, 127, 131–32, 138–
  40, 181, 190, 213, 219–22, 233, 247–
  48, 251, 279–80, 284, **285–87,** 293–
  94, 305–6, 314, 337, 403, 404, 405,
  407, 434–35
Nguyen Viet Thanh, 71, **287–88**
Nguyen Xuan Oanh, **288,** 404
Nha, Vu Ngoc, 190
Nham, Nguyen Trong *see* Xuan Thuy
Nhu, Madame, 109–10, 277, 432
Nhu, Ngo Dinh *see* Ngo Dinh Nhu
Nitze, Paul, 435
Nixon, Richard, xxxix, xlii–xlv, 17, 21,
  25–26, 56, 68, 70–71, 80, 87, 101,
  125, 133, 144, 162–63, 167, 201,
  212–13, 236–37, 245, 252, 255–56,
  261–62, 287, **289–94,** 306, 308, 340,

# Operations Index

Page numbers in bold type indicate an entry for the operation or project.

# About the Author

Edwin E. Moïse (B.A. Harvard; M.A. University of Michigan; Ph.D. University of Michigan) is a Professor of History at Clemson University. He began his career studying the political and economic history of modern Vietnam and China, especially the processes of Communist revolution. But in recent years his interests have shifted toward military history, particularly the Vietnam War. He is the author of *Land Reform in China and North Vietnam; Modern China: A History;* and *Tonkin Gulf and the Escalation of the Vietnam War.* He is a member of the Association for Asian Studies, the Society for Historians of American Foreign Relations, the American Historical Association, and the Society for Military History.